The Livery Companies of the City of London.

The Queen Margarete Hitþ
me wyff and Spolþse to kyng
Narry the sexthe.

Reproduced from Mr J.F.Wadmore's account of the Skinners Company
published by the London and Middlesex Archæological Society

THE

LIVERY COMPANIES

Of the City of London

*THEIR ORIGIN, CHARACTER, DEVELOPMENT, AND SOCIAL
AND POLITICAL IMPORTANCE*

BY

W. CAREW HAZLITT

Of the Inner Temple, Barrister-at-Law

BENJAMIN BLOM  New York/London

First Published 1892
Reissued 1969 by
Benjamin Blom, Inc., Bronx, New York 10452
and 56 Doughty Street, London, W.C. 1

Library of Congress Catalog Card Number 68-56529

Printed in U.S.A. by
NOBLE OFFSET PRINTERS, INC.
NEW YORK 3, N. Y.

CONTENTS.

———◆———

Voluntary Associations Which Have Disappeared, or have Merged in the Livery Gilds.

CONTENTS. vii

viii CONTENTS.

LIST OF ILLUSTRATIONS.

ix

PREFACE.

I.

The Royal
Commission. I. NOW that every public institution begins to think it necessary or fit to be ready on demand with its credentials, and to be prepared to exhibit its *raison d'être*, it seems to be an opportune moment for bringing within a convenient compass an account of all the Gilds and Livery Companies of London. In the old days, customs and bodies survived from generation to generation without inquiry and challenge; and even within our own recollection calls for scrutiny and reform have been parried, or, if answered, have been practically inoperative. But the Royal Commission of 1880, and the returns thereby requested and obtained, marked a new era in the question, as well as in the relations between the Companies and the public.

Considering that the former enjoyed, even in the face of such a Commission, great and varied facilities for evasion, and that there was no legal power of enforcement, the response on their part may be fairly described as remarkably cordial and frank. At the same time, all the returns were accompanied by a respectful protest; in a few cases very little information was given, and in two or three no return was made.

Although there was at first, especially on the part of the

I

minor associations, a strong feeling of distaste and distrust toward the Commission, it may be questioned whether the disclosures to which it led did not operate beneficially on the bodies and individuals primarily concerned. For the Report went, as a whole, to shew and establish in a conclusive manner, and under the most authoritative auspices, that the Gilds were far from justifying the strictures passed upon their management and financial economy by many influential public men, and that, whatever might have been the directing impulse or motive, their property was, at the period when the Commission sat, extensively utilized, not only for charitable purposes, as to which there have been conflicting opinions, but for purposes directly and indirectly connected with education, social science, and human progress.

Commission not directly operative.   Some surprise and dissatisfaction prevailed at the time, it may be remembered, because the Government did not found on the Report any proposal to Parliament ; nor has any step been since taken, beyond the slight redistribution of administrative powers under the County Council system. The hostile critics of the Corporation and the Companies made a good deal of the serious loss to the Imperial revenue from the enormous amount of property held in mortmain and exempt from succession-duty in perpetuity, as well as of the large fees paid to members of the Courts for attendances in the case of a few of the wealthier Gilds. There was also a contention, that the Companies were independent of the Corporation, and were, at least no longer, what they nominally or ostensibly professed to be—representatives, guardians, and promoters of various trades and callings.

The Corporate Tax.   The charge, which almost amounted to a reproach, that by their constitutions they intercepted a large sum, which in ordinary cases would be available at certain intervals for succession-duty, and thus inflicted a wrong on the general community, has been met since 1884 by the CORPORATE TAX of five per cent., which assesses these bodies on a basis so calculated that they pay their quota to the revenue in the same manner as ordinary individuals. Of course they were expressly entitled under their charters to hold in mortmain ; but when other modes of taxing them had become incompatible with our laws, and antagonistic to public opinion, it seemed desirable, no doubt, to devise some fresh expedient for disencumbering them, if only of a percentage of their incomes. The corporate tax yields the Exchequer many thousands a year.

The plea, after all, can only apply to their corporate property, since their trust estates are purely eleemosynary ; and the argument appears to possess all the less validity, that a fair proportion of the annual receipts pass to the members, and indirectly become liable to taxation, while, if it were not so, it is within the competence of the Companies at any time to dissolve themselves as regards their corporate possessions and divide the assets. Whether an equitable apportionment of the funds is made among the several grades is a question, again, for the Gilds themselves ; but the complaint that extravagant amounts are voted to the Courts may be met by pointing out that the greater the output in this or any other direction the greater is the presumed gain to the imperial exchequer from normal property-tax.

The Common Hall. Trust and Corporate Estates separable.   Two other points deserve to be noticed. The Companies and the Corporation, as the matter has stood time out of mind, are intimately and inseparably bound up together by the usage of the Common Hall and otherwise ; and, secondly, it has been established on the highest authority, that the alienation of their Trust Estates would not affect their integrity or their title to their acquired and absolute property, while it might in some leading instances form a source of advantage to them and of loss to the public.

Ostensible object of foundation.   It is not requisite to enter into the question of the diversity of object or motive which professedly led these bodies to make common cause; but, confining ourselves to those of native origin, which established themselves within the City of London from the twelfth century downward, we see that the main ostensible justification for their sufferance was, not trade, but charity and alms ; and they owed their freedom from molestation during the earlier stages to their comparative insignificance, politically and financially, and to their municipal franchises, until, when their resources expanded, and their pretensions grew respondent, a prescriptive title and a full purse befriended and preserved them. This middle period was the season of ripening investments in land and of active connexion with manufacture and commerce, culminating in widespread ruin, attendant upon the Civil War, the troubles in Ireland, and the Great Fire ; and the modern annals of the surviving Companies tell a story of abandonment of old mercantile traditions in the face of changed times and of a return, but on a basis commensurate with immensely augmented power for good, to that benevolent and religious mission which first procured them toleration and power.

The Royal Commission advantageous.   These institutions may be fairly considered as having taken a fresh lease of their existence, and they mainly owe the renewal of political life to their own foresight, energy, and munificence. We know that it is a common error to suppose that an enormous proportion of their revenues is consumed in entertainments, and that civic feasts are nothing but phenomenal spectacles of *gourmandise*.[1] In the first place, the amount spent on them is relatively

---

[1] A curious illustration of the harm done to these bodies by ignorant and indiscreet persons occurred in the case of the late surveyor to one of the great Companies, who used to tell his friends that he thought they spent all their money in eating and drinking.

small; and, further, they are almost the only survivals of ancient English hospitality. So far from being limited to the municipal bodies themselves, there is scarcely a member of English society of any recognised status who is not on the *rota* of invited guests.

The Companies have reason, we think, to consider that the report of the Royal Commission was decidedly advantageous to them, in shielding their independence and property from the extreme reformers in the Liberal ranks in Parliament, who, it must be within recollection, openly spoke of the propriety of a complete reorganization, involving the virtual extinction of the original bodies.

Danger averted by disclosure. This danger has been averted, in the first place by the evidence collected in 1880 and following years; and, secondly, by the proofs which so many of the Companies continue of their own accord to evince of their lively and intelligent interest in the cause of culture and in the welfare of the community. A dispassionate estimate of the position, as it now stands, with the Companies as trustees *de jure* or *de facto* of very large charitable funds, may lead to the impression, or even the deliberate belief, that, if the estates were taken over by the Government, no appreciable gain would accrue to the existing or any other beneficiaries; and assuredly it is the clear and urgent interest of the civic bodies in possession to work more and more in the direction of justifying sympathy and support on their behalf. It should be always borne in mind, besides, that we have here a case in which the burden of proof lies exclusively on the shoulders of the reformer.

We are of opinion that the Companies, and the Corporation itself, are infinitely more secure from molestation at this moment than they were ten years ago. Their best, if not their sole, policy is to march abreast with the times; and no Government in the future will venture to approach Parliament with a proposal for a readjustment of their revenues.

Moreover, we apprehend the best friends of the City and its venerable customs and privileges to be on our side, when we assert that, had the bulk of the Companies stood on their strict legal rights, and refused disclosure, the position of the entire body would ere this have become very critical. A judicious and graceful deference to public opinion has been their best security ; as, in a converse way, it was said of Queen Elizabeth, that her greatest art as a ruler lay in knowing when and where to yield. By studying contemporary feelings and wants, the municipality in all its length and breadth may, and will, continue to prosper ; but by a misinterpretation of its relationship to the State it would incur a danger not to be possibly over-rated. No earthly power—not even Lord Salisbury's omnipotent Upper Chamber—could save the Corporation and allied bodies from destruction, if they should leave the path which most of them are treading, and wherein their true salvation lies.

Agitation for disendowment.   Some of our public men in and out of Parliament have propounded and agitated the desirability of taking back the City charters, and appropriating the funds of the Corporation and Companies, on utilitarian grounds ; and there has been, and indeed is, a fear that, if a dissolution should impart to the legislature a more pronounced democratic character and feeling, and a Government pledged to a Socialist policy should be installed in office, the ancient and time-honoured constitution of the City of London would be among the earliest objects of attention and attack.

Civic bodies valuable as general social factors.   We do not hold this view to be well-founded, because the very education which the City has from the outset contributed to foster, and of which in its broader and higher forms it is one of the most zealous and munificent promoters, will gradually and steadily raise up a vast democratic community, inimical, it may be, on the one hand, to the retention of many abuses still lingering among us, but, on the other, adverse to the disappearance of institutions which have learned to throw down their roots deep into the popular sympathy, and to identify themselves with some of the most important and costly improvements of recent days. Nor are we to forget that the Municipality of London at large is a most potential and unique factor in knitting together the classes, and in preserving from decay and oblivion the ancient hospitality of our kings. The seat and centre of princely bounty have been transferred from Whitehall to Guildhall.

The civic banquets were anciently and originally analogous to those of the monarch, and were only held at fixed seasons, the interval being marked by a more frugal domestic economy and a more sparing diet than at present prevails among those attached to the Gilds. The feast was at one period a purely exceptional event, and was the most pleasant of the bonds of fellowship which connected trades, classes, and families.

The City and the Peerage. It has been most decisively shown to what a great extent our ennobled families derived their extraction and the means of acquiring and maintaining their honours from the City. A list of those whose origin was municipal and mercantile embraces some of the most distinguished names in the peerage; and to those who have not been led to study this aspect of the matter it is apt to be a source of surprise when they discover how the Corporation and Gilds have formed an immemorial link between commercial life and the aristocracy.

The pages of the *Remembrancia* testify to the solicitude of almost all classes to acquire a standing in the City by membership of one of the Gilds or by freedom of the Municipality itself. Letters of application from the king, nobility, and other personages of station and influence, to the Lord Mayor flowed in without interruption at one period. Sometimes the request was granted ; at other times regret was expressed at the inability to comply, from the absence of vacancies or an analogous plea.

Gain of the aristocracy from municipal alliances. We hardly know how deeply and how repeatedly our aristocracy has been indebted for its maintenance and renewal to the robust and energetic life, and the pecuniary subsidies, of the City. The wealth of the early London merchant was tolerably amerced by the Crown under irresistible pressure ; but through two channels of a different class immense strength was imparted to the Upper Chamber during some centuries : firstly, by the elevation of citizens to the peerage ; and, secondly, by the espousal of their daughters to noblemen. Of the six daughters of Sir William Cockaine, Lord Mayor of London in 1619, all married peers or their immediate kindred.

The dismemberment of the City Gilds, and confiscation of their estates, must appear on deliberate reflection almost an impossibility, when we consider that such a proceeding would shake the basis of the entire corporate structure, and would reduce to inanition a feature of English political and social life which has grown up with us, and forms no mean part of our constitutional fabric and our historical traditions.

The Companies an indefeasible element of London life. 2. The Livery Companies of London are, in truth, part and parcel of a grand municipal machinery, which is indivisible, and ought to be indissoluble. It is not only in this case that the common plea, *quieta non movere*, may be urged, but, as we have mentioned, a very grave question must arise under present conditions, whether these organizations, as they are now constituted on an improved basis and to a considerable extent in harmony with the views of the Imperial executive, are not preferable *media* for carrying out the undertakings and responsibilities which they silently and practically recognise as appertaining and essential to their existence.

They are emphatically appurtenances of the City. Their property, their associations, and their centres are equally within the municipal frontier. But there is between them and a large class of men, whose occupations and interests lie in the same narrow area, the broadest and clearest dividing line. With the modern school of speculative enterprise, so often tainted by dishonour, the Gilds have neither kinship nor sympathy ; and this may be predicated, perhaps, with peculiar force of the greater ones, which not only hold themselves aloof from dubious principles and undertakings, but exclude from their fellowship and their table thousands of individuals who are conspicuous figures in London commercial life. These two types are like two streams, which flow side by side, and do not mingle.

General survey of the question. Speaking generally, and stating the case broadly and fairly, the City Gilds offer themselves to our notice and criticism as communities which started under colour of being, above all things, eleemosynary in their constitution and spirit, yet which were, at the same time, essentially mercantile in their constituent parts and corporate feeling. Their religious and charitable programme recommended them, in the eyes of pious or benevolent testators, as the most appropriate and secure trustees or recipients of legacies, large or small ; and for centuries, while they dispensed alms and relief pursuantly to their professions and to the terms of bequests, they amassed wealth by commerce, and acquired an enormous property in reserve at inconsiderable cost. Their rise in financial and political importance made the ratification of their acts and *status* by our kings little more than a question of toll. It was a compact between the Crown and these associations for their mutual advantage. The unlimited nature of the royal prerogative left out of account the prospective or even the current interests of the general community ; nor was it humanly possible to foresee the progressive advance in the value of metropolitan land and sites, which confers on the City Companies, in spite of the most serious and repeated misfortunes, their actual vantage-ground. The treaties made in former days were, after all, agreeable to contemporary policy, custom, and convenience.

Cui bono? A judicial consideration of the relationship of the City Gilds to the general community, and of their public obligation in respect of a revision of their constitution, leaves us with a very narrow argument and a very poor one, if it should happen to be our cue or our mission to advocate such a change. Indeed, when we see that it can only be a question of the corporate income, since of the trusts the Companies are mere unpaid administrators at a pecuniary sacrifice, and that of this private revenue a very large quota is annually devoted to the augmentation or extension of trusts, it is difficult to know on what ground a new scheme could be introduced and defended ; for all individual opinions as to the modes in which the Companies think fit to bestow their money are really irrelevant and futile from an official and statutory point of view. It has to be ever borne in mind that the Companies are in lawful possession, and that the burden of proof lies with others ; and no Parliament which is likely to sit at Westminster would or could, in the face of the most positive evidence as to the indefeasible character of the Companies' non-trust property, listen to any factious cry for confiscation under the cloak of reform, even assuming that the system of management could be shown to be in some respects defective or unsatisfactory.

A word with Parliament.   With how much greater force the argument which has been more than once brought into employment against the Corporation and the Gilds applies to those members of both Houses of Parliament to whose inspiration, or at any rate, to the concurrence of many of whom, the Royal Commission was due! These noblemen and gentlemen, in such cases as are most noteworthy, acquired their property under circumstances precisely analogous to those which placed the civic bodies in possession of theirs. In both instances the pecuniary value was comparatively, if not absolutely, trifling at and long after the date of entrance upon it; and in both cases the national industry and prosperity made it and them what it is, and what they are. The difference occurs, when we compare the stewardship of the City with that of the great capitalists and owners in Parliament. "*Physician, heal thyself!*" Let a Royal Commission issue to report to the nation upon the property of the Dukes of Westminster, Bedford, and Portland, the Marquis Camden, Earl Cadogan, Lord Portman, and a few more. For if redistribution is to be granted, it must be granted all round.

Adaptation to changed circumstances. The times have changed, and the Corporation of London, with all that is attached to it and interconnected with its life, has perceived the need of moving forward, as those who stand still in an advancing crowd are liable to be trodden down and left behind. But the principle of admission to the Gilds by purchase had already caused those bodies to assume a modified complexion, and had strengthened their hands by the admixture of foreign blood, so to speak, and by the broadening of their constitutions. For Parliament, in dealing with them, began to find that it had to reckon upon the opposition of a large number of influential persons, many of them members of one or other of the Chambers; and even the practice of enrolling honorary Gildsmen in consideration of their literary, artistic, or royal pretensions, operated to a certain extent in a similar way, in lending an atmosphere to

the ancient *régime*, and identifying it with the existing age
and with general society. The City *scored* prodigiously when
it threw aside its invisible mantle and ceased to be altogether
a close borough. This, if we may be permitted to say so, is
likely to prove the safety-valve of the Corporation and the
Companies. The less mysterious and exclusive they shew
themselves, the greater will be their prosperity and longevity.
Such a policy will be the best barrier against Socialism.

Public opinion should be cultivated and welcomed by the
Companies in the time before us, as the sweet air, which will
alone keep them green and flourishing. There is always the
danger, where information is withheld, of something more than
the truth being suspected, and of a sentiment of distrust and
resentment being employed by a party or a clique for their
own particular purposes. A liberal policy and a frank and
open hand are the clear safeguards of these institutions
hereafter.

II.

Conditions
favouring and
influencing
establishment.
3. The period within which the majority of the
Gilds had their first rise was one in which protection and companionship were apt to be eminently
conducive to the successful pursuit and development of commerce. In an imperfectly organized society, and with the
authority of the Crown far from thoroughly consolidated, union
and co-operation among men of the same calling were great
sources of security ; and these fraternities, existing, as we find,
in an unofficial state long before they obtained recognition
and rank as chartered bodies, enjoyed the means of affording
each other mutual assistance and support, more especially
where, as was usually the case, their hands were still further
strengthened by the accession of persons of standing, who

were not craftsmen, but sought membership on independent grounds.

Germ of the Gilds.   The rudimentary nucleus or germ of the Gilds was undoubtedly that principle of the old law, which exacted a guarantee for his good behaviour from every free-man on the attainment of his fourteenth year, or from his guardians, and which seemed to necessitate, not only for the payment of this *geld*, but for any contingencies arising out of apprenticeship or servitude, the formation and maintenance of a common purse.

Its constitution.   The graduated constitution of the Gild was an almost necessary corollary of its mode of development. Its mercantile and adventurous attributes were a super-structure on its primitive object and function as an industrial union and safeguard. It happened, no doubt, in this, as in numerous other instances, that the original promoters of the idea in London did not entertain any notion of overstepping the limits at first laid down, and would have viewed with excessive surprise the advance beyond them which had been made even in the time of the Edwards (1272–1377), when the aristocratic element, in the form of the municipal dignitary and capitalist, had already assumed supreme control over the movement, and converted what was in its inception a scheme of humble pretensions and narrow scope into a prominent constitutional feature and an important agent in the financial transactions of the realm.

Protectionist spirit.   Throughout the ordinances and regulations framed by or for the various Companies, it can be no source of astonishment to meet with a consistent and uncompromising protectionist spirit. This was the policy and feeling on the part of all traders in former days, and has not even yet lost its weight in England, while on the Continent and in the United States it survives in undiminished force and

repute.   As the eye runs through the proclamations, acts of
Parliament, and the bye-laws of the Gilds themselves, it is one
unvarying cry of exclusion of the foreign competitor or of
his admittance at a disadvantage, which we encounter ; and we
believe that, if the Government of the present day would go
with it, the City is sufficiently conservative to return, in certain respects and to some extent, to the old-fashioned platform.

But the law of supply and demand is among ourselves
supreme, and it merely resolves itself into the dual question of
production and consumption.   The time may come, however,
when education will teach the community something in this
direction, and when the low-priced continental fabrics of all
kinds will not find so free a sale.   They represent all that is
unwholesome and false in social and commercial economy.

The rigorous protectionist principle, however, which governed
these associations, and which in the course of centuries was
temporarily relaxed only under urgent or special circumstances,
rendered such an alliance and brotherhood among the followers
of the same calling, as would at present prove a hindrance and
an anachronism, expedient and advantageous from every point
of view.

Causes condu-   The need for approximation and fellowship, which
cive to asso-
   ciation.   appear in almost all cases to have preceded the
prayer for a charter, naturally followed the absence of ready
means of intercourse with distant persons and places and with
each other in times of imperfect and rudimentary legislation,
scanty appliances of all kinds, and general illiteracy ; and these
formed the causes of a resort to common, in preference to
personal, action.

Again, membership of a Gild produced a natural bond of
affection and confidence on the part of each man toward his
fellows ; and where there were no representatives he turned, as
a matter of course, to the corporate and perpetual institution

whereto he had belonged during life, and perhaps his father before him, and saw in it the means of transmitting his name and securing the application of his property to its appointed objects.

Its benefits. The tie thus created gave facilities, keenly appreciable in those days, for commercial and private intercourse ; and when enfranchisement and endowment were gradually conferred on the Companies, there was a tolerably efficient machinery for keeping at a distance the domestic, and still more the foreign, interloper. The leagues or trades' unions were offensive as well as defensive, and for a long season acted their part, and operated beneficially. Their original *rôle* is mere matter of history. Our country has left them in this sense behind, and has laid down other lines for all of us. The rest of the world retains its old traditions, and has to consider whether it will hereafter follow our leadership. But the Gilds stand on an equally solid, though on a different, basis as part of our polity and life ; and the trades have found other methods of promoting their interests and vindicating their pretensions.

Balancing drawbacks. The means of self-defence which this species of combination supplied were of course at the best very inadequate to resist forcible encroachment and spoliation. Union in some shape was indispensable from causes which have been explained ; and it followed that, in unsettled times under an arbitrary monarchical government, the very machinery and fellowship which on so many accounts proved a source of strength and success was apt, at critical conjunctures, to prove an element of danger and weakness. When the Crown learned the easy lesson of treating the Gilds as milch kine, bodies were found to be more vulnerable than individuals ; and our kings were wholly exempt from scruple when money was required, and unblushingly ignored the charters which they or their lawful predecessors had granted, and for which pecuniary consideration had been obtained. No pirate or sharper was more callous, more mean, and more cruel than sacred majesties of bygone days ; and among them the " Merry Monarch " and his brother may be probably regarded as having borne the bell.

The two chief impediments to the progress and welfare of the Gilds, as the trade and wealth of the country developed in the time of Elizabeth, were indeed the extortions of the Crown and Court, in the shape of benevolences, loans, and disbursements for unprofitable speculations, on the one hand, and on the other the system of patents and monopolies, which, during the rule of the heartless, profligate, and venal Stuarts, crippled legitimate commerce. No form or channel of plunder escaped the harpies who surrounded the throne, and who usually farmed to others their share of the prey.

Foreign source of our Gilds. 4. The rise of a vast number of civic and provincial associations, with their subsequent partial evolution into chartered Gilds, was probably due to continental influence and example, more particularly to the precedents set in the Low Countries and in Italy, with which the relationship of our English traders was, from a very remote epoch, constant and extensive. With a view to the establishment of commercial industries and *entrepôts*, involving unavoidable and large pecuniary risk, the primary need of union and protection was very soon discerned. The merchants, who transacted their affairs in what was then the business centre, the neighbourhood of Thames Street and East Cheap, were in many cases not even denizens, but French, Italian, Dutch, or German settlers, Jews included, among us ; and those who were English by birthright claimed by the nature of their employments an exemption from the various feudal services imposed on ordinary civilians in the Middle Ages. They therefore necessarily clustered in those places which were suitable, at once by position and privileges, to their wants and callings, and they thus constituted throughout the free ports of the kingdom a vast community, independent of military and other kindred obligations, and internally governed by their own ordinances.

The ancient trading Companies.

An interesting and profitable subject for investigation and study would be the relationship between the Gilds, at and long after their commencement, and those other commercial unions which monopolized the import and export trades, and constituted an indispensable adjunct to the manufacturers and salesmen at home. All these associations, such as the Easterlings of the so-called Steelyard in Thames Street, the Hanse colony in Bishopsgate, the Merchants of the Staple, the Merchants Adventurers, and others which we have elsewhere enumerated, had their headquarters in the heart of the City proper. The vicinity of the river side was a great centre of activity; Billingsgate is mentioned as far back as 1299 as a point whence goods were shipped abroad; Queen-hithe was another lading and landing stage; and it was doubtless through the foreign and English mercantile communities, whose vessels touched at all then known or frequented ports, that the London Gilds, as a rule, engaged in speculative enterprises, rather than deal in their own bottoms with distant countries. A knowledge of foreign navigation and languages conferred in this respect an advantage on the Easterlings and their successors, who were formerly, to a large extent, the proprietors of the "petty traffickers" and "rich burghers of the flood."

London life. The more special student of this one side or aspect of earlier London life rises from his task with a very powerful impression of the vast multiplicity and complication of interests, which in bygone days perpetually engaged the attention of the municipal government, and rendered the conduct of public affairs infinitely more onerous and delicate than at present, when changes in the law, in the structural condition of the metropolis, and in the habits of the people, have done so much to improve and simplify the working machinery, and of course to lighten the responsibilities of the Corporation. The pulse of London cannot have beaten less quickly and proudly, but it was differently regulated.

A new era in our commercial history.   With the reign of Edward III. (1327–1377) a very marked impulse was given to our commerce, and the necessity for organizing on a clearer and firmer basis the existing trading fraternities followed as an inevitable consequence. Between the opening and close of that long reign an immense improvement and expansion were witnessed in all branches of manufacture and industry.

Foreign wars beneficial to the Gilds.   It is not difficult to see how the rise and consolidation of the Gilds, as part of a great municipal system, were largely aided by the feebleness of the Crown as a central executive authority, arising, through the reigns of the Plantagenet kings, from their constant habit of changing their headquarters, and from their long series of foreign wars.

Enfranchisement of the London trades.   The successive enfranchisement of the trades of London, with the concession in due course of *inspeximus* or new charters, is found to run parallel with the chronic financial embarrassment of the Crown through misgovernment or through lavish expenditure on military equipments ; and the City became, and remained during centuries, when all other channels had failed, the great resource of monarchs in straits. From a very early date, the Corporation and Gilds adopted the principle of receiving security in some shape or other for money lent or given ; and it would be an enormous total, if we could put down on paper the aggregate cost to London from first to last of its privileges and property.

Obscurity of origin.   All such associations as those which we are considering and describing have a natural difficulty in tracing their primary starting-time and the exact circumstances which first gave them distinct form and being. Their obscurity and insignificance during the earlier stages of development, and their peaceful employment within a limited area, help to account for the absence of records of their transactions and progress, till they arise to our notice as institutions professedly of lengthened standing and prescriptive rank. Their establishment "out of memory" was almost invariably accepted as a ground for the eventual concession of a charter or letters patent; the expression signified the inability of the applicants to adduce precise legal evidence of their title beyond common tradition and report, the very vagueness of which had its virtue.

Constitution of the Gild.   5. The normal constitution of a Livery Gild embraces a Master, Wardens, a Court of Assistants, a Livery, and the general body of Freemen. To them used to be added the Apprentices, making altogether six grades.

The MASTER was originally nothing more than the Master or Upper Warden; and the Fishmongers and Goldsmiths still retain this notion or principle, and term their chief executive officer *Prime Warden*. The Cooks' charter gave them two masters. The Vintners long remained without one, and were governed by four Wardens : the *Upper* and *Junior*, the *Renter* and the *Swan*, Wardens. Some Companies have only three, some only two, of these functionaries.

The ASSISTANTS derive their appellation from their original and existing duty as an auxiliary committee to co-operate with the Wardens.

The LIVERY is so called from the ancient practice of periodical delivery of clothing to this body. In some cases the junior members are called *Bachelors*.

The Yeomanry.
The general or, as they are designated in the Clothworkers' Gild, *diffusive* body of freemen are otherwise known as the *Yeomanry* or *Commonalty*, and occasionally succeeded in putting sufficient pressure on the Court to obtain independent Wardens for the management of all minor points of detail and discipline. But the experiment was rarely of long duration.

Although the freedom or yeomanry in many cases formed in course of time a numerous body, and preponderated in extent over the rest of the Gild, it was in its practical origin, if not in the spirit of the movement, an outlying portion of the semi-religious, semi-commercial congregation, not only destitute of executive authority, but unentitled to vesture ; and the express mention in several of the charters and in all the Ordinances of these brotherhoods of the livery of clothing, and the emphasis laid on its pattern and colours, with the very particular reference to it in an ancient chronicle of the reign of Edward II. as marking an era in the history and progress of the Gilds, satisfy us that it was regarded by the leading members alike as a distinctive emblem and as a constitutional boundary. The apparel was an article of faith and a token of caste ; it at once served as an element of union and a medium of control. Those outside the clothing might by election be lifted up into it, but the recruiting process was slow and limited ; and we see that in some of the larger Companies the yeomanry became so much an independent class, that they sought to have their own separate administrative officers, and sometimes proved so grave a source of inconvenience and discomfort to their oli-garchical superiors, that the latter mooted the expediency of a thorough and permanent severance.

Source of their discontent.
These remarks may amount to another mode of saying that at a very early stage in the annals and career of the Gilds an attentive observer might have detected

an inherent tendency on their part to diverge from their original gospel and *rôle*, and, whereas the incidence of apprenticeship was the very essence and foundation of their being, to develop a cliental and charitable principle into a sub-municipal auto-cracy, and to spurn, when its support was no longer needed, the ladder by which they had climbed to power.

A plea for the governing bodies.

At the same time we must keep in sight the growing changes in social feeling and mercantile life, which tended, as years passed, to loosen the old bond between the class to which the upper sections of the Gilds belonged and that from which the yeomanry sprang ; and the progress of legislation, following the impulse of more modern thought, favoured the revolt of the inferior and less privileged branches of each of these Companies from a type of jurisdiction, which was apt to survive longer among such as exercised than among such as were asked to obey it.

Patrimony disadvanta-geous to the yeomanry.

Again, the admittance of females or sisters to the freedom, and to succession by patrimony, had a natural tendency to deprive of its faculty of coherence and organization a body incessantly and progres-sively increasing by the ordinary law of nature, and to trans-form the yeomanry of both sexes into a body of such incalcu-lable dimensions, that the Company itself was unable to furnish exact figures. It is not extraordinary that an element in the constitution, so incompact and unwieldy, parted with its signi-ficance and weight, and resolved itself into a passive object of nominal membership and charitable relief.

The Ordinances.

6. The letters patent, licences, and charters obtained by the Gilds were as between them and the Crown. But, independently of them, for the due control of their internal affairs and the protection of their class or corporate interests, Ordinances invariably followed at a shorter

or longer interval, and were periodically renewed. These regulations were originally framed by the Associations on their own authority; but we shall see that this practice grew inconvenient and invidious, owing to clauses being inserted contrary to the public welfare, and that the sanction of the Court of Aldermen was made imperative. This precaution, however, notwithstanding, several statutes, commencing with 15 Henry VI., restrained the governing bodies under penalties from making any rules in diminution of the royal prerogative or against the common profit of the people.

Licences in Mortmain. The exemption from the Statute of Mortmain, which forms a clause, in the majority of instances, in the charters, and variously occurs with and without a limit, or with a progressive power in successive grants, could only apply to freehold lands not subject to military service; but the principal bequests or devises of this character occurred at a period when the feudal system had been relaxed, the early acquisitions being almost exclusively within the confines of the City, and being independent of such obligations. The Gilds were disqualified from taking copyholds, or even customary freeholds, where there was a reserved rent of any kind, although at the Reformation the Crown in some cases sold or handed back their property to these Corporations at precisely such a rent over and above the purchase-money. On the other hand, the Colet estate at Stepney, being copyhold, the heirs successfully contested the title of the Mercers to it; and it was ultimately re-conveyed to the Company by a circuitous process and, no doubt, at considerable expense.

The Power of Search. The power of Search, which was an almost invariable incidence of the grant of Ordinances even to an unchartered brotherhood, though of questionable legality, led, in cases of discovery of improper practices, to the presentment of the offence by the overseers to the Mayor's Court, and to the issue of a summons to attend in answer. The faculty did not generally extend farther than the freedom, but in a few exceptional cases it was general ; while, on the contrary, some of the Companies never possessed it in any measure.   It naturally differed in its scope according to the residential and other features of the craft ; but it was, as may be readily conceived, an outgrowth from the primitive and long-continued practice of operatives carrying on their work within a certain radius in their own homes, as we have seen in our time the weavers do both in London and the provinces. The visiting duties or surveillance of the Wardens of the Gild were superseded, when home-labour gave place by degrees to factories and sheds.

Feudalism.   The exoneration from ordinary feudal services was qualified and more than balanced by various forms of commutation, both municipal and imperial.   The Plantagenets, to a certain extent, and after them in heavier measure the Tudors and Stuarts, considered that the Corporation and Companies were banks, on which they might draw at will.   It was possible, while the system prevailed, to enforce the performance of certain duties as an equivalent for the tenure of property ; but the City, which claimed the right of holding in free burgage, was viewed, as the wealth of its denizens became conspicuous, as a collateral factor of special value in another direction, and as peculiarly amenable to pressure from the immense stake which it held under the sufferance of an arbitrary monarchy.

The municipality and its adjuncts, however, if they did not discharge the duties of subjects resident outside the boundaries in a direct and personal manner, did not escape even this kind of tribute ; for it was levied in the shape of periodical requisitions from the sovereign for the equipment and support of a quota of soldiers, and even of ships and seamen, on all emergencies.   At home, so to speak, in addition to normal burdens,

the Gilds were taxed from a very remote date for the purpose
of laying up stores of grain against a bad harvest, and of
husbanding coal between Lady Day and Michaelmas, in order
to re-sell it to the poor of the City at a loss ; while several,
if not all, had calls made upon them to take their turns in
providing the armed watches for the respective gates. The
Ironmongers and others, as we shall find, maintained their own
armoury chiefly on this account.

III.

The word mistery.

The ordinary orthography of the term *mystery*
is calculated to favour an erroneous impression on
the part of those who do not remember that the true word
is mistery, the old French *maistre* and *maistrie* having been
translated indifferently into English *master* and *mister, mastery*
or *mistery*. Mistery, mester, maistrie, are all closely allied to
mestier or *métier*, a trade. These trading unions were in fact
expert craftsmen, and were totally distinct from the mysteries
of the ancients and of the mediæval period. The enrolment of
them under the tutelary patronage of the Saviour, the Virgin,
or a saint, was a common form of sanction and security from
the earliest period, and one which has not yet, in the eyes of
some, parted with its significance. Commercial and religious
life was bound up together in a far greater degree among our
forefathers ; and it was unusual to undertake transactions or to
decide on any measure without the presumed approbation of
the Unseen. We note how vestiges of this feeling linger in
the municipal habit of assembling in prayer prior to certain
electoral ceremonies.

Apparel. The distinctive apparel of the Gilds, to which
Chaucer refers in a familiar passage, was a symbolism pic-
turesquely characteristic of the old time, when all arrangements

were in keeping with the conservative sentiment discernible throughout the entire costume of these commercial brotherhoods. The dress formed part of the prevailing spirit of freemasonry, which dictated a rigid adherence to external insignia as much as to other prescribed or customary usages. A vintner did not presume to wear the livery of a grocer, or a freeman of a warden, any more than either ventured to infringe the ordinances of his craft, or to cross the lines of his charter. The vesture was part of the constitution of the Gild, the outward and visible sign of membership and graduated dignity; nor, when we find two of these Corporations exchanging vestures on special occasions and to a limited extent, was it other than a token of that fraternal reciprocity and affection which knit yet more closely the bond between these societies by one of the most sacred of trusts and most exalted of privileges, a community of garb?

The language of many ancient documents corroborates the view that the mere uniformity of garb or vesture which conferred on the Gilds the designation of Livery Companies may be taken to have an underlying religious significance, and to have been, perhaps unconsciously and intuitively, adopted in imitation of the practice of monastic bodies, with the modification suitable to groups of laymen dedicating themselves only in part to the service of God. At the same time, it is more than doubtful whether in their inception the Companies, as voluntary societies, adopted such a method of distinguishing themselves from the ordinary community and from each other. In the original grants there is no reference to them under the style of Livery Companies; but it is on record that the practice of attiring themselves similarly began to gain favour even so far back as the reign of Edward II. Such external symbols of identity have become superfluous; yet the state of society and education once and long rendered them essential.

Amalgamating   When the first or initial stage had been reached
movement.   and completed by the embodiment of the industrial
world of London City under certain divisions, each governed
and fortified by its own charter or bye-laws, or both, a second
process is found to have gradually matured and accrued, by
which the several branches of a department of business were
consolidated in one great executive and municipal *integer*, and
the conduct of the affairs was at once rendered less costly and
more effective.

Thus the Armourers knit together in a single fraternity the
minor contributory crafts, such as the Bladesmiths on the one
hand and on the other the Braziers and Potters; the Shearmen
and Fullers reconstituted themselves under the name of Clothworkers; the Marblers and Lapidaries on the one hand and the
Paviours on the other were lost in the Masons; the Sheathers,
if not the Furbishers, became incorporated with the Cutlers, the
Spurriers with the Loriners, the Silkmen with the Mercers, the
Tawyers and White Tawyers with the Skinners or Curriers,
the Stringers with the Bowyers; while the Drapers or
Haberdashers took over, so to speak, the Hosiers, Hatters,
Cappers, and Brace-makers. The Grocers gradually absorbed,
so far as independent concerted action went, the group of
subsidiary interconnected industries, originally represented and
protected by the Pepperers, the Spicers, the Soap-makers, the
Starch-makers, the Cheese and Butter-mongers, the Sugar-
bakers, and the Druggists. The last severed themselves in
1617 under the title of Apothecaries, and during a long period
monopolized the trade in tea, coffee, and other dear specialities, as they continued in certain places abroad to do down
to a recent date. But of course no single craft, even in its
amplified shape, undertook either the manufacture or sale of
articles outside its legitimate province, except the Haberdasher
and Grocer, whose shops became general emporia, even in

Plantagenet days, for all sorts of minor miscellaneous wares, and the Upholder, who was *ex officio* a second-hand dealer in the earlier stage, according to the testimony of Stow.

Its advantages. The simplification and economy of management and control, where the interests concerned were sufficiently cognate to be capable of becoming or being made common, naturally recommended themselves to communities forced to stand for ever on their defence, and exposed to all kinds of vexatious requisitions and embarrassing ordinances. Experience must have shown them their chronic liability, under an arbitrary government and a somewhat vacillating and timid municipal system, to oppression, impoverishment, and even ruin, and the urgent need for consolidation and unity.

Incorporation. The final consummation was the evolutionary development of limited survivals into corporate bodies, more or less removed from their primitive functions and traditions by the force of unforeseen circumstances, which launched them on a new carecr, as beneficiaries in fee or trust under numberless wills, as well as by a happy concurrence of events, and which left it optional on their part whether they would sever themselves from their ancient callings and employments or otherwise. The majority, as we know, sooner or later elected to dissolve old ties, and to enter upon a new life, in which the wealth, fortuitously accumulated by vast internal changes in a very narrow area, and by judicious husbandry, experienced redistribution in a variety of ways, mainly equitable and benevolent. A few of the Gilds, on the contrary, and most notably the Clothworkers, have not deserted their former associations, and appropriate princely sums to the advancement of the industry over which they once exclusively presided. This Company stands in the peculiarly honourable and special position of having, irrespectively of its own direct pecuniary interests, stepped forward as the patron and friend of the Yorkshire

wool and cloth trade, rather than as having merely fostered
it from local inducements.

The Ulster   7. Circumstances of a political character in fact
Plantation.   combined, after a while, to impart to these civic
organizations far more important functions than those with
which they at the outset charged themselves. For not only
the spirit of commercial and maritime adventure afforded scope
for the employment of capital, but the transfers of landed
estates, especially in the north of Ireland, in Londonderry and
Coleraine, during the reign of James I., formed an outlet for
money and a field for speculation which proved in the end
fairly satisfactory, but lay long dormant and unprofitable.

Origin of the   As far back as 1608, James I. and his advisers,
Revenue.   having to deal with the question of settling or
colonizing the counties of Armagh, Tyrone, Coleraine, Done-
gal, Fermanagh, and Cavan, which formed the theatre in the
latter part of the reign of Elizabeth of a rebellion against the
English Crown on the part of certain prominent and powerful
Irish noblemen or chieftains, had published a schedule of orders
and conditions to be observed by the undertakers, as well as
a statement of the nature of the property to be allotted. The
pamphlet was for general circulation, and originally all his
majesty's subjects were at liberty to enter into the scheme.
Several offers were made in consequence by private persons ;
but the king changed his purpose so far as to decide upon seeking to persuade the City of London to embrace the project,
and caused a second statement to be prepared for this special
purpose, under the title of " Motives and Reasons to induce the
City to Undertake the Plantation in the North of Ireland."

This counter-proposal was at first rejected ; but as James
proved importunate, the twelve great Companies were invited
to select a competent number of their most substantial members,

each choosing four persons, to deliberate on the question, and report their views to the king in writing. There was still considerable backwardness in entertaining the question; committees were formed, and visited Ireland to judge the value of the speculation on the spot; certain interrogatories were addressed to the Lord Deputy in relation to the estimated outlay and profit; and the end was, that on January 28, 1609–10, a preliminary contract was signed in London, and was read at Guildhall on the 30th.

At the outset, it was arranged that the Plantation should be administered by a Governor, Deputy-governor, and twenty-four Assistants, following the lines of the Gilds; that the Recorder and five of the Aldermen of London for the time being should be *ex officio* members of the court; and that the Deputy-governor and the remainder of the court should be free of the City.

Change of Plan. The Irish Society.　This was the body subsequently known as the Irish Society. For some time it carried on the management of the estate with funds supplied by the several Companies interested; but there seems to have been some difficulty, which led to the transfer of the property in 1613 to the Companies and the concession of a charter. Under this fresh departure all the moneys were to be divided into twelve portions; each Company was to represent a portion, and if so desired might associate with it one or more of the minor Companies, the interest being reckoned proportionably; and a new survey of the lands was to be undertaken, with a view to equalizing the twelve shares as nearly as possible. For these shares the Companies drew lots.

Undivided Residue.　But a residue of the estate, having been pronounced not easily apportionable, was never vested in the Companies, and remained under the control of the Irish Society for their common and several benefit. Under the charter of 1613 this body received a licence to hold and grant lands and hereditaments, and was described as the " Society of the Governor and Assistants, London, of the New Plantation in Ulster within the Realm of Ireland." The territory over which its jurisdiction extended was erected into a new and independent county of Londonderry.

Licence in Mortmain.   Two years later (September 30, 1615) the king, by letters patent, granted the Society and the Companies a licence in mortmain, that the latter might be encouraged to proceed and finish the Plantation, and in future time reap some gain and benefit from their trouble and expense.

Value and purchase-money.   The lands thus transferred to the twelve Livery Gilds, were estimated to produce at the time (1608–15) 1,800*l.* a year. The price was 60,000*l.* = 5,000*l.* for each subscriber, or about twenty-nine years' purchase.

Revocation of Charter by Star Chamber.   The unprincipled and cowardly despotism of the Stuarts was exemplified in the decree of the Star Chamber which repudiated and annulled the charter of 1615, and necessarily crippled the power of the proprietors, until the act was rescinded as unlawful and unjust by the Long Parliament in 1641.

Restoration by Cromwell.   On March 24, 1656, the grant was restored by letters patent of the Protector Cromwell, and the Companies' estates were re-conveyed to them by the Society. The latter, shortly after the Restoration, was re-incorporated, with another re-grant of the property to the several feoffees (April 10, 1662).

Later history.   Since that time, such Companies as have not parted with them have remained in peaceful enjoyment of their possessions, which, however, have in no case been, on the whole, very advantageous or profitable, owing to the immense expenses incurred in litigation and improvements. The Merchant Taylors, who let their Irish venture go, it appears, in 1727, stood alone, we believe, in subscribing for one full manor and a portion of another. The Clothworkers sold their Irish property for 150,000*l.*, and the Grocers for about the same amount, redemption of tithes inclusive. The Ironmongers have quite recently parted with theirs under less advantageous conditions.

The Sub-shares. In several cases, the detachment of sub-shares made the original outlay less onerous to the great Companies; but when they disposed of their possessions at a fortunate juncture, they suffered through the natural claim of the smaller contributories to participate proportionably in the advantages of the sale.

Of all the Companies, even after reckoning the drawback of 40,000*l.* paid over to the Stationers to extinguish their claim and the Girdlers' share, the Skinners seem to have succeeded best in turning the Ulster speculation to good account, judging from the increase in the rents returned in 1882. This may have arisen from the Company enjoying the benefit of having had in its members many practical surveyors, who visited the domain personally. But the Salters also found it possible and expedient to buy out the Dyers and the Saddlers for 83,000*l.*, and to expend a very large sum in improvements. These, with the Mercers, are almost the only survivals of the Ulster Plantation as it was originally constituted and apportioned.

Litigation. Owing to litigation, very little has been received by the Companies from the surplus undivided property retained in trust by the Irish Society, comprising portions of the towns of Londonderry and Coleraine, woods, fisheries, ferries, and waste.

The venture, from which in some respects the Companies would have done well to have kept aloof, agreeably to their first determination, continued to afford them ground for anxiety and a constant outlet for money, until, as we have said, some of them parted with their shares under fairly auspicious conditions, and others succeeded in rendering the speculation at length reproductive, while at least in one instance the opportunity was missed, and the sale was effected on less favourable terms.

Difference between the Gild and the Trades'Union. 8. We have described these Gilds as Mutual Benefit associations, at first voluntary, then governed by Wardens and a code of bye-laws alike

approved by the Corporation, and eventually established under the protection and control of a charter. But while they answered in some respects to the modern trades' union, in two important particulars they differed from it, inasmuch as they did not presume to regulate the hours or price of labour, and had a restricted jurisdiction over the selling scale of commodities, in which they were interested as manufacturers or retailers. There they were bound by the law, as interpreted by acts of Parliament, by royal proclamation, or by civic usage.

Wages. As regarded wages in very early times (1350), the masons, carpenters, and plaisterers appear to have stood on the same footing, and to have had from 5d. to 6d. a day, without food, according to the season; the tilers earned from 4$\frac{1}{2}d$. to 5$\frac{1}{2}d$.; and the ordinary labourer 3d. This scale was laid down by the Mayor, and any one not observing it was liable to a penalty of 40s.

Plurality. Originally persons followed more than one trade, or changed their line of business. In 1402, Thomas Dufhous, brewer, was admitted of the fellowship of Fishmongers, on the ground that he had long followed the latter trade, and was known for a reputable citizen. Some few years later, in 1416, Alderman Richard Merlawe, who represented that he had for some time past belonged to the two trades of ironmongery and fishmongery, and had taken livery or vesture of both crafts, now, in accordance with a new ordinance of the Mayor and Aldermen, that no one should be of more than a single fraternity, elected and prayed to be of the Fishmongers' brotherhood alone, and was therefore admitted to the freedom and vesture or Livery of the same.

Admittance of Strangers.   But the practice of admitting other than members of the trade which the Company represented was of very early date, even among some of the greater Gilds ; and the persons so introduced were strangers as well as followers of different vocations.   This class of freemen was practically honorary, or at all events outside the scheme ; and as this departure from the original design is shown by records to go back to the first half of the fifteenth century, we seem to be entitled to presume that a more ambitious programme and basis struck the municipal authorities as practicable and expedient, even within the Plantagenet epoch, and that from what had been first a purely commercial idea of a rather humble type evolved in process of time one of the most opulent, influential, and enduring political federations in the world.

The Gild the forerunner of the Poorhouse and Hospital.   The source and explanation of the moneys and properties left to the Gilds to charitable uses are obviously to be found in the deficiency of our early municipal institutions and the absence of any system of poor relief.   At the time when many of the benefactions had been devised to these fraternities, even the hospitals, such as Bethlehem and Bartholomew's, which afterward sheltered the lower grades of vagrant and beggar, and gave them temporary aid or sustenance, were neither numerous nor efficient for the purpose ; and of accommodation and help for persons of both sexes in a somewhat more reputable sphere there was an absolute want.

Reasons for confidence in it.   The financial and social aggrandisement of many of the Companies, and their consequent divergence from their original *raison d'être*, may be readily traced to the development of a feeling on the part of citizens, and even strangers, in the old state of the laws affecting benefactions and charities, that these institutions formed the safest depositories for money left in trust or otherwise for superstitious, eleemosynary, and educational purposes.   There were no bodies formerly existing, when nearly all the Gilds were successively established, so well calculated to administer and protect funds lodged in their hands for periodical distribution and specific benevolence ; and this was as much the case in the provinces as in the metropolis, and without the City as within its confines.

Acquisition of real property.   It was not from the amount in specie, however, that the Gilds derived their chief advantage, but from lands and tenements of small worth at the period, and which it required the lapse of centuries and patient endurance of successive vicissitudes and reverses to ripen into what they appear to us all in modern balance-sheets.

IV.

Departure from original design and professions.   We see that it is only those Companies which succeeded in removing themselves to a long distance from their original *rôle* as trade guarantee and protection societies, and in holding their ground in the presence and spite of all imaginable difficulties and discouragements, that remain to-day in the foremost rank.   The rest have to be satisfied with a secondary position and influence ; and a few have, even within a measurable period, suffered extinction. The conditions of apprenticeship and commercial supervision, under which they first rose, have gradually undergone so organic a change, that these institutions could not possibly preserve much vitality or general usefulness in adhering to the primitive lines ; and it would not be difficult, of course, to point out some which depend for their survivorship on one or two modest rentals, on a scanty revenue arising from fees and fines, or even on private subscriptions.

Exceptional success of certain bodies.   While they yet preserved their ancient attributes, it was those bodies which ministered to the embellishment of the person and to female vanity which the most signally prospered. The Mercers, the Drapers, the Merchant Taylors, the Goldsmiths, the Cloth-workers, the Skinners, the Haberdashers survived and overcame the most stupendous reverses, and remained possessed of great wealth. Then, again, the Grocers represent a federation of trades, most of which have always been highly remunerative, appealing to manifold daily requirements ; and finally, by way of example, the Fishmongers, trafficking during centuries, even before they were incorporated, in an industry of a national character, when our diet was more modified than at present by religious observances, found themselves, in the middle of the fourteenth century, second only to the Mercers in opulence and consideration.

Suggested Consolidation of the minor Companies. The position of such of the minor Companies as do not possess a place of meeting and business is sufficiently unfortunate and unsatisfactory to warrant a respectful suggestion that some concerted movement might be made by them for forming a federal union for official and representative purposes, and of employing a Common Clerk, who should be a gentleman capable, by his training, knowledge, and experience, of managing their affairs and protecting their interests.

The present executive officers of a few of these smaller corporations form a painful and striking contrast to the urbane and straightforward attitude of the greater, and of many indeed of the less leading, Companies. These gentlemen may have nothing to communicate ; but their address is apt to foster a suspicion that they have something to conceal.

Assuming that no such combination is possible, however, the next best plan will be for them to profit by the example set by the preponderating majority (at least in weight and consequence) of the Companies.

Further modification possible. 9. The decay of apprenticeship, and other fundamental changes in commercial life and sentiment, may ultimately lead to still further modifications of the Livery Companies, and to a thorough divestment in many instances of the attributes and claims with which they began and justified their existence. Those which possess both trust and corporate estates of considerable and permanent value will resolve themselves into virtual oligarchies of a philanthropic character, in which even the Liveries will find their influence by little and little abridged ; while such as have no estates, or property of insignificant extent, will become little more than social clubs under an old-fashioned name. Nor is it by any means impossible that the Gilds may hereafter elect to dissolve, and to divide their private possessions among the members, leaving the Imperial Government to manage the remainder at the public expense. We do not say that they would do unwisely.

Such a contingency the outcome of external changes. We do not allege or imply that the Gilds would have acted more discreetly and advantageously by popularizing their constitutions in compliance with modern ideas and demands. For the whole current of feeling and opinion has been diverted into new channels ; and their sole resource and best defence are undoubtedly to be found in the policy on which so many of them have entered, of rendering their surplus revenues applicable to existing social objects and needs on the latest lines.

The City Freeholds. 10. A majority of the Companies have been fortunate in the ownership of freeholds in the City, which of late years have risen in value to a wholly unforeseen extent, and have not always reached their climax. This has undoubtedly been the leading element and cause of prosperity, and of the power to enjoy and maintain it by

nobly and wisely sharing it with the community by a fundamental revision of their traditional scheme; so that, instead
of remaining in the bàckground, and standing on their ancient
rights and prescriptive claims, they, or an overwhelming
majority of them, have come forward with unreserved frank-
ness, and have at once disarmed public hostility and jealousy,
and enlisted public confidence.

Their various   For the acquisition of the greater part of their
sources.   corporate possessions the Companies have been
indebted either to private generosity and good fellowship or
to the incessant political commotions and the vicissitudes of
private fortune in earlier times. Their estates, not merely in
London, but in the provinces and out of England, were frequently obtained in mortgage or as security, at all events, for
pecuniary advances to the Crown; and in many instances it
has only been within the last half or three-quarters of a
century that the expansion of value in civic property has com-
pensated the Gilds, which were strong enough to wait, for
long years of slender returns, unjust treatment, and calamitous
reverses, and has at the same time enabled them to withstand
the depression in their agricultural rents, and to keep pace
with the age by constituting themselves promoters of almost
every department of humanizing and elevating science.

Prostration of   When we regard the wholesale devastation
strength by   wrought by the Fire, the probable loss of private
the Fire of   property by the members of Gilds, and the para-
1666.
lysis of business, side by side with the ruin of the corporate
estates and the absence of any system of insurance, we may
entertain a grave doubt whether such crushing reverses
could have been stemmed by any but bodies of loyal and
united men, acting together for the common honour and
welfare. Many of the less opulent fraternities probably never
rallied from the blow in any appreciable measure; even their

more fortunate brethren staggered under it, and felt its effects for more than a century.   It fell on the City, at a point of time when that narrow area embraced well-nigh the whole wealth of the kingdom, with tenfold the force that it would at present, when our industries, our commerce, our resources, and our specie are more widely distributed ; and what dismay and disorganization a far less grave event of the same character would create to-day!

Causes of revival.   During actual centuries the destinies of many of the Gilds trembled in the balance ; and it was in those instances where they were strong enough to hold their ground, or rich enough to propitiate the party in power, that they outlived the bad old times, and saw themselves and their property at last, after the Revolution of 1688, comparatively out of danger.   Then, when they had been so fortunate or farseeing as to secure estates in the City, came the slow but steady reaction, the flow of the tide toward prosperity and opulence which has never ebbed.   Yet we must remember that they owed their salvation and well-being to commercial principles totally opposed to their own traditions and prejudices, to the overthrow of the archaic views of trade and industry in which they had had their first rise and a long career of success, and to the broadening of English policy and sentiment in every direction. Whatever danger the City Companies may apprehend from more advanced Radicalism, the diffusion and triumph of Liberal ideas have made them what they are to-day, has alone enabled the Mercers, the Grocers, the Merchant Taylors, the Clothworkers, and the other societies which stand preeminent, to publish magnificent statistics of revenue and still prouder statistics of expenditure.   The *ratio* of financial importance is that of the ownership of freeholds within a radius of two miles from the Mansion House.

It perhaps happened fortunately for the Gilds, that the

diversion of English commerce from its original channels and centres did not occur until they had acquired their estates, and consolidated themselves, so as to be enabled to retain their position and power when the agencies which had favoured and justified their institution were gradually superseded by the organic change in the condition and relationships of the English-speaking folk.

V.

The present work. The object of the present publication is to offer, in a tolerably succinct and compact shape, a comprehensive description of all the Gilds, for the use and information of those who cannot afford the leisure to study the subject more at large ; and it is our wish to introduce as far as possible illustrations of some of the most remarkable objects in the hands of the Companies.

Its design. The undertaking has been planned on the basis and principle of exhibiting to the fullest extent the public utility and spirit of these ancient and interesting institutions, of which some trace back their origin almost to the Middle Ages, and most of which existed for a considerable period prior to their incorporation.

The Returns of 1882. The absolute necessity for publishing, or privately issuing, narratives of this description was very sensibly affected by the parliamentary returns of 1880, which, with very few exceptions, furnished to the Legislature and the public a view of the origin, character and objects, and income and expenditure, of the London Companies. But a separate and independent record of each Gild remains the sole means of laying before the public an adequately full and clear view of its origin, benefactions, and conformity to modern demands.

Existing accounts of the Companies.
It is by no means the fact that, of the seventy-five Companies, even a majority has hitherto thought fit to follow the example set by the Grocers, Haberdashers, Ironmongers, Leathersellers, Merchant Taylors, Skinners, and Vintners, by putting into circulation a more or less comprehensive history of their formation, constitution, and property. Only about four-and-twenty out of the seventy-five have taken such a course, and of these we have what may be termed exhaustive memorials from not more than half a dozen or so. The remainder have been content to appear in pamphlet shape, as it were, and to limit their narrative to a summary or outline, usually accompanied by a selection of graphic embellishments from objects of historical value in their possession. An account of the Mercers on a satisfactory scale is, we understand, in preparation by their clerk; one of the Weavers is shortly to be expected; and monographs of the Barber-Surgeons and Gold and Silver Wire-Drawers have quite recently appeared, the former being among the most sumptuous of the whole series.

Our own text.
Our accounts of the respective Companies have been drawn up on the basis of the official returns, with such additions as it was practicable to supply, and were thought likely to prove interesting, in each instance. The response of many, if not of most, of the Gilds to the parliamentary requisition may be said almost to err on the side of copious minuteness, especially in statistics and supplementary papers of various kinds; and for such a purpose as the present there is an enormous body of detail, which is undeniably of immense permanent value, but which appeals to the student of blue-books rather than to the general reader.

Statistical details.
The details of income and expenditure, which form part of the returns made by the Companies to Parliament in 1882, are in the main of no great public

interest and concern, beyond the figures which occur in our general introduction ; and it would be unadvisable, in the present case, to enter into such statistics, where they possess no historical bearing, and are purely financial. They are accessible at large in the Blue-Books, if reference is desired for special purposes. They may be taken with a moderate allowance to represent the actual positions of the several bodies in this respect ; from causes which are elsewhere explained, the receipts of the Gilds would now, as a rule, exhibit an increase on the returns of ten years ago.

The returns were in their very essence official, and what might have been expected ; it was a strict matter of business ; extraneous topics were only incidentally and, as it were, unconsciously introduced ; and any information of a miscellaneous character has consequently to be sought elsewhere. At the same time, there is no dearth of archæological and literary particulars, and the true aim in the present case seemed to be to provide such as does not occur in the separate histories, in Herbert's work, and other more or less accessible sources.

Trade usages and pretensions. We have entered into certain details in connexion with the Gilds, as well as with the unincorporated bodies, where trade usages and claims are treated, because they seemed to possess a more or less important measure of relevance to modern commercial economy and doctrine. But a glance even at one or two of the less elaborate monographs in print will suffice to demonstrate the impossibility, if it were desirable, of affording space for more than the salient facts and features relative to each Gild.

Permanent value of the Returns of 1882. Men of letters and research, however, owe a lasting debt of gratitude to the Returns, which brought a veritable *terra incognita* within general reach, and cast a flood of light on an unique body of material for study and use.

The present book a comprehensive synopsis.

It is obvious enough that an entrance into more particular detail might sometimes have been advantageously undertaken ; but exigencies of space debarred the writer from assigning to any of the seventy-five bodies described more than a limited and fair proportion of the book, of which the fundamental plan and aim, after all, were a concise and comprehensive view of the entire subject, accompanied by such introductory matter as would, it was hoped and thought, assist altogether the formation of a fairly clear and correct general idea of a question of standard importance and interest.

Normal periodical incidence.

One group or succession of features in the annals and fortunes of these associations commences with the reign of Henry VIII., and embraces the unscrupulous and exorbitant calls on the Companies for financial aid and pecuniary assessments on a wide variety of occasions and pretexts by the royal houses of Tudor and Stuart, the practice of compelling them to maintain stores of grain at a heavy cost in the City against the periodical dearths, the disastrous incidence of the Civil War and the Great Fire, the vexatious and harassing *Quo Warranto* business in 1625 and 1684, and the changes in commercial polity and practice, whereby the practical advantages of the charters have been rendered a dead letter.

The writs of *Quo Warranto*.

The aim of the writs of *Quo Warranto* by Charles I. and Charles II. against the City charters, was, under colour of declaring the privileges and powers exercised by the Corporation and Gilds illegal and void, to raise money by fines, to establish a royal jurisdiction, and to convert the Mayor, the Court of Aldermen, and the governing bodies of the Livery Gilds, into nominees and tools of the Crown. But the Act of William and Mary equally repudiated the writ of 1684 and the subsequent conditional re-grant of powers.

Order of arrangement.   The arrangement of the Companies has been made on the common basis of placing the twelve great bodies in their precedence, and the remainder in alphabetical order.   The principle of priority or sequence was settled before 7 Henry VIII., when a precept of the Lord Mayor was published by reason of the long-continued dispute for superiority in this respect between the Clothworkers and the Dyers.

Executive Staffs.   It did not seem to be of any service to particularize in each case the exact nature and extent of the executive staff maintained by the Gilds ; since the system does not materally vary, and has no bearing on the historical, social, or literary aspect of the matter.   The official machinery naturally differs according to requirements, and several of the minor bodies are limited to a clerk, who keeps the archives at his own address.

Literary memorials.   To the account of each Company is annexed a list of the civic pageants performed by it, and of the books, tracts, and broadsides relating to it with which we happen to have met ; but the latter by no means claims to be exhaustive.   Nor is it an easy matter to determine where the line should be drawn, as there are many works relevant to the Corporation and the City which do not specifically concern the Gilds, and a large body of literature upon industry and trade which is of too general a tenor to be ranged under any particular head.

But in the Guildhall Library, British Museum, and other accessible public collections, the reader whose requirements lead him to researches beyond the ordinary limit, will find an extensive assemblage of publications and privately issued pieces bearing upon this topic.   As a rule, in this bibliographical accompaniment we have limited ourselves to those items which are of historical or technical complexion, and have passed over all the merely indirect literary products, which have grown round the respective branches or divisions of the question, an infinite profusion of facetious trifles included. These have no bearing on the municipal or the industrial aspect of the matter in hand, and therefore appeared to be foreign to our purpose.

But while we have restricted ourselves to the earlier literature, leaving more recent productions to others, we have thought it useful to include much outside the strict historical boundary, which illustrated the incidence of each particular calling and association.

It may not be disrespectful to intimate that there will be probably found here many items which are new even to those specially interested in the municipal antiquities of London.

Mr. Welsh's Bibliography. Mr. Charles Welsh, librarian to the Corporation, recently read before the Library Association a paper on the "Bibliography of the City Livery Companies"; but this restricts itself to an indication of the works which have been printed on the history of the several Gilds; and Mr. Welsh proposes to follow it up by a similar account of those preserved in MS.

The radical and complete change which has taken place in the relationship of the several departments of commercial industry to each other, as well as in the distribution of the sale of commodities among certain of them, will readily account for the arrangement of articles under what would otherwise appear unsuitable heads.

The City pageants. As regards the City pageants, or Lord Mayors' shows, the honour and expense of setting them forth were of course limited to the very narrow proportion out of the whole number of Companies among which the choice of Mayor lay; and the distinction, during the period from Elizabeth to Anne (1566-1714), was principally enjoyed by the Drapers, Goldsmiths, Haberdashers, Mercers, Merchant

Taylors, Ironmongers, and Skinners. Many wealthy and important Gilds have never returned a Mayor, and others have been successful only on a single occasion. The great Companies have, in fact, almost monopolized the chief magistracy; and Stow[1] goes so far as to say that the Lord Mayor is to be chosen yearly out of them, "because those of inferiour rancke are not capable of such dignitie."

Loss of many of the printed copies. The printed accounts of these solemnities seem to commence (if we leave out of account the lost Ironmongers' one of 1566) with the Skinners' in 1585, and there are several gaps in the series down to 1639. None from 1640 to 1654 inclusive is known. The missing years prior to 1639 seem to be 1586–7–8–9, 1592–1604, 1607–8, 1610, 1625, 1630, and 1636. The account for 1588 was licensed for the press, and probably published. The earliest detailed description of one is perhaps that prepared to celebrate the investiture of Sir Christopher Draper, Ironmonger, in 1566.

We have not carried our bibliography of the pageants beyond 1700; but they continued to appear some years subsequent to that date.

Unpublished narratives. The existing printed pageants are far from representing the entire series, or even all which passed the press. From time to time a discovery is made of some piece, of which the existence had remained quite unknown, as was the case with the Fishmongers' Show for 1590, being the second relic of the kind hitherto recovered, and six-and-twenty years prior to that of Munday in 1616; and there is absolute evidence that the device of the Ironmongers' pageant for 1566 was privately issued by the Company. But in Herbert's *Livery Companies* and elsewhere many notices

---

[1] *Survey of London*, 1633, p. 599.

occur of similar displays by the principal Gilds, alike before the invention of printing and before the practice of committing the descriptive ac⌐ounts to type. The most ancient solemnities were not by any means confined to Lord Mayor's day, but perhaps even more frequently took place on occasions when the Companies were required, by precept or otherwise, to meet the Sovereign or his guests on their entry into the City from Westminster or from abroad. From the circumstance that they originally assumed the form of cavalcades, they were termed *ridings*; the members of the procession were on horseback, and so late as 1710 the Lord Mayor rode in this way to wait upon the judges. During some time, however, the passage was by water, and must have presented an imposing and attractive spectacle, while the river-side was still largely occupied by Gild-halls and private residences.

The Halls.	A tour of visits to the Halls of the Gilds is an experience which becomes very impressive from the powerful contrast which these scenes of dignified repose offer to the bustle and din prevalent without and on every side. Although the buildings themselves are rarely, if ever, contemporary with the origin of the institution, the site and soil are frequently unchanged; but even where it is not so, and the Hall occupies what may be termed cold ground, the interior is apt to transport you in fancy to immeasurably different conditions of life, thought, and locomotion.

Absence of Archæological interest.	The Halls themselves are too frequently void of attraction to the historical student. Where they are not absolutely modern, the ancient features are generally either superficial or fragmentary. Their restoration, after the Fire of 1666, was peremptory, where the means existed; but the more recent replacements of the work of Wren, Jarman, and other seventeenth century artists seem rather questionable in point of taste and judgment.

It is to be said, however, on the other side, that the future of the Companies is indissolubly identified with modern ideas and institutions, and we find substantially little, *as a rule*, in their places of assembly to remind us of the nature of their origin or of the causes of their prosperous longevity.

And of characteristic memorials. Their successive departure, with very few exceptions, from their original structure and pleas for existence and encouragement, is answerable for the at first rather surprising dearth of typical and characteristic objects in their hands. The early Gildsmen seem to have attached no value to historical relics other than portraits or decorative articles in the shape of tapestry and arras. You are met, as a rule, by a smile, when you ask the clerk or other officers whether his Gild can shew you anything of the kind; and you learn that there are at the best only a few early registers and account-books, the charters, the bye-laws, the grant of arms, one or two pieces of elderly furniture, and some antique plate. The Fire of 1666, which the historian of the Apothecaries' Society terms *beneficent*, swept away much, no doubt; and neglect and indifference have, we fear, accomplished the rest.

Obligations to helpers. While we have occupied ourselves with this subject, we have necessarily been placed in communication with a numerous body of gentlemen connected with the Livery Companies and the City of London; and it is our simple duty, as it is a pleasure, to acknowledge the assistance which has been rendered to us in a great variety of ways, both for our text and illustrations, as well as the courteous reception which has awaited us from the official representatives of the Companies. In a work of this kind the amount of minute detail, which has to be collected or verified, makes the labour, no less than the encroachment on the time of others, peculiarly heavy.

But we have very particularly to thank the clerks to the

Grocers', Fishmongers', Merchant Taylors', Salters', Drapers', Clothworkers', Coopers', Haberdashers', Saddlers', Stationers', Fan-makers', Shipwrights', and Loriners' Companies ; and Mr. John Welsh, Librarian to the Corporation ; Mr. J. A. Kingdon, of the Grocers' Company ; Mr. John Addison, Past-Master of the Clockmakers ; Mr. Frederick Clarke, Master of the Cordwainers ; Mr. George Elkington, junr. ; Mr. F. J. Cox ; Mr. John Jarvis, junr. ; and our old schoolfellow, Dr. Sharpe, Keeper of the Archives at Guildhall, for personal attention and assistance.

The graphic part of the volume.   The illustrations of various kinds which accompany the volume have been of course selected with a view to their characteristic interest and significance. Seeing the enormous amount of treasure in the shape of plate and other objects in the possession of the Companies, or the major part of them, it was out of the question to reproduce more than a limited number of representative specimens ; and the difficulty, by the exercise of this line of choice, at once sensibly decreased, since in typical antiquities and curiosities these bodies are, as we have said, by no means rich.

The Armorial Bearings which we give possess a certain symbolical and typical value, as the distinguishing badges and ensigns of these industrial corporations, when such an emblem on a coat, on a banner, or over a portal, spoke a language perfectly intelligible to thousands, who were neither heralds nor scholars. External and figurative tokens constituted the best method of appeal to persons of illiterate character conversant with the alphabet and mechanical appliances of the chief industrial arts. In ancient commercial life these blazonries played the same part as in that of the religious and chivalric orders ; their actual speech and significance are of the past, and their retention by the Companies, especially where they are unfaithful to the old design, is a matter of mere form. Both the early and current representations in print are apt to be inexact from an imperfect study of the original grant, or from an advised change in some of the detail; but if the shield is to be of any worth and authority, it should be set forth in accordance with the Herald's own delineation.

The kind and liberal use of many of the graphic embellishments of the book has, we are sure, largely tended to render it more acceptable and attractive.

Our genuine purpose. Whatever we may have done in the direction of criticizing some of the proceedings and tendencies of the City Gilds, our primary motive has been, and is, not to bear a part in pulling down these few remaining old stones of London, but to preserve them. The Gilds have, to a large extent, their future in their own hands; and they seem, on the whole, fairly sensible of the responsible position which they occupy, and of their changed relationship to the community.

In 12 Richard II. (1388) letters mandatory were directed by the king from Cambridge to the Mayor of London, to make proclamation that all the masters and wardens of Gilds and fraternities within the City of London, or the suburbs thereof, should deliver to the king and council in the Chancery a full, distinct, and proper account in writing of the manner and nature of such foundations, together with their rules and ordinances, and an account of all their lands, goods, and chattels, and to produce their charters, under pain of having all their grants revoked or annulled. The text of the commission is extant, but no record has yet been discovered of the results as regards the Livery Companies of London. Only the returns of some of those belonging to the provinces have come to light, and have been edited by the late Toulmin Smith.

In 1 Edward VI., after the passing of the act which vested all lands held to support chauntries, or obits, or for other superstitious purposes, in the Crown, the Companies of London were called upon to make returns (which are still extant) " of any such establishments existing within their bodies, with particulars of the estates left to support them, and of all other property to which the Crown became entitled."

The " Municipal Commission " was appointed in 1833, " to inquire as to the existing state of municipal corporations in England and Wales." The Commission prosecuted the inquiry in divisions, and five commissioners, of whom the late Sir Francis Palgrave was one, inquired into London and Southwark. Their report, drawn by Sir Francis Palgrave, is a long and careful one.

It is obvious that a City Company is not a city or a borough, and it was not therefore clear that the Companies of London were within the scope of the Municipal Commission. The commissioners, however, probably felt that as they were historically connected with the municipality, it was desirable to inquire into their constitution ; and with this view they administered a number of queries, and also sat at the Guildhall to receive information. Many of these bodies sent in answers to the queries of the commissioners. These related, not only to the constitution, but also to the corporate property and their mode of expending their corporate income. No questions were asked as to the trust property, for the reason that that was then undergoing an inquiry by a Charity Commission.

The Charity Commission between 1818 and 1880 made a series of elaborate inquiries into the charities administered by the Companies. The results are to be found partly in the Reports of the Commission, and partly in the Appendix to that of the Royal Commission of 1880.

In 1868 Lord Robert Montagu moved in the House of Commons for a return of the charities administered by the City Companies. This was promptly supplied by the Charity Commission; but the return is not always accurate, and is too condensed to be very useful. Between 1876 and 1879 the educational endowments committee of the School Board for London was engaged in an inquiry into the charities administered by the Companies; and the Royal Commission of 1880 was furnished by the Board with copies of the Report.

In the Record Office, duplicates of many of the charters and licences in mortmain granted to the Companies are preserved. Many judgments of the courts of law and decrees of the courts of Chancery concerning them are also recorded there, and there can be no doubt that the office contains many other documents relating thereto. In the Hustings Court of the City, many of the acts of the courts of Aldermen and Common Council under this head are enrolled, and thousands of the wills [1] under which the Companies hold property, and many of their other title-deeds, are to be found in this ancient office. In the Guildhall library there is a considerable collection of books and pamphlets relating to this topic.

Shortly after the appointment of the Municipal Commission of 1834, the great Companies employed Mr. Herbert, librarian to the Corporation of London, to write an account of their history. Several of the great Companies had given little information to the commissioners, whose proceedings they conceived to be *ultra vires*. They were willing, however, to give it to the public voluntarily, and for this purpose they placed their archives at Mr. Herbert's disposal. The result

---

[1] A calendar of wills is in course of publication under the care of Dr. Sharpe, Curator of the City Archives.

was the *History of the Twelve Great Companies of London*, 1836, which contains some information as to their trust, but none as to their corporate, estate.

Herbert's *History of the Twelve Great Companies* necessarily contains only very incidental notices of the others ; and it must be confessed that, from an historical point of view, the latter offer to us a volume of information and material quite equal in importance, and sometimes even superior in curiosity and interest. Of the so called *minor* Gilds, many are divided from the foremost twelve by little more than an imaginary and customary line ; and a limitation to the twelve great fraternities shuts out many of the most valuable industries of the country, and much of that illustrative and picturesque light which this side of London life sheds on the ancient condition and genius of the metropolis.

By no means the least valuable feature in Herbert's book, is the "Historical Essay" which forms an introduction to the accounts of the Gilds. This preliminary matter is full of interesting and important information, which it would be perfectly futile to condense. But occasional use has been made of it in the notices which we have given of the ancient Hanseatic and other fraternities, which from the Anglo-Saxon times began to form settlements in the vicinity of the Thames bank by Dowgate and Queenhithe.

The *White Book* of the City of London is one of the storehouses of information which the late Mr. Riley threw open to us all in a series of volumes, which comprehended that, the *Liber Custumarum* and the *Liber Horn*, with very curious Appendices of the *Assisa Panis*, etc.

The *White Book*, traditionally compiled by John Carpenter, founder of the City of London School, and Sir Richard Whittington, citizen and mercer, deals with a variety of topics connected with civic government and police, and includes rates of

customs, with the modes of payment, regulations as to forestallers, bakers, vintners, brewers, taverners, skinners and
furriers, butchers, and others, and lays down the scale of wages
for different classes of operatives, and the lines on which they
should work. The volume seems to be a compilation into a
more or less methodical form from the then existing records,
which had gradually accumulated at Guildhall as separate
documents or papers. It certainly, with its companions and the
Addenda, constitutes material for forming a fairly correct judgment of the internal condition of London proper, commercial,
social, and sanitary, in the old time. It was a book of reference
and authority alike for the official dignitary, the merchant, the
lawyer, and the tradesman.

Mr. Riley's *Memorials of the City of London and of
London Life*, printed by order of the Corporation in 1868 ; the
Chronicle of Old London, 1089–1483, 4to, 1827 ; *Munimenta
Gildhallæ Londinensis, Liber Albus, Liber Custumarum, et
Liber Horn*, published in 1859, under the direction of the
Master of the Rolls, contain many allusions to the early history
of the Companies. The Corporation of London has published
an index to *Remembrancia*, which contains much relevant detail.

It is deserving of remark that, while copious notices of
many or most trades present themselves in the City archives,
of others which must have existed from the most ancient
period in some shape we meet with no trace ; and this is so
much so, that it would be far easier to enumerate the bodies
to which references exist.

Serjeant Pulling's *Laws of London* and Mr. Norton's
Commentaries on the City of London may be consulted.

The only monographs of authority in English are Mr.
Gross's elaborate and valuable one on the Gild merchant, and
the late Mr. Toulmin Smith's *Original Ordinances of more
than One Hundred English Gilds*, published by the Early

English Text Society. The latter contains an introduction by Miss Toulmin Smith, author of the article on "Gilds" in the *Encyclopædia Britannica*, and a preliminary essay on the subject of these corporations by Dr. Brentano, of the University of Aschaffenburg. The essay of Dr. Brentano is much relied upon by Dr. Stubbs in his *Constitutional History of England*, a work which, with the same author's *Annales Londinenses* and *Annales Paulini*, the late Mr. J. R. Green's *History of the English People*, and the brilliant description of the Companies with which Mr. Froude's history commences, constitutes a summary of the history of the Gilds from their foundation to the period of their decadence as industrial corporations. Mr. Freeman's studies have been limited to the early "Knighten Gild."

The principal authorities in German on the subject of the Gilds of mediæval Europe are the works of Wilda and of Gierke (*Geschichte des Deutschen Genossenschaftwesens.* Berlin, 1868).

For the Gilds of France the authorities are Raynouard's *Histoire du Droit Municipal en France*, published in 1829 ; M. A. Thierry's *Récits des Temps Mérovingiens*, published in 1840 ; M. Delpit's *Collection de Documents Inédits* ; M. Gustave Fagnier's *Études sur l'Industrie à Paris au* 13ème *et* 14ème *Siècle* ; and a valuable paper by a Belgian antiquary, M. Wauter, entitled *Les Gildes Communales à l'Onzième Siècle*, published in the *Bulletin de l'Académie de Belgique* (2me série, t. xxxvii., p. 874).

The Grocers' Company, the second in order of civic precedence, appointed a committee in that year "to search their records and prepare a report upon the constitution and income and expenditure of the Company, and the general management of the Company's business." This was presented to the court on February 2, 1881, and was drawn up with great ability, and in a form which made it serviceable to the Royal Commission. These were the earliest returns received from the great Companies.

The above were the sources of the preliminary report of 1880.

A few of the minor Companies either declined to make returns or made returns which were not satisfactory. These Companies were the Broderers, Dyers, Distillers, Glovers, Tinplate Workers, and Weavers.

The royal commissioners received statements from some gentlemen, who suggested that it was desirable to disestablish and disendow the Companies, or to materially alter their constitution. Three academical bodies, University College, London, King's College, London, and Magee College, Londonderry, and the University Extension Society sent deputations to urge their respective claims to recognition by the Government as candidates for endowment, should the commissioners determine to recommend to the Government a redistribution of the revenues of the Companies. The School Board of London came before them to enforce the views expressed in the report of the educational endowment committee mentioned above; and a deputation, consisting of the Lord Chancellor, the president of the Royal Society, and Sir F. Bramwell, F.R.S., attended to explain the constitution of the City and Gilds of London Technical Institute.

During 1883 they received a number of deputations from the Companies, and addressed to the Companies an invitation to appoint a representative or representatives to give evidence before and confer with them. In reply the Companies sent before the Commission several gentlemen of great experience in the conduct of their affairs, from whom it received valuable information; and several of the statements laid before it displayed much learning and ability.

VI.

The General Introduction which succeeds is a careful digest and synopsis of the elaborate parliamentary return of 1882, prefixed to the returns furnished by the Companies. The official authority of the statements contained therein was judged to be a strong ground for preferring it to any compilation of a normal literary character. But while it is unquestionably of extreme value as a record, the length to which it extends, from the absence of any necessity for studying space or expense, renders it tedious and unattractive ; and there has been no great difficulty in reducing the matter within reasonable limits, and at the same time omitting nothing essential to a proper view of the whole subject. In the Report, however, the object being different, the method pursued was naturally at variance with ours, and the consequence has been that the material has unavoidably undergone a certain amount of rearrangement and modification.

This body of information will serve to prepare the reader for the historical sketches and other particulars of the several Companies which follow.

A revised *précis* of these valuable preliminaries seemed to be as much as could be reasonably expected or required ; and the task of condensation was the more feasible that, without omitting any material fact or circumstance, a large amount of space was capable of being saved by eschewing redundancies, contradictions, and irrelevancies so often found in records un-trammelled by literary exigencies, and a fairly lucid and full view of the whole question presented in a far more moderate com-pass. Besides, it was found that the arrangement of the matter was faulty and confused, and that an entire reconstruction of the report was calculated to render it far more intelligible and satisfactory. It will probably not surprise any one conversant with official composition to learn that it has been necessary throughout to reduce the text to grammatical English. A competent knowledge of their native language ought to be a compulsory part of the training of all lawyers and public servants. In many cases we have felt to be justified in correcting errors of statement of various kinds.

The parliamentary return of 1884, as it is hereinafter set forth, assumes the shape which it would have presented in the first place, had it emanated from a literary, instead of an official, source. The draughtsmen of these papers are usually chosen from the same class of personage as those of bills and statutes, and with the same unhappy results.

Except in one or two instances, no changes of consequence have occurred in the constitution and general position of the Gilds since 1884, when the report of the Royal Commission was published.

As in a work of the present character it is obviously impossible to include all the minute particulars and lengthy documents in print or MS., a table of the miscellaneous and supplementary papers annexed to the Report of 1882 may be useful for reference. The four volumes of the *City of London Livery Companies Commission* Report contain, in addition to the accounts of the Companies, historical and statistical, the following items :

Text of Commission.

Report signed by the Earl of Derby, the Duke of Bedford, Viscount Sherbrooke, Lord Coleridge, Sir Sydney H. Waterlow, Mr. Pell, Mr. Walter James, Mr. Firth, and Mr. Burt; with Appendix and Notes by Messrs. Horace Davey and F. Vaughan Hawkins.

"Dissent" Report, signed by Sir Richard Cross, Sir N. de Rothschild, and Mr. Alderman Cotton.

Protest of Mr. Alderman Cotton.

Observations and Memorandum by Mr. Firth and Memorandum by Mr. Burt.

ORAL INQUIRY, PARLIAMENTARY SESSION, 1882.

Evidence of Mr. Thomas Hare, Senior Inspector of Charities, and his Memoranda.

Evidence of Mr. Henry Longley, Commissioner of Charities.

Evidence of Mr. James Beal and Mr. J. R. Phillips (who appeared to support the views of Mr. Firth), Mr. E. J. Watherston, Mr. W. H. Williamson, and Mr. W. Gilbert (all of whom requested to be examined).

Evidence of Sir George Young, Dr. Wood, Dr. Williamson, F.R.S., and Mr. Henry Morley (a deputation from University College, London).

Memorial of University College, London.

Evidence of the Lord Chancellor, Mr. W. Spottiswoode, F.R.S., and Sir F. Bramwell, F.R.S. (on behalf of the City and Gilds of London Technical Institute).

Prospectus of Technical Institute.

Memorial of King's College, London, and Evidence of the Rev. Canon Barry, Professors Adams, Shelley, and Wiltshire, Mr. Serocold, treasurer, and Mr. Cunningham, secretary (on the behalf of the College).

Evidence of Dr. Todd, the Rev. Mr. McCay, Mr. Andrew Brown, Mr. Robert Stewart, Mr. Robert Dunn, the Rev. Mr. Brown, and Professor Dougherty (a deputation claiming to represent the tenants on the Ulster estates), and Appendix.

Evidence of the Rev. Mr. Rogers, Mr. Cooke, and Professor Dougherty (a deputation from Magee College, Londonderry).

Evidence of the Right Hon. G. J. Göschen, M.P. (a deputation from the London Society for the Extension of University Teaching).

Evidence of Mr. Lucraft (a deputation from the School Board of London).

ORAL INQUIRY, PARLIAMENTARY SESSION, 1883.

Letter from the Mercers' Company.

Memorandum of the Merchant Taylors' Company (as to certain statements made by Mr. Beal, Mr. Phillips, and other witnesses examined during 1882 with reference to the Company).

Statement by Grocers' Company (as to certain statements made by Mr. Beal, Mr. Phillips, and other witnesses examined during 1882 relating to the Company, and as to certain views expressed by Mr. Firth in *Municipal London*).

Evidence of Mr. J. H. Warner (on behalf of the Grocers' Company).

Evidence of Sir F. Bramwell, F.R.S. (on behalf of the Goldsmiths' Company).

Letter of Mr. Prideaux, on behalf of the Goldsmiths' Company, to the Commissioners (criticizing certain statements made by Mr. Beal, Mr. Phillips, and other witnesses during 1882, and also the views expressed by Mr. Firth in *Municipal London*). Statement of the Company (with reference to the same matters), and evidence of Mr. Prideaux (on behalf of the Company).

Evidence of Mr. T. H. Fordham, Mr. W. C. Venning, and Mr. J. T. Smith (representing the Fishmongers' Company), and statement of the Company (with reference to statements made by witnesses from Ulster in 1882).

Evidence of Mr. Graves and Mr. Beaumont (representing the Cutlers' Company), with reference to a passage in Mr. Firth's *Municipal London.*

Evidence of Mr. E. Gregory, Mr. W. H. Townsend, Mr. White, Mr. Wyld, Mr. Neate, and Mr. Owen Roberts (representing the Clothworkers' Company).

Observations and Further Observations by the Clothworkers' Company (with reference to statements made by Mr. Beal, Mr. Phillips, and other witnesses examined during 1882, and also as to the views expressed by Mr. Firth in *Municipal London*).

Evidence of Mr. Dalton, Mr. Jennings, and Mr. Sawyer (representing the Drapers' Company).

Evidence of Mr. Hill, Mr. le Gros Clark, Mr. Hicks, Mr. Eaton, M.P., Mr. Alderman Fowler, M.P., and Mr. E. L. Scott (representing the Salters' Company); and statement by the Company (as to the evidence given by the Ulster witnesses in 1882).

Evidence of Mr. Barron, Mr. Bevan, Mr. Horner, Mr. Price, Mr. Gribble, and Mr. Beck (representing the Ironmongers' Company and certain Companies associated with it in the management of Ulster estates).

Evidence of Mr. Miles, Mr. John Miles, Mr. Layton, and Mr. Rivington (representing the Stationers' Company).

Statement by the Society of Apothecaries, and Evidence of Mr. Sauer and Mr. Upton (representing the Society).

Evidence of Dr. Ramsay and Major Harding (representing the Needlemakers' Company).

Statement by the Horners' Company, and Evidence of Mr. Compton (representing the Company).

Statement by the Ironmongers' Company, and Statement by the same (as to the Company's Irish estate and the evidence given by the Ulster witnessses in 1882).

Statement of the Skinners' Company and Memorial (as to the Ulster estate of the Company and the evidence given by the Ulster witnesses in 1882).

Letters from the Coachmakers' and Barbers' Companies.

CHARITY COMMISSION PAPERS.

Observations by the Armourers' and Braziers' Company as to evidence of Mr. Lucraft.

Detailed accounts of Mercers' Company, and Charitable Accounts of same ; Mr. Hare's Report on the Charities administered by the Company, with an Appendix.

Mr. Hare's Report on the Charities administered by the Grocers' Company, with an Appendix, and Charitable Accounts of the Company.

Mr. Hare's Report on the Charities administered by the Drapers' Company, with an Appendix, and the Charitable Accounts of the Company.

Mr. Hare's Reports on the Charities administered by the Fishmongers' Company, with an Appendix, and the Company's Charitable Accounts.

Mr. Hare's Report on the Charities administered by the Goldsmiths' Company, with the Charitable Accounts of the Company.

Mr. Hare's Report on the Charities administered by the Skinners' Company, with an Appendix, and the Accounts.

Mr. Hare's Report on the Charities administered by the Merchant Taylors Company, draft Report on Boone's Charity, administered by the Company, Mr. Skirrow's Report on Donkin's Charity, administered by the Company, and the Accounts.

Mr. Hare's Report on the Charities administered by the Haberdashers' Company, with an Appendix, and the Accounts.

Mr. Hare's and Mr. Simmons' Reports on the Charities administered by the Salters' Company, and the Accounts.

Mr. Hare's Report on the Charities administered by the Ironmongers' Company, and the Accounts.

Mr. Hare's Report on the Charities administered by the Vintners' Company, and the Accounts.

Charitable Accounts of the Vintners' Company.

Mr. Hare's Report on the Charities administered by the Clothworkers' Company, with two Appendices, and the Accounts.

Minor Companies.

Mr. Simmons' or Simons' Reports on the Apothecaries', Armourers', Bakers', Barbers', and Blacksmiths' Charities, with the Accounts of each.

Mr. Simmons' Report on the Charities of the Bowyers' Company.

Reports on the Charities of the Broderers' and other Minor Companies by Mr. Hare, except the Upholders', for which there is no Report.

Reports on the Continental Gilds in communications to the Foreign Office, and Memoranda by persons resident abroad.

Tables of Income (Trust and Corporate) and Expenditure of the Gilds.

Amounts contributed by members and amounts spent on internal objects.

GENERAL INTRODUCTION.

THE Companies of London appear to have sprung from a number of Gilds, which were associations of neighbours for purposes of mutual assistance. Such associations were very numerous in the Middle Ages, both in town and country, and they appear to have abounded in London at a very early period. A Frith Gild and a Knighten or Knights' Gild seem to have existed in London in Anglo-Saxon times,[1]

---

[1] The Cniighten, Knighten, or English Knighten, Gild was no more than a similar association in its origin, consisting of thirteen military persons, to whom, according to the received tradition, King Edgar (958–68) granted certain waste land in the east of London, toward Aldgate, for prescribed services performed. The concession, which does not seem to have been committed to writing, was confirmed by Edward the Confessor in a charter at the suit of certain burgesses of London, the successors of these knights; but there was no trading privilege, and the Prior of Holy Trinity, Aldgate, became the sovereign of the Gild and the Alderman *ex officio* of Portsoken Ward. He rendered an account to the Crown of the taillage paid by the men of the Ward, presided over the Wardmotes, and in Stowe's time still rode in procession with the mayor and other aldermen, but clad in a purple, instead of a scarlet, gown. The term *portsoken*, as Herbert suggests, doubtless signified the soc-en or franchises at the port or gate.

and at the Norman Conquest there were probably many other bodies of a like nature there. Their main objects were the relief of poverty and the performance of masses for the dead.

These Gilds present a close analogy to the Collegia Opificum which existed under the Roman empire—institutions arising out of the urban life of the period, the primary objects of which were common worship and social intercourse: the secondary objects, the protection of the trades against unjust taxes and their internal regulation. They also served as benefit clubs, defraying the expenses of burial and funeral sacrifices for deceased members, in some cases out of legacies left for that purpose. It has been suggested that mediæval Europe borrowed this part of the industrial organization of the Roman empire, as it did portions of the Roman juridical system.

Hallam describes the Gilds as "fraternities by voluntary compact, to relieve each other in poverty, and to protect each other from injury. Two essential characteristics belonged to them: the common banquet and the common purse. They had also in many instances a religious, sometimes a secret, ceremonial, to knit more firmly the bond of fidelity. . . . They readily became connected with the exercise of trades, with the training of apprentices, with the traditional rules of art."

A vast number of such fraternities existed throughout Europe during the Middle Ages. Every hamlet had a Gild of some kind. In the towns they were very numerous.

The passage cited suggests a classification of the fraternities which has been adopted by subsequent writers. The Gilds have been divided into social or religious Gilds and Craft Gilds. But the Gilds of the former class, those which were not industrial corporations, by no means limited their purposes to mutual relief and protection. They shewed much public spirit, and undertook public burdens of every kind. The repairing of roads and bridges, the relief of pilgrims, the maintenance of schools and almshouses, the periodical exhibition of pageants and miracle-plays, are a few of the objects which they promoted.

Another community, differing from these, but which also was of importance during the Middle Ages, was the Gild Merchant. It existed in the towns, and was, as compared with the Craft Gilds, an aristocratic body, of which the members were originally prosperous traders, and became in course of time, by purchase or otherwise, landowners. Many of these patrician families, especially abroad, acquired oligarchical and even sovereign power in the towns, through the Gilds Merchant. But eventually, in nearly every case, the aristocratic municipality had to give way, though sometimes not till after a long and fierce struggle, to the general body of the citizens as represented by the Craft Gilds. In

London the victory of the popular party had become assured as early as the reign of Edward II.

The Gilds Merchant and the Craft Gilds were thus the germ of the municipalities of Europe. Speaking of the English communities from this point of view, Hallam says: " They are frequently mentioned in our Anglo-Saxon documents, and are the basis of those corporations which the Norman kings recognised or founded. The Gild was, of course, in its primary character, a personal association ; it was in the State, but not the State ; it belonged to the city without embracing all the citizens ; its purposes were the good of the fellows alone. But when the good was inseparable from that of their little country, their walls and churches, the principle of voluntary association was readily extended ; and from the private Gild, possessing already the vital spirit of faithfulness and brotherly love, sprang the sworn community, the body of citizens bound by a voluntary but perpetual obligation to guard each other's rights against the thefts of the weak or the tyranny of the powerful."

The trades of London had in early times their recognised quarters in the City, and the Gilds undertook the regulation of them. They appointed overseers to inspect the wares produced or sold, and also umpires to adjudicate in cases of dispute between masters and workmen. They generally had halls, at which meetings of the principal members took place for purposes of inspection, arbitration, and consideration of claims to charitable relief ; and at these halls banquets were frequently given. Being purely voluntary associations, they required no licence from the State.

"Ordinances" were framed for internal government by the most influential members. Such ordinances were (1) religious ; (2) social and charitable ; (3) industrial. They comprised rules for the attendance of the members at the services of the Church, for the promotion of pilgrimages, and for the celebration of masses for the dead ; and regulations as to common meals and the relief of poor brethren and sisters, the hours of labour, the processes of manufacture, the wages of workmen, and technical education.

The Inns of Court and Chancery and Serjeants' Inn were probably at first bodies in some respects similar to the Gilds, though not corporations.

Charters were granted by Edward III. or Richard II. to many of the Companies for valuable consideration. Succeeding sovereigns renewed them down to the time of the accession of the House of Hanover. The sums paid by the Companies to the national exchequer in respect of the original and *inspeximus* charters were very considerable.

The terms of the charters are in most cases obviously founded on the ordinances. They recognise the Gilds as existing, "administered," to quote the words of Dr. Stubbs, "by their own officers, and administering their own property in the usual way, the Aldermen of the Gilds holding the estates, when the Gilds possessed estates, direct from the king." The hospitals and Inns of Court of London and many provincial Gilds received their first charters about the time of the incorporation of the London Companies, and *inspeximus* charters afterwards in the same way at the commencement of each reign. At a certain interval from their incorporation the then existing members formed "bye-laws" to control details.

On their incorporation the Companies, like all similar bodies, became amenable to the processes of *Scire Facias* and *Quo Warranto* ; but there is nothing in their history to warrant the supposition that they could ever have been legally dissolved. From the time when the State recognised their existence, the only obligation of the governing bodies, which succeeded the "Aldermen," has been to carry out, so far as has been practicable, having regard to change of times, the terms of the charters and bye-laws, and to apply the trust-funds to the purposes for which they were bequeathed. The corporate property of the Companies has always been, in the eye of the law, their own, just as much as the property of individuals.

A licence in mortmain was contained in most of the charters, and some of the charters of *inspeximus* contain lists of the lands held by the Companies at the time they were granted, and expressly recognise the title thereto ; but by the immemorial custom of the City "free burgage" lands, *i.e.* lands held "direct from the Crown," could be devised to corporations without any limitation as to value. During many centuries land was throughout England the principal kind of property ; and it was only natural that, having the advantage of this custom, the Companies should soon become large holders of real property within the walls of London.

Their constitution was usually aristocratic. The administrators, who are generally named in the first charters, were the principal capitalists and employers of labour, or else distinguished citizens not connected with commerce or manufactures, and by the terms of the charters these boards had complete control over the associations. Some, such as the Mercers and Grocers, appear to have consisted, to a great extent, of merchants and wholesale dealers ; others, such as the Fishmongers, and the other Companies deriving their names from trades, of shop-keepers and their apprentices ; others, such as the Goldsmiths and the Clothworkers, deriving their names from "arts and misteries," of master-manufacturers and artisans. But the names of the Companies are misleading, for the reasons that from time immemorial (1) the privileges of membership have been hereditary, one mode of admission having always been by patrimony, which causes the right to the freedom to descend to all the lineal representatives, male and female, of every freeman ; (2) a system of apprenticeship has entered into the constitution of the Companies, under which members, irrespective of their membership of the respective trades, were privileged to receive apprentices. These reasons have caused the Companies to consist largely of non-craftsmen from the earliest times ; and the proportion of non-craftsmen seems always to have been particularly large among the governing bodies.

It has been suggested that these corporations, by their power of admitting to their freedom, were one of the causes of the disappearance of villeinage. There is no doubt that the custom of the towns by which freedom was obtained by means of residence for a year and a day within the walls was, along with manumission and the growth of copy-hold tenure, an instrument of enfranchisement, and that this custom obtained in London ; but Dr. Stubbs is of opinion that the influence exercised by the civic Companies was not in this respect considerable.

The charters, particularly the later, generally extend the area of control assumed by the Companies in their original state as Gilds. Under some, the Companies acquire power to prevent persons other than freemen from carrying on callings, and the right of searching for and destroying defective wares within a radius of several miles from Cornhill. It is needless to say that monopolies and powers of this description are contrary to law ; yet both by their charters and by letters patent the Companies received such from the Crown. From the time of their incorporation down to the present period, they have exercised them in certain cases, as hereinafter mentioned, within the City and its liberties ; never, probably, in the more extended area over which, by virtue of some of the more recent charters, they acquired a nominal control.

During the whole period from the Plantagenet dynasty to the Restoration, the Companies, probably because they constituted a convenient division of the citizens for purposes of taxation, were forced to contribute large sums to the national exchequer, chiefly for the purpose of defraying the expenses of wars ; and under a custom of the City which has long been obsolete, they were at one time bound to lend money to the municipality with which to purchase corn and coals for the poor in times of scarcity.

Their decay as trade organizations had certainly commenced at the outset of the sixteenth century ; and probably by the end of it they had practically ceased to be of any use for industrial purposes, prior to the revival which has taken place within living recollection.

The period of the cesser of their original connexion with the trade and manufactures of London is approximately that of the Reformation ; and as Catholicism was of the essence of their religious rules at the time when they ceased to have any such control, they also ceased to be in any real sense religious fraternities. Thus, of their three original functions, two, those of common worship and association for commercial purposes, became obsolete about four centuries ago. Their remaining function, the dual one of hospitality and charity, became the only one which it was possible for them during a great length of time to discharge. It appears that during the last four hundred years, and until recently, the Companies were mainly associations identified with hospitality and benevolence.

The returns discovered by Toulmin Smith present a vivid picture of the state of the Social Gilds and Craft Gilds of the provincial towns of England during the fourteenth century. They are the answers of the Gilds to an inquisition directed by Richard II. and his Parliament sitting at Cambridge in 1388. Two writs were ordered to be issued to the sheriff of each county, the first calling upon "the masters and wardens of all Gilds and brotherhoods" to send up to the king's council all details as to the foundation, statutes, and property of their Gilds ; the second calling upon the "masters, wardens, and overlookers of all the mysteries and crafts" to send up in the same way copies of their charters or letters patent. These writs are in Latin. The returns are in Latin, Norman-French, or English, chiefly the last.

It has been computed that at this time there were about 40,000 such associations in the provinces. From the mention of sisters in almost all the returns, it may be inferred that women were equally eligible with men for membership, and that they attended the masses, specially solemnized for the benefit of the associations, and their banquets. The number of members varied indefinitely from a very few to 15,000. An oath of obedience to the ordinances was administered to each member as he or she joined. The officers and servants consisted of an alderman, several stewards, a clerk, and a dean or beadle. The members met from once to four times a year, either in the Gild-hall or Gild-house, if the Gild possessed a hall or house, or at the houses of different members in rotation. They arrived clad in a costume or vesture, the colour and pattern of which had been selected by the founders. At the meetings officers were appointed, new brethren were admitted, and relief was voted. It does not appear whether all the members were summoned for the transaction of ordinary business,

or whether the aldermen or wardens and stewards practically themselves managed the affairs of the Gilds.

On the " Gild day," generally the day of the saint to whom the Gild
was dedicated, the brethren and sisters, arrayed in their vesture, and
carrying candles, went in procession to church to hear mass performed
at an altar, the light before which was maintained by the Gild. One of
the ordinances of many consisted in a bidding prayer, which was said
on this occasion, and in some cases at the commencement of all the
meetings of the fraternity. After the conclusion of the mass alms
were distributed to the poor by the stewards, and the Gild returned
in procession to their hall to enjoy the anniversary banquet or common
meal.

The brethren and sisters also attended in their garb at the funerals of
members and at the performance of masses for the repose of the souls
of their dead. The Gild provided the customary wax lights and the
pall.

An entrance fee, a fixed annual payment to the common purse, and
dues to the aldermen and officers, were the contribution made by
members to the funds of the Gild. In some, each member on joining
had to undertake to leave the Gild a legacy at his decease. Many such
were left, chiefly of lands, where the Gilds had, as was commonly the
case, licences in mortmain. Usually these legacies were coupled with a
condition that an obit should be annually performed for the soul of the
testator. The Gilds themselves also invested their savings in lands.
Many of them by these means became large holders of real property.

The incomes of all the Gilds were up to a certain point expended in
much the same way. The maintenance of the hall, the expense of the
entertainments, the payment of salaries, the relief of poor members and
of their widows and orphans, the portioning of poor maids, and the
payments for funerals and obits were the purposes to which the common
funds were primarily applicable. The funds of the Craft Gilds were
secondarily applicable to the binding of apprentices, loans to young men
starting in business, the purchase of new receipts and inventions, and
the prevention of adulteration. Both the Social and Craft Gilds also
relieved the poor, supplied the place of highway boards and bridge
authorities, maintained churches, endowed schools, colleges, and hospitals,
and exhibited pageants. The rules of all the bodies were such as to
inculcate respect for the law, commercial honesty, and a high standard
of conduct, together with kindness and consideration for the brethren
and sisters, and for the poor. They also breathe a spirit of very simple
piety.

The urban Craft Gilds were subject to the jurisdiction of the municipal

authorities.   Their regulations were liable to annulment if inconsistent
with the franchises and liberties of the towns ; and the mayors and town
councils frequently issued precepts to them with respect to the hours of
labour, the methods of manufacture, the education of apprentices, and
the relations of the different trades to each other.

The Gilds of Norman London were voluntary associations, precisely
similar to the provincial institutions.   They have had a double history ;
(1) a history in connexion with the municipality of London ; (2) a
domestic history, as industrial, mercantile, and charitable corporations.

1. By the time of Edward II., the government of London had
assumed, partly in consequence of the terms of the City's charters,
partly as the result of civic revolutions, a popular form, composed of
Anglo-Saxon and Norman elements, and substantially identical with
the present constitution.   The old manorial jurisdictions had been
swept away, a civic court of law had been established, and the servile
tenures had been replaced by "free burgage," the urban analogue of the
rural free socage.

The Craft Gilds of London, which appear by this time to have
absorbed the Knighten Gild and other similar bodies, represented the
popular party in the contest, and in the result substituted themselves,
though for a short time only, for the wards as the constituent parts of
the Municipality.   The trades, having in many cases their recognised
quarters in the City, the temporary substitution of the bodies which
represented them for the wards still left the representation local.   This
arrangement, however, lasted only till the next reign, when the wards
were permanently restored, with the differences consequent upon the
abolition of all feudal or semi-feudal privileges.

2. As regards the domestic history of the Companies as industrial,
mercantile, and charitable corporations, their present constitution, involving three grades of membership—the Court electing itself by
co-optation, the Livery, and the Freemen—was evidently a development
of the more pristine system of government, under which these distinc-
tions of rank and authority were less broadly and strongly marked.
The probability seems to be, that their present framework, one obviously
of great advantage to the Courts, dates back before the reign of Edward
III., in which, as it is well known, they received their parent charters.
The origin of the distinction between the Great and the Minor Companies is not so clear.

A craftsman, a member of the Mercers' Gild, became Mayor in 1214,
and before the end of the thirteenth century the Mayors were always
members of the Craft Gilds, particularly (1) of the Mercers, Grocers,
and Goldsmiths, which were from the earliest times largely composed

of wealthy merchants and shipowners; and (2) of Companies such as the early Woolstaplers and Sheermen, which represented the trade in wool and cloth.

Having regard to the fact, that about a century after this period the leading men of the Gilds were generally Aldermen, and that the Corporation exercised a minute supervision over the trade and manufactures of London, we regard the Companies as having become in effect a *municipal committee of trade and manufactures.* Soon after they had arrived at this position they were incorporated, and thereupon became practically a *State department for the superintendence of the trade and manufactures of London.*

Long before their incorporation, the Gilds had held the sites of their halls and almshouses and other real property, houses, shops, and warehouses. The tenure in time became "free burgage." An incidence of this tenure, and an important one as regards the Companies, was that it supplied the means of going beyond licences in mortmain. By the custom of the City, public bodies could accept lands held by citizens in free burgage and devised to them while so held without any limitation as to amount. The Companies appear to have become large purchasers of lands under the fiction of holding them by devise in free burgage. A Company found the money, and had the land purchased and conveyed to trustees in trust to convey it to some one person in trust to devise it to the Company by his will. The association then obtained the purchased land under the will of the nominee of their nominees.

Legacies for religious and benevolent purposes, some internal, some external, were early bequeathed to the Gilds. Their large trust-estate dates from the fourteenth century. It for some time constituted, in conjunction with the monastic and parochial endowments of the City, an organization of eleemosynary and educational charity, which was of great importance in the absence of a poor law.

By their charters, and also by grants from the Municipality of London, between the Crown and which there was much jealousy, the Companies obtained (1) monopolies, and (2) powers of search. They assumed to prevent non-members from trading and manufacturing, and they visited shops, manufactories, and houses for the purpose of testing wares, which were required by Act of Parliament, municipal precepts, or their own private regulations, to be of a certain standard or quality. They also enforced a strict system of seven years' apprenticeship.

As regards powers conferred by statute upon the Companies or at present exercised by them by virtue of custom or in reliance on the terms of their charters:

1. The Fishmongers, relying on their charters, but without authority

of any statute, appoint and pay " fish meters," who attend at Billingsgate
Market, examine the fish offered for sale there, and condemn any which
may be proved to be unsound.   The Company defrays the expense
of deodorizing and removing the fish thus condemned.   It also dis-
charges the duty of prosecuting offenders against the provisions of the
" Fisheries (Oyster, Crab, and Lobster) Act," 40 & 41 Vict., c. 42, with
respect to the sale of undersized fish or of fish during close time.

2. The Goldsmiths, under the acts 12 Geo. II., c. 26 (an act obtained
at the instance of the Company themselves) and 7 & 8 Vict., c. 22, were
till recently empowered to assay and mark plate, and to prosecute
persons who in any part of England sold plate requiring to be marked
which is below standard, or who forge the Company's marks or utter
wares bearing counterfeit marks.   Also under the Coinage Act of 1870
provision is made for an annual trial of the pyx ; and this trial, in
accordance with a practice which has prevailed since the reign of
Edward I., takes place at Goldsmiths' Hall.

3. The freemen of the Vintners who have become such by patrimony
or by apprenticeship, and the widows of such freemen, enjoy by custom
the right of selling foreign wines without a licence throughout England
on certain ancient highways.   They also, by virtue of an ancient custom,
employ a staff of tackle porters, who unload wines at the London Docks.
The Vintners' and Dyers' Companies are by ancient custom associated
with the Crown as joint protectors of the swans of the Thames.

4. The Apothecaries have powers under the Apothecaries Act, 1815,
and the Apothecaries Act Amendment Act, 1874, to examine candidates for licences to practise as apothecaries, to confer such licences,
and to recover penalties from persons so practising without licence.
They also maintain extensive chemical and pharmaceutical laboratories
in connexion with their hall, and keep up a botanical garden in Chelsea,
in respect of which they employ a botanical demonstrator to give
instruction in botany.

5. The Founders' Company stamps weights under the acts 5 & 6
Will. IV., c. 63, and 41 & 42 Vict., c. 49, s. 67.

6. The Gunmakers have a proof house in London, and have powers
under the Gun Barrel Act, 1868 (31 & 32 Vict., c. 113), for enforcing
the proving and marking of guns, pistols, and small arms, and the
prosecution of offenders against the act.

7. The Scriveners, under the act 41 Geo. III., c. 69, s. 13, conduct an
examination for admission to the office of a notary, and can prevent
any person practising as such who has not passed such examination.

8. The Stationers, who are exclusively craftsmen, have kept a register
of all publications since 1557 ; and this is legal evidence under the

Copyright Act of 1842, although the entry is not compulsory. The register from 1557 to 1640 has been printed. This Company also carries on in its corporate capacity the trade of a publisher, its principal publications, however, at present being Almanacks.

The attendance at Bartholomew and Southwark fairs of representatives or members of some of the Companies was in some instances not discontinued till a comparatively recent time; and, besides those chartered or customary functions which we have just mentioned, there were privileges, such as the charge of the City Beam by the Grocers' Company, and the superintendence of Blackwell Hall by the Drapers' Company, which were continued after the Gilds had ceased to represent the trade and commerce of London. The date at which they definitely ceased to do so may be fixed at the Restoration.

London was during all this time a great manufacturing town, in or near which clothworking, the smelting of iron, the making of armour and bows, the working of silk and leather, the manufacture of the precious metals, and other minor industries were practised with much success. It was also the chief port of northern Europe, and as all the merchants of the Staple were members of the Gilds, and corresponded with the merchants of the Staple in the provincial towns and on the Continent, there can be little doubt that the halls of the Gilds were practically exchanges. The leading members seem also to have given advice to the Privy Council as to the mercantile policy of the Crown.

Throughout the same period, the State and the Municipality sought to regulate, not only the manufactures and commerce of London, but also the wages, habits, and even the dress of the citizens to a degree not always consistent with personal liberty; and this system of statutes and precepts was to a great extent administered through the agency of the Companies. Artisans and tradesmen who made or sold bad articles were tried by the wardens, and if found guilty were punished by the civic power, or occasionally by distresses levied by the Companies themselves.

As early, however, as the reigns of Edward III. and Richard II., the mediæval theory of *status* as the basis of the relations of master and servant and of employer and employed was being gradually undermined as villeinage disappeared, and the Reformation began to make progress. The Gilds, which had their origin in an earlier conception of society, appear to have gradually excited the hostility of the artisans of London, who naturally viewed the monopolies and other privileges obtained from the Crown with jealousy, as they were apt to be beneficial to a limited number or a favoured grade. The constitution of the Gilds was only suited to a limited area, to the inspection of factories and shops in one

street or one quarter, so that the spread of London beyond its walls
and the growth of the great suburbs, particularly those of Westminster
and Southwark, must have seriously interfered with their efficiency as
superintendents of production. The later charters generally extend the
local limits of the trade control, in order to meet this difficulty.

These causes tended to cripple the Gilds in the capacity of a State
department and municipal committee. Yet they continued to receive
charters at the beginning of every reign for a long time after this date.
Indeed, some were founded, both in London and in the provinces,
as late as the time of Anne ; and the term of apprenticeship sanctioned by the London and provincial Gilds, *viz.* seven years, was adopted
in an act of 1662, which was not repealed till 1814.

For a long time, however, after the seventeenth century, these bodies
were an important element in the City. The wealthy bankers, merchants, and shipowners who traded in the City had houses there, and
belonged to the Companies. The first quarter of the present century
is the approximate date of the cessation of the residential connexion
of the Companies with the City.

Provincial and Continental Gilds.

Turning now to (1) the provincial Gilds of England, (2) the Gilds of
continental countries.

1. It is certain that of the 40,000 communities which are alleged
to have existed in the provincial towns and rural districts of England
during the Middle Ages, only a very few survive. Many were of
course monasteries, nunneries, or chauntries ; these were suppressed, and
their lands confiscated, at the Reformation. Many, again, though not
altogether clerical institutions—for instance, schools or hospitals—were
so connected with the dissolved orders, or had so much property settled
to superstitious uses, that they perished along with the monasteries.

It does not appear that all the property of the Gilds in these towns
was confiscated ; and there is evidence that one Company at least was
allowed to redeem confiscated lands in the same way as the City
Companies redeemed theirs. Their halls also are not likely to have
been held to superstitious uses.

In the histories of some of the old towns of England, an account,
though not a full one, is to be found of their early Gilds. We may
take the cases of (1) Bristol, (2) Coventry, (3) Newcastle-on-Tyne,
(4) Norwich, (5) York.

In these five places there existed upwards of 150 Gilds, corporations
in every way resembling the London Companies, and some of them,

such as the Merchants' Company of York, the Merchant Adventurers' Company of Newcastle, the Merchant Adventurers' Company of Bristol, and the Gild of St. George of Norwich, bodies of great dignity and opulence. These and the rest have disappeared, except the Merchant Adventurers' Company of Newcastle, the Merchant Adventurers' Company of Bristol, which has, at this day, a large amount of house-property at Clifton, and a few insignificant Companies containing only a few members.

There are historical traces of the existence of many of these bodies down to a period long after the Reformation, and indeed till the present century ; of sales by them of their halls ; of transferences of their alms-houses ; and of sales of their estates, particularly houses, as the number of members decreased.

We assume that the surviving members divided the proceeds of these sales, as there can be no doubt that they were entitled to do, unless they held the property subject to some trust. A similar course has been taken in London in the cases of Serjeants' Inn, Doctors' Commons, Clement's Inn, Barnard's Inn, and Staple Inn. So too the few surviving members of the Fullers' Gild at Newcastle obtained an order from the Master of the Rolls to divide the remaining property and dissolve the association. But many corporations, which were trustees of charities, appear to have dissolved themselves without making provision for the future maintenance of their charities.

It seems not improbable that some of the London Gilds may have taken a similar course. At the time of the revival of the Needlemakers' Company, the number of members had become very small, and, but for the influx of new members, the survivors might have divided the assets. But we have not met with any actual proof of a London Company so doing.

2. The Royal Commission obtained information, through the Foreign Office and otherwise, as to the history of the Gilds of France, Belgium, the Netherlands, Switzerland, Germany, Austria, Norway, Sweden, Italy, Spain, Portugal, Russia, and Turkey.

Two learned archæologists, M. Pigeonneau, Professor at the Sorbonne, and M. Levasseur, of the French Institute, sent interesting communi-cations on the subject of the French Gilds. These gentlemen, like the English and German antiquaries, adopt the classification of the mediæval Companies into Merchant Gilds, of which they choose the Parisian Company of Mercers as an example, and Craft Gilds. We learn from them that all such bodies in France were suppressed during the third year of the Revolution, 1791. They had existed from a period prior to the twelfth century. They were reorganized by Colbert in 1673, and their suppression was attempted by Turgot, during his short ministry in 1776. They were very numerous. At the Revolution, fifty still existed in Paris. They possessed halls, almshouses, and chapels, but not much other real property. Their funds consisted chiefly of accumulations of dues and fines, and during the eighteenth century they had become impoverished. At their suppression, their property was devoted to State purposes; but compensation was in some instances paid to existing members. Patrimony appears to have entered, though to a limited extent, into their constitution.

In Belgium the Gilds were suppressed, and their property confiscated in 1794.

In the Netherlands the trade Gilds were suppressed in 1798; their property was vested in commissioners. In 1820 the municipalities were directed to sell the property and hold it in trust for the relief of indigent members and of the poor of the communes.

In Switzerland many of the trade Gilds still exist under the names of "abbayes" or "zünfte," and have—especially, it is believed, at Berne—considerable real property. Some have been dissolved, either dividing the estate among the survivors, or applying it to public purposes, particularly education.

In Germany, under the "Gewerbe-Ordnung" of 1869, an act depriving the ancient Gilds of their privileges, placing them under communal or State control, and rendering them incapable of acquiring land without the consent of the communal authority, these bodies began rapidly to disappear. An act of 1878 reversed the policy of the "Gewerbe-Ordnung," and in 1881 one was passed for the encouragement of the Gilds. They have now power "to create industrial schools, to make rules for advancing the technical education of masters and journeymen, to establish a system of examinations, to create tontine and sick and invalid funds, and to appoint tribunals of arbitration."

In Austria-Hungary the "Innungen" (Trade Gilds) were abolished, and their monopolies repealed, by a law of 1859. The act establishes in their stead "Genossenschaften," local bodies representing the master-manufacturers and the journeymen — apparently trade-councils and tribunals of arbitration, and having in some cases technical schools attached to them. The act provides for the sale of the halls of the "Innungen" and for the payment of the proceeds, after settlement of the debts of the suppressed bodies, to the Genossenschaften.

In Norway and Sweden the old trade corporations, which are described as having been a serious drawback to the development of the native industries, were dissolved in 1846.

In Italy, the ancient Gilds, with a few exceptions, were abolished during the present century, prior to the union of the Kingdom. In 1878 and 1879 acts were passed abolishing all monopolies; but provision is made for the regulation of certain trades by the municipalities and for "institutions of mutual assistance," *i.e.* benefit societies, in connexion with such trades.

In Spain many of the mediæval Craft Gilds (*Gremios*) still exist. Their rules as to apprenticeship were cancelled in 1836; but they were not dissolved, and still survive as benefit societies and trade councils. They possess halls or houses of meeting, but no other real property. In Portugal the Craft Gilds were suppressed in 1834. They appear to have possessed little real property. In Russia and Turkey, there are at the present day many institutions resembling the Craft Gilds of the Middle Ages. In all these countries the Gilds seem to have been much more exclusively associations of members of trades than was ever the case with the London Companies.

There appear to have been always three grades of membership of the London Livery Companies: (1) mere membership, the possession of the Freedom, which makes a freeman or freewoman; (2) membership of what is called the Livery; (3) a place on the Court or governing body.

The Freedom has been from time immemorial obtainable in four ways: (1) by apprenticeship or servitude; (2) by patrimony; (3) by redemption; (4) by gift. The last is purely honorary.

A system of apprenticeship was an essential element in the Gilds from which the Companies sprang. After their incorporation, the term of service, the premium, and the *status* and duties of apprentices, were regulated by bye-laws framed by the Courts, and submitted by them (1) to the judges, (2) to the Municipality. The youths were articled on these terms as apprentices to freemen for a period of seven years, at the expiration of which, upon proof that they had duly served their masters during the seven years, they became entitled to the Freedom of the Company.

Two ceremonies were involved in this method of admission: (1) that of binding; (2) that of conferring the Freedom at the expiration of the articles. Each took place at the hall of the Company, or, if the Company had not a hall, at the Guildhall, a name which is itself a memorial of the importance of the Gilds of London in early times. The father or guardian of the apprentice paid the Company a nominal fee and some small sums to the officers and servants in respect of the binding; and when the apprentice was admitted to the Freedom, he also paid a nominal fee to the Company, and some small sums to the officers and servants in respect of his admission.

Of patrimony we have already spoken.   Every son or daughter of a person who has been duly admitted to the Freedom has always been entitled to claim, when of age, his or her admission to the Freedom upon proof of (1) his or her legitimacy, (2) the membership of his or her father at the time of his or her birth.   The ceremony of admission took place at the hall of the Company, or at the Guildhall, and the novice paid an entrance fee and small charges of about the same amount as in the case of admission by apprenticeship.   It was far more usual for sons to follow their fathers' occupations during the Middle Ages than it is at present ; but Gilds into which members were admitted by patrimony must always have contained persons of no occupation, or of occupations different from those from which the Gilds derived their names.

Apprenticeship also seems to have been by no means confined to the trades of the Gilds.   From an early period a practice prevailed of bestowing the freedom on persons who had been bound to any of the members, irrespective of their callings.   Such bindings were foreign to the ordinances of most of the Gilds, and involved an infringement of the rights of the Gilds which represented the trades, if any, of the apprentices.   Also from an early period purely colourable bindings were allowed ; that is, youths were bound as a matter of form to persons whose trades they did not mean to follow, and who undertook no obligations in respect of their protection or education, in order that they might on coming of age be able to claim the Freedom of the Companies of their nominal masters.

This colourable apprenticeship was no wrong, it being one of the modes of admission, and enabled a man of moderate means to obtain for his son a position in the Company, which otherwise he would not have been able to do, and which might be to his advantage in after life.   It must be remembered that this has been the custom of centuries.

The Freedom has been (1) sold, (2) conferred, like that of the City, as an honour upon personages of distinction, from a very early period. The former method of admission is called admission by redemption ; the latter, admission *honoris causâ*.   Redemption does not at present exist in the Grocers' Company, but does so (with a limitation to members of the trade in those few Companies which still have a trade, such as the Apothecaries and the Stationers) in all the others.   The Court is and has for centuries been the admitting authority both to the Freedom and the Livery.

The entrance-fee paid in respect of admission to the Freedom by redemption seems to have always varied with the civic and general standing of the several Companies.   At present the maximum seems to be about 108*l.*

Above the mere freemen and freewomen have always been the members of the Livery, those who, as it was technically expressed, had the clothing of the brotherhood. They were either (1) craftsmen, employers of labour ; or (2) non craftsmen, persons of some wealth and position, who had joined the Company by patrimony or by purchase.

From very early times down to the present day the Court of Aldermen, in the exercise of a sort of visiting jurisdiction, has claimed the right of authorizing the Companies to organize a Clothing or Livery ; two terms which custom made synonymous, but of which the latter was originally tantamount only to the delivery of the Gild suit. By an act of the Court of Aldermen, dated July 27, 1697, it is enacted " that no person shall be allowed to take upon himself the clothing of any of the twelve Companies unless he have an estate of 1,000*l.*, of the inferior Companies unless he have an estate of 500*l.*" ; and the spirit of this property qualification is still generally observed.

On admission to the Livery, larger fees are payable than in the case of admission to the Freedom. A distinction is always made between the case of persons who have entered by patrimony or by servitude and that of persons who have entered by purchase, the latter class being compelled to pay far higher for the new privilege. In addition to the fees and fines, each freeman and liveryman has always paid quarterly to the common purse a quarterage or quarterwage. It is estimated that there are about 7,300 liverymen altogether, and about 1,500 of these constitute the respective Courts.

The Courts consisted originally of the founders. As vacancies took place by death, these persons elected members of the Liveries to fill them. The Courts at an early stage consisted of a master or prime warden, and two or more other wardens, and a number of " assistants." [1]

At the present day the governing bodies are called the Courts of Assistants. A new member, on election by co-optation, generally took office as renter-warden, an onerous position. He was promoted from wardenship to wardenship till he became prime warden or master. After having " passed the chair" he became an ordinary Assistant for life. At nearly all the steps a fee or fine was charged. At the present time the system is similar, and most of the Assistants have served as wardens, and have passed the chair.

---

[1] " Assistants are to be traced in the councils of twelve of the Saxon Gilds, and in the *eschevins* and elders of the Norman era. The first hint of them in the Livery Companies occurs in the records of the Grocers, under the year 1379, when six persons were chosen to aid the wardens in the discharge of their duties."—*Herbert on the Companies*, vol. i., p. 53.

The fees payable in respect of the several promotions are considerable. A person joining a prominent London Company as a liveryman by purchase might, in his progress from the position of a mere
freeman to the mastership, have to pay 200*l.*, or even upwards of 300*l.*
in fees and fines. The numbers of the Courts vary from about twelve
to between thirty and forty.

The privileges which the members of the City Companies at present
possess, apart from their position as voters on the municipal register of
London, are as follow :

I. Freemen and freewomen (of the latter of whom, however, there
are now scarcely any), and the widows and orphans of freemen, are
entitled in case of poverty and in old age (1) to be received into the
almshouses of the Companies which have almshouses ; (2) to pensions
and casual relief out of the trust funds which have been left to the
Companies for that purpose. They are also commonly relieved out
of the Companies' corporate income.

The charters granted frequently refer to the relief of the poor
members of the Gilds in such way as to shew that a main object of the
grant of power to hold land in mortmain was the maintenance of almshouses. For instance, the preamble of the Mercers' charter is as follows :
" In consideration that several men of the mystery of mercery of the
City of London often by misfortunes of the sea and other unfortunate
casualties *have become so impoverished and destitute* that they have little
or nothing in consequence to subsist on unless from the alms and
assistance of the faithful." The Grocers' charter grants to the wardens
and commonalty of the mystery that they may " acquire lands " in the
City and its suburbs " to the value of twenty marks per year, to have
and hold to them and their successors towards *the support of the poor
men of the said commonalty.*" The Fishmongers' charter similarly contains a grant of power to hold land " *for the sustentation of the poor men
and women of the said commonalty.*"

The Goldsmiths' charter recites that " many persons of that trade by
fire and the smoke of quicksilver had lost their sight ; and that others
of them by working in that trade *became so crazed and infirm that* they
were disabled to subsist but of relief from others ; and that divers of
the said City, compassionating the condition of such, were disposed to
give and grant divers tenements and rents in the said City to the value
of twenty pounds per annum to the Company of the said craft *towards
the maintenance of the said blind, weak, and infirm.*"

Some of the charters do not contain clauses of this benevolent kind ;
but during this period a religious or benevolent object may generally be
presumed as regards mortmain lands.

All the great and several of the small Companies have endowed alms-houses. Originally, in many cases, the almshouses adjoined the halls ; nearly all were within the City or its liberties. But as the value of building land in the City has rapidly increased during the present century, the Companies have sometimes found it profitable to let the sites of these foundations for the construction of warehouses and offices, and to rebuild the almshouses on less expensive sites in other parts of London or in the country. The trust-funds for their support and the relief of poor members, their widows and orphans, are very ample, and often partly consist of contributions from the corporate income.

As a rule, a claim to relief in case of poverty is the only privilege which the possession of the mere freedom of a Company confers. In a single case, that of the Clothworkers, the almspeople are invited to an entertainment. In that Company, also, and in two or three others, the freemen are enabled to educate their children on advantageous terms, owing to admissions to Christ's Hospital, which some of the Companies have bought for the purpose, and to the Companies' own schools.

The privileges of liverymen as regards charitable relief are similar to those of freemen ; but the pensions voted to them and their widows and orphans are larger. They have also generally a legal right to a place at those banquets which are chartered franchises, and they are invited by the Courts as a matter of favour to other entertainments, sometimes, in the more opulent Companies, to two or three banquets in the course of a year. In most of the Companies, when a liveryman petitions successfully for relief from the trust or corporate funds, he has to resign his position on the Livery, and has the amount of his livery-fine returned to him. The pensions voted to decayed liverymen, their widows and orphans, vary, according to the wealth of the Companies, from 50l. to 150l. a year. There are a few Companies, the Iron-mongers and Joiners, and for some purposes the Mercers and Coopers, in which the Livery (and not merely the master wardens and assistants) constitute the governing body.

The Courts have in their hands, as a rule, the entire control of the Companies' affairs, the appointment of the staffs of salaried officials which the Companies employ, the management of the Companies' corporate property, the admissions to the Freedom, Livery, and Court, the administration of the Companies' charitable trusts, the appoint-ments of the incumbents of livings and of the masters of schools. They are also the entertainers, and have, as of course, a place at all the Companies' banquets. In the great Companies a member of the Livery is seldom elected to the Court till he has been on the Livery for fifteen or twenty years ; but seniority is not the sole criterion

of fitness.   Regard appears to be paid to social position, business
capacity, and interest in the charities of the Companies.   Also in some
of the Companies a liveryman is at once promoted to the Court on
his election as an Alderman.

Members of the Courts, their widows and orphans, are, like freemen
and liverymen, eligible for pensions and charitable relief out of the trust
and corporate funds of the Companies in case of poverty.   The highest
pensions commonly voted to such persons amount to 200*l*.   The
average amount is from 50*l*. to 100*l*.   Formerly it was not necessary
for a member of the Court to retire on making an application for a
pension.   But at present the same course is followed as in the case of
liverymen ; the applicants are removed from the Court, and their fees
are returned to them.   With rare exceptions, all the proceedings of the
Courts are secret.   Their accounts are not published, and the liverymen
and freemen have not access to the records of their proceedings.

The substitution of the Companies for the wards as divisions of the
Municipality of London lasted only a few years in a very early epoch.
The householders in the wards, being freemen of the City, are now and
have always been, except during this short interval, the electors to the
courts of Aldermen and of Common Council respectively.   But till
1835 the Freedom of the City could only be obtained through a Livery
Company.   In that year the Municipality of London decided to confer
it irrespective of the Companies on certain terms through the City
Chamberlain.   But the freemen of the Companies have still the right to
claim as such the Freedom of the City; and it is not uncommon for them
to pay the City fee to the officers of the Company, on joining, for payment over to the Chamberlain.   On promotion to the Livery, this is still
more usual.   However, since 1835, the Freedom of a Company and the
Freedom of the City have not been convertible terms ; and so far back
as 1837 the Corporation possessed a very slight, hardly more than a
nominal, control over the Companies.

This control was due to the " Common Hall," which consists of
those liverymen of the Companies who are also freemen of the City.
It still proposes to the Court of Aldermen two Aldermen, one of
whom the Court elects Lord Mayor, and itself elects the Sheriffs, the
Chamberlain, the Bridgemaster, and the auditors of the City and
Bridge-House accounts.   The election of the Lord Mayor takes place
on September 29, that of the other officers on Midsummer Day.

Prior to the Reform Bill (2 Will. IV., c. 45), the liverymen of the
Common Hall constituted the parliamentary constituency of London.
Every voter had to be a freeman of the City and a liveryman of a
Company.   The Reform Bill preserves the franchises of the liverymen

in conjunction with those of the ordinary electors, with the limitation that, in order to vote as a liveryman, it is necessary to have taken up the freedom of the City prior to March 1, 1831, or to have obtained it subsequently by servitude or by patrimony through a qualified person, and also to have been resident within seven miles of the Mansion House for the six months preceding registration.

In addition to the vote in Common Hall and the parliamentary suffrage, those members of the Companies who have become free of the City possess the other rights of citizens. These were formerly much more important than they now are; but even at the present day none except freemen can claim the benefit of the custom of the City of London.

The part played by the leading Companies in early times in civic pageants is well known. The ceremony of inauguration formerly took place on October 29, or if that fell on a Sunday, on the 30th. Lord Mayor's Day is now celebrated on November 9. The Companies to which the Lord Mayor and the Sheriffs belong usually join in the procession; and the former for the time being takes precedence over all the others.

Number of Members.

There is great difficulty in forming an estimate of the number of freemen. They are often never heard of after they have taken out their freedom. They change their residences and cease to pay quarterage, when their names are erased from the lists. Sometimes, years after this has been done, the Companies are reminded of their existence by a claim to charitable relief. It seems not improbable that there may be 10,000 freemen altogether. There are perhaps upwards of 1,000 connected with the Goldsmiths and Drapers respectively. The number of those belonging to the other great Companies is much smaller.

Some of the minor Companies are in point of numbers and wealth equal to the less opulent of the great Companies. Such are the Armourers, Carpenters, Leathersellers, Brewers, Saddlers, and Cutlers.

The Companies named in the Second Report of the Commission appointed to inquire into Municipal Corporations in England and Wales are eighty-nine in number, twelve great Companies, seventy-seven minor Companies. Out of these latter[1] thirteen proved to

---

[1] These were the Companies of Combmakers, Fishermen, Gardeners, Hat-band Makers, Longbow String Makers, Paviours, Pinmakers, Silk Weavers, Silk Throwsters, Soapmakers, Starchmakers, Tobacco-pipe Makers, and Woodmongers. The names of some supposed members of these Companies were discovered by reference to

have become extinct since the date of the Report, while four[1] turned out not to be Livery Companies. The Needlemakers, Basketmakers, Turners, Shipwrights, and Fanmakers, the charter of the last of which was recently recovered by accident, have been resuscitated of late years.

Two of the largest liveries are those of the Loriners and Spectacle-makers, bodies membership of which appears to entail little advantage beyond the municipal and parliamentary franchises. So far as the number of votes is concerned, the Loriners stand at the head of all the Gilds in the regulation lists of 1891, and appear to have always occupied a prominent rank in this respect. The liverymen, from whom the members of the Courts are selected, are a body consisting chiefly of persons following professions, persons engaged in commerce, or persons who have retired from business. A considerable number are men of some eminence. Many members of the House of Commons are liverymen. The City is represented by the Aldermen, most of whom belong to several Companies, and the Common Councilmen. The Courts consist, speaking generally, of liverymen of some fifteen years' standing, mostly promoted according to seniority. We have observed too, that admission by patrimony produces a natural effect on the constitution of the Liveries and on that of the Courts. Where a family continues prosperous from generation to generation, it acquires a position of considerable importance on the Court and Livery of a Company. A remarkable instance is that of the Mercers' Company, the Court of which is recruited from a Livery of ninety-seven, on which certain families are represented by as many as nine or ten members.

It cannot be of any real importance whether the Courts be composed of ten, twenty, thirty, or forty members, when their surroundings and social positions are considered. It must be remembered that every liveryman aspires to attain the Court, and that to enable a fair proportion of the Livery to do this, it is absolutely necessary that the Courts be large. It may also be pointed out that each member has paid a sum according to the *status* of his Company for his seat, and that he does not reach this till he is far advanced in life, that some die before and some soon after their election on the Court, before they

---

the City registers, and communications were sent to these persons with a view to discovering the circumstances under which the Companies had been wound up, and what had taken place with respect to the property, if any, remaining at the date of the dissolution. We did not in any case receive an answer to these communications. The Paviours' Company has left some papers deposited in the Guildhall Library, and these we caused to be examined. No reference was, however, found in them to the circumstances under which the Company had been dissolved.

[1] These were the Carmen, the Fellowship-Porters, the Parish Clerks, and the Watermen and Lightermen.

have received even a return of the fines and fees paid by them to their Company.

Although only 1,500 of the Livery out of a total of about 20,000 liverymen and freemen are members of the Courts of the Companies at any one time, each qualified liveryman and freeman in rotation, if life allowed, would become a member. The whole of the remaining 18,500 members have a vested interest in the properties of the Companies, and enjoy advantages and privileges as such. There is no evidence, and not even a suggestion, of a contemplated payment of any dividend or of any misappropriation or division of the funds ; and nothing of the sort could legally take place without the consent of each and every member, be he liveryman or be he freeman.

Three great events have exercised an important influence on the history of the Companies ; *viz.* (1) the Reformation, (2) the Fire of London, (3) the Plantation of Ulster.[1]

(1) In the course of the suppression of the religious houses, many lands held by the Companies to superstitious uses, such as the performance of masses for the dead and the maintenance of chauntries, were confiscated. The Companies were, however, allowed to redeem the lands, on a representation that they were required for the purposes of the eleemosynary and educational charities of which they were trustees.

(2) The halls, almshouses, and house property of the Companies suffered severely in the Fire of 1666. Its effects for a time greatly impoverished them, and large sums were raised by the governing bodies for rebuilding. In many cases they were never restored.

(3) At the time of the colonization of Ulster certain of the Companies united to purchase and undertake the settlement of a large tract of country in the county of Londonderry.

The growth of the great municipal estate, which is hereinafter described, may be traced down from the twelfth century. The Companies have been purchasers of land in the City of London and elsewhere, and many hundreds of legacies of land, or of money to be converted into land, have been left to them for charitable purposes. Their wealth has probably increased with each century ; but the chief increase has taken place during the present one, as a consequence of the recent rise in the value of house-property in the City of London

---

[1] Long before this movement on the part of the Crown in 1608, Robert Payne, a surveyor and land-agent, and twenty-five partners, undertook a settlement of lands in Ireland, subsequently to the so-called pacification in Elizabeth's reign under Sir George Carew ; and another of the company published an account of the good success of the project, in order to encourage colonists, in 1589.

Within the next twenty years the lapse of old leases will still further tend to augment the aggregate.

On the whole, we estimate the trust and corporate income of the Companies for 1879–80 as between 750,000*l.* and 800,000*l.*, a sum exceeding the income of the two Universities of Oxford and Cambridge and of the colleges therein at the time when a Royal Commission inquired into these learned bodies.

Taking the real property at a number of years' purchase, which we are informed cannot be excessive, and the income of their personal property as representing an ordinary percentage on the capital, we are of opinion that the capital value of the Companies' property cannot be less than fifteen millions sterling.

The income arising from this property is partly (i.) corporate income ; (ii.) trust income ; *i.e.* income which the Companies or their Courts are bound to apply in accordance with (*a*) the wills of founders, (*b*) Acts of Parliament, (*c*) the decrees of the High Court of Justice, and (*d*) schemes framed by the Charity and Endowed Schools Commissions.

The following list shews the income of the great Companies in order of civic precedence and of the minor Companies in alphabetical order, as it was returned in 1882 ; and it is (with very few exceptions) substantially the same at present. We should state that the balance in hand at the beginning of each financial year is excluded, as not being income. Such sum is considerable ; and we have made an addition to the corporate income, which may be supposed approximately to represent the annual interest thereupon.

GREAT COMPANIES.

	Income (*for* 1879–80) £	Corporate. £	Trust. £
Mercers	82,758	47,341	35,417
Grocers	38,236	37,736	500
Drapers	78,654	50,141	28,513
Fishmongers . . .	50,713	46,913	3,800
Goldsmiths . . .	54,297	43,505	10,792
Skinners	28,927[1]	18,977	9,950
Merchant Taylors . .	43,311[2]	31,243	12,068
Haberdashers . . .	29,032	9,032	20,000
Salters	21,040	18,892	2,148
Ironmongers . . .	21,647	9,625	12,822
Vintners	10,887	9,365	1,522
Clothworkers . . .	50,458[3]	40,458	10,000

[1] In 1891 the income, according to Whitaker, was 39,000*l.*
[2] In 1891, 50,000*l.*   [3] In 1891, 55,000*l.*

The rateable value of the halls of these Companies is about 35,000*l*., that of their schools and almshouses is probably about 15,000*l*. The value of their plate and furniture is approximately about 270,000*l*. The annual income of the livings in their gift is about 12,000*l*. a year.

MINOR COMPANIES.

	Income.	*Corporate Income.*	*Trust Income.*
	£	£	£
Apothecaries	3,898	3,398	500
Armourers	8,086	8,026	60
Bakers	1,911	1,591	320
Barbers	1,720[1]	1,120	600
Basket-makers	61	61	None.
Blacksmiths	684	684	None.
Bowyers	590	550	40
Brewers	18,640	3,157	15,482
Broderers	No return.	—	70 (?)
Butchers	2,021	1,389	632
Carpenters	11,318	10,378	940
Clockmakers	—	—	—
Coachmakers	1,179	1,179	None.
Cooks	2,560	2,380	180
Coopers	7,120	2,420	4,700
Cordwainers	7,754[2]	6,154	1,600
Curriers	1,295	1,245	50
Cutlers	5,387	5,337	50
Distillers	No return.	—	—
Dyers	7,000	6,000	1,000
Fanmakers	250[3]	250	None.
Farriers	240	240	None.
Feltmakers	362	172	190
Fletchers	150[4]	150	None.
Founders	1,943	1,853	90
Framework Knitters . .	310[5]	180	130
Fruiterers	470	467	3
Girdlers	4,306	2,932	1,374
Glass-sellers	190	100	90
Glaziers	300	260	40
Glovers	150	150	None.
Gold and Silver Wyre Drawers	65	62	3
Gunmakers	2,565	2,565	None.

[1] In 1891, 2,600*l*.   [2] In 1891, 9,300*l*.   [3] In 1891, 50*l*.
[4] In 1891, 100*l*.   [5] In 1891, 440*l*.

	Income. £	Corporate Income. £	Trust Income. £
Horners	100	100	None.
Innholders	1,547	1,327	220
Joiners	1,312	1,312	None.
Leathersellers	18,728	16,395	2,333
Loriners	1,267	1,267	None.
Masons	400[1]	400	None.
Musicians	400	400	None.
Needlemakers	250	250	None.
Painters	3,100	800	2,300
Patten-makers	300	286	14
Pewterers	3,850	3,610	240
Plaisterers	900	867	33
Playingcard-makers . . .	50	50	None.
Plumbers	900	882	18
Poulters	1,050	620	430
Saddlers	11,243	10,243	1,000
Scriveners	856	846	10
Shipwrights	833	833	None.
Spectacle-makers . . .	1,134	1,089	45
Stationers	4,746	3,170	1,576
Tallow Chandlers . . .	No return.		220
Tinplate Workers . . .	No return.		37
Turners	718	718	None.
Tylers and Bricklayers . .	834	664	170
Upholders	353	333	20
Wax Chandlers . . .	1,005[2]	1,375	230
Weavers	No return.		360
Wheelwrights	319	319	None.
Woolmen	300	300	None.

The rateable value of the halls of the minor Companies is about 20,000*l*. a year ; that of their almshouses, schools, etc., is about 3,000*l*. a year. The value of their plate and furniture is approximately about 50,000*l*. Their ecclesiastical patronage is limited to one or two Companies which appoint to preacherships.

It will be noticed that there is great disparity in the amount of the trust incomes of the Companies. In some cases it is nominal or even nothing. The strongest instances are those of (1) the Grocers' Company, the trust income of which is 500*l*. out of a total income of 38,000*l*. ; (2) the Armourers' Company, the trust income of which is

---

[1] In 1891, 550*l*.   [2] In 1891, 1,600*l*.

60*l.* out of a total income of 8,000*l.* Other, though less striking, examples are those of (1) the Fishmongers' Company, the trust income of which is 3,800*l.* out of a total income of upwards of 50,000*l.* ; (2) the Leathersellers' Company, the trust income of which is 2,300*l.*, out of a total income of nearly 19,000*l.* ; (3) the Saddlers' Company, the trust income of which is about 1,000*l.* out of a total income of upwards of 11,000*l.*

On the other hand, the trust incomes of the two wealthiest Companies, the Mercers' Company and the Drapers' Company, are respectively above one-third and two-fifths of the total income : in the case of the Mercers' Company 35,000*l.* out of 83,000*l.*; in that of the Drapers' Company 28,000*l.* out of 79,000*l.* Also in several cases the trust income greatly exceeds the corporate income. Thus (1) the trust income of the Haberdashers' Company is probably 20,000*l.* out of a total income of 30,000*l.* ; (2) the trust income of the Brewers' Company is 16,000*l.* out of a total income of 20,000*l.* ; (3) the trust income of the Painter-stainers' Company is 3,000*l.* out of a total income of 4,000*l.* ; (4) the trust income of the Ironmongers' Company is 12,000*l.* out of a total income of 21,000*l.*

The above table also shews that some of the minor Companies are not trustees of charities. These are the Basketmakers, Blacksmiths, Coachmakers, Fanmakers, Fletchers, Glovers, Gunmakers, Horners, Joiners, Loriners, Masons, Musicians, Needlemakers, Playingcard-makers, Shipwrights, Turners, Wheelwrights, and Woolmen. The total income of these eighteen Companies is, however, only about 8,000*l.* a year ; and several of them, particularly the Loriners and Spectacle-makers, the recently resuscitated Companies of Turners, Needlemakers, Fanmakers, and Shipwrights, as well as a few others, chiefly depend on the fees and fines paid by existing members. On the whole, of the sum of from 750,000*l.* to 800,000*l.* which constitutes the annual income of the Companies, (1) about 200,000*l.* a year may be trust income, (2) from 550,000*l.* to 600,000*l.* corporate income.

As to the trust-estate of the Companies, it supports upwards of a thousand charities ; and the authorities in 1882–3 were of opinion that no charities in England were better administered.

As regards both classes of property, not only did financial difficulties continue down to a comparatively recent date, but the income probably did not become considerable till about 1830, when a large number of building leases in the City fell in, and it became possible for the Gilds to raise the ground-rents so as to participate in its increased value.

The Irish estate of the Companies, in the purchase of which they sank in the reign of James I. about 60,000*l.*, exclusively of subsequent working expenses, did not become really remunerative till quite lately. Nothing can be more admirable than the conduct of the Companies with respect to these Ulster lands. They found them a desert, and by their care and munificence they have made them one of the most prosperous parts of the United Kingdom. Indeed, they may be said to have founded at their own expense the loyal province of Ulster, a service to the Crown perhaps without a parallel, except that rendered by the East India Company.

In times past, the chief Companies always devoted a substantial portion of their funds to public objects; and their expenditure upon such objects appears to have grown in proportion to the growth of their revenues. Thus, in 1822, the Goldsmiths, whose income was not then large, founded six exhibitions of 20*l.* a year, three tenable at Oxford, three at Cambridge. The Company gradually increased. the number and value of its exhibitions, till it had in 1882 endowed seventy-five exhibitions, each of the value of 50*l.* a year, tenable at the two Universities. Many examples of the same steady increase in their annual contributions to public objects can be found in their recent history. The Fishmongers, Grocers, Ironmongers, Clothworkers, and several of the minor Companies have similarly increased existing exhibitions, or have founded new out of their private means. Indeed the Companies largely subsidize in this respect the Universities of Oxford and Cambridge, including Newnham and Girton Colleges for the higher education of women, University and King's Colleges, London, and the London School Board.

They also support, to a considerable extent, out of their private income between thirty and forty schools: St. Paul's, Merchant Taylors', Tonbridge School, Aldenham School, and Great Crosby School, besides those admirable institutions, Bancroft's Hospital, the Aske Schools, and the Grocers' Middle-class School at Hackney Downs. These schools are distributed over fourteen or fifteen counties, and not fewer than 12,000 scholars are educated at them. Mr. Matthew Arnold has stated his opinion that the Companies have done much useful service in this respect. The Cambridge Local Examination Board has also given a favourable account of their management and fruit. On Merchant Taylors' School, a school without endowment, the Merchant Taylors' Company proves to have expended in recent years, out of its private income, a sum of no less than 140,000*l.*

The support given by some of the Companies to Technical Education, and to the City and Gilds of London Technical Institute, deserves special commemoration. This body was founded in 1878 by a committee sitting at Mercers' Hall, and composed of Lord Selborne, Sir

F. Bramwell, F.R.S., and Sir Sydney Waterlow and other members of the principal Companies, together with representatives of the City of London. In the autumn of this year the committee communicated with and received reports on the subject of technical education from six gentlemen of great scientific or practical knowledge of the question ; *viz.* Sir William Armstrong, F.R.S., Mr. G. T. C. Bartley, Lieut.-Colonel Donnelly, Captain Douglas Galton, F.R.S., Professor Huxley, F.R.S., and Mr. H. Trueman Wood.

In the same autumn, the Mercers, Drapers, Fishmongers, Goldsmiths, Salters, Ironmongers, Clothworkers, Armourers, Cordwainers, Coopers, Plaisterers, and Needlemakers agreed to provide about 12,000*l.* a year out of their private funds for these purposes ; and the " City and Gilds of London Institute for the Advancement of Technical Education" was provisionally constituted with the following objects : *viz.* (1) the foundation of a central institute in London for technical education ; (2) the establishment of or assistance to trade schools in London and the provinces ; (3) technological examinations ; (4) grants in aid of existing institutions having for their object technical education.

In the year 1879 the Institute was incorporated, and it has ever since continued to prosper, with the most beneficial results to the community at large. Between 1881 and 1884 the Gilds contributed about 120,000*l.* to this object alone. The Companies have thus founded in England a system of technical education, a service to the State which it is difficult to over-value, and an undertaking strictly in accordance with their original constitution. Moreover, the Clothworkers' Company has promoted the establishment of Yorkshire College at Leeds, where instruction is given in the manufacture of woollen goods, and similar institutions at Bradford, Huddersfield, and other places, the present seats of its former trade.[1]

The Companies contributed 13,000*l.* to the Royal College of Music. The Fishmongers bore the brunt of the labour of organization in respect of the " International Fisheries Exhibition," and this and other Companies made a large contribution to the expenses. They also materially assisted the " International Health Exhibition." The Grocers have founded a scholarship for scientific research.

The real estate of the Companies is situated partly (1) in the City of London proper, in other districts of London, and in the suburbs of London ; (2) in various parts of England ; (3) in the county of Londonderry, Ireland.

1 *Metropolitan Estate.*—The metropolitan estate of the Companies

---

[1] See further particulars under the account of the Company.

consists (1) of the Halls, and such of the almshouses, schools, and other institutions maintained by the Companies as are within the metropolitan area ; (2) of some thousands of houses in the City of London proper, many of them in excellent situations, and let as warehouses, banks, counting-houses, salerooms, offices, and shops, and also of some wharves with warehouses attached to them situated on the banks of the Thames, some on the City side, some on the Surrey side ; (3) of house property outside the City of London proper, but within the metropolitan area : *viz.* in Stratford,[1] West Ham,[2] Fulham,[3] Hackney,[4] Hammersmith,[5] Lambeth,[6] Islington,[7] Notting Hill,[8] Stoke Newington,[9] Stepney,[10] Walworth,[11] Hoxton,[12] Finsbury,[13] St. Pancras,[14] Southwark,[15] and Whitechapel.[16]

2. *Estates in English Counties.*—The Companies of London are owners of agricultural land or of house property or of rentcharges in the following English counties : Bedfordshire,[17] Buckinghamshire,[18] Berkshire,[19] Derbyshire,[20] Durham,[21] Essex,[22] Gloucestershire,[23] Herefordshire,[24] Hertfordshire,[25] Kent,[26] Lancashire,[27] Lincolnshire,[28] Middlesex,[29] Monmouth,[30] Norfolk,[31] Northumberland,[32] Northamptonshire,[33] Oxfordshire,[34] Staffordshire,[35] Shropshire,[36] Surrey,[37] Wiltshire,[38] Yorkshire,[39] Sussex.[40]

---

[1] Carpenters.
[2] Ironmongers, Carpenters, and Salters.
[3] Carpenters.
[4] Farriers and Clothworkers.
[5] Brewers, Girdlers, and Clothworkers.
[6] Butchers.
[7] Clothworkers, Brewers, Mercers, and Glaziers.
[8] Barbers.
[9] Masons and Barbers.
[10] Coopers.
[11] Fishmongers.
[12] Haberdashers.
[13] Blacksmiths.
[14] Brewers.
[15] Coopers, Cordwainers, Girdlers, and Saddlers.
[16] Gunmakers, and Tylers and Bricklayers.
[17] Drapers and Mercers.
[18] Mercers, Girdlers, and Brewers.
[19] Fishmongers and Salters.
[20] Goldsmiths.
[21] Mercers.
[22] Drapers, Goldsmiths, Haberdashers, Salters, Brewers, Coopers, Feltmakers, Pewterers, Saddlers.

[23] Haberdashers.
[24] Grocers.
[25] Drapers, Merchant Taylors, Clothworkers, Brewers, and Leathersellers.
[26] Mercers, Drapers, Fishmongers, Skinners, Merchant Taylors, Haberdashers, Vintners, Clothworkers, Coopers, Leathersellers, and Saddlers.
[27] Merchant Taylors.
[28] Mercers and Drapers.
[29] Goldsmiths, Salters, Brewers, Blacksmiths, Coopers, Cordwainers, Leathersellers, Musicians, and Saddlers.
[30] Haberdashers.
[31] Drapers and Fishmongers.
[32] Mercers.
[23] Grocers.
[34] Ditto.
[35] Haberdashers.
[36] Ditto.
[27] Drapers, Fishmongers, Skinners, Merchant Taylors, Haberdashers, Ironmongers, Clothworkers, Carpenters, Cooks, Coopers, Musicians.
[38] Clothworkers.
[39] Drapers and Ironmongers.
[40] Goldsmiths and Merchant Taylors.

☞ The Clothworkers' and Brewers' estates at Islington, the Fishmongers' at Walworth, the Haberdashers' at Hoxton, the Clothworkers' at Hackney, are very large.

Two Companies[1] possess estates in Wales, and one[2] lands in the Isle of Man.

3. *Irish Estate.*—Some of the Companies still possess a considerable amount of real property in the county of Londonderry, which they, with the Irish Society, were led to purchase at the commencement of the seventeenth century.

A large proportion of the Companies' estates in the City and in the metropolitan area is at present let on long building-leases, on the termination of which there is a certainty of an increased ground-rent. We regard this circumstance as conclusive evidence that the value of the Companies' estates is at present increasing, although the value of their agricultural property in England is at present depressed.

About 60,000*l.* a year arises from trust property invested in consols and other securities ; (2) some of the small Companies, which do not own land, derive their whole permanent income from savings, accumulations of fees and fines, similarly invested ; (3) a part of the sum is derived from the purchase-money of houses in the City of London, in some cases corporate, in other cases trust property, which the Companies have been compelled to surrender, under the provisions of the Lands Clauses Consolidation Act, for the purposes of railways, docks, and other public undertakings.

The contributions of existing members, consisting of quarterages, entrance-fees, livery-fines, and fines on promotion to the Court or to office, appear to amount to from 15,000*l.* to 20,000*l.* a year. In other words, existing members contribute from $\frac{1}{50}$th to $\frac{1}{37}$th or thereabout of the total income.

Expenditure: (1) Trust, (2) Corporate.

The income of more than 200,000*l.* a year derived from trust property arises from about 1,100 benefactions, the earliest certainly not less ancient than the fourteenth century, the latest under wills proved within the last few years. Of this sum about 140,000*l.* a year arises from rents and rentcharges, the remainder from dividends.

It appears from official sources that in 1862 about one-half the trust income was expended upon the inmates of almshouses and poor members, about one-quarter on schools, apprenticing charities, and exhibitions at the Universities, and about one-quarter on charitable objects of a general kind ; the two principal charities of this third class being endowments for the relief of the indigent blind and a fund for the sustentation of elementary schools connected with the Church of England.

Since 1862 there has been a considerable alteration in the distribution

[1] Grocers and Drapers.   [2] Clothworkers.

of the charitable income of the Companies, owing to the increase of the rents of certain of the educational foundations. In 1882 it was estimated that (1) about three-eighths, or 75,000*l.* a year, was expended on the support of almshouses and the relief of poor members ; (2) about three-eighths on education, as above defined ; (3) about one-quarter on charitable objects of a general kind.

Some of the charities of the third class are bequests for purposes which are obsolete, such as the relief of the inmates of debtors' prisons ; others are bequests for purposes which seem to have become impracticable, owing to the difference between ancient and modern times ; as for instance, portions to poor maids and loan-charities for advances to young men commencing business.

Many of the Companies' charities are for the benefit of the inhabitants of provincial towns and villages. In early times persons from the provinces came to London to engage in business, and when they had amassed fortunes, left legacies, not only to the Gilds to which they belonged, but to their native places.

1. As regards the sum of 75,000*l.* which is spent on almshouses and poor members. Most of the great Companies, and several of the minor Companies, maintain almshouses for their poor. Probably as early as the fourteenth century they possessed several in the City of London. The principal now existing are Whittington College in Islington, maintained by the Mercers ; St. Peter's Hospital at Wandsworth, maintained by the Fishmongers ; the Goldsmiths' almshouses at Acton, Middlesex, and Hackney, the Merchant Taylors' at Lee, Kent, the Skinners' at St. Helen's and Mile End, the Salters' at Watford, the Ironmongers' in Kingsland Road, the Vintners' at Mile End, the Clothworkers' at Islington, the Armourers' in Bishopsgate, the Bakers' in Hackney, the Brewers' at South Mimms, the Carpenters' at Twickenham, the Coopers' at Stepney, the Dyers in the City Road and in Spitalfields, the Framework-knitters' in Shoreditch, the Girdlers' at Peckham, the Leathersellers' at Barnet, the Saddlers' in Isleworth, the Tylers' and Bricklayers' at Islington, and the Weavers' at Wanstead.

These institutions have in almost all cases been largely endowed by bequests of land or money of a date subsequent to their foundation. Upwards of 500 of the 1,100 charities administered by the Companies relate to the sustentation of the almshouses, or to the relief of impoverished members, or that of the widows and orphans of members by gifts of money, food, or clothing. Very many trusts of this kind have been created during the last century, and not a few during the present, the benefactors having been in every instance, it is believed, members of the Companies.

All these foundations from a very early period have been assisted by grants from corporate income. In many cases existing members have subscribed toward them out of their private means. During the past and the present centuries, moreover, almost all the almshouses have been rebuilt, to a large extent out of the Companies' corporate estates.

The almshouses vary in size, some being mere cottages, others, like Whittington and St. Peter's Colleges, large establishments, managed by a governor, a chaplain, and a considerable staff of servants. Besides the almspeople, a large number of pensioners, decayed liverymen and freemen, and widows and orphan daughters of former members, who are in an indigent condition, are supported or assisted out of the trust income of the Companies. More than 600 charities exist for this purpose. There are far more female than male inmates, and a large majority of the pensioners are the widows and orphans of poor members who have never been called to the Livery.

The number of almspeople, pensioners, and persons otherwise relieved by the Companies may be about 2,500. There have been exceptional cases where the recipient was a member of the Court of one of the larger Companies, or where the relief went to the family of a deceased liveryman, in which as much as 400*l.* and 250*l.* a year respectively have been granted. But there are very few pensions of more than 100*l.*, or at most 150*l.*, a year, and the great majority do not exceed 50*l.* a year, while many consist of much smaller sums. The expense of maintaining the almspeople may be estimated at about 60*l.* a year each.

2. As regards the sum of 75,000*l.* which is spent on education, the objects supported are (1) the Universities of Oxford and Cambridge, (2) certain schools.

(1) The Arabic Professorship at Cambridge derives a portion of its endowment from the funds of one of the Companies. Several of the great Companies, and a few of the minor, are trustees of funds for the maintenance of scholarships or exhibitions at each University. The number of such foundations at Cambridge is considerably larger than that of those at Oxford. The trusts are generally in terms for the benefit of "poor scholars," and candidates, the means of whose parents are small, are sometimes preferred. At the two Universities there are generally upwards of 100 undergraduates who derive assistance from the Companies. As a rule, no preference is shown to members of the Companies or to their relatives.

(2) Five schools of high repute, at which a classical education is given, are managed by the Mercers, Merchant Taylors, Skinners, and Brewers. These are St. Paul's, founded by Dean Colet in 1510, Merchant Taylors', founded in 1561, Tonbridge, founded in 1553, Aldenham, founded in

1599, and Great Crosby, founded in 1618. St. Paul's and Tonbridge Schools are two of the most richly endowed schools in England. Merchant Taylors' has no endowment. The three first-mentioned schools have a large number of valuable exhibitions at the Universities, of some of which the managing Companies are themselves trustees.

St. Paul's School has been rebuilt at Hammersmith, pursuant to a scheme of the Endowed School Commissioners issued in 1879. Merchant Taylors' School has recently been removed to the Charterhouse. Tonbridge School has also been rebuilt, pursuant to a scheme sanctioned by the Charity Commission in 1870. The total number of scholars receiving their education at these schools, assuming them to be full, may be estimated at upwards of 2,000.

The Merchant Taylors' Company have spent on the Merchant Taylors' School a very large sum out of their corporate income. The Reports of the Charity Commissioners and inspectors of charities shew that the Mercers' and Skinners' Companies have in the past spent considerable sums from the same source on St. Paul's and Tonbridge Schools respectively.

The Companies are also trustees and managers of several middle-class schools for children of both sexes. The principal foundations of this kind are (1) in London the Mercers' School, founded in 1542; the Grocers' Middle-class School at Hackney Downs, founded in 1873; Bancroft's School at Mile End, founded in 1728, and maintained by the Drapers; the Greencoat School at Greenwich, founded in 1685, and maintained by the same; Aske's Schools at Hatcham and Hoxton, founded in 1688, and maintained by the Haberdashers; Dame Owen's School at Islington, founded in 1609, and maintained by the Brewers; the Ratcliff schools at Stepney and Bow Road [1] and the Stationers' school. [2] (2) In the provinces,—a school at Horsham, Sussex, [3] at West Lavington, Wiltshire, [4] at Oundle, Northamptonshire, [5] at Colwall, Herefordshire, [6] at Witney, Oxfordshire, [7] at Tottenham, in Essex, [8] Sir John Gresham's school at Holt, Norfolk, [9] a school at Cromer, in Norfolk, [10] at Bromyard, in Herefordshire, [11] at Stockport, Cheshire, [12] at Ashwell Hertfordshire, [13] at Wallingford, Oxfordshire, [14] at Newport, Stafford-

---

Founded
[1] 1540; managed by the Coopers.
[2] 1858, in pursuance of a scheme established by an order in Chancery.
[3] Managed by the Mercers.
[4]   Ditto   ditto.
[5] 1556; managed by the Grocers.
[6] 1612;   ditto   ditto.

Founded
[7] 1670; managed by the Grocers.
[8] 1617;   ditto   Drapers.
[9] 1554;   ditto   Fishmongers.
[10] 1505;   ditto   Goldsmiths.
[11] 1656;   ditto   ditto.
[12] 1487;   ditto   ditto.
[13] 1655;   ditto Merchant Taylors.
[14] 1659;   ditto   ditto.

shire,[1] at Monmouth,[2] at Bunbury, Cheshire,[3] at Landrake, St. Erny, Cornwall,[4] at Peel, in the Isle of Man,[5] at Sutton Valence, Kent,[6] and at Isley Walton, Leicestershire.[7]

The number of children of both sexes who are educated at these schools was in 1882 upwards of 10,000. It will be seen from the returns of the Companies which manage them, as well as from the Reports of the Charity Commission and the inspectors of schools, that considerable sums have been voluntarily spent on them out of corporate income.

Of the total sum of 75,000*l.* a year applicable to classical and middle-class education, including in the former category the contributions to the Universities, the proportions are about 35,000*l.* and 40,000*l.*

3. Of the 50,000*l.* a year, which forms the division of the trust income devoted to charitable objects of a general kind, about 9,000*l.* a year is applicable to the sustentation of primary schools under the management of clergymen of the Church of England in England and Wales;[8] about 5,000*l.* is applicable to the relief of indigent blind persons;[9] the remaining 36,000*l.* a year (arising from nearly 500 legacies, bequeathed during a period commencing in the fourteenth and ending in the present century) is applicable (1) to the relief of the poor of the City of London by doles of money and food and gifts of clothing, to the relief by the same means of the poor of parishes outside the City, and of the poor of many urban and rural parishes throughout England; (2) to clerical objects connected with the Church of England, such as lectureships of a general or special character at churches in the City, or in connexion with certain of the charitable institutions maintained by the Companies in the provinces; and to annual subscriptions to medical charities, particularly the London hospitals.

The reports of the Inspectors of Charities, which accompany the returns of 1884, contain detailed accounts of all the charities above-mentioned, setting forth the names of the founders, abstracts of the deeds or wills constituting the charitable trusts, the property which is charged therewith, and the mode in which the trusts are administered; and where a private Act of Parliament has been obtained, the terms are set forth. In the numerous cases in which the Court of Chancery or the Charity or Endowed Schools Commissions have decreed new schemes,

---

Founded

[1] 1656; managed by the Haberdashers.
[2] 1614; ditto ditto.
[3] 1594; ditto ditto.
[4] 1703; ditto Ironmongers.
[5] 1653; ditto Clothworkers.
[6] 1876; ditto ditto.
[7] 1625; ditto Bowyers.

[8] The Betton Charity, founded 1723, administered by the Ironmongers.
[9] The principal charities for this purpose were founded respectively 1717–24 and 1790, 1795, 1808, 1860, and 1889, and are administered by the Clothworkers and the Painterstainers.

the particulars are set forth. The amount of charitable property here involved is very considerable.

We believe that, except in cases where the terms of the charitable bequests authorize the Companies to charge for administering them, or where the conditions of a new scheme expressly authorize them to do so, the Companies act gratuitously.

Corporate Income.

Including an allowance in respect of the Halls and other buildings used by the Companies, and of their plate, furniture, and other property not producing income, we estimate the corporate or non-trust income of the Companies at from 550,000*l.* to 600,000*l.* a year. Taking the smaller sum as a basis, and deducting from it 125,000*l.*, which may be taken to represent (1) such allowance, (2) a sum representing the interest of the debt of the Companies, and (3) a sum representing the average proportion of income saved annually, about 425,000*l.* remain to be accounted for. Of this sum we compute that about 175,000*l.* is annually spent on "maintenance," about 100,000*l.* on entertainments, about 150,000*l.* on benevolent objects.

In maintenance we include sums spent in the payment of rates and taxes, in rebuilding, repairs, and other charges connected with the Halls, almshouses, schools, and other buildings and improvements, in the payment of fees to the governing bodies for attendances, in the salaries of officers and servants employed in London and in Ireland. Of the 175,000*l.* thus spent, (1) about 75,000*l.* a year is spent on rates, taxes, rebuilding, repairs, and improvements ; (2) about 40,000*l.* a year is paid to members, (3) about 60,000*l.* a year is spent on the salaries of officers and servants.

(1) Of the above-mentioned 75,000*l.*, rates and taxes, which include the tithe rentcharge on the Ulster estates, form the least considerable item. A large proportion of the income derived from Ireland is annually spent on improvements, in which term are included not only drainage and farm buildings, but the construction and maintenance of roads and bridges, and the support of places of worship, schools, and dispensaries for the use of the tenants. Part of the fund is expended on repairs and improvements in connexion with the urban and rural English estates of the Companies. The largest item, however, is that which is annually expended on the restoration and decoration of the Halls, thirty-four in number. In 1862, the Clothworkers rebuilt their Hall at a cost of £68,000. Several other bodies have taken the same course on a smaller scale.

(2) Court fees are payments to such members for attendance at the

meetings for admissions to the freedom, calls to the Livery, elections to the Courts, appointment of officers and servants, management of the corporate and charitable estates, elections of almspeople and pensioners, superintendence of schools, invitations to entertainments, and the consideration of charitable offerings.

The Courts of the chief Companies meet about once a month, those of the minor Companies about once a quarter. Where the business is large and complex, committees are appointed for special purposes.

(3) A clerk and a beadle have been attached to each gild from time almost immemorial. As the estates have increased, a number of additional offices have been created, such as those of accountants, surveyors, and assistant clerks, and a staff of domestic servants has been engaged. Those of the Companies which retain their lands in Ulster have employed resident agents since they ceased to let to middlemen.

The highest salaries paid to clerks amount to about 2,000*l*. a year. The salary next in amount is one of 1,500*l*. a year. The clerks of most of the important Companies receive about 700*l*. a year. The salaries of those attached to the minor Companies are small; some receive no stipend. The clerks are mostly' solicitors, who in some cases are allowed to carry on a private practice at the Halls of the Companies which employ them or (their recompense being nominal) transact the Companies' business at their own offices. In a few instances, the same gentleman acts for two or even three bodies. There are, besides, the salaries of the masters of the Companies' schools, those of the governors, matrons, and medical officers of their almshouses, and those of the chaplains and clerical lecturers whom they employ in connexion with their charities.

The entertainments given by the Companies are of two kinds : Court dinners and Livery dinners. Two or three banquets of the former kind are held annually in the more considerable Companies. In those of less importance not more than one Livery dinner is annually given ; and in some cases, owing to want of funds, the members of the Liveries are not entertained. It is the practice of most of the Companies to invite guests on these occasions. Royal personages, members of the reigning Continental houses, and persons of distinction generally, are frequently entertained by the Companies, which thus assist the Corporation in dispensing the hospitality of the City. Entertainments to persons of eminence are frequently preceded by the ceremony of conferring the freedom of the Gild, *honoris causâ*. In many cases guests are also invited to its Court dinners.

4. The part of the corporate income which is devoted to public objects we estimate at 150,000*l*. a year, of which about 10,000*l*. is ex-

pended on the relief of poor members, in addition to the 75,000*l.* a year out of trust income. If to this sum be added the trust income of 200,000*l.* a year, it follows that about half the income is distributed between benefaction and public or benevolent objects. About 50,000*l.* appears to be expended on education.

5. About 90,000*l.* a year appears to be devoted to benevolent and public objects of a general character. Besides the contributions to churches, schools, and dispensaries in Ulster, the Companies subscribe largely to other Ulster charities, both religious and secular, and also have of late subsidized new railways by grants of land and loans. These sums taken together amount to a deduction from the rents greatly exceeding the sum commonly allowed for such purposes by private landlords. On their English estates the Companies generally support the religious and secular charities connected therewith. As regards London, where the bulk of their property is situated, they make annually a very large contribution, one probably amounting to 70,000*l.* or 80,000*l.*, to public and benevolent objects. The London Hospital, during the ten years 1869–79 received 26,500*l.* from the Grocers alone. The hospitals for special diseases, the dispensaries, and other medical charities, not only of the City, but in other parts of London, receive a very large sum annually. Religious charities and societies having for their object the building and endowment of churches and schools in connexion with the Church of England, secular objects, orphanages, refuges, and funds for the relief of distress, such as the poor-boxes at the Metropolitan Courts, are all supported by the Companies, which are large subscribers to the Mansion House Funds set on foot under special circumstances by the Lord Mayor and the Corporation. Of late also, and particularly since the movement in favour of technical education began, some of the Companies whose names represent existing trades, have given exhibitions at their Halls or elsewhere of works of art or of the processes of manufacture, and have become supporters of trade benefit-societies.

Mode in which the Corporate Estate was Acquired.

A large proportion of the lands in the City held by the Companies in their corporate right was acquired by them outside their licences in mortmain under the custom and tenure of free burgage, under wills constituting trusts for the maintenance of obits, chauntries, or for other superstitious uses. This land the Companies recovered from the Crown, at the time of the dissolution of monasteries, for valuable consideration, in the reigns of Edward VI. and James I.

The terms of the grants have been held by the Court of Chancery to have vested in the Companies the same absolute property in these lands which the act of Edward VI. vested in the Crown, and they have thus been since the Reformation in the eye of the law the corporate property of the Companies, free from any trust. The lands were allowed to revert, because the Companies represented to the Crown that the rental was required for the support of their almshouses, schools, and exhibitions, many of which depended for their existence on these superstitious benefactions.

It appears that the Companies have not been always able to prove from their archives that the trust to purchase lands had ever been executed, and that they have been in the habit of simply crediting the charities with the annual interest of the sums originally bequeathed on this condition. The deeds and minutes of Court which perished in the Fire of 1666 might have thrown light on this matter.

For the purpose of the repurchase of their forfeited estates, and of the rebuilding their Halls and house property after the Fire, and of the Ulster Plantation, the Companies raised very large sums of money between the years 1547 and 1670. The sum paid to the Crown in respect of the Irish estate seems to have been levied as a civic impost. It would seem that part of the money expended in rebuilding and redemption was raised by mortgage, part by the contributions of existing members, or members who were persuaded to join for the purpose of helping the Companies out of their difficulties.

As regards the interpretation put by the Court of Chancery on wills, where the question has been whether the charities, or the Companies which administer them, were to become entitled to the increased income resulting from the rise in value of house property in the City, and also the schemes framed by that Court in accordance with the principle of *cy-près* to which it has recourse in the case of obsolete or impracticable benefactions, it may be said that the function of a Court can only be accurately to interpret the terms of the wills and to carry out the founders' intentions ; and no doubt the rules as to interpretation adopted by the Court of Chancery are judicious, while, in framing *cy-près* schemes, the Court has shown a wise and liberal spirit, and has done its utmost to recognise changes in the circumstances. But we think it impossible to pursue many of the cases without seeing that the Companies have made good their title to unexpected increment as corporate income when there was really an intestacy with respect to the fund, or under circumstances where there is no proof that the testator ever intended to constitute them beneficiaries.

The corporate or private property and income of the Companies have been declared by the highest legal authority to be as absolutely the Companies' own as those of any private person ; and we may refer to the circumstances under which this property was acquired, partly by purchases made out of the private incomes of the Companies, partly by gifts "intended to be for their absolute use :" to the public spirit shown by the Companies in past times and at present, in the good use which they have made of their incomes : in past times in saving their charities from bankruptcy and in the colonization of Ulster : at present in their support of useful objects and, in particular, in the establishment by them of technical education, a movement which has revived in the only way now possible the connexion of the Gilds with the arts and manufactures which they formerly represented.

Their property being at law the Companies' own, the product partly of their own savings, partly of absolute gifts to them, and the income from it being in great part spent for the public good, we deprecate any State interference with this property or with the Companies in their administration of the income arising from it.

As regards the trust-property of the Companies and the charities, above 1,000 in number, of which they are the gratuitous managers, under the control of the Court of Chancery and the Charity Commission, the existence of several great and many small schools and of eleemosynary foundations, in the benefits of which almost every county in England participates, is due to the liberality and public spirit shown by the Companies from the earliest period to the present moment.

The Companies easily defeated Mr. Firth as regards every part of the case set up by him in his work called *Municipal London;* and a motion by him in favour of disestablishing and disendowing the Companies was rejected in the deliberations of the Royal Commission by a majority of ten to two. The gentlemen who appeared before the Commission to support Mr. Firth's views were not, in the Commissioners' opinion "competent by reason of their situation, knowledge, and experience to afford correct information on the subjects of the inquiry" within the meaning of the terms of the Commission.

So far as we can judge, no valid or weighty objection whatever exists in London either against the City or against the Livery Companies ; and Mr. Firth and the few persons who were associated with him were never appointed by the citizens of London to act as their representatives in this or any other matter.

VOLUNTARY ASSOCIATIONS
WHICH HAVE DISAPPEARED, OR HAVE MERGED
IN THE LIVERY GILDS.

VOLUNTARY ASSOCIATIONS
WHICH HAVE DISAPPEARED OR HAVE MERGED IN THE LIVERY GILDS.

NUMEROUS callings formerly existed in a separate and exclusive form, as will be readily perceived on a glance at Stow's *Survey*, Herbert's *Historical Essay*, Riley's *Memorials*, 1868, and Mr. Kingdon's *Introduction to the Grocers' Records*, without having developed into Associations. Some became known under different names, and were absorbed in other trades, while some grew obsolete, and passed into disuse and oblivion.

These small communities or unions long contributed to influence the municipal life and society of London, and existed side by side with others which at the outset possessed no larger share of vitality and justification; but from a variety of agencies they failed to become a permanent parcel of the wide and complex machinery of metropolitan government.

The most striking characteristic features of ancient commercial policy were the almost endless subdivisions of labour and employment and the larger measure of initiative right; and the tendency grew concentrate or centralize, and thus to extinguish many of the minor groups of artificers as independent bodies.

The White and Brown Bakers.

MAITLAND says that the Bakers (*Bolangerii*, Fr. *Boulangers*) are charged in the Great Roll of the Exchequer in 1155 with a debt of one mark of gold, on account of their Gild, and thence deduces the fact that they then held their rights in fee-farm of the Crown. But he adds that they appear to have been incorporated about 1307 by letters patent of Edward II.

We must once more quote Maitland for another very early notice, as well as an extremely curious one, in connection with the Good Friday bun :— " The Bakers, probably perceiving that great Profits arose to the Clergy by the Use of the Symbols of the Cross, *Agnus Dei's*, and name of Jesus, to oblige their Customers (for their own Interest), began to imprint upon their Bread the like Representations : which induced Henry the Third, by his mandate from St. Edmund's Bury, of September 1, 1252, strictly to injoin all Bakers thenceforth not to put any of those sacred representations upon their Bread."

In 30 Edward 1 (1301–2), the Bakers were allowed to hold four hall-moots yearly, to determine all offences committed in their business ; and the same ordinance restrained them from selling bread save in the market, on the site of the modern Bread Street. It elsewhere appears that in Basinghall Street, near the spot afterward, at least, known as Bakewell (or Blackwell) Hall, stood a building called the *Bakehouse*, doubtless the general bakery for the City within the walls.

The bread consumed in London in former times was, however, to a considerable extent made, not in the City itself, but at Bromley-at-Bow and Stratford-at-Bow. In 1310 several bakeries of Stratford were presented for selling halfpenny loaves of short weight ; and we learn from the consequent proceedings that the bread was weighed in a hot state, and that in the price paid by the customer allowance was made for the shrinkage on cooling.

In 1312 a baker was arrested for selling bread made of putrid wheat ; and in the following year the loaf of French bread of John de Bledelow was found to weigh 29s. 2d., the shilling being equal to three-fifths of an ounce, whereas it should have weighed the same as the halfpenny loaf of Wastrel bread, and it was short by 12s. 10d.

There is perhaps no vocation which so often fell under the unfavourable cognisance of the Court of Aldermen as that of the baker. The regulations for the craft in the *Liber Albus* and elsewhere are both numerous and stringent ; but the purveyors of bread evidently laboured a good deal to the intent that the law might be more honoured in the breach than the observance. The cases of conviction and punishment for selling loaves of short weight or impure material are innumerable ; and one of the drawings in the fourteenth century *Assisa Panis* depicts a baker drawn on a hurdle by two horses, with his fraudulent loaf tied round his neck.

Among the Harleian MSS. is a poem by John Lydgate, a versifyer of the earlier part of the 15th century, wherein he lays deceit to the charge of the Millers and Bakers of that time, and suggests that they might do well to band themselves together, not merely for their common benefit, but in order to enable them more effectually to despoil the public :—

' Let mellerys and bakerys gadre hem a gilde,
And alle of assent make a fraternite."

In 1580 we meet with a letter from the Earl of Leicester to the Lord Mayor, pointing out the hardship upon Humphrey Nichols, a Brown Baker, by reason of the temporary inhibition to bake twopenny wheaten loaves ; and Lord Burghley himself intercedes for some one who had made bread below the assize. But it was shown that the bread was for a private household, and not for public sale.

In 1376 the Bakers sent two members to the Common Council, and in 1469 supplied 44 men-at-arms to the muster for watching the City gates. In both cases there appears to have been only one fraternity and one trade, although, according to Stow (ed. 1633, pp. 624, 642), the Bakers *originally* formed two such, with differing arms as below.

WHITE BAKERS.

BROWN BAKERS.

We at all events become aware of their dual existence when they are amalgamated by Henry VIII. in 1509. But this formal union was not thoroughly consolidated till the middle of the 17th century ; and in 1622 the Brown Bakers obtained a distinct charter.

The unsoundness and insincerity of the alliance are exemplified by the fact that in 1594 the Brown Bakers are found with a separate meeting-place in the basement of Founders' Hall, Lothbury, and voluntarily contributing £6 to the paving of the yard and kitchen, as though they were tenants of some standing. The basement became generally known as Brown Bakers' Hall, a name which it retained even in 1654, when it was converted to other uses at a rent of £8, and when the trade was perhaps at length under one government.

The Bladesmiths, or Bladers.

A GOOD deal of difficulty and friction was created about 1406-8 by the deceptions and malpractices in cutlery on the part of foreigners and other interlopers, who manufactured goods in unrecognised quarters and offered them for sale, whereby, among other matters, the Blade-smiths as a body incurred discredit and loss. In 1408, therefore, the Association of Bladesmiths solicited and obtained the assent of the Court of Aldermen to a code of articles, by which the sale of blades was restricted to Gracechurch Street, the pavement near St. Nicholas' Shambles in Newgate Street, and the Tun on Cornhill, and which compelled the workers, under pain of forfeiture, to make the points and edges of lance-heads, swords, daggers, knives, and axes hard enough to bear the assay ; that the masters or wardens of the trade should oversee all articles made, and that each man should to the larger pieces affix his own peculiar mark. The Gild occurs down to 1532. In 1469 it found twenty men for the City Watch. In 1502 it had a prescriptive Livery of twelve.

Stow's Continuator (1633) mentions William Palmer, a Blader, as a great benefactor to the church of St. Mildred, Bread Street, under 1356.

The Block-makers.

THIS Association, which was in alliance with the SHIPWRIGHTS, and which did not obtain a charter, was at one period both numerous and important. Its members were the manufacturers and salesmen of the pulleys for ships' rigging and tackle, and had their centre in the purlieus of the Docks. During many years it was a practice with the Block-makers to go in procession, the first Friday in July, down the Mile-End Road to Epping, where they attended Fairlop Fair. The cavalcade in-cluded a ship or ships on wheels, with streamers and a band, and often extended nearly a mile in length. The usage originated in the circum-stance that Mr. Day, a member of the trade at Wapping, had a property in the neighbourhood of Epping, where he entertained the whole Com-pany on beans and bacon.

The Braelers, or Brace-makers.

THIS Association had Wardens and an organized system of govern-ment in 1354, when the earliest bye-laws were submitted to the Court of Aldermen and approved. This code is of the usual character on the whole, but, as is always the case, contains one or two provisions special to the particular craft, as, for instance, the admittance of strangers (or other than freemen) to work after examination as to fitness and position, and the enforcement of imprisonment in cases of fraud. It is stipulated that the trade shall not employ sheep-leather.

The Burillers.

THIS Association, which was evidently at one time of considerable weight and note, was a branch of the great family of communities engaged in the production of woollen cloths, and was probably of equal antiquity with that of the Weavers. It received incorporation by letters patent of Henry III. (1216–72), the terms of which indicate the vocation as one of established character.

The Burillers are frequently noticed in an incidental manner in the municipal archives and in the early chronicles as concerned in some dispute with the other Fraternities, particularly the Weavers, with whom their relations were necessarily very intimate and constant. In 1298–9 a serious difference arose between these two bodies in consequence of the Burillers having chosen two Bailiffs from their own ranks to hold Courts, and having presented them to the Mayor, who approved them ; and it was settled that, where any matter could not be arranged in the Bailiffs' Court, it was to be referred to Guildhall.

In the succeeding year another circumstance arose, of which the ulterior value is to illustrate the extremely ancient standing of the Burillers, as well as the archaic government of that community. The Weavers appeared at Guildhall (1299–1300) by their Bailiffs to answer the Burillers "upon certain articles, points, and establishments, whereof there was no memory, and in respect of which, and other things, it was alleged that the defendant Association had committed trespass and wrong. The controversy was referred back by the Mayor to a committee of arbitration composed of three members of the Burillers' Fraternity and their Alderman, and an equal number of the other craft ; and the result was that certain heads of agreement were submitted. We hence infer that the burthen of the grievance was the old story of blending of foreign with English wools.

But the Alderman of the Burillers was, even at this distant date, growing an obsolete designation. He was in fact the Master Warden of the body, which gave its name to the soke or ward adopted as its head-quarters, and had a proprietary and seigniorial *status* as distinguished from a mere electoral one, so long as he held office ; and indeed we may see how in one case, that of Farringdon Ward, feudal rights were acquired some time prior to these transactions by an influential goldsmith on payment of a nominal tribute.

A special function of the craft of Burillers was the inspection and measurement of cloth, and the summons to the Mayor's Court of all such as were found on search made to have exceeded the prescribed and lawful width from list to list of two ells, which, according to

Herbert, were known as *burrells*. This duty to some extent subsequently devolved on the Merchant Taylors. In 50 Edward III. (1376), the Gild was represented by two members only on the Common Council, a proportion significant of its commencing decline as an independent Society.

It appears that the worsted manufacturers in Norfolk had been accustomed to make their cloth at pleasure and without hinderance until 2 Edward III., when some one came into those parts with a commission from the king to require them to conform to a certain assize ; and we gather that the trade was at that period extensive and important, since a committee, with the Bishop of Norwich at the head of it, was appointed to report upon the matter.

The Cappers.

THIS Fraternity, which (like the Hatters) was eventually engrossed by the Haberdashers, received letters patent from Henry III.   Its members are frequently mentioned in the City archives in conjunction with the allied crafts.   In the charter of Henry VII., incorporating the Haberdashers, the Cappers are identified with the Hurers.

The incorporation by patent of this and other minor industries serves to illustrate the tendency to decentralize labour and distribute as equally as possible the details and profits of manufacture.

The Carmen.

THE Carmen of the City of London were incorporated by letters patent, 15 Henry VIII., and were limited to 400, including those who belonged to the King's Borough of Southwark, which was within the same jurisdiction.

By a reference to what is said under the account of the Woodmongers it will be observed that the control of the operative members of this Gild was claimed at a later period by the Governors of Christ's Hospital and by the Woodmongers.   The authority of the former was overruled by the Court of King's Bench.   A conflict on this, as on so many other, points of municipal policy arose, and the natural consequence was, that there was a considerable amount of anarchy and confusion.   The correspondence and dispute lasted during several years with intermissions.

It is difficult to discern where the independence of the Carmen as a Gild lay, for they were certainly under the supervision of the Woodmongers for some purposes, and of Christ's Hospital for others. The deficiency of vehicles outside the City led to incessant requisitions upon them from the Court and nobility, more especially when some special circumstances called for an unusual number of conveyances, both for passengers and luggage.

The proposition of the City in 1608 was, that whereas each carman used time out of mind to pay a duty of four nobles a year in addition to a quarter-wage of four shillings for a single cart and so rateably in progression, now he should pay two nobles as duty for a single cart and four shillings quarter-wage, the number of carts being limited to that in the charter.

The arrangement seems to have been accepted by the Common Council, and about 1620 the matters in controversy were brought to a conclusion for the time, the last incident being the resistance of the Woodmongers and Carmen to assessment by the Justices of Surrey.

The Carmen were incorporated with the *Fuellers* in 1606 by letters patent under the name of Woodmongers, and so continued till 1668, when the Company was charged by Parliament with fraudulent practices in the sale of coals and other fuel, and threw up its charter, the Carmen reverting to their former grade as a Fellowship under a resolution of the Common Council by the name of the Free Carmen of the City of London, and with a governing body composed of a Master, two Wardens, and forty-one Assistants.

In 1739 the now separate Company is mentioned as still flourishing, and as having in the hands of its freemen 420 carts or cars for the con-veyance of all descriptions of goods, coals and coke included, to and from all parts of London and its Liberties, at a tariff fixed by the City.

But the working carmen were placed under the control of the Governors of Christ's Hospital, and each paid for his licence to the Hospital 17s. 4d. a year. The heaviest load mentioned is 2000 lbs.

The Gild yet survives, and as recently as 1891 possessed four votes for the City in respect of its Livery.

The Courtier and the Carter. A ballad licensed in 1566.
The World runnes on Wheeles; or, Oddes betwixt Carts and Coaches. By John Taylor. 12mo, 1623, 1635. With an engraving.
The Carmen's Remonstrance against the Woodmongers. 4to, 1649.
A Proclamation to restrain the Excessive Carriages in Wagons and four-wheeled Carts, to the Destruction of High-ways. 1661. A broadside.

The Cheesemongers.

"THE reputable men of the trade of Cheesemongers" occur as successful applicants to the Court of Aldermen in 1377 for the sanction of bye-laws drawn up by themselves for their internal government. They sold cheese and butter; and it appears that these came into the City by water, in carts, and by men on horseback. The articles sought to restrain those who brought them by land from selling them otherwise than at Leadenhall Market or in that between the Shambles and Newgate, and before the stroke of noon, and to render it unlawful for those who came by water from selling them to hucksters, regraters, forestallers, and others. Special allusion is made to Welsh cheese, called *talgar*, which is said to have been carried to London, and surreptitiously sold in Fleet Street, Holborn, and elsewhere. Cheese engrosses the entire text of the code; and we learn that the Cheesemongers had been required to revise their scale of prices.

In 1379 regulations were first formally made as to the sale of butter within the City. The price differed with the season. No butter was saleable without the porringer, which held half a quart butter-measure.

The Cheesemongers concentrated themselves in the vicinage of Breadstreet Hill in the time of Stow or at least of Howes (1633) for the convenience of their trade, and Thames Street has always continued to be the great landing place for foreign cheeses. The earlier factor in this commodity at the river-side was probably a wholesale merchant.

The importation of the Dutch cheeses was probably of great antiquity. In the *Abridgement of the City Charter*, 1680, the waterside porters are authorized to charge 12*d.* for unloading two cwt. of Holland cheese, being the scale for foreigners, or those who were not free of the City.

Cheesewright, which is at present only the name of a person, was obviously in the first instance that of a craft, and indicates those who made the article, as the cheesemonger does those who sold it.

The Comb=makers.

THIS Society was incorporated by letters patent of Charles the First, in April, 1636, under the name of the Master, Wardens, and Fellowship of the Comb-makers of London.

Maitland (1739) says that its government was a Master, two Wardens, and thirteen Assistants, but that it had neither Hall nor Livery.

The Corders of the Ropery.

THE Ropery adjoined the Steelyard, or rather Staple-yard or House, and was originally a seat of the distinct industry in which the Corders engaged. The sale of ropes, cord, and other similar appliances for sails and shipping was naturally allocated to the water-side; and the Corder gradually added, according to the prevalent usage, where no other separate craft undertook the business, the canvas and sail-cloth trades.

The Ropers and Canvassers (with the Pepperers) eventually merged in the GROCERS.

The Free Fishermen.

THIS Company was incorporated, according to Maitland (1739), in the third year of James II., under this style; but no further particulars are forthcoming, except that there is a series of petitions extant, addressed by the body to the Government, and that, from a reference by Maitland in his second edition (1756), there seems to have been an antecedent charter.

The Case of the Company of Free Fishermen of the River of Thames, and other Fishermen of this Kingdom, using the Lobster Trade. A broadside. [About 1700.]

The Forcers, or Casketmakers.

THE manufacture of caskets, formerly called *forcers*, was evidently one of great antiquity and of special importance in regard to the skill and taste demanded in such as were of costlier workmanship.

The bye-laws or ordinances, of which the good folk following this trade solicited official approbation, apparently for the first time, in 1406, stated in the premises that divers persons, both freemen of the City and foreigners, were in the habit of making and vending forcers of defective material and fabric, in great deceit of the people, and so forth ; and accordingly the petitioners asked to be allowed to appoint from year to year two Wardens, and to have certain articles for their stricter governance and greater security. It is hence ascertained that the usage of the trade was to make nine different sizes, of the second of which only the distinctive name, a *quarlet*, transpires.

These caskets were originally of wood, lined with linen cloth. Like the salvers and trenchers of the same material, they were the precursors of others formed of the precious metals, and elaborately tooled and chased.

By the Act 1 Richard III., dealing with the importation by foreigners of a variety of goods, " painted forcers," doubtless of wood, are enumerated in the list of prohibited merchandise.

The Fullers.

A CHARTER of incorporation was granted to the Fraternity or Gild Perpetual of the Mistery or Craft of Fullers, April 28, 1480, 20 Edward IV. The Company was ordained to consist of three Wardens and a commonalty of freemen and freewomen, with a licence in mortmain and a common seal, and the right of pleading and being impleaded. The charter conferred the power of making ordinances for the internal government of the Society, under the advice of the Lord Mayor, but to be exempt from the jurisdiction of the King's courts.

This was followed by a deed executed in the name of the three persons, members of the trade, who had been instrumental in obtaining the charter, John Britte, Henry Lee, and Thomas Wymonde, and dated October 18 in the same year.

Doubtless, the Fullers caused ordinances or bye-laws to be framed by virtue of the liberty above given, but they do not seem to survive. For a considerable period they remained an influential and numerous association, and gave much trouble to the City by the disputes which arose as to the methods of fulling and other points.

The Fullers had, long prior to this date, concentrated themselves, it appears, in the neighbourhood of *La Blanche Chapelle*, or White-Chapel, where in ancient times the matfellon,[1] or fuller's teasel, largely used by the trade in their operations, grew to such an extent that the district became known as *Villa Beatæ Mariæ de Matfellon.* They had at one period a Hall in Billiter Square. Their successors, the Clothworkers, adopted from them the Virgin as their tutelary saint.

The question of irregular fulling in water-mills and walk-mills, instead of by hand, was mooted in 1404 ; and the Mayor and Aldermen were instructed to come to the aid of the Hurers and Cappers in this matter, and to enlarge the powers of their Wardens, so as to enable them to cope with the grievance, which damaged their reputation and business.

Similar fellowships existed down to a much later time as separate bodies in the provinces. The Fullers of Newcastle-on-Tyne, by dissolving themselves and dividing their corporate property, created the test case, by which it was ruled by the Master of the Rolls that there was a right and power resident in such societies to determine their existence, and distribute the corporate estate.

The Furbishers.

THE code of bye-laws by which this Craft, no longer recognised in a separate form, was regulated, bears date 1350 ; but it then already possessed Wardens, and had doubtless been some time in existence as an unchartered Fraternity or Association. These articles relate to the manufacture of pommels or hilts and scabbards of swords, and to the repair of old weapons of that class. They are few in number, and chiefly of normal character.

---

[1] In ancient times, somewhat nearer the city, in St. Botolph's parish, Bishopsgate, lay Tazel Close, so called because before it was let as an archery ground the teasel used to be regularly cultivated there. The area was eventually enclosed, and became the Artillery Garden.

The Gardeners.

OLD ARMS.   PRESENT ARMS.

ALTHOUGH not now numbered among the Livery Gilds, the Gardeners were twice incorporated ; namely by letters patent in 1605, September 18, and by charter in 1616, November 9. In the first instance, the Company obtained enrolment in the Chamber of London ; but in 1616 the civic authorities seem to have offered difficulties, as happened in other cases. It does not appear under what conditions the Gardeners lost this original grant, which may have applied, like that of 1616, to those occupied in the City or within two miles thereof; but the Court of Aldermen proved obdurate, and the King wrote from Scotland to endeavour to induce that body to relent, with what success we do not learn.

The disappearance of the Gild may be ascribed to its lack of industrial importance, and to the uncommercial character of those who, beyond the working members of the craft, felt an interest in such matters.

It seems from a petition presented by the "Gardeners of the Earls, Barons, and Bishops, and of the Citizens of London," that it was in 1345 regarded as a prescriptive usage for them to be permitted to offer for sale, in front of the church of St. Martin, at the side of the gate of St. Paul's church, their masters' garden-produce for their profit. But the practice was represented to the Corporation as being attended by such grave inconvenience to the frequenters and officials of the churches and others, that, by way of compromise, the petitioners were allowed to stand in future on the space between the south gate of St. Paul's and the garden-wall of the Friars Preachers at Baynard's Castle.

The style of the Company was The Master, Wardens, Assistants, and Commonalty of the Company of Gardeners of London. There were a Master, two Wardens, and eighteen Assistants, but no Livery.

The Haberdashers of St. Katherine the Virgin and of St. Nicholas.

Two Brotherhoods so named existed in London long before the acquisition of corporate dignity by the Gild now known under the name of Haberdashers. It was not till 1448 that the Haberdashers of hats and those of small wares, the Hurers or Cappers, and the Hatters strictly so termed, were finally combined in one society and under one constitution. The most ancient references to the unincorporated Haberdashers do not state whether they were of St. Katherine or of the other Fraternity.

In 1311 divers haberdashers and hatters were convicted of selling false hats, black, white, and gray, made of wool and flocks, and the goods were burned in Cheapside. It seems to have been an inquisition undertaken at the request of certain hatters, who are named.

The earliest bye-laws of the Haberdashers are dated 1371. They are comparatively few and simple, and merely rehearse that none of the trade should take a journeyman save as an apprentice for seven years, that no sales of wares should take place on Sundays or holy days, or elsewhere than in the dealer's own shop or stall, and that the fraternity shall every year choose four overseers to protect the trade and present defaulters to the Guildhall.

All that we are enabled to understand is, that these persons were "the reputable men of the trade of Haberdashers."

Under the date 1378 we have, in Mr. Riley's *Memorials*, an exceedingly curious and edifying schedule of the contents of a haberdasher's shop. They comprise (1) 12 dozens of laces of red leather, value 8*d.*, and a gross of points of red leather, value 18*d.* ; (2) one dozen of cradlebows made of wool and flax, 18*d.* ; (3) three ditto, 3*d.* ; (4) red, green, and white caps, the last called *nightcaps*, the coloured at 2*s.* 8*d.*, and the white at 2*s.* 3*d.* a dozen ; (5) two dozen of woollen caps of divers colours, 16*s.* ; (6) six ditto of black wool, 4*s.* ; three of blue and one of russet, 2*s.* 6*d.* ; (7) five children's caps, red and blue, 2*s.* 1*d.* ; (8) one dozen of black hures [caps], 4*s.* ; one ditto, 4*d.* ; (9) two hair camises [coats of camlet], 12*d.* ; (10) one hat of russet, 6*d.* ; one white hat, 3*d.* ; two papers covered with red leather, 12*d.* ; (11) one purse called *hamondeys* [or hamodeys] of sea-green colour, 6*d.* ; four pairs of spurs, 2*s.* ; one double chain of iron, 10*d.*, and another iron chain, 6*d.* ; (12) one wooden gaming-table, with a set of men, 6*d.* ; (13) one cloth painted with Him crucified and other figures, 2*s.* 4*d.* ; (14) eight white chains of iron for ferrets ; one set of beads of jet, 6*d.*, one other set of black alabaster, 4*d.*, and three of wood, 3*d.* ; (15) two pairs of pencases with ink-horns, 8*d.* ;

(16) one pair of children's boots of white woollen cloth, 2*d.* ; (17) one osculatory, called a paxbread, 3*d.* ; (18) four combs of boxwood, 4*d.* ; (19) two wooden boxes, 3*d.* ; (20) two wooden pepper querns, 3*d.* ; (21) two lbs. of linen thread, green and blue, 2*s.* ; (22) two wooden frames for cushions, 2*d.* ; (23) six purses of red leather, 4*d.* ; (24) four eyeglasses, 2*d.* ; (25) eighteen ink-horns, 18*d.* ; (26) one black girdle of woollen thread, 2*d.* ; (27) thirteen quires of paper, 6*s.* 8*d.* ; (28) other paper, damaged, 6*d.* ; (29) one wooden block for caps, 2*d.* ; (30) six skins of parchment, called *soylepeles*, 6*d.* ; (31) one wooden whistle, 2*d.* ; (32) seven leaves of paper, 1*d.* ; (33) three pieces of whipcord, 3*d.*

The preceding inventory, when we consider its date, is of singular interest and pertinence. It probably represents the remainder-stock of a dealer, insolvent or deceased, and is remarkable enough for the diversity and range which the business had at that time assumed. It further proves that the haberdasher was accustomed to keep miscellaneous goods of almost every description for domestic use other than apparel and furniture.

The Hatband Makers.

THIS Society was incorporated by letters patent of 13 Charles I., 12 December, 1638, as the Master, Wardens, Assistants, and Fellowship of the Mistery of Hatband-Makers of the City of London. The government was by a Master, two Wardens, and twelve Assistants. There was no Livery.

The Company flourished so long as the fashion prevailed of wearing rich and costly hatbands; but even in Maitland's time (1739) had dwindled down to two or three members. It has long been extinct.

The Hatters.

THESE existed as a separate body down to the fourteenth century, but appear to have been eventually amalgamated with the Haberdashers.

The bye-laws of the Hatters were approved by the Corporation in 1347, and included the usual provisions and safeguards, with power of search and of appointing six overseers. They prohibited the sale of foreign hats, except in gross and to freemen.

The Heaumers.

THE men of the trade of Helmetry, eventually merged in the Armourers, submitted their Articles or bye-laws to the Mayor and Court of Aldermen for approval in 1347, and they were passed. Besides the habitual conditions as to freedom, apprenticeship, and such points, the Heaumers were empowered to elect Wardens or supervisors, to prevent the employment of unskilful workmen, to the discredit of the craft and the common deceit ; (2) to make assay of all helmets of foreign fabric, and mark them before they could be sold ; (3) to see that all helmets whatsoever were properly stamped with the sign of the maker.

The Hostelers and Haymongers.

THESE are cited in a petition of 1327, as if they formed one and the same body, in connexion with a grievance as to the misdemeanour of certain foreigners who, whereas they were entitled to sell only in gross, brought their hay in small bottles in carts, so concealed as not to be readily observable, and retailed it for half-pence and farthings, not only in the forenoon, but in the later part of the day.

On the 12th December, 1446, certain men of the Mistery of Hostelers of the City preferred a petition to the Mayor, which prayed for the confirmation of their ordinances ; and the same was granted, and the ordinances entered on record. Here there is no mention of the Haymongers ;—and about twenty-seven years later (October 28, 1473) we detect a further development of the organization in another address to the Court at Guildhall, in which the Wardens and other men of the Mistery of *Innholders* represent that they had been heretofore improperly designated *Hostelers*, which Hostelers were verily their servants, and begging that in this renewal of their ordinances and henceforth they might be called Innholders ; whereto the City assented.

This incident closes therefore the annals of the Hostelers, whose future career may be found narrated under their correct appellation or style. But we see in these passages the origin of the modern *hostler* or *ostler ;* and it may be the fittest opportunity of pointing out the need of remembering, when we consider the subject of English Inns and their keepers or holders, the primitive nucleus of the principle and institution, and the transitional stages through which they passed, before they attained even the form assumed by them in the days of Chaucer.

THE ANCIENT HOSTELER.

At the outset, the Inn was merely a lodging for travellers, not necessarily a public one, on or near the wayside along the principal routes for pedestrians, riders, or packhorses throughout the kingdom. Private householders, who had sufficient accommodation or a desire to earn money by such means, received strangers under their roofs for the night, or at most,— if they had satisfactory credentials,—for two or three days. Ordinarily, all that was offered was the shelter for man and beast, and perhaps the bait for the latter ; but the guest was supposed to bring his own commissariat. From certain persons thus placing their dwellings at the disposal of casual visitors, when there was no other refuge, and where it was not a party carrying its own tent, or where, again, there was an absence of facilities afforded by ancient ruins or dense sylvan cover, it became a natural evolution to the professional host, who adapted his premises to public and general requirements, and soon learned to find in the purveyance of refreshments, both liquid and solid, an additional and leading source of profit. The growth of the Inn was at once the cause and consequence of an increased habit of travelling, through the extension of inland commerce and the rise of provincial towns into greater importance and into more regular inter-course with the metropolis ; and the houses of public entertainment in London and in other chief centres, especially sea-ports, were fostered and multiplied by the floating population, which gradually rendered the City itself so cosmopolitan.

The original combination of the hay-dealer with the Hosteler or Hostler simply had in view the habitual demand for the article on the part of ordinary customers and the incidental sale to others. We do not accept without reserve the statement of the Innholders in

1473, that the Hostelers were subordinates. In the official returns of 1469, touching the City Watch, the Hostelers are charged with furnishing eighteen men, and there is no reference to the Innholders ; but it may be the fact that, when inns became of greater importance and dimensions, the office of hosteler, and the term, acquired a new and modified meaning, and that the individual, who kept the rudimentary establishment, transferred his name to the superintendent of the stable under the innholder. But by whatever title he was known, the hosteler has never become an extinct type ; he was the keeper in the Stuarts' time of the *petty ostery*, or cheap lodging-house and restaurant ; and he still survives among us.

From the mention of the Hostelers and Haymongers in very early records as a branch of trade and as a recognised association, almost before we meet with the Innholder, it seems possible that the latter was an aftergrowth,[1] and that the accommodation of travellers at bed and board in town or country, especially in places off the high roads, followed the supply of mere entertainment for man and beast on their way from point to point. The person who kept the inn not unnaturally acquired an importance superior to the person who kept the stable, hay-loft, and brewery-tap or *brasserie ;* and these premises became a subsidiary portion of the establishment ; but the still not unfrequent separate tenure of the outbuildings may be viewed in the light of a survival, and as shewing the germ of the inn.

In not a few of the Ordinances of the other Gilds we meet with injunctions against the sale of goods by craftsmen in hostels in lieu of the open market ; and this irregular practice was discountenanced, because it was held to be a vehicle and facility for fraud, where the Wardens had no opportunity of control. But it was also the origin of the later usage of employing inns as a rendezvous for travellers and itinerant dealers, and the foundation of the Commercial Room.

Within the confines of the City itself, however, the practice of furnishing entertainment and sleeping accommodation for the traveller more speedily followed than elsewhere ; and in 1365 the *herbergeour* or keeper of the *auberge*, subsequently known as the *innholder*, was already a familiar institution, around which sufficient time had elapsed for the growth of abuses. For we encounter about that period, when Chaucer must have been intimate with such resorts, and was studying character with rich profit to us all, that the authorities had to put pressure on certain herbergeours to restrain them from baking their own

---

[1] Somewhat on the same principle that the Frenchman's shirt is said to have been an aftergrowth from his wristband.

bread, and from selling ale, except to stranger guests,—the *bonâ fide* traveller of those days,—or unless the landlord was also a common brewer; and all loaves supplied to customers were to come from the baker, and to bear his mark.

The ordinances of 1365 prescribe the scale at which the innkeeper should charge for his hay and oats, whether the former was sold by the bottle or otherwise.

The Hurers, Hurriers, or Milliners.[1]

THIS Fellowship, with those of the Hatters and Cappers, was perhaps at one period associated with the Mercers, while the latter still retained their small-ware trade. The Hurers and Hatters were united by letters patent of Henry VII.; and this body, again, with the Cappers and two Fraternities of Haberdashers, constituted the Gild of *Haberdashers*, incorporated under that title in 1447. The Court of Aldermen found it imperative to devote a considerable share of time and attention to the trades' unions and Gilds, among which questions of law or right were continually arising. In 1376, the Hurers or Hatters complained that certain persons fulled caps or *hures*, or hats, in the same manner as clothes, at a certain water-mill, and shewed that these things so fulled with the clothes were very inferior to those done by hand; and, on sufficient proof being given, the Court acceded to the Hurriers' prayer for a restraint of the practice.

The Hurers recur in 1398, under the first mayoralty of Sir Richard Whittington, as receiving an official sanction to supplementary articles for the government of their trade. These prescribed that caps or hures, or other matters, should not be scoured in the public thoroughfares, but on private premises—a provision occasioned by the practice of hurers sending their assistants, and even children, down to the river side to scour their goods, and great dissension and even bloodshed arising, to the great scandal of the trade, besides that they were often sent thither "amid horrible tempests, frosts, and snows."

The Milliner seems to have been recognised as a separate employment and denomination, and to have occasionally become one of great importance and wealth, for in 1552 Baptist Borrow, milliner, in St. Giles's Cripplegate, is recorded as being buried "with a pennon, a coat-armour, and a herald;" and there were twenty-four torch-bearers, the Company of Parish Clerks, and many other mourners; and the church was hung with black.

---

[1] The word *milliner* is usually derived from Milan, Milaner, a dealer in Milanese goods.

The Linen Drapers.

In the notice of the Drapers' Company some account will be found of the somewhat slow and tardy development of a branch of business which is at present so universal and lucrative. The introduction of linen fabrics from abroad was long opposed by vested interests here ; and we have to wait till the latter half of the 15th century before we gain any tidings of this industry as the foundation of a Fellowship or Fraternity. In 1469 the Linen-Drapers, then evidently of humble rank, gave a quota of four men-at-arms to the City Watch, the *maximum* being 210. In 23 Henry VIII., they are enumerated among the bodies which sent representatives to a municipal banquet ; and whereas the Drapers themselves were allowed to fill twelve places besides those of their Wardens, the Linen-Drapers were obliged to be content with two. They had at this period no Livery, and apparently never achieved any other progress toward independence.

One of the most distinguished followers of this calling was James Heyward, whose place of business was on Fish Street Hill. He died in 1776 in Austin Friars, in his seventieth year. He had in his younger days contributed to the *Spectator*, and he bore a name which, during centuries had been associated with letters—nearest to his own time in the person of Mrs. Eliza Heyward or Hayward the novelist.

The **Merchant's Warehouse laid open**; or, the Plain Dealing Linnen-Draper. Shewing how to buy all sorts of Linnen and Indian Goods. By J. F. 12mo, 1696.

The Marblers.

Stow says : " The Company called by the name of *Marblers*, for their excellent knowledge and skill in the Art of Sculpturing personages for Tombs, Grave-stones, and Monuments in Churches and elsewhere in Religious places : their antiquity and what respect they have carried is unknown to me, nor can I find them to be incorporated ; but [they]

hold some friendship with the Masons, and are thought to be esteemed among them in Fellowship."

In the list of burials in the Priory of Blackfriars occurs, under date of June 6, 1527 : "Thomas Raynton, citizen *and marbler*." This Raynton must have been a person of some consideration, as he directed that he should be interred here " within the cloister, nigh as may be to the grave where Dr. Morgan, late Prior, lies buried, if he fortunes to decease within the City." Hugo Marleberer, one of the Sheriffs of London in 13 Edward III. (1339–40), may be probably claimed as a member of the same calling. That was a period when the avocation still bestowed the patronymic or surname.

Other Gilds, which have disappeared from observation, are never-theless more or less fully recorded and known, as we shall point out elsewhere ; but this is the only reference to the Marblers with which we recollect to have met, beyond the passage in the *Survey of London* and two notices in Riley's *Memorials* under 1281 and 1284. They merged perhaps in the Masons.

This obsolete or amalgamated Gild must have been for a length of time of very considerable eminence and wealth ; and to its members or the followers of the vocation we doubtless owe great part of those fine monuments of deceased celebrities which were erected in former times in London, Southwark, Westminster, and elsewhere, and of which many perished in the Fire of 1666.

The pages of Camden (Latin account of the *Royal and Noble Burials in St. Peter's, Westminster*, 1600 and 1606), Payne Fisher (*Tombs and Monuments in St. Paul's*, 1684), Weever (*Ancient Funeral Monuments*, 1631 and 1767), and Dingley (*History from Marble* and *Welsh Journal*) afford some idea of the extent and rank of this industry, when during centuries such a succession of costly tombs was demanded by our wealthy and powerful families, and the art was confined to a few individuals, bound together by ties of fellowship and reciprocity.

That a good deal of their work has disappeared, we need not doubt for an instant. Successive improvements and other changes, and fires, have done their part ; and in certain cases the monuments have been removed for the sake of the material, as when, in 1564, Sir Martin Bowes, a member of the Goldsmiths' Company, and then Lord Mayor, sold for 50*l.* the grave-stones and monuments at the Greyfriars—of course only one instance out of many, where a person of such station could be guilty of such an act.

The Marblers are pretty clearly identical with the LAPIDARIES. Speaking of the Gildhall of the Merchants of the Hanse of Germany in Thames Street, Stow's Continuator (1633) mentions that the Gild

hired in 6 Richard II. a house adjoining, some time belonging to Richard
Lions, a famous Lapidary, one of the Sheriffs of London in 49 Edward
III. and in 4 Richard II., taken forcibly from that house by the rebels
under Wat Tyler, and beheaded in Cheapside.

The Parish Clerks.

PRESENT ARMS.

THIS Brotherhood was incorporated by letters patent of 17 Henry
III., in the year 1233, by the name of the Fraternity of St. Nicholas,
and again by patent of 9 James I., 19 January, 1611–12, under their
present designation.   The grant was renewed 11 Charles I., 27
February, 1636–7.

In 27 Henry VI. certain tenements at Bishopsgate, on the left hand
side of the street from the gate, were granted to the fellowship for the
purpose of endowing and maintaining two chaplains in the chapel of
St. Mary Magdalen, near Guildhall.   In this concession the property
is described as having formerly belonged to "a Brotherhood of St.
Nicholas"; but it may be presumed that that was the germ of the later
body.

The Parish Clerks were bound under the old law to register the
weekly christenings and burials in their respective parishes by six
o'clock p.m. on each Tuesday; but the time was changed to two
o'clock, to enable the authorities to have knowledge of the figures and
facts in advance.

A decree of the Court of Star Chamber in 1625 gave the Parish
Clerks liberty to have on their premises a printing-press for the purpose
of the periodical Bill of Mortality, and the Primate assigned them a

printer to superintend it.   But the list was confined to deaths within
the City bounds, and is consequently very defective.

The charter of 1637 conferred jurisdiction over the Cities of London
and Westminster, the Borough of Southwark, and fifteen out-parishes ;
and the corporation consisted in 1739 of a Master, two Wardens,
seventeen Assistants, and all the Parish Clerks *ex officio* within the
Bills of Mortality.

In 1391 the Fraternity, consisting of the clerks of the various parish
churches of the metropolis and others of a similar calling, performed
at Skinners' Well, Clerkenwell, the *Creation* and the *Passion* before the
King, Queen, and nobility, and received under writ of privy seal 10*l*. for
their pains ; and in 1409 there was a second representation before Henry
IV. and his Court of the same kind, but of ampler extent, which lasted
seven days.   In his *Miller's Tale*, Chaucer makes jolly Absolom, the
parish clerk, take the part of Herod in exhibitions of this character.

This Fraternity seems to have borne a part in those frequent religious
ceremonials which marked the life of former days.   In the Corpus
Christi procession of the Skinners, described by Stow, no fewer than
two hundred are said to have attended.

In the Founders' accounts for 1497 there is, in connection with the
celebration of a mass, a payment to two parish clerks of eightpence, or
a groat each.

Maitland states in 1739 and again in 1756, that the Hall of the Company was in Wood Street, Cheapside ; it is at present in Silver Street,
a turning out of that thoroughfare.

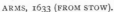

ARMS, 1633 (FROM STOW).

EARLY ARMS.

But their earlier, if not their original, seat was at Bishopsgate, where
at the very beginning the Clerks were established.   As we have above
mentioned, houses near the gate were vested in them in the reign of
Henry VI. to found a religious service with two chaplains near Guildhall, and this circumstance doubtless led to their eventual migration to

that vicinity. One of the houses so devised was the Wrestlers' Inn, and another, the Angel; the Parish Clerks' Hall lay behind, and was approached by a court. The premises consisted of the Hall itself and seven almshouses, and at the Dissolution were granted to Sir Robert Chester. The former owners took legal proceedings against the intruder, and anticipated a successful issue; but Chester determined the suit by pulling down the Hall, and disposing of the materials.

The Paviours.

OLD ARMS.

PRESENT ARMS.

STOW (ed. 1633, p. 641), says: "The Company of the Paviours no doubt have beene a Company of antiquity, and maintained a Community or Brotherhood among themselves, but for incorporation no Record doth testifie it to me, and therefore I have lesse to say of them."

It seems reasonable to conclude that this Association could not have acquired much importance in early times, when the use of pavement, or even of paved stone ways, was excessively limited.

By the regulations as to wages. of various trades, set down in the *Liber Albus*, paviours were not entitled to charge more than twopence for making seven foot and a half of pavement of the foot of St. Paul in breadth. This was termed a toise; and the workman was further bound to conform to the Assize.

No paviour might lay his work at a different level or elevation from that of the neighbouring premises.

In 1739 and 1756 Maitland refers to this as a Company by prescription, and as consisting of three Wardens and twenty-five Assistants, without a Livery.

Ube Ipepperers.

A COMPARATIVE examination of the records and notices relative to this most ancient Fraternity seems to lead to the conclusion, that they were the descendants of the "Emperor's men," or Teutonic Society, which in the tenth century obtained a grant of land or a site at Dowgate by the river's bank, and held it by a sort of feudal custom, namely, by a half-yearly delivery to the Crown of ten pounds of pepper. They may well have derived their appellation from this source ; but they soon began to extend their transactions, and united with the Corders and others in forming a more or less irregular Gild, which doubtless made it a primary business to supply and monopolize the riparian trade in that quarter. In 1180, according to an entry in the Pipe Rolls, they had attained sufficient eminence to find a place among the eighteen "adulterine" Gilds, which were fined because they had not sought a royal licence. They were required to pay sixteen marks. The same thing happened to some of the bodies which now form the twelve great Companies.

The Pepperers and Corders (with whom were subsequently associated the Farriers, Apothecaries, and others) obtained the nomination of the keeper of the King's Great Beam at the Staple-Yard or Steelyard, the goods brought or shipped there being almost exclusively such as fell under the heavy standard. The importance of accurate determination of weight was far greater when the state of the currency necessitated a large resort to barter.

The earliest ordinances of the Pepperers with which we are acquainted are those which they made, with the assent of the Lord Mayor and Aldermen, in 1315–16, wherein they are described as "the good folks of Soper Lane of the trade of Pepperers," and credit themselves with the desire to settle certain undermentioned points for the common benefit.

They are ranged under four heads : namely, That no one of the Craft shall directly or indirectly mix or adulterate goods of different quality and price. That no one shall tamper with bales, so as to change or transfer the contents of any bale, or place false wares beneath true ones. That no one shall moisten saffron, alum, ginger, cloves, and such other merchandise, in order to increase the weight. That every vendor shall have true uniform measures and weights, shall sell by the hundredweight of one hundred and twelve pounds, fifteen ounces to the pound, save confections and powdered goods, which shall be sold by twelve ounces to the pound.

This shews that, prior to their combination with the *Spicers* under

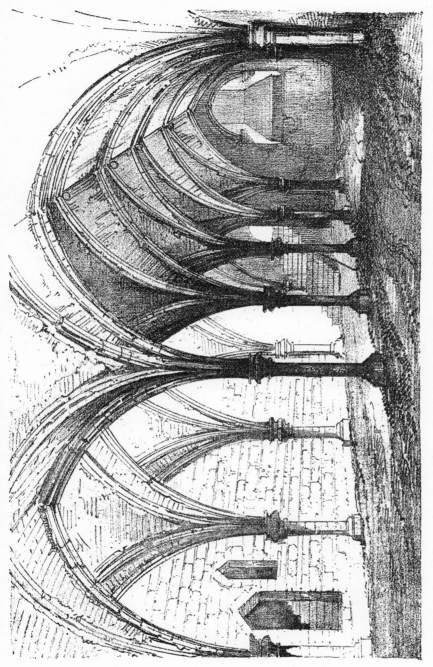

CRYPT OF GERARD'S HALL, BASING LANE.
The residence of Sir John de Gisors, Citizen and Pepperer. (Destroyed in 1852.)

the name of *Grocers*, the Pepperers had in use both the avoirdupois and troy or tron weights.

The Pepperers steadily rose in wealth and dignity. On the decline of the influence of the Jews and Italians, they gradually added to their functions those of bankers and pawnbrokers, before the Goldsmiths' Gild made those departments of business their particular province. The Fraternity had strengthened its ranks indeed by admitting to membership some of the more eminent merchants of foreign origin, whose experience and connexions were apt to prove of essential service in an industry of varied character and incidence. Among these we may mention Andrew Bokerel and Sir John de Gisors.

Bokerel in 1225 farmed the revenues of the King's Exchange, near St. Paul's, where all transactions in the precious metals were once conducted. He was succeeded at intervals in this responsible and honourable office by other Pepperers, and in 1231 was chosen Mayor, holding that position till 1237. Between the latter date and 1345, the year of the incorporation with the Spicers, eight other brethren of the Gild filled the mayoralty. In 1312, of the twenty persons specially charged by Edward II. in his letters from York to hold the City in his obedience, nine were Pepperers. It was the frequent absence of our kings from London, and the weakness of the central authority, which favoured the growth of municipal power.

Some suppose that Bucklersbury, to which the followers of the mistery shifted somewhat later from Sopers' Lane, owes its name to Bokerel, who had his mansion house there. We observe that in the Coroner's Roll of Edward I. for 1278 Broad Street Ward is described as the Ward of William Bokerel. He was the proprietary or feudal Alderman, and as in the case of the Faringdons the estate remained some time in his family. Isabella Bokerel, whose will, dated 1280, is enrolled in the Court of Husting, was doubtless of this ancient stock ; she appears to have possessed property in the Saddlery adjoining Cheapside. This illustrious municipal family first presents itself to our notice in the person of Thomas Bokerel, Sheriff in 1216–17, 2 Henry III. He was probably related to Andrew, who was Sheriff, 8 and Mayor, 15–21, of the same reign. In the 11 and 12 Henry III. Stephen Bokerell was one of the Sheriffs in the mayoralty of Roger Duke, and in 40 of that king Matthew Bokerell filled the same office.

The Fraternity migrated at a later period, perhaps about the first quarter of the fourteenth century, to Sopers' Lane, where they continued to rise in importance and reputation as dealers or factors in an extensive choice of necessaries for consumption or use, as bankers, and as financiers.

Riley prints an indenture as to a sale of jewels by Walter Adryan, Pepperer of London, in 1338, to Margery Randolf; which jewels were presumably his private property, and must have represented a considerable money-value.

The Pepperers, with whom were associated the Spicers of Cheap, a second opulent body, both of whom may have felt the need, as their business and resources expanded, of some system of defensive co-operation, though ostensibly for the maintenance and increase of love among themselves, formed themselves on St. Anthony's Day (May 9) 1345, into a fraternity, called the Fraternity of St. Anthony, "to the honour of God, the Virgin Mary, St. Anthony, and All Saints," and agreed to dine together, being two and twenty persons, on June 12 following, at the palace of the Abbot of Bury [Bevis Marks] in Threadneedle Street, near St. Anthony's Hospital, when two Wardens were elected for the government of the body, and certain ordinances were settled among themselves, providing for conditions of membership, the payment of fees, the maintenance of a priest, the choice of a common livery, arbitration between brethren in cases of dispute, attendance at mass and at a banquet on St. Anthony's Day, when the Wardens were required to wear chaplets, and crown their successors for the year next ensuing, the rules of apprenticeship, and the relief of the poor of the Brotherhood. The Wardens of 1346 delivered to those of 1347 all the property of the Association, namely, 6l. 6s. in money, the Halliwell chalice, and a vesture.

The assemblies at the Abbot of Bury's, a house exempted by charter from episcopal, and perhaps from other save regal, interference, and contiguous to the hospital and church of the patron-saint of the Pepperers, were purely temporary, and the new Gild returned shortly after to quarters in Sopers' Lane, their former centre, by St. Antholin's Church, at the junction of the lane with Watling Street and Budge Row ; but we shall see that, during a lengthened period, the Fraternity had no fixed abode or address, and occasionally met in St. Antholin's, or whither the Wardens summoned them.

Mr. Kingdon has taken singular pains to trace and establish a link between St. Anthony's in Threadneedle Street (a presumed cell of St. Antoine de Vienne in Dauphiny) and the long commercial relationship of the Pepperers with Alexandria, the seat of the worship of the Coptic personage of the same name, who is commonly known as St. Anthony; and that gentleman ascribes the Association of the Pepperers with the Hospital or Hospice in the City of London to their espousal of the Alexandrian anchorite as their tutelary saint.

Sopers' Lane, Cheapside, the modern Queen Street, appears to have been from the most ancient times a busy and noisy spot. It owed its name to the Soapers or Soap-makers, who, at a period when Cheapside was still a comparatively open space, were left at liberty to pursue their calling here. The Pepperers, a far more important, influential, and respectable body, perhaps succeeded them. In 1297 we come across an ordinance of the City to forbid evening "cheapings" here and to abolish what is termed the New Fair. At this time, and till some centuries later, Cheapside extended only from Sopers' Lane to Foster Lane. On the removal of the Pepperers, or rather Grocers, to Bucklersbury, the Curriers and Cordwainers settled here.

In the time of Stow's Continuator (1633), a chain was drawn across the middle of this lane, which was, no doubt, just such a narrow thoroughfare as many yet remaining thereabout.

In 1348, the widows of free Pepperers were allowed to preserve their membership, to apply for relief, and to attend the dinners, so long as they remained in that state, or did not remarry out of the Fraternity; and in the same year a beadle was appointed to summon the members.

The Pepperers and Spicers, as an independent Gild, may be considered as having determined their career some time previously to 1373, when they had apparently enlarged their sphere of activity and influence, and designate themselves *Grocers*, otherwise dealers in whole-sale or gross ; for the contention of Mr. Kingdon, that they were so called because they adopted the avordupois standard is rebutted by the evident circumstance that they used both standards.

It is certain, however, that anterior to 1345, namely, in documents of 1310 and 1328, the appellation *Pepperer* is rendered by the Latin word *Grossarius,* as if they were beginning to gain recognition under the latter, which found its way into our language through the mediæval form *Grocere*.

The Pinners or Pin-makers.

IN 1376 the Pinners returned two members to the Common Council, and in 1469 supplied twenty men to the City Watch—a fair quota, as the Salters made themselves answerable only for a similar number, while many of the minor Companies contributed no more, or less, than half.

By the charter granted to the Girdlers, 10 Elizabeth, the *Pinners* and Wire-workers,[1] who had been one body at least since the time of Edward IV., and kept their accounts together, were united with them ; and this is the last intelligence which we gain of the present Association, until 1598 or thereabout, when it appears to have abandoned its Hall in Addle Street, rented from the Plaisterers, through a depression in the industry, and to have removed elsewhere.

After existing during three centuries, perhaps, by prescription, or as a subordinate member of the Girdlers, the Pinners obtained separate letters patent of incorporation, 11 Charles I., August 20, 1636, when the home manufacture of this article of constant use began to grow more extensive and regular, and to supersede the foreign trade, which is said to have been so large in the previous reign that 60,000*l.* a year left the country to pay for our imports. Its style was, The Master, Wardens, Assistants, and Commonalty of the Art or Mistery of Pin-makers of the City of London. The government was a Master, two Wardens, and eighteen Assistants. There was no Livery.

We have already traced the Pinners to Addle Street as lessees ; and from a broadside in the library of the Society of Antiquaries, ascribed to 1619, we learn that the Company then had a Hall at St. Mary at Hill, but were on the point of migrating to a new one at St. Katherine Crie, where they were prepared to supply customers. Here there is evidence to shew that they continued to exercise their trade, and to hold

---

[1] See the account of the *Tin Plate Workers* in the next division of the book.

periodical assemblies until 1723, when the Hall was diverted from its purpose, and let as a Presbyterian meeting-house. Like that of the Founders, it lay back from the thoroughfare in Old Broad Street, and was approached by an alley still known as Pinner Court. It was taken down in 1797. But over the building at the end of the court *Pinners' Hall* is inscribed in bold characters. The whole group of modern brick and mortar is a nest of offices. The footfall of a Pinmaker has not been heard there these hundred and fifty years passed.

Prior to the happy discovery of the notion and art of making this diminutive essential, thorns, stone, bone or metal skewers, brooches, and bodkins, the two latter often of silver or gold, were employed by all classes.

This was a part of the primitive mercer's occupation, which he eventually relinquished to the hurer or milliner, and which became in turn one of the lucrative specialties of the haberdasher of small wares.

Here the retailer acquired a footing more advantageous than that of the manufacturer ; for the corporate privileges of the Pin-makers appear to have lapsed, and very little is heard or known of them as a Company or Gild after their original incorporation. The combined influence of the bodies interested in keeping them under normal mercantile control was very strong.

***

Account Books of the Pinners and Wire-makers, temp. Edward IV. Egerton MS. Brit. Mus. 1142.

Minute Book of the Pin-makers, 1710–23. MS. in the Guildhall Library.

To all Haberdashers and other Tradesmen whatsoever, buyers and sellers of Pinnes within the Cité of London and suburbs thereof. [Notice by the Master, Wardens, Assistants and Companie of Pin-Makers, of the Removal of the Hall heretofore on S. Mary Hill, to near S. K. Crie Church, where the Companie have in readinesse all sorts of Pinnes. [1619.] A broadside.]

***

The Planers.

A NOTICE of this Craft Gild will be found under the account of the Joiners in the following section. Like the Sawyers, they long maintained an independent position as a trade's-union, and were manifestly recognised as such so late as 1629, in which year they contributed 4*l.* 6*s.* to the civic expenses connected with a coronation, against 8*l.* 16*s.* demanded from the Joiners, and 10*l.* 15*s.* from the Carpenters.

The Planers must have constituted a regular and important organization, distinct from both, and were constructively of great antiquity, although their rise into prominence doubtless resulted from the development of the special branch of the art which they professed. They, equally with the Sawyers, however, failed to hold their ground.

The Potters.

THIS Brotherhood probably merged in the Armourers and Braziers. It is to be concluded that it possessed no constitution or governing body.

In proceedings which took place in 1316 before the Mayor and Aldermen, "the good folks of the trade of Potters in London" made plaint of abuses and frauds committed to their detriment by persons who sold pots of bad metal by setting them on the fire and thus making them look like vessels of good material ; and these offenders aggravated their delinquency by offering the goods for sale in West Cheap on Sundays and festival days.

The Mayor's Court directed that steps should be taken by honest men of the trade to make assays, and determine in what proportions lead and copper ought to be employed in the manufacture. But the record, whence these particulars are taken, was left incomplete.

The Pouch-makers.

WE first hear of this Fraternity in 1339, when overseers were appointed to order the trade, and detect fraudulent or irregular practices. From new articles or ordinances framed for them in 1371 it is readily inferable that they had obtained antecedent regulations. Those of 1371 pre-scribed an exclusive right of sale for purses and straps of leather in the City, but during the day and in their shops only, and not privily in *hostels;* that no serving-man or apprentice of the trade should work under any person of another trade, lest he might teach him the craft ; that no apprentice should be received who was a common brawler or otherwise of evil fame ; and that an infringement of the rules of the Society should be punished by a fine. Here they are termed "the reputable men of the trade of Pouch-makers," and it is expressly mentioned that the articles have not yet been "enrolled" among the archives of the Fellowship.

In the following year a fresh code of bye-laws was drawn up for the Pouch-makers and Leathersellers jointly ; and we shall find that the latter ultimately absorbed the former and more ancient union.

In 1400 the Pouch-makers obtained from the Court of Aldermen the supervision of galoches of wood, which they shewed to the Court that they had invented and established. These were apparently clogs or pattens with leathern straps, to lift the wearer above the kennels of the City, and were probably a foreign fashion temporarily brought into use here.   As early as 1469 a Society of Patten-makers existed, as we shall see hereafter, but was not incorporated till 22 Charles II.

In 1488 and 1501 the Court of Aldermen made further ordinances for the regulation of the craft.   In 1501–2 they are reckoned in an official list as the fifty-sixth Gild, coming between the Broderers and the Woodmongers ; in 23 Henry VIII., at the Lord Mayor's banquet, they ranked fifty-third, following the Carpenters ; and they appear to have then possessed a Livery, though in 1501–2 they are classed with the bodies which had none.   But, on the other hand, it is stated that in 1517, by virtue of an order of the Court of Aldermen of November 17, they had joined the Leathersellers.

They long continued, however, to be an influential body.   Under March, 4, 1503–44, among the burials at Blackfriars, occurs that of John Burton, Citizen and Pouch-maker, who directs that he shall be buried where God shall provide ; but if he deceases within seven miles or thereabouts, in the body of this church, as nigh as may be to the image of our B. Lady.   He bequeaths 6s. 8d. to the Prior and Convent to fetch his corpse to sepulture, and for their accustomed divine services.

On their union with the Leathersellers, the Pouch-makers brought into the common chest a large and valuable assortment of plate, pewter, masers, and table-linen, besides a picture of the Assumption ; shewing that they were a substantial and thriving Fellowship.   The inventory of their goods is still extant.[1]

The Pursers or Glovers Pursers.

SOME notice of this Fellowship, which was incorporated with the Leathersellers in 1502, will be found under the accounts of that and the Glovers' Companies.

The Shearmen (Pannarii) or Retunders.

IN 1527–8 these, with the Fullers, were constituted a Company under the name of Clothworkers.   They first occur to notice in 1180, among the eighteen adulterine Gilds, and are described as Pannarii.

Although the Shearmen existed so much earlier, and formed a member of the group of industries represented by them, the Weavers, Fullers, and Dyers, there is no trace of any charter of incorporation prior to that of January 24, 1507–8, 23 Henry VII., under the Great

---

[1] *History of the Leathersellers' Company*, by W. H. Black, 1871, p. 48.

Seal, in which licence is given to the men of the mistery of the Shearmen within the City of London and their successors to found a Mistery or Gild in honour of the Assumption of the Virgin, with power to elect from year to year out of their own body a master and two Wardens, with the rights of mortmain, of pleading and being impleaded, of having and using a common seal, and of framing ordinances.

The Shearmen, however, under the name of *Pannarii*, occur among the eighteen unlicensed Gilds, fined by the Crown in 1180, but paid, or became liable to pay, only one mark. Their Alderman was then John Maur. This is the only explicit allusion to them, till we find them in possession of bye-laws in 1350, under the approval of the Corporation; and indeed the Telarii, or Weavers, who were closely associated with the Shearmen during the employment of unmixed woollen fabrics or the Old Drapery, had them before the reign of Edward I., since in these latter there is an express reference to anterior ordinances not at present known. Those of Edward I., as they more particularly concern the Weavers, may be better reserved for another place.

The code of 1350 does not essentially or greatly vary from that in force among the other early brotherhoods. But it may be noted (1) that none should engage a foreigner to be a partner with him in his business; (2) that all disputes arising between man and man were to be referred to the Wardens, and that no more strikes among the members, in the way of conspiracy and combination, were to be suffered.

We learn that the Shearman at this period received, according to the season, from 3*d.* to 4*d.* a day and his table, and nothing extra in the winter for night-work.

The labour of the Shearman in the middle of the 14th century is elucidated by the entry among the City Regulations of 1350, where the prices chargeable by him are specified and fixed, namely, for a short cloth, 12*d.*; for a long one, 2*s.*; and for a cloth of rayed or striped soy, and shearing the same, 2*s.* This scale was applicable to piece-work only.

Prior to their union with the Fullers in 1528, this Society seems to have had its bye-laws at least twice renewed, namely in 1452-3 and in 1507-8. In the former they are described as the *Shermen-Craft* of the House of the Augustine Friars in the City of London; and the code is stated to be acknowledged in the presence of the Official of the London Consistory Court in a certain upper hall called Lombard's Hall, within the said House of Augustines. It is curious that in the date not only the regnal year of Henry VI., but that of the pope, is furnished.

In 1453 the Shearmen seem to have numbered sixty, the Wardens inclusive, but not reckoning the sisters, who formed part of the Society, and joined, if not in the labour, at least in the ceremonial observances, as they shared its privileges and obligations. The ordinances of this date cite a Council of twelve persons to advise and control the Wardens, the prototype of the more modern Court of Assistants ; and they contain a curious provision, interdicting the acceptance of anything in payment of labour from a Lombard or stranger but coined money, to some extent in forestalment of the Truck Act. The remainder of the code is occupied by injunctions as to religious observances, quarter-wages, fines, and methods of regulating work.

A very short time after this date, in 35 Henry VI. (1456–7) and while the Shearmen yet preserved their individuality, John Hungerford and others, Citizens and Shearmen of London, acquired by deed from John Badby "a tenement and mansion-house, shops, cellars, and other the appurtenances lying in Minchin Lane, to the use of themselves and their heirs for ever." The grantor of this property, which is still vested in the Shearmen's successors, was perhaps related to the person of the same name, of Taplow, Co. Bucks, who had rights over Boveney Lock, near Eton, in 1375.

The ordinances of February 18, 1507–8, were approved by the Lord Chancellor, Lord Treasurer, Chief Justice of the King's Bench, and Chief Justice of the Common Plea, at Westminster, and mainly follow the lines of 1452–3. But here we find the twelve Councillors of 1452–3 explicitly called *Assistants*, and one of the Wardens distinguished as the *Upper* or *Master Warden*, the origin of the later office of Master ; this functionary must have served twice the office of Lower Warden. The seat of the Company is now termed its Common Hall, and the Livery occurs by name as a body entitled to receive from the common purse at intervals new clothing of the same colour and hooding. We perceive that it is indifferently, here and elsewhere, cited as the Livery, the Clothing, and the Vesture, and special officers were set apart to attend to the provision of it from time to time.

One of the articles of 1507–8 deals with the relief of poor members out of the common box and alms of the Craft, while in another is the direction, at the obsequies of a member, that all his brethren shall follow him to the grave in their proper dress.

These are by far the most elaborate and exhaustive regulations with which we have met at so early a period, and they embrace the oaths to be administered to new comers, as well as to the officers of the Company.

The Sawyers.

UNDER the account of the Joiners we have taken occasion to notice the origin of that Craft Gild as an offshoot from the Carpenters. In 1670, the latter drew up a series of objections to the incorporation of the Sawyers, and were seconded in their resistance to the proposal by the Joiners and Shipwrights. The main argument was, that the Sawyer was a labourer, whose work was necessarily overlooked by masters, and who sought independent jurisdiction as a method of still further enhancing the price of his work, which used to be 5s. and 6s. per load, and since the Fire had risen to 8s. and 9s.; and that the Carpenters themselves in their shops used the long or whip saw, and sometimes employed their own journeymen or apprentices, sometimes the class which now made pretension to become a Company.

The matter did not probably proceed beyond a preliminary stage or a tentative discussion.

The Sheathers.

THESE were absorbed in the Armourers, but for a length of time, like the Bladesmiths, Furbishers, etc., constituted a distinct, though unchartered Society.

The Shivers.

FOR a brief period, while commercial intercourse with the Peninsula was interrupted by the war between the French and ourselves (1809–12), the manufacture of wooden bungs for casks developed into an important industry; and a short-lived Association, called the Shivers' Company, sprang into existence. But the inconveniences arising from the want of flexibility and elasticity in wood naturally led to a prompt disuse of the new custom and to the early dissolution of this modern and most fugitive of trade misteries.

Oaken shives are still made and used to a limited extent, but by far the greater part of the immense quantity of shives required by British brewers and others is supplied from America, the soft wood used being compressed by the process of manufacture, and becoming perfectly liquor-tight on contact with fluid.

The Silkmen.

IN 1611 the Commissioners for Suits referred a petition from the Silkmen of the City, praying incorporation, to the Lord Mayor by command of his Majesty; and the Corporation reported that the Company was neither profitable nor necessary, and would entail great and sundry inconveniences. They alleged that the step would lead to abuses in working, in dyeing, and in weighing; and for all the purposes which it set forth provision was already made by custom of the City or by statute.

The Silkmen, who, as we perceive, had their own arms, and were plainly a numerous and important body, are named in the course of the controversy and correspondence which took place between 1607 and 1616 in relation to the dyeing of silk. We hence learn that there was a certain description of silk then sold under the designation of *London* or *light-weight* silk, and that many other abuses existed in the trade, which the King or his nominee thought should be remedied by some new machinery, but with which the City declared itself competent to deal.

This Fellowship obtained letters patent, 7 Charles I., May 23, 1631. The government consisted of a Master or Governor and twenty Assistants. But it possessed neither a Livery nor a Hall.

The Silk=Throwers or Throwsters.

IT appears that, at some considerable period prior to the institution of this Company, the trade was chiefly in the hands of foreigners ; but their descendants by intermarriage and naturalization acquired a sufficient footing to obtain in 1622 recognition as a Fellowship by the City, and in 1630 (April 23) a regular charter, with a government consisting of a Master, two Wardens, and twenty Assistants. There does not seem to have ever been a Livery or a Hall.

In an Act of Charles I., the Silk-throwsters are described as broad-silk weavers, and are declared admissible into the Weavers' Company, provided that they were "conformable to the laws of the realm and to the constitution of the Church of England." But the evidence goes rather to establish that this proposed union did not take place, inasmuch as subsequently to the Restoration the Throwsters still appear to have been an independent body, and no one was at liberty to engage in the trade, unless he had served his seven years' apprenticeship to the Gild, and been admitted to the freedom.

A very Considerable and Lamentable Petition to the Honourable House of Commons, February the 12th, 1641. **The Humble Petition** of the Master, Wardens, and Commonalty of the Mistery or Trade of the Silk Throsters of London. A broadside. [1642.]

The Soapers or Soap=makers.

UNDER the notice of the Pepperers we have introduced a reference to Sopers' Lane in Cheapside, which was successively occupied as a seat of trade by the Pepperers and by the Curriers and Cordwainers. But, prior to either of these, and constructively at a period of extreme antiquity, the spot formed the centre of the soap manufacture, of the origin of which we do not hear much, but which, during the reign of the later Tudors and the Stuarts, became an object of profitable employment, and consequently a prize for the patentee and monopolist, who bought his right from the Crown or its agents, and then farmed it to others.

In 1579–80 we come across the Soap-makers, and discover them in a dilemma, by reason that the Lords of the Council pressed upon them the sole purchase of oils from one Laurence Mellow, whereas the trade demonstrated, to the apparent satisfaction of the Court of Aldermen, that Mellow's oils were of the worst quality, and unfit for their purposes. The matter ended by the Lord Mayor sending samples of the stuff to the Council, and leaving Mellow to shift as he could.

The term *soap-boiler* occurs among the trades which were admitted to membership of the Merchant Taylors' Company at a somewhat late date. They are named in the Ordinances of 1661.

Many years after, the Soap-makers obtained a charter (13 Charles I., May 22, 1638), and had a government composed of a Master, two Wardens, and eighteen Assistants. But they never possessed a Livery or a Hall, and in the last century transacted their affairs at Guildhall.

A Proclamation concerning Soape and Soape-makers. 1633. A broadside.
A Proclamation for the Well Ordering and Settling the Manufacture of Soape. 25 Jan., 1633-4. A broadside.

A Proclamation concerning the Well-Ordering the Trade of Making and Selling of Soape. 13 July, 1634. A broadside.

A Short and Trve Relation concerning the Soap-business. 4to, 1641.

Tvstin's Observations, or Conscience Embleme. . . . By me, John Tustin, who hath benne plundered and spoyled by the Patentees for white and gray Soape. Aug. 27, 1646. A broadside.

The Soap-Patentees of London's Petition Opened and Explained. By Richard Wilkins. 4to, 1646.

A Looking-Glasse for Soap-Patentees. 4to, 1646.

The Soap-Makers' Complaint for the Losse of their Trade. 4to, 1650.

The Soap-Makers' Petition : Whipt and Stript. 4to, 1650.

The Spicers.

THE Spicers of the Ward of Cheap are coupled with the Pepperers of Sopers' Lane in an instrument of 1345, which practically laid the foundation of the Grocers' Company, and which in its unincorporated state was known and recognised as the Fraternity of St. Anthony. Of the Spicers (Fr. *espiciers* or *épiciers*) as a separate body we do not gain much intelligence prior to their union with the perhaps more wealthy and important Merchant Gild of Pepperers. Their subsequent history is bound up with that of the GROCERS.

It seems to be thought that the Spicers of Cheap did not confine themselves to spices and other fine goods, sold by the troy weight, or Goldsmiths' measure of twelve ounces to the pound, but had trans-actions in sundry choice and costly specialties, such as precious stones, jewellery, and other Oriental products or merchandise of a portable and luxurious character.

The Spurriers.

THIS Brotherhood, which subsequently merged in the Loriners, obtained a set of Ordinances in 1345, by which, among other usual stipulations, it was prescribed (1) that no one of the trade shall work longer than from daybreak till curfew rung out at St. Pulcher's, Newgate, by reason of deceptions practised, as the use of false or cracked iron, and the laying of gilding on false copper, and further, because certain would wander about all the day, and go to their work at night drunk, and blow up their forges to the peril and discomfort of all ; (2) that none shall expose his spurs for sale on Sundays or double feasts, but only his sign, and shall, if he then sell, do so within ;

(3) that all Spurriers shall be freemen ; (4) that none shall offer old spurs regarnished, or change them for new ones ; (5) that no foreigner shall be admitted, unless he has been enfranchised ; (6) that none shall work on Saturdays after noon till the Monday morning ensuing.

In 1501–2, the Spurriers were the seventy-sixth Company, and are marked as having a Livery.

In 1509, they were the last in order of the forty-seven Companies which lined Cheapside at the coronation of Henry VIII. They were still a separate Gild in 23 Henry VIII.

Stow says (1633) that Huggin Lane, in Queenhithe Ward, was formerly called Spuren, or *Spooner*, Lane ; but the name *Spuren* seems rather to indicate the seat of the Spurriers—*the lane of spurs.*

The same writer informs us that Water Lane in Tower Street Ward was once known as Spurrier Lane. Both thoroughfares were within a short distance of each other, and doubtless owed their designation to a similar circumstance—the selection of the locality as a seat of the Craft.

The Starchmakers.

ON February 5, 1607–8, the Grocers' Company represented to the Lords of the Council, through the Lord Mayor, the evils likely to arise from the incorporation of " certain persons allowed and using the trade of starchmaking" by letters patent. The petitioners alleged that the price of the article would be increased, and great inconvenience and annoyance caused to the public. As we hear no more of them, the Starchmakers did not probably then obtain their charter, even if they paid for it.

They were, however, afterward incorporated by letters patent of May 13, 1622, 20 James I., and consisted of a Master, two Wardens, and twenty-four Assistants, without Livery and Hall.

Stow (*Annals*, 1615, p. 869,) notices the coming to London in 1564 of Mistress Dinghen van den Plasse, a Fleming, with her husband. She was the daughter of a man of good position, and they removed to England for greater security. The wife started in business as a Starcher, and acquired a large custom from her own country-people here. Her fame as a starcher led to the more general use of cambric and lawn ; and she took pupils, whom she charged from 4*l.* to 5*l.* for instruction, and 20*s.* for initiating them into the art of seething or boiling the starch.

A **Proclamation** for the Well-Ordering the Making of White Starch within this Realm, and for Restraint of the Importation thereof from Foreign Ports. 1661. A broadside.

The Stock=fishmongers.

IN the patent granted to the Fishmongers' Company in 1364, this other Fraternity is described as enjoying an exclusive right of selling stock-fish in such places as were set apart for the purpose. They are frequently mentioned by Stow and others ; but we do not learn at what precise date they acquired the King's licence and the recognition, which are indistinctly stated in Edward's patent to the Salt-fishmongers.

It is clear that they had their own places for transacting business and displaying their goods. In the charter to the Salt-fishmongers in 1399, we meet with a notice for the first time of *Stock-fishmongers' Row*, that part of Upper Thames Street between the Water Gate or Oyster Gate and Old Swan Lane. One of the wharves in that thoroughfare was known as Fresh-fish Wharf ; and the members of the Fraternity possessed a station at or near St. Botolph's, Bishopsgate. They were debarred from selling before morning mass.

In 1406, Peters, who brought fresh fish for sale in the City, were allowed to stand in Cheap, and nowhere else.

Several distinguished men raised themselves to eminence by a successful career in this species of business, and among them Sir William Walworth, whose gallantry displayed itself in the rebellion of Wat Tyler.

But at length, in 24 Henry VII., September 20, 1508, after perhaps two centuries of life as a single Association, and five years after their actual union and employment of a common Hall, " Le mester de stok-fisshmongeres," as they are termed in the charter of 1399, was statutorily incorporated by the name of the Wardens and Commonalty of the mistery of Stock-fishmongers of the City of London, with perpetual succession, a common seal, a licence in mortmain, and the power of pleading and being impleaded.

The two Gilds were amalgamated 27 Henry VIII. Among the

municipal archives of this year is an order of the Court of Aldermen, under December 12, giving precedence to this then new Gild after the Vintners; and a further one of July 2, 1509, places them next to the Grocers, when the Companies assembled on public solemnities in St. Paul's Churchyard, and in processions next to the Vintners, as in 1508, and before the Dyers.

Stock-fishmongers' Hall stood in Thames Street, a few doors eastward from the other Company's seat, on one of two pieces of ground belonging, 42 Edward III., to Sir John Lovekyn and others, and then the site of four tenements. Lovekyn's residence is described in an inquisition, 22 Richard II. (1399), as " one tenement on the Oyster Hill, in the parish of St. Magnus, London," and is valued at 11s. 4d. a year. The Hall was built at the back of Lovekyn's house between 1368 and 1399. Contiguous to it were premises on a part of which stood one of the common privies, then and long after a not very picturesque or sanitary feature in the landscape.

The Stringers.

THE good folks of the trade of *Strengers,* that is, bow-string makers, represented to the Court of Aldermen in 1416, a period of great military activity in connexion with our French wars, that grave inconvenience and loss had accrued by the use of defective strings; and that whereas complaints have been made to them by persons in authority, officers of the King and others, that some remedy ought to be found for this evil, they prayed that they might have Wardens and Ordinances, as other trades had, to see well that the material and workmanship were good. This requisition was granted.

This appears to be the same body which, under the name of *Long Bow-String-Makers,* is described by Maitland as a Company by prescription, yet in possession of a coat of arms as given above. Its governing body consisted of two Wardens and nineteen Assistants; but there was no Livery.

The Surgeons.

THIS appears to have been a short-lived association, arising out of the grant in 1461 of a charter to the Barbers, and the evident feeling of the necessity for a higher grade of practitioner in difficult cases, or indeed in almost all outside phlebotomy and dentistry. Its name occurs in 1469 among the Companies then liable to participate in guarding the City gates ; but it is described as contributing nothing, and in 1501–2 was one of the twenty-eight bodies without a Livery. The other official lists contain no reference to it. But the two bodies were, as we shall hear, united by Act of Parliament in 1548, and remained so till 1745, when the Surgeons were erected into a new and independent Company from consideration of the great increase of knowledge among them, and the peculiar importance of their calling, as well as from a widely-diffused persuasion that the Barbers were playing a double part, incompatible with the public interest and security.

The Surgeons' Company was appointed to consist of a Master, two Wardens, twenty-one Assistants, and ten Examiners ; and the same privileges and powers were conferred on the governing body as were contained in the charters of Henry VIII. and Charles I., and in the Act of 1548.

Under the account of the BARBERS some further details of the original Surgeons' Society will be found.

LITERARY NOTICES.

The Noble Experyence of the Vertuous Handy Warke of Surgery Practysed and Compyled by Jherome of Bruynswyke. Folio, 1525.

The Practyse of Cyrurgeons of Mount-piller [Montpelier]. 4to [about 1525].

An Act Concernyng Barbers and Surgeons to be of one Companie, within the Citie of London. Sm. folio (with other Acts), 1540.

The Byrth of Mankynde, Newly Translated out of Latin into English. 4to, 1540, 1545, 1549, 1552, 1613, 1626, 1634.

The Questionary of Cyrurgyens. With the Formulary of a Lytell Guide in Cyrurgie. 4to, 1541.

Compendiosa totius Anatomie Delineatio, ære exarata per Thomam Geminum Londini. Folio, 1545. With copper-plates.

A Most Excellent and Learned Woorke of Chirurgerie, called Chirurgia Parua Lanfranci. Translated and Published (with Additions) by John Hall, of Maidstone, Surgeon. 4to, 1565.

The Historie of Man, Sucked from the Sappe of the most Approved Anathomistes. By John Banister, Master of Chirurgerie, etc. Folio, 1578.

The French Chirurgerye, or All the Naturall Operations of Chirurgerye, with divers and sundrye Figures. By Jaques Gyillemeau. Folio, Dort, 1598 ; 4to, London, 1635.

A Discovrse of the Whole Art of Chyrvrgerie. . . . Compiled by Peter Lowe, Scottishman, Doctor in the Facultie of Chirurgerie at Paris : . . . The Second Edition corrected, and much augmented and enlarged, by the Author. 4to, [1605] 1612, 1634. With woodcuts.

The first portion is inscribed to James Hamilton, Earl of Abercorn, and others ; the second, to John, Archbishop of Glasgow. There are verses by Thomas Churchyard, Esquire, John Norden, Physician, and G. Baker. The author dates the second edition from his house in Glasgow, Dec. 20, 1612.

Description of the Body of Man, with the Practise of Chirurgery. By Alexander Rhead. 4to, 1634. With engravings.

The Surgeon's Mate; or, Military and Domestique Surgery. By John Woodall, Master in Chirurgery. Folio, 1639.

In this book the use of lemon-juice in cases of scurvy is first recommended.

The Chyrurgeon's Store-House. Furnished with Tables cut in Brasse. By Johannes Scultetus [Schultz] of Ulm. Translated by E. B. 8vo, 1674 With 43 copper plates.

Compendium Anatomicum, Novo Methodo institutum. By John Case, M.D. 12mo, 1695. With copper plates.

Orang-Outang, sive Homo Sylvestris; or, the Anatomy of a Pygmie Compared with that of a Monkey, an Ape, and a Man. By Edward Tyson. 4to, 1699. With engravings.

The Judicial of Vryns. Folio [about 1510].
** Two or three editions.

The Seynge of Urynes. 4to [1525 ?].
** Several editions.

The Ivdgement of all Urynes. 8vo [about 1540].

The Differences, Cavses, and Iudgements of Vrines. By T. F., 8vo, 1598 ; the same, by J. Fletcher. 8vo, 1641.

The Urinal of Physick. By Robert Recorde, M.D., of Tenby. 8vo, 1548. Dedicated to the Wardens and Company of the Surgeons of London.
** There are several later editions, down to 1665.

The Arraignment of Vrines: Wherein are set downe the manifold errors and abuses of ignorant Vrine-monging Empirickes, cozening Quacksaluers, womenphysitians, and the like stuffe : Confining the vrines within their owne lists and limits, . . . Collected and gathered together . . . and written first in the Latine Tongue, and diuided into three Bookes by Peter Forrest D. of Physicke, and natiue of the Towne of Alcmare in Holland. . . . Translated into our English Tongue by Iames Hart D.r in the foresaid Faculty. 4to, 1623.

The Anatomie of Vrines. Containing the Conviction and Condemnation of them. Or, the second Part of our Discourse of vrines. Detecting and vnfolding the manifold falshoods and abuses committed. . . . Neuer heretofore published. By James Hart of Northampton. 4to, 1625.

The Tapissers or Tapestry=makers.

THE ordinances of "the good folks" of this trade were made and approved by the Corporation in 1331. They refer to the removal from the Fellowship of any misdoer or thief, to the tapice being of the lawful assize used in ancient times, and if of the common assize, four ells in length and two in breadth; and if of the smaller assize, three ells in length, and $1\frac{1}{2}$ ells in breadth. No tapice or carpet was to be made with arms thereon, unless it were wholly of wool. No cushion or banker[1] was to be made with arms thereon, unless it were all wool, and half an ell square, and at least an eighth of an ell deep. No one not free of the City was to keep any handiwork belonging to the trade, on pain of forfeiture. No material was to be used henceforth in the trade but good English or Spanish wool. Of course cases often occurred in which spurious material was used by the original Fellowship, and if the fraud was detected the goods were burned.

The Tapissers probably became absorbed in the Broderers. They are specially mentioned by Chaucer in his *Canterbury Tales*, written about 1388, as a separate and conspicuous body; but it may be surmised that they had branched off from the Tapestry Weavers.

The Grey Tawyers or Tanners.

THIS was a minor craft immediately in connexion with the Pelterers or Skinners, being the mechanics who flayed the animals; and its byelaws, made in 1365, chiefly relate to its obligations to the more important and powerful body. Some of the provisions were sufficiently drastic. They recite, besides other matters, that no Tawyer should deal in any peltry; that he should not act as broker between one dealer and another; that he should not make old budge into new leather, and that he should not cut off the head of any work; and the penalties were almost always in the form of imprisonment, in addition to a fine.

The oath to be administered to the Tawyers is found in the *Liber Albus*. It solely concerns the prohibition from flaying horses within the City and its then suburbs, and belongs to the fourth year of Edward III.

The Grey Tawyers appear to have had no Livery. In 1469 they were sufficiently prosperous to equip twenty guards for the City gates; and in 1531–2 they were represented by two members, besides their Wardens, at the Mayor's feast.

---

[1] A cushion for banks or benches.

The White Tawyers.

BOTH this community and the fore-mentioned are shown to have been in close relations with the Skinners and Upholders, of whom accounts are given elsewhere.

The White Tawyers acquired by-laws in 1346, and are there described as "the good folks the Megucers, called *Whittawyers*." This code is rather lengthy, and comprises some unusual provisions : (1) That they would find a wax candle to burn before Our Lady in the church of All Hallows, London Wall, and put money in the Box to support the same. (2) That if any of the trade should fall into poverty, he should, if he were a man of fair repute, receive 7*d*. out of the Box weekly, and his widow after his decease during her widowhood and good behaviour. (3) That one who died, and had not wherewithal to bury him, should be buried out of the Common Box, and that all the Brotherhood should attend the vigil, and make offering on the morrow. (4) That Overseers should be elected once a year with the customary powers and duties. (5) That none shall take for his work more than the fixed price: namely, for the dicker of Scots or Irish stags, ½ mark ; for the dicker of Spanish stags, 10*s*. ; for the hundred of goats'-fells, 20*s*. ; for the hundred of roe-leather, 16*s*. ; for the hundred of hinds'-calves (young female deer) or kids'-fells, 8*s*. These are the persons who are described in 1311 as preparing white leather with alum, salt, and other materials. Some further account of them is given under that of the LEATHERSELLERS.

The Tobacco-Pipe Makers.

THIS Fraternity obtained letters patent 15 Charles II., April 29, 1663, incorporating them as the Pipe-makers of the Cities of London and Westminster, with a Master, two Wardens, and eighteen Assistants, but with no Livery.

Nothing appears to be known of them except that they still existed in needy circumstances in 1826, when they applied without success to the Founders (and probably to other Companies) for assistance.

The Makers of Vinegar, Aqua Vitæ, and Aqua Composita.

THIS was evidently an unendowed Fellowship of recognised standing in 1594, when the Court of Aldermen supported it against a patent granted by the Queen to Richard Dickes, to the prejudice of the civic body. It doubtless eventually merged in the Distillers' Gild, which was incorporated in 1638, but not enrolled till 1658.

The Watermen.

IN 1372 the City authorities enacted that no boatman should take for his fare between London and Westminster more than two pence ; and the same, until his boat is full of people, when he shall take three pence at the highest for his boat, himself, and his partner, on pain of imprisonment as well in London as in the Staple of Westminster, and that no boatman should withdraw himself from serving the people on the same pain.

From extant printed monuments we learn that there was in 1559–60 an established scale of fares for passengers between London and Gravesend and London and Windsor ; and in 1641 the Watermen are expressly described as a Company, possessing ancient Overseers, Rulers, and Assistants, or, in other words, a government of long continuance.

By the Act 2 and 3 Philip and Mary, the Court of Aldermen was invested with the duty and power of electing, out of the whole body plying between Gravesend and Windsor, eight Overseers ; and beyond the regulations made by this statute we find others under 1 James I. cap. 16.

The Watermen (with whom were subsequently, but before 1700, associated the Lightermen) of London and Westminster were never formally incorporated ; but under the government of their Overseers the provisions of the law were enforced, as may be judged from a long account in Maitland, who appears to have taken particular pains to ascertain all that was possible about the Society ; in his time, the number of boats and barges belonging to the Free Watermen was computed at about 7,000.

By the 11 and 12 William III. cap. 21, the Watermen of London and Westminster were at liberty to ply for hire on Sundays ; and in the case of those of Westminster, who appear to have been independent of the London body, the proceeds were applied to charitable purposes. It was officially stated that in 1701 this fund amounted to 800*l.* a year. The interests and resources of the Fraternity were fatally affected by modern improvements.

The tariff, originally fixed in 1559, was revised from time to time. Maitland prints that in force in 1671, including the " Rates for carrying of Goods in the Tilt-Boat between London and Gravesend."

The Table of Fares " from London to places on the River Thames without the Bill of Mortality " contains the charges for the boat and the Company as far as Gravesend one way and Windsor the other. The payment to Chelsea, Battersea, or Wandsworth was 1*s.* 6*d.* and 3*d.* for the Company ; that to Putney, Fulham, or Barn- Elms, 2*s.* and 4*d.* ; that to Hammersmith, Chiswick, or Mortlake, 2*s.* 6*d.* and 6*d.* The rate of course increased with the distance ; Twickenham cost 4*s.* and 6*d.* for the Company ; Hampton Court, 6*s.* and 1*s.* ; Weybridge and Chertsey, 10*s.* and 1*s.* ; and finally Windsor, 14*s.* and 2*s.* It was almost a monopoly.

An Act was framed in 1729 to amend the previous Acts relating to Watermen, Wherrymen, and Lightermen, working on the Thames.

The Watermen, although we do not find any trace of a charter, constantly describe themselves as a Company ; and in an order of 1701, to check the use of bad language on the river, the Hall is expressly named, but without an indication of its locality.

It was first and long situated, however, in Lower Thames Street, near the Three Cranes, in Vintry Ward, on the site of Calvert's Brewery, was burnt down in 1666 with most part of the contents, and rebuilt twice, in 1667–8 and 1722. But in 1776 the Company parted with the property to the brewing-house, and transferred its quarters to St. Mary-at-Hill, near at hand.

The Company was particularly honoured by the eminent literary qualifications and special standing of John Taylor, called the Water-Poet, one of the most prolific writers of his time, both in prose and verse. His publications range in date from 1612 to 1653, and in subject over the whole field of social and political life. He was a zealous and staunch Royalist, and after the death of Charles I. confined himself to the production of fugitive pieces on miscellaneous topics. Two engraved portraits of Taylor exist.

He was certainly a man of unequalled versatility with his pen; and his writings shed a remarkable light on contemporary usages and events.

LITERARY NOTICES.

The Prices of Fares and Passages to be Paid unto Watermen from London to Gravesende, and likewise from Gravesende to London, and to every Common Place betwene: and also between London Bridge and Windesoure. [1559.] A broadside.

The Prices and Rates that every Particular Person ought to Pay for his Fayre or Passage vnto Watermen or Whyrrymen from London to Gravesende. . . . [1559–60.] A broadside.

Cas Merveilleux d'un Bastellier de Londres, lequel, sous ombre de passer les passans outre la rivière de Thames, les estrangloit. 8vo, Lyon, 1586.

To the Right Honourable Assembly, the Lords, Knights, Esquires, and Burgesses of the Honourable House of Commons in Parliament: The Humble Petition of the Ancient Overseers, Rulers, and Assistants of the Company of Watermen. Written by John Taylor. 4to, 1641, 1642.

To the Right Honourable the Lord Mayor, Aldermen and Commons of the City of London, . . . The Humble Petition of the Sea-men and Watermen in and about the said City . . . 1659. A broadside.

To the Supreme Authority of the Parliament of the Common-wealth of England. The Humble Address and Congratulation of many Thousands of Watermen belonging to the River of Thames. 1659. A broadside.

The Woodmongers.

THE sole very early reference to this Association occurs in an indenture of 1375 between the Woodmongers of London and John Baddeby, of Taplow, in the county of Buckingham,[1] whereby the latter renounced his alleged right to a toll on all vessels passing through Baddeby's Lock, probably, as Mr. Riley suggests, Boveney Lock, near Eton.

Hence it is to be inferred that the Woodmongers brought this commodity from a distance in various directions by water for sale in the metropolis. From an order of Common Council in 1379, it is clear that buyers of billets, and perhaps firewood generally, brought by water were bound to go direct to the wharves, and that middlemen were not

---

[1] See the account of the Shearmen, *suprâ*.

allowed.   Two persons, presumably forestallers, who were found in this year to have 6,000 billets stored up for re-sale, forfeited them to the authorities.

But in the case of large contracts for timber for building purposes, the Companies' archives and other authorities combine to establish that the contractor or architect bought his material direct from the estate, as when, in the restoration of Goldsmiths' Hall in 1666, a negotiation is conducted with Colonel Nevill, near Windsor, for the required supply.

In 1501–2 the Fellowship is returned as fifty-seventh in order, and stands between the Pouchmakers and the Turners.   In 23 Henry VIII., where the precedence is not strictly marked, it is forty-eighth, and is said to have no Livery.

We learn from Stow (ed. 1633, p. 642) that "the Company of the Woodmongers, being a very ancient Fellowship, and of good and amiable agreement together for long time, became to be incorporated the nine and twentieth day of August, in the third yeare of the Reigne of our Sovereigne Lord King James ; " but in this statement the old historian is not perfectly explicit, as will be seen on a reference to the account already given of the Carmen.

John Dyer, Citizen and Woodmonger of London, is named as the plaintiff in a case of alleged forgery in 1412.

From some correspondence between the Lords of the Council and the City in 1601, it appears that the Woodmongers had the supervision of the Carmen within the civic boundaries, and that the Mayor found difficulty in dealing with both.   The City was expected to find at short notice carts and hackney carriages for the purposes of the Court, and the payment was evidently irregular and precarious.   Two hundred two-horse carts were demanded to convey the King's effects to Greenwich in 1604.   The hackneymen and coachmen who served the King of Denmark during his visit to England in 1606 were furnished by the civic authorities.

It is remarkable that in 1615 this Society subscribed as much as 200*l.* to the Ulster Plantation scheme, as sub-sharers with the Vintners.   The sum was equal to that given by the Carpenters, and far in excess of the quota found by several bodies still surviving.   The *minimum* was 20*l.*

As we perceive from the language of a tract quoted below, it was still in existence in 1649, and was then engaged in defending its interests against hostile encroachment.   Elsewhere we take an opportunity of shewing that there were at one period relations between the Woodmongers and the Clockmakers, through the call for the old-fashioned cases for coffin-clocks.

But after a troubled and chequered career, the Woodmongers abandoned their charter in 1668, in consequence of charges preferred against them in Parliament.

In 1694, however, they were resuscitated by a resolution of Common Council on a smaller basis, with the right to keep 120 carts, independently of those maintained by the Carmen for the conduct of their own business.

The Woodmongers' Remonstrance, or, The Carmen's Controversie rightly stated ; Wherein the present Jurisdiction and Corporation of the Woodmongers is vindicated ; (2) the Original and Nature of Cars and Car-rooms ; (3) the Inconveniences attending the Erroneous Conceit of accounting them Goods and Chattels ; (4) the Mistake concerning Sea-coal Sacks rectified. By W. L. 4to, 1649.

The Wool=packers.

IT is to be presumed that this was no more than a voluntary unchartered Association, and was superseded by the WOOLMEN. Stow observes (ed. 1633, p. 640) : " The Company of Wooll-packers, I know not what to say of them, because it seemes that there were such men in the Haunse dayes, when the Wooll-Staple flourished, and that our Wooll-merchants had their eminency." In 1588 we find a stationer established in Hosier Lane, Smithfield, at the sign of the Woolpack.

The Wool-packers were probably not an union of the operatives or yeomen of the trade employed by the woollers or woolmen ; but the masters who conducted that branch of the business, and it is highly questionable whether they were, at least originally, connected with the Wool-winders. The Association, of whose history Stow avowedly knew next to nothing, long continued to be a distinct and respectable one, under that name ; although, in 1416, John Russell, one of the members, was sentenced to the pillory for slandering an Alderman.

It is evident that this was a very ancient body, for it is not only mentioned in a return of 1469, but among the forty-eight Gilds enumerated and placed in order of priority in 1515, it stands forty-fifth.

Proposed Corporation or Society of Retail Traders of London and the Suburbs.

IT appears that in 1636 a charter was in readiness to pass the Great Seal for incorporating both freemen of the City and others resident within three miles' compass, as well as foreigners (by special payment to the Crown), being Dealers by Retail, except weavers, tilers, and bricklayers, who were reserved for future consideration. But as we hear no more of the scheme, which was set on foot, of course, as a method of raising funds for the King, it probably dropped, although considerable efforts were made to give effect to the charter.

VOLUNTARY ASSOCIATIONS WHICH SURVIVE IN THAT FORM.

The Fellowship Porters.

THIS is a body of some length of standing, and still preserves the form of an Association, but has never, we believe, been chartered or incorporated. The members, all of whom appear to be practical working craftsmen, discharge the duties of loading and unloading at the Docks and the vicinity, and occasionally have collisions with rival unions. The Porters possess no arms, and use those of the City of London, whence their authority arises.

This community does not appear to possess any distinct organization, and is the only survival of many attempts on the part of the journeymen, yeomen, or denizens in trades in former days, to combine for something more than self-defence. But the resources of the Porters are too insignificant to render their influence sensible. The Fellowship Porters appear to have consisted of more than one body, as we hear of the Billingsgate section, about 1620, as having, "time out of mind," attended to that particular service. The Fishmongers' Company used to appoint two of its freemen Tackle-Porters, as they were termed, to attend to the lading and unlading of its vessels at the water-side.

Some light is cast on this Fraternity by the City Regulations of 1350, where their tariff between certain distances is laid down, and by the entries in the *Remembrancia*, wherein it is set forth that the charges made by them for portage or porterage had been so settled by Act of Common Council, and that the employment was a very ancient

one, whereon a great number of poor freemen of the City depended
for their livelihood. Among others who complained of the unreasonable demands of the Porters were certain maltsters of Henley-on-
Thames.

The tariff chargeable by the Packers' Water-side Porters for landing
or shipping goods and persons, not freemen, was regulated by the City
authorities, and a table of rates is appended to *An Abridgement of the
Charter*, 1680.

Maitland (1739–56) speaks of the Porters as consisting of Tackle and
Ticket Porters, and says that they constituted a Fraternity by Act of
Common Council in 1646, with the power of annually choosing from
among themselves twelve Rulers, six of each denomination (two of
whom must be registrars), for the good government of the whole and
the settlement of all differences, but with a right reserved to the Court
of Aldermen to intervene and arbitrate.

The church of St. Mary-at-Hill, between Billingsgate and East-Cheap,
is the annual scene of an ancient ceremony or usage performed by this
Fraternity, of which the members, on the Sunday next after Midsummer
Day, attend here in the morning, and while the psalm is being sung,
march up, two and two, to the rails of the communion table, where, in
two basins placed there for the purpose, they make their offerings. The
rest of the congregation follow the example, and the fund thus collected
is applied to the relief of the aged and sick of the body.

There were, as in the case of other Associations, similar bodies in
the provinces, and more especially at the sea-ports. Among those at
Faversham some were known as *backers*.

To the Honourable the Knights, Citizens, and Burgesses, in the Commons
Hovse of Parliament now assembled. The humble Petition of 15,000 poore
labouring men, known by the name of Porters, and the lowest Members of the
Citie of London. 1641. A broadside.

Other unincorporated Societies, whose names occur in early official
lists as of recognised position, were the Foisters, Netters, Mailmakers,
Corsors [Horse-dealers], Cartwrights, Box-makers, and Instrument-
makers. The three last are mentioned in 1672 as branches of the
Carpenters. The Corsors were incorporated with the Innholders, the
Mailmakers with the Pouchmakers, and the Foisters (perhaps) with the
Watermen.

FOREIGN CORPORATIONS.

The Alien Weavers.

R EGULATIONS for this Union or Fellowship were made in 1362 at its own request, and three Overseers appointed to be chosen, to control all proceedings, to maintain peace, and to adjudicate in certain cases, as for instance, where a workman purloined from his master the first time, and both were willing to have the matter amicably settled.

The Flemish Weavers.

HOW far this evidently very ancient body was identical with the Alien Weavers just mentioned, or, again, with the Easterlings of the Steelyard, with which riparian vicinity they were apparently connected, we hardly know. The bye-laws proposed in 1366 for formal acceptance by the Corporation speak of their long establishment in London ; but the oldest mention of them seems to be the royal protection accorded to John Kemp, a Fleming, on his coming to London in 1330 to follow the art, and to teach it to others. The encouragement thus given led to an influx of seventy families, it is said, from Flanders and Brabant, who quartered themselves in the Ward of Candlewick or Cannon Street.

The draft code of 1366 seems to point to a good deal of habitual discord among the members of the colony. It also contains a provision that all existing ordinances may remain in force. Certain questions, if in dispute, are to be referred to a committee of four-and-twenty members, chosen or approved by the Mayor and Aldermen. This was a large number, and if it was not disproportionate, indicates a very extensive assemblage of artificers and a very prominent industry.

It elsewhere appears that the Flemish Weavers and those of Brabant were distinct communities, and that in 1370 the serving-men of the former stood for hire in the churchyard of St. Lawrence Pountney, and those of the latter in that of St. Mary Somerset at Queenhithe. They were placed thus far apart, because they were addicted to fighting each other. But no opposition was offered by either or by the authorities to the common employment of workmen by the two Associations.

OTHER RIVERSIDE TRADING COMPANIES.

ALLIED to the Livery Gilds and other Fellowships of a mercantile character by community of origin and aim were certain other Associations, which arose to meet the gradual development of commercial enterprise, and to co-operate with such bodies as the London Companies at home in carrying native products or manufactures abroad, and exchanging them for those of other countries.

These cognate corporations were :

1. The Easterlings of the so-called Still or Steel yard [*Stabile Emporium*, or Staple-Hof].

Of the members of this Gild probably the best known name is that of George Gizen, whose portrait by Holbein is preserved at Berlin.

2. The Almaines [Germans], belonging to the Hanse or Gild of the merchants of Almaine, first in Thames Street, and then at Bishopsgate, or perhaps, for some time concurrently at both.

This body was possibly connected with the Hamburgh merchants, who in the time of Elizabeth had quarters in Lothbury at Founders' Hall.

MERCHANTS OF THE STAPLE.

3. The Merchants of the Staple, incorporated by Edward III.

*** Their original Staples seem to have been at Calais and Antwerp.

MERCHANTS ADVENTURERS.

4. The Merchants Adventurers, incorporated by Edward IV.

*** Their privileges, etc., were confirmed and enlarged by Elizabeth in 1564. This body had been originally a branch of the Mercers, and had sprung from the ancient Fraternity of St. Thomas à Becket ; but it eventually severed itself from that tie, and became an independent trading body in London and elsewhere. Its members simultaneously belonged, in some cases, to the City Gilds. The principle of dividing a vessel into shares, which was older than this Society, and is a feature in the story of Richard Whittington, still prevails. A sixty-fourth part is, we believe, the *minimum*.

MERCHANTS OF ELBING.

5. The Merchants of Elbing, incorporated by Elizabeth.

MERCHANTS OF RUSSIA.

6. The Moscovite Company, incorporated by Edward VI.

*** Their privileges were confirmed and enlarged by Elizabeth.

MERCHANTS OF THE LEVANT.

7. The Levant, or Turkey Company, incorporated by Elizabeth.

*** Their charter was confirmed by James I.

THE VIRGINIA COMPANY.

8. The Virginia, Bermudas, or Sommers Islands Company

THE AFRICAN COMPANY.

9. The African Company, incorporated in 1588 by Queen Elizabeth, again in 1662 as *The Company of Royal Adventurers of England to Africa*, and a third time in 1672, under the title of *The Royal African Company*. This scheme, owing to opposition, chiefly by the Dutch, was by no means successful, even with parliamentary support and the prestige of having the King himself as its honorary Governor.

A passing mention of its foundation and scope may prove of interest on more than one account, however, as we have at this moment all sorts of similar speculations on foot for the ostensible betterment of our fellow-creatures.

In 1791 English coins were struck for a body designated the Sierra

Leone Company for local currency; and in 1818 an ackey and half ackey were issued, with the head and titles of George III. and the words *Ackey Trade* below the bust, and on the reverse the arms of the African Company, with the legend: Free Trade to Africa by Act of Parliament, 1750.

MERCHANTS OF EAST INDIA.

10. The Merchants of East India.

✱✱✱ Incorporated in 1600. In 1603 they are described as "the Governours and Assistants of the East Indian Marchants in London," in a pamphlet printed in that year. In 1628 they term themselves "the Governour and Company of Merchants of London, trading to the East Indies."

11. New East India Company.

✱✱✱ Amalgamated with No. 10 in 1699 as the United East Indian Company.

MERCHANTS OF SPAIN.

12. The Merchants of Spain, incorporated by Elizabeth.

12*. The Foreign Shipwrights without the Liberties, incorporated in 1612.

NEW FRENCH MERCHANTS ADVENTURERS.

13. The New French Merchants Adventurers.

⁎ Arms were granted to them in 1616.

FRENCH MERCHANTS.

14. The Company of French Merchants.

HUDSON'S BAY COMPANY.

15. The Hudson's Bay Company, incorporated in 1670.

₊ This important enterprise and institution led, among other matters, to the substitution of beaver-skin for felt in the hat and cap trade, and injured the Feltmakers.

THE SOUTH SEA COMPANY.

16. The South Sea Company, 1710–20.

Of nos. 1–3 of these corporations some account may be found in a small pamphlet by the Rev. W. H. Jones, M.A., published about 1825, 8vo, pp. 24 + title, called, "The Merchants of the Staple; or, The Wool Trade in England in the Olden Time."

17. The Royal Lustring Company.

Charles Knight, in his *London*, 1842, in an excellent account of the Weavers of Spitalfields, says :—

"The silk manufacture at Spitalfields, having received an extraordinary impulse from this occurrence [the arrival of the Huguenots], began to acquire considerable importance. The refugees introduced the weaving of the various silk fabrics then known by the names of lustrings, alamodes, brocades, satins, black and coloured mentues, black Padua-soys, ducapes, watered tabbies, and black velvets ; but no sooner had the strangers made a firm footing in England, than, like their predecessors, they cried out for protection, and under the name of the Royal Lustring Company, obtained an Act, prohibiting the importation of foreign lustrings and alamodes. The Lustring Company was, however, defeated, not by Acts of Parliament or foreign competition, but by a change of fashion, which drove lustrings and alamodes out of the market."

It was the practice of eminent commercial and other public men in former days, as now, to belong to two or three of these bodies. Beyond them, however, and independent of their control, was at least one other Association, which is proved by documentary testimony to have existed in London from the beginning of the fourteenth century : the Venetian Vice-Consulate and the Standing Committee of Trade of that Republic, which possessed a settlement of some kind in the metropolis. It was from this source and channel that we derived, at and long after that time, supplies of wine, silk, drapery, sugar, confectionery, alum, glass, and other commodities, and either paid for them in cash or in kind, exchanging the foreign goods for tin, wool, iron, hides, and other staples, which, our foreign friends contended, were not invariably of the best quality or of true weight.

The Venetian Company is noted as having contributed 200*l.* to the expedition of Henry V. for the recovery of Guienne, and it had a second call in 1415, when Henry was preparing for another French campaign, with a threat that, if it proved contumacious, its rulers would be committed to the Fleet.

It may be added, that the " Flanders galleys " of Venice were in the habit of calling, not only at London, but at Dartmouth, Plymouth, Sandwich, Southampton, Rye, and Lynn.

In his *Historical Essay*, 1836, Herbert supplies a very adequate view of the singularly curious development and evolution of the commercial movement, which began at least as early as the tenth century in the neighbourhood of Thames Street, and which resulted, first, in the establishment of a group of traders, chiefly of foreign origin, between the Tower and Queenhithe ; and, secondly, in their gradual disappearance, by amalgamation or decay, as our native industries and industrial societies gained importance, efficiency, and strength.

The Hanseatic League may be treated and received as the forerunner and model of all those Fraternities which followed it in steady succession in other parts of the Continent and in England. It was represented here by the Teutonic Gild, probably the most venerable of all the bodies

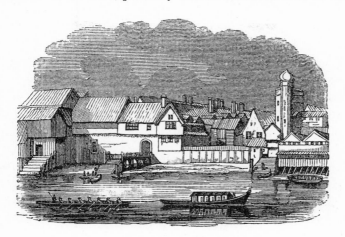

HALL OF THE TEUTONIC GILD.

of that kind, and an establishment which had its seat at Downgate or Dowgate. This Gild seems to have been identical with the "Emperor's men" to whom Ethelred II. in 979 accorded the right of settling in Thames Street on payment of ten pounds of pepper half-yearly to the Crown. This site is supposed, by a distinguished member of the Court of the Grocers' Company, Mr. Kingdon, to have been the spot afterward known as the Steelyard or Stillyard, otherwise and more accurately called *Staple-yard* or *Staple-Hof*, being the wharf where the King's Great Beam was kept for the weighing of avoirdupois merchandise. When Howes published his edition of Stow, in 1633, the *Old Hall*, as it was then called, was still standing ; and we are told that it "is large, builded of Stone, with three arched gates towards the street, the middlemost whereof is farre bigger than the other, and is seldome opened, the other two be mured up : . . ."

It is very likely that the custody of the two Beams, the Great one for avoirdupois, and the Small one for troy, standard, was always entrusted to denizens ; but the Pepperers and Corders are the earliest persons of whom there is any certain record in connexion with this matter. As we have stated, the Woollers or Woolmen subsequently attended to the troy balance, and the Grocers to the avoirdupois. In Scotland, the term *Tron*, if it was identical with Troy, signified the weighing-machine for heavy goods also.

It was through the temporary influence of Richard Earl of Cornwall, brother of Henry III., when he was, in 1257, nominated King of the Romans, that the Teutonic Gild gained a stronger footing in London and throughout the kingdom.   But this colony seems to have finally transferred its headquarters to the neighbourhood of Bishopsgate ; for in 10 Edward I. arose the dispute between the Germans and the Mayor respecting the repair of the wall in the latter quarter, to which they would scarcely have been liable, if located on the riverside.   In the thirty-third year of the same reign the Teutonic Gild is quoted as well established at Bishopsgate.

Stow tells us that the Merchants of Almaine, whom we apprehend that he confounds with the Flemings, imported wheat, rye, and other grain, cable, ropes, masts, pitch, tar, flax, hemp, linen cloth, wainscot, wax, steel, and other profitable commodities.

The Hithes hereabout, Edred's Hithe, Queen-hithe, etc., were all landing places for goods, both from English and foreign ports, and stations where custom was payable.   The receipts from the vessels un-loaded at Queenhithe belonged in the time of Henry III. to his queen, or were usually farmed by some adventurer, who paid his composition at Clerkenwell half-yearly.

In 5 Edward VI. the Crown sequestered the privileges of the foreign Merchants of the Staple and the other alien communities carrying on trade in that vicinity, in consequence of complaints made as to their interference with the rights and interests of denizens.   But of course a strong element of this character survived, as it continues to do.   Custom and prescription have always offered obstacles, a kind of *vis inertiæ*, to the literal execution of a country's laws.

THE GREAT COMPANIES.

THE GREAT COMPANIES.

The Mercers.

THIS Gild, at present acknowledged to be the premier one in ceremonial precedence, is also probably one of the most ancient, and doubtless, like many or most of the others, existed by royal licence some centuries before it acquired a charter and a fixed constitution. The origin of this and other communities of the same class is seldom traceable beyond a point of time when they are accidentally brought to light by some fortuitous or indirect means.

The genesis of the Mercers is almost lost in myth. It is associated with the Hospital of St. Thomas of Acon, founded at the end of the twelfth century by the sister of Thomas à Becket and her husband on the site of the birthplace of St. Thomas. The founders, as well as Gilbert à Becket, St. Thomas's father, are reputed to have belonged to the Fraternity of Mercers ; and the latter is supposed, prior to the Reformation, to have been intimately allied to the religious establishment, simultaneously dedicating itself, on the common principle and law of all these mediæval secular bodies, to the conduct of trade and the performance of almsdeeds.

We have nothing better than presumption and tradition to guide us until we reach the close of the reign of John, when the Mercers gave their first Mayor to the City in the person of Robert Searle, although the two earliest magistrates, Henry and Robert FitzAlwyn are equally claimed by the Gild as members.

The fortunes of the Mercers remained bound up during a very lengthened period with those of the Merchants Adventurers, and down to 1526 the two bodies registered their transactions in the same books. The Adventurers, in fact, conducted the export and import trade in alliance with the London firm or body ; and the goods in which they dealt were multifarious enough about the middle of the fifteenth century, comprising linen cloths, buckrams, fustians, satins, jewels, fine woollen and linen wares, cottons, threads, drugs, wood, oil, wine, salt, copper, and iron. In other words, the Gild at first engrossed the sale by retail of an assortment of items which subsequently became separate industries and employments.

In 1393 the first charter was obtained, probably through the agency of Sir Richard Whittington, from Richard II., at a cost to the recipients of over 87*l.* out of a total income of less than 300*l.* ; and shortly after a licence in mortmain was granted by the same prince, enabling the Mercers to hold land to the value of 20*l.* a year. In this parent charter they are described as the " Men of the Mistery of Mercery of the City of London."

But large as was the outlay, the incorporation of the Mercers undoubtedly repaid them, and bore indeed early fruit, not only in the confidence in their stability which it imparted, but in the distinction which it brought in its train. We shall probably never know to the full extent the obligations under which the then young Company lay to Whittington, through his benefactions to it after his death and during his lifetime, as well as through his good offices with the King. It is evident from existing documents that his standing with Richard II. was exceptionally influential ; and it is equally clear that Dean Colet and others were favourably induced, by the relationship between him and his sovereign, to give a preference to the body to which he belonged as one of the founders, in making their testamentary and other dispositions. For we find that with the fifteenth century the bequests to the Mercers for charitable, religious, or corporate purposes began to flow steadily in ; and, from their prevailing nature as freeholds in the central portion of the City, laid the foundation of that princely estate which now belongs to the Gild either in fee or trust.

Foremost in the long series of the benefactions of Sir Richard Whittington, curiously enough, however, was his purchase in 1408 or 1409 of Leaden Hall,[1] a private residence of the Nevilles and De Bohuns, and his presentation of it, not to the Mercers, but to the City authorities. The second charter of 1424-5, dated from Westminster, February 14, 3 Henry VI., was accorded at the express request of the four executors of Whittington ; and besides being an *inspeximus* of that of 1393, bestowed on the Company the right of a common seal, and of suing and being sued in all courts.

---

[1] A front view of Leaden Hall, as it appeared in 1756, is given in Maitland, second edition, vol. ii., p. 999. The market is said to have been established by Sir Simon Eyre in 1446.

Some years elapsed after the concession of the first charter before the Company proceeded, so far as our present knowledge extends, to the formulation of Ordinances or bye-laws for the internal management of its affairs and the proper control of its officers and members. Such a code was framed in 1407, and again in 1410; and in 1424, consequently on the important Whittington benefactions, Ordinances were made for his almshouses.

The ordinary bye-laws above mentioned, and those which succeeded them at intervals, provided for the trial by the Company's officers of all weights and measures belonging to freemen; and a few years prior

THE DEATH OF WHITTINGTON (from his MSS. *Ordinances*, 1424).

(1403) the Company purchased on its own account two brass measures, an ell and a yard long respectively, and a pile of brass, with a coffer to hold them. But neither in these more ancient bye-laws nor in those of later origin was the power of search, which was the usual accompaniment of them, bestowed; nor do the Mercers seem to have ever possessed any legal title of this description, although they at one time exercised it in some particulars.

Sir Richard Whittington had died in the beginning of 1423-4 at his house in the parish of St. Michael Paternoster in the Royal [Reole], and his will was proved by his four executors in March of the same year.

All his foundations and bequests were confirmed by Act of Parliament in 1432. The Mercers did not enter into possession of the income till 1424, or at least the earliest accounts bear that date. The revenue was at that time 280*l.* 11*s.* 1*d.*,[1] and the expenditure 265*l.* 11*s.* 5½*d.*, while the aggregate corporate revenue of the Company appears to have been very little, if at all, in excess of 300*l.* ; and indeed in 1448 it is returned at only 261*l.* odd. A distinction, however, is to be drawn and understood between the estate of the Mercers as a Gild and the personal property of the members. For a levy of 500 marks on the Mercers, toward the expense of the king-maker Warwick in his expedition to the North in 1461, was explicitly raised from 145 freemen of the Gild ; and in the statute of 1 Edward IV. for the quieting of titles, the City Companies are only indicated in general terms, whereas the Mercers stand alone in being mentioned by name.

Unquestionably the capital incidents in the early annals of the Mercers were their appointment, under the will of Whittington (September 5, 1421), as trustees of the charities which he established, and their selection by Dean Colet to the permanent care and control of the new school of St. Paul's, founded and endowed by him after his father, Sir Henry Colet's, death in 1510. It is almost needless to point out, that in each of these cases the eleemosynary spirit was paramount ; that the value of the foundations at the period, and very long after, was comparatively small ; and that the vast expansion of the rentals or other income has partaken of the influence and benefit of the revolutionary change in the estimation of land and tenements in London. It is not more than equitable to state, that not only was Colet the third person who had instituted an educational seminary in St. Paul's Churchyard, but that the notion had been broached so early as 1456 by the Master and Brethren of St. Thomas of Acon, in Cheapside, who petitioned Parliament for power to found a grammar school " to teach all that will come."

The whole of the Whittington estate amounted, as we have said, in 1425 to 280*l.* a year ; the Colet, when it had been augmented by supplementary grants under his will, represented no more than 112*l.* and a fraction ; and both, the former more especially, included leading sites in prominent City thoroughfares. A portion of the Dean's posthumous benefaction consisted of property at Stepney, which was claimed by his heirs, because the testator was not entitled to amortize copyhold ; but the difficulty was arranged, and this property is at present, next to that in the City itself, the most lucrative part of the

---

[1] The present income appears to be over 12,000*l.* a year.

bequest, the character of the locality having undergone of late years an entire transformation through buiding leases and railway enterprise.

The Whittington estate seems to have lain exclusively in the metropolis, and to have been distributed among the parishes of St. Martin's Outwich; St. Mary-le-Bow; St. Lawrence, Old Jewry; St. Mary Magdalen, Milk Street; All Hallows, Barking; St. Dunstan's in the East; St. Leonard, Eastcheap; and others—all in the vicinity of Cornhill and such now busy and densely built neighbourhoods.

The present writer has elsewhere [1] entered into some particulars of the life of Whittington and of his charitable foundations, partly carried out by his four executors. He was a just and upright man, but toward the close of his career seems to have contracted the character of being a somewhat severe and even arbitrary reformer of abuses. His personal influence and prestige lent his views and aims peculiar weight ; and so long as he lived he was a law to the City. One of the ordinances of his college was, that the almsmen should pray in perpetuity for the souls of Sir Richard Whittington and

CREST OF WHITTINGTON.

---

[1] *Tales and Legends*, 1892, p. 406 *et seqq.* But it may be suggested that the rough portrait inserted above is a comparatively late reproduction of an earlier print or likeness, when the cat myth had acquired currency. The assignment of the prodigy was, perhaps, topographically unfortunate, as there is no ground for supposing that in that part of Africa the domestic cat was unknown or uncommon even in the fifteenth century.

wife, Sir William Whittington and his wife, father and mother of the said Sir Richard, and King Richard II., *promoter of Sir Richard Whittington;* and the solidity of his reputation led to the Mercers, after his death, appⅼⱱaching Henry VI., through his executors, with a prayer for a new charter.

ORIGINAL ARMS.

The youthful and somewhat feminine physiognomy of Richard II., who may be treated as with Whittington the co-founder of the Mercers, possibly favoured the notion, when the Company transferred its allegiance to the blessed Virgin, that a very slight modification of the portrait in the old arms, as they are given in the folio edition of Stow, 1633, would answer for an effigy of the new patron. We should rather have seen the king retained. The Mercers owed more to him than to Our Lady.

The original foundation of Colet, whose father, as well as himself, belonged to the Company, consisted of lands in Buckinghamshire and Hertfordshire; and had he not added by will the residuary devises, and been followed by others, particularly Sir Baptist Hicks, Viscount Campden, who had amassed a fortune as a mercer, the school could not have assumed its actual proportions without substantial assistance.

By the scheme removing the building elsewhere, all the old atmosphere and association have been necessarily sacrificed. As a modern piece of machinery for the public instruction of boys, the great seminary at Hammersmith is, no doubt, incomparably preferable. Its historical ties were completely severed, when it ceased to stand under the shadow of the cathedral of which its founder was Dean.

Before we quit the subject of Colet's St. Paul's, to which we can obviously devote no more than a passing notice, we may call attention to the statutes which the Dean established for this charity, of which all are conceived in that spirit of frigid austerity which distinguished scholastic training down to modern days, and of which some, again, are curious as demonstrating the primitive arrangements for the comfort of the boys.

For the period which witnessed its institution, in 1512, the school, with its high-master, under-master, and chaplain, must have been regarded as a great advance and improvement, preceding by so many years Christ's Hospital and the other Edward the Sixth schools. Nor, when we take into account the experimental or tentative character which belonged to the new St. Paul's (for there had been at least two antecedent places of instruction close at hand), are we at all to blame Colet for the harshness, narrowness, and barbarism, from our point of view, of many of his injunctions.

On the contrary, let us always remember his answer to those who expressed surprise at his not placing the school under clerical super-intendence : " That there was no absolute certainty in human affairs ; but, for his part, he found less corruption in such a body of citizens (as the Mercers) than in any other order or degree of mankind." This manly secularism placed him immeasurably in advance of his time.

In connexion with St. Paul's School, though at a period posterior to the founder's time, it is to be remembered that the boys, like those of Merchant Taylors', occasionally, in the reign of Elizabeth, performed plays before the Court and otherwise. The Merchant Taylors' boys are often called Mulcaster's, or Munkester's children, from the name of the first head-master, Richard Mulcaster, under whom (a man of some literary taste) they were trained.

It is so far curious, that with both their earliest acquisitions out of their own funds they afterward parted. These were the Pye at Bishops-gate, consisting of three messuages and eight shops, valued at 10*l.* a year, and the Crown-field in Westcheap, being a meadow and shops, valued at 7*l.* 13*s.* 4*d.* a year. It had been to enable them to hold the former that they sought and obtained the licence in mortmain.

But the most signal and tantalizing example of unlucky miscarriage occurred to the Mercers in a case, where some land in the suburbs of London was devised to them, and subsequently allowed to pass from their possession.

In 1513, the widow of Thomas Bradbury, Mercer, and late Lord Mayor of London, gave to the Company in trust for certain superstitious and charitable uses land of the then estimated value of £20 a year, being the Conduit Mead and appurtenances. This was the ground on which New Bond Street and the adjoining thoroughfares were eventually built ; and, as Herbert remarks even in 1836, had the Mercers kept the property, " it would have more than quadrupled the value of all their present estates."

By deed of October 18, 1618, the Irish Society erected a portion of the County of Londonderry, the whole of which had been vested in it by letters patent of March 29, 1613, into a Mercers' manor, and con-veyed it to the Company by feoffment two days later, subject to the usual conditions. The Company associated with it as sub-sharers the Innholders, the Cooks, the Broderers, and the Masons. Upon the re-incorporation of the Society in 1662, the Mercers commenced a system of letting their manor for successive terms of years at a rental and fine. The first lease (1663–1713) was at 300*l*. a year and 500*l*. fine ; the second was raised to 420*l*. a year and 6,000*l*. fine ; and the third, which was for sixty-one years and three lives, realized to the Mercers the same rent, with a fine of 16,500*l*. The last life expired in 1831, and the Mercers have since managed the property through an agent.

The present may be the most suitable place for presenting a view of the mode in which the property was apportioned among the fifty-five corporations then existing, and in which the manors were constituted. The Companies marked with an asterisk have parted with their interest.

MERCERS.	SKINNERS.	Pewterers.
Innholders.	Stationers.	Barber Surgeons.
Cooks.	White-Bakers.	Carpenters.
Broderers.	Girdlers.	
Masons.	———	———
———		VINTNERS.
GROCERS.*	MERCHANT-TAYLORS.*	Residue of Grocers'
(No sub-sharers.)	*See Clothworkers.*	Share.
———	———	Woodmongers.
DRAPERS.	HABERDASHERS.*	Weavers.
Tallow-Chandlers.	Wax-Chandlers.	Plumbers.
———	Turners.	Poulterers.
FISHMONGERS.*	Founders.	Tylers and Bricklayers.
Leathersellers.	———	Blacksmiths.
Plaisterers.	SALTERS.	Fruiterers.
Glaziers.	Dyers.	Curriers.
Basket-Makers.	Saddlers.	———
Musicians.	Cutlers.	CLOTHWORKERS.*
———	Joiners.	Overplus from Merchant-
GOLDSMITHS.	Woolmen.	Taylors' share.
Cordwainers.	———	Butchers.
Painter-Stainers.	IRONMONGERS.*	Brown-Bakers.
Armourers.	Brewers.	Upholders.
———	Scriveners.	Bowyers.
	Coopers.	Fletchers.

Herbert furnishes an interesting account of Mercery, with an explanation of the ancient meaning and scope of the term, and he also refers to the early state of the corresponding industry in France. " Mercerie," he says, " comprehended all things sold by retail by the little balance or small scales, in contradistinction to things sold by the beam or in gross." He adds that the mercers who in 1299 attended the French fairs, if they sat on the ground to sell their wares paid a halfpenny toll, but if they occupied a stall they paid double. As early as the commencement of the eighth century, merceries are mentioned as dutiable in France. But we seem to have very little information about them prior to the notices in the Charta Mercatoria of Edward I. (1302). The ancient mercer was a pedlar; but he was so at a period when such a mode of conducting inland business was almost the only one available. His multifarious stock and transactions, with his relatively limited expenditure, favoured the growth of his trade; and circumstances eventually detached from it those branches which became by natural development separate vocations, until at last the mercer reserved to himself only the higher and costlier class of goods in his own department, and allowed the rest to devolve on the draper and the haberdasher.

As the butchers with bad meat, the fishmongers with putrid or fore-stalled fish and unlawful nets, the bakers with bread of light weight or unwholesome quality, and the vintners with wine unfit for use, were a constant source of trouble to the authorities, so the mercers come under our notice at regular intervals as vendors of false blankets and other cognate wares, the haberdashers and hatters of spurious head-gear, and the shoemakers and cordwainers as purveyors of commodities fashioned out of defective or fictitious material. But it is the individual manufac-turer or retailer who is in all cases the delinquent, and who is brought to justice by the Fraternity or Gild.

One of the circumstances which stimulated the demand for silk goods was the presentation to Queen Elizabeth in 1560 by her silk-woman, Mistress Montague, of a pair of silk stockings; and it is said that Eliza-beth thereafter never wore any other material. She had always used cloth.

It may be inferred from the terms of the dedication prefixed to a popular tract of 1607, that Elizabeth appointed a special Mercer to supply her wardrobe. Sir William Stone at one time held this position.

The Mercers profited by the increasing taste for expenditure and show under the later Tudor and the Stuart rule, not merely in the intro-duction of silk as a substitute for cloth in articles of apparel, but in the demand for other commodities on sale by them. Stow's Continuator mentions stockings of Spanish silk as worn both by Henry VIII. and his son; but they were exceptions to the prevailing custom, and, in the former case at least, were a gift from Spain. The same writer remarks that gowns of Bruges satin, cushions and window-pillows of velvet, which at one period were considered suitable only for persons of the highest rank, had come into use in the City at last.

Occasional complaints were addressed by the Crown to the Corporation, accompanied by threats of revocation or forfeiture in reference to the alleged exorbitance of charges made by the mercers for their goods, even when the prices had generally receded ; and in one instance, when the Lords of the Council intervened (1551), the Mayor prayed the Mercers to sell as cheaply as they could, " although to their loss," which may have been no more than the commercial parlance which is so often heard among us still. For among all the manifold forms of business, larger fortunes were probably made by mercery than by any other, as it comprehended such a wide variety of articles in constant demand, and appealed to all classes, till the draper and haberdasher constituted separate departments, and subdivided the trade.

The earliest vestige of a seat of business, rather than a Hall, occurs under 1413–14, when the Company hired or borrowed from the Master of St. Thomas of Acon a small room, which at once served as an office and a chapel. But in 1517, at a date more or less posterior to the evacuation of that locality by the Ironmongers, whose spacious quarter

THE OLD HALL.

had been immediately contiguous, what is termed the New Hall was commenced, and was finished in 1552, although the new chapel had been consecrated so far back as 1523. In 1538 the Company, on the suppression of the college of St. Thomas of Acon, purchased the site and buildings, including the church, cloister, chapter-house, burial-ground, and other houses, with the church, parsonage, and advowson of St. Mary Colechurch, and other properties, for 969*l.* 17*s.* 6*d.*, and a reserved rent of 7*l.* 8*s.* 10*d.*, afterward redeemed. The transaction involved the necessity of borrowing the money, which was partly obtained by loan from Sir Richard Gresham and others, and partly from St. Paul's School Chest. But it was a wise and fruitful investment.

The site of the Hall and the buildings attached is of very peculiar interest, as it not only represents the earliest settlement of the Mercers in London, but, according to tradition, was once occupied in part by the shop of Gilbert Becket, Mercer and Portreeve of London, the father of the future Archbishop. Becket's place of business, before the Hospital of St. Thomas was erected on the ground, is supposed to have stood near the present entrance to the Company's hall in Cheapside. It is deserving of mention that in 1660 the Council of Trade was allowed to hold its meetings at Mercers' Hall, and that in 1694 the Company lent the apartment for the first meeting of the newly established Bank of England, and in 1698 for the reception of the subscribers' names to the United East India Company.

THE MODERN HALL, 1842.   ENTRANCE IN CHEAPSIDE.

The story goes that, many years since, the Mercers felt some anxiety as to the soundness of the woodwork of their Hall and the durability of the general structure, and asked their then surveyor for a report. He pronounced that it might last ten years; but a second opinion was fortunately taken, and this guaranteed the building for a century. The latter professional gentleman superseded the utterer of the rash view by which the hall was nearly sacrificed. A similar incident occurred to the Clothworkers, who were less cautious, and let their old place go.

The Court of Assistants was established in 1463, in consequence of the
expansion of the volume of business demanding constant and anxious
attention, and of a feeling that the responsibility was too onerous for
the Wardens. The Court was appointed to consist of twelve sad and
discreet persons to be assistant to the Wardens ; but its meetings were
at first designated *assemblies*. This new body steadily acquired great
power and ascendency, and obtained the virtual right of electing the
executive of the Gild.

This momentous development of the constitution carried with it the
necessity of providing for the more complex administrative machinery
a fuller and more comprehensive body of ordinances for mutual and
common observance ; and in 1504 a code framed by the Company was
approved by the Primate, the Chancellor, and the two Chief Justices.
This new code extended to fifty-one Articles, and contained at the end
the oaths to be administered to apprentices, freemen, servants going

beyond sea for their masters, and shop-holders. These oaths were practically mercantile contracts.

The Mercers have always remained a comparatively limited Company
in point of numbers, and this feature is ascribable to the ancient regulation, arising out of the disputed admittance in 1403 of the freeman
of another Gild, that in future no stranger should receive the freedom
without the consent of the whole commonalty.

In 1474, the Freemen, householders, and Livery of the Company
amounted to seventy-four ; in 1537, there were fifty-three only ; in
1573, they represent themselves as having shrunk in number, partly by
reason, no doubt, of the incessant exactions of the Crown ; in 1701,
they had more than quadrupled ; in 1722, the number was considerably
reduced ; in 1742 the figures again stood within three of those of 1701 ;
in 1833, the total was 120 ; but in 1880, the figures had considerably

risen, as the returns of that year shew : Freemen, 166 ; Livery, 157 ; Court, 28 ; Master and Wardens, 3 ; total, 354. In 1892 the Livery numbered 185. The exact computation of numbers in the earlier period is rendered difficult by the inability in every instance to ascertain whether the statistics given are inclusive. The returns made to the Royal Commission of 1882 are often conflicting.

The figures given on page 180 are supposed by Herbert to represent liverymen of a City Gild ; but the spirit and *pose*, and even the fall of the dress, appear to be borrowed from the familiar group of Venetian senators or decemvirs in the work of Vecellio, published in 1590. We apprehend the subjoined representations to be truer to English costume.

LIVERYMEN TEMP. HENRY VI. (A.D. 1444.)   LIVERYMAN TEMP. JAMES I.

With the exception of Richard II., its first patron, whose portrait formed part of its arms, till he was displaced by the Virgin, the present Prince of Wales, and a few of the nobility, this Gild is far from being so rich as many in its roll of eminent honorary members, although in its own ranks it has counted a long array of distinguished individuals, who have risen by successful careers in the business, including Sir Richard Whittington ; Sir Godfrey Bullen, a mercer in the Old Jewry and Lord Mayor in 1451, and great-grandfather of Queen Elizabeth ; the Greshams ; Sir Henry Colet ; and Sir Baptist Hicks, afterward Viscount Campden.

The Gresham family is mentioned in the person of William Gresham as belonging to the Gild in 1537 ; this gentleman traded with the Levant, and in some early account books, 1521–39, cited by Mr. Burgon,[1] is described as a factor on the *Mary George*. Sir Thomas Gresham, founder of the Royal Exchange and Gresham College, the confidential and trusted servant of princes, in his way, and Sir Richard Whittington and Dean Colet in theirs, make ample amends by their noble acts and self-sacrificing careers for the general deficiency of the

---

[1] *Life and Times of Sir Thomas Gresham*, 1839, vol. i. p. 8.

Mercers in famous members. We cannot fail to observe how Sir Thomas, in his letters to Queen Mary, proclaims his pride of his calling and his Gild by subscribing himself *Mercer*.

SIR THOMAS GRESHAM, CITIZEN AND MERCER.
From the Painting by Sir Antonio More.

In addition to the lustre shed on the Mercers by the names which we have enumerated, it must be remembered that by far the most illustrious of our early printers, William Caxton, served his apprenticeship to Robert Large, a distinguished and philanthropic member of this Gild, and thus indirectly honoured it ; and Maitland tells us that John Iwyn or Ewin, a London physician, gave the ground on which the monastery of the Greyfriars by Newgate was built, and enrolled himself a lay brother thereof. His fair and honourable repute was long preserved in the designation of the church of St. Nicholas, which was more properly called St. Nicholas Iwyn, and only by popular habit St. Nicholas Flesh-Shambles.

A peculiarly interesting association with the chapel formerly attached

to Mercers' Hall remains to be noticed. It was in the porch that Thomas Guy, founder of Guy's Hospital, was bound apprentice to a bookseller in 1660.

The Mercers were obliged to go to the Crown for new charters at least at each change in the succession ; this was, in fact, among the devices of our sovereigns for raising funds. They surrendered their old grants in the customary fashion in 1558, 1560, 1615, and 1684. In 1652, the Long Parliament commanded the attendance of the governing body with their charter ; but nothing was actually done. Cromwell left the Companies unmolested, where he did not reinstate them, as happened in one or two instances, in their franchises or possessions.

So early as 1658, notwithstanding a long succession of rich bequests and donations, and a commencing advance in the value of existing properties, the Mercers had found their affairs gradually growing more and more embarrassed. From this date forward their practical command of the market, through industrial and legislative changes, particularly the impulse received from the Huguenot settlement at Spitalfields, had declined, if not determined. On the other hand, the endless series of subsidies, contributions, and assessments to which they, in common with all the other great Fraternities, had been subjected during the Tudor and Stuart reigns, both within [1] and without the civic jurisdiction, the commercial depression attendant on the Civil War, and the shrinkage in their internal income from the decline in their numbers, united to shake the Company's stability ; and the Great Fire completed and crowned the catalogue of disasters, and brought matters to a climax. In that holocaust perished the Company's Hall and Church, nearly all the premises belonging to it in the City, the Mercers' and St. Paul's Schools, and the Royal Exchange. Gresham College escaped the flames ; and the governing body temporarily used it as a place of meeting and business. Everything was suddenly paralysed, and the greatest distress prevailed among the officials, servants, and almspeople dependent on the Company's employment or charity. Moreover, the work of restoration was retarded by the want of funds, and even the money obtained was borrowed. This incident, in short, was a blow which it occupied the Mercers nearly a century and a half to retrieve. The details are of no general interest ; but at the commencement of the present century (1804) the Company was out of debt.

The pecuniary difficulties in which the Companies, and conspicuously the Mercers, found themselves still entangled long after the Fire, naturally tended to relax their conditions of entrance, in order to obtain funds ; and the Common Council considered it necessary in 1697 to pass an Act whereby no one was qualified to be a liveryman of one of the great

---

[1] From the early part of the fifteenth century the Gilds were required to furnish their quota toward the storage of grain and coal against the ever-recurring contingency of a dearth.

Companies, unless he had an estate of £1,000, or of the minor bodies, if he was not worth a moiety of that sum.

At the present moment, it stands at the head of all the Gilds, not only by civic precedence, but by virtue of its splendid revenue, which is fast approaching 100,000*l.* a year.

The staff consists of a numerous and liberally paid body of officers and servants, including the Irish Agent and Clerk, of whom the former resides in the manor house at Kilrea, the latter in London. The Irish Agent and the Land Agent are nominated by the Court of Assistants, the Chaplain by the House-warden, and the other officers by the general Court. The Clerk receives emoluments amounting to about 2,100*l.* a year, besides a residence.

MERCERS' COMPANY SALT-CELLAR (17th Century).

LITERARY NOTICES.

Reasons Humbly offered for the Passing a Bill for the hindering the Home Consumption of East-India Silks, Bengals, etc. And an Answer to the Author of several Objections against the said Bill, in a book, entituled An Essay on the East-India Trade. With a Postscript containing the French King's Decree concerning India Manufactures. By T. S., Weaver in London. 8vo, 1697.

An Account of Dr. Assheton's Proposal (as improved and managed by the Worshipful Company of Mercers London) for the Benefit of Widows of Clergymen and others. 12mo, 1699.

Dr. Assheton was Vicar of Beckenham.

A Full Account of the Rise, Progress, and Advantages of Dr. Assheton's Proposal. 12mo, 1710.

The History of Richard Whittington, of his low birth, his great fortune, as yt was plaied by the Prynce's Servants.   Entered at Stationers' Hall, February 8, 1604–5.

A Ballad, called The vertuous Lyfe and memorable Death of Sir Richard Whittington, mercer, sometymes Lord Maiour of the honorable Citie of London. Entered at Stationers' Hall, July 16, 1605.

The Famous and Remarkable History of Sir Richard Whittington. By T. H. 8vo, 1656 ; 4to, 1678 and n. d.   With woodcuts.

London's Glory, and Whittington's Renown : Or, A Looking-Glass for Citizens of London.   A ballad. [About 1650.]

An Old Ballad of Whittington and his Cat. [About 1700.]   A broadside.

Absolutissimus de octo orationis partium constructione libellus. Per Joannem Coletum. 8vo, 1533–4, Mensis Martii.

Joannis Coleti Theologi, olim decani diui Pauli, æditio. 8vo, 1534.

This includes some of Lily's *Rudiments of Grammar.* It was reprinted with the Grammar Rules, etc, for Wolsey's School at Ipswich, 8vo, 1535, 1536.

A right fruitfvll monition, cocerning the ordre of a good christian mans Lyfe. By the famouse Doctour Colete. 8vo, 1563.

A Sermon of Consecrating and Reforming, made [in 1511] by John Colet. 8vo, 1661.

Preces in Usum Antiquæ et Celebris Scholæ juxta D. Pauli apud Londinates. 12mo, 1677.

Sir Thomas Gresham his Ghost. 4to, 1647.

On the title-page is a woodcut of Gresham rising full-dressed from his shroud.   The tract refers to certain alleged abuses in connexion with his benefactions.

CIVIC PAGEANTS.

Charity Triumphant; or, the Virgin Show : Exhibited on the 29th of October, 1655, being the Lord Mayor [Alderman Dethicke's] Day. [By Edm. Gayton.] 4to, 1655.

London's Yearly Jubilee : Performed on Friday, October 29, 1686, for the Entertainment of the Right Honourable Sir John Peake, Knight, Lord Mayor of the City of London.   With a Description of the several Pageants, Speeches, and Songs made proper for the Occasion.   All set forth at the proper Costs and Charges of the Right Worshipful the Company of Mercers.   Composed by M. Taubman. 4to, 1686.

London's Anniversary Festival : Performed on Monday, October 29, 1688, for the Entertainment of the Rt. Hon. Sir John Chapman, Knight, Lord Mayor of the City of London ; being their great Year of Jubilee : with a Panegyric upon the restoring of the Charter ; and a Sonnet provided for the Entertainment of the King. By M. Taubman. 4to, 1688.

The Grocers.

THE Grocers, eventually one of the wealthiest, most important, and most beneficent of the City Gilds, trace their descent and origin from an amalgamation between the Pepperers of Sopers' Lane and the Spicers of Cheap in 1345. The former community is found, as we

OLD ARMS.

have elsewhere noted, in the enjoyment of a high and influential position in the earlier moiety of the preceding century, and probably absorbed the Corders, Canvassers, and other bodies; so that the final union of 1345 amounted to the formation of a great commercial federation, embracing in itself several once separate and thriving industries. But somewhere about 1370 an extension of the business of the Fraternity of St. Anthony, as the united Pepperers and Spicers styled themselves, led to the adoption of the more modern and more com-

prehensive name, which obviously signifies engrosser, or dealer in miscellaneous articles of consumption, as the haberdasher, and indeed the
primitive mercer, were in articles of dress or ornament.

The development of business in retail forms a subject which has
never been hitherto very attentively considered.   In the provinces it
was long conducted beyond doubt, to a large extent, by the pedlar
and traveller ; and even in the streets of London the hawker soon becomes a familiar figure as well as an early ground of complaint.   Fairs
and markets were formerly more frequent and more generally diffused,
and many of the trades chiefly depended on them for their miscellaneous custom.   The Grocers, Haberdashers, Drapers, and others,
until the fashion set in for converting many of the religious and secular buildings into shops or warehouses after the Reformation, must have
been almost exclusively merchants in gross, who reached the community through itinerant middlemen.

In 1373 we first meet with the current designation in the records of
the Company ; and it then consisted of 124 members.   Three years
later a new set of Ordinances was drawn up, directing the two Wardens,
now called Masters, to convene four meetings or common congregations
in the year, appointing six persons to assist them—in other words, a
Court of Assistants—and a common box, to which every member of the
Fraternity should contribute tenpence a quarter for the relief of the
poor brethren.   These regulations further prescribed, that no freeman
or member of another mistery should be admitted without the common
assent, and should then pay 10l. at least—an almost prohibitive scale.

The Grocers—still, be it recollected, only a voluntary unchartered
Association—are included under the operation of the Ordinances made
and published by the City in June, 1386, for the general control of
the trades of London ; and among these occur a grant of the power
of search to the Wardens or Masters of the Grocers over all spicers,
whether freemen or not, and likewise a stipulation that every member
of the mistery shall be entitled to have his weights and measures
assayed by the Wardens on bringing them to their hotel for the time
being.   Eight years afterward, in consequence of a joint complaint
by the Grocers and certain Italian merchants, the Court of Aldermen
sanctioned the appointment by the former of a garbler or inspector
of spices and other " subtle wares."

We have here an outline of the history of the Grocers anterior to
the concession of their parent charter, February 16, 1428–9, 7 Henry
VI., wherein they are specified as " the Freemen of the Mistery of
Grocers of the King's City of London."

By this instrument the new Company was made one perpetual commonalty, and was authorized and empowered to appoint a governing body for the supervision and control of its affairs and businesses for ever, to hold a common seal, to receive and enjoy quietly lands and other possessions within the City of London to the value of twenty marks by the year in free burgage, and to have the right of pleading and being impleaded in all courts : provided always that there was nothing in the premisses tending to the diminution of the honour or authority of the Crown.

In a Patent Roll of 1447 the power of search, conferred by the civic Ordinances of 1386, was revoked so far as the City liberties were concerned, but was enlarged so as to comprise the whole kingdom with that exception, the Court of Aldermen having perhaps preferred to retain this jurisdiction, yet occasionally delegating it to members of the trade as experts. These letters patent amount to a supplementary charter, and are extremely interesting and valuable, as shewing the wide variety acquired at that date in the business of a Grocer. For we perceive that purchasers resorted to their emporia to obtain an almost endless assortment of domestic necessaries. The articles on sale included all kinds of spices, drugs, medicines, oils, ointments, and plaisters, confectionery, syrups, and waters ; and we may particularize (i.) pepper, ginger, cloves, mace, cinnamon, rosin ; (ii.) rhubarb, senna, electuaries, syrups, turpentine, annis, ammonia, wormseed, wax, spikenard, waters, ointments, oils, plaisters, powders ; (iii.) green ginger, succade, cardamums, dates, almonds ; (iv.) canvas and alum. Many of these articles of commerce had been imported from the shores of the Mediterranean, Asia Minor, and from the East by the Pepperers and Spicers time out of mind. The last-named produce, which was brought from Egypt and elsewhere, formed the subject of an attempt in London in 1627 to supersede it by a home manufacture, to which a reference will occur again, and about 1660 alum works were established in Lancashire by James Benson.

The enumeration of the groceries supplied for the Goldsmiths' Feast in 1498 embraces cinnamon, sugar, comfits, ginger, carraways, loaf-sugar (6 lbs. at 2½d. per lb.), pepper, English saffron, dates, almonds (16 lbs)., *milk*, raisins, prunes, cloves, mace, aniseed, rice, great raisins, broken sugar, and thirty-eight messes of wafers at 3s. 4d. In statements of a somewhat later date oranges occur ; they had been introduced in the reign of Edward I. through his consort Eleanor of Castile, but they are not frequently mentioned in early entries. Loaf-sugar had become much commoner, since in the reign of Henry III. the King desired the Sheriffs of London to send him four loaves to Woodstock, if they could procure so many. Later charters include tobacco, while they omit drugs and

medicines on account of the separate enfranchisement of the Apothecaries in 1617.

The right of search practically determined at the end of the seventeenth century, when the Company seems to have largely discontinued
its direct association with commerce, which was distributing itself into
new channels and becoming a machinery composed of wholesale and
retail dealers.

In the reign of Charles I., when Stow's Continuator wrote (1633), the
Grocers and Apothecaries made Bucklersbury their centre, as the
Drapers did Watling Street, the Goldsmiths Cornhill, and so on.

The charter of 1607 did not foresee the imminent severance of the
Apothecaries from the Grocers, and in it the Company is explicitly re-
incorporated as " the Freemen of the Misteries of Grocers and Apothecaries of the City of London " ; whence it is perhaps inferable that the
latter vocation had grown of sufficient importance to be specially named
in conjunction with the other.   The Apothecaries were in fact ripe for
secession ten years before that event occurred.

An incident of capital interest in the history and affairs of the present
Company was its participation in the Irish scheme of 1613.   The
Grocers did not join, however, till 1617, when they paid 5,000l. for a
share, less a portion which was taken over by the Vintners.   Between that date and 1622 they expended a further sum of 2,000l. on
improvements, and the five years' receipts shewed a loss of 6,150l.
During a long series of years, which embraced the Civil War, nothing
was obtained in the shape of rents, and in 1658 an agent, sent over to
make inquiries, remitted 100l.

In 1675 matters had so far improved that the Grocers' manor in
Ireland could be let on a thirty-one years' lease at a rent of 10l. and
a fine of 3,660l. ; but in 1689 political disturbances again threw the
country back, and although great expense was incurred from time to
time in repairs and works, in 1810 the Company took the management
into its own hands from dissatisfaction with the system of leases for
lives.   In 1872, at a fortunate juncture, the resolution was definitively
formed to part with the whole property ; the tithe-charge was redeemed
for 7,358l. and the estate was submitted to auction in eleven lots, producing 157,256l.   The total net rental at the time appears to have
been about 2,500l. only, but ten lots out of the whole fell into the hands
of outside investors.   It should be borne in mind that the former owners
had laid out very large sums in the endeavour to improve the lands ;
and indeed, not merely was the income in 1872 nearly treble the returns
of 1831, but the deductions in future years for expenses were found to
decrease.

The Great Fire, succeeding the long series of political troubles in England and Ireland, prostrated the Grocers' Company, which lost, like the Mercers, nearly everything which it possessed in the City, its muniments being saved by their storage in a tower which escaped the flames. The disaster was not fully retrieved within a century, and the Gild was brought to the verge of ruin. Its plate was melted in the fire ; but the metal was recovered, and was sold toward the relief of the prevailing distress. It is said to have weighed 200 lbs. It had been gradually accumulating since 1346, when Geoffrey de Halliwell, pepperer of Sopers' Lane, presented to the Fraternity a silver chalice and cover, weighing twelve ounces goldsmith's weight, and other things of value.

Nothing short of the most generous conduct on the part of individual members of the Company could have averted a catastrophe in 1666 and the following years. Funds were necessarily provided by the Court and Livery out of their own pockets for a lengthened interval, as the corporate estate was in abeyance.

The Grocers had received from time to time, in the usual way, renewals or re-grants of their charter from Charles I. and II., James II., William and Mary, and George I. Here again, in the case of the negotiation with the advisers of Charles II. in 1675, the Company suffered great anxiety, as it had been served with a writ of *quo warranto*, and it was feared that there was a scheme on foot to seize into the King's hands the estates of all the City Gilds. The Grocers deemed it wise to surrender their grant, and to pray for a new one, which was conceded with certain limitations. But James II., desirous of conciliating the City, restored the former privileges ; and in 1690 matters were placed on a still more secure footing by the charter of William and Mary, the King honouring the Company, as indeed Charles II. had done before, by serving the office of Master in 1689, and by directing an annual present of three fat bucks to be sent from Enfield Chase in perpetuity to Grocers' Hall. The royal bounty did not survive the reign.

The embarrassments continued, however, down to 1721, the Company experiencing continual difficulty in meeting the most ordinary engagements, and the greater part of its charities being suspended. In order to raise money, facilities were afforded to persons desirous of joining ; the ranks of the Court were enlarged from fifty-seven to eighty ; and the Hall was let, first to the Lord Mayor, and then to the Bank of England, on a repairing lease. In 1700 there was an unsuccessful attempt to pay the Company's creditors 6s. 8d. in the pound.

From 1721 an improvement in the affairs seems to have set in, and in 1730 there was a cash balance of 3,000l. available for investment. It was put into East India Stock. This period proved a permanent turn-

ing-point in the Company's career, and the termination of the long
series of misfortunes, which it shared with all bodies similarly situated,
until the Revolution of 1688 effected a revival of tranquillity and confidence.   In 1759 affairs wore a still brighter aspect, and since that date
there has been no retrogression.

The Grocers appear to be legally independent of their bye-laws ;
but those of 1711, founded on the preceding code of 1690, form the
basis of their present internal government.   The provisions are of the
usual character ; and although there is a reference to the right of search,
the Company had now practically abdicated its position as a trading
corporation, and was becoming what we see it to-day, and what it had
indeed been on a humbler and narrower scale in its origin, a philanthropic
Gild of the first rank.

The later history of the Grocers constitutes a narrative, of which they
may justly be proud, since in nearly all the charitable or benevolent
foundations entrusted to their management their corporate estate has
been largely expended from year to year, in an ever-increasing ratio, in
enlarging the original bequests or in adapting them to modern demands
and views.   Nor has their bounty limited itself to a conscientious maintenance and spontaneous extension of ancient trusts.   For large sums
have been devoted to the endowment of scholarships and exhibitions, to
purposes of education outside their own schools, and to the support of
hospitals.   This sort of stewardship has characterized during many
passed years not only the policy of the great Companies, but that of
several of the so-called minor ones, on which the levies for such objects
are naturally apt to bear a more than proportionate relationship to their
total incomes.

The number of members has fluctuated at different periods.   In the
first place, when the Pepperers and the Spicers were originally amalgamated in 1428–9, only twenty-two persons seem to have been concerned in the step.   In the time of Charles I. (1640) the Court alone
consisted of fifty-seven, and in 1688 it was increased under urgent
financial pressure to eighty.   In 1795, the entire Company numbered
between two and three hundred, and of these only forty were grocers ;
the influx of new members in 1688 had modified the complexion of the
body, and the influence and tendency proved permanent and growing.
The present figures are about 630.   In 1880 there were 397 freemen,
214 assistants and liverymen, and 21 honorary associates.

The Company remained nearly a century after its informal establishment in 1345 without a Hall.   The governing body first assembled, as
we have shown, at the Abbot of Bury's house or hotel in St. Mary Axe.
They subsequently seem to have used as a place of business and meet-

ing the house of one Fulgham, called the Ringed Hall in St. Thomas, Apostle; and as a matter of evidence and authority the accepted address was "the hotel of the Wardens for the time being." But in 1427, as if the Fraternity then felt itself strong and rich enough to apply for the charter actually obtained shortly after, the Wardens purchased for 320 marks the chapel with other portions of the demesne of Lord Fitz-walter, in what was then known as Conyhope Lane, and proceeded thereon to erect a building, which became the permanent seat of the

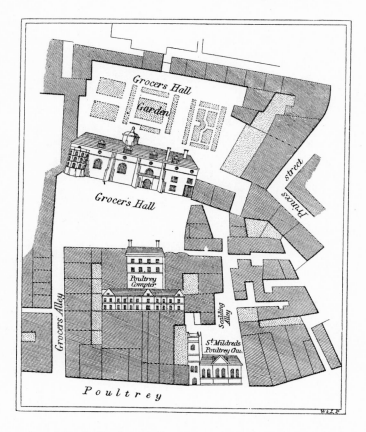

then unenfranchised Society. It is supposed that No. 8, Old Jewry marks the site of the entrance to the Old Hall.

The structure, with the rest of the City estate, perished, with the sole exception of a tower containing the archives, in 1666; and the Grocers have consequently no ancient plate or other relics of the remote past. Their staff, in early days limited to a Beadle, now corresponds to the magnitude of their business and the splendour of their position.

The Histories of the Company furnish lists of distinguished freemen and honorary members. Among the former we have to mention

Andrew Bokerell, Pepperer, who held the mayoralty uninterruptedly from 1231 to 1237 ; Sir John de Gisors,[1] Pepperer, and Mayor in 1244-5, 1245-6, and 1258-9 ; Sir Alan de la Zouche, a member of an ancient and illustrious stock ; Andrew Aubery, Mayor in 1339-40 and 1351 ; Sir Thomas Knollis ; Sir Robert and Sir Thomas Chicheley ; Sir John Crosby ; Thomas Lord Coventry ; Charles II. ; Sir Heneage Finch, first Earl of Nottingham ; William III. ; and others.

The honorary Grocers comprise Sir John de Londres, parson of St. Anthony, admitted (evidently *honoris causâ*)[2] in 1349 ; Sir Philip Sydney, whose obsequies at St. Paul's, February 16, 1586-7, the Company attended ; George Monk, Duke of Albemarle ; William Pitt, George Canning, Sir Robert Peel, Lord Napier of Magdala, Sir James Paget, Mr. Anthony Trollope, and Sir Frederick Roberts.

GROCERS' COMPANY.   WARDENS' GARLANDS.

LITERARY NOTICES.

The Case of the Company of Grocers Stated. And their Condition in their present Circumstances Truly Represented, Together with a short Account of their Original ; How Eminent they have been in the City, and also of some of their Ancient Privileges and Usages. Designed for Information and Satisfaction of the Members, and Vindication of the Company. By William Ravenhill. Folio, 1682.

A Short Account of the Company of Grocers, from their Original. Together with their Case and Condition . . . As also how their Revenue is settled. By William Ravenhill, Clerk of the Grocers' Company. 4to, 1689.

A Short Discourse of the three kindes of Pepper in common use, and certaine special medicines made of the same. By Walter Bailey, M.D. 8vo, 1588.

A briefe and short discourse of the Vertue and Operation of Balsame. By the same. 8vo, 1585.

---

[1] This very eminent man resided at a mansion in Basing Lane, subsequently known as Gerard's Hall, and for a very long period prior to its demolition in 1852 converted into an hotel. Several members of the family of Basing appear in the early records.

[2] Unless he acted as Chaplain, in which case he may have been on the Livery. The Chaplain to the Drapers' Company is still a liveryman.

A Discovrse of the medicine called Mithridatium. By the same. 8vo, 1585.
This was a confection of opium, otherwise called Theriacum.

The Metamorphosis of Tobacco. 4to, 1602.
Works for Chimney Sweepers: Or, A Warning for Tobacconists. 4to, 1602.
A Defence of Tobacco. By Roger Marbeck. 4to, 1602.
Perfvming of Tobacco, and the great Abvse committed in it. With many other ancient and modern Perfumings. . . . Taken out of the new Historie or Illvstration of Plants, written by Matth : de L' Obel. Translated by I. N. 4to, 1611.
De L'Obel was keeper of Lord Zouch's Physic-Garden at Hackney.

A Proclamation touching Tobacco. 1625. A broadside.
The same. . . . 1626. „
A Proclamation for the well ordering of Tobacco. 1627. A broadside.
The Armes of the Tobacconists. 1630. A broadside with a woodcut.
Tobacconist originally signified not a vendor, but a smoker, of the weed.
An Ordinance concerning the Excise of Tobacco. December 23, 1643. 4to, 1643.
⁎⁎⁎ Two editions.

An Ordinance of the Lords and Commons for the Regulating of the Rates on the Customes and Excise of Tobacco. 4to, 1644.
A Proclamation, prohibiting the Planting, Setting, and Sowing of Tobacco in England and Ireland, according to an Act of Parliament therein specified. 1661. A broadside.
The Venimous Qualities of Tobacco. 4to, 2 leaves.
The Women's Complaint against Tobacco. 4to, 1676.
The Touchstone or Triall of Tobacco, whether it be good for all Constitutions. 4to, 1676.
A Proclamation restraining the abusive Venting of Tobacco.
A true Report concerning the worthy accompt of Tobacco, approved in experience ꞌby the Party and Reporter himself. By R[ichard] B[rowne], Clerk of the Green Cloth.—*MS. Ashmole.*

A Proclamation for prohibiting the Importation of Allvme, and the buying and spending thereof, in any His Maiesties Dominions. 1625. A broadside.
A Relation of James Benson's Undertaking the Allum at the Allum Work, in Lancashire (1660).
See Bright's Catalogue of books sold at Sotheby's, 1845, No. 3346.

A Curious Treatise of the Nature and Quality of Chocolate. By Anthonio Colmenero, Doctor in Physic and Chirurgery. Translated by James Wadsworth. 4to, 1640.
The Nature of the drink Kauhi, or Coffe, and the Berey of which it is made. 12mo, Oxford, 1659.
A Cup of Coffee. 4to, 1663.
The Vertues of Coffee. Set forth in the Works of the Lord Bacon . . . 4to, 1663.
A Satyr against Coffee. A folio leaf. [About 1680.]
The Natural History of Coffee, Thee, Chocolate, Tobacco. 4to, 1682.
An Essay upon the Nature and Qualities of Tea. By John Ovington, M.A. 12mo, 1699.
Wholesome Advice against the Abuse of Hot Liquors. Particularly of Coffee, Chocolate, Tea, Brandy, and Strong Waters. By Dr. Duncan, of the Faculty of Montpelier. 8vo, 1706.

A Description and History of the Coffee Tree. By Sir James Douglas. Folio, 1727.

An Answer to the Sugar-Bakers or Sugar-Refiners Paper. Folio, 1695.

A profitable and necessarie Discourse, for the meeting with the bad Garbling of Spices, vsed in these daies. And against the combination of the workemen of that office, contrarie vnto common good. Composed by diuers Grocers of London, where in are handled such principall matters as followeth in the Table before the booke. 4to [1591].

CIVIC PAGEANTS, ETC.

The Triumphs of Honor and Industry: A Solemnity performed through the City, at the Confirmation and establishment of the Right Honorable, George Bowles. In the Office of his Majesties Lieutenant, the Lord Mayor of the famous City of London. Taking beginning at his Lordships going, and proceeding after his Return from receiving the Oath of Mayoralty at Westminster, on the morrow next after Simon and Judes day, October 29, 1617. By Thomas Middleton. 4to, 1617.

The Triumphs of Honor and Virtue: A Noble Solemnity performed through the City, at the sole Cost and Charges of the Honourable Fraternity of Grocers, at the Confirmation and Establishment of their most worthy Brother, the Right Honorable Peter Proby, in the high office of his Majesty's Lieutenant, Lord Mayor and Chancellor of the famous City of London. Taking beginning at his Lordship's going, and perfecting itself after His return from receiving the Oath of Mayoralty at Westminster, on the morrow after Simon and Jude's Day, being the 29 of October, 1622. By Thomas Middleton. 4to, 1622.

London's Triumph, Celebrated October 29, 1659, in honour of the much honoured Thomas Allen, Lord Mayor of the said City, presented and personated by an European, an Egyptian, and a Persian, and done at the Costs and Charges of the ever to be honoured Company of Grocers. By J. Tatham. 4to, 1659.

London's Triumphs Presented in several delightful Scœnes, both on the Water and Land, and celebrated in Honour to the deservedly honored Sir John Frederick, Knight and Baronet, Lord Mayor of the City of London. At the Costs and Charges of the Worshipfull Company of Grocers. By John Tatham. 4to, 1661.

London Triumphant; or, the City in Jollity and Splendour: Expressed in various Pageants, Shapes, Scenes, Speeches, and Songs: invented and performed for Congratulation and Delight of the well-deserving Sir Robert Hanson, Knight, Lord Mayor of the City of London. At the Cost and Charges of the Worshipful Company of Grocers: His Majesty gracing the Triumphs with his Royal Presence. Written by Thomas Jordan. 4to, 1672.

Some copies do not mention the King's presence. His Majesty dined after the proceedings at Guildhall.

London in its Splendour: Consisting of triumphant Pageants, whereon are represented many Persons richly arrayed, properly habited, and significant to the Design. With several Speeches, and a Song, suitable to the Solemnity. All prepared for the Honour of the prudent Magistrate, Sir William Hooker, Knight, Lord Mayor of the City of London: at the peculiar Expenses of the Worshipful Company of Grocers. As also a description of his Majesties Royal Entertainment at Guildhall, by the City, in a plentiful Feast, and a glorious Banquet. Written by Thomas Jordan. 4to, 1673.

The Triumphs of London, Performed on Tuesday, October 29, 1678. For the Entertainment of the Right Honourable, and truly Noble Pattern of Prudence and Loyalty, Sir James Edwards, Knight, Lord Mayor of the City of London. Containing a true description of the several Pageants, with the Speeches spoken on each Pageant. Together with the Songs sung in this Solemnity. All set forth at the Costs and Charges of the Worshipful Company of Grocers. Designed and Composed by Tho. Jordan, Gent. 4to, 1678.

London's Joy ; Or, The Lord Mayor's Show : Triumphantly Exhibited in Various Representations, Scenes, and Splendid Ornaments, with divers pertinent Figures and Movements. Performed on Saturday, October 29, 1681. At the Inauguration of the Right Honourable Sir John Moore, Knight, Lord Mayor of the City of London. With several Speeches and Songs which were spoken on the Pageants in Cheapside, and sung in Guildhall during Dinner. All the Charges and Expenses of the industrious designs being the sole Undertaking of the Worshipful Company of Grocers. Devised and composed by Tho. Jordan, Gent. 4to, 1681.

The Triumphs of London : Performed on Monday, October 29, 1683. For the Entertainment of the Right Honorable and truly noble Pattern of Prudence and Loyalty, Sir Henry Tulse, Knight, Lord Mayor of the City of London. Containing a Description of the whole Solemnity, with two new Songs set to Music. [By Thomas Jordan.] 4to, 1683.

The Triumphs of London : Performed on Saturday, October 29, 1692. For the Entertainment of the Right Honourable Sir John Fleet, Kt., Lord Mayor of the City of London. Containing a true Description of the several Pageants, with the Speeches spoken on each Pageant. All set forth at the proper Costs and Charges of the Worshipful Company of Grocers. Together, with an Exact Relation of the most Splendid Entertainments, prepared for the Reception of Their Sacred Majesties. By Elkanah Settle. 4to, 1692.

The Triumphs of London : Performed on Tuesday, October 29, 1695. For the Entertainment of the Right Honourable Sir John Houblon, Kt., Lord Mayor of the City of London. Containing A true Description of the several Pageants, with the Speeches spoken on each Pageant. All prepared at the proper Costs and Charges of the Worshipful Company of Grocers. To which is added, A New Song upon His Majesty's Return. By Elkanah Settle. Published by Authority. 4to, 1695.

Hosanna ; or, A Song of Thanksgiving sung by the Children of Zion ; and set forth in three notable Speeches at Grocers' Hall, on the last solemn day of Thursday, June 7, 1649. The first was spoken by Alderman Atkins, the second by Alderman Isaac Pennington, the third by Hugh Peters (no Alderman, but) *Clericus in Cuerpo.* 4to, 1649.

The Drapers.

THE Drapers, like many or most of the other Gilds, had a lengthened existence antecedent to their formal confirmation. In or about 1215, Henry FitzAlwyn, Draper and premier Mayor of London (1189–1215), bequeathed to them his estate at St. Mary Bothaw, a small parish north of Queenhithe, which modern changes have almost effaced. In 1252 and 1253 the Mayor was successively chosen from this Society. It is perhaps to be regarded as flattering to FitzAlwyn that, he being nominated by the Crown, and the latter in 1208 conferring on the City the future right of election, he retained the dignity till some years later. The Drapers formed one of the branches of the clothing trade, of which the Weavers, Tailors, Shearmen, Fullers, and Dyers were other component parts; and all these sub-divisions of industry frequently occur as engaged in differences respecting the details and dividing lines of their respective businesses.

The Drapers judiciously propitiated the Crown in 1363 by contributing the liberal quota of fifty marks toward the King's French wars, and in the very following year approached his grace with a prayer for a charter, which infallibly cost them a further considerable amount. By this, so far as we can make out, they specially and by right chiefly, if not exclusively, confined themselves to the retail department; and the instrument just quoted was indeed professedly executed for the purpose of enabling them to exercise a stricter and more authoritative control over the retail trade, and to see the provisions of the Statute of the Staple more punctually and efficiently carried out.

The preamble recites that it had been shown to the King and Council that great numbers of persons belonging to divers misteries, who had not properly learned the trade of drapery, *according to the good, ancient custom of London*, meddled therewith; and not only was the quality of cloth offered for sale consequently uncertain, but it was in the hands of interlopers and forestallers who enhanced the price.

The italicized words in the foregoing paragraph may be deemed sufficient to establish that the peculiar province of the Drapers was one of great antiquity and recognised standing in 1364. The charter of Edward prescribed that hereafter no one should follow or exercise the calling until he had served his apprenticeship to it, and that the sale of cloth should be limited to persons of this mistery, save where it was purveyed to lords and other in gross and not for retail. In order to enforce this and other regulations, four Wardens were to be elected, subject to the approval of the Lord Mayor, and nothing in the charter or in any Ordinances was to be in prejudice of those who had the right

OLD ARMS.

of holding fairs in the suburbs of London, or of the merchant-vintners of England and Gascony.

Not merely the sale, but the making, of drapery is mentioned in this charter of 1364. Whence it may be deduced that the early drapers were also tailors and dressmakers or milliners, the so-called merchant-taylors being at the outset rather linen-armourers, and paying attention to a class of employment which was perhaps more lucrative, as well as more technical.

The reservation of the existing privileges of the Vintners had reference to the charter obtained by that Gild just before, wherein, for the sake of preventing the excessive efflux of money for the purchase of wines, they were left at liberty to exchange their commodities for cloth, and buy the same freely.

It may be more correct to describe the grant of 1364 as a patent, for it really went little, if at all, beyond a ratification of certain remedies for current abuses and grievances. The first actual charter was that of November 30, 17 Henry VI., which conferred on the Drapers the right of forming themselves into a Company, under the name of the " Master, Wardens, Brethren, and Sisteren of the Gild or Fraternity of the blessed Mary the Virgin of the Mistery of the Drapers of the City of London."

This instrument recites the several statutes of Edward III. and his successors relating to the subsidy on cloth, the sealing of cloth by the Alnager, the fixture of the dimensions of cloth, the farm of the alnage and subsidy, and of a moiety of forfeitures of unsealed cloth, and re-enforces their provisions, appointing certain persons to carry out the law, with the power of search over all houses and shops in the City and its suburbs.

The charter of 6 Edward IV., besides being an *inspeximus* of the earlier one, granted a licence in mortmain to the extent of 20*l.* a year for the professed purpose of enabling the Gild to support two chaplains, to pray for the souls of the King and Queen and divers other noble personages, and for the well-being of the Gild. The next instrument, of the nineteenth of the same reign (1479), is so far curious, that it so closely follows, and that it guarantees the Drapers against any concession of a charter to the Shearmen, as solicited by the latter. It also withdraws from the Shearmen for the future any right of search, correction, and authority over other trades, especially the Drapers and Taylors, except in so far as such right might be conceded by the Lord Mayor and Aldermen. The seizure of cloth illegally shorn by the two other crafts is particularly forbidden, but the Shearmen might enforce or recover the penalty attached.

The frequency of a renewal of grants is of course explained by the course of political events. The accession of Richard III. almost necessitated an approach to him with a view to confirmation and indemnity, and the charter of May 21, 1484, is found accordingly to be of a peculiar and special character. It releases the Gild from all transgressions, forfeitures, etc., prior to February 21 preceding, condones all acts done without licence to the same date, as well as all fines, aids, etc. before Michaelmas, 22 Edward IV. But this grace did not comprise accounts with the Staple of Calais, the Staple of the Treasury of Calais, the Chamberlains of Chester, Northwell, and Southwell, the Keepers of the Royal Wardrobe, the Clerks or Keepers of the Hanaper of the Chancery, their executors or administrators, the Clerks of the Royal Works, the Treasurer of Ireland, or the Receivers of the Duchies of Lancaster and Cornwall.

The *inspeximus* of Philip and Mary (1558) recites only those of 17 Henry VI. and 6 Edward IV.; and that of 1560 follows the same course, adding the previous *inspeximus*.

The language and tenor of the charter of 1607, which is next in the rather long series, shews that the Drapers had meanwhile experienced a very considerable development in regard to their possessions and prosperity. It may conveniently, for our present purpose, be bracketed with that of 1619 of the same King, which now particularly bears on the Hall of the Company and other property held by it in London and the Borough.

Under the instrument of 1607 the government of the Gild was appointed to consist of a Master, four Wardens, and twenty-four Assistants, the Master and Wardens to be annually re-elected, but the Assistants to be for life, unless for some special reason removed. This principle imparted to the constitution an unusually oligarchical cha- racter, which was still further confirmed by the regulation that the Master and Wardens should be chosen by a selected body of twelve of the Assistants, all of whom must have been past Masters or Wardens. Each past Master or Warden was *ex officio* an Assistant for life. The charter of 1607 also bestowed the right to have a perpetual succession, to use a common seal, with power to change and alter the same, to hold lands, tenements, etc., to the value of 200*l.* a year, and to exercise as heretofore the power of search.

When we come to the charter of a few years' later date, we find that it is exclusively devoted to a rehearsal of the several properties then held and enjoyed by the Gild with *or without* licence in various parts of London and Southwark, and we are confronted with a marvellous picture of the aggrandisement during the period intervening between 1364 and this transaction. The estates of the Drapers, for which they now obtained the royal acknowledgment, with peaceful occupation for ever, and a full indemnity for all passed acts done, on payment of a fine of 206*l.*, reserving only such rights as were already held of the Crown by others ; and the whole of this splendid property was vested in them in free burgage, and not by knight's service or any other feudal tenure.

It may be of interest to enumerate the particulars of this confirma- tion. The lands, tenements, and hereditaments consisted of (1) the capital messuage with appurtenances called Drapers' Hall, with the gardens, buildings, curtilages, messuages, and tenements thereto belonging, in the parish of St. Peter-le-Poer, in the ward of Bread Street, with ten messuages adjoining the Hall and a garden ; (2) ten messuages lying together in St. Margaret, Lothbury, and two others ; (3) eight messuages lying together in St. Stephen, Coleman Street ; (4) four messuages, nine stables, and a garden, near London Wall ; (5) a capital messuage and three others, in St. Mary, Bassishaw ; (6) ten messuages or tenements, formerly eight, in Beech Lane, St. Giles Without Cripplegate, and eight tenements, messuages, or almshouses adjoining ; (7) ten messuages or tenements, with appurtenances, formerly one messuage known as the Bull, in West Smithfield, and five other messuages, formerly one, in the same parish ; (8) two messuages in St. Nicholas Shambles, Christ Church ; (9) two messuages in the parish of St. Michael-le-Querne ; (10) two contiguous messuages, a third called the Goat, and another, all in the parish of All Saints, Honey Lane ; (11) two messuages in Bow Lane, otherwise Cordwainer Street ; (12) a corner house in Watling Street and Soper Lane [Queen Street] ; (13) three messuages, formerly two, in Walbrook ; (14) sixteen messuages, a capital messuage, called the Herber, and an inn called the Chequer, in St. Mary, Bothaw ;[1] (15) four messuages at or near Dowgate ; (16) three messuages formerly two, a corner messuage in Candlewick [Cannon] Street and Abchurch Lane, and a capital messuage[2] with eight other messuages adjoining, in St. Swithin's Lane ; (17) two messuages or tenements in Sherbourne Lane ; (18) four messuages adjoining to Bearbinder Lane ; (19) thirteen messuages in Cornhill and the immediate neighbourhood, including the advowson and patronage of St. Michael, Cornhill ; (20) three messuages, including a corner one, in Birchin Lane ; (21) four messuages in the parish of St. Nicholas Acon, or St. Mary Abchurch ; (22) five messuages lying together in Lawrence Pountney Lane and Thames Street ; (23) a messuage on New Fish Street Hill ; (24) six-and-twenty messuages and a wharf in the parish of St. Olave, Southwark ; (25) two messuages in Botolph Lane, Billingsgate ; (26) a messuage in Petty Wales, in the parish of All Hallows, Barking ; (27) four tenements lying together in Mark Lane ; (28) two messuages near the end of Tower Street ; twelve messuages and a shed near Tower Street, in the parish of St. Margaret Pattens ; (29) seventeen messuages near Little East Cheap and Philpot Lane ; (30) a messuage in Grace-

---

[1] Probably their most ancient possession, having been left to them by their associate, Henry FitzAlwyn, first Mayor of London, about 1215.

[2] The former Hall of the Company, before they removed to Throgmorton Street in 1543. The site still belongs to the Drapers ; it is opposite Salters' Hall, and the houses, including the Surveyor's office, bear the Company's arms.

church Street ; (31) an annuity or yearly rent of 52*l.* 10*s.* from messuages, etc., in the parish of St. Leonard, Shoreditch.

From this instructive schedule, forming part of the charter of 1619,
and virtually its only subject-matter, we derive some conception of the
steady accumulation of investments, which had been made in the course
of about a century ; and if we turn to the balance-sheets published
in 1884 we perceive the enormous increase in the value of the land and
tenements acquired.   Many buildings specified in 1619 have been long
removed under various improvement Acts or schemes.[1]   A new one was
contemplated or proposed in 1684, but was not carried out.[2]

The oldest Ordinances for the government of the Brotherhood are
referred to 1322 ; but no text of them seems to be extant.   Others were
made in 1405 and 1418.   Some of the articles in the former are new ;
those laying down that a freeman and his wife shall pay a composite
quarterwage of 7*d.*, that the allowance to the Warden for rushes, minstrels, players, and other petty items shall not exceed 20*s.*, and that when
the Mayor attends the dinner, being a member, 40*s.* shall be chargeable
for his mess.   There is also the rule for observance in sitting at table,
which has not occurred before.   All such as had been Masters and
Wardens were appointed to sit apart at the high table next the
cupboard, unless it were otherwise directed by the Master and Wardens
for the time being ; but at a table next the parlour door guests of
the Master and Wardens might sit.   No brother of the Fraternity,
liveryman or freeman, was entitled to seat himself at the general board,
till those at the high table had washed and taken their places.

The following code of 1418 commences with directions as to internal
affairs and religious or charitable observances, and concludes with a
series of articles of a more practical complexion relevant to the conduct
of trade and the protection of financial interests.   The latter portion
includes rules for attendance at Westminster, Bartholomew, and Southwark Fairs ; but first of all the most noteworthy points are the obligation
on the part of the Wardens to render yearly accounts, which is still
continued, and the settlement of the order of precedence at banquets.

More elaborate bye-laws were drawn up in 1663.

The earliest accounts of the Company are of the year 1415, when the
income was below 38*l.*, and the expenditure below 24*l. per annum.*
The members then numbered ninety-six, of whom thirteen were in arrears

---

[1] Philip and Mary and Elizabeth conferred *inspeximus* charters.   We do not meet
with any notice of renewals or re-grants by Charles I., James II., or William and
Mary.

[2] How the Drapers escaped from the almost inevitable incidence of each fresh
monarch and dynasty, it is useless to conjecture.

with their quarterwages. Some of the items of outlay are curious and even historically interesting, comprising payments for attendance at fairs, to minstrels with the charges for their hoods and entertainment, for horse-hire for some of the Company to ride in the civic procession to meet the King and Queen Dowager on their entry into London after the Battle of Agincourt, and disbursements for table-cloths and garlands, and for the Lord Mayor's mess, his lordship (Sir Nicholas Wotton) this year being a Draper.

In 1397 Blackwell, or rather Bakewell Hall,—possibly so named from the *Bakehouse* in the vicinity,—had been established in Basinghall Street, as a central and general emporium for the sale of woollen cloths of all kinds, the sole condition of admittance being the payment of certain reasonable tolls and dues. There was a vigorous attempt to convert it into a monopoly in favour of the free drapers of London ; but the municipality interfered, and opened its doors to all comers. It was under the first mayoralty of Sir Richard Whittington (1397–8) that the Ordinances of Bakewell Hall were first drawn up by the authorities for the proper control of the foreign drapers or clothiers, who resorted thither for the sale of their cloth. These regulations seem certainly to imply that very serious abuses had hitherto prevailed in regard to this matter, and that the foreigners imposed both on the English and on each other. It was now laid down that the foreign drapers should offer their goods nowhere else, and only from noon on Thursday till noon on Saturday, and nothing save whole cloths and half cloths. In 1405 the Company obtained the right of nominating the Keeper, subject to the approval of the Court of Aldermen ; and during more than two centuries the London Drapers enjoyed profitable facilities here for the disposal of their goods. The old-fashioned machinery gradually broke down under a variety of adverse influences, particularly the gradual withdrawal of the members of the Gild from an active share in business, the indirect operation of the Orphan Act of 1697, and the development of commerce outside the jurisdiction of the City on more modern lines.

When the City Companies finally agreed to take over, with certain reservations, the Ulster estates, the Drapers paid for one full manor, and admitted only one sub-sharer—the Tallow-Chandlers.

The Draper presents himself as the salesman—as the Clothier in contrast to the Shearman or Clothworker—in the *Little Gest* of Robin Hood (1508), in a passage where Much, the miller's son—as he watches Little John measuring out the cloth for Sir Richard at the Lea, without very nice regard to the quantities—asks what devil's-kin draper he is, that he uses no better rule ? This merchant-gild, as it probably may upon the whole be considered, sold the goods in the piece or by the yard, as well as in a made-up form. They purveyed the new clothes for both sexes, as the upholder did the second-hand.

During the twenty years and upward that Robin Hood passed in the forests of Yorkshire and Nottinghamshire, it is once or twice casually shown that the hero kept by him a store of cloth in the piece, for the use of himself and his men. It was probably bought at Nottingham, if it was not by possibility acquired from some trader passing through Barnsdale or Sherwood. Even in such case, Robin would have paid for it, as that was not the class of men whom he plundered.

The Linen-Draper,[1] though it has become a familiar term, and has gained by degrees a wide and vague significance, was, at the beginning, an important departure and a distinct line of business. The general employment of linen and the free currency of the fabric here were long restrained by the failure of the foreign manufacturers to obtain the same footing in our country as their brethren who dealt in wool. A predilection long survived among us for the older textile on sanitary and other grounds ; and the Act for Burying in Woollen passed as late as 1678. Even in 1730, it was noted as a remarkable circumstance, that Mrs. Oldfield the actress was interred in Westminster Abbey in a Holland shift trimmed with lace and a Brussels lace head-dress. There is quite a little group of tracts illustrating the resentment of some persons at the legal requirement, which was no doubt often evaded.

In the time of Stow's Continuator (1633) Watling Street was the principal centre for drapers and retailers of woollen cloths, both broad and narrow.

The Drapers virtually severed their practical connexion with the industry which had given them their name and their wealth, as constitutional changes rendered the ancient principles of commerce untenable, and the growth of their estate, as well as the modification of their constituency, rendered mercantile pursuits, and even the task of superintendence, foreign to their needs and views. This is the story of all the leading Companies.

That under immediate consideration has prodigiously expanded its resources of recent years, and is among the most opulent of the Fraternities. It seems to have rallied with unusual rapidity from the effects of the Fire of 1666, and to have remained uninterruptedly solvent. It contributes out of its corporate funds very large sums, year by year, to educational objects, while more than a third of its total revenue is under the control of the Charity and Endowed Schools Commissions.

The original "Fraternity of the Drapers of Cornhill," as it was

---

[1] Compare the preceding Section.

termed, realized the idea pervading the institution and nonage of all these organizations, when the Brethren adopted the practice at the outset of assembling in council in the adjacent church of St. Mary Bethlehem, Bishopsgate, with the assent of the Prior and on payment of a fine and a quarterwage. The fixture of the weaving business in the neighbourhood of Cannon Street led to a drift in that direction of the woollen-tailors and cloth-sellers, and eventually the Drapers met at a house in St. Swithin's Lane, purchased or otherwise obtained from John Hend some time anterior to 1405, when we hear of the Ordinances of that year having been settled " at John Hend's house in Swithin's Lane." This personage was Mayor in 1405, and the repairer of St. Swithin's Church.

In a document of 1445–6, 24 Henry VI., the building is specified as Drapers' Hall, and in 1479, after a grand hunt in Waltham Forest, when the Mayor, Sir Bartholomew James, Draper, and others accompanied the King, the Lady Mayoress afterward entertained in St. Swithin's Lane the Aldermen's wives and other ladies, Edward IV. having sent a present of venison and wine and particularly desiring that the City ladies should receive every attention. There are several entries of charges for work done and other outlays incurred at this first Hall of the Company.

During the remainder of the fifteenth century, and far into the reign of Henry VIII., Drapers' Hall in St. Swithin's Lane was periodically the scene of good cheer and generous hospitality; and the fair sex was invariably remembered at the great feasts. The entertainments in 1515, 1516, 1521, and other years were extraordinarily sumptuous and costly, and among the guests were all the civil and ecclesiastical notabilities on friendly terms with the Company, especially the Master of St. Thomas of Acon, the Prior of St. Bartholomew's, and the Prior of St. Mary Overy. When exalted or highly important visitors were asked, the Master and Wardens, or some of them, personally waited on the individual. There is an entry under 1496 of 4*d.* for boat-hire, to bid the Lord Treasurer (William Paulet, first Marquis of Winchester) to a feast. In 1521 the Midsummer celebration cost no less than 64*l.* 8*s.* 2*d.* But the grand Election dinner of 1516, when a large number of distinguished persons and many ladies (who appear to have dined in a separate apartment) were present, may be judged, from the description of it, to have been still more magnificent. Leland the antiquary was among the guests; and there were two players, who had their messes and rewards. The account of the Company's plate shews a total of 98 pieces, exclusively of 16½ dozens of plain silver spoons.

The early association of the Drapers with the neighbourhood of

Cornhill and the bequests of members in trust for the performance of obits at the adjacent Austin Friars, may have had some share in drawing their attention to the opportunity of securing a more commodious Hall, when the princely residence of Thomas Cromwell, Earl of Essex, escheated to the Crown by his attainder in 1540; and in 1543, after a good deal of negotiation, the Company purchased the whole, with its appurtenances and certain supplemental matters in the shape of fixtures.

The circumstances under which it was enabled to place itself in a position to treat with the Crown for this splendid property are not generally known. But the fact is, that in 1540, under the will of Thomas Howell, a Monmouthshire gentleman and an English merchant at Seville, 12,000 ducats of gold,—of which only 8,720 (about 4,300*l.*) seem ever to have been paid,—were left to the Drapers, in trust to

DRAPERS' HALL. THE CROMWELL HOUSE.

buy 400 ducats annual rent to provide 84*l.* every year for four orphan maidens of the testator's kindred, if they could be found,[1] or if not, of four such outside his kindred, each of whom was to receive 21*l.* Out of this money the Drapers bought for 1,200*l.* the Cromwell mansion and its appurtenances, which, not reckoning the house, was estimated at that time to produce 105*l.* a year. There was some delay in the completion of the business; for Howell had made his testamentary dispositions at Seville, and appointed residents there his executors.

As early as 1559 the scheme adopted by the beneficiaries was judged unfair and improper, and it was considerably modified by the Court of Chancery after an investigation extending over six months.

The abstract of the case is, that Thomas Howell in 1540 left about 4,000*l.*, more or less, in trust to the Drapers for eleemosynary and secular purposes within certain defined limits; that the Drapers, desiring to invest money in a new direction, made a compact with Henry VIII., under indentures dated March 31, 1543, confirmed by letters patent

[1] See a curious entry in Burn's *Star-Chamber*, 1870, p. 52.

of July 4, 1543, whereby they became proprietors of the attainted favourite's seat or inn in the City for 1,200*l.* + 10*s.* 4*d.* a year payable to the Court of Augmentations; and that, the property yielding nearly enough even at that period to carry out the two conditions involved, namely, the yearly payment of 84*l.* and the execution of necessary repairs from time to time on the premises, the purchasers had their Hall and certain appurtenances into the bargain, although the testator expressly stipulated that the more his money would command in the way of land, the more the trustees were to apply to the same purpose, by enlarging the scope of the charity in a corresponding ratio. Therefore it followed that the dedication of any part of the fund to the Hall was as foreign to the mind of Howell as its submission to ecclesiastical control.

This was the place in connection with which Stow narrates the familiar story of the injustice done to his father, who occupied a house in the rear; and also that to which James Howell, writing to his father, September 30, 1629,[1] refers, where he speaks of apprenticing his brother Ned to the Company, and seeing the portrait of Thomas Howell over the chimney-piece in the great room. That portrait, no doubt, disappeared in the fire. But the clerk, when he ascertained Howell's name, told him that, if his brother could prove his descent from that stem, he would have 300*l.* given to him on completing his articles, on loan for five years without interest, and that any poor maid, who was of the right blood, might claim 50*l.* for a portion. Which indicates a favourable revision of the arrangement at that date. The new owners had held their first meeting in the Hall on the 7th August, 1541, and their first Court on the 10th, although they were not in legal occupation, and had not paid the stipulated amount.

Herbert[2] furnishes from the Company's archives the following schedule of the contents of Cromwell's late residence :—

"*Imprimis,* a fair great gate ; a fair yard, paved ; a fair low gallery on the north side of the yard ; a great winding stair with bay glass windows leading into the hall ; *Item,* over that stair fair leads ; *Item,* a fair hall with two bay windows and clerestories, with a buttery, a pantry, a cellar for wine, ale, and beer ; *Item,* a dark chamber with lattice over the said buttery and pantry to look down into the hall ; *Item,* a fair great parlour with bay glass windows and a fair chimney ; *Item,* a buttery with a clerestory, and within the same buttery a jewel-house ;[3] *Item,* a fair kitchen, with two great chimnies, dressing boards, a great cistern of lead, with conduit-water coming thereinto and two clerestories ; *Item,* a pastry-house with three fair ovens, moulding boards and shelves, and a clerestory ; *Item,* a scullery-house with a chimney and a clerestory ; *Item,* two

---

[1] Letters, ed. 1754, p. 212.

[2] *Twelve Great Livery Companies,* 1836, i. 471.

[3] In the Founders' Books, under 1647, there is an entry shewing that the treasure chest or trunk was kept in the inner buttery.

larder-houses, with clerestories ; *Item*, a coal-house ; *Item*, a winding stair from the kitchen into the hall, and over the same fair leads ; *Item*, on the east side of the great gate two low chambers, the one with a chimney and an office to wait in, and three clerestories, the other with a clerestory under the pantry ; *Item*, in the second storey, a fair chamber for the ladies, ceiled and matted, with a chimney ; *Item*, in the third storey, three little chambers with bay windows and one chimney ; *Item*, a garret over them ; *Item*, under the great stair a little dark room ; *Item*, under the great parlour a fair cellar paved, for wine or ale ; *Item*, the great garden and an entry thereto."

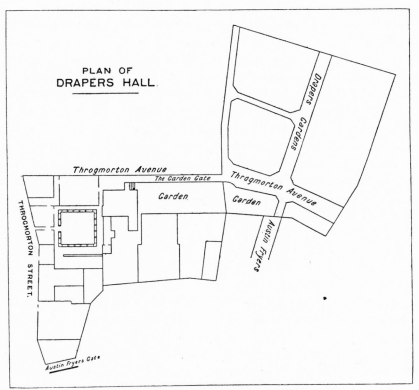

GROUND-PLAN OF THE CROMWELL PREMISES.

The Great Fire laid waste all this proud domain, whose garden and orchard were open in those days to the north as far as Hampstead. But the muniments were saved by lying in one of the out-buildings, and the plate by being deposited in the sewer. The Hall was rebuilt in 1667, by Jarman, and again partly destroyed in 1774. It subsequently underwent great alterations, and in 1846, under the 9 & 10 Vict. cap. 19, when the same Court, which in 1559 disposed of the question in six months, had occupied about *six years* in coming to a conclusion, the Hall and grounds were sold in pursuance of a decree in Chancery, which, without imputing fraud to the Company, charged it with mis-appropriation of the Howell trust, and directed an entirely new principle

of management.   The Drapers virtually remained owners as before ;
but a large portion of the open space was let on a building lease, and
forms the block known as Drapers' Gardens.[1]   There was further
legislation on the subject in the Act 15 & 16 Vict. cap. 14.   The
charity is now so framed as to befriend the general cause of female
education in Wales.

The Hall was entirely rebuilt in 1870.   The existing garden and
the old mulberry orchard are shown on the plans at the Hall.   The
former is a small oblong plot ; but the orchard was a square piece of
considerable area, stretching down to London Wall.

The Plan-books comprise ground-sections on parchment of the
premises and of all the Company's estates at successive dates, and form
two large folio volumes.   The earliest appear to belong to a period not
more remote than 1609, two years after the first charter of James I.

The Company is elsewhere said to have consisted in 1415 of 96
members.   In 1557 the "Freemen Householders" are set down at 77.
During the eighteenth century the Livery varied from 150 to 180 ; in
1835 it reached 344, the fine being then 35/. ; but in 1879, including
the Court, it counted only 302.   Between 1820 and 1879, 1,583 were
admitted to the freedom, the major part by patrimony, three only by
gift.

Herbert prints from the original records a series of extracts in
chronological order, illustrative of current historical events and the
share taken by the Drapers in them.   It has been stated that this Gild,
in the person of Sir John Norman, Mayor in 1453, took the initiative
in acquiring a barge for its use ; but the Grocers had possessed one
many years before.   It may be the case, however, that Norman, who
built the first Drapers' barge at his own expense, was the earliest Mayor
who went by water to Westminster to be admitted.   But the ancient
usage of proceeding on horseback was not finally discontinued till 1710.

This ancient and honourable Society has contributed to our nobility
several distinguished families ; the Pulteneys, Earls of Bath, the Capels,
Earls of Essex, the Brydges, Dukes of Chandos, the cadets of which
have intermarried with the Berkeleys and the Lords Wotton.   But
perhaps the brightest ornaments on the roll are the numerous benefactors to municipal objects from the beginning of the fourteenth to
the end of the seventeenth century.   Among these were John Hend,
Mayor in 1405, restorer of St. Swithin's Church, whose house, in the

---

[1] A detailed account of the Howell charity would occupy too large a space in such
a volume as the present.   It belongs rather to the Annals of the Drapers, when they
are written.

cognominal lane, was the first Hall of the Gild, and is still its property ; Sir Simon Eyre (1446), founder of Leadenhall Market, and donor of 8,000 marks for the relief of the poor ; Sir George Monnox (1515), who expended large sums in good works at Walthamstow ; Thomas Howell, whose bequest to the Company was immediately instrumental in enabling it to secure the Cromwell premises in 1543 ; Alderman William Lambert, who instituted and endowed Queen Elizabeth's College at East Greenwich ; Sir Robert Clayton (1680), Lord Mayor, originally a Scrivener, who built a portion of Christ's Hospital ; and others.

Nor are we to forget that Anthony Munday, son of Christopher Munday, Citizen and Draper, was by patrimony of this Company. He was the celebrated Elizabethan dramatist, prose-writer, and pamphleteer, a composer of many of the City Pageants from 1605 to 1623, Editor of Stow's *Survey* in 1618, and the coadjutor of Humphrey Dyson, notary, antiquary and book-collector, in the second posthumous edition in 1633.[1]

The members of the Fraternity, possibly to some extent from the nature of the industry with which they were connected, varied their livery or vesture with remarkable frequency, and prescribed with great strictness the mode in which it was to be bought, valued, and worn. Beginning with 1405, there is a curious sequence of regulations on this subject.

The colour and fashion were originally changed every year ; and then, as that practice may have been found too troublesome or expensive, every second year. In the colour the whole Fellowship was to be consulted ; and the purchase devolved on the Wardens. But eight valuers, chosen by the whole Council, were to appraise the cloth, when selected, to price and to seal it. If the livery was of one colour, the hood was to be such as the Fellowship at large might approve ; but if the dress was party-coloured, there was to be no hood. Should any one prefer to supply his own cloth, the Wardens claimed eight shillings from him for every yard, grained or cut. In 1483, the dress was violet and the hood crimson ; in 1495, both gown and hood were half murry and half violet ; in 1498, the gowns were murry and the hoods blue and crimson ; and in 1503 violet and scarlet were the hues. In 1516 we hear of sad blue and crimson, in 1520 of violet gowns and violet and scarlet hoods ; and from time to time, until a uniform pattern was fixed, of other

---

[1] A copious account of Munday's publications will be found in my *Collections and Notes*, 1876–92, and the pageants which he wrote for the Companies are described under their several heads.

colours, such as puce and scarlet, and brown, blue, and scarlet. The hood, which was almost universal among these Fraternities, was a symbol of their affinity to the Church, just as the differences in the patterns and tint of their dress formed distinguishing marks of the respective Arts or Trades quite as unmistakeably as those denoting the various monastic orders.

The painted glass windows at Merchant Taylors' Hall remind us that the Skinners and Taylors also had a taste for brilliant and striking costumes of a distinctive character ; and it was an article of faith with all these good folks ; but we do not meet with such minute notices of these particulars where the question had not, as it were, a professional significance and bearing.

LITERARY NOTICES.

An Epitaph of the Vertuous Life and Death of Dame Helen Branch, of London, widow, late the wife of Sir John Branch, Knight, sometime the Right Honourable Lord Maior of London, and daughter to Mr. William Nicolson, sometime of London, Draper. 4to, 1594.

A true Copie of a Writing Testimonial, by aucthority devised and commanded, to satisfie the worlde, and to cleere Zechary Dow, of London, Draper, and his children, from the reproach of a hand wryting, falsely compacted and maliciously published in Blackwell Hall and elsewhere against him [Nov. 28, 1610]. A broadside.

CIVIC PAGEANTS, ETC.

Himatia-Poleos : The Triumphs of Old Drapery, or the Rich Clothing of England. Performed in affection, and at the charges of the right worthy and first honoured Company of Drapers, at the instalment of Sir Thomas Hayes on Saturday, being the 29 of October, 1614. Devised and written by A[nthony] M[unday], Citizen and Draper of London. 4to, 1614.

Metropolis Coronata, The Triumphs of Ancient Drapery : Or, Rich Clothing of England : in a Second Year's Performance. In Honour of the Advancement of Sir John Jolles, Knight, to the high Office of Lord Mayor of London, and taking his Oath for the same Authority, on Monday, being the 30 Day of October, 1615. Performed in hearty affection to him, and at the bountiful charges of his worthy Brethren the truly Honourable Society of Drapers, the first that received such Dignity in this City. Devised and written by Anthony Munday, Citizen and Draper of London. 4to, 1615.

This pageant concludes with the Speech spoken by Earl Robert de la Hude, commonly called Robin Hood, and the song of Robin Hood and his Huntsmen.

The Sun in Aries : A Noble Solemnity Performed through the Cittie, at the sole cost and charges of the Honourable and ancient Fraternity of Drapers, At the confirmation and establishment of their most Worthy Brother the Right Honourable Edward Barkham, in the high Office of his Maiesties Lieutenant, the lord Maior of the famous Citie of London. Taking beginning at his Lordships going, and perfecting it selfe after his returne from receiuing the Oath of Maioralty at Westminster, on the morrow after Simon [and] Jvdes day, being the 29. of October, 1621. By Tho. Middleton, Gent. 4to, 1621.

Reprinted in Nichols's *Progresses*, and in the editions of Middleton.

The Triumphs of Integrity : A Noble Solemnity, performed through the City, at the sole Cost and Charges of the Honorable Fraternity of Drapers, at the Confirmation and Establishment of their most worthy Brother, the Right Honorable Martin Lumley, in the high Office of his Majesty's Lieutenant, Lord Mayor and Chancellor of the famous City of London. Taking beginning at his Lordship's going, and perfecting itself after His Return from receiving the Oath of Mayoralty at Westminster, on the Morrow after Simon and Jude's Day, being the 29 of October, 1623. By Tho. Middleton, Gent. 4to, 1623.

The Triumphs of the Golden Fleece : Performed at the Cost and Charges of the Ancient and Honourable Society of the Drapers : For the instalment of their worthy Brother, Mr. Martin Lumley, in the Mayoralty of London. On Wednesday, being the nine and twentieth day of October, 1623. Written by A. Munday, Citizen and Draper of London. 4to, 1623.

Munday, as a citizen of London and a member of the Drapers' Company, may have recollected some of the older pageants prepared by that Society for its Midsummer and other Feasts, when minstrels and players were usually engaged as part of the proceedings. In 1521, it was resolved by the Court of the Company to renew all the old pageants for the house, including the new pageant of the *Golden Fleece* for the Mayor against Midsummer ; also the giant, Lord Morrispike, and a man's dance, as was used the last year. In that year a sum of 13s. is charged in the account for "Glee and his company, for two plays for Monday and Tuesday."

The Triumphs of Health and Prosperity : A noble Solemnity performed through the City, at the sole Cost and Charges of the Honourable Fraternity of Drapers, at the Inauguration of their most Worthy Brother, the Right Honourable Cuthbert Hassket, Lord Mayor of the Famous City of London. By Thomas Middleton. 4to, 1626.

Porta pietatis ; Or, the Port or Harbour of Piety : expressed in sundry Triumphs, Pageants, and Shows, at the Initiation of the Right Honourable Sir Maurice Abbot, Knight, into the Mayoralty of the famous and far-renowned City London. All the Charge and Expense of the laborious Projects, both by Water and Land, being the sole Undertaking of the Right Worshipful Company of the Drapers. By Thomas Heywood. 4to, 1638.

Londini Status Pacatus ; or, London's Peaceable Estate. Exprest in sundry Triumphs, Pageants, and Shews, at the Initiation of the Right Honourable Henry Garway into the Majoralty of the famous and far renowned City London. All the Charge and Expence of the laborious Projects, both by Water and Land, being the sole Undertakings of the Right Worshipful Society of Drapers. Written by Thomas Heywood. 4to, 1639.

The Triumphs of London : Performed on Friday, October 29, 1675, for the Entertainment of the Right Honourable and truly noble Pattern of Prudence and Loyalty, Sir Joseph Sheldon, Knt., Lord Mayor of the City of London. Containing a true Description of the several Pageants, with the Speeches spoken on each Pageant. Together with the several Songs sung at this Solemnity. All set forth at the proper Costs and Charges of the Worshipful Company of Drapers. Designed and Composed by T. Jordan. 4to, 1675.

London's Triumphs : Express'd in sundry Representations, Pageants, and Shows. Performed on Monday, October 30, 1676, at the Inauguration and Instalment of the Right Hon. Sir Thos. Davies, Lord Mayor of the City of London. Containing a true description of the several scenes and habits of the Representors, with the Speeches spoken on each Pageant. All the Charge and Expenses of the Industrious Designs being the sole undertaking of the Ancient and right Worshipful Society of Drapers. Being the Second year without Interruption. Devised and Composed by Tho. Jordan. 4to, 1676.

London in Lustre: Projecting Many Bright Beams of Triumph : disposed into several Representations of Scenes and Pageants. Performed with great Splendor on Wednesday, October 29, 1679. At the Initiation and Instalment of the Right Honourable Sir Robert Clayton, Knight, Lord Mayor of the City of London. Dignified with divers delightful Varieties of Presentors, with Speeches, Songs, and Actions, properly and punctually described. All set forth at the proper Cost and Charges of the Worshipful Company of Drapers. Devised and composed by Tho. Jordan, Gent. 4to, 1679.

London's Royal Triumph for the City's Loyal Magistrate: In an Exact Description of several Scenes and Pageants, Adorned with many Magnificent Representations. Performed on Wednesday, October 29, 1684. At the Instalment and Inauguration of the Right Honourable Sir James Smith, Knight, Lord Mayor of London. Illustrated with divers delightful objects of Gallantry and Jollity, Speeches and Songs, Single and in Parts. Set forth at the proper Costs and Charges of the Worshipful Company of Drapers. By Thos. Jordan. 4to, 1684.

The Triumphs of London: Performed on Thursday, Octob. 29. 1691. For the Entertainment of the Right Honourable Sir Thomas Stamp, Kt.; Lord Mayor of the City of London. Containing A true description of the several Pageants, with the Speeches spoken on each Pageant. All set forth at the proper Costs and Charges of the Worshipful Company of Drapers. By E. S. 4to, 1691.

A Speech made to his Excellency the Lord General Monck, and the Councell of State, at Drapers' Hall in London : the 28th of March, 1660. At which time they were entertained by that honourable Company. Spoken by Walter Yeokney. 1660. A broadside written by T. Jordan.

A Dialogue betwixt Tom and Dick: The former being a Countryman, the other a Citizen, Presented to his Excellency and the Council of State, at Drapers'-Hall in London, March 28, 1660. (To the Tune of *I'll never love thee more.*) [1660.] A broadside. Written by T. Jordan.

> Apparently a spurious impression or text of the former.

The Fishmongers.

THE PRESENT ARMS.

Pol.—Do you know me, my lord?
Ham.—Excellent well ; you are a fishmonger—
Pol.—Not I, my lord.
Ham.—Then I would you were so honest a man.—*Hamlet,* iii. 2.

THIS Company originated in the same manner and under the same circumstances as the other Fraternities of London, appointed and

THE OLD ARMS.

authorized, first by common usage, then by licence of the king, and finally by a succession of charters, to exercise a monopoly as regarded the conduct of the trade in salt fish within the City and its Liberties.

But in one respect the Gild presented an important variation from nearly all the more ancient bodies of the kind which we are describing, inasmuch as, in the *extant* grants at all events, there is no reference to any religious or charitable motives ostensibly influencing the formation of such an union of members of the trade ; and the sole object put forward is the protection of the interests of those concerned from a commercial point of view.

The Fishmongers, in common with others, were amerced in the time of Henry II. (1154), for carrying on trade as a community without the royal licence. This is apparently the earliest specific mention of them ; but it involves a piece of circumstantial testimony, which justifies the persuasion that they were then of more or less lengthened customary prescription, which is in the highest degree likely ; and in fact, from the immense comparative demand for fish of all kinds, but especially for those which were chiefly preferred for use during Lent and on fast-days,[1] we may securely refer the genesis of a system of supervision and restraint to a time immemorial, as the Patent of 1364 actually puts it. The Company lost nearly the whole of its muniments in the Great Fire ; but it is generally understood that it received a confirmation of its rights, as recognised in 1154 on payment of a fine, from Edward I. in 1272, from Edward II. in 1307, and from Edward III., concurrently with so many others, in 1327.

Long prior to the grants of 1364–5, legislation had intervened to prevent what were then considered abuses and irregularities in this industry. The 1 Edward I. prohibited the partnership of denizens with foreigners bringing fish in their ships to London, and the storage of it in cellars, or beyond the second day, save salt-fish. The Act further reserved a right of pre-emption to the King's purveyors. The clauses in respect to storage aimed at the forestallers and regraters, and had perhaps a more direct bearing on the dealers in stock-fish. The *Assize of a Fisher*, published in consequence of this law, limited the profit of dealers to a penny in the shilling, forbad forestalling and regrating

---

[1] The origin of fasting, which formerly divided the week into two dietetic sections, as Wednesday was also observed as a day of abstinence from flesh, must be sought in those regions where, on sanitary grounds, too large and continuous a consumption of animal food was apt to be prejudicial ; but, as in other matters, neither the Mosaic nor any other code established for communities existing under totally different conditions from ourselves ought to have the least binding force on Western Europe. As for the reasons which were assigned for the practice by the old theologians, they are neither more nor less foolish than such pleas are usually found to be ; but the main argument that the use of flesh without intermission was productive of religious laxity, may just as well be employed to support the physical source of the custom, before it was clothed with a ritualistic attribute, to suit the diplomatic objects of the Church.

in enhancement of prices, and obliged vendors to expose their goods for sale openly in the markets. No fishmonger might water his fish more than twice.

The same reign witnessed an evident proof that the Fraternity had made considerable progress in wealth and importance, and discerned the wisdom of propitiating the Crown ; for in 1298, when Edward I. returned from Scotland, the Fishmongers were foremost among the civic bodies which celebrated the auspicious occasion on St. Magnus's Day. Stow tells us that they passed in solemn procession through the City, having, amongst other pageants and shows, four sturgeons gilt carried on four horses, followed by four salmon of silver on four horses, and after these eight-and-forty knights on horses resembling salt-water luces, and then another knight habited like St. Magnus, and these were succeeded by more horsemen. It was, no doubt, an imposing spectacle, as it was the earliest of which there is a definite account.

The fish trade seems to have been not less open to fraud and to disregard of municipal regulations than the rest of those with which we deal ; but the caterers for the daily necessaries of life and perishable commodities were unusually prone to dishonest practices. There was a periodical necessity for revising, enlarging, and renewing the ordinances governing the craft, within as well as without. The *Liber Horn*, written in or about 1290, by Andrew Horn, a member of the Gild, who died in 1328, furnishes some additional precepts which then had force ; they declared, among other points, that no fishmonger should buy fish beyond the bounds, namely, the Chapel on London Bridge, Baynard's Castle, and Jordan's Quay, lest they, or some of them, should forestall by meeting the boats, before they reached the landing-stages, to which all the fish was to be brought, before it could be sold. The limits within which the Fishmongers of London were at liberty to sell, varied under different reigns and circumstances. The grant of all import-dues at that point by Henry III. led to a concentration of the industry near Queenhithe in order to increase the Queen-gold from taillage ; but the spot was afterward allotted to other uses. But during the reign of Edward IV., while London Bridge was under repair, the unlading of cargoes was permitted at Queenhithe. Sprats, eels, whiting, plaice, cod, and mackerel are particularized in this temporary ordinance.

The trade, however, from the most ancient times, has localized itself in the neighbourhood of Billingsgate ; the old fish-market extended east and west from Bread Street to Old Change, and north and south from the northern extremities of those streets to Old Fish Street ;

and before the two Companies or Associations of Fishmongers were united by Henry VIII., the vendors of salt and fresh fish had their distinct quarters. There was Salt Fish Wharf and Fresh Fish Wharf.

Knightrider Street, in the immediate vicinity, was celebrated for fish dinners; and Friday Street, just by, is reputed to have owed its name to its site having been occupied by the Friday market.

Salt fish was to be sold only after prime. But it appears that in 1320 certain dealers on Fish Wharf successfully maintained their title to dispose of herrings and other fish to any that would buy, even to hawkers.

In the early catalogues of fish, with which we meet in tables of fare at great feasts, in the household books, and in the statutes, occur nearly all the species which are now used as food, and several, including the whale and the sturgeon,[1] which have fallen into disuse. Salmon, herring, eels, haddock, mackerel, soles, turbot, oysters, were common and generally cheap. The tariff fixed in the time of Edward I. limited the best soles to 3*d.* a dozen, turbot to 6*d.*, the best mackerel, in Lent, to 1*d.* each, the best pickled herrings to twenty the penny, fresh oysters to 2*d.* per gallon, a quarter of a long hundred (30), of the best eels to 2*d.* At this time we hear of lampreys being fetched from Gloucester for the royal table; at a far earlier period an inordinate partiality for them had proved fatal to one of our kings.

In 1311, Hugh Matfrey, a fishmonger of London, having bought lampreys of Nantes of Thomas Lespicer of Portsmouth, and stored them, in lieu of exposing them for sale publicly under the wall of St. Margaret's, Bridge Street, according to the ordinances of the City, was prosecuted, but escaped without punishment on entering into a bond not to offend again in the like manner.

Salted haddock, mackerel, and sturgeon are mentioned in the days of Edward I. as paying pontage, when carried over London Bridge. Herrings were reckoned by the last of 10,000, and there was a brisk trade in them, both fresh and cured, between Hull, Yarmouth, and London; and there is special provision for them in the 31 Edward III., called the *Statute of Herrings*. Besides cloth, the Merchant Vintners trading with Gascony, in order to save the currency, were allowed to purchase herrings for export on favoured terms. Eels of various sorts

---

[1] By 17 Edward II. whales and great sturgeons, taken in the sea, save in privileged places, were to be reserved to the King's use. Salted whale seems to have been occasionally served at the King's table. In 1515, porpoises (which are not, however, strictly fish) were sold at Newcastle-on-Tyne for food.

were largely used during Lent in the monasteries; and preserves for them, called *Anguillonia*, were placed on our rivers. Herbert acquaints us that carp was also extensively propagated in ponds, and that in the King's Pike Ponds on the Bankside, Southwark, were long kept the pike for the royal table.

Under 1247, mackerel are cited as allowed for diet to certain religious bodies on the third day of Rogation Week.

The statute 13 Edward II. prescribed strict regulations for preserving salmon in those rivers which it then frequented.

The Norfolk coast is shown to have been at all times a rich field for the fisherman; and the ports of Blakeney, Clay, Cromer, and of course Yarmouth, possessed many doggers, lodeships, and other craft for carrying on the commerce. There seems to have been a general provision, that the fish taken and offered for sale should be "good and covenable"; and a later statute (23 Edward IV.) expressly refers to the package of small fish.

Unlawful nets were frequently seized and destroyed. In 1313, one belonging to the Abbot of Lesnes, near Erith, suffered this fate. These nets were called kidels, and were too close in the meshes. In 1344, at length, to prevent or check this nuisance, Inspectors of Nets were appointed.

Dorsers of defective measurement were also liable to seizure, and in 1315 certain conger, plaice, and gurnard, trussed in these false dorsers, were brought into Guildhall, and their owners summoned. Curiously enough, one was Andrew Horn, above-mentioned, afterward Chamberlain of London, and then a fishmonger in Bridge Street or New Fish Street; but he was one of two acquitted.

The Company adroitly ingratiated itself with the Crown, when Edward III. stood in need of money for the support of his wars in France, and in 1363 contributed 40*l.* to that object, being, with one exception, the highest amount given, the Mercers heading the list with 41*l.* In the very year following, the Fishmongers obtained their new charter from the King.

This Patent set forth that it was a custom in London beyond the memory of man, that no fish should be sold except by fishmongers, and that these fishmongers had had leave given to them by the King's progenitors, to elect yearly certain members of the mistery to rule the same for the general commodity of the people. Two further instruments, both dated in the succeeding year, dealt with points, overlooked perhaps in the previous one, fixing the number of Wardens of the mistery at four, and specifying a Lay Hall-moot, where we understand that these officers were chosen half-yearly, approved, and sworn in the presence of the Mayor or Sheriff, or their deputies, and where likewise questions affecting the trade were to be discussed and arranged. The latter was a very unusual prerogative, and we shall see that it was productive of some inconvenience.

In 1377, the Fishmongers returned six members to the Common Council, and occupied the fourth place among the Gilds of London, a rank which was confirmed in 1515, and which they have since uninterruptedly enjoyed.

But it happened only three years later, 3 Richard II., that an Act of Parliament passed, opening the trade in fish to all persons in amity with the King, and that the Mayor, John de Northampton, exacted from the Fishmongers an admission that their trade was no craft, and consequently not entitled to rank as a mistery. In 1380, Parliament went still further, and, on the plea of fraudulent practices by certain of the Company, enacted that in future no Fishmonger should be admitted to the mayoralty. This severe and injurious disability was soon rescinded, and the Company was invited to state its case in the House of Peers. The particulars are chiefly curious as illustrating the primitive manners of the time, the delegates of the Company presenting themselves in Parliament, and holding a free altercation with their opponents. The difficulty was overcome by a fresh Patent, 7 Richard II., which restored their commercial privileges, but compelled them hereafter to refer all cases of dispute to the Mayor's Court.

It appears that the charges against the Company related to the forestalling and retailing of fish; and it was alleged by the defendants that their accusers acted through malice, some of them having been formerly imprisoned at the instance of members of the Gild.

In 1418, the Corporation called on the Masters of the Fishmongers on Fish Street Hill and in Old Fish Street to see well that the lowest price was set on fish for the easement of the people, and that the whiting taken in the Thames should be sold in gross at the quay where the vessel bringing it in was moored, and then carried to Fish Street for sale by retail.

At the same time, it was ordered by the Mayor that oysters and mussels should be sold at 4d. per bushel, 2d. the half-bushel, one penny the peck, a halfpenny the half-peck, according to the assize.

The Fishmongers seem to have exercised or claimed the sole right of exporting salt to foreign parts. In 1632, the Eastland merchants of Newcastle-on-Tyne are found petitioning against this monopoly without success, the civic authorities siding with the Fishmongers for reasons shown in their certificate forwarded to the Government.

The extent of the business of the Company at the end of the fourteenth century, when the above-mentioned troubles arose, is proved by the existence of no fewer than six of the Hall-moots, where matters were settled among members of the craft for a considerable period ; and when the Fishmongers were ultimately required to resort to the Mayor's Court in the usual way, these buildings naturally fell into disuse. It is to this that the following extract has reference :—

"On the east side of Old Fish Street Hill," says Stow's Continuator (1633), "is one great house, now letten out for rent, which house sometime was one of the Hals pertaining to the Company of Fishmongers at such time as they had sixe Hal-motes, or meeting-places ; namely, twaine in Bridge Street, or New Fish Street, twaine in Old Fish Street, whereof this was one, and twaine in Stockfishermonger Row, or Thames Street, as appeareth by a record, the 22 of Richard the second."

It was in that same year, that the Company are shown by an *inspeximus* of 6 Henry VI. (July 10, 1427), to have received a further charter from Richard II. (May 9, 1399), in which six Wardens (the existing number), in place of four, are allowed, and the right of holding the old lay Hall-moot is restored. "Our well-beloved liegemen of the mistery of Fishmongers" procured, however, a regular Patent from the former prince (11 Henry VI., Feb. 8, 1433), in which they are recognised as one body perpetual, with a common seal for the errands and business of the said mistery and commonalty ; a licence in mortmain, and the other usual powers ; and this was confirmed by the Patent of 23 Henry VII., July 3, 1508.

As we have elsewhere stated, the Stock-fish Mongers were incorporated by the same sovereign, Sept. 20, in the year just cited ; and in 1536, 27 Henry VIII., the two Companies were united by a royal charter and by Articles of Agreement, which contain some points of interest. Among them were stipulations :   1. That the Stock-fish Mongers shall convey to the other Gild for the joint benefit of the two.   2. That such arms as Garter and Clarencieux, kings of arms, have appointed and granted to the crafts, shall be for ever continually kept, and never be extinguished, altered, or defaced, otherwise than in manner and form as is in their letters patents declared.   3. That all assemblies of Courts, as well for the good politic guiding and order of the same craft, and for the amendment and reformation of misdemeaned persons of the same craft, to the good orders and rules of the same, as for any other cause concerning the mistery, shall be holden, kept, and used in the place commonly called the Fishmongers' Hall in the parish of St. Michael, Crooked Lane, London, and not in any other place ; and, 4. That the chapel of St. Peter and St. Sebastian, standing in the parish church of St. Michael in Crooked Lane, shall be made, built, and finished in all things by the said Fellowship of Fishmongers and Stock-fish Mongers, at their cost and charge, in length to the church-porch of the churchyard there, and shall be considered the joint endowment and property of the united Company.

The charter of 1536 was confirmed by Edward VI., July 2, 1548, and in his fourth year he gave liberty to the Companies, the Fishmongers' inclusive, to redeem for a sum of money (18,744*l*. 11*s*. 2*d*.) the possessions which had been ceded by them at the dissolution of religious establishments.

This act of repurchase formed a very valuable and a permanent piece of evidence in behalf of the City Gilds, as it virtually purged all antecedent irregularities, if any, in the acquisition of their corporate estates.

We may embrace the present opportunity of remarking that the Crown displayed some tact in divesting itself of the distasteful and troublesome duty of negotiating with all the individuals and bodies involved in the suppression of religious foundations of various classes, and in farming the business for a stated amount to a syndicate, which undertook all the labour and bore some of the odium.

The committee of assignees held their meetings at Skinners' Hall, where they made the best bargains in their power with the owners of the property, who were practically the victims of a rather shallow trick for raising money under colour of Protestant zeal and purism.

The levy of money by indirect means yet remains one of the amiable characteristics and stratagems of the Church, where it is a question of raising tribute from the laity under the name of tithe, or tithe rent-charge. In these and a few other matters, we have not shaken off our mediæval predilections.

The Fishmongers hold further charters of 1 Mary (May 18, 1553), 1 Elizabeth (October 6, 1559), and 11 Elizabeth (November 20, 1569), reciting and confirming the prior grants. But in 2 James I., August 30, 1604, the Company was re-incorporated with a governing body of six Wardens and twenty-eight Assistants, on which the power was conferred of making ordinances for the guidance and control of the members of the mistery, and the management of its affairs in London, Southwark, and the suburbs and liberties thereof, with the right of search over all fresh and salted fish, and seizing such as was unwholesome or illegally taken.[1]

---

[1] In a test-case, which was heard at the Mansion House, October 1, 1891, and in which the Company prosecuted, Mr. Alderman Phillips ruled that oysters taken from the waters of a foreign State and placed for a time in English waters could not be sold during the close season in England. He held that the saving words, " taken

This and a second grant of 4 James I. also dealt with the question of indemnification for all acts previously committed or done, and acknowledged the title of the Company to all its lands, tenements, etc., as secured by the instrument of 4 Edward VI.

The *Quo Warranto* issued against the City Gilds by the Government of Charles II. in 1684 of course touched this Company, which, however, succeeded in obtaining a second re-incorporation (January 14, 1685). All the proceedings under the writ of 1684 were annulled by the Act 2 William and Mary, c. 8 (1690), and the Company suffered no further molestation. Yet in 1815, 55 George III., it thought fit to apply for an *inspeximus*, which was conceded under writ of privy seal.

The Fishmongers shared with a limited number of the Gilds the dubious honour of being requested by James I. to assist him in settling the Ulster Plantation. The matter occupied some years before it was finally arranged, in 1617–18, when the present Company took over from the Irish Society, to which the whole territory had been assigned by the Crown, a Fishmongers' manor, which was productive of the same kind of unfavourable experience as those forced on the other Companies, generally held by them at great loss and small profit, and eventually, whenever the fortunate opportunity offered, sold. The Fishmongers admitted five other Gilds as sub-sharers.

The returns made in 1882 to the Royal Commission of 1880 are in this case remarkably copious and exhaustive, and present a view of the Fishmongers' extensive charities and educational endowments. It is understood that the current figures (1891) are approximately similar.

Herbert supplies a good deal of information respecting the successive Ordinances framed by the government of the Company for observance, agreeably to the powers conferred in the charters. But it may be necessary to repeat that the Fishmongers have a Prime Warden and five others, who, with the Assistants, constitute the Court. As regards the statement of the writer quoted, that they have never had a Master, the fact is, that the officer so called is no more in any instance than the Master or Prime Warden.

A still more interesting point is quoted by Herbert, where he, in relation to the loss of the Fishmongers' earlier records in the Fire of 1666, derives from the Goldsmiths' archives the singular piece of information that that Fraternity and the Fishmongers, in token of the amity between them, yearly exchanged with each other at one time eight newly-made suits and hoods, and wore the same respectively.

---

within the waters of some foreign State," applied only to oysters intended for immediate consumption, and that a "term of residence" made the oyster British. He therefore imposed a nominal penalty.

It appears that they formerly had their livery renewed, in part or wholly, every year, on the Feast of SS. Peter and Paul, and kept it two years, but in no case were at liberty to part with the old suits, either to their apprentices or to strangers.

Old Fishmongers' Hall, before the Fire, occupied an oblong plot of ground in Thames Street, which had been the site of four or five tenements, and on which was subsequently erected the mansion of Sir John Cornwall, Lord Fanhope.   This building was given by him to the Company in the reign of Henry VI., when, long prior to the ultimate

PLAN OF OLD FISHMONGERS' HALL AND ITS ENVIRONS.

union with the other Fraternity in 1536, the two for general purposes already acted in harmony.   In 19 Henry VII., five years before the ratification by the Crown, the two bodies were practically united, and used one Hall.

The area of Lord Fanhope's premises was 120 feet frontage to Thames Street by 200 feet of depth toward the river.   At the period when John, afterward Sir John, Lovekyn removed thither, in the reign of Edward III., the place was little more than an open strand on the river bank. Lovekyn, who was a Stock-fish Monger, held this land in free burgage ; and through failure of issue it descended after his death to one of his executors, the famous Sir William Walworth, and was subsequently purchased by Lord Fanhope, from whom it was conveyed through trustees in 1435 to the Fishmongers, who about this time acquired some of the adjoining properties. But it was not till several years later that Fanhope's house was adopted as a Hall. The premises were subject to an annual rent of 40 marks, equal to about 45s., presumably for the support of a chantry, since, on the suppression of these establishments, the Company commuted the payment, and made the place freehold.

The Company, then, in 1502, eventually agreed to settle at Fishmongers' Hall, Fanhope's former dwelling, and the other Halls were let out to several tenants, though subsequently taken back from time to time, and added to the original structure. All the arrangements were not finished, it is supposed, till 1513, when the pile assumed the aspect of a large square block of masonry, with turrets at the angles and

FISHMONGERS' HALL ABOUT 1650.

a central gateway facing the river. It must have gradually absorbed several of the minor tenements which once abutted on it at different points.

But alterations seem to have been introduced when Hollar engraved his view of the Hall about 1647, unless it is that the earlier plans by Agas and Hogenberg are inaccurate in detail. For here we perceive a partition of the court-yard by a refectory running across the quadrangle. The river front, which probably lay back some forty feet from the bank, is plain, and consists of two projecting wings, and a centre with a balconied first-floor, two rows of windows, and a lofty octagonal domed tower rising above the roof. There is a terrace between the building and the river, reached by an arched doorway.

Jarman's Hall stood more forward than the present one, and was on the site of the northern foot of the bridge. In the interior, the various

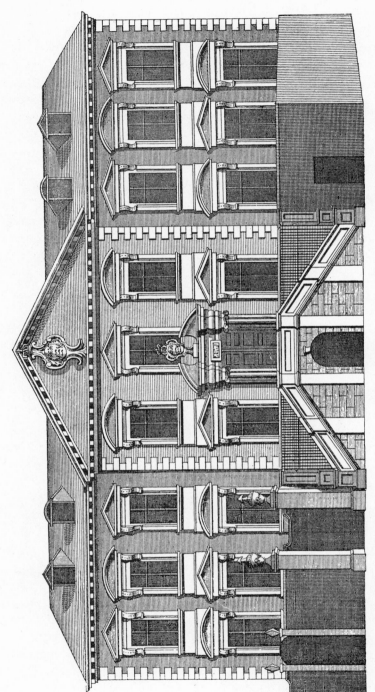

FISHMONGERS' HALL IN 1739.

portions of the structure enclosed a square paved court ; the dining apartment, which, as we are to see, was ordered to exceed that in the original room in dimensions, lay on the south side ; the court and withdrawing rooms on the east, and the business premises on the west. The dining-hall had a Grecian screen, a gallery, and a statue of Sir William Walworth by Pierce. The walls of the reception chambers were decorated with emblematical representations of fish, and other paintings.

The present Hall is a modern erection, and, like that of the Goldsmiths, is chiefly remarkable for its splendour. It has of course no historical interest.

A long roll of excellent and philanthropic personages, including many Mayors, especially Sir John Lovekyn and Sir William Walworth, can be shown by this Gild, which played its part in the series of pageants by land and water which usually signalized the installation of each chief magistrate. These commenced centuries before any separate description of them was or could be published. The earliest with which the Fishmongers were directly identified, was the ceremony at the admission of John Allot in 1590 as Mayor of London and of the Staple ; and in the printed account by Thomas Nelson there is a curious reference to the scarcity and dearness of fish at that point of time. The Company did not return its second Mayor till 1616.

The Gilds, as we know, participated in other festivities and inaugural occasions besides the Lord Mayor's initiation ; and Cheapside witnessed a constant succession of spectacles, which, from the habit of going on horseback, gained the name of *Ridings*. Chaucer depicts the apprentices neglecting their employers' affairs, and running to the doors to gape at these cavalcades.

There is nothing particular to record under this head till the Great Fire came, and in a neighbourhood which abounded in combustibles, oil, pitch, tar, hemp, flax, cordage, wines, spirits, reduced everything speedily to a wreck. The Hall was not very far westward from Pudding Lane, and the flames crossed the bridge-end by St. Magnus, and enveloped the whole precincts. The Hall itself, with its high roof and turret, was left a shell. Only the stone part of the Oyster or Water Gate escaped.

The governing body met, under these circumstances, at Bethlehem Hospital, and Jarman was employed to construct a new Hall. On the 30th July, 1667, 200,000 bricks, 4,000 deals, 40 standards, and 100 putlogs were ordered as a commencement. It was decided to enlarge the proportions of the refectory to thirty-three feet wide by sixty-six feet deep. On April 8, 1668–9 the ground-plan was deposited at Guildhall. On

November 11 it was resolved by the Court that the Clerk's office should be finished first of all. Between December, 1669, and June, 1671, the work was completed ; but in the former month the Court began to sit in the new quarters, perhaps in the Clerk's room.

The government of the Company has been already stated to consist of a Prime or Master Warden, five other Wardens, and twenty-eight Assistants, who form the Court. But there is a practice of referring matters of special business or inquiry to a series of standing committees, viz. :—

The Committee of Wardens.
      ,,   for General Purposes.
      ,,   ,, Accounts.
      ,,   ,, Audits.
      ,,   ,, Irish Estate.
      ,,   ,, Wine.

In addition to which there is a sub-Irish Committee. The Committee of Wardens is composed of the whole body of six. That for General Purposes includes the Wardens and the six senior Assistants. The Account Committee has seven members, one of which is the Prime Warden. The Audit Committee consists of the Prime and Renter Wardens, the past Prime and Renter Wardens, and one Assistant, who has served or fined as Prime Warden. Twelve members, of whom five must have visited the estate, constitute the Irish Committee, namely, the Prime and second Wardens, and ten others, Wardens or Assistants ; and the sub-committee is a selection of those persons from the larger body. The Wine Committee is formed of the Renter Warden and four others, Wardens or Assistants.

The bye-laws of the Company at present in force appear to be those of 1843 and 1860, founded on those of 1668. The most ancient code is that of 35 Edward III.

Of the pageant for 1616 the Company possesses the original drawings made for the order of procession and the costumes, and reproduced them in a folio volume several years ago with a descriptive text. In one of the apartments at the Hall are two excellent paintings in oil by Scott, of London and Westminster Bridges, as they appeared about the middle of the last century. The statue of Walworth in wood, which stood in Jarman's Hall, is still preserved on the staircase : there is also an ancient pall, reputed to have once covered his bier, and the identical dagger with which he stabbed Wat the Tyler. The last-named relic has been in the possession of the Fishmongers ever since that time, and is probably another small salvage from the flames in 1666. It is of plain and coarse fabric, without a sheath, and with only a portion of the ancient wire covering to the wooden handle remaining.[1]

A very curious account of the Wat Tyler episode, differing from that usually received, may be found in *A Chronicle of London*, 1089- 1483, 4°, 1827, p. 73, and the text of Sir William Walworth's will, dated 20 December, 1385, is given *in extenso* in *Excerpta Historica*, 1833, p. 134 *et seqq.* The instrument breathes a spirit of piety and benevolence, and no one is forgotten. The spiritual welfare of Sir John Lovekyn, once master of the testator is particularly safeguarded by provision of masses and prayers for his soul. There are large bequests of money, plate, and MS. books. His widow, his chaplain, the Bishop of Winchester, and another, are appointed his executors. He left the bishop 40*l.* for his trouble.

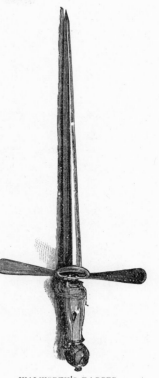

Among the MSS. bequeathed occur *Vitæ Patrum, Rationale Divinorum Officiorum, Legenda Sanctorum*, a Psalter, the Epistles of St. Paul, with a gloss, and others of a similar character.

WALWORTH'S DAGGER.

With the Bishop of Winchester Walworth had been brought into relationship as the farmer of the Stews in Southwark, which formed part of his lordship's estate.

This Company, in its present state of disconnection from the branch of commerce which it at first and long pursued and controlled, and in its substituted function and rank as a benevolent and charitable community, tells the common story of these unions, composed of men who grew wealthy according to the prevailing standard, and by the fortunate purchase of town and other sites, of which they could not have foreseen the prodigious advance in pecuniary value, laid the basis of noble estates, and made possible a complete revolution on the part of their beneficiaries in character and policy. At the same time, a certain representative proportion of the Fishmongers yet belongs to the trade ; while, as we have

---

[1] The inscription round the glass case in which the dagger lies runs as follows : "With this dagger Sir William Walworth, Lord Mayor of London, Citizen and Fishmonger, slew the rebel, Watt Tyler, in Smithfield. Anno Domini 1381.

remarked, the governing body occasionally intervenes for the public protection in regard to irregularities committed.

Herbert has collected peculiarly ample notices of the eleemosynary trusts and other charitable foundations of the Company, and these are, again, very fully set forth, with all the statistics at large, in the Returns made to the Royal Commission of 1880.

LITERARY NOTICES.

A Dietarie. Writtes published after the ordinance of Earles and Barons. Anno Domini 1315. A broadside. [Mary.]

*** Extracts from Laws and Ordinances, from 1315 to 1555, respecting the flesh and fish diet allowable to certain classes.

A Proclamation set forth by the Kynges Maiestie with the aduise of his highnes moste honorable counsaill, the ix. day of Marche, in the fifth yere of his highnes most prosperous reigne, forbidding the eating of flesh in the time of Lent. A broadside. [1552.]

A Briefe Note of the benefits that growe to this Realme by the Obseruation of Fish-daies. By Edward Jennings. 4to, 1593.

A True Narrative of the Royall Fishings of Great Britaine and Ireland. Instituted Anno 1632. By Simon Smith, Agent. 4to, 1641.

The Herring-Bvsse Trade : Expressed in Svndry Particulars, both for the Building of Busses, . . . By the same. 4to, 1641.

London's Blame, if not its Shame : Manifested by the great neglect of the Fishery. 4to, 1651.

A Proclamation for restraint of Killing, Dressing, and Eating of Flesh in Lent, or on Fish-days, appointed by the Law to be observed. 1660. A broadside.

Icthyothera, or, The Royal Trade of Fishing. Discovering the inestimable profit the Hollanders have made thereof, with the vast Emolument and Advantages that will redound to his Sacred Majesty, and his three Kingdomes by the improvement of it. 4to, 1662.

The Trade and Fishing of Great Britain Displayed. By Captain Iohn Smith. 4to, 1662.

The Royal Fishing Revived. By the same. 4to, 1670.

A Plea for the bringing in of Irish cattel . . . Together with an Humble Address to the Honourable Members of Parliament of the Counties of Cornwal and Devon, about the advancement of Tin, Fishery, and divers Manufactures. By John Collins, Accomptant to the Royal Fishery Company. 4to, 1680.

Salt and Fishery. A Discourse thereof, Insisting on the following Heads : 1. The several ways of making Salt in England and Foreign Parts. . . . By John Collins. 4to, 1862.

The only Design of the Company of Fishermen. By the Bill depending in the Honourable House of Commons, as far as relates to themselves. A broadside. [About 1690.]

A Collection of Advertisements, Advices, and Directions, Relating to the Royal Fishery within the British Seas. 4to, 1695.

Reasons Humbly Offered for passing the Bill for preventing the Importation of Fresh Fish caught by Foreigners, and the Preservation of the Brood and Fry of Fish. A broadside.

Reasons of several Owners of Fishing-Vessels, Humbly Offer'd against a Clause proposed by some Fishmongers, to repeal the Law now in Force, prohibiting Lobsters being Imported by Foreigners. A broadside.

An Answer to the Allegations of the Fishmongers, in their Paper, intitled, Reasons humbly Offered for passing the Bill for preventing the Importation of Fresh Fish caught by Foreigners. A broadside. [About 1700.]

Remarks Humbly Offer'd by some of the Fishmongers in Answer to the other part of the Fishmongers' Reasons for repealing that part of the Billingsgate Act which relates to the prohibiting Lobsters being caught by Foreigners. A broadside.

Farther Reasons Humbly Offer'd for passing the Fish Bill. A broadside.

The Case of the Coasting Fishermen of the Kingdom of Great Britain. A broadside.

An Answer to the same. A broadside.

A Brief Detail of the Home Fishery from early time ; particularly as relates to the Markets of London and Westminster. In Three Letters. 8vo, 1763.

The Booke called The Mirrour of Justices : Made by Andrew Horne. With the Book called, The Diversity of Courts. . . . 8vo, 1646.

*** Andrew Horne was City Chamberlain and Fishmonger. Ob. 1328. This work by him was written in French, of which the present was an English translation. He was also the compiler of the *Liber Horn*, edited by Mr. Riley.

New England's Trials. Declaring the Successe of twenty-six Ships employed thither within these sixe yeares. By Captain John Smith. 4to, 1620. Dedicated to the Master, Wardens, and Company of the Fishmongers.

CIVIC PAGEANTS, ETC.

The Device of the Pageant : set forth by the Worshipful Company of the Fishmongers for the right honorable John Allot, established Lord Mayor of London, and Mayor of the Staple . . ., 1590 : By T. Nelson. 4to, 1590.
Reprinted entire in the *Antiquary*, xiii. 54–56.

Chrysanaleia : The Golden Fishing : Or, Honour of Fishmongers. Applauding the Advancement of Mr. John Leman, Alderman, to the Dignity of Lord Mayor of London. Taking his Oath in the same Authority at Westminster on Monday, being the 29 Day of October, 1616. Performed in hearty love to him, and at the Charges of his worthy Brethren, the ancient and Right-worshipful Company of Fishmongers. Devised and written by A[nthony] M[unday], Citizen and Draper of London. 4to, 1616.

A Speech Made to His Excellency the Lord General Monck, and the Council of State at Fishmongers' Hall in London the Thirteenth of April, 1660. Written by Tho. Jordan . . . Spoken by Master Yeokney. 1660. A broadside.

The Triumphs of London, for the Inauguration of the Right Honourable Sir Thomas Abney, Knt., Lord Mayor of the City of London ; containing a Description of the Pageants, together with the Publick Speeches, and the whole Solemnity of the Day. Performed on Tuesday, the 30th day of October, Anno 1700. All set forth at the proper cost of the Honourable Company of Fishmongers. By Elkanah Settle. Folio, 1700.

The Goldsmiths.

THIS ancient, important, and wealthy body first comes under notice in 1180, as one of the so-called "adulterine" Associations, which had been founded, and had assumed certain rights, without the royal licence; it was amerced 45 marks, a comparatively high assessment; but there is room to suspect that the fine in this and other similar cases, amounting in the aggregate to about 120*l.*, was never paid, as the above-named sum is entered in the records as a debt so late as the 10th year of John. The Alderman of the Goldsmiths in 1180 was Radulph or Ralph Flael.

The next appearance of the *Gilda Aurifabrorum* is under even less satisfactory circumstances, as it connects them in March 1267–8,[1] with the Merchant-Taylors in an armed affray at night between the two Fraternities in the open street. The rioters were not parted or pacified without the forcible interference of the Sheriffs at the head of a *posse comitatus*, when many arrests took place, and thirteen of the delinquents were executed. In 1299–1300 (28 Edward I.) the Wardens of the Goldsmiths are mentioned.

But since all leading members of a mistery were in former days constituent parts of a Brotherhood, we have only to conclude from the almost immemorial citation of the industry and manufacture and of eminent followers of the business from Anglo-Saxon times, whatever may be the origin of some of the specimens of antique work in our collections, that the present Company existed long before any record of it in its corporate capacity.

Two points combine in testifying to its rank and resources in 1180: the heavy amount of the fine imposed for unlawful acts, and the lofty position of its Alderman, Ralph Flael, who, like the Alderman of the

---

[1] Herbert says, in 1226.

Burillers elsewhere cited and (to some extent) the Alderman of Faringdon Ward, under the primitive civic *régime*, was practically the lord in
demesne *ex officio* of the Ward of Aldersgate, in which the members of
the Goldsmiths' craft concentrated themselves. Their quarter, except
so far as the retailer was concerned, was then, as their Hall is at the
present moment, in the precincts of Foster Lane, and they principally
inhabited the eastern side of that narrow thoroughfare, which derived
from them the name of Goldsmiths' Row. The district is, in proceedings under the year 1339, called the Goldsmithery or *Aurifabria*, as
we shall observe hereafter that the Saddlers' contiguous quarters were
named *the Saddlery ;* and a man was hanged there in that year for steal-
ing a cup, apparently of glass, value 8*s.*

OLD ARMS.

Returning to the case of Farringdon Ward, this division or soke was
bought in 1279 by William Farringdon, Goldsmith, was held by him
and his heirs by the presentation of a gilliflower at Easter, and remained
in that family eighty years. This strikes one as being a somewhat
different matter from the assumption of independent authority within
the precincts of the soke or ward by Ralph Flael and by the Alderman
of the Burillers, which arose from the quasi-feudal localization of their
trades and their command of paramount influence over the respective
Fraternities. It was a life-tenure, whereas that of Faringdon was of a
more directly seigniorial complexion, being unconnected with his own
Gild, and surviving him.

We shall not be far in error, if we assume from a comparison of authorities and notices, that the Goldsmiths, like the Weavers, continued to be an unincorporated community during several centuries, and were unexceptionally members of the trade ; saving perhaps the official staff, although we find even the Chaplain in some instances admitted to the Freedom.

In 1275, Gregory de Rokesley, Goldsmith, was chief Assay-master of the king's Mint and keeper of the Exchange [1] at London ; and it was only three years posterior to this date that the relationship to these institutions proved fatal to many members of the craft ; for in the *Chronicle of London*, 4to, 1827, under 1278, we read that " all the Gold-smiths of London, and all those that kept the Change, and many other men of the City, were arrested and taken for buying of plates of silver and of change of great money for small, and were indicted therefor, and that on the Monday next after the Epiphany a large number of the offenders, principally Jews, were condemned at Guildhall to death by drowning and hanging."

The Goldsmiths in the reign of Edward I. (1272-1307) had clearly attained great consequence and extensive custom, and reckoned among their patrons royalty itself.   In 1303, Thomas de Frowick, afterward a Warden of the Gild, received an order under the Great Seal to make a new crown for Edward's second Queen, having previously supplied the King with divers silver cups and vases.   It was perhaps no unusual circumstance, that the merchant met with serious delay in getting his bill satisfied ; and the character of the transactions which these traders had with exalted personages, may be judged from the fact that Frowick, in praying the King, for God's sake and for the soul of his father Henry, to settle the demand, proposed to accept 440*l*. on account, if necessary.

The statute 28 Edward I. originally vested the right of assay in the Company, and directed that no vessels of gold or silver should leave the maker's hands, till they had been tested by the Wardens, and stamped with the leopard's head ; and in consequence of this law, an Office of Assay was established in the beginning of the fourteenth century.   But it may be supposed that it was not universally operative or effectual ; and as late as 1505 it required heavier penalties to enforce the law.

The taste or need of the Crown for costly articles of goldsmith's work, and the, no doubt, chronic incidence of procrastination in honouring accounts delivered, placed the Gild at all events in an unusually favour-able position for seeking a more distinct acknowledgment of its rights. The earliest of a series of fifteen charters was granted to it in 1327, a

---

[1] The present Old Change marks the site.

year marked by the number of similar concessions made to these civic communities, but still more so by the magnificent display which Richard de Bettoyne, Goldsmith, made as Mayor of London at the coronation of Edward. In his official capacity he claimed and was allowed to serve the office of Butler, and appeared with 360 valets all clothed in the same livery, and each carrying in his hand a silver cup ; and at the conclusion of the ceremony, as his fee, he received a gold cup and cover and an enamelled gold ewer. There was a dispute, it seems, about the title to these articles, and ten years later an estreat for 89*l.* 12*s.* 6*d.* in respect of them issued from the Exchequer on the late Mayor's goods. He was evidently a wealthy man, as he offered to satisfy the claim if enforced.

This person was perhaps related to William de Bettoyne, to whom the Court of Aldermen in 1291 granted the lease of the Small Beam for weighing silk and spices, and declined to cancel the decision on receiving the King's writ, recommending some one else. But in 1310, on a fresh vacancy, the City elected the royal candidate, who was supported by letters both from the King and the Queen.

The patent of 1327 empowered the Gild to elect a properly qualified governing body to superintend its affairs, and reform subjects of just complaint ; and prescribed, as a safeguard against a prevailing fraud and abuse, that all members of the trade should have their standings in Cheapside or in the King's Exchange, and that no gold or silver should be manufactured for export, save such as had been bought either in the Exchange or of the trade openly. For it transpires that it had been a common practice to purchase gold and silver in the bye-streets and other obscure places without inquiry, and forthwith to melt the whole down, and convert the metal into falsely-wrought objects of sale for the foreign market.

Two other patents of the same reign are confirmatory, but add a licence in mortmain to the value of 20*l.* a year for the relief of poor or infirm brethren. In 16 Richard II. (1393) a fourth instrument sanctions a Chaplain to perform daily mass for the faithful departed, confirms the Gild as a perpetual Society, and fixes the number of Wardens at four. The charters of Henry IV. and Henry VI. are *inspeximus.* But Edward IV. in his second year (1462–3), besides allowing the acts of his predecessors, conferred on the Goldsmiths a common seal, with the power of pleading and being impleaded under the name of the Wardens and Commonalty of the Mistery of Goldsmiths of the City of London, of making bye-laws, and of exercising search and oversight of goldsmiths' work throughout the kingdom.

A corroboration of their privileges and power was obtained 20

Henry VII. (1504–5), when the Company, having represented the insufficiency of the present right of search, the King vested in them the faculty of fining and imprisoning at their discretion all defaulters in the trade, of seizing, condemning and breaking unlawful work without rendering account to the Crown, and of compelling makers to bring all articles to the common Hall to be assayed and stamped, before they could be sold, which last requirement had been nominally in force since the 28 Edward I.

This charter was, from a commercial point of view, the most valuable yet accorded to the Goldsmiths, as it placed them on the footing which they till recently continued to enjoy. Its terms were ratified by *inspeximus* patents of all the sovereigns down to William and Mary. James II. reserved to himself the nomination of the Wardens and Clerk ; but this claim was annulled by his immediate successors.

There was a peculiar circumstance associated with the renewal of the charter by Henry VIII., which was accomplished to a large extent through the instrumentality of a member of the Court, Sir Martin Bowes, who had pointed out to his brethren that the then existing charters incorporated them merely as the Four Wardens and Commonalty of the Mistery, and an additional inducement was perhaps to endeavour to assure to themselves their chantry funds and other fiduciary property. Bowes seems to have shown great zeal in the matter, and frequently saw the Lord Chancellor upon it, before it was finally settled. For it appears that while the negotiation was pending, Henry conceived the idea of using the proposal as a leverage for obtaining money ; and on the plea that the applicants had been guilty of misdemeanours in regard to the Assay, refused to grant their prayer, unless they paid a fine of 3000 marks and defrayed the expenses of the Assay Office.

The Company not only submitted, but consented to regard their governing body as acting on behalf of the King, and to admit two Assayers, a Haberdasher and a Grocer, nominated by the Crown.

The expenses of confirming their charter on this occasion seem to have amounted to 9*l.* 12*s.* 8*d.*, of which 2*l.* was a fine to the King, 2*l.* the cost of the writing and confirmation, and 1*l.* 6*s.* 8*d.* of the enrolment. The green wax and silken lace are entered in the account at 2*s.*

In common with several of the Companies, the Goldsmiths regained 4 Edward VI. by purchase all the bequests made to them, prior to the Dissolution, of properties to be held to superstitious uses, and forfeited to the Crown, which through intermediary grantees reconveyed them to their owners. In the present case, twenty-four separate benefactions of great present value were involved ; and by the process of recovery in the ordinary way of purchase the property naturally changed its nature from fiduciary to corporate or private estate.

But the Company had had the mortification some time previously,—under the inquisition for destroying or defacing all superstitious and idolatrous objects,—of melting down two of their principal pieces of plate, adorned with images of St. Dunstan. Of these one appears to have been a sort of statuette, which was kept in one of the rooms of the Hall.

These proceedings were followed by a declaratory (private) Act of James I., by which certain doubts were set at rest as to whether the properties just referred to, or only the rents therefrom, belonged to the Company ; nor did this entirely dispose of the difficulty ; for it was subsequently discovered that the Goldsmiths were entitled to more than they had claimed, namely, 379 houses and tenements in the City of London ; and after a negotiation with the agents of the Crown the whole was finally confirmed to the Company by an exemplification under the Great Seal in 1619.

The Company exercised its former rights under a succession of Acts of Parliament from the reign of Henry VI. to that of Victoria, but chiefly under 12 George II. (1739), cap. 26, and 7 & 8 Victoria, cap. 22.

The Ordinances passed in the fifth year of Henry VIII. seem to be the earliest regular code extant. At that period the Company was in full working order and in the plenitude of its power and prosperity.

They provided for the election of the Prime and three other Wardens a month before St. Dunstan's Day [1] and for the winding-up of the accounts by the retiring officers ; for the yearly reading of the said Ordinances on St. Dunstan's Day and for the keeping of that day ; for due respect to the Wardens and to each other ; for the exercise of the right of search by the Wardens in divers cities, boroughs, and fairs ; for the use of Troy weight and the prohibition of the employment of bad gold and silver ; for the assay and stamping of goods ; for the regulation of apprentices ; for the exaction of testimonials or sureties from stranger workmen and shop-keepers.

There were also clauses to guard against the use of laten except for tools, against the gold-beater beating fine gold, and to enforce an uniformity of assize in all moulds of gold and silver.

The necessity for the right of search and the presentation of delinquents is exemplified by the occurrence of cases of fraud of every description, even embracing the manufacture of counterfeit jewellery within the precincts of St. Bartholomew's Priory. The particulars of

---

[1] Formerly the day of election ; but in 1550 it was changed to Holy Trinity Monday.

the visit of the Goldsmiths' Wardens on the 20th April, 20 Henry VI., to the Prior, and of their seizure in his presence, on the premises of John Tompkins in the Close, of copper plated with silver and of pieces of laten, one of which v.:s in the bed-straw, intended for conversion into goblets, are still preserved ; and the account concludes with narrating how at last " the false harlot stole away out of the place, or else he had been set in the stocks."

The extension of the industry and those engaged in it beyond the original narrow limits of Foster Lane and its immediate neighbourhood was bound to afford facilities for deception and roguery, even in the presence of increased vigilance and more stringent regulations ; and as the Wardens probably had fixed periods for making their rounds of inspection, nothing but an accidental discovery or special intelligence was, as a rule, likely to be effectual in bringing fraudulent practices to light and punishment.

This point is abundantly illustrated by the usage which seems to have prevailed of attending Bartholomew and Sturbridge fairs in solemn state, so that the " mis-worker" had an ample opportunity of preparing for his visitors. The Wardens, we perceive, went to these fairs in the daytime or the evening in their livery gowns and hoods, accompanied by two of the Clothing or Livery, the Renters, the Clerk and the Beadle. The only detective machinery was the clue furnished by an informer or by some chance. It was a period when greater stress was laid on oaths and sureties than at present. In 1468-9 a suit in Chancery was instituted for the recovery of a false diamond set in gold; and considerable trouble and expense were incurred in the matter. The individual charges were moderate enough ; a petition or "bill" to the Lord Chancellor is set down at 2s. But a good deal in this and other cases went in boat-hire and refreshments.

So far as the foreign members of the Craft were concerned, the Company could of course do nothing beyond the requisition for a testimonial from the authorities of the locality whence they came, unless they had been sufficiently long in residence in London to gain a footing and a character.

We have mentioned the power of Assay and the early institution of an Assay Office, which was eventually established within the Hall. There was at first one Assayer ; but subsequently three were employed. By the 7 & 8 Victoria, the Company was debarred from making any profit on the operation or on the stamping process, and were entitled to charge only the actual cost ; and the system has since fallen altogether into disuse as a compulsory observance.

Connected with the Assay was the ceremony known as the Trial of the Pix, which was, in point of fact, the assay of a new coinage. The practice is, and has been from time out of mind, for the Lord Chancellor to issue a precept to the Company to form a jury of the Assay-master and eleven other persons. These assemble in the court-room of the Duchy of Lancaster, where the coins to be tested are delivered to them by officers of the Mint in the pix, a small box so denominated. The indenture, under which the Master of the Mint acts, is first read ; the pix is then opened, and the coins are taken out and enclosed in paper parcels, each under the seal of the Wardens, Master, and Comptrollers. From each 15 lbs. of silver, or *journies*, two pieces at least are taken at random for the trial ; and each parcel having then been opened, and the contents found to answer to the endorsement, the coins are mixed together in wooden bowls, and afterward weighed. From the whole collection the jury takes a certain number of each kind of coin, to the aggregate weight of 1 lb., for the assay by fire ; and, the indented trial-pieces of gold and silver of the specified dates having been produced by the officer appointed, a sufficient quantity is cut from each of them to enable a comparison with the pound weight of either metal. The result is certified by the jury in a written verdict to the Lord Chancellor for preservation among the archives of the Privy Council. If the weights are found good, the Master of the Mint receives his *Quietus*, or discharge.

The trial by fire is carried out by the deposit of a small quantity of the silver in the fire by the Assayer, who at the end of a fixed time takes it out again, and with his scales, which are adjusted to the hundredth part of a grain, computes and reports the quality of the metal.

The Company appears to have incurred considerable loss by the obligation incurred by it under statutes of conducting the Assay and maintaining an office and staff for the purpose, as all the functionaries were necessarily skilled and confidential.

The business of finance and exchange was always one in which the foreign element made itself more than usually conspicuous and influential. We know at how remote a date the so-called Lombards settled in London ; but not merely Italian merchants, bankers, brokers, money-lenders, became numerous and found a profitable market in a city which from the outset was essentially cosmopolitan, but Germans, Venetians, Netherlanders, Spaniards, Frenchmen, naturally and instinctively gravitated to a centre where money was realizable in such a multiplicity of ways. The Goldsmiths, who to some extent succeeded the Pepperers as financial agents, were peculiarly apt to experience an early and increasing intermixture of blood in the composition of their ranks ; and the foreigners, who were generally willing, or at least were required, to pay rather liberally for their freedom, largely contributed to improve our taste and the style of the work produced in England.

One passage in the accounts relative to the custom of taking security for pecuniary advances, notices the appropriation of certain plate left in pawn, where it had remained with the Wardens a certain space of time and no one claimed it.

The extension of the employment of goldsmiths to plating or harnessing the inferior metal is recorded as early as 1376. It was an art of great antiquity ; but it involved this craft in great and constant trouble, as the plating process was frequently made a vehicle for the fraudulent sale of copper-gilt and other false wares for the real article, and the workmen even fabricated the mark. It was also not an unknown device to gild silver and set the gold stamp upon it.

In connection with the composite character gradually assumed by the Company, and the large influx of foreign goldsmiths or craftsmen into London, we have to take cognisance of a singular trial of skill or competition in 4 Edward IV. between the goldsmiths of London on the one part and the alien workmen of the same City, of Westminster and of Southwark on the other. The contest arose from a contention by one Whit Johnson, a foreigner, with Oliver Davy, a London goldsmith, that the English were less proficient in the art than the strangers ; and the wager was laid between the parties before a mixed jury at the Pope's Head tavern in Cornhill, on the 21st November in the aforesaid year. The task assigned was the making, working, and graving by an English operative or apprentice, and by an alien operative or apprentice (the latter to be of any foreign nationality), of a cat's face and a naked man, both inward and outward, with four puncheons on two plates of steel of the size of a penny sterling ; and the native work was adjudged, by great deliberation, good avisement, and sad oversight of the said puncheons on the part of the jurors, to be the better and more cunningly wrought. The puncheons were ordered to remain at Goldsmiths' Hall in perpetuity, as a record and for reference, in case any such debate should again arise.

For retail purposes, the goldsmiths of London spread themselves at an early period over the whole area between St. Paul's, or even further westward, and Lombard Street or Cornhill. But the manufacturers probably remained in the old quarter near St. Vedast Foster Church, where, in the neighbourhood of the modern Hall, Goldsmiths' Alley and Silver Street still indicate the ancient industrial site. It is curious that, in his *Relation of England*, about 1500, an Italian of rank speaks of the numerous goldsmiths' shops in the Strand ; he specifies 52 ; and he tells us that they were so rich and full of silver vessels, great and small, that in all the shops of Venice, Milan, Rome, and Florence put together, there were not so many.

But from a remote date we meet with other trades in this immediate locality, namely the printing establishments of John Scot and John Waley, in the reigns of Henry VIII. and his successors; and in 1622 and later, the shop of John Bartlet, at the Gilt Cup, bookseller, whose sign, however, implies a recollection of the vicinity or of the abandoned premises of a member of the goldsmiths' craft. *The Three Gilt Cups* was another stationer's sign. During many years, Charles Hoole, a well-known teacher and writer of educational works, kept a private grammar school in Goldsmith's Alley. We find him there in 1649.

In 1629 a movement first arose for making Cheapside, Lombard Street, and the immediate vicinity the exclusive seat of the goldsmiths' and other sumptuous shops. His Majesty had noticed certain mean houses interspersed among the rest, and an Order in Council directed the attention of the City to the matter. His Majesty's eye was offended by the spectacle. Yet some time elapsed before the reform took effect ; and even then the authorities had to reckon with those who had been dispossessed and were aggrieved by the increasing difficulty of securing accommodation at a reasonable rent. The Government of Charles I. acted in a characteristically arbitrary manner by threatening the Corporation with penal consequences if all the shops in the quarter were not let to goldsmiths and the like, or closed till suitable tenants presented themselves.

The Goldsmiths participated in the characteristics common to all these Fraternities dependent on internal resources and action for the support of their poor and the maintenance of religious observances. They had a chapel dedicated to St. Dunstan, their patron saint, in St. Paul's Cathedral near at hand. It was at St. Dunstan's in the East that the brethren and sisters, with their wax lights in their hands, attended the obits of those whom they had lost, and who had left funds for the purpose ; and on St. Dunstan's Day the general yearly feast was long held. Even in 1367 it cost over 21*l.*, when the corporate revenue must have been very inconsiderable.

The accounts and other records of the Company extend from 5 Edward III. to the present time, and include plans of the estates and of the old Hall.

In 1335, when the Wardens' accounts open, the body and its revenue were equally insignificant, although it counted among its members individuals who were prosperous and wealthy. There were then only 14 apprentices, whose fees were 28*s.* ; and the corporate income mainly

depended on subscriptions and fines.   The beginning of the following
century witnessed a marked progression, and we see the Gild taking a
part in public affairs, receiving special attention from Royalty, and contributing a liberal quota to current emergencies.   It found 34*l*. 19*s*. o*d*.
in 1451 for two spearmen and 12 archers fully equipped for the army
sent over to the siege of Calais.

In 1477 the members of the Company had greatly increased, and
amounted to 198, including 41 foreigners, who are returned as residing
in Westminster and Southwark as well as in St. Clement's Lane,
Abchurch Lane, Brick Lane, and Bearbinder Lane, in the City itself.
But in 1483 the total had shrunk to 149.

The Goldsmiths, like the Mercers, have always remained a relatively
small Company.   The Livery is now limited to 150, exclusive of the
Court of Assistants of 21 members, and the Prime and other Wardens,
making a total of 175 only.

In 1537, the numbers are given as 52 in a paper printed by Herbert from the original then in the Chapter House.   But in 1540, when
Anne of Cleves entered London, the Company took a prominent
part in the procession appointed to meet her ; and the delegates are
described as riding in black velvet coats, with gold chains round their
necks, and velvet caps with gold brooches, attended by their servants
clad in coats of good russet cloth.

The entries in the accounts are too numerous to cite in a work of the
present scope, and more properly belong to a monograph.   But they
form an index to the progress, development, and fluctuations of the
Company under a succession of dynasties and domestic events, as well
as a picture of opinions, prejudices, and manners ever changing with
the times.   We there discern the strange combination of financial
frugality and humble religious fervour with splendid hospitality, sump-
tous display, and loyal offerings in aid of public objects.   There are particulars of intestine disagreement as to the jurisdiction of the Executive,
of transactions between distinguished brethren and clients desirous of
raising money on pledges, and even passages between priests and the
Gild, respecting the application of Chantry funds.

At one period scarcely any one belonged to the Company who was
not of the Craft.   Now it is the case that the connection with the trade
is purely nominal, and that the aims with which it was founded have
completely determined.   But, on the other hand, the Company has of
late years heartily responded to the always increasing demand for
money, either in the form of payments or annuities, in aid of technical
and general education, and has proved itself a good friend to a wide
circle of public institutions and objects, as well as a generous contri-

butor to the incessant appeals for the relief of sudden or unforeseen contingencies.

The fortunes of Goldsmiths' Hall have been fairly diversified and historically curious. In the days of Edward II. the site belonged to Sir Nicholas de Segrave, brother of Gilbert de Segrave, Bishop of London in 1316, both of whom were of the Segraves of Leicestershire. On the death of this personage the Company bought the premises, and a copy of the deed of sale, dated May 19, 1323, is preserved among the archives. No clue appears to exist to the date of the erection of the first Hall ; but since in 1366 we find the Company assembling in their "common place" in the parish of St. John Zachary, and in 1380 a new parlour and cellar were built, we judge it to be most probable that at the outset the Goldsmiths used the old house of Sir Nicholas de Segrave, and made certain additions to it. In 1401 the Hall in Foster Lane is explicitly cited. The conclusion that the original structure occupied by the Fraternity was the Segrave house is strengthened by the circumstance that in 1407 Sir Drue Barentyn began to carry out his scheme for refounding the Hall, or, in other words, for replacing the first building by another more suited to the requirements of a public body. It is tolerably clear, however, that Barentyn did not complete the project, as notices occur periodically, and till long afterward, of works in hand for the structure. It was evidently a place of some pretensions and extent, as we hear of the Chamber, probably a Court Room, the Hall, the Armoury, the Granary, the Assay-Office, the Vaults, the Chapel, and the Court-yard or garden, with the entrance-gate. The Hall had bay windows, that toward Huggin Lane being adorned with the armorial bearings of the Gild, and having a roof surmounted by a lantern and a vane. The process of furnishing this establishment proceeded gradually and slowly, and was mainly accomplished by donations ; but the arras, made expressly in Flanders for the Hall, and illustrating the history of St. Dunstan, was no doubt a corporate item, and cost no less than 263*l.* 6*s.* 8*d.*

Stow, writing in 1598, speaks of the Hall as "a proper house, but not large," and discredits accordingly the received tradition of Sir Bartholomew Read having entertained here in 1502 more than one hundred persons of great estate. For he says : "For the messes and dishes of meates in them serued, the paled parke in the same hall, furnished with fruitfull trees, beastes of venery, and other circumstances of that pretended feast well weighed, Westminster Hall would hardly have sufficed . . . ."

During the Civil War, the Parliamentary party made the Hall their head-quarters for meetings and their treasury. Numerous entries in the books refer to these transactions, more particularly to an unsuccess-ful attempt on the part of the Upper Chamber in 1647 to obtain the premises as part security for a sum of money then being raised for public purposes.

The building erected in and after 1407 was seriously damaged by the Great Fire ; but the Company's archives and plate escaped, and were temporarily deposited in a house at Edmonton. The plate was sub-sequently lent to Sir Robert Vyner for his use during his Shrievalty. Until the Hall was restored by Jarman, a house in Grub Street, formerly the residence of Sir Thomas Allen, Grocer, and Lord Mayor in 1659, was leased for twenty-one years at 60*l.* a year, and 100*l.* fine.

Jarman laid his ground-plan for the repairs and other works before the Court on the 17th March, 1666-7 ; but difficulties presented them-selves in the shape of periodical falls of parts of the building months subsequently to the date of the disaster ; and the whole summer passed away without seeing more than the erection of a new Assay House, which was an urgent need, and therefore specially expedited.

The Hall was not ready for occupation till 1669. The Company had been impoverished by the Fire, and was obliged to part with a portion of its plate to defray expenses, thoughtfully registering in its books the inscriptions on such pieces as had been presented by brethren in the hope of their perpetual preservation. One standing cup and cover, the gift of Robert Sherley the Elder in 1612, weighed 93½ ounces.

The structure, as it stood about this time, with Jarman's alterations and repairs, was a red brick building, encompassing a small paved quadrangle, with a broad arched doorway and a space above for the Company's Arms. The Livery Hall, on the east side of the yard, was paved with black and white marbles, finely wainscoted and stuccoed, and elegantly furnished. The Court-room was also very handsome and sumptuous, and the balustrade of the staircase was beautifully carved. It was, no doubt, in some respects less imposing than the present block of building, which is a product of the last quarter of a century ; but it was infinitely more in keeping with the old-time associations and traditions of its owners.

The Accounts enter with much minuteness into the question of the Livery or Clothing, or rather, perhaps, into the rule to be observed in respect to the Livery of the Clothing. The colour and pattern varied from time to time, as in the case of the other Fraternities. In 13 Edward IV. violet and scarlet are named, and payments are sanctioned for the cloth of these colours given to the Fishmongers, of whom, on solemn occasions, a certain number wore the Goldsmiths' Livery, and *vice versâ*, as a token of good fellowship and ancient amity. In 3 Henry VII.

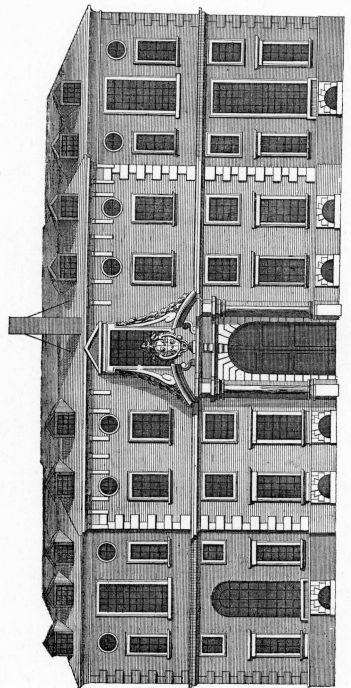

GOLDSMITHS' HALL IN 1739.

the gowns remained of violet and scarlet ; but the hoods were changed
to blue and murrey.   In 8 Henry VII. puce and fine violet in grain
for the gowns went with black hoods.   But in 10 Henry VIII. the
gowns were violet, the hoods violet and scarlet.   The members were
at liberty to buy their vesture where they pleased.

Among the constant ordinances of the Gild was the yearly visit in
procession on St Dunstan's Eve to that saint's chapel in St. Paul's ;
and on this occasion and on the morrow the Goldsmiths and Fishmongers exchanged complimentary visits, and entertained each other
with a great deal of formality and cordiality combined.

GOLDSMITHS' HALL.   THE PRESENT STAIRCASE.

Of the distinguished members of the Gild we may enumerate William
Fitzwilliam, founder in the beginning of the 13th century of the House
of Black Nuns, at St. Helen's, Bishopsgate ; Gregory de Rokesley,
perhaps the most illustrious person associated with it ; Sir Nicholas
Faryngdon, whose name is familiar as at one time feudal proprietor
of the agnominal Ward ; Sir Martin Bowers, who performed good
service at the period when the difficulty arose as to the charter in the
reign of Henry VIII. ; and Sir Francis Child, the member of a family
identified with the early annals of banking and the currency.   Jasper
Fisher, one of the Clerks in Chancery, and a justice of the peace, who

built what was known as *Fisher's Folly*, in Bishopsgate, was a Goldsmith by freedom.

GOLDSMITHS' HALL. EWER OF THE 18TH CENTURY.

LITERARY NOTICES.

The valuacyō of golde and syluer, made ī ȳ yere M.CCCC.lxxxix., holde ī the marke unce englice quart troye, dewes and aes . . . . 8vo (about 1520). Printed at Antwerp. With engravings.

An Advice touching the currancie in payment of our English Golde. 8vo, 1627.

To the Right Honourable the Lords and others of His Maiesties most Honourable Privie Counsell, the Humble Petition of Thomas Crosse, Goldsmith, on the behalfe, not onely of himselfe, but of the whole body of Goldsmiths within the Realme of England. A broadside, about 1630.

⁎ Relating to interlopers.

Perfet Directions for all English Gold now currant in this Kingdome. 8vo, 1632.

By the King. A Proclamation concerning Gold-weights. 1632. A broadside.

A Proclamation for the restraint of the consumption of the Coyne and Bullion of this Realme. 1635. A broadside.

A Brief and Easie way by Tables, To cast up Silver . . . and Gold. . . .
By John Reynolds of the Mynt in the Tower. 8vo, 1651.

A True Discovery to the Commons of England, How they have been cheated of
almost all the Gold and Silver Coyn of this Nation. By Thomas Violet
[Goldsmith]. 12mo, 1650.

The Advancement of Merchandize. By the same. [With a reprint of the above.]
Folio, 1651.

Narrative of Some Remarkable Proceedings, Concerning the Ships *Samson
Salvador,* and *George.* Folio, 1653.

Mysteries and Secrets of Trade and Mint-affairs. Folio, 1653.

A most humble Remonstrance of Peter Blondeau, concerning the offers made by
him to this Commonwealth for the coyning of the monie by a new invention not
yet practised in any State. 12mo, September 9, 1653.
An account of Blondeau's trial of his scheme at Goldsmiths' Hall is here given.

A Proclamation declaring the Rates at which Gold shall be current in Payments,
and to prohibit the transportation of the same. 1661. A broadside.

A Proclamation for the Calling in of all Moneys of Gold and Silver, Coyn'd or
Stamped with the Cross and Harp, and the circumscription, *The Commonwealth
of England.* 1661. A broadside.

A Proclamation against Exportation, and Buying and Selling of Gold and Silver at
higher rates than in our Mint. . . . 1661. A broadside.

His Majesties Gracious Patent to the Goldsmiths, for Payment and Satisfaction of
their Debt. Published by His Majesties command, For the Information of their
several Creditors. Folio, 1677.

A Touchstone for Gold and Silver Wares, Or, A Manual for Goldsmiths. By W.
B. of London, Goldsmith. 8vo, 1677. Second Edition, 8vo, 1678.
The second edition includes John Reynolds of the Tower Mint's *Tables of Gold and Silver.*

The Tryal of William Stayley, Goldsmith; for speaking Treasonable Words against
His Most Sacred Majesty. . . . Folio, 1678.

The Tryal and Condemnation of Mr. William Staley, a Papist, 4to, 1678.

The Behaviour of Mr. William Stayley in Newgate. . . . 4to, 1678.

The Execution of William Staley. 4to, 1678.

An Account of the Digging up of the Quarters of William Stayley. 1678. A
broadside.

CIVIC PAGEANTS, ETC.

Chryso-Thriambos: The Triumphs of Gold. At the Inauguration of Sir James
Pemberton, Knight, in the Dignity of Lord Mayor of London, on Tuesday the 29
of October, 1611. Performed in the hearty Love, and at the Charges of the Right
Worshipful, worthy, and ancient Company of Goldsmiths. Devised and written
by A. M., Cittizen and Draper of London. 4to [1611].

The Triumphs of Truth: A Solemnity unparalleled for Cost, Art, and Magnificence,
at the Confirmation and Establishment of that worthy and true Nobly-minded
Gentleman, Sir Thomas Middleton, Knight; in the Honourable Office of his
Majesty's Lieutenant the Lord Maior of the thrice famous City of London.
Taking Beginning at his Lordships going, and proceeding after his Return from
receiving the Oath of Mayoralty at Westminster, on the Morrow next after Simon
and Judes Day, October 29, 1613. All the Showes, Pageants, Chariots; Morning,
Noone, and Night-Triumphs. Directed, written, and redeemed into Form, from
the Ignorance of some former Times, and their common Writer, by Thomas

Middleton. Shewing also his Lordships Entertainment upon Michaelmas Day last, being the Day of his Election, at that most famous and admired Work of the Running Stream from Amwell Head into the Cestern at Islington ; being the sole Cost, Industry, and Invention of the worthy Mr. Hugh Middleton, of London, Goldsmith, 4to, 1613.

There are two editions of this pageant in 1613, one wanting the Entertainment at the New River Head. Reprinted in Middleton's Works.

A Speech made to his Excellency the Lord General Monk and the Council of State, at Goldsmiths' Hall in London, the 10th day of April, 1660. At which time they were entertained by that honourable Company. After a Song, in four parts, at the conclusion of a Chorus, Enter a Sea-Captain. [By T. Jordan.] 1660. A broadside.

Two editions. The other gives the name of Yeokney, or Young, as the spokesman, and has a shorter title.

The Goldsmith's Jubilee: Or, London's Triumphs. Containing a Description of the several Pageants : On which are Represented Emblematical Figures, Artful Pieces of Architecture, and Rural Dancing : With the Speeches spoken on each Pageant. Performed October 29, 1674, for the Entertainment of the Right Honourable and truly Noble Pattern of Prudence and Loyalty, Sir Robert Vyner, K^t and Bart., Lord Mayor of the City of London : At the Proper Costs and Charges of the Worshipful Company of Goldsmiths. The King's Most Sacred Majesty and his Royal Consort, their Royal Highnesses the Duke and Duchess of York, Prince Rupert, the Duke of Monmouth, several Foreign Embassadors, Chief Nobility, and Secretaries.of State, honouring the City with their Presence. Composed by Thomas Jordan. 4to, 1674.

London's Triumph, Or the Goldsmith's Jubilee : Performed on Saturday, October xxix., 1687. For the Confirmation and Entertainment of the Right Honourable Sir John Shorter, Knight, Lord Mayor of the City of London. Containing a Description of the several Pageants and Speeches . . . together with a Song for the Entertainment of His Majesty. . . . All set forth at the proper Costs and Charges of the Worshipful Company of Goldsmiths. By M. Taubman. Folio, 1687. With four etchings illustrative of the ceremony.

Glory's Resurrection; Being the Triumphs of London Revived, For the Inauguration of the Right Honourable Sir Francis Child, K., Lord Mayor of the City of London. Containing the Description (and also the Sculptures) of the Pageant, and the whole Solemnity of the Day. All set forth at the proper Cost and Charge of the Honourable Company of Goldsmiths. Published by Authority. Folio, 1698. With four copperplate engravings.

The Skinners.

The passage in *Hamlet*, where the virtues of tanning are mentioned, is almost too well known to call for repetition :—

"*Ham.*—How long will a man lie i' the earth, ere he rot ?

1 *Clown.*—Faith, if he be not rotten before he die . . . he will last you some eight year, or nine year ; a tanner will last you nine year.

*Ham —*Why he more than another ?

1 *Clown.*—Why, sir, his hide is so tanned with his trade, that he will keep out water a great while ; and your water is a sore decayer of your whoreson dead body."

THIS Craft-Gild ministered to a taste which, in its origin, was a natural resource in colder climates, and a necessity of life, but became, as the variety of choice extended, and more beautiful and costlier furs were introduced from other countries, an article of luxury and an object of legislation.

We receive rather imposing accounts of the richer furs, which were used by Anglo-Saxon men and women of rank as personal ornaments ; but the habit was of course in those days of extremely narrow observance ; and the recorded cases may perhaps chiefly serve to prove the contrary. rule. Even in the time of Edward I., when we begin to acquire a better knowledge of our history, the use of furs was limited, both in extent and character ; and it was only as our relations with foreign regions, through the development of commercial enterprise at home and abroad, grew more habitual and general, that our merchants enjoyed facilities for obtaining the commodities of this class, which rendered their business at once more varied and more lucrative. During a lengthened period, the skins of coneys and other indigenous fur-bearing animals were exclusively employed and worn by all but individuals of high rank and great wealth.

Supervisors of hides were appointed to make search for those that were false and badly tanned, and on conviction, the offenders forfeited them to the Sheriffs. A case is noticed in 1320, where hides of this sort had been brought to the City to be made into boots and shoes, and

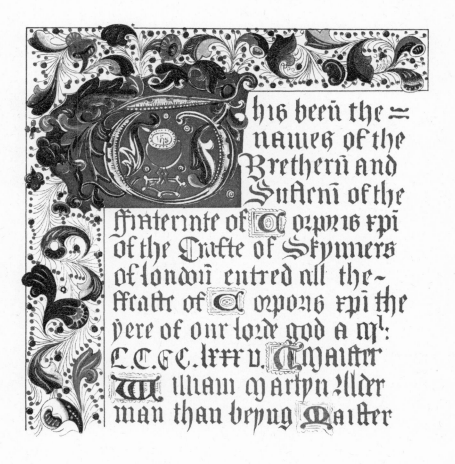

his beeū the =
naūes of the
Brethern and
SuΛcnī of the
ffraternite of Corpris xpi
of the Crafte of Skynners
of londoū entred all the-
ffeaftre of Corpons xpi the
yere of onr lorde god a m̄ᴸ:
C.C.C.C. lxxx v. Ωꝭaistr
William ꝯartyn Aldr
man than beyng Ωaister

Reproduced from Mr. J.F. Wadmore's account of the Skinners Company
· published by the London and Middlesex Archæological Society ·

were seized, and, after the inquisition of a jury of thirteen, condemned. Such frauds were common.

Anciently the tanners, not freemen of the City, were required to offer their hides for sale in a shed erected for the purpose in Friday Street, and to pay a penny by the dicker of ten ; and it was a subject of complaint and redress, that in 1370 these dealers did not comply with the law, but sold hides in their own dwellings or in the public thoroughfares.

The several descriptions of fur or peltry recited in the Tables of Excise at the end of the *Abridgement of the City Charter*, 1680, are badger, beaver, cat, calf, coney (black and grey), elk, fox, genet, kid, lamb, mosker, otter, rabbit (distinguished from coney), sheep, and

OLD ARMS.

squirrel. In the same work occur the package duties payable on beaver-skins, namely eighteen-pence per cwt. of five score. Beaver was already probably beginning to supersede felt as a material for hats among richer persons.

The Skinners received their first charter in the first year of Edward III. (March 1, 1327–8), concurrently with several other associations. It is addressed to "Our beloved men of our city of London, called Skinners," and was partly an outcome from the more general use of furs in this reign, and the consequent growth of abuses in connection with the trade. The instrument is declared to be executed by reason of a petition laid before the Crown with the advice and assent of all the men of the mistery, "for the common utility of the commonalty of the realm to the said city resorting." It rehearses the ordinances which had lately been made for the regulation of the fashion of furs, and for the prevention of the fraudulent sale of old furs as new by hawkers ; and the Company is empowered to elect overseers to make search for deceitful and spurious wares, and to present delinquents to the Lord Mayor. The right is also accorded of attending the fairs at St. Botolph's, Winchester, St. Ives, Stamford, St. Edmund's Bury, and elsewhere within the realm, and making search for false goods in like manner.

The two most ancient books in the hands of the Company are the original records of the two Fraternities of Corpus Christi and the Virgin respectively, prior to their incorporation as one Gild. In the former appear the Ordinances which were drawn up for the guidance of the members and the executive in 39 Edward III., and approved by the Court of Aldermen.

The articles related to the separation of old and new peltry, so that no man should work both, lest he should mix them ; to the view of all goods by the Wardens prior to sale or removal out of the City bounds, furs brought from abroad inclusive ; to the attendance at religious rites ; to fines for refusal to serve offices ; to observance of hours by workmen ; to apprentices ; to oaths ; and to pleas of Court, which were not to be made by freemen without the leave of the governing body.

These bye-laws shew that the necessity was felt for an unusual degree of stringency and vigilance in preventing fraud or abuses. The grey furs of Flanders are stated to have been often stuffed with chalk. The freemen of the Craft were limited at this period in their abode to Walbrook, Cornhill, and Budge Row ; but this restriction can scarcely be taken to affect their mart at Leadenhall.

The Company has a later code of Ordinances, dated 1676, partaking of the usual character, and substantially following the lines of that of 1365–6.

The second charter of the Company, 16 Richard II., April 20, is partly an *inspeximus*, and recites that, " We, for the devotion of the said Skinners in this behalf, which seems good and holy, having consideration of our special grace and for sixty pounds, which the same Skinners to us had paid into the hanaper, the said letters of him our grandfather . . . approve and ratify." Here the Gild is described as, " The Skinners and the men of the Mistery ; " and the grant proceeds to state as one of its objects the increase of the fraternity of Skinners, *and other persons, whom to the same they will receive*, to authorize the yearly election for ever of a Master Warden and four others from the body for the government thereof, to enact that the brethren and sisteren shall receive a new livery annually of one and the same pattern, and shall make procession at the feast of Corpus Christi, and afterward celebrate an entertainment in any competent place within the City of London for the same assigned. Finally, the Gild had licence in mortmain to the value of twenty marks by the year, both within and without the City, for the support of two chaplains to perform all necessary acts of piety.

It had been between 1327 and 1392 that the two branches of the Fraternity, that first settled on Dowgate Hill, in Walbrook parish, and then at St. Mary Bethlehem, and the other belonging to St. Mary Spital, consolidated themselves into one body, and therefore the charter of Richard comprehended the whole Craft for the first time.

There seems to be some basis for the supposition that between the charter just cited and that of Henry VII., one of 16 Henry VI. ought to find a place in the series. Herbert states that such an one is specified in the calendars of the Patent Rolls, and that it prescribed ordinances. But there is some confusion between it and that of Henry VII., which immediately succeeds in order ; and it is worthy of notice that in her *inspeximus* Elizabeth names nothing between 1392 and 1500, the reputed grant of Henry VI. of course belonging to 1438.

The charter of the 16 Henry VII. (Feb. 22, 1500–1) recites that of 1392, and emphasizes the recognition of the Gild as one united brotherhood, that is to say, as the amalgamated Fraternities of Corpus Christi at St. John in Walbrook, and that of the Virgin at St. Mary Spital, between Moorfields and Bishopsgate. It specifies the governing body as the Master and Wardens of the Gild or Fraternity of Corpus Christi of the Skinners of London, confers the power of pleading and being impleaded, and renews the rights connected with the supervision of the trade in the City and at fairs, subject to the Master and Wardens being sworn at Guildhall, on election, to execute faithfully the trust reposed in them.

This grant enters with particular nicety into the regulations concerning the treatment of furs and the prevention of frauds commonly perpetrated by members of the mistery and others. The details prove that at this time a vast advance had been made in the variety and choice of these articles, and that a very extensive trade existed in them between this country and the Continent or even more distant regions.

This was succeeded by *inspeximus* instruments of June 8, 1558, 4–5 Philip and Mary, and March 22, 1560–1, 2 Elizabeth, in the latter of which still more elaborate details are given of the modes for importing and dressing furs ; and it is stated that it had been shown how it would be to the general advantage, if furs were brought into the country in a way suitable to their several kinds. Hence it appears that there was a principle of calculating by "beasts, tiers, and bellies"; and we hear of fur of minever of seven tiers or 100 bellies, and of 8 tiers or 120 bellies ; fur of biso of eight tiers or 72 beasts, fur of popell or squirrel of 7 tiers or 60 beasts, hoods of minever pure of forty bellies, and of super-pure of 32 bellies, and so on.

The charter of 2 Elizabeth was confirmed and enlarged by that of 4 James I. (Dec. 2, 1606), which is the Company's acting one. It recites that of the late Queen Elizabeth and the Act of Parliament 3 James I., November 5, entitled, "An Act for the relief of such as lawfully use the trade and handicraft of Skinners," and proceeds to lay restrictions on the exportation of coney-skins and such matters, but is principally occupied by the formulation of a new governing scheme for the Company, necessitated, it may be concluded, by a certain amount of unfairness and illegality in the election of persons not belonging to the craft to responsible offices. The King therefore prescribes, that where the Master is not a professional skinner, the Wardens shall be so, and that the mastership cannot be held by any not a skinner in two years successively; while, where the Master was a skinner, the Wardens, or two of them, might be unprofessional members of the Gild. The King approves of the appointment of Assistants, but directs that one half of them should be skinners by calling, and nominates certain persons, citizens and skinners of London, to be added to the existing body during life. The instrument likewise creates two Deputy-Searchers, to serve under the Master and Wardens in exercising the powers of the Gild in that behalf.

This grant ought to be read with the knowledge that during the latter part of the reign of Elizabeth, and down to 1606, serious discontent and complaint had prevailed among the working men of the Gild through an insufficient recognition of their rights and interests ; and the present attempt on the part of James to popularize the constitution by the admittance of supplementary members to the Court from the body of freemen, and the restraint laid on the future preponderance of members of other crafts or private individuals in the administration, was naturally viewed by the oligarchy in power as a dangerous blow to its influence and prospects.

The charter of 1606 has been characterized as clandestine and *ex parte;* but from the tenor, of the Act of November 5 just previous, it is almost obvious that the renewal had been sought by the Company itself in the usual manner, and that the democratic features in it were inserted in compliance with representations addressed to the King and with notorious facts.

The Company, however, when the truth transpired, and the royal nominees presented themselves for acceptance, refused to acknowledge the instrument and its operation, and laid a case before the Privy Council, in which it was set forth that the proposed innovations in the electoral and executive systems were entirely contrary to its wishes and welfare, and had been conceded without its privity ; and by two orders of Council, February 8 and March 22, 1606-7, the obnoxious clauses of the charter were revoked.

After the accession of Charles I. in 1625, the Skinners, who, by reason of the miscarriage of the Artisans' Charter in the previous reign and its withdrawal, had had no confirmation of their grant since 2 Elizabeth, found themselves involved in the despotic *Scire Facias* writ of Charles I., directed to the Corporation itself and all the privileged bodies in the City. The Skinners accordingly surrendered their charter and title-deeds, and the matter remained in abeyance till 1641, when, the Long Parliament having reversed the writ of 1625, the King assented to the restitution of the forfeited possessions and securities, but failed, in consequence of the perturbed condition of affairs, to proceed farther. The Skinners therefore continued as before to act on their charter of 2 Elizabeth, which substantially upheld all their pretensions, and indeed on the valid portions of that of James I., which constituted, outside those conditions ultimately withdrawn, little more than an *inspeximus* of that of 1560-1.

After the Restoration, the Skinners waited several years before they approached the Crown with a prayer for a new charter. But in 19 Charles II. (June 28, 1667) they obtained one, which rehearses some of the familiar points, but which is curious and exceptional, inasmuch as it states that the trade was then in a fairly flourishing condition, and that not only certain technical phrases had become obsolete and unintelligible by process of time, but the methods pursued in the manufacture were different. The charter recites the Act 3 James I. for the relief of Artisan Skinners, and lays stress on the encouragement of the trade in those skins which could be procured in England, especially those of rabbits of various colours. It deals with the lax observance of certain statutes made for its control, particularly the practice on the part of persons not out of their apprenticeship of making muffs, furring garments, gloves and other articles, with the questions of dividing the wools from the skins of rabbits and others, and of hiring journeymen to work for them, all these matters being in contravention of the charters. It was now accordingly declared that the power vested in the Master and Wardens of the Skinners and their successors, in the nature of privileges, exemptions, and jurisdiction was continued to them ; that their title to all their acquired possessions was confirmed, to be held by such tenures as they had been accustomed ; and that the Master and Wardens were at liberty to frame ordinances for the good government of the Gild.

The writ of *Quo Warranto*, issued in 1684 against all the City franchises, applied of course to the Skinners, who again surrendered their charter; and in 1 James II. (April 4, 1685) received a fresh one, following the lines of that of 1667 in some respects, but embracing some very arbitrary and unconstitutional provisions, while it gave liberty for the use of a common seal, the erection of a Court of Assistants, and the appointment of a Clerk. The King, in fact, reserved to himself and his heirs the nomination of the Court, the approval of the Clerk, and the right of removing any or all of the governing body at pleasure, prescribed that the Master, Wardens, and Assistants should be under the jurisdiction of the Court of Aldermen, and that no Catholic or Dissenter should be admitted to the Company.

But the whole of the extraneous matter introduced into this grant was, as usual, rescinded and annulled in the first year of the following reign by an Act of Parliament passed, " for Reversing the Judgment in a *Quo Warranto* against the City of London, and for restoring the City of London to its ancient Rights and Privileges."

Leadenhall Market, where the Skinners formerly possessed a considerable amount of house property, known as Skinners' Row, was the ancient centre of their trade, and had probably owed its connection with the Gild to the neighbourhood of the separate Fraternity of St. Mary Spital to that emporium, previously to the union of the two bodies in the fourteenth century.

The Skinners, as originally constituted, were, of course, a Craft Gild; even in the charter of 1667, only "such as use the trade, mistery, and occupation of handicraft Skinners" are recognised; and the operative element was bound to be more or less influential, and to prove a chronic source of friction and trouble, when the executive body and the leading members of the Company gradually obeyed a tendency to detach themselves from practical relations with trade, as the trust and corporate estates grew in importance, and alone formed an amply sufficient employment and dependence.

We do not find in the charter the customary terms of description applied to the Gild. Its members are at first addressed as the " Men called Skinners" (1327), or the "Skinners and Men of the Mistery" (1392), or the " Mistery of Skinners" (1558). In 1501, in the charter of Henry VII., and in 1685, in that of James II., they occur as the "Master and Wardens of the Gild or Fraternity of Skinners." But the phrase "commonalty" is never employed.

This apparent anomaly may have something to do with the tendency of the journeymen to alienation, which we detect as early as 1606, when they tried without success to gain a footing on the Court.

The Artisans or Freemen always maintained a certain share of authority and consideration; and in 1733 they were joined and supported by the Master and Wardens in a petition to Parliament against the duty on rabbits' skins. It was a common cause. Yet by that time the Company must have arrived at a stage when the details of commerce were a matter of indifference.

The dissatisfaction of the Artisans with their standing in the Gild manifested itself once more in 1744, in a remonstrance to the Court in which the complainants represented their grievances and the concession made to them by James I. in the cancelled charter of 1606. But the Court, while expressing its willingness to afford the Artisan Skinners all reasonable aid in the redress of their hardships, adhered to the view that the charter of 1606 was clandestinely obtained, and constutionally and properly revoked.

The aggrieved body, however, persisted in their contentions, and in February, 1744-5, served the Court with a copy of a rule for a mandamus to choose a certain number of their class for seats on the Court. A return was ultimately made to the writ, and the plaintiffs lost the day. The proceedings did not end there ; and in 1748 a trial in respect of an alleged false return to the writ of 1744 took place in the King's Bench, and terminated in the acquittal of the defendants.

This verdict brought the contest, if not the quarrel, to a close ; the issue was so far not very material, since the Company was at this time, as we know, emerging from its pristine condition and structure into an organically new life as an uncommercial, fiduciary and benevolent corporation.

The earliest home of the Skinners appears to have been in the parishes of St. John upon Walbrook and St. Martin Orgar, and is perhaps to be identified with the spot on Dowgate Hill in the former parish where the premises of the Company now stand. But a second community belonging to the same craft, and eventually incorporated with those at Dowgate Hill, is found in St. Mary Axe and at St. Mary Spital, in the latter of which quarters they contracted a liability to contribute to the restoration of London Wall between Aldgate and Bevis Marks.

The site on Dowgate Hill purports to have been purchased by the Skinners in the time of Henry III., who granted them licence in mortmain for the power to hold the same, with buildings thereon, namely, four tenements in the former, and two in the latter, parish, five being apparently shops. The value by the year was 12*l*. 6*s*. 8*d*., which argues a somewhat important area. In the 19 Edward II. (1326), however, this property had left the hands of the Gild, which seems to have removed to St. Mary Bethlehem, between Bishopsgate and Moorfields, and belonged to the celebrated soldier, Ralph de Cobham ; and owing to the circumstance that he demised his estate to the Crown, the place reverted in the reign of Edward III., as it is supposed, to the former owners, who thus returned to their old Walbrook seat. Yet in 1392 no progress seems to have been made toward the erection of any suitable place of assembly, as the yearly feast of Corpus Christi was then to be held in any competent spot within the City for it appointed. Very little is to be learned about the origin of a Hall and its customary appurtenances,—except that the Fraternity of Corpus Christi and the Virgin, which had a chapel annexed to St. Mildred's in the Poultry down to the Reformation, was probably this united Gild,—from 1392 down to the period when it is described by Stow as "a fair house sometime called Copped Hall," a name which reminds us of the old Conyers' seat in Essex ; nor do we know whether the premises were the old tenements altered or a new building, beyond the statement in Stow (1633), that during the occupation of Ralph Cobham or De Cobham the property consisted of his house and five shops. But possibly some of the ancient tenements had been converted into places of business since Cobham's time.

After the fall of the Commonwealth, General Monk was entertained at several of the Halls of the Companies ; and he attended at the Skinners' on the 10th April, 1660, when Pepys, under date of the 11th, notes that the General found the Parliament arms already supplanted by the Royal. Whatever stood on the ground evidently perished in the fire of 1666 ; and of the structure erected after that calamity there are several accounts. Strype speaks of it as situated in Dowgate, fairly built since the fire of London, at an expense of above 1,800l., and adds that the Lord Mayor sometimes kept his official residence there, on account of its good accommodation, and that the New East India Company held their general courts there, while it remained a separate body, paying 300l. a year rent. It had a large quadrangle, says Strype, paved with freestone. The *New View of London*, 1708, terms it "a noble structure built with fine bricks and richly finished, the hall with right wainscot, and the great parlour with odoriferous cedar." It was subsequently much altered, both within and without, by Jupp, who destroyed some of the original characteristic features of the place, including the cedar wainscot.

We do not meet with many notices of the effect of the Fire on this Company ; yet it must have wrought terrible damage to the City property, and we are aware how it reduced the strongest of these bodies to the brink of ruin. But we perceive that not many months later the

Skinners applied for a fresh charter, in which it seems to be shown that their affairs were then tolerably prosperous.

The Skinners boast an unusually proud list of royal personages who have been honorary members of their fellowship. It opens with Edward III. and his queen, and comprises the Black Prince, Richard II. and his queen, Henry IV. and his queen, King Henry V. and his queen, Henry VI., Edward IV. and his queen, and a long series of noble and distinguished men and women.

The principal figure in their early history, however, is Sir Andrew Judd, the founder of Tonbridge School, whose endowment was afterwards augmented by other members of the Company. Judd was four times Master, and Mayor in 1550. He was a native of Tonbridge and a distant relative of Archbishop Chichele. He died September 4, 1558, and was buried at St. Helen's, Bishopsgate, with great splendour.

The Skinners came into possession of the management and control of Tonbridge School under the provisions of his will in 1558, in connection with the general scheme of the Government of Edward VI. for establishing grammar schools throughout England. The school at Tonbridge was originally limited to instruction in the rudiments under one master and one usher. The estate supporting the charity consists of property in the City of London, and of the Sandhills estate on the south side of the New Road in the parish of St. Pancras. This is described in the devise of 1558 as "a close of pasture, with the appurtenances called the Sandhills, situate, lying, and being on the back side of Holborn . . . being of the yearly value of 13*l*. 6*s*. 8*d*." This land at present comprises the area extending from Tonbridge Street on the east to Burton Street on the west, and Leigh Street on the south.

In consequence of some litigation in and about 1825, a varied scheme was settled, and the Company made certain exchanges of property, including premises in Leadenhall Market. These arrangements were completed in 1841.

The St. Pancras estate above mentioned was let on building leases for ninety-nine years in 1807 to James Burton, Esq., at 2,500*l*. a year; and the Company has since that period largely profited by the constantly rising value of land and demand for railway and other public purposes, the Midland line having paid 32,000*l*. for a portion of the St. Pancras estate. But, on the other hand, the Skinners have expended large sums on their school and for other beneficial objects, as appears in the elaborate accounts presented to Parliament in 1882.

The order of precedence among the Livery Companies is at present settled beyond the likelihood of any fresh disturbance or controversy,

The mode in which civic processions, of which they formed part, were to be regulated, was insensibly fixed and recognised by custom; but in cases where the priority was doubtful or close, questions were apt to arise, and twice in the annals of these Associations serious commotions arose on this point. In 1339 there was a dispute between the Skinners and the Fishmongers, which assumed the proportions of a riot in the streets, and resulted in the ringleaders being executed; and in 1483 a second altercation, which was amicably arranged, occurred with the Taylors.

Stow graphically describes the Skinners' Corpus Christi procession. He observes: "This Fraternity had also once every yeare on Corpus Christi day, after noone a Procession which passed through the principall streets of the City, wherein are borne more than one hundred torches of Waxe (costly garnished) burning light, and above two hundred Clerkes and Priests in Surplesses and Coapes, singing. After the which were the Sheriffes' servants, the Clerkes of the Compters, Chaplaines for the Sheriffes, the Major's Serjeants, the Councell of the City, the Maior and Aldermen in Scarlet, and then the Skinners in their best Liveries."

The same authority furnishes a list of twenty mayors between 1348 and 1698, who were of this Fraternity. Below will be found a list of the printed pageants, commencing with that of 1585, which is, next to that of the Ironmongers, 1566, the most ancient of the published series.

It has been seen that by the charter of 16 Richard II. it is reserved to the Gild to admit other than followers of the vocation, with a view to the fuller and more speedy development of it. But it was probably in contemplation that the outsiders should at any rate belong to other branches of the same industry. In 23 Henry VI., of the entire Fraternity, which was doubtless not large, nineteen are described in the Company's books as: doctors (1), gentlemen (3), of no trade or description (9), butchers (2), dyers (1), joiners (1), grocers (1), and silk-wives (1).

The numbers in 1537 of the "Freemen Householders" were 141. In 1699 the Livery counted 180; in 1724, 192. At a poll in 1722, only 124 voted. In 1742, the figures were 137; in 1796, 150; in 1834, 200; and in 1892, 150.

In 1738, the calls to the Livery, 27 in number, exhibited a continuance of the hybrid character of the Company. They included six skinners, one gentleman, one grocer, two linen-drapers, two upholsterers or upholders, one glover, one tallow-chandler, one butcher, one plaisterer, one victualler or innholder, one mum-merchant, one watchmaker, one feltmaker, one haberdasher, one wharfinger, one taylor, one timber-merchant, and three not described.

In the ten years 1870-9 both the income and expenditure of the Skinners considerably increased, the former, partly owing to a rise in the value of the Irish property, and partly to improvements in the London estate ; the latter, chiefly by reason of an enlargement of grants and donations for charitable and other allied purposes.

The Skinners eventually bought the shares held in the Irish plantation by the Stationers and Bakers, and assumed the management of that of the Girdlers ; and they seem to have succeeded of late years in raising the income from this source very considerably. In 1879 the aggregate revenue of the three subshares was upward of 2,500*l.* The new owners borrowed 60,000*l.* to enable them to carry out these arrangements. The Girdlers receive the nett rent of their portion, the other Company undertaking the administration and agency.

LITERARY NOTICES.

The Generall Greeuance of all England, Man, Woman, and Child: To the High and Honourable Court of Parliament. [In relation to the transportation or export of raw hides. About 1625.] A broadside.

This document more especially refers to the injury sustained by curriers, shoemakers, and cobblers.

Schola Tunbridgiensis. By John Stockwood. 8vo, 1619.

The Case and Condition of R. Tichbourn, Late Alderman, and now Prisoner in the Tower of London. Presented to the Consideration and Compassion of his Fellow-Citizens. 4to, 1661.

CIVIC PAGEANTS, ETC.

The Device of the Pageant borne before Sir Wolstone Dixie, Lord Mayor of London, October 29, 1585. By George Peele. 4to, 1585.

Reprinted in Strype's edition of Stowe's Survey, folio, 1720, book v., pp. 136, 137 ; in Nichols' Progresses of Queen Elizabeth, ii. 221, and in the editions of Peele's Works. This pageant is curious and valuable ; not only for the poetry, but because it describes the flourishing state of the metropolis in the days of Queen Elizabeth. The *dramatis personæ*, represented by the children of the pageant, are, London, Magnanimity, Loyalty, the Country, the Thames, the Soldier, the Sailor, Science, and first, second, third, and fourth Nymphs, who have all appropriate speeches assigned to them.

The Device of the Pageant borne before the Right Hon. Martyn Colthorpe, Lord Mayor of the City of London, 29 October, 1588 : Licensed for the press this year, but not at present known.

See my *Handbook*, 1867, p. 450.

The Triumphs of Love and Antiquity: An Honourable Solemnity performed through the City, at the Confirmation and Establishment of the Right Honourable Sir William Cockayn, Knight, in the Office of his Majesty's Lieutenant the Lord Mayor of the Famous City of London : Taking beginning in the morning at his Lordship's going, and perfecting itself after his return from receiving the oath of Mayoralty at Westminster, on the morrow after Simon and Jude's Day, October 29, 1619. By Thomas Middleton. 4to, 1619.

Britannia's Honor: Brightly Shining in seuerall Magnificent Shewes or Pageants, to Celebrate the Solemnity of the Right Honorable Richard Deane. At his Inauguration into the Majoralty of the Honourable City of London, on Wednesday, October the 29th, 1628. At the Particular Cost, and Charges of the Right Worshipfull, Worthy, and Ancient Society of Skynners. By Tho. Dekker. 4to, 1628.

London's Triumph; Or, The Solemn and Magnificent Reception of that Honourable
Gentleman, Robert Tichborn, Lord Mayor : After his return from taking the
Oath at Westminster, the morrow after Simon and Jude day, being October 29,
1656. With the Speeches spoken at Fosterlane-end and Soperlane-end. By
J[ohn] B[ulteel]. 4to, 1656.

London's Triumphs: Celebrated the 29th day of this present month of October,
1657, In Honour of the truly Deserving Richard Chiverton, Lord Mayor of the
City of London, at the Costs and Charges of the Worshipful Company of Skinners. By J. Tatham. 4to, 1657.

A Speech made to his Excellency, Lord General Monck, and the Council of State,
at Skinners' Hall, on Wednesday, being the fourth of April, 1660, at which time
he was nobly entertained by that honourable Company. [1660.] A broadside
by T. Jordan.

A Speech made to his Excellency, the Lord General Monck, at Skinners' Hall, on
Wednesday, being the 4th of April, 1660. . . . [Another edition purporting
to have been spoken by Walter Yeokners.] 1660. A broadside.

A Song to his Excellency the Lord General Monck, at Skinners Hall on Wednesday, Aprill 4, 1660. At which time he was entertained by that Honourable Company. 1660. A broadside.

Londinum Triumphans; or, London's Triumph : Celebrated in Honour of the truly-
deserving Sir Anthony Bateman, Knight, Lord Mayor of London, and done at
the Costs and Charges of the Worshipful Company of Skinners, on the 29th of
October, 1663. By John Tatham. 4to, 1663.

London's Resurrection to Joy and Triumph : Expressed in sundry Shewes, Shapes,
Scenes, Speeches, and Songs in Parts. Celebrious to the much-meriting Magis-
trate, Sir George Waterman, Knight, Lord Mayor of the City of London. At
the peculiar and proper Expenses of the Worshipful Company of the Skinners.
The King, Queen, and Duke of York, and most of the Nobility being present.
Written by Thomas Jordan. 4to, 1671.

 *** Some copies were printed without a mention of the Court being present, and without the con-
cluding leaf on which the account is given.

London's Great Jubilee, Restored and Performed on Tuesday, October the 29th,
1689, for the Entertainment of the Right Honourable Sir Thomas Pilkington,
Kt., Lord Mayor of the City of London. Containing a Description of the several
Pageants and Speeches, together with a Song, for the Entertainment of Their
Majesties, who, with their Royal Highnesses the Prince and Princess of Denmark, the whole Court, and both Houses of Parliament, honoured his Lordship
this Year with their Presence. All set forth at the proper Costs and Charges
of the Right Worshipful Company of Skinners. By Matthew Taubman. 4to,
1689.

 *** This pageant was revived in 1761 on the occasion of the visit of George III. to the City, when
Sir T. Fludyer entered on office, and it was printed the same year in 8vo.

Accompanying the Drapers' Pageant for 1679 by Thomas Jordan, is an Address to
the Skinners' Company by John Tatham.

Sir Humphrey Edwin, Citizen and Barber-Surgeon, was elected Mayor in 1698, and
thereupon, agreeably to custom, translated himself to this Company. But owing to his
opinions as a non-juror there was no show, although in Halliwell's *Dictionary of Old
English Plays*, 1860, it is stated that a descriptive account—perhaps of what was intended—was written by Elkanah Settle, and printed, folio, 1698.

The Merchant Taylors.

CONCORDIA PARVÆ RES CRESCVNT.

THE annals of the Taylors before their elevation into a Fraternity are principally remarkable for the legend of the devil making his way, accompanied by Pride, into their haunts in Birchin Lane, where he had hoped to have received a friendly welcome, but was so sharply set upon by the linen-armourers and their very prentices with their Spanish needles, that he wished himself well out of their reach. The locality named afterward became the quarter of the second-hand clothes' dealers.

The Company's books commence with the year 1299–1300, the date of their licence from Edward I., and give the names of the Masters and Wardens thenceforward; but some are missing. The *Gild of Pilgrims*, of which Warner le Tournour was then Alderman, is enumerated, however, among the eighteen unlicensed bodies in 1180, and was required to pay 40s., which was apparently never done; and we can have no hesitation in concluding that this was the present Company.

It has been already shown, under the account of the GOLDSMITHS, that the present Gild was engaged in 1267–8 in a dispute with them; and this is, in fact, the next earliest clue which seems to survive. It is even doubtful whether the date of the affray has been correctly given: Stow, in his *Chronicle*, 1615, assigns it to 1268; but Herbert places the incident under 1226. In 1304 another very serious disturbance arose, and also at night, on the same spot, in which the Taylors were again implicated. The occasion or cause is not stated in either case.

The licence accorded by Edward I. in 1299 to the Gild to assume the name and title of Taylors and *Linen Armourers*, is not only one of the earliest references extant, but importantly and decisively indicates the operative functions of this Society, in connection with the lining and quilting of armour, as well as with the more ordinary forms of industry with which we associate the calling. The Merchant-Taylor of the Plantagenet era was naturally a product of contemporary fashions and requirements ; the use of armour was universal among a very large section of the community in all parts of the kingdom ; the warlike policy pursued by Edward I. and III. at home and abroad made the call and market for military appliances and outfits immeasurably more active than it had ever been before ; and the linen-armourer of that time must, as a privileged monopolist, have found his vocation busy and lucrative.

THE COMMON SEAL.

We rely on the voucher of Stow for the statement that on St. John the Baptist's day, 1300, the Taylors and Linen-Armourers chose a Master and four Wardens, the former entitled the *Pilgrim*, as being the traveller for the whole Company, and the latter "the purveyors of alms or quarterages." Hence, as well as in the far more ancient record above cited, we perceive that here there was a strong desire from the outset to communicate to the movement a distinctly religious tone and side.

The Gild, a few years later, addressed a petition to the Crown, representing the wish for incorporation, whereas "from the time whereof there is no memory" they had held their assemblies once a year to govern the mistery and settle its affairs ; and in March, 1326–7, the first charter, an instrument of limited scope, was received from Edward III., enacting that only freemen should follow the craft within the City, and that none should have the freedom, unless he were vouched by honest and lawful men of the mistery to be honest, faithful, and fit for the same.

The succeeding grant of Richard II. in 1390 conferred the power of creating a Master and four Wardens at their pleasure, and entitled this body to draw up ordinances for the management of the whole Fellowship.

In the course of the reign of Henry IV. the Company obtained no fewer than three grants ; the first and second confirmatory in the second and sixth years (1400–1 and 1404–5), and a third, in 1407–8, addressed to the Wardens, who are named, whereby the privileges were amplified, and the use of a common seal sanctioned. Here the Gild is successively addressed as The Taylors and Fraternity of St. John the Baptist in London, the Taylors of London, Wardens of the Fraternity of St. John the Baptist, where the religious attribute and function are strikingly prominent, and as the Fraternity of Taylors and Linen-Armourers of St. John the Baptist.

The broad distinction between those two great manufacturing and trading bodies, the Drapers and Taylors, was, that the former dealt in the woollen goods, and the latter in linen, either for apparel or the garniture of armour. Our Government resisted the effort made to place the foreign dealers and workers in linen on the same footing as those of alien blood or origin carrying on business in the more ancient and more widely-employed material, who were exonerated by Edward III. from tribute to the native Gild of Weavers ; and when the question was carried into the Court of Exchequer, the claim of the strangers was formally disallowed. All branches of this industry were then beginning to assume a new and freer phase ; we were growing independent of our continental instructors ; and the native Taylor and Linen Armourer was already a busy and profitable employment, in the presence of an inexhaustible call for the warlike appointments which we suppose to have been their principal source of labour and profit, and which occupy a proportionately conspicuous position in the earliest and at the same time most characteristic grant of arms to the Gild.

In addition to the interior garniture of the armour, of which each several component portion was separate with its technical name, as set out in the dictionaries, the Taylor-Armourer made the doublets and other articles of apparel belonging to civil life ; the quilting and padding of which sometimes rendered them almost weapon-proof, especially when leather was introduced to strengthen the joints or seams. The care, skill, and art involved in making these accoutrements, either preparatorily to the addition of the metal-work or otherwise, and the extensive demand for such articles of apparel or protection by soldiers of all grades and by the wealthier citizens of London and other leading

places, may elucidate the growth of the craft and its eventual recognition by the Crown as a corporate Fraternity.

Very probably, before the rise of the Draper as a separate craft or
industry, the Taylor, the more ancient institution, provided for the wants
of both sexes ; and those attached to royal and noble establishments
undoubtedly attended to the whole department, and employed labour to
carry out orders.

The Linen-Armourer of an age when the horse, as well as his rider,
was protected by iron or steel work, the precursor of the merely ornamental caparison, found a further channel for his enterprise in that
direction ; and it was the more artistic skill, if not the more advantageous
conditions, involved in this class of commerce during some centuries,
which may have relaxed the interest of the Linen-Armourer in the
other branch of his business, and have opened the way to the Draper,
who confined himself to the details of every-day civil apparel.

Some slight difficulty has been made by Herbert and others in respect to the question, whether the Taylor of old days was a salesman as
well as a manufacturer.   But there seems to be barely any ground for
doubting that he filled both parts, so far as his own craft was concerned,
as the Draper was a dealer in woollen cloths, and also retailed them in
the shape of apparel.   But, at the same time, the unique distinction
conferred on them by Henry VII., and maintained through subsequent
reigns, may tend to shew that the Company, at the close of the fifteenth
century, was already segregating itself from petty trade, and in the
course of less than a hundred years had relinquished to the yeomanry
all active interest in the craft, unless it was in the way of wholesale
merchandise.

In 1351, the Company admitted their first honorary member, and
about two years after came into possession of a chapel at the north
door of St. Paul's, where prayers and obits might be offered daily for
the spiritual welfare of those of the Fraternity present and to come.   In
1455, Pope Calixtus III. granted leave for the celebration of masses on
the altars in this edifice, which probably superseded the ancient one in
Threadneedle Street.

The Saracen's Head, in Friday Street, is believed to have been the
first purchase of real property made ; it was bought in 1401 out of the
common box.   Houses in Bread Street were devised to the Company
in 1404 ; and in 1406, John Churchman, Merchant Taylor, gave his
brethren others in Bishopsgate and Threadneedle Streets with the advowson of St. Martin Outwich.   The foundation of its trusts was a
bequest by Peter Mason of property in the Poultry for eleemosynary
objects.

Successive renewals and enlargements of the privileges and powers were made by Henry VI. in his eighteenth and thirty-first years, by Edward IV. in 1465, and by Henry VII. in 1502; which last is the present acting charter. The charter of Henry VI. accorded the right of search; but by writ of Privy Seal directed from "The King's Parlour[1] at Sheen," August 21, this faculty is revoked; it was restored in the following reign. In the charter of Henry VII. the Company is first described as that of the Merchant Taylors; a concession due (it is said) to the personal interest of Sir William Fitzwilliam, a member, but not until a proclamation had been issued, inviting the Corporation or others to shew cause against the change within a fixed date;[2] and the governing body is authorized to admit any person to the Freedom or otherwise without the let or hinderance of any other mistery. This grant is also remarkable inasmuch as it not merely reinstates the right of search, but contains a clause, vesting in the Merchant Taylors the monopoly of working, cutting, or making men's apparel within the bounds. But no reference occurs to female dress.

Our Sovereigns from Henry VIII. to James I. renewed the grants by *inspeximus,* and by two licences of the last prince the faculty of the Company of holding in mortmain was extended. The liberty to frame and enforce ordinances at an earlier date notwithstanding, there appears to be no record of any code anterior to 1322, which more directly affects the Armourers, as it interdicts their interference with the lining of armour.

The first series of Articles for the internal regulation of the body, consequent on incorporation, and periodically revised and renewed, was drawn up and approved by the City shortly after 1327, and is termed, "Articles of the Armourers." In 45 Edward III., a second edition of these is described as "Articles of the Taylors." There was nothing fresh till 9 Henry VII., July 10, when new "Ordinances of the Taylors" were presumably prepared and submitted to the Court of Aldermen by reason of the recent amplification of privileges and the apparent settlement of the Crown under a new dynasty.

These Ordinances of 1487–8 remained, like the charter of the same

---

[1] The discontinuance of this genuine old English term for a conference-chamber at most of the Gild Halls, and in its secondary sense in private houses, is to be regretted. The Directors of the Bank of England still retain the good old-fashioned phrase. Nor can we help thinking, when we read about the parlour of Henry VI. at Sheen, of the famous nursery tale of the four-and-twenty blackbirds, and of the queen, in that delightful fiction, sitting in her parlour eating bread and honey.

[2] The Haberdashers were similarly honoured during a brief period; but the privilege was withdrawn, although in official lists of 1509, 1515, and 1531–2, the Company still bears the ampler and more dignified title.

king, the standard text ; but they were confirmed in May, 1613, and in May, 1661.   They chiefly relate to commonplace internal details. There is also a series of mere forms of adjuration for various purposes.

But a curious precept, reciting a former one, had been made in 1310 by the common authority of the City and Crown, that the tailors who had the furs—probably the fur collars and cuffs—of good folks to scour, should only perform the work in Cheap by night or just before day-break, so that great lords or other passing by might not be hindered or annoyed ; and if they were so busy as not to be able to do this at the prescribed times, they were to scour in some dead lane behind St. Martin's le Grand or London Wall.

The Ordinances of 1661, however, comprise several clauses relative to those members of the Company who were not also members of the trade ; and we are permitted to conclude that they formed at this period a numerous section, having been admitted, perhaps, rather more freely by reason of the straitened circumstances of the Merchant Taylors at this juncture.   For it includes nearly every industry then followed in London, and even discloses several not elsewhere specified ; namely, a butter-seller, a cruet-seller, a milliner, a mealman, an oilman, a sempster, a sailsman, a retail tobacconist, a feather-maker, a perfumer, and a gilder.

One of these items refers to the payment of a fee of thirty shillings to the Company's chest for the binding and registration of any one as apprentice to a freeman of the Merchant Taylors, who is also a Merchant Adventurer, a Turkey Merchant, a Spanish Merchant, a French Merchant, or the member of any other Association trading beyond the seas.

This Gild does not appear to have solicited a charter from Charles II. or James II.; but it shared the inconvenience of the writ of *Quo Warranto* in 1684, the operation of which, however, was short-lived, as it suited the interest of James to rescind his brother's obnoxious and unreasonable proceedings.

Of the 24,731*l.* due to the Merchant Taylors at the close of the troubles, not more than 2,250*l.* ever returned to their hands.   This occurred in 1668.   The reduction of rental was very prolonged, since it was necessary to re-grant the lands on which the tenements had perished in 1666, at very low ground-rents, to tempt and enable old or new tenants to rebuild.

In connection with the advances of the Merchant Taylors to the Government on the Public Faith, we find, under date of 1650, a reference to the purchase by them of certain Dean and Chapter's lands, which had formerly belonged to the prebend of Finsbury Moor.   This property which is frequently cited in the earlier records as a source of trouble to the City, was for some time laid out in gardens and tenter-grounds for the tailors, drapers, and other workers and vendors of cloth; and it anciently extended to the very walls of London toward the north.

The Reformation obliged the Merchant Taylors to surrender their trusts and other property applicable to superstitious uses; the rental amounting to 102*l.* 0*s.* 10*d.* a year, besides an assortment of apparel and other chattels connected with their chapel at the north door of St. Paul's. They redeemed only a portion for 2,006*l.* 2*s.* 6*d.* Very ample particulars of this branch of the estate are published by Herbert, who adds that the Company, in order to secure part of the forfeiture worth 98*l.* a year, as an investment, was obliged to sell lands and tenements of the annual value of 124*l.*

Some estimate may be formed of the comparatively slender available corporate resources of the Merchant Taylors in 1549-50, when we thus see that they were unable to raise about 2,000*l.* to redeem a portion of their Chantry estate, after its forfeiture to the Crown, without sacrificing other property, with which they were less reluctant to part; yet at this point of time the Company seems from inventories to have been in possession of a very large and valuable collection of silver plate.

But in some extracts from the books ranging from the fifteenth to the eighteenth century, as given by Herbert, we readily perceive that, while the revenue of the Company was incomparably smaller than at present, the demands upon it for public objects, legitimate or otherwise, were incessant and heavy, and that long subsequently to the Great Fire, the corporate finances were still in a very depressed state. A more constitutional Government had succeeded to that of the Stuarts; but immense damage was inflicted by the Fire; the connection of the Gild with trade was of little or no value; and the rental from City property still remained stationary or very slowly progressive. The great stride forward was reserved for the present century, and was due to agencies almost wholly external.

The Merchant Taylors, in providing the gross total of 5,000*l.* for the purchase of a twelfth share in the Irish Venture pressed upon the City by James I., arranged with the Clothworkers to take over a certain proportion, as the Grocers did with the Vintners. We hear very little of the mode in which the Company conducted the management of the estate, or of the measure of success which attended their stewardship; but in 1727 the property was sold to William Richardson, Esq., for 20,000*l.* 6*s.* 6*d.*, with a reserved rent of 150*l.*

Both Herbert and Mr. Clode supply very copious and adequate

extracts and illustrations of the unceasing part borne by the Merchant Taylors in all descriptions of public occurrences, with the inevitable feature of a call for pecuniary outlay, differing in amount from a few pounds to a few hundreds. Some of these items of expenditure were compulsory, in the shape of requisitions from the Crown for subsidies and loans, or from the City for participation in some royal ceremony; others were optional and voluntary. In 1469 the Company ranked

THE ORIGINAL ARMS.

second or third in the muster of men-at-arms for the City Watch, supplying 200 men, while the Mercers found the same number, and the Brewers 210.

The earliest entry of much significance is in reference to the steps taken by two of the Court in 1480 to arrange with the Heralds' College for the grant of arms, of which we furnish an illustration. The records under 1483 of course mention the difference with the Skinners on the question of precedence, sent for trial to the King's Bench, and referred back for settlement to the Lord Mayor, who seems to have proved the difficulty and doubt existing on the subject by his suggestion of a friendly compromise.

But the order in which the Companies placed themselves was, as a matter of fact, quite uncertain and irregular till 8 Henry VIII., when the Court of Aldermen formulated what was intended to be a definitive rule for observance. In this List the Taylors are sixth and the Skinners seventh, and the succession is in short the same as at present, except that the Clothworkers are described as *Shermen*, and the catalogue embraces no more than forty-eight bodies, concluding with the Fruiterers.

In the settlement of precedence at the coronation of Henry VIII. and Catherine of Arragon the Merchant Taylors stood even before the Mercers.

In 1563 it deserves notice that William Fleetwood, steward of the Taylors' manor of Rushed, being chosen Recorder of London, a hogshead of wine was voted to him by the Merchant Taylors. In the following year the Company was approached with respect to some of its property in Lombard Street and Cornhill, in view of the erection of an Exchange. Under 1571 the Lord Mayor issues his precept that ten men of this Gild, and as many of the Vintners', shall watch each of the City gates every tenth day. In 1579–80 there is a requisition from the Crown for the supply and training of 200 men at the Company's charge. In 1586 soldiers are provided to attend the obsequies of Sir Philip Sydney. Thirty-five men-at-arms have to be found to assist in repelling the Spanish invasion. A precept regarding plays and playhouses is received, March 22, 1591–2.

On July 5, 1597, John Stow presents a copy of his *Annals* to the Company, and the Court grants him thereupon an annuity of 4*l.*, successively increased to 6*l.* and 10*l.*[1] On October 21, 1600, curtains are ordered for the Queen's arms and for the maps given by Mr. John Speed. In 1594, 60*l.* are demanded as a second contribution to the pest-house, and 296*l.* 10*s.* toward the equipment of six ships for her Majesty's service. In 1602–3 and 1603–4 the Company takes the lead with 936 quarters and a sum of 37*l.* 8*s.* 9*d.*, in contributing to the storage of corn for the use of the poor, and to the expense for receiving James I. on his entry into London. A Merchant Taylors' boy reads an address to the King at his coronation. In 1607 the visit of James to

---

[1] The Company also restored Stow's monument in the church of St. Andrew Undershaft, originally erected by his widow.

the Company costs upward of 1,000*l.*, and Ben Jonson writes the dramatic entertainment. 1608. On consideration, French and Dutch tailors are admitted to employment. 1609. The Virginian adventure is discussed. 1610. John Churchman, from whose benefaction the Company derives some very valuable property, and who had served as Master, becomes an almsman through reverses of fortune. Besides usual allowances, a pension of 20*l.* a year is settled on him, and he is permitted special privileges. July 16, 1614. No Knights are to be put up for the wardenship, as it is not thought to be consistent. 1625–6, March 21. The Persian Ambassador is allowed to walk in the Company's garden for his recreation, and is invited to dinner on May 10, 1629. The Merchant Taylors give the *maximum* quota (225*l.* 15*s.*) toward the cost of celebrating the coronation of Charles I.

1635, July 14. Certain tenants, bound by their leases to furnish bucks to the Master on the renewal, refuse to perform the covenant, and have the sealing of their new leases postponed till they submit. 1640. October 7. The Merchant Taylors contribute £5,000 to the £200,000 demanded by the King from the City for the maintenance of the army in the North. 1642, April 16. The Company has to furnish arms and ammunition in aid of the defence of the City. 1645–6, March 11. 40*l.* are paid toward the expenses of the Scottish troops under the Earl of Leven. 1654. The Company is obliged to sell property to the value of 180*l.* a year, and to retrench, in order to meet the drain on its funds, yet votes 13*l.* 6*s.* 8*d.* to John Ogilby, a freeman, in recognition of his literary services and merits. 1666, September. The Great Fire. 1684, April 9. The writ of *Quo Warranto* is served. 1684–5, February 9. The Company requests permission of the Court of Aldermen to put up the statue of James II., ordered by them from Grinling Gibbons. 1687, September 25. The Master and Wardens surrender their office. October 3. They and the other Gilds are re-admitted by letters patent under the Great Seal, directed to the Lord Mayor from Windsor.

1688, May 22. It is ordered that the silver yard be delivered to the Wardens of the Yeomanry, as occasion requires.

1689, October 18. The whole Court, or any five of them, are appointed to consider and examine *of what use and benefit the Yeomanry are to this Company, and what advantage they have brought, or damage they have done, to this Company since their restoration.* 1702–3, February 7. The Hall and rooms, except the little parlour, the rooms over it, and the Clerk's house, are let to the East India Company at a peppercorn rent and a fine of 500*l.*, till Midsummer, 1709; and on March 12, 1706–7 notice is given of the willingness of the Company to take another tenant on the expiry of the term. The East India Company take the premises, however, for another year at a rent of 200*l.* The Merchant Taylors subsequently again let their Hall, between this date and 1721 or later, to the South Sea Company. 1727. The Irish estates are sold.

From this time to the reign of George III. we do not hear much of the domestic history of the Company ; but its circumstances were probably beginning to improve.

We have been tempted to offer the preceding extracts as a sort of outline, by way of sample of the manner, in which an important and wealthy body of men, possessing in freehold a landed estate and other property of great and growing value, were subjected during centuries to the most trying and humiliating vicissitudes and extortions ; for the light which this glimpse into the records from 1469 to 1727 affords us is a peculiarly representative one, owing to the community of origin, basis, and constitution. *Mutatis mutandis*, the archives of all the Gilds, especially of course the greater and richer, tell the same chequered tale, and to meet these calls the personal estate of members necessarily paid heavy toll.

Before the Merchant Taylors acquired, 1331, the site of the present Hall in Threadneedle Street, they possessed a place of meeting in Basing Lane, behind the Red Lion, in Cordwainer Street Ward, which still existed in 1593, and is explicitly described as "the old Hall," for which a tenant then offered himself. When they used the premises in Basing Lane, they were still, at least until 1327, unincorporated ; but the removal to what was more properly called Three-Needle Street, indicates a prosperous condition and strong confidence in the future.

For the property represented an important investment and a considerable dormant rental. It is described as a dwelling-house, formerly occupied by Sir Oliver de Ingham—who was summoned to Parliament 2 Edward III. as Lord De Ingham, and who died in 1344 without male issue—with its abuttals or easements, and two great gates, one toward Broad Street, the other toward Cornhill.

The Merchant Taylors appear to possess the scantiest possible information concerning the circumstances under which the present building, or even that which stood in 1588, after having undergone extensive repairs, evolved from the structure once owned by Lord de Ingham. Judging from a variety of *data*, the Ingham mansion was a detached one with approaches from two thoroughfares, Cornhill and Broad Street, and a certain area of garden. The new proprietors, who came into possession of it from the immediate owner, "a worshipful gentleman," as Stow terms him, Edmund Crepin, were scarcely in a position to rebuild ; and the probability may even be, that they found the premises too large for their requirements. The history of the transformation is divisible into two distinct periods: from 1331 to 1666, and from 1666 to the present time. The latter is a subject of inferior interest, though of less obscure character. But it would be very desirable, no doubt, to be able to trace with greater exactitude the successive stages in the work. Almost every point is conjectural; and as one piece of guess-work is

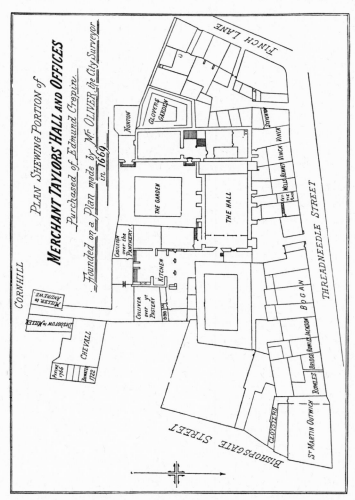

as good as another, perhaps, we may hazard a speculation that the Fraternity continued for a long time to use the Ingham house, or a portion of it, unaltered, and merely executed repairs or slight alterations as they were needed. The partial, piecemeal method in which the Company worked at a much later period, ought to reconcile us to the view that at first they were still more deliberate and conservative.

From certain authoritative statements and indications it may be presumed that the existing Hall stands partly on the lines of that before the Fire, but that the latter had been rebuilt at some uncertain date (between 1406 and 1450) on fresh ground, and quite apart from the Ingham Hall and its underlying crypt, which remained little changed, may-be, from Norman times. Where new work had been introduced, was most likely to be in the offices and dormitories—in those portions used for every-day purposes. It must have been a somewhat ill-appointed and uncomfortable domicile or even meeting-place; for down to the Elizabethan age the windows of the Hall were unglazed, and admitted the rain, and the floors of the rooms were of the most primitive description.

We know that by the gift of John Churchman, in 1406, of seventeen shops and other messuages at St. Martin's Outwich or Otewich, belonging to William and John Otewich, whose executor he was, facilities were afforded for the enlargement of the premises on that side; but we seem to have no evidence when this occurred, or how long the process occupied. In short, so many alterations were effected by degrees in the ground-plan and by the almost indubitable absorption of the Churchman or Otewich group of shops by the church of St. Martin, Outwich, succeeded by the demolition of the church itself, that there is little room for wonder, if those most conversant with the matter are at a loss here.

One rather material point in connection with the Churchman gift, thus presumably merged in the Hall, is, that it was "in perpetual alms" for the benefit of the poor brethren and sisters of the Society.

From a variety of scattered entries we may just collect that the New Hall, or Taylors' Inn, as it was long termed in distinction from the old house in Basing Lane, was in course of time adorned with costly arras depicting the history of St. John the Baptist, and furnished with a screen surmounted by a gilt image of the patron saint in a gilt tabernacle or portico. The windows were gradually glazed, and many of them embellished with armorial bearings of the donors; sweet rushes were strown on the floor; tables on trestles ran the whole length of the apartment, and on feast-days were covered with choice table-cloths and the Company's plate; and from the ceiling were suspended flags and streamers.

Besides the Hall or Refectory and the offices, the block of buildings may be taken, in the early Tudor era, to have consisted of the Parlour, the Long Gallery, containing portraits of benefactors, the Bachelors' Gallery for the junior members of the Gild, the King's Chamber, which was used when Henry VII. served as Master, but was rebuilt in 1593, and the garden, with alleys and a terace, and a back-way into Cornhill. In this plot of ground lay the old Ingham Hall, with a crypt beneath it and a chapel annexed, and the Treasury, where the muniments and plate are said in 1491 to be kept.

In the parlour was part of the arras, some oil paintings presented by Mr. Vernon in 1616, a portrait of Sir Thomas White, a picture by Gerard Dow with a silk curtain before it (a practice still followed), and the set of Speed's maps given by him to the Company, similarly protected.

This description must be received with caution and indulgence as

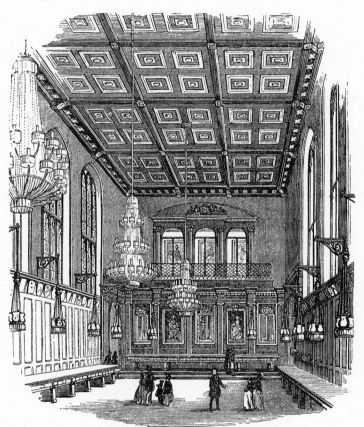

INTERIOR OF MERCHANT TAYLORS' HALL, 1842.

answering to the arguable aspect of the place during the Tudor and Stuart times, and substantially down to the occurrence of the grand catastrophe of 1666.

Yet that the Hall anterior to the Fire was entirely distinct from the Ingham house, and on another site, there is no question; and indeed we perceive that in 1646 the Merchant Taylors leased the latter, with its crypt or cellar, for twenty-one years to L. Newman, but reserved the passage into Cornhill, inhibited the tenant from building so as to overlook the garden, and required him to furnish a fat buck annually against the Election dinner.

At present, after the expenditure of vast sums of money in rebuilding and redecorating, the Hall has become one of the most splendid edifices of the kind in London. The ancient Ingham crypt survives ; but the chapel has been converted into a kitchen. Ingham's Hall has doubtless long disappeared.

Merchant Taylors' Hall well repays a visit and a study. It is old-fashioned, ample, sumptuous ; and it is stored with a variety of

ROSE-WATER DISH OF THE EARLY PART OF THE 17TH CENTURY.

interesting and historical remains, besides the portraits of eminent men of more modern date and the collection of antique plate. The most remarkable feature is the series of stained-glass windows in one of the corridors, commemorating the momentary feud for precedence in processions between the Taylors and the Skinners in 1483–4, which terminated in a friendly compromise and a dinner. The successive stages in the quarrel are depicted with great skill and spirit and with all the impressive accessories of costume and colour ; they exhibit the first hustling and skirmish in the streets, the arrest of some of the rioters, the award of the Mayor, the hand-shaking, and the pacificatory banquet.   The whole is a striking, realistic *tableau*, forming part of the modern buildings erected between 1878 and 1881.

The Company also possesses two magnificent Palls of early embroidered work, attributed to the fifteenth and sixteenth centuries, and very ineffectively reproduced in Mr. Clode's *Memorials ;* the silver Seal of the Fraternity, engraved in Mr. Clode's book, and the solid oaken poop of the barge, with the Arms, as well as a coloured drawing of the vessel, now no longer used.

The constitution of the Company vests in the Master and four Wardens for the time being all the corporate power and property ; a principle which was, no doubt, adopted in the first place as a matter of convenience and necessity, but which, alike in this and in other parallel cases, has created the anomaly of no title to a share of the assets of the Company belonging, in the event of realization, to the members at large, although their standing has been acquired by a pecuniary payment, and they are partakers of many of the immunities and advantages of association.   Should a partition at any period be arranged, it might be difficult to settle in whom the estate is really lodged.

The governing body is composed, as usual, of the Master, Wardens, and Assistants ; and there are three standing committees of members of the Court : the Estates, the Charities, and the Schools.   There are other occasional committees.   The Court must consist of at least thirteen members.

In 1501-2 the Livery of the Gild amounted to 84 ; in 1534, to 97. In 1699 it is returned as 600.   In 1710 it had receded to 481.   At the parliamentary poll in 1722, 346 voted ; in 1724 the return was 473 ; but the *New and Complete Survey*, 1742, reckons 394.   The *History of the School*, 1812, speaks of the Livery as consisting of 300.   The printed lists of persons entitled to vote in 1832 gave only 265 inclusive, and in 1834, 320.   The Returns of 1882 reduce the figures to 226 inclusive ; but those of 1892 give them as 270.

The Merchant Taylors, in common with the Mercers, Goldsmiths, and other eventually prominent Gilds, do not figure much in the registers and records of the Corporation in connexion with early trade disputes and scandals.   In 1415 the journeymen or yeomen of this calling, who proved a very troublesome element, and one which became at a later period of dubious value, were forbidden to occupy dwellings apart, or to wear any special livery, without the leave of their Wardens.   This restriction had reference to a tendency on the part of the working operatives of certain businesses, about and before the commencement of the fifteenth century, to combine together against their principals, and initiate " strikes."

Looking at these matters with our modern eyes, we see that there was blame on both sides. From an early date many of the Companies conceived an intolerance of the mere holders of the Freedom, with whom the tie of the rest was apt to be more or less loose and more or less purely eleemosynary ; and we have the beginning of a spirit of revolt on the part of the Yeomanry against the overbearing attitude of the Executive, and of a widening estrangement in the sentiments of the governing section toward those who had been an integral and essential part of the fundamental constitution of these Societies. In this particular case, the recalcitrant workmen were found dwelling in Three Shears Court at Garlick Hill, without official inspection, and were presented to the Lord Mayor, who reprimanded them, and ordered them to withdraw within bounds.

In the 4th of Henry VII. the freemen, or Yeomanry, addressed a petition to the Court of Aldermen to be allowed their ancient suffrages in the election of Master and Wardens ; and the municipality fenced the prayer or demand by granting them the exercise of all honest customs as theretofore. The movement indicates a stealthy tendency on the part of the Executive to take the whole government into their own hands.

Two years later, the Yeomen Taylors petitioned the Court of Aldermen to be suffered, agreeably to ancient usage, to assemble at the Church of St. John of Jerusalem in Smithfield, on the Feast of the Decollation of St. John the Baptist, to make offering for their brethren and sisteren deceased, and for other purposes. But the record is imperfect, and we do not hear what was decided.

As the affairs of the Company grew more complex and extensive, it was found that the Yeomanry required a larger share of attention in points of detail and discipline than the normal governing body could afford them ; and some time previously to 1596–7 the Court of Assistants resolved, mainly on this account, but partly too, perhaps, to meet the spirit of discontent and insubordination among the lower grades of the Society, to appoint annually thenceforward four Warden Substitutes and sixteen Assistants from the Yeomanry to manage certain matters laid down for them by the Court, and to have the privilege of meeting in the Hall subject to convenience and approval. In some instances, the retiring Wardens were taken up into the Livery.

This was an entire innovation on the prevailing practice of the Gilds, and was doubtless adopted in the interests of peace and efficiency. But the experiment did not answer ; the Wardens of the Yeomanry and their colleagues gradually overstepped the limits of their particular jurisdiction ; and in 1661, the Company, after a good deal of sufferance, abolished the affiliated officers, and proceeded to remodel their internal government.

The ascendency of the Court and Livery of the Merchant-Taylors appears to have steadily increased toward the latter part of the seventeenth century, if we may judge from a question, which was seriously raised and discussed in 1689, whether the Yeomanry was a feature in the system worth preservation. The Company must at this period have almost severed its practical tie with the trade.

Until the abolition of Bartholomew Fair, in 1854, after an existence of seven hundred years, it was customary for the representative of the Company to proceed to Cloth Fair, and to test the measures used for selling cloth there by the Company's silver yard, of which a specimen is still preserved at the Hall.

With this exception, we believe that the direct intervention of the Company in trade matters determined in 1691, upon the abolition of the Wardens of the Yeomanry.

The official supervision of Cloth Fair formed part of prescription enjoyed since the charter of 1439, by which the Company exercised the general right of search ; there are registrations of cases, in which possessors of unlawful measures and other culprits were proceeded against under this authority ; and Professor Morley points to an entertainment held at the Hall on the eve of the search, as if considerable importance was then attached to the process, and others beside the Beadle attended on the occasion. The original practice, while the custom was in full force, was, that the Wardens and Clerk should also attend ; but the Merchant-Taylors during a lengthened period delegated this task to the Wardens of the Yeomanry. When the association with trade and the Fair grew less particular, and these functionaries were abolished, the duty devolved on the Beadle.

The cloth-yard arrow, of which we hear in the Robin Hood and other ballads, had its origin here ; and it is worth remarking that in the *Little Gest of Robin Hood*, printed in or before 1508, where Little John measures out the scarlet and green cloth for the Knight, he employs his bow for the purpose, that being, when bent, perhaps approximately a yard or ell in diametrical length.

SILVER CLOTH YARD.

It is curious that among the eminent members of the Fraternity the name of Sir John Hawkwood occupies the foremost place, although his connexion with it is excessively doubtful. A distinguished brother, and one of the governing body, was Robert Dove, the friend of Stow.

An account of him was published in 1612. In 1604 he gave his fellow-gildsmen twenty gilt spoons marked with a dove. He was very probably connected with Thomas Dove of Exeter, the rich clothier, whom Deloney commemorates in his *Six Yeomen of the West*, published before 1600. Sir William Fitzwilliam, founder of the noble house still extant, belonged to this body, as we have already seen, and is said to have been immediately instrumental in procuring from Henry VII. the more honourable designation of Merchant-Taylors for his Gild. Fitz-william, who had been in the service of Wolsey, and stood firm to him in his fall, left to it in trust a sum of 7*l.* to find a priest to say masses for his soul in the Church of West Ham, Northamptonshire; but the bequest was for a long time "concealed" by the Company, which was ordered in 1578 to pay the arrears, amounting to 103*l.* 5*s.* by instalments. This Fitzwilliam was doubtless the descendant of William Fitzwilliam, citizen and goldsmith, who, in 1210, founded the Benedictine Nunnery of St. Helen's, Bishopsgate. One of the benefactresses is Dame Thomasine Percival, of whom there is so romantic a story John Webster the dramatist was a freeman, and was employed to write the Taylors' Pageant in 1624. There is in one of the rooms at the Hall a long catalogue of royal and noble personages who have been from time to time enrolled as honorary associates.

Of those who have belonged to the Gild, however, Sir Thomas White [1] is *facile princeps*. But to John Churchman and Richard Hills it owes much.

It may be generally observed, that at the present moment the temper and tendency of the Merchant-Taylors are in the direction of extending their eleemosynary and educational grants, and of reducing their sumptuary expenditure. On their schools and other charities, and on the advancement of culture, they are laying out very large sums. Merchant-Taylors' School alone has cost them within a limited period about 150,000*l.*

In 1555, previous to the institution of the school, Sir Thomas White, a member of the Court of the Merchant-Taylors' Company, established St. John's College, Oxford, and reserved forty-three of its fifty endowed fellowships for the scholars; and in 1561 Mr. Richard Hills, Merchant-Taylor, provided the first payment (500*l.*) toward the institution of Merchant-Taylors' School and purchase of the site in Suffolk Lane. Sir Thomas White co-operated at a somewhat later date; and Hills

---

[1] In the dedication of his *Brief Chronicle of the Success of Time*, 1611, to the Merchant-Taylors, Anthony Munday gives an interesting account of Sir Thomas White's benefactions.

and himself are usually regarded as the co-founders of this charity. It was originally intended for 250 boys ; but in 1616 there were as many as 389. The numbers had receded in 1625 to 131, and in 1665 to 112. The endowment has been greatly enlarged and entirely remodelled within the last thirty years ; and the old house in Suffolk Lane, where the present writer received his education, *or a part of it*, between 1842 and 1850, has been abandoned for an entirely new building on the site of the Charterhouse.

Great Crosby School, near Liverpool, founded by John Harrison, Merchant-Taylor, in 1618, for 100 boys, and placed under the care of the Company, has also been rebuilt on an improved and more commodious scale.

The Almshouses of the Company, which once stood in Threadneedle Street by the Hall, and were afterward removed to Tower Hill, are now at Lee in Kent, and accommodate thirty-two inmates, widows or daughters of freemen, being not less than fifty-four years of age. The cost of rebuilding in 1825 was upward of 11,000*l*.

The Company has lately undertaken to subscribe 2,000*l*. a year to the City and Gilds of London Technical Institute.

LITERARY NOTICES.

The Enquirie and Verdite of the Quest Panneld of the Death of Rychard Hune, Wich was founde hanged in Lolars tower. 8vo, [1514.]
Only two fragments are known. It is reprinted by Fox ; and see Stow, *Annales*, 1615, p. 497. Hune was a member of the Merchant-Taylors' Company.

Londons Dove : Or, A Memoriall of the Life and Death of Maister Robert Doue, Citizen and Merchant Taylor of London. By Anthony Nixon. 4to, 1612.

The Honorable Prentice ; Or, This Taylor is a Man. Shewed in the Life and Death of Sir John Hawkwood. By William Vallans. 4to, 1615, 1616.

The Honour of Merchant-Taylors, wherein is set forth the Noble Acts, Valliant Deeds, and Heroick Performances of Merchant-Taylors in former Ages. By William Winstanley. 4to, 1668. Dedicated to the Merchant-Taylors' Company.

The Honour of the Taylors ; Or, The Famous and Renowned History of Sir John Hawkwood, Knight. 4to, 1687.

An Elegie Raised to the immortall Memorie of the trulie noble, and most accomplished, with all reall perfections Elizabeth Lady Ducey. By Robert Codrington, M.A. [About 1648]. An unpublished MS., English and Latin.
This lady was the wife of Sir Robert Ducie, who was Lord Mayor in 1630, and who was the son of Henry Ducie, of London.

The Prentize Indentures. Entered at Stationers' Hall, Feb. 6, 1594–5, to be printed for the Merchant Taylors' Company.

A Prayer to be said by the Poor, Needy and Aged Almesmen of the Company of the Merchant-Taylors, for the blessed charity of a good brother of that Company. [1625]. A broadside.

Positions Wherin those primitive circumstances be examined, which are necessarie for the training up of children. By Richard Mulcaster, first headmaster of Merchant Taylors' School. 4to, 1581.

The First Part of the Elementarie. By the same. 4to, 1582.

In Mortem Serenissimæ Reginæ Elizabethæ. By the same. 4to, 1603. English and Latin.

A New Balade. O Dere Lady Elysabeth. By R[ichard] M[ulcaster]. A broadside.

Catechismus Paulinus. By the same. 8vo, 1599, 1601, etc.

Poemata. By the same. 8vo, 1599.

The Scholars Petition for Play-dayes instead of Holy-dayes: Exhibited to the Right Worshipfull the Master, Wardens and Assistants of the right Worshipfull Company of Merchant-Taylors by the Scholars of their School. Martij 31. An. 1644. [1644–5.] A broadside.

The School's Probation; Or, Rules and Orders for Certain Set-Exercises to be Performed by the Scholars on Probation-daies. Made and approved by Learned Men, for the Use of Merchant-Tailors' School in London. 8vo, 1652, 1661.

This work, it appears from Wilson, was compiled as early as 1608.

The English Rudiments of the Latine Tongue. By William Du-Gard. 8vo, 1656.

An Humble Remonstrance Presented to the Right Worshipfull Company of Merchant-Tailors, Maii 15, 1661. By William Du Gard. 4to, 1661.

** In relation to his dismissal from the head-mastership of the school.

CIVIC PAGEANTS, ETC.

The Triumphs of Reunited Britannia: Performed at the Cost and Charges of the Right Worshipful Company of the Merchant Taylors, in Honor of Sir Leonard Holliday, Knt., to solemnise his Entrance as Lord Mayor of the City of London, on Tuesday the 29 of October, 1605. Devised and written by A. Munday, Citizen and Draper of London. 4to, 1605.

A Speech, Music, and other Inventions, by Ben Jonson, 1607.

In July, 1607, James I. dining with the Court of the Merchant Taylors' Company, Ben Jonson was employed to prepare "a speech, musique, and other inventions."—Wilson's *History of M. T. School,* i. 171. It appears that the speech consisted of eighteen verses delivered by a child " clothed like an angel of gladness" (Fleay, p. 180).

Troia-Noua Triumphans. London Triumphing : Or, the Solemne, Magnificent and Memorable Receiving of that Worthy Gentleman, Sir John Swinnerton, Knight [Merchant-Taylor,] into the Citty of London, after his Returne from . . . Westminster . . . the 29 of October 1612. By Thomas Dekker. 4to, 1612.

The Freeman's Honour: A play by Wentworth Smith.

It is only mentioned in the epistle dedicatory of his *Hector of Germany,* 1615. This play, however, is said to have been " acted by the servants of the King's Majesty, to dignify the worthy Company of Merchant Taylors." It was possibly a mere civic pageant.

Monuments of Honor, Derived from remarkable Antiquity, and Celebrated in the Honourable City of London at the sole magnificent Charge and expenses of the Right Worthy and Worshipful Fraternity of the Eminent Merchant Taylors. Directed in their most affectionate love at the Confirmation of their right worthy Brother John Goare, in his high Office of His Majesty's Lieutenant over this royal Chamber. . . . Invented and written by John Webster, Merchant Taylor. 4to, 1624.

Mars his Triumph : Or, The Description of an Exercise performed the xviii. of October, 1638, in Merchant Taylors Hall, By certain Gentlemen of the Artillery Garden, London. By W. Barriffe. 4to, 1639.

Huntington Divertisement, Or, An Interlude for the Generall Entertainment at the County Feast, held at Merchant-Taylors' Hall, June 20, 1678. By W. M. 4to, 1678.

London's Glory ; or, the Lord Mayor's Show : Containing an Illustrious Description of the several Triumphant Pageants on which are represented Emblematical Figures, Artful pieces of architecture, and Rural Dancing, with the Speeches spoken in each Pageant : also Three new Songs ; the first in Praise of the Merchant Taylors ; the second, the Protestants' Exhortation ; and the third, the plotting Popish Litany ; with their proper Tunes, either to be sung or played. Performed on Friday, October 29, 1680, for the Entertainment of the Right Honourable Sir Patience Warde, Knight, Lord Mayor of the City of London. At the proper Cost and Charges of the Right Worshipful Company of Merchant Taylors. Invented and composed by Tho. Jordan, Gent. 4to, 1680.

War Horns, Make Room for the Bucks with Green Bowes. 4to, 1682.
This refers to the Entertainment of the London prentices and others at Merchant-Taylors' Hall.

The Lord Mayor's Show : Being a Description of the Solemnity at the Inauguration of the truly loyal and Right Honourable Sir William Prichard, Knight, Lord Mayor of the City of London, President of the Artillery Company, and a Member of the Worshipful Company of Merchant-Taylors. Performed on Monday, September 30, 1682, with several new loyal Songs and Catches. [By Thomas Jordan.] 4to, 1682.

The Triumphs of London : Performed on October 30, 1693. For the Entertainment of the Right Honourable Sir William Ashurst, Knight, Lord Mayor of the City of London. Containing a True Description of the several Pageants, with the Speeches Spoken on each Pageant. All set forth at the proper Costs and Charges of the Worshipful Company of Merchant-Taylors. Together with the Festival Songs for his Lordship and the Company's Diversion. By Elkanah Settle 4to, 1693.

The Haberdashers.[1]

THE Haberdashers may be considered as an offshoot of the Mercers, whose original small-ware business they took over, and at the same time as a fusion of the United Hurers and the Cappers and Hatters, who have been noticed in the former division of the present work.

The term *Haberdasher* was applied to two Brotherhoods, one of St. Catherine, the other of St. Nicholas ; and it was agreeable to the ancient commercial polity and economy, that side by side with them existed other Societies of Hurers, Cappers, and Hatters, with independent interests and administrative systems. In 1376 the Haberdashers of St. Catherine and the Hurers were entitled to send two members each to the Common Council.

In 26 Henry VI., the branch of St. Catherine received a charter under the style of "The King's beloved Subjects the Men of the Mistery of Haberdashers within the City of London," and had licence thereby to establish a Gild or Fraternity in honour of the blessed Katherine the Virgin of the men of the mistery aforesaid, to have perpetual succession, with power to add to their numbers, to elect four capable and sufficient Wardens among themselves for their government, and to acquire in fee and perpetuity lands, tenements, and other possessions, to make and use a common seal, and to plead and be impleaded in all courts. The instrument further sanctioned the claim for the brethren and the sisters

---

[1] Some information respecting these bodies will be found in the preceding section.

of one livery or vesture of a suit, and the celebration of a Gild-feast on the day of St. Catherine.

The association thus formed must at this period have attained considerable prosperity and eminence, since twelve of the Gild attended the coronation in 1466 of Elizabeth of York. It was then ranked as the eighth in precedence. In 1469, it contributed the large quota of thirty freemen to the City watch, it then counting as the eleventh Company ; and at the coronation of Richard III., the Haberdashers', in common with the other Fraternities, was represented by its Master.

The St. Nicholas branch apparently coalesced with the other in the

OLD ARMS.

same or following reign, and in 17 Henry VII. the whole corpus of once separate callings was consolidated.

But the charter of Henry VII. is in its structure very peculiar, since it commences by incorporating the Fraternity of Hurers, otherwise Cappers, and Hatters, as a Gild in honour of St. James the Apostle, and settling their constitution ; and at once proceeds to declare that this newly-created body may, again, be united with the Haberdashers under the style of the Fraternity of Merchant Haberdashers in the City of London, *and not otherwise*. The two operations were thus most unusually carried out under one seal.

The *inspeximus* of 1511 specifies them as Haberdashers only ; and under date of April 1, in that year, we find that the Court of Aldermen ordered the payment by the Chamberlain of 40 marks to the Company toward their costs in negotiating with the King's Council on this

point, as if the Corporation had intervened in the question of relinquish-
ing the additional title, a process which the language of the former one
rendered somewhat embarrassing.

The fairly prompt revocation—in the next following charter—of the
special privilege which placed the Haberdashers on the same titular
footing as the Taylors, may be thought to establish two points : the
stricter interpretation then placed on the term *merchant* in our language,
and the understood and accepted compliance with it on the part of
the more favoured body at a more advanced stage in its career. For,
as we elsewhere state and hold, the Taylors at one time were alike
manufacturers and salesmen.

There is no doubt that the relinquishment of the designation was
official and absolute. Yet although in the City records under 1501–2
the Company is cited as the Haberdashers simply, in later lists down to
23 Henry VIII. they occur with the more honorific style.

This grant was confirmed by successive Governments.

The amalgamation by Henry VII. of the Hatters and Hurers, and his
simultaneous digest of the entire trade into one Company, did not affect
the standing distinction between the vendor of hats and caps and the
vendor of small wares, who were respectively known down to a far later
date as Haberdashers of hats and Haberdashers of small wares. For
executive and defensive purposes, the Company undertook to compre-
hend both divisions, and was a sort of joint-stock concern, trafficking
precisely in those articles of dress and use which were in universal
demand.

It is further to be remarked, that the trade in pins was at this time
beginning to prove an important element in the haberdasher's stock ;
but they were principally imported from the Continent, and did not constitute an English industry, till the extraordinary demand led to the
establishment of factories in London, which soon competed successfully
with the foreign article. The makers organized themselves in process of
time into a chartered body in consequence of the great development of
their Craft ; but from some unexplained cause they failed to maintain
their corporate rank.

The aggrandizement of the Haberdasher, both of hats and small wares
is represented to have produced a strongly marked change in the aspect
of many of the City and suburban thoroughfares, which exhibited a far
gayer and more attractive appearance toward the time of Elizabeth than
formerly, and involved a much more profuse expenditure on trifles and
knick-knacks, especially those of Continental fabric.

The Haberdashers' earliest bye-laws, subsequently to their incorporation, are supposed to have perished in the Fire ; and they do not possess

any anterior to 1675. They treat of 1. The Election of Master and Wardens ; 2. the choice of Assistants and Liverymen ; 3. Quarterages ; 4. Apprentices ; 5. the Wardens' Courts and Assistants' Courts. The freeman's quarterage was then 2s. a year.

These Articles are set out at large in the Returns of 1882. The only one of special relevance and curiosity is that which deals with the choosing of *Bachelors*, a designation likewise used by the Merchant-Taylors, but which seems to be intended here in a different sense. The clause ordains that at the election of a new Mayor, a convenient number of freemen shall be appointed bachelors of the Company, and shall serve in foins and budge, when the Mayor goes to take oath at Westminster, and shall contribute to the charges of the Company in attending the pageant a sum not exceeding 6l. 13s. 4d. each, under certain prescribed penalties.

The text does not state so much ; but it is inferable that the persons thus selected became permanent members of the Livery. The amount of assessment appears to demonstrate the affluence of members who were merely holders of the Freedom. But the governing body would naturally choose such as were known to be in a position to disburse the quota.

The Haberdashers, associating with themselves the Wax-Chandlers, Turners, and Founders, took one of the manors under the Irish Plantation Scheme of James I. But they were foremost in parting with the property, so far as they were concerned, the co-parceners not apparently joining in the transaction, as the tenants-in-chief sold their interest in 1675, and the Founders at all events retained theirs till 1686.

As early as 1639 the Haberdashers appear to have made a movement toward a realization of their Irish property. In that year the Crown, through the Star Chamber, declared the purchase of the Ulster Plantation, from which James I. had obtained so large a sum, to be illegal and void, and in lieu of reimbursing the purchasers, demanded a fine of 110,000l., or, in other words, aimed at a second despotic extortion. But the House of Commons voted the levy to be an usurpation and an act of injustice ; and the City and Companies were saved from the threatened blow. It was not strange, however, that those who held such a sterile and precarious investment should be anxious in some cases to divest themselves of it ; and had not the Long Parliament, very shortly after, curtailed the royal power, and swept away many tyrannical enormities, it is eminently probable that the Companies would have been compelled to part with their property, and forfeit all the outlay so far incurred.

The Hall is first specifically mentioned in the charter of 20 Elizabeth, where the power is conferred of having one, and of convoking assemblies.

The site on which the modern building stands in Gresham Street, formerly Maiden Lane, was bequeathed to the Company by William Baker, Citizen and Haberdasher, in 1478, and occupied about half an acre.   An accurate plan of this important area is preserved among the Company's archives; but of the Hall there seems to be nothing beyond the tradition.

The Hall by Wren, which Herbert describes in 1836 as in need of reconstruction, was almost completely destroyed by fire about two years later, and rebuilt.   The Court Room, or part of it, is all that remains of the second edifice.   The old courtyard is covered by warehouses, which immediately flank the present Hall to the south, and form an element of considerable danger.[1]   The compass of the premises has been contracted by the temptation to let off superfluous space.

There are several large portraits in oil on the walls of the Hall, and with two of them,—those of George II. and Queen Caroline,—a singular anecdote is connected.   They had been lost during a long series of years when a member of the Court recognised them in a house in the West of England in 1879, and purchased them as a present to his Company. Beyond the feeling of association, however, they possess no importance.

Of the building burnt down in or about 1846, Brayley gives an account in *Londiniana*, 1829, and tells us that the refectory was a lofty and spacious room, with a wainscot twelve feet high all round, and a music or minstrels' gallery over the screen at the lower end.   He also

---

[1] Within the last few years the premises have had one or two narrow escapes, and have been seriously injured.

supplies a view of the exterior, while the courtyard still remained, and the footway in front was paved with rough flagstones.

The Company has four groups of almshouses : Aske's Hospital at Hoxton, the Jones charity at Monmouth and at Newland, Gloucestershire, and Adams's benefaction at Newport, Salop. They have also under their management four schools : Trotman's in Bunhill Row for 100 boys belonging to the parish of St. Giles, Cripplegate, Jones's at Monmouth for 100 boys belonging to the town or county, Adams's at Newport for 30 boys, and a fourth at Bunbury in Cheshire, instituted in 1594–5.

Mr. William Jones, Haberdasher and Merchant Adventurer, the founder of the Jones charities in Monmouthshire and Gloucestershire, was a native of Newland in the latter county. Sir Francis Jones, Lord Mayor in 1620, was of a different family, being the son of John Jones, of Claverley, Salop. It is said of the former, that when he became rich he visited his native town *incognito*, and was not very hospitably received, and that he subsequently waited on the Mayor of Monmouth, to which place he left a considerable share of his fortune. The Haberdashers received 18,000*l*.

His will is dated Dec. 26, 1614 ; and Letters Patent, granting the trusteeship to the Haberdashers, issued on the 19th March following, the testator having evidently died in the interval. A fine full-length life-sized portrait of him hangs in the Hall.

They have several Exhibitions at the two Universities and a share of ecclesiastical patronage.

The Returns and information supplied to the Royal Commission in 1882 were very copious, frank, and satisfactory. Owing to the loss of certain property at Old Change, and the pressure of the Corporate tax, the income has since that time declined, and the expenditure is correspondingly curtailed.

A peculiar distinction appertains to the Haberdashers, in having had among their number, in the reigns of Edward VI. and his two royal sisters, a man who was a familiar figure in the City, and who after his decease was judged to be sufficiently prominent and famous to become the hero of a story-book and a character in a play. We refer of course to William Hobson, whom Thomas Heywood, writer of several of the City pageants, has introduced among the *dramatis personæ* of his "Troubles of Queen Elizabeth," 1605. Two years later, a pamphleteer, in search of material for a fugitive *brochure*, published the *Pleasant Conceits* of Hobson.

In the play he is depicted as a kind-hearted, charitable man, who had begun life as a haberdasher in the Poultry, and had acquired wealth, of which he made good use. Both productions, in which he is commemorated, shew him to have been a rather eccentric character, full of quaint phrases and turns of thought, and to have kept his apprentices in good order. Heywood makes him rate one of them for squandering his master's money on pies at the Dagger in Cheap, and in guzzling at ale-houses.

In 1 Edward VI., after the suppression of monastic and other cognate bodies, Hobson is said to have purchased the Chapel of Corpus Christi and the Virgin at the end of Cony-hope Lane (Grocers' Hall Court), annexed since 1394 to St. Mildred's in the Poultry, and to have built on the site a warehouse and shops, facing the street, with lodgings or chambers over them. In this chapel, according to Stow, was the seat or meeting-place of a Gild or Fraternity, which had a licence to acquire lands and tenements of the value of 20*l.* a year or upward. But the brotherhood associated with it was that of the Skinners, who in their later charters were described as the Gild of Corpus Christi, and in fact received out of the sale of the chapel a yearly rent of 2*s.*

CIVIC PAGEANTS.

The Triumphs of Peace: τῆς εἰρήνης τροφεῖα, Or, The Triumphs of Peace, that celebrated the Solemnity of the Right Honourable Sir Francis Jones, Knight, at his Inauguration into the Mayoralty of London, on Monday, being the 30th of October, 1620. At the particular Cost and Charge of the Right Worshipfull and Ancient Society of the Haberdashers. With an Explication of the severall Shews and Devices. By John Squire. 4to, 1620.

At the House of the Right Honourable Sir Francis Jhones, the first Entertainment at the first Great Feast preparde to giue Welcome to his Owne Noble Fraternitie the Company of Haberdashers. 1620.

This forms part of a volume in 8vo, by Thomas Middleton, entitled *Honorable Entertainments Composde for the Seruice of this Noble Cittie,* 1621.

Londons Ius Honorarium. Exprest in sundry Triumphs, pageants, and shewes : At the Initiation or Entrance of the Right Honourable George Whitmore, into the Maioralty. . . . All the charge and expence of the laborious proiects and obiects, both by Water and Land, being the sole vndertaking of the Right Worshipfull the society of the Habber-dashers. By Thomas Heywood. 4to, 1631.

Londini Artium et Scientiarum Origo : London's Fountain of Arts and Sciences ; expressed in sundry Triumphs, Pageants and Shews, at the Initiation of the Right Honourable Nich. Raynton, in the Majoralty of the famous and far-renowned City of London. All the Charge and Expense of the Laborious Projects both by Sea and Land, being the sole Undertaking and Charge of the Right Worshipfull Company of Haberdashers. Written by Thomas Heywood. 4to, 1632.

Londini Speculum : or, London's Mirror, expresst in sundry Triumphs, Pageants, and Shewes, at the Initiation of the Right Honorable Richard Fenn, into the Maioralty. . . . All the Charge and Expence . . . being the sole undertaking of the Right Worshipful Company of the Habberdashers. By Thomas Heywood. 4to, 1637.

London's Triumphs : Celebrated the 29th of October, 1664 ; in Honour of the truly Deserver of Honour, Sir John Lawrence, Knight, Lord Maior of the Honourable City of London ; and performed at the Costs and Charges of the Worshipful Company of Haberdashers. Written by John Tatham, Gent. 4to, 1664.

The Triumphs of London. For the Inauguration of the Right Honourable Sir Richard Levett, K^t Lord Mayor of the City of London. Containing A Description of the Pageants, together with the Public Speeches, and the whole Solemnity of the Day. Performed on Monday the 30th Day of October, Anno 1699. All set forth at the proper Cost and Charge of the Honourable Company of Haberdashers. Published by Authority. [By Elkanah Settle.] Folio, 1699.

The Salters.

SAL   SAPIT   OMNIA

The universal practice of fasting, which prevailed in our country in Popish times, not only in Lent, but on Wednesdays and Fridays, and on special occasions fixed either by the Church or the Government, assisted in rendering the vocation of a Salter a very busy and profitable one. But he also derived much advantage from the indispensable storage of winter provision and from the constant and large demand for salted victual for the Navy and Merchant Services. The consumption of salt fish in former days was unquestionably enormous ; and where our vessels of all kinds occupied in their passage from place to place an infinitely longer period, and victualling stations or depôts were scarcely known, the dependence of every class of seafarer on cured fish and meat was almost complete.

It might not be rash to set back to the remotest antiquity the existence of this craft as a Brotherhood in some shape or other. In the Household Expenses of Edward I. a Salter is mentioned as one of the officers of the kitchen ; and at that time it seems to have been usual to serve up the fish during Lent in the form of bread or loaves. Salmon, herring, sturgeon, eels, are named among the sorts so treated. This description of viand was placed on the table at breakfast as well as at dinner in the houses of the nobility; and its exclusive use throughout the country at stated seasons supplies us with an estimate of the aggregate sale of the article.

The Salters obtained a patent, 37 Edward III., granting them, in common with the members of the trade elsewhere, certain liberties; and in the following year the London Fraternity itself received letters of protection. According to the official return, they sent members to represent them on the Common Council in 1376. In 1394 they had the grant of a Livery from Richard II., with the confirmation of his grandfather's patent; and in 3 and 24 Henry VI., and 3 Edward IV., their privileges were again renewed by *inspeximus.* The instrument of 1394 is of this importance and interest, that it shews the Fraternity to have been then known as established and existing under the name of the Brotherhood of Corpus Christi in All Hallows, Bread Street.

It happened in 1454, previously to this last concession, that under the will of Thomas Beamond, Citizen and Salter, and sometime Sheriff of London, he left to the Wardens of the Brotherhood and their successors in perpetuity land in Bread Street, on which stood at tha time the Hall of the said Gild and other property, of the proceeds of which some were to be applied to the repair or restoration of the said premises, and part to superstitious and charitable uses in connection with the Salters. There was a suit at law at some subsequent date to establish that Beamond intended the religious body to be benefited by his dispositions; but judgment was given that the Gild of Corpus Christi and the Salters were one and the same.

At the Dissolution of religious houses under Henry VIII. there was the usual surrender to the Crown or its nominees of all the property held to superstitious uses, according to the language of the time; and this escheat was followed by the redemption of such possessions at a considerable price. Whoever was actually responsible for these proceedings was responsible for an act of sheer robbery and fraud.

In the first of Elizabeth, July 20, 1558, the Salters obtained enlarged powers, including a licence to hold and grant real property, and to exercise the right of search within the Freedom, and were constituted a body corporate and public, and one perpetual commonalty, with two Wardens on the same footing as other bodies corporate within the City; and in 2 James I. all existing rights and privileges were acknowledged by *inspeximus,* and for the first time the Executive is amplified by the appointment, in addition to the two Wardens, of a Master and twenty-four Assistants. The charter, which may be treated as the earliest complete institution of the Company, nominated the

Master, Wardens, and Court, and fixed the elections thereafter for the Monday sevennight following Trinity Sunday, vesting the function in the Livery ; the Assistants were to hold their places for life, unless they were removed on some reasonable ground.

The Salters contributed to the purchase of the Irish Plantation in 1613, and are one of the few Companies which still keep their interest. They have laid out large sums in improvements since 1853, when a ninety-nine years' lease of the whole, granted by them, expired. In 1876 they acquired the Saddlers' share for 33,000*l.*, and in 1879 the Dyers', for 50,000*l.*, both amounts payable by instalment over fifteen or twenty years.

In 1620, some controversy having arisen respecting property held by the Company in the City, owing to alterations or misdescriptions of names and particulars, letters patent were purchased for 600*l.* from James I., vesting all such estate in the Master, Wardens, and other governors, the title notwithstanding, to be held by them and their successors for ever in free burgage.

As early as 6 Henry V. (1418) the Court of Aldermen ordained that two Salters, who had purchased salt within the City bounds, should sell it at cost price for the common good. This was a species of benevolence in kind akin to those which the Crown exacted in money. But as one at least of the parties involved was a prominent and rich man, the proceeding was possibly a matter of mutual understanding at some moment of scarcity.

The Salters, however, shared the fate of the other Gilds in having to contend against the arbitrary exercise of authority on the part of the Crown and its dependents. In 1611 Sir George Bruce obtained a patent for the manufacture of White Salt to supply Lynn, Boston, and Kingston-upon-Hull on better terms than former holders, and he represented that he was employing 1,000 hands in the business. The Company was consulted, and delivered their certificate ; but it does not appear what was its purport.

Such, with the exception of a charter of James II. (1684–5), which temporarily abridged the franchises and powers of the Salters, but was revoked by the Act of William and Mary, is the brief history of this Gild in its relationship to the Crown during two centuries and a half.

Three sets of Ordinances are said to have been framed by the Salters prior to 1507, namely : (1) Ordinances of the Salters ; (2) Ordinances between the Masters and Servants of the Mistery of Salters ; (3) Ordinances of the Salters and Tallow Chandlers ; (4) Ordinances of the Salters (7 Edward IV.). In 1507 a fifth set of Articles was approved by the Lord Chancellor, the Lord Treasurer, and the two Chief Justices, in which the Company is described as the Wardens and Fellowship of the mistery and craft of Salters in the City of London, and Keepers of the Fraternity of Corpus Christi in the Church of All Hallows, Bread Street.

James I., by his charter in the second year of his reign, permitted the governing body to make bye-laws, provided that they were reasonable and not contrary to the laws of England—a stipulation made as far back as Henry VI., and formulated by Act of Parliament, 19 Henry VII. The Articles were again approved by the Lord Chancellor and Judges in 1676.

The arms of the Company were originally granted by Thomas Benoist Clarencieux in 1530, John Cage and Christopher Webbe being then

OLD ARMS.

Wardens ; and the original document is preserved among the archives. The crest and supporters were added by Robert Cooke Clarencieux in 1587. In the "Heralds' Visitation of London" by Sir Henry St. George in 1634, and again in 1687, they were approved, as appears from the certificate of the Clerk of the Gild attached to the latter. Some doubt has been expressed as to the true intention and significance of the supporters, which have been variously explained and indeed drawn as otters, ounces, and lions. But there can be little question that the otter, which was with peculiar fitness associated with a body so primarily interested in fish, is at any rate the correct symbol.

The particulars obtainable of the successive Halls of the Salters are sufficiently scanty and imperfect. There is not much risk in assuming that their first home or place of meeting was in Bread Street, and that in 1394, when they acquired a somewhat extended patent from Richard II., they already possessed on that spot, unless they assembled in the church itself or in the vestry, some convenience for transacting business and accommodating muniments.　It seems, however, to be a matter of clear record that, at some date antecedent to 1454, when, as we have noted, Beamond left them the fee, the Fellowship had actually built a house independent of the church.　Beamond is said to have erected on the same ground during his life the six tenements for almspeople, equally left to his brethren ; and possibly he was the founder of the Hall itself.　Herbert found among the books two papers, one belonging, as it is supposed, to 1394, and containing a receipt for a game pasty at Christmas, and the other the bill of fare at a feast in 1506, when fifty of the Company were present.

In 1539 this structure was so seriously damaged by a fire, that it was found necessary to rebuild it.　In the will of Sir Ambrose Nicholas, Salter and sometime Lord Mayor, another benefactor of the Gild, the second edifice is specified as "the common Hall of the said Wardens and Commonalty, called Salters' Hall in Bread Street ; " it was totally destroyed by fire in 1598.　There is explicit testimony that the same site was used once more, and served the Company, until in 1641, having purchased of Captain George Smith and Catherine his wife, "the great house," called London Stone, or Oxford House, otherwise Oxford Place, through their feoffees,[1] they transferred themselves in due course thither.

Oxford House had been at one epoch the town inn or residence of the Priors of Tortington, in Sussex ; and in the rear were two houses, where Sir Richard Empson and Edmund Dudley used to live, and might have once been seen in consultation in the garden, while the mansion belonged to the Earl of Oxford.　Before it passed to the Smiths, Alderman Stapylton lived there.

What amount of reconstruction Oxford Place underwent at the hands of its new owners, in the face of their different requirements, we do not hear.　But the old Hall in Bread Street probably continued for some time to be used ; and the committee appointed to organize the trained bands of the City are mentioned as meeting there from 1641 to 1643. Even after its desertion by the Company, it preserved its former appellation, as we find the Judges holding sittings in the Hall so late as 1654.

The building, being the fourth, in which the Company had made their seat, perished in 1666, and was replaced by a small structure of brick, the ancient garden still remaining ; and finally, in 1821, the whole of the

---

[1] The fine was paid in Hilary Term, 16 Charles I.

materials *in situ* were sold by auction to make room for a new and the present place of assembly, which was not completed till 1827. The almshouses were more recently (1863) removed to Watford.

LITERARY NOTICES.

A Proclamation for the maintenance and exercise of the Mines of Saltpeter, and the true making of Gunpowder. 1625. A broadside.

A Proclamation for preservation of Grounds for making of Saltpeter, and to restore such grounds as are now destroyed, and to command Assistance to be given to His Maiesties Saltpeter-makers. 14 March, 1633–4. A broadside.

A Draught of the Contract about Salt, on the behalf of Nicholas Murford ; also a Proposition made by Thomas Horth, Merchant, and other owners of Salt-pans at South and North Shields, and another Petition on the behalf of the Town of great Yarmouth. [1638–9.] A broadside petition to Parliament.

A true Remonstrance of the state of the Salte-business, undertaken (for the furnishment thereof between Barwick and Pool with the Ile of Wight and members inclusive) by the Societie of Salt-makers of South and North Shields, and of Scotland. [1638.] A broadside.

Tracts Consisting of Observations about the Saltness of the Sea. By the Honourable Robert Boyle, F.R.S. 8vo, 1674.

CIVIC PAGEANT.

Descensus Astrææ : The Device of a Pageant borne before M. William Web, Lord Mayor of the City of London, on the Day he took his Oath, being the 29 of October, 1591. Whereunto is annexed, a Speech delivered by one clad like a Sea Nymph, who presented a Pinnace on the Water, bravely rigged and manned, to the Lord Mayor, at the time he took Barge to go to Westminster. Done by G. Peele, Master of Arts in Oxford. 4to, 1591.

Reprinted in the editions of Peele.

The Ironmongers.

PRESENT ARMS.

THE venerable antiquity of this Craft Gild is deducible from the existence of the art of working iron, which was a legacy to us from our Roman conquerors and civilizers. The Forest of Dean, in Gloucestershire, appears to have been one of the earliest fields of activity in this direction ; and the mineral riches of that region were discovered or

EARLY ARMS (FROM STOW, 1633.)

recognised by the Romans. But the London market, in the earliest times of which there is any clear and continuous record, was supplied with products in this valuable metal by the furnaces of the Wealds, which enjoyed the advantage of proximity and short water-transit, so peculiarly great in the case of heavy goods. We are aware that, later forward, there was even an attempt to soar to a higher pitch at Buxted, in Sussex, where a cannon-foundry was established, but did not prosper.

The first extant direct reference to the iron trade between London and the Wealds of Sussex, Surrey and Kent is, as not unfrequently happens, the result of some exposure of an abuse ; and we have to consider ourselves under obligations as historians to these irregularities, which so introduce to our knowledge and study features and elements of commercial life which would otherwise, perhaps, have maintained still longer and further the undisturbed tenor of their existence.

According to the *Liber Horn*, under 1300, complaint was made in the Chamber of London to the Court of Aldermen, that the smiths of the Wealds and other merchants brought down the iron parts of cart-wheels to London of much shorter dimensions than formerly, to the great loss and scandal of the whole trade of ironmongers ; and this proceeding immediately throws light on the fact that Wardens or overseers of the Craft were then in vogue, and consisted of three persons, an Ironmonger of the Bridge, who doubtless superintended the process of unlading from ships in the Pool or at the wharves, and two of the Market, who exercised surveillance over goods brought from all quarters and over the multifarious incidence of quality and measurement, purchase and sale.

These officials possessed a standard rod, sealed by the Chamber, for the verification of all iron-work belonging to cart-wheels ; and the Chamber kept two duplicates of the same.

IRONMONGERS' MARKS.

We depend, as usual, on retrospective inference in our formation of an estimate of the growth of the Craft and its initiation as a Gild. We see, in the first place, that the accidental glimpse under 1300 reveals the industry in an advanced stage of development, and in possession of some kind of executive government, namely, two Wardens of the Market and (subordinated to them, as we collect from a document of 33 Henry VI.) one of London Bridge. Now, it is curious that among the eighteen Gilds fined in 1180 are two designated *Gilds of Bridge*, of which we may perhaps take the present to be one and the Pursers the other. But there was a great disparity in their relative importance ; for the first paid only one mark, while the second, of which Robert Wood was Alderman, paid ten. The minor body, if our guesswork is worth anything, would be the Pursers of the Bridge, who merged in the Leathersellers.

There is room for suspicion that so important a vocation, comprising a large and profitable traffic, and numbering among its followers men who rose to the highest civic honours, did not remain till the second half of the fifteenth century, the date of its first charter, destitute of some patent or grant from the Crown to protect its external interests, and to facilitate and legalize its management. In 1348 the Ironmongers sent, by virtue of a precept from the Mayor, four "good people, the wisest and most sufficient, to represent them at the Common Council. In 1376, they deputed a similar number ; and meanwhile, in 1363, they subscribed 6*l*. 18*s*. 4*d*. toward the French war. From the middle to the latter end of this century, the Gilds or Misteries, owing to their development and local centralization, had obtained a principal share in the electoral power, and down to 1384 returned most of the officers and dignitaries of the City. In the last year of Edward III. they numbered forty-eight without any settled order of precedence. Their relative consequence and weight are ascertained by the graduated scale of representation, which varied from six to two. The Ironmongers are the thirty-fifth on the roll, and sent four councillors.

These various particulars and indications combine to prove the solid position of the Ironmongers as a voluntary body under two Wardens, when, in 1464, they obtained their parent charter from Edward IV., and cause a passing surprise that they should have waited so long before they took steps to place themselves on a footing of equality with the other Fraternities ; when it is made clear by the preceding official entries that they took high rank among the misteries, and were influentially represented at the Common Council.

By this instrument, in which the Gild is specified as " our well-beloved and faithful liegemen, all the freemen of the mistery and art of

COMMON SEAL.

Ironmongers of our City of London and suburbs thereof," it was constituted in effect and name one body and one Commonalty corporate for evermore, of one Master and two Keepers or Wardens, and the Commonalty ; and Richard Flemming, Alderman and past Warden, was hereby appointed the first Master, and Nicholas Maxhall and Robert Toke the first Wardens, with perpetual succession, a licence in mortmain to the extent of ten marks a year, the power of pleading and being impleaded, the use of a common seal, and the right of holding lawful assemblies and making ordinances not prejudicial to the laws and the prerogative.

Contrary to the usual practice, this Company is largely governed by bye-laws anterior to its first charter, namely, by the Articles granted in 1455, 23 Henry VI. By this code it was laid down that thirteen persons, beside the Wardens, made a quorum; that the Yeomanry should pay their quarterages four times a year; that persons nominated Stewards should be fined 10*l.* for refusal; that the Wardens, once a year or oftener, should make search of weights and measures; that persons admitted to the Livery should pay 6*s.* 8*d.* for their pattern, and wear such decent apparel as the Wardens might approve, and other normal details.

There were, in addition to these ordinances for the Gild at large, "The Orders of the Yeomanry;" for, as we find, the freemen were so termed in this, as well as in the Merchant Taylors' body; and the younger sort of liverymen were similarly designated *Bachelors*. There was also a Capitulary, or set of rules for the officers of the Gild, from the Senior Warden to the Under Beadle's wife. About 1590 the Beadle is said to have under his care the velvet garlands em-

ELECTION GARLAND.

ployed in elections and five tobacco dishes. The bye-laws were renewed and enlarged in 1498, and supplementary clauses from time to time added.

In 1456 Lancaster Herald granted "to the honourable Craft and Fellowship of the franchised men of Ironmongers of the City of London a token of arms," namely, a chevron, gules, set between three gads of steel, azure, on the chevron three swivelles of gold, with two lizards proper, encooped with gules on the helmet.

The original *maximum* imposed on the Ironmongers' licence in mortmain had been ten marks a year, which was gradually extended to 300*l.*, and under the charter of James II. was made unlimited. But the Company obtained special licences to buy lands for Betton's estate, to 1,000*l.* a year value, and for Geffery's estate to a similar amount.

By none of its charters has the Company acquired the right of search; and in cases where abuses existed in the trade, it was bound to have recourse to the Court of Aldermen to take the initiative in the matter. Other of these bodies were similarly situated; and the question was more than once raised as to the constitutional right to confer this power, insomuch that we meet with cases where our Kings, having granted a Gild the right, subsequently retracted it. But a great deal of uncer-

tainty and irregularity prevailed on the point, and the inquisitorial function, when trade became less exclusive, often led to unforeseen friction
and inconvenience through the claim of one craft to exercise in such a
respect a supervision over another, or where, as in one peculiar instance,
authority was temporarily vested in the Haberdashers to control the
Fishmongers.

A curious incident, which may be thought to reflect honourably on
the Ironmongers, happened upon the occasion of the great dearth of
1597, when an Order in Council enjoined a suspension for that year
of all expenditure on civic entertainments, and the money, which such
festive indulgences would have involved, was to be applicable to the
relief of the poor, and to be collected by Thomas Wood and Richard
Wright, Citizens and Ironmongers, on behalf of all the Companies of
London.

The estimation of the ranks of the Ironmongers is affected by the
principle that all members of the Livery belong to the Court or governing
body, from which the Master and Wardens are annually chosen.   There
are only therefore the Livery and the Freemen or Yeomanry.   At one
time women were admitted to the freedom.

In 1502 the Livery is given as 25.   In 1524 the Yeomanry are returned at 56, and in 1537 the " Freemen householders" at 59.   In the
official lists of 1699 and 1724 the Liverymen are stated to amount to
100 and 109.   In 1882 the Freemen numbered 156, and the Livery
52.[1]

A reference to the municipal and other returns between 1469 and
1629 shew this body in the possession of a more than average stability
of position.   In the first-named year it supplied forty guards for the
City gates, and in 1502 and 1509 appears as the eighth Company ; but
in 1515 it was officially set back to its present rank as the tenth.
Through the reigns of the earlier Stuarts it seems to have well maintained its ground.[2]

The Yeomanry, as early as 1497, prayed the Company to be permitted
to have their own executive in the shape of two Wardens, to whom they
might pay eightpence a year each man for the expense of government
and for a feast on the day of Corpus Christi.   At what precise date the
demand was conceded is not quite certain ; but the petitioners gained
their object, and separate Ordinances, as well as Wardens, for them were
provided.

---

[1] According to Whitaker, the Livery in 1892 was reduced to forty-two.
[2] In 1603-4 the Ironmongers were assessed at 17l. 12s. toward the reception of
James I., and in 1629 it contributed 76l. 19s. 6d. to the expenses attendant on the
coronation of his son.

The regulations for the Livery and choice of vesture were passed in the time of Edward IV., just at the time when the charter was received. The main principle was, that no change in the pattern or colour was to be made without the assent of the whole Company; and four persons of the Livery were to accompany the Wardens to the draper's shop or to Blackwell Hall, to witness the purchase of the material. A new suit was customary every third year, and, as with the other Companies, the colour generally underwent a change from time to time. It is noticeable that the Chaplain's gown and hood cost 2*l*. 6*s*. 9*d*., six or seven times as much as those of an ordinary liveryman.

The earliest Ironmonger who served as Sheriff was William Dykeman, in 1368. Sir Richard Marlow, Citizen and Ironmonger, filled the mayoralty in 1410 and 1417. In 1442, Sir John Hatherley, Ironmonger, was Mayor. In 1566, Sir Christopher Draper, a benefactor, and in 1609, Sir Thomas Campbell or Cambell, filled the office.

Of the more eminent members of the Company we may specify Robert Byfield, Sheriff in 1479, Merchant of the Staple, Richard Chamberlain, Citizen and Ironmonger, one of the Sheriffs, a Merchant Adventurer and of the Muscovite Company, interred at St. Martin's, Ironmonger Lane, in 1562, and Sir James Campbell, Mayor in 1629, and son of Sir Thomas above-mentioned, to whom his brethren were under obligations for important charitable bequests. Of these his clerk, Edward Browne, who is known as a verse-writer and pamphleteer of the Civil War era, has left a curious account and remembrance in a little volume quoted below. The celebrated Beckford, author of *Vathek*, was an Ironmonger, and served the Mayoralty in 1752 ; and the Master of the Company in 1769 was John Shakespear Esquire, Alderman, and Rope-maker at Stepney, where his Walks were long famous.

The Ironmongers once followed, in common with the Grocers, Fishmongers and Carpenters, a dramatic usage at the election of their Wardens, as we may remember from a passage in Evelyn's Diary, when he was present at the banquet on the following day in 1671. On August 20, on the eve of the Council Feast—at first each fifth year, then in alternate years, and finally, in and after 1527, year by year—a Court of the whole Fellowship was called together, and proceeded to nominate a Master and six other persons, from whom the old Wardens selected two at their discretion as their successors ; and the next day, when the feast was, the old Wardens crowned the new with garlands. The re-election of the Wardens for a second term of office was in 1527 left to the pleasure of the Master.

The practice and solemnity were formerly picturesque enough. At the dinner, the old Wardens at a given juncture rose and left the room, and shortly returned, with the Beadle bearing the garlands for the new officers, and minstrels playing before them ; and, making obeisance to the Master, the Wardens delivered to him the garlands, that he might place them on the heads of certain there present, esteemed by him the most worshipful. The coronation of the Master and Wardens elect then followed.

The Ironmongers have suffered this custom to fall into desuetude.

The law of analogy warrants an hypothesis, if not a conclusion, that the Ironmongers sheltered themselves, agreeably to the usage and feeling of primitive times, under the protection of St. Martin's, Ironmonger Lane, while they yet remained a voluntary Society of Corpus Christi, and possibly met in the church or church-house, before they acquired a residence there or elsewhere.

The first recorded obit performed on behalf of a member belongs to 1511, however ; and in 1479 the Company was already in its quarters in Fenchurch Street, which it may have made a special exertion to acquire upon incorporation thirty years previous.

The most ancient seat of the Ironmongers was by general allowance in the lane leading out of West-Cheap or Cheapside, which still retains its proprietary name ; and the adjoining churches of St. Olave, Old Jewry, and St. Martin, Ironmonger Lane, received the ashes of many of the early members of the Fraternity from the reign of Edward III. to that of James I. ; long prior to which latter epoch, however, the settlement of the trade had been removed to the neighbourhood of the river, and its place of assembly and business was on the existing site in Fenchurch Street, in the parish of All Hallows Staining.

The original colony in Ironmonger Lane, beneath the shadow of St. Martin's, necessarily rendered that precinct, during its lengthened tenancy, busy, populous and noisy, and involved the possession by those of the Craft of an extensive area for their warehouses, yards, and shops, where they kept the stock of manufactured goods brought from the foundries, and sold them by retail and wholesale. It was much the same with them as with the Soap-makers in Sopers' Lane opposite. As space in the City became more in demand, and the observance of order in the streets grew stricter, they found it convenient to emigrate riverward, where accommodation was more ample, and cartage was saved.

The most ancient indication of the present site of the Hall is a grant to Richard Attemerke in 1344 by Robert de Kent, Citizen and Horse-merchant of London, and Felicia his wife, daughter and heiress of John Rosemound, Citizen, of a vacant plot of ground surrounded by their tenements, with a certain part of a certain great gate and a solar built thereon, opposite the highway of Aldgate Street, on the south side, in the parish of All Saints, Staining. These premises passed through several hands before, on the 20th October, 1457, under the will of Alice Stiuard, widow, her executors sold the property, with all its appurtenances, to Richard Flemming and others, Citizens and Ironmongers of London.

One of the earliest steps taken after the purchase was the acquisition of the exemplification of arms from Lancaster Herald; and another call on the corporate funds was the repair of the premises, which became of course a chronic source of outlay, as well, perhaps, as their adaptation to the wants of the new proprietors.

The first allusion to a Hall in the parish of All Hallows, Staining, is due, curiously enough, like our first knowledge of the Gild itself, to a matter in dispute. In this case it was a claim for church-dues made upon the Company in respect of their Hall, and after some litigation eventually compromised.

It was prior to 1481, seventeen years after the insertion in their charter of a licence in mortmain, that the Company came into possession, by what means or under what circumstances is not stated, of the Manor of Norwood in Middlesex, once appurtenant to the See of Rochester, but formerly attached to the Primate's Manor of Hayes; and in the year cited the Master of the Ironmongers held his first Court there. This manorial property, which is a peculiar feature in the annals of a Livery Gild, had been granted by the Bishop of Rochester in 1241 to Matthew de la Wike in fee farm; and then and in later records it is valued at seven marks a year, so that it probably, even in 1481, fell within the powers of the Company under their charter. The scantiest particulars exist on this, which might have formed a very interesting point; and we merely possess a list of feoffees, members of the Company, who held the estate on its behalf, down to 1580 or thereabout, when it was alienated to Lord Dacre.

Ironmongers' Hall, as it stood in the Tudor era, occupying the entire area between Fenchurch and Leadenhall Streets with the exception of a few tenements with a frontage to the former, ultimately added by gift, was entered on the Leadenhall side by a gate-house surmounted by a little chamber or solar. The pile was quadrangular, and it contained the large refectory, roofed with lead, with a wooden floor strown with rushes and a wainscot dado; a little gallery; a court chamber, partly hung with tapestry and wainscoted; a stone parlour, a parlour, the counting-house, the great and little garret, the kitchen with a paved entrance, the buttery, the larder, the armoury, and the yard leading to the garden.

In the counting-house the books were kept, and oaths were admin-

istered. The smaller garret formed a receptacle for the priest's vestments and other canonical requisites. It was apparently the Chaplain's
room.

In the inventory of 1556 we find the following articles specified as
part of the furniture and contents : a suit of vestments of cloth of gold,
a hearse-cloth or pall of gold in a box, another of black worsted with
a white cross of Bruges satin, six dozen of wooden trenchers, a book on
which to administer oaths, a dozen silver spoons with lions, weight 16
oz., the gift of Mr. Downs ; six cushions of green sey, or silk, with
feathers ; two great carpets for the two tables, of tapestry work, one
lined ; two pieces of tapestry that hang at one end of the court of
entry, a small carpet of tapestry for the window.

This is a modest stock enough, and seems, among other points, to
imply that the collection of plate had not been recovered or redeemed
at this time.

In 1578 the Company formed the project for a new Hall, which was
finished in 1587 at an initial cost of nearly 600*l*. This did not possibly
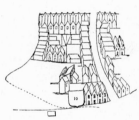
THE HALL ABOUT 1560.
It is the building marked 10.

encroach much, if at all, on the garden, which
was maintained, as the accounts shew, with
great care. The ordinary working gardener
had 8*d*. a day for his wages, and the Company
found all that was necessary. We perceive
that this plot, stretching behind Leadenhall
Street and Fenchurch Street, was planted
with roses, vines, lavender, marjoram, rose-
mary, camomile, and pinks, and that a
certain portion was in lawn ; for in 1610 there is mention of mowing
the grass and cutting the hedges. In 1656 a penalty was payable by
any one drying clothes in the garden.

For the new Hall the Company gradually bought fresh furniture and
other appointments ; and we hear of an old banner with the Ironmongers
arms, which had been, no doubt, in the former house ; and an inventory
taken in 1643 exhibits á grand advance in all branches of useful and
ornamental effects, including a very respectable assemblage of plate,
though whether it was the original or a new collection we cannot say.
One "ale-pot," presumably of silver, purports, however, to have been a
prize in a lottery. But all these lists are open to the suspicion of being
imperfect or partial, as others of or about the same period disclose an
armoury, an assortment of fine table-linen and pewter, and other symptoms of comfort and prosperity.

It is assumed, probably with correctness, that the second Hall on the
Fenchurch site had its frontage on the southern, instead of the northern,

side, and faced the street as the building does at present ; but it should be added that this course was facilitated by the bequest of Sir Christopher Draper, Mayor in 1566, who left his brethren the land on which the Elizabethan Hall was partly erected, and that the possession of the supplemental ground was an inducement to rebuild with an abuttal nearer to the river.

In the days of Mary (1556) the armoury possessed seventeen back and breast plates, seventeen sets of splints, twelve gorgets, twelve swords, eleven daggers, white soldiers' coats of kersey with red crosses on them, four coats of russet frieze, corslets, skull-caps, bills, morris-pikes, and sheaves of arrows.

There was an armourer to keep the articles in proper condition. His fee was 20s. a year.

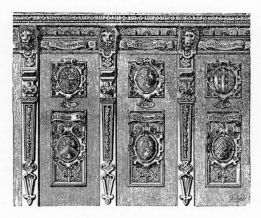

DADO AT IRONMONGERS' HALL.

This feature of the Hall, eventually removed, was to a certain extent of a practical character in two respects : in the first place, as illustrative of metal-work, and secondly as containing the weapons and body-furniture, which members of the Fraternity might have occasion to use in ceremonial observances, in their official attendance by rotaticn upon the City gates, and at critical junctures. The collection of weapons and armour was calculated to equip a dozen men or so; its scope was municipal.

We shall find that the Carpenters and others founded a similar insti-tution for their own use.

The 1587 dining-room is described as furnished with seven long wainscot tables, one mahogany table, six dozen leathern chairs, and five larger chairs for the Master and Wardens ; there were some portraits of benefactors on the walls ; and the windows exhibited commemorative coats or shields, which might have been, and indeed doubtless were, transferred from the first house of the Company in this quarter.

One of the portraits in the windows was a small whole-length of Sir Christopher Draper above-mentioned.

The Company's noble premises in Fenchurch Street still remain intact, and occupy a considerable area in the rear of the main thorough-fare. Fewer entertainments are now given than of old, and the Company does not possess much plate. It has nothing whatever, we believe, emblematical of the Craft.

The entries in the Ironmongers' books afford many interesting illus-trations of the part taken by the Company in current public events, and in the tyrannical proceedings of the Crown for the levy of supplies for all sorts of purposes. In 1523 the Company had to deliver part of its plate as security for the speedier payment of the quota toward the sum of 20,000*l.* peremptorily demanded by Henry from the City, and pawned the remainder, besides handing over the whole of the cash in hand, 25*l.* 14*s.* The expenses of meeting the Queen on her entry into London in 1541 from Greenwich in their barge were nearly 9*l.*, which may have included the refreshments taken on board : a kilderkin of ale, claret, ling, gurnets, fresh salmon, great eels, bread and cheese, and other items. In 1542 the imposing City pageant of setting the Mid-summer Watch on the Eve of St. John the Baptist cost the Gild 38*s.* ; and two years later some of the plate had to be again pledged to furnish ten billmen and four archers, fully provided, for the expedition to Boulogne. In 1545 40*l.* were allotted as the Ironmongers' proportionate amount for storing grain against a season of dearth.

Other charges appear for repairing the Church of All Hallows, Staining ; for erecting a stand to witness the passage of Mary I. through Cheapside to her coronation in 1554; for "fetching in" of Elizabeth in 1558 ; for the expense of the "May-game" which preceded her Majesty to Greenwich ; for the cost of the Royal Exchange (75*l.*) ; for supplying men-at-arms and seamen for the Queen's service, at various times from 1562, fully armed and equipped ; for contributing to ten ships of war and a pinnace for the defence of the realm (1591) ; for finding their quota of a loan of 20,000*l.* to Elizabeth on her bond for six months (1599) ; and for meeting the fine of 1,000*l.* levied on the City for negligence in not having discovered the murderers of John Lamb.

Under 1579 occur two singular remembrances : one being a letter from the Queen herself to the Company, praying them to grant a lease of premises to William Sparke, to which they accede ; and the other, an arrangement under which two Ironmongers and two Grocers were required to station themselves from 7 a.m. to 6 p.m. at Bishopsgate to take note of the habits or dress of all persons passing through in the course of the day.

All through the period of the Civil War, and from the Restoration to the Revolution of 1688, the fortunes of the Ironmongers were more or less chequered and dark. They had absolutely refused to participate in the advance of 200,000*l.* asked by Charles I. in 1640, to enable him to oppose the Parliament, but subscribed to a loan of 40,000*l.* for the King's use. In 1665 a new form of internal impost manifests itself in the requisition to the Companies to lay up coal, between Lady-Day and Michaelmas annually, for retailing to the poor below cost price. Then in 1684 came the *Quo Warranto.*

It would be difficult to name any device which was not put into force all round for rendering the funds of this and other like bodies little more than fiduciary, whether they chose or not, and for neutralizing any natural tendency on their part to accumulate wealth, save the actual land in fee, which did not represent immediate value.

WHIFFLER.　　　　HENCHMAN.

In the Preface to the present book we have pointed out how very imperfectly, on more than one account, the printed pageants represent the long series of commemorative solemnities on the occasion of the advent of members of the various Gilds to the mayoralty. Of those Shows, which fall within the time when periodical publication had become, at all events, the rule, there are records among the Companies' muniments, in many instances, where no printed copy has been yet recovered. But the idea of registering such particulars at large does not seem to have been generally adopted, and the somewhat elaborate description of the Ironmongers' spectacle for 1566, for Sir Christopher Draper, may therefore be worth noticing in detail.

We start with the singular fact that the contract for supplying the twenty boats and their crews, and the music, all properly fitted and equipped, was accepted by John Candish, haberdasher, at 10*l.* There were to be two trumpeters, a drum and a flute, eight single and eight double basses, and squibs sufficient for the time. Candish was evidently expected to attend, as two ells of sarcinet are allowed for his cassock, and 10*s.* in money for his hose, and he was to wear a silk night-cap and a scarf. The master and gunner of the foist, from which the salutes and fireworks were sent, were also dressed in sarcinet cassocks, silk night-caps, and scarves. The torches were furnished by Richard Sharpe, wax-chandler. They were an ell long, and cost 15*s.* the dozen. Richard Baker, painter-stainer, agreed at 16*l.* for the carpenter's and painter's work, and to have 40*s.* more, if necessary.

The banners and streamers of course formed a prominent feature in the display and in the expense. There were two long streamers of crimson taffeta, twenty-four trumpet-banners, a banner with the Mayor's arms, another with the Queen's, and many more.

CRESSET.

Mention occurs of the apparel borrowed for the children from Thomas Giles of Lombard Street, probably an upholder ; of the breakfast given to the children before the business of the day, by the good man of the *Bell* in Carter Lane, where they were lodged and dressed ; of the drink given to the children at the *Bell* in Mincing Lane ; of the subsequent erection of the pageant in the Company's Hall, and of the payment for the white staves borne by the whifflers, who cleared the way before the Show, and were frequently members of other Companies.

John Tailor, master of Westminster School, accepted 40*s.* for his pains and cost in sending six of his boys to take part in the procession. The Lieutenant of the Tower contributed the ordnance, ammunition, and arms, probably for a consideration. The device of the pageant was written by James Peele,[1] who had 30*s.* as his fee.

Sixteen of the junior members or bachelors of the Company attended in satin cassocks, crimson satin hoods, and furred gowns. Thirty more wore gowns furred with budge, coats or cassocks of satin or damask,

---

[1] Probably the father of George Peele the dramatist. He is also known as the author of a work on Book-keeping, 1553, 1569. He was possibly a glover, either by trade or freedom, as he supplied seven pairs at 6*d.* a pair for the children.

and the same hoods. Stewards were appointed, to see that all these had their breakfasts against the starting-time.

The pageant was carried by porters, for whom hogsheads were placed at intervals to enable them to lay their burden down occasionally.

The several members of the Company paid their proportion toward the charges, and also sent in their plate to embellish the table at the banquet.

The total cost was 63*l.* 11*s.* 8*d.*

LORD MAYOR'S SHOW.
Wild or Greenwood Men clearing the way.

In the time of Elizabeth, the vast and increasing demand for wood-fuel for domestic purposes was held to justify legislation in order to preserve for the use of the City and suburbs all timber within twenty-two miles of the metropolis, and to prohibit the erection of any new furnaces, mills, or forges inside that radius, with a special exemption of the woods of Christopher Darrell, gentleman, in the parish of Newdigate, Surrey, who had planted for the use of his own works there. Two years later, a second statute was enacted to prohibit the establishment of any new foundries, even in the Wealds, on account of the great number already thereabout, and possibly, besides, in view of the large quantities of imperfectly smelted ore, which improvements in the bloomeries gradually enabled the undertakers to re-smelt with profit.

No explicit account seems to be discoverable of the position and origin of the London Locksmith. The Continent, especially Antwerp, supplied us in ancient days with locks, as well as with chests of safety for treasure. But there were necessarily native craftsmen in this kind of industry from a very remote date ; and they were in the time of the Plantagenets known as *Lockyers*. In a sworn inventory of goods under 1356 two of this trade appear on the inquest. The Lockyers probably formed a branch of the Ironmongers, but never attained sufficient numbers and influence to aspire to a separate constitution. Down to a much later period, the bolt did duty for both methods of fastening doors and apartments, and strong-boxes were principally imported.

The Ironmongers have practically sold their Irish estate, of which the income had recently declined. There is no doubt that delay was prejudicial in this case to realization. In the account of the Scriveners' Company some reference will be found to the sub-share taken by the latter and the misunderstanding which arose in respect of it, as in other analogous cases. The other Companies associated with the Ironmongers were the Brewers, Coopers, Pewterers, and Carpenters.

As the Skinners christened their manor the manor of *Pellipar* from their own craft, so the Ironmongers' estate was denominated the Manor of *Lizard*, from the supporters of their coat of arms, as granted by Lancaster in 1456.

The reply tendered by the Ironmongers to the inquiry of the Royal Commission of 1880, under the head of Reform, was one which might have been with equal propriety made by most of the other Gilds, certainly by those possessing regular organization. The Clerk, in whose name the Report was forwarded, stated that he knew of no body of men more capable of managing the affairs of the Ironmongers' Company than the members of the Court, who consisted of naval, military, legal, and medical gentlemen, of bankers and merchants, and of persons connected with various businesses, many of them landed proprietors, and all qualified by their pursuits and knowledge to decide upon such matters as are brought before them. The accounts, he added, were kept in the clearest and simplest form, and there was no official routine and unnecessary delays ; and he considered that it would be a great misfortune, if the conduct of the affairs were transferred to a public department.

LITERARY NOTICES.

Metallica; Or the Treatise of Metallica : briefly comprehending the Doctrine of diverse new Metallical Inventions, but especially how to neale, melt, and worke all kinde of mettle-oares, Irons, and Steeles, with Sea-coale, Pit-coale, Earth-coale, and Brush-fewell. By Simon Sturtevant. 4to, 1612.

A Treatise of Metallica. But not that which was published by Mr. Simon Sturttvant upon his Patent, which is now by order cancelled and made voyd. Whereupon Privilege by Patent is granted . . . to John Rovenzon Esquire for the making of Iron and other Mettals . . . 4to, 1613.

Letters of Deputation, by William Elliots and Matthias Meisey of London, gentlemen, for the searching and seizure of all foreign Steel unlawfully imported. March 27, 1627. A broadside.

Panzoologicomineralogia; Or a Compleat History of Animals and Minerals. By Robert Lovell, of Corpus College, Oxford. 8vo, 1661.

Dud Dudley's Metallum Martis: Or, Iron made with Pit-coale, Sea-coale, etc. 12mo, 1665. With a plate.

Metallographia; Or, An History of Metals. By John Webster, Physician and Surgeon. 4to, 1671.

The Art of Metals. By A. A. Barba. Translated in 1669 by the Earl of Sandwich. 8vo, 1674.

Fodinæ Regales; Or the History, Laws, and Places of the Chief Mines, and Mineral Works in England . . . By Sir John Pettus. Folio, 1670.

Fleta Minor. The Laws of Art and Nature. In Knowing, Judging, Assaying, Fining, Refining, and Inlarging the Bodies of Confin'd Metals. By Sir John Pettus. Folio, 1686. With engravings.

An Epitaph on the death of the Vertuous Matrone, the Ladie Maioresse, late wyfe to the Right Honorable Lorde (Alexander Auenet) Lord Maior of the Citie of London. Who deceased the vii. Daie of July, 1570. By John Philip. A broadside.

An Epitaph on Sir Alexander Avenet. By the same. Entered at Stationers' Hall, July 13, 1580.

The Whole Life, and Progresse of Henry Walker the Ironmonger. By John Taylor. 4to, 1642.

　*** It may be observed that in Hazlitt's *Collections and Notes,* 1876-91, are notices of several tracts by Walker, who also wrote under the name of *Mercurius Morbicus.*

A rare Paterne of Justice and Mercy; Exemplified in the many Notable and Charitable Legacies of St. James Cambel Knight, Alderman of London, deceased : Worthy imitation . . . By Edw. Browne. 8vo, 1642.

Browne was also a member of the Ironmongers' Company, and describes himself as sometime servant and clerk to Cambel or Campbell.

Time Well Spent; Or, Opus Iræ et Labor Benevolentiæ, In Seven Bookes. By the same. 4to, 1643. With portraits of the Author and his second wife.

　*** Book IV. contains a list of the Legacies of Sir James Cambel, who was son of Sir Thomas Campbell, Mayor in 1609.

CIVIC PAGEANTS.

[The Device of the Pageant borne before Sir Christopher Draper, Ironmonger, at his initiation into the Mayoralty, 29 October, 1566. At the cost of the Worshipful Company of Ironmongers. By James Peele.]

　No printed copy of this work is known ; but it appears that Peele or Pele received 30s. for it, and whereas he also supplied the Company with seven pairs of gloves for the children in the Show at 6d. a pair, he may have been of the Glover's Company. There is very little doubt that he was the father of the dramatist, who received from him his literary bent.

　Like that of 1590, this pageant may hereafter be found. That it was printed is established by the following entry in the Ironmongers' books :

> " Paide to the prynter for printing poses, speeches, and songs, that
> were spoken and songe by the children of yᵉ pagent ... ... vˢ."

　Whence we are entitled to infer that the tract was, in the same way as the Fishmongers' above referred to, privately printed for the Company, and perhaps only a few struck off.

Camp-bell, or the Ironmongers' Fair Field, at the installation of Sir Thomas Campbell, October 29, 1609. By Anthony Munday. 4to, 1609.

Only a fragment of this pageant is at present known.

Sideto-Thriambos. Or Steel and Iron Triumphing : Applauding the Advancement of Sir Sebastian Harvey, Knight, to the Dignity of Lord Mayor of London. Taking his seat in the same authority at Westminster on Thursday, being the 29th day of October, 1618. Performed in hearty love to him, and at the charges of his kind brethren, the Right Worshipful Company of Ironmongers. Devised and written by A[nthony] M[unday], Citizen and Draper of London. 4to, 1618.

London's Tempe; Or, The Feild of Happiness. In which Feild are planted severall Trees of Magnificence, State, and Beauty, to Celebrate the Solemnity of the Right Honourable James Campebell, at his Inauguration into the Honorable Office of Prætorship, or Maioralty of London, on Thursday the 29 of October, 1629. All the particular Inventions . . . At the sole Cost, and liberall Charges of the Right Worshipfull Society of Ironmongers. By Tho. Dekker. 4to, 1629.

Londini Sinus Salutis ; or, London's Harbour of Health and Happiness : Expressed in sundry Triumphs, Pageants, and Shows, at the Initiation of the Right Honourable Christopher Clethrowe into the maioralty of the far renowned City London. All the charges and expenses of this present ovation being the sole undertaking of the Right Worshipful Company of the Ironmongers. The 29 of October, 1635. Written by Thomas Heywood. 8vo, 1635.

An interesting and curious account of the negotiation with the Ironmongers' Court for the production of this show, for which Heywood and another person, named John Christmas, received 180*l*. inclusive, may be found in the History of the Company by Nichol, edit. 1866, pp. 222–3. The Company was to have 500 copies of the printed account.

London's Annual Triumph : Performed on Thursday, October, 29, 1685. For the Entertainment of the Right Honourable Sir Robert Jeffreys, Knight, Lord Mayor of the City of London. With a Description of the several Pageants, Speeches, and Songs, made proper for the Occasion. All set forth at the proper Costs and Charges of the Worshipful Company of Ironmongers. Composed by Matt. Taubman. Printed and Published by Authority. 4to, 1685.

The Vintners.[1]

THE prevalent notion that the followers of certain vocations are limited in their worldly aims to an exceptional extent by the sordid desire of gain, and by the life-long endeavour to conduct a profitable traffic to the vital detriment of the community, has its chief seat of strength in those businesses which concern the sale of liquors of an intoxicating nature ; and this circumstance may be possibly attributable to the survival among us of Puritan traditions and prejudices, coupled with the inevitable liability of an abuse of stimulants to become a public scandal and a statutory offence.   Many misdemeanours and vices of a far graver character have failed to attract the same amount of general notice, or to receive an equal degree of juridical attention, owing to the fact that they fail to come within the official cognisance of the local or other government of the country.   A man may not expose himself in a state of inebriation in the Queen's high-way ; but he may within certain (and very wide) bounds do much worse things in his own house.   The sin of drunkenness is, no doubt, a social crime also ; and it is that alike, whether it is committed in view of others or in private, except from two points of view—the mischievous example and the unhappy consequences.   The legitimate application of drink, however, is vastly in excess of its misuse ; and the injury likely to accrue from its suppression must be regarded as infinitely greater, even if we keep the want of equity out of sight, than any benefit which could possibly be received under existing social and sanitary conditions.

Not merely is it the case that those who have been, and are, engaged in the liquor-traffic suffer from unjust and untrue criticism as regards the political and moral bearings of their occupation ; for we find by looking into ancient records that, among the authors of philanthropic

[1] See a volume entitled : *The Vintners' Company, their Muniments, Plate, and Eminent Members, with some Account of the Ward of Vintry.*   Revised and Edited by Thomas Milbourn, Architect.   4to, 1888.   With Illustrations.   The matter represents an enlarged text of Papers originally read by three or four gentlemen before the London and Middlesex Archæological Society.

benefactions from remote times, the men who have devoted their lives to this industry and merchandise may claim a distinguished rank ; nor ought we to overlook the fact that their wealth has contributed during centuries, as it does still to-day, to support and cherish that very Church which is so loud in its condemnation of the brewer, the wine-merchant, and the publican—so loud in its condemnation, because it happens to be its cue to see only one side of the question.   For otherwise, of course, no amount of money bestowed on alms for ecclesiastical purposes could atone for the evils of intemperance.   But every one, who desires to enjoy the reputation of possessing average intelligence, should be willing to allow that society at large is not to be brought down to the standard of the fool or the sot, and that because a proportion of the people cannot restrain their desires, the whole world is not to be debarred from reasonable indulgence and tonic repair, any more than we are to cease to eat grapes because one or two folks have been choked with a grape-stone.

The trades which at present interest themselves in the importation or manufacture of liquors of various kinds, with all the accessory appliances requisite for their sale and use, have in some cases descended from antiquity, and possess historical records and traditions, while others are of modern growth and of a different constitution.   The changes of taste or the progress of science have rendered a few obsolete.   We hear no longer of the Horners, who used to be associated with the Bottle-makers, nor of the Pewterers, nor of the Shivers, who carried on for a short time the business of supplying the wine and beer trades with wooden bungs. But, on the other hand, a gigantic unincorporated commerce has arisen by the immense development of the spirit industry, especially in whisky, and by the call for a numerous assortment of miscellaneous beverages, of which the two most important are, perhaps, cider and perry—drinks formerly made on the farm or in the kitchen for domestic consumption.

Our ancestors, however, almost exclusively applied their attention to the shipment of wine from abroad and to the production of ale and beer ; and we find, as a consequence, that the persons engaged in these callings were the first to seek from the Crown security and encouragement.   It was absolutely essential in former times for all who aimed at conducting mercantile transactions with safety and profit to shelter themselves under royal protection, and to forestall competitors.   Monopolies were generally recognised, and the prize was to the highest, or at all events to the earliest, bidder.   In the same manner as the vassals of a powerful baron grouped themselves round their lord's castle, and looked to him for succour in the hour of need, so the members of a trading fraternity procured their charter, which guaranteed them immunities and privileges, and defined their powers.

These corporations multiplied, and into their number gradually entered some which were connected, directly or indirectly, with the liquor-business. The Vintners, or, to follow the earlier and more correct orthography, Vintonners, took the lead. Their origin is so ancient as to be involved in considerable obscurity ; they formed a large and influential body long before they were formally recognised by letters patent of 37 Edward III. (July 15, 1364), followed by an *inspeximus* of the same, 6 Henry VI., November 8th, 1427, and they eventually became one of the Twelve Great Livery Companies. It was perhaps fit that the Gild which trafficked in the most dignified and costly sort of drink should take precedence over the rest.

OLD ARMS.

This Patent forbad any to trade for wine to Gascony, except such as were enfranchised of the craft of Vintners, and obliged the Gascons, when they imported their wines, to sell them in gross, so as to exclude retailers. It conferred on the Company the right of search over the trade, and four persons were to be annually presented to the Lord Mayor of London or his deputy for approval, and to take the oath, in order to discharge this duty, such being no keepers of taverns. These officials were invested with full discretionary power to see that dealers conformed to the law in respect to measures, prices, and other particulars, and to provide for the punishment of defaulters. Stow tells us that the wine measures employed in old times were the gallon, pottle, quart, and pint.[1]

The vintner did not by any means invariably dispose of his wines absolutely, but consigned them to a taverner or tavern-keeper on sale. This appears in various extant transactions from the fourteenth century. A tavern at the head of London Bridge, in the parish of St. Olave, Southwark, was let by Thomas Drinkwater, a taverner, to James Beau-fleur, Citizen and Vintner, mainly with a view to the retailing by Drink-water of the wines of the other party, and the rendering of a proper account from time to time by the vendor. Twenty shillings were allowed for the gown of Drinkwater ; but he was expected to find necessary furniture and drinking vessels, as hanaps of silver and wood.

The regulations for the delivery, taxation, and sale of wine in London naturally preceded the existence of any systematic organization for the control of those engaged in the industry, and the protection of the rights

---

[1] That is to say, for retail transactions. The pipe, tun, and hogshead (oxhide) were employed for shipments and for sales in gross.

of the Crown and the interests of the community. In 1257 the King claimed to be entitled to prisage from every ship bringing wine into the port of London, and subject to full custom of two tuns, at 40s. the tun. The earliest vestige of a Gild specially dedicated to this branch of commerce occurs in the shape of the grant of Botolph Wharf in 1282 to Henry de Kingston, for the use of the Vintners of London, at a penny rent.

In 1301 there were four societies of *Wine-Drawers* in London : the New Meyne, or New Gathering ; the King's ; the Shipup ; and another not named. These bodies, of whose corporate history we only casually and temporarily hear, grew prominent and substantial enough to secure a charter, to which the Vintners offered strenuous opposition, but seem to have eventually merged in the general Gild and vocation.

The year 1311 marked an important era in the London wine-trade ; for it witnessed the issue of a writ, whereby none but the King's butler might thenceforth value or buy wines coming by ship toward the City until the same had been unladen and warehoused, with the additional provisos, that, before they were stowed away, each tun should be marked with the gauge mark at both ends, that they should not be touched for three days, and that no wholesale dealer or grosser of wines should be a taverner, or *vice versâ*. Parties utilizing the lees and droppings to the prejudice of health were liable to exemplary punishment.

The same writ of 4 Edward II. lays down other regulations and re-commendations, and fixes the selling prices for the year at 5d., 4d., and 3d. per gallon, according to quality.

In 1342, additional regulations and restrictions were set forth by the Corporation, and these were from time to time renewed and augmented. It appears from a precept of 1351, 25 Edward III., that the mistery had become sufficiently important to send four representatives to the Common Council. In 1364 a signal example was made of a vintner who sold unwholesome wine "in deceit of the common people, in con-tempt of our lord the King," etc. ; he was compelled to drink some of the liquor, the residue being poured over him; and he was disfranchised as a member of the Craft. But at a very early date a distinction was drawn between "unsound and unwholesome wines" and those which were merely "medled" or blended. The latter was an allowable and recognised process.

In 1370 the Mayor and Court of Aldermen agreed to certain regula-tions for tavern-keepers, drawn up by the Vintners, and involving wide powers of search and inspection, and considerable amercement in cases of contumacy or fraud. The tavern-keepers were supposed to proceed to the appointment of four Overseers to secure observance of these rules.

Wine seems to have been a popular article in certain cases of fines inflicted on culprits. In a quarrel between the Saddlers and certain other craftsmen in 1327 twenty tuns of wine formed the penal payment by the former on breach of the terms of agreement, and two years later Robert le Bret, Goldsmith, was amerced in one tun because he forsook his brethren, who had been sent on a message to the King at Windsor. The same person and another Goldsmith had to agree to lose two tuns to their fellows, if either of them was proved to have taken the initiative in any fresh dissension.

Stow, speaking of the Vintry and Vintry-ward, describes it thus :—

"A part of the banke of the River of *Thames*, where the Merchants of *Burdeaux* craned [1] their Wines out of Lighters, and other Vessels, and there landed and made sale of them, within forty dayes after, untill the twenty-eighth of *Edward* the first, at which time the said Merchants complained, that they could not sell their wines, paying poundage, neither hire houses or cellars to lay them in ; and it was redressed by vertue of the King's Writ, directed to the Maior and Sherriffes of London, dated at Carlaveroke or Carlile. Since the which time many faire and large houses (with Vaults and Cellars for stowage of Wines, and lodging of Burdeaux Merchants) have been builded in place where beforetime were Cooks houses : for *Fitzstephen* in the reign of *Henry* the second, writeth, that upon the Rivers side, betweene the Wine in ships, and the Wine to be sold in Tavernes, was a common Cookes Row, &c., as in another place I have set down whereby it appears, that in those daies, (and till of late time) every man lived according to his owne professed Trade, not any one interrupting another. The Cookes dressed meat, and sold no wine ; and the Taverner sold wine, but dressed no meat for sale. . . ."

Referring to Galley Quay, he proceeds to state that the Gallies of *Italy* and other parts did there discharge their wines and merchandises brought to this city ; and in like manner, in course of time, he adds, that the merchants of Bordeaux built at the Vintry tenements for their use, made of stones brought from Caen in Normandy, which soon presented a worn appearance, and needed constant repair ; and when the place was no longer required for the original purpose, the premises became dilapidated, and were let out to other tenants.

Stow's Continuator, in speaking [2] of the growth of luxury after the accession of the Stuarts, observes :—

"In the time of Henry the eight, and Edward the sixt, Vinteners and Tauernors houses were not in any such measure, manner, nor plentious store and variety of wines of all Nations in any one mans house, as now at this time, there is in every vinteners house, for in those dayes whosoever drew White, Clarret, and red Wine, sould no more kindes of Wine. The Dutch then sold onely renish wine, as now they doe, and at that time, when an Argosey came with Greeke, and Spanish Wines, viz. Muscadell, Malmsey, Sacke, and Bastard, the Apothecaries of Londun then went vnto those

---

[1] The Three-Craned Wharf stood here, and near at hand was the printing-office of William Copland, whose imprint cites his address.

[2] *Annals*, 1615, p. 867.

marchants, and euery man bought such Rundlets, vessels, and quantities of those rich
Wines, as they thought they should retayle in the citty, vnto such as vsually bought
of them only for phisicke, and for the communion Table, and for speciall countrey
chapmen that dwelled in Cittles, or speciall good Townes."

The Company was not formally incorporated till 15 Henry VI.,
August, 23, 1437, when it received the ordinary privileges and endowments as to perpetual succession, the right of using a common seal, and
of pleading and being impleaded in all courts, the title to appoint a
governing body of four Masters or Wardens, and a licence in mortmain
to the extent of 20l. a year.   The style of the Gild was, The Freemen of
the Mistery of Vintners of the City of London.

The licence in mortmain was somewhat differently framed from those
conceded to the other bodies ; for it was limited to the City of London
and the suburbs thereof, and the lands or other hereditaments were to
be held of the Crown as well for the support of the poor of the commonalty as for the celebration of prayers for the King, his ancestors, and
successors, and for the men of the said mistery and all the faithful
deceased.

It is further noticeable that merely Wardens are mentioned, and no
person clothed with authority over them.

This instrument was confirmed and renewed by *inspeximus* of 24
Henry VII., October 2.   But a grant of arms had been made by
Clarencieux, King-of-Arms, in 1447, and was certified in 1530 and
1634.

The Act 7 Edward VI., March 1, embodied a series of very stringent
and injurious provisions in regard to the sale of wine in London by retail under any circumstances whatever ; and the Vintners immediately
after the death of the King, which shortly followed, approached the
Government of Mary with a prayer for a special exemption in their
favour from the operation of the statute.   They obtained three successive
patents from the Queen between 1553 and 1555, enabling them to conduct their business as heretofore.   But the Company appears to have
laboured for some time under considerable disadvantages, and to have
suffered a lengthened interference with their franchise, as the patent of
Philip and Mary emphatically refers to criminal informations, bills, and
suits as commenced against the Gild corporately or individually, and to
forfeitures, penalties, and losses as either incurred or imminently hazarded.
So much was this the case, that it was deemed expedient to apply for a
new charter, which was granted in a most copious and elaborate form,
July 30, 1558 (5 & 6 Philip and Mary).

The main feature in this grant was the re-incorporation of the Vintners
of London proper as a separate mistery, which must be supposed to

signify an exclusion of the suburbs, as well as of the provinces, and the enlargement of the licence in mortmain from 20*l.* to 40*l.* a year ; and we perceive that a *Master and three Wardens* are named for the first time.

The Vintners' charter was renewed by Elizabeth in 1567 and 1577, by James I. in 1603 and 1619, and by James II. in 1685. The last varied in certain particulars from the preceding, and was not only declared void by the Statute 2 William and Mary, but was revoked by James himself, when he found it judicious to disarm the resentment of the City.

By the earlier charter of Elizabeth liberty to possess a Hall was first accorded ; and in the later charter, the widow of a Vintner, if she remarried within the Freedom of London, or the wife, apprentice, or servant of a Vintner or his widow, was entitled to keep a tavern for the sale of wines.

In the preamble of the second charter of Elizabeth there is a curious reference to the right of every one to pursue such lawful calling, whereby he may gain his living, as is most agreeable to his choice or taste.

There are bye-laws drawn up by the Company, and approved by the Primate and others, of 1507, 1581, 1594, and 1607. In 1829 the Court devised a supplementary ordinance for removing from the Freedom any member who allowed the sale of wines, by retail or otherwise, on his premises by a person who was not free, or not the widow or apprentice of a Vintner ; which seems to exclude ordinary servants.

The bye-laws of the Vintners emulate their charters in length and prolixity, and testify to the troublesome and disorderly incidence of the industry, no less than the multifarious detail connected with it. One of the provisions, under which a free Vintner held his house, was, that he should not sanction or connive at any bawdry on the premises, and should enforce good and honest conversation by frequenters thereof.

By 19 Elizabeth a special charter had been granted to the Company, empowering any free Vintner to sell wines ; and this faculty was renewed and enlarged by her successor. It transpired, in a case which came before the courts in February 1888, that the privilege was exercised only by about fifty out of 450 members of the Gild ; and while the later charter of James I. laid down the principle that the law was to be construed liberally, it lent no countenance to delegation by a Vintner to any third party, or to any colourable pretext, by which the trade was carried on under exemption from licence by a person purporting to be the servant of a Vintner. Nor does the law recognise dispensation with a certificate, except in such places and under such conditions as come within the meaning of the Company's charter, or the immunity of free Vintners from any statutory enactment not directly overriding the terms of their grant; since it is not agreeable to the spirit of the law that a prescriptive title, which favours a limited section of the community, should be strained or extended beyond its express provisions.

The privilege or exemption was, and is, narrowed in fact to the lines of the old highways to and from leading ports, and is not a general inland franchise.

It may be presumed,—in face of a continuous series of royal and parliamentary enactments controlling the sale and price of wines,—that the authority and function of the Company were merely administrative, and that at most it had power to make bye-laws for the guidance and protection of the Trade. What is known as the "Wine Project" was one of the incidences of the Civil War, and arose from a patent or monopoly procured by sundry persons, especially Alderman Abel and Richard Kilvert. These farmed the wine business, paying to the Government 40s. per tun; but the system did not enjoy a long duration. This is no place for discussing such a question, which can only interest us here in its relation to the jurisdiction of the Company; doubtless the latter experienced, in common with many other institutions, a temporary deadlock from the disturbance of political tranquillity and the intro-duction of parliamentary and military power.

The authority of the Vintners in early times was apt to be continually traversed and curtailed by the grants from the Crown, as a matter of requital or favouritism, of patents and monopolies to uncovenanted persons independent of the Gild. Queen Elizabeth conferred such a grant on Sir Walter Raleigh; and from a licence issued by him *ex officio* in 1584 to Jeffery Bradshaw, of Bradford, Yorkshire, to keep a wine tavern, and stamped with Raleigh's name by his deputy or clerk, we learn that the price of French wines wholesale was then about 12*l.* a tun, and the retail price 16*d.* a gallon, and that sack, malmsey, and other sweet sorts were 8*l.* the butt or pipe, and about 2*s.* the gallon.

From time immemorial, the Vintners enjoyed the exclusive right of loading and landing, rolling, pitching, and turning all wines and spirits imported into or exported from the City of London and all places within three miles of the same. The Company employed its own tackle-porters, and held itself answerable for their defaults. But modern legislation has gradually reduced this system and privilege to a nullity.

The governing body is composed of a Master, Upper Warden, Renter Warden, Swan Warden, twelve past Masters, and two other members. The Swan Warden has under his charge, in concert with the Dyers' Company, a certain proportion of the swans on the Thames. Thirteen constitute a quorum. Of the aggregate total of 450 members about one moiety is on the Livery.[1]

During the ten years 1870–80 the income seems to have had a prevailing tendency to exceed the expenditure! A large sum is annually laid out on entertainments, and about the same amount on charitable objects outside the trusts. There had not then manifested itself a very strong feeling in the direction of applying surplus funds to educational and benevolent purposes; but the movement shewed symptoms of commencing vitality; and in the hands of a capable Executive this Association would doubtless prove itself worthy of its municipal rank and obligations.

So early as 1357, Sir John Stody, a member of the Fraternity, then unincorporated, left the Vintry and its appurtenances, comprising Stody's Lane, to his brethren, and thus afforded them the opportunity of securing on easy terms the site for a residence and place of business. It was, no doubt, there that the earliest house or Hall stood; but whether it was an old structure or a new one, we do not hear. On Nov. 7, 1446, Guy Shuldham devised to them part of his lands in the parishes of St. Martin's in the Vintry and St. James, Garlick-Hithe, subject to a rent of 5l. a year to superstitious uses inherited from a former owner, his immediate predecessor, John Micole or Michel; and Shuldham charged the property with a further payment of 6s. 8d. a year to like uses, requiring the Vintners to maintain thirteen almshouses[2] in proper repair and to appropriate them to thirteen poor of the commonalty rent-free for ever.

This second gift led to the determination to erect a new Hall, with the almshouses on the Stody and Shuldham sites, so peculiarly convenient in the case of a body whose functions were so intimately and constantly identified with the water-side; and the block of buildings then constructed, and perhaps completed at intervals, exhibited a broad frontage to the Thames with a garden in the rear, and abutted to the North on Thames Street, when that thoroughfare was narrower, and had not encroached on the premises of the Gild in that direction. In 1446 the Hall is described as consisting of the refectory, parlour, counting-house, with two rooms over it, kitchen and coal-house, pantry, buttery, and a yard with a well therein. The parlour is said to be on an upper floor, and to possess a leaden roof. The yard was then a piece of waste ground, probably toward the river, and may be perhaps identified with the subsequent garden.

---

[1] In 1892 the Livery was returned as 198.
[2] These have long been removed to the Mile End Road.

The formal licence to have a Hall occurs only in the charter of 1567, which, however, merely sanctioned something already long in existence ; for the licence in mortmain dated back to 1364, and it could have been requisite to vest the property in feoffees only down to that time, unless we are to understand the statutory force of acts done on the spot as so far wanting.

The historian of London enumerates several freemen of the Company, who held the mayoralty from 1341 downward, especially Henry Picard, who, in 1356, entertained on the same day the Kings of England, France, Scotland, and Cyprus, and Sir John Stody, his immediate successor, and other great personages. This signal circumstance is the presumed origin of the health, drunk to this day, of *Five Times Five.*

VINTNERS' HALL ABOUT 1650.

The incident is thus narrated by Stow :—

"*Henry Picard*, Vintner, Maior, 1357. In the year 1363, did in one day sumptuously feast *Edward* the third, King of *England, John*, King of *France, David*, King of *Scots*,.the King of Cipres, then all in *England ; Edward*, Prince of *Wales*, with many other Noblemen, and after kept his Hall for all comers, that were willing to play at dice and hazard ; the Lady *Margaret* his wife kept her chamber to the same effect," etc.

The allusions to the Hall in early documents and accounts are very few ; but two curious exceptions occur in the mention under 13 Henry VII., January 10, 1497, of an official view of the premises for the purpose of assessing the fine for amortizing them pursuant to the licence ; and in 1609 it was directed that a pair of stocks should be placed there for the punishment of refractory members.

In 1660, shortly before the Restoration, General Monk accepted the invitation of several of the City Companies to partake of their splendid hospitality ; and he attended at Vintners' Hall on April 12. An address was delivered to him "shadowing forth his illustrious virtues as the printed copy expresses it, "under the emblem of a vine," and a musical entertainment was specially prepared for the occasion.

Six years later, the building, where these proceedings had taken place, was lost in the Great Fire, with the bulk of the contents ; and the Company met, first at the Hall in St. Nicholas Lane, and subsequently at the Fleece in Cornhill. The new Hall, erected in part on the old foundations, was not ready for occupation till April, 1671 ; and the wainscoting of the Court-room was completed only in 1676. The whole outlay was defrayed by private subscriptions.

At a much later period, in 1702, Sir Samuel Dashwood, Vintner, being elected Lord Mayor at the accession of Queen Anne, gave a banquet at which her Majesty and the Court were present ; and that year's show was produced at the cost of the Fraternity. The Hall in which the Queen and her suit dined was, doubtless, that described by Hatton below, and was the third which has occupied the same precincts. The Company possesses a remarkable piece of tapestry, executed in 1466, and illustrating the history of St. Martin ; an embroidered pall or hearse-cloth, and a fine collection of Queen Anne and other plate. The oldest relic of this kind belongs to the year 1518 ; but from the records it is gathered that much was sold in 1545 and 1548, as well as at other times, without any note of the date. The so-called "Milkmaid Cup" seems to be only a copy of one of the numerous varieties of double cups of foreign, usually German, fabric, belonging to the sixteenth and seventeenth centuries. The Vintners used to be famous for their cellar of port.

It used to be a custom at the Vintners' banquets to present each of the guests with a silver spoon bearing the Company's arms.

Hatton, in his *New View of London*, 1708, furnishes an interesting account of the Hall, as it then existed. He tells us that it was situated on the south side of Thames Street, near Queen Street, and was a large and commodious brick edifice. The chamber, called the Hall, was paved with marble, and wainscoted with an enrichment of carved fruit and leaves, more particularly the screen at the east end, "where," he says, "the aperture into the Hall is adorned with columns, their entablature and pitched pediment ; and over acrosters are placed the figures of Bacchus between several Fames, and these between two panthers ; and there are other carved figures, as St. Martin, their patron, and the cripple, . . . there are also other embellishments of several coats of arms, etc."

The present aspect of the Hall and premises is still very striking, and except that some of the decorations of the wainscot have been repaired or renewed, and modern stained glass windows introduced (including an additional one), and that on a portion of the old garden a spacious smoking-room has been built, the place is substantially much the same as it was in Hatton's time. There are persons living who remember the mulberry-trees which used to stand in the garden of the Vintners' premises before its absorption by Hambro' Wharf and other structures.

Stow specifies the numerous gifts made to the Vintners from time to time by members of the Brotherhood ; but their charity was by no means confined to home, as the copious gifts bestowed upon all kinds of benevolent objects abundantly testify :—

"In 1357, *Sir John Stody*, Citizen and Vintner, gave the Vintry, with Stody's Lane, and all the tenements adjoining, to the Brotherhood.

"*Richard Chawcer*, Vintner, gave to St. Mary Aldermary Church his Tenement and Taverne, with the appurtenances, in the Reóle or Royal,[1] the corner of *Kirion Lane*, and was there buried, 1348.

"*Simon Eyre*, 1459, gave the Taverne, called the *Cardinals Hat* in *Lombard Street*, with a Tenement annexed on the East part of the Taverne, and a mansion behind the East Tenement, together with an Alley from *Lombard Street* to *Cornhill* with the appurtenances, all which were by him new builded toward a Brotherhood of our Lady in Saint *Mary Wolnoth's* Church.

"*Richard Jacob*, Vintner, gave a gift of sixteene pounds for ever, that it should be distributed to *Christs Hospitall*, Saint *Bartholomews*, *Bridewell*, and Saint *Thomas* in *Southwark*, forty shillings to each house yeerely : and the other eight pounds to be given to certain appointed poore Parishes in *London*.

"He gave moreover (for so long time as two hundred yeeres should last) the summe of twenty-eight pounds yeerely. Of which portion of money, sixteene pounds was appointed for poore Prisoners, that lay imprisoned in any of the eight Prisons in and about *London* yeerly ; to each Prison forty shillings : as the *Gatehouse*, the *Fleet*, both the *Compters* of the *Poultry* and *Wood Street*, *Ludgate*, the *Marshallsea*, the *Kings Bench*, and the *White Lion*.

"What remained of the over-plus of the money, was to be distributed to the poore of divers appointed Parishes.

"Mistris *Sibilla Jacob*, widdow unto *Richard Jacob*, Vintener, gave unto Christs Hospitall, three pounds, and to Saint *Thomas*, three pounds.

"Master *Henry Prannel*, Vintner, and Alderman of *London*, gave among the Hospitals the summe of 50 pounds yeerely.

"*Boniface Tatam* of *London*, Vintner, buried in the Parish of Saint *Peter* upon *Cornhill* the third of *February*, 1606, gave 40s. yeerely to the Parson, for preaching foure Sermons every yeere, so long as the Lease of the *Marmaid* in *Cornehill* (a Taverne so called) shall endure. He gave also to the poore of the Parish thirteene penny loaves every Sunday, during the foresaid Lease.

"Roger Mason, *of the Parish of Saint Giles without Creplegate, Citizen and Vintner of* London, *gave to the poore of the freedome of this Parish,* 200 *pounds, wherewith an yeerely rent of* 16 *pounds or thereabout, is purchased for ever ; to be bestowed on ten Gownes of black Cloth lined, to bee distributed yeerely upon tenne poore men of this Parish, upon* All Saints *day, at the discretion of the Vicar, and* Churchwardens for the time being. He died the 3 day of Septemb. 1603.

"1623. *Jasper Underwood*, Vintener, gave 10 pounds to bee distributed.

---

[1] This locality, so called from its selection as a quarter by the wine-trade of Bordeaux, is named in the grant of land by Sir Richard Whittington in 1411 for the rebuilding of the church of St. Michael Paternoster, near which he resided.

"*George Clarke*, Citizen and Vintner of *London*, gave unto the use of the poore of the Parish of Saint Leonard's, Shoreditch, the summe of 100 marks in money.

"*Stephen Skidmore*, Vintner, gave a gift of forty foure pounds yeerely, and ordered in this manner :

"To seventeen poore Parishes in *London*, appointed by nomination, seventeen pounds.

"To the poore of the Parish of *S. Stephen* in *Coleman-street*, twelve pence weekly in bread.

"To the poore of Corke in Ireland (where it seemeth he was borne) being twelve in number, to each poore body forty shillings.

"Master *William Day*, Vintner, gave fourescore pounds : with the which sum are to be provided twelve coates, for twelve poore mens children, for ever yeerely, and to bee distributed at the said Feast of *All Saints*."

STONEWARE JUG (16th Century).

But the most munificent donor belonging to this ancient and honourable Gild remains to be mentioned :—

"*Robert Gale*, Vintner, out of his Lands lying in divers places, gave the summe of one hundred and forty pounds yeerely, to be imployed in manner following after the decease of *Dorothy* his wife.

To six of the poorer sort of Scholars in *Corpus* Christi Colledge, in the University of Oxenford, usually commorant and residing in the said Colledge, and yeerely to be chosen on the Feast day of Saint *Thomas* the Apostle, by *George Lacocke*, his heires or assignes, under his or their hand and seale : To each Scholar he gave three pounds six shillings eight pence yeerely for ever, to be paid by the said *Lacocke*, his heires or assignes for ever, out of his lands in *Claipoole*, in the County of *Lincolne*, and *Brassington*, in the County of *Derby*.

To the poore in the towne of *Chippenham* in *Wiltshire* he gave twenty pounds.

To the Preacher there, 20 shillings.

To the Bailiffe and Burgesses, as a friendly remembrance, yeerely twenty shillings.

To *Christs Hospitall* in *London*, twenty pounds.

To the Company of Vintners, twenty pounds.

To the poore in *Lincolne*, 20 pounds.

To a Preacher there yeerely, ten shillings.

To the Maior and Chamberlaine, twenty shillings.

To the Minister of S. *Markes* Church there, ten shillings."

The eminent or noteworthy members of the Company also include the names of John Adrian, Lord Mayor in 1270 and 1271 ; Reginald atte Conduit, Mayor in 1334 ; John de Oxenford, Taverner, Mayor in 1341 ; Henry Pickard, Mayor in 1356 ; Sir Samuel Dashwood, M.P., Mayor in 1702 ; Sir Gilbert Heathcote, mentioned by Pope, and said to be the Sir Andrew Freeport of the *Spectator*, Mayor in 1710, and the last who rode to Westminster, to be admitted, on horseback, and (above all) Benjamin Kenton, the distinguished philanthropist, in his youth a waiter at the Crown and Magpie in Aldgate, and who left 400,000*l*.

LITERARY NOTICES.

The Vintners' Licence to Retail Wine. 1561.

Mentioned in the Coopers' Accounts as having been enrolled ; but whether printed or not is not clear.

A New Boke of the natures and properties of all Wines that are commonly vsed here in England. . . . By William Turner. 8vo, 1568.

The Proofe and Prayse of Wine, taken in measure and due time. Licensed for the press in 1582.

A Ballad, called the Vntymely End of Master Page, a vintener in London, who was murthered by a mayde servante of his house. Entered at Stationers' Hall, September 8, 1613.

A Ballad, being the second parte of the murder of Master Page by his mayd, and of her execucon by burninge in Smithfield for that fact 11 Septembris, 1613. Entered the same day.

Wine, Beer, Ale and Tobacco, contending together for superiority. 4to, 1629, 1630, 1658.

_**_* In the first edition this tract is ascribed to *Gallobelgicus*.

A Proclamation for the Prizing of Wines. February 1, 1634–5. A broadside.

The same. February 21, 1636–7. A broadside.

The same. February 8, 1637–8. A broadside.

The Tree of Hvmane Life ; or, The Blood of the Grape. By Tobias Whitaker, M.D. 12mo, 1638, 1654.

A Health to all Vintners, Beer-brewers, and Ale-taverners, Tapsters. . . . Constituting a Jury for the Regulating of Drinking and Drunkenness. [About 1640.] A broadside.

The Petition of the Retailing Vintners of London, and their Propositions and Demaundes contrived and made amongst themselves at their Hall, in Novemb., 1637, whereby it may appear who projected the penny a Quart on Wines. [1641.] A broadside.

A Trve Discovery of the Proiectors of the Wine Proiect, and of the Vintners owne orders, made at their Common-hall. 4to, 1641.

A Trve Relation of the Proposing, Threatning, and Persuading the Vintners to yield to the Imposition upon Wines. 4to, 1641.

A Reply to a most untrue Relation made and set forth in Print, by Certaine Vintners, in excuse of their Wine Proiect. 4to, 1641.

A Dialogue or Accidental Discourse betwixt Mr. Alderman Abell and Richard Kilvert,[1] the two maine Proiectors for Wine, . . . contayning their first manner of their acquaintance, how they began to contrive the Patent it selfe, how they obtayned it, and who drew the patent. 4to, 1641.
The Same in Dutch. 4to, 1641.

The Last Discourse betwixt Master Abel and Master Richard Kilvert. 4to, 1641.

Resolutions of the House of Commons concerning the Prices of Wines, etc. May 26, 1641. A broadside.

The Humble Remonstrance of the Farmers and Adventurers in the Wine-farme of fourty shillings per tun, to the honourable House of Commons. . . . 1641. A broadside.

An Exact Legendary Compendiously containing the whole life of Alderman Abel, the maine Proiector and Patentee for the raising of Wines. His apprentiship with a Vintener, . . . 4to, 1641.

The Copie of a Letter sent from the Roaring Boyes in Elizium to the two arrant Knights of the grape in Limbo, Alderman Abel and M. Kilvert. 4to, 1641.

Good Newes for all true-hearted Subjects. Videlicet, the Parliament goes on. Written by Francis Mussell, Vintner. 1641. A poetical broadside.

The Prisoner's Observations by way of Complaint. Printed February 4, 1645. By the same. A poetical broadside.

The Vintners' Answer to some Scandalous Pamphlets Published (as is supposed) by Richard Kilvert; And abetted in some points by his Brother Roger, and Alderman Abel. 4to, 1642.

An Ordinance . . . for Freeing and Dischargeing the Vintners from any Demand for, or concerning any Delinquencies, concerning the Imposition of forty shillings per Tuune on Wines or anything concerning the same, except the persons herein excepted. May 12, 1645. 4to.

A Ternary of Paradoxes. By Johannes Baptista Van Helmont. Translated by W. Charleton. 4to, 1650.
*** One of the paradoxes is the Nativity of Tartar in Wine.

The English Rechabite; or, A Defyance to Bacchus and all his Works. By Robert Whitehall, of Merton College, Oxford. Folio [about 1660].

A Proclamation for the Publishing of an Act of Parliament late made for the better Ordering and Selling of Wines by Retail, etc. 1660. A broadside.

A Proclamation concerning the Granting of Licenses for Selling and Retailing of Wines. 1661. A broadside.

A Proclamation, prohibiting the Importation of divers Foreign Wines and Merchandizes into this Realm. 1661. A broadside.

---

[1] Kilvert had been a proctor in the Court of Arches.

A Proclamation for Prizing of Wines.   February 4, 1661–2.   A broadside.

A Proclamation concerning Wine Licences.   1662.   A broadside.

The Art and Mystery of Vintners and Wine-Coopers.   8vo, 1682.

A Proclamation for Prizing of Canary Wines.   December 16, 1687.   A broadside.

A New Treatise of Artificial Wines.   By W. Y.-Worth.   12mo, 1690.

The Britannian Magazine; or, A New Art of Making above Twenty Sorts of English Wines.   By W. Y.-Worth.   The Third Edition.   12mo.   [About 1690.]

A New Art of Making Wine, Brandy, and other Spirits, compliant to the Act of Parliament concerning Distillation.   By the same.   12mo, 1691.

The Search after Claret; or, a Visitation of the Vintners.   In verse.   By Richard Ames.   4to, 1691.   Second Edition.   4to, 1691.

A Further Search after Claret; or, A Second Visitation of the Vintners.   4to, 1691.

The Last Search after Claret in Southwark; or, a Visitation of the Vintners in the Mint.   4to, 1691.

The Bacchanalian Sessions; or, the Contention of Liquors : with a Farewell to Wine.   By R. Ames.   4to, 1693.

Miscellanies over Claret; or, The Friends to the Tavern the best Friends to Poetry.   4to, 1697–8.   Four Parts.

In Vino Veritas; or, A Conference betwixt Chip the Cooper, and Dash the Drawer, discovering some Secrets in the Wine-brewing Trade.   8vo, 1698.

The Juice of the Grape; or, Wine preferable to Water.   .   .   .   With a Word of Advice to the Vintners.   By a Fellow of the College [of Physicians].   8vo, 1724.

The Order for Swannes both by the Statutes, and by the Auncient Orders and Customes, used within the Realme of England.   4to, 1570.

Several of these Books of Orders, etc., were once in existence.   There are also extant many MSS. Collections of Swan-marks for different parts.

The supervision of the City swans devolves by custom on the Skinners and Dyers jointly.

The Orders, Lawes, and Ancient Cvstomes of Swannes.   Caused to be printed by John Witherings, Esquire, Master and Governour of the   Royall game of Swans and Signets throughout England.   By John D'Oyly.   4to, 1632.

D'Oyly refers to older orders in print.

Bacchus Festival; or, A New Medley, being A Musical Representation at the Entertainment of his Excellency the Lord General Monck at Vintners' Hall.   April 12, 1660.   A broadside.   By T. Jordan.

A Speech made to his Excellency George Monk, General, and [the Council of State] on the twelfth day of April, 1660.   At a Solemn Entertainment at Vintners' Hall.   Wherein his illustrous virtues are shadowed forth under the Emblem of a Vine.   [By Thomas Jordan.   1660.]   A broadside.

Two editions the same year.

The Clothworkers.

OLD ARMS.

THE parentage and foundation of this, in some respects the most important of all the Gilds of London, are to be found in our preceding account of the SHEARMEN and the FULLERS, of whom the Clothworkers were an amalgamation, as certain primitive minor Crafts already noticed had been fused at an earlier stage with those other two bodies. It may be true that the history of this Association was at one time closely interconnected with that of the Weavers; but the rise into independent recognition and rank, not only of the Clothworkers under their original styles as Shearmen and Fullers, but the severance from them of the Drapers and Taylors demonstrates the great antiquity of this branch of the cloth trade as a distinct industrial art.

This separation of the various processes and steps in manufacture was partly due to the steady and enormous development of the demand for goods employed for personal, domestic, and even decorative purposes, and to the changes which took place in the material of certain fabrics. But, of course, the period of signal prosperity for the Weavers themselves, who were doubtless the pioneers in this direction, was when the market was free from competition, and they enjoyed the monopoly of sale to the draper and the tailor of the produce of their looms. Every reform and improvement in their Craft tended to their disadvantage; the community, as it became more populous and less

simple in its tastes, encouraged every novelty, which was introduced
either by our countrymen or by foreigners established in London ; in
the statutes framed for their relief we easily discern a trace of this commencing decline ; and nothing but the principle of Protection sustained
archaic methods of workmanship and old-fashioned schools of design.
The English, or at least the London, artisan soon discovered that, if he
desired to occupy a favourable position, and to hold his ground, it was
necessary for him to be an apt scholar in learning the lessons taught
by our continental visitors, and to make that a starting-point for further
progress.   There is no doubt that, if we read aright the municipal
expansion of the several departments of the woollen and linen cloth
industries, we must interpret it as directly symptomatic of a parallel
growth in our enterprise, skill, and success in establishing by sure
degrees a machinery in our own capital, which long remained adequate
to our wants and worthy of our national character.

   One striking piece of testimony to the independent magnitude of the
Shearmen and Fullers, anterior to their embodiment as a single Gild,
seems to lie in the comparatively late date of final union, inasmuch as
the individual interests of two prosperous and influential Fraternities
would be less readily accommodated or adjusted than those of two or
more minor fellowships.

   The Charter of 19 Henry VIII., January 18, 1527–8, commences by
rehearsing the circumstances under which Henry VII. and other

sovereigns had previously
accorded privileges or incorporation to the Shear-
men and Fullers respec-
tively, proceeds to transfer
and change the said two
Gilds of Shearmen and
Fullers into " the name of
one Master and four War-
dens of the Gild or Fraternity of the Assumption of
the Blessed Virgin Mary
of the Art or Mistery of
Clothworkers in the City of London," to be one Body and one Commonalty corporate, with the power of acquiring, holding, and alienating
rents and other possessions whatever, with perpetual succession and a
common seal.   It likewise provides for the election from time to time
of the governing body, for the Livery of clothing of one suit or pattern
to the brethren each year, or each alternate year, at the pleasure of the

Executive; for the exercise of a common right of search over denizens and aliens, and punishment of offenders or defaulters according to the law of England or the custom of London, in all matters pertaining to the misteries of Shearmen and Fullers, and to woollen cloths and fustians, and all other goods, used in the same; and for the restraint of foreign workmen, not admitted to the Freedom of the Clothworkers.

This large grant, which forms the groundwork of the present constitution, was confirmed by *inspeximus* of 4 & 5 Philip and Mary, June 4, 1558, and of 2 Elizabeth, July 8, 1560.

Charles I. in a charter dated April 24, 1633, recites the former grants, and renews the Gild under the name of the Master, Wardens, and Commonalty of Freemen of the Art or Mistery of Clothworkers of the City of London, and appoints the existing functionaries, that is to say, Thomas Byard to be the first and modern Master, and other four persons to be the first and modern Wardens, *ad interim* and until the period for the ordinary elections of officers, namely, the first Monday in the next ensuing August. The royal letters further released and purged the beneficiaries from any doubts or inadvertences whatever in former proceedings and acts.

Charles II. by letters patent under the Great Seal, February 5, 1684–5, gave the Clothworkers a new charter, in which their privileges were considerably abridged, the king assuming a right to nominate the Assistants and Clerk, as well as the Master and Wardens *ad interim* as before, and to debar the governing body from entering on office, unless they took the oaths of allegiance and supremacy, and subscribed to the Test and Corporation Acts. In other respects the Company was left undisturbed.

The reign of James II. was short enough to prevent any protracted inconvenience and loss, and long enough to occasion a great deal of vexation and trouble. The period of more than three and a half years, between February, 1684–5 and October, 1688, when James revoked his arbitrary, intolerant, and strategic infringement of the civic rights at large, was an interval during which the Clothworkers and their contemporaries suffered equal anxiety and discomfort. But the Revolution of 1688 permanently cleared the atmosphere.

The Ordinances, commencing with those of 1531–2, approved by Sir Thomas More as Lord Chancellor, the Lord Treasurer, and the Chief Justices, followed in a certain measure those previously drawn up for the government of the Shearmen and the Fullers as separate Fraternities. They dealt, as usual, with the election of officers, the livery of clothing, the rendering of accounts, the relief of necessitous brethren and their burial, if necessary, out of the common box, with the dirges and masses

to be said for their souls, the attendance of members at the obsequies
of a brother in their best apparel, and the treatment of apprentices,
journeymen, and foreigners. There are provisions regulating the details
of work and hours of attendance, forbidding men of the mistery to play
at unlawful games or resort to riotous practices, and imposing fines for
misdemeanours.

This Code, which is unusually lengthy, was renewed 29 Elizabeth,
July 2, 1587, and 15 Charles I., April 18, 1639. It would be impossible
to furnish more than an outline of the contents. But some of the rules
and conditions are very curious, more particularly in respect to the conditions and hours of labour.

In common with the Taylors, Skinners, and other Gilds, the Clothworkers admitted sisters to the freedom ; and as the children of both
succeeded to the privilege as an inheritance, the ranks of the Yeomanry,
as it was generally termed, increased from time to time to such an
extent that the bond between them and the Livery and Court had a
natural tendency to slacken. The bulk of freemen and freewomen by
birthright have consequently long ceased to exercise any control over
the government ; but the Clothworkers preserve the ancient usage of
permitting their Hall to be occasionally employed by the Yeomanry for
their sports and recreations during good behaviour and subject to convenience, to the extent of inviting the whole body of almsfolk to an
annual feast. Provision is also made on a very liberal scale for the
relief of all the poor of the Company, and even for the payment of
funeral expenses.

At a former period, however, the Court experienced the same kind
of disposition to aggressive encroachment or self-assertion on the part of
the freemen as we have had occasion to notice in other instances. A
successful effort in obtaining concessions had a contagious influence ;
and the Clothworkers, like the Merchant-Taylors, temporarily acquiesced
in the institution of Wardens of the Yeomanry. But they were discontinued in 1754. It is worth remarking, that one of the points of
debate between the Court and the operative class was the legality of the
seizure by the Wardens of ill-wrought goods ; for this entered into the
very questionable power of search conferred by the majority of the
charters.

The disaffection to the autocratic jurisdiction of the Court and Senior
Liverymen may be traced back a long way, since it furnished the
subject-matter of a pamphlet (apparently a reply to another), in which
the whole constitutional question is ventilated, and the pretensions of the
Diffusive Body or Commonalty to a share in the control are shown to be
groundless and at variance with the meaning and spirit of the charters.

The present aggregate numbers of the Company may be about 500, of which the Livery represent about 150, the Court inclusive. The latter is estimated at 44 with the Master and Wardens. Every precaution is taken to secure respectability on the part of the Livery, and on that of the Executive section able and substantial persons. The general temper and feeling are emphatically tolerant and reasonable.

The Company was one of the twelve contributories of 5,000*l.* toward the total of 60,000*l.* eventually paid to the Government of James I. for the forfeited Irish estates, of which we have given particulars in several earlier places. In this instance, the Clothworkers, as proprietors in chief, found 2,260*l.*, the remainder being found by the Butchers and five other bodies. But considerable difficulty was experienced, even under these conditions, in raising the amount. In 1610 or the following year, at the request of the Lord Mayor and Court of Aldermen, Lord Compton (ancestor of the Marquis of Northampton) contributed 200*l.* toward the Ulster Plantation "to the ease of the poor Company of Clothworkers," whereof his father-in-law, Sir John Spencer, knight, was a member and principal upholder.

In 1769 the Clothworkers' Irish estate was let by public auction on a lease of sixty-one years and for three lives at a rental of 600*l.* and a fine of 28,000*l.* But it has since been sold for 150,000*l.*

In 1316 the Aulnage, a word derived from the old French *aulne*, ell, the common standard of measurement, was granted to. John Peacock of canvas, linen cloth, napery, as well English as foreign, kerseys, worsted, and all kinds of cloth of Lincoln, Essex, Norfolk, Suffolk, Kent, Stamford, Beverley, St. Osyth, Devon, and Cornwall.

The cloths offered to foreign dealers in exchange for wine and other produce were found at a very early period to be not unfrequently false in dimensions, colour and substance, and fraudulently mixed with wool ; and in 13 Richard II. (1389) it was enacted that "no plain cloth, tacked or folded, shall be set to sale within the counties of Somerset, Dorset, Bristol, and Gloucester, but that they shall be opened, upon pain to forfeit them, so that the buyers may see them and know them, as it is now in the County of Essex, and that the workers, weavers and fullers shall put their seals to every cloth."

The great abuses represented to Queen Elizabeth as being practised in connection with the " draping of cloth," led her Majesty in 1581, in concert with Lord Burghley, to recommend a suitable person for the post of Alnager, Searcher, or Surveyor to the City. It was an office which was created by the most ancient statutes, and was finally abolished in 1700, ten years after the appearance of published Reasons for commuting aulnage for a custom or excise. We find John May, Deputy-Alnager, who had been a servant of the Duke of Lenox, publishing a vindication of the functionaries discharging the duty ; and a good deal of discontent and irritation was produced from time to time by this surveillance over the trade, which in its turn was attended by tyranny, espionage, and extortion.

It can only be pointed out generally, that henceforth there was an almost uninterrupted series of correspondence and discussion on this subject among the parties officially or commercially interested, and that the question of the manufacture, oversight, and sale of this commodity awakened the attention of the highest legal and other authorities.

The exclusive use of woollen cloth of the old-fashioned texture was discontinued in 1567 or thereabout, in consequence of the introduction of serges and other lighter fabrics, as it is held, by manufacturers at Norwich and elsewhere in the provinces. This new material, which of course tended to break the monopoly of the London Clothworkers, and of what became known by distinction as the Old Drapery, was called the *New Drapery*, and was probably designed for wear during the warmer season.

The John May above mentioned obtained a lease from the Corporation in 1612 of a site for a proposed market for the sale of strained cloths and other stuff of the *New Drapery*, but was hindered in carrying out his plan. Perhaps he was invested as a *solatium* with the office of Deputy-Alnager.

The early cloth trade was divided between Yorkshire and the North of England, Shropshire and North Wales, Gloucestershire and Devonshire. It is now almost exclusively restricted to Yorkshire and North Wales. We possess literary and other records of its flourishing condition in those districts where it has ceased to be a prevailing or leading industry ; and a popular writer of the reign of Elizabeth produced a novel, of which the six great clothiers of the West are the heroes and central figures. They belonged to Reading, Gloucester, Salisbury, Worcester, Exeter, and Southampton. But three like eminent characters of the Midland and North country are also particularized in connection with Manchester, Halifax, and Kendal. Still more curiously, the Six Clothiers of the West formed the subject-matter of a drama in two parts, which was written and acted in 1601—the only performance of the kind, perhaps, ever brought on our stage.

One of the earliest symptoms of a tendency to revolt against the imposts laid on trade in the metropolis under various heads and pretences was the proposal to establish a Staple of North-Wales cottons and frieses at Chester in 1582, with liberty to export the same direct abroad ;

and one ground of objection offered by the City was the loss imminent thereby to its hospitals through the failure of the charges leviable at Bakewell or Blackwell Hall, amounting by estimation to about 100*l.* a year. Curiously enough, the bailiffs of Shrewsbury appear as opponents to the scheme, of which we do not hear further, save the attempt of the drapers of Shrewsbury and Oswestry to hamper the London dealers by way of reprisal in procuring their goods, as theretofore, from North Wales, agreeably to their power under the City Charter of trading with all parts of the kingdom.

Our knowledge of the original Hall of the Shearmen on the east side of Mincing Lane, subsequently occupied by the united Gild, is

limited to a very rough outline in the map of London published by Agas about 1560, and figured in the text. It is said that in the stained glass windows of the refectory were the arms of ten Lord Mayors and sixteen Sheriffs, who had belonged to the Fraternity; and mention occurs of an upper-hall window, and of parlours also embellished with stained glass.

General Monk, in the early part of 1659–60, paid a series of ceremonial visits to the Halls of the principal Gilds ; he was at Clothworkers' Hall on the 13th of March ; and a speech or address, prepared by Thomas Jordan, the City poet, was delivered to him in the course of the entertainment given in his honour by the Company.

Pepys notes, under September 6, 1666 : " Strange it is to see Clothworkers' Hall on fire these three days and nights in one body of flame, it being the celler full of oyle." The *London Gazette* of September 8, 1666, refers to the arrest of the flames at this point.

In 1668, the house opposite the Hall was burnt down, but fortunately without injury to the surrounding buildings. Yet Pepys, under June 19, notes that the fire broke out at between two and three in the morning, so that the danger was all the greater.

The ground-plan and frontage of the second Hall are now given, and will be found to differ very essentially from those of the building erected in 1862, on a report that the former one was insecure from the ravages of dry rot. In the rear of the demolished structure lay a large garden, with a fountain in the centre.

Hatton, in his *New View of London*, 1708, describes it as " a noble rich building." " The Hall," he says, " is a lofty room, adorned with wainscot to the ceiling, where is a curious fretwork. The screen, at the south end, is of oak, adorned with four pilasters, their entablature and compass pediment of the Corinthian order, enriched with their arms, palmbranches, etc. The west end is adorned with the figures of King James and King Charles I., richly carved as big as life in their robes, with regalia all gilt with gold, where is a spacious window of stained glass, and the Queen's arms ; also those of Sir John Robinson, knight and

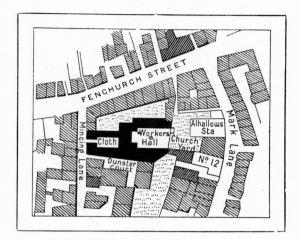

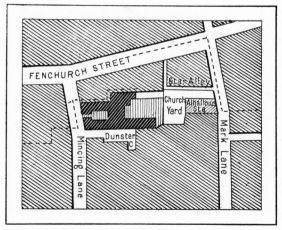

TWO PLANS SHEWING THE SITE AND AREA OF THE HALL DEMOLISHED IN 1862.

baronet, his Majesty's Lieutenant of the Tower of London, Lord Mayor of this honourable City, anno 1663, and president of the Artillery Company, who kept his mayoralty in this Hall, in which year he entertained their majesties, the King, Queen, and Queen's mother, and their royal highnesses, the Duke and Duchess of York, and towards the re-edifying of this Hall a worthy benefactor. His coat of arms, 6th and 4th *gules* and *or* quarterly embattled, the 2nd and 3rd *vert* semi of trefols : a buck trippent *or* : and the like buck for the crest." Here were also the arms of Samuel Pepys, Master in 1677, those of William Howard, Master

in 1687, and those of Sir Joseph Williamson, principal Secretary of State, Master in 1676, all benefactors of the Company. In two small windows were the arms of the City and of the Clothworkers, the latter with the motto, *My trust is in God alone.* The exterior of the house had fluted brick columns with Corinthian stone capitals.

There are engraved representations of the exterior of the late Hall ; but the general effect does not essentially vary from that of the one now existing.

Clothworkers' Hall stands on a far larger area than the block taken down in 1862, of which an appreciable part was occupied by a garden. But the mansion-house now covers the whole ground, and abuts in the rear on the Churchyard of All Hallows, Steyning. It is a spacious and splendid edifice, planned on a scale commensurate with the wealth and wants of the Company, and so far resembles it, that its modern side is principally conspicuous, although not more so than is the case with many others.

Before their removal to Islington, where, as early as 1640, the Company already possessed a similar endowment of the gift of John Heath, the Clothworkers' almshouses were situated in Whitefriars, on part of a garden belonging to Margaret, Countess of Kent, who held the ground under a demise from the Prior of the Friary.

Among the celebrities who have belonged to the Clothworkers, may be mentioned William Lambe, a benefactor of this and other institutions, and a man of high public spirit ; he was Master in 1569-70, and died in 1580. His name survives in Lambs-Conduit Street. The Company also boasts Samuel Pepys, F.R.S. ; Sir John Spencer, ancestor of the Marquis of Northampton, and a great upholder of the Company ; James the First ; Sir Thomas Trevor, Baron of the Exchequer ; Sir John Robinson, nephew of Archbishop Laud, Lord Mayor in 1662-3, and Lieutenant of the Tower ; Sir Godfrey Webster ; the Countess of Kent, freewoman and widow ; and William Hewer of Clapham, Esquire, sometime Pepys's clerk, and like him a book-collector. But there is a long and honourable roll of generous and philanthropic members, the fruits of whose beneficence assist in enabling this excellent and noble Association to carry on its industrial and eleemosynary schemes ; and a tolerably convincing proof of the vitality of the Company, no less than of the reliance on its probity and administrative machinery, lies in the most recent trust-estate left to it—that of 70,000*l.* under the will of Mr. Thomas William Wing, of Piccadilly, 1884 (proved in 1889) for the Relief of the Blind.

In 1677 Samuel Pepys was Master of the Company, and signalized his year of office by the presentation of a Bowl and Cover of silver gilt, enriched on the exterior with frosted work, and weighing 166 ounces. His brethren also received from him a gilt ewer and bason weighing 196 ounces. Both of these memorials of him are still in the Clothworkers' possession. Pepys's and Hewer's arms used to be in the eastern window of the Hall.

CLOTHWORKERS' COMPANY. ROSE-WATER DISHES AND EWERS (1593–1880).

*** No. 4 represents the Pepys Gift.

Let us recollect, too, that no less a man than Geoffrey Chaucer, though not a member, discharged official duties in connection with the cloth and leather trades, having been appointed in 1374 Comptroller of the Subsidy of Wools, Skins, and Tanned Hides. The poet received the not inconsiderable emoluments; but in 1385 he was permitted to fulfil the functions, as well as those of the Comptrollership of the Petty Customs of the Port of London, by deputy.

The relative importance of the Clothworkers was recognised by Herbert, when he wrote his work, about 1836; for he speaks of them as having a very large estate, out of which they annually paid to the poor 1,400*l.* "It is," says he, "a rich, eminent Company." It goes almost without saying that not only these figures, but even those in the parliamentary return of 1884, are ancient history, since the annual amount at present devoted to educational and charitable purposes does not probably fall short of 50,000*l.*, irrespectively of the New Wing Fund.

Annexed are the latest statistics connected with the Company's Yorkshire College at Leeds, as furnished to us by the courtesy of Sir Owen Roberts :—

Technical Education.
CLOTHWORKERS' COMPANY.

	Annual Subscriptions for Maintenance.	Building Equipment.
Yorkshire College, Leeds— Textile Industries, Dyeing and Art Departments wholly Founded and Maintained by the Company	£2,000	£30,000
Bradford Technical College . . .	500	4,100
Huddersfield Technical School . .	300	2,000
Halifax „ „ . .	Not Settled	2,000
Keighley „ „ . .	150	1,300
Dewsbury „ „ . .	50	800
Salt Science, Art and Technical Schools, Shipley	100	
Bingley Technical School . . .	50	350
Ossett ,, „ . . .	20	200
Morley „ „ . . .	20	
Wakefield „ „ . . .	—	100
Yorkshire Union of Mechanics' Institutes— (583*l.* 10*s.* Contributed to Technical Prize Fund. Grants of Books to Village Library of Value of 14*0l.*)	25	
University College, Bristol— (Grants from 1876 to 1886 = 3,700*l.*)	100	1,000
Trowbridge, Wilts, Technical School	—	105
Glasgow Technical School— (Grants from 1878 to 1884 = 1,050*l.*)	50	200

Yorkshire Clothworking Districts.

City and Gilds of London Institute for the Advancement of
    Technical Education   .   .   .   .   4,000*l.* per annum.
Special Donations to Building and Equipment .   .   .   .   12,000*l.*   „
Total Grants to City and Gilds of London Institute to 31 December, 1891, 57,600*l.*

    The Clothworkers' Company expend on " Technical Education " in London, York-
shire, and other Provincial Districts connected with the Clothworking Industry alone,
upwards of 12,000*l.* per annum.
    CLOTHWORKERS' HALL,
        October 14, 1891.

Above all the Companies, perhaps, on the whole, the Clothworkers'
are to be considered as having preserved a continuity of existence and
approbation in their former warrantable espousal and protection of
the trade and their present generous and intelligent patronage of it.
They have thus strengthened their own hands and have become a source
of power and security to others ; and this proud result is largely due to
the efficiency of the Executive.

LITERARY NOTICES.

A profitable booke, declaring dyuers approued remedies to take out spottes and
    staines in silkes, veluets, Linnen, and Wollen Cloths. With diuers colours how to
    die Veluets and Silkes, Linnen and Woollen Fustian and Threade. Also to dresse
    leather, and to colour fells. How to Gild, Graue, Sowder, and Vernishe. And
    to harden and make soft Yron and Steele. . . . 4to, 1588, 1596, 1605.
             A translation from the Dutch by L[eonard] M[ascall].

A Declaration of the Estate of Clothing now vsed within this Realme of England.
    . . . With an Apologie for the Aulneger, shewing the necessarie vse of his
    Office. Written by Iohn May, a deputie Alneger. 4to, 1613.

To the Most Honorable Assembly of the Commons House of Parliament. The
    humble Petition of the Artizan Cloth-workers of the Citie of London. [1624.]
    A broadside.

An Ordinance to prohibite the transporting of Wooll and fuller's earth. 1647. A
    broadside.

The Golden Fleece: The Riches of English Wool in its Manufacture. By W. S.
    8vo, 1656.

A Proclamation for the preventing of the Exportation of Wools, Wool-Fells, Woollen-
    Yarn, Fuller's-Earth, and other Scouring-earths, out of this Kingdom. 1660. A
    broadside.

A Proclamation for the free Exportation of Woollen Manufactures of this Kingdom
    from the Twentieth day of May until the Five and Twentieth day of December
    next. 1662. A broadside.

Reasons for a Limited Exportation of Wooll. 4to, 1677.

A Treatise of Wool and Cattel. 4to, 1677.

An Act for Burying in Woollen. 1678. A broadside.

The Golden Fleece: Or, Old England Restored to its old Honest Vocation. By J. F.
    4to, 1679.

The Trade of England Revived. [By John Blande.] 4to, 1680.
        ⁎ This tract deals with Wool, Woollen Cloth, Linen Cloth, Silk, Silk weavers, etc.

A Treatise of Wool, and the Manufacture of it. 8vo, 1685.

An Abstract of the Proceedings to prevent Exportation of Wooll Unmanufactured from the year 1667 to this present year, 1688. By William Carter, Clothier. 4to, 1688.

The Aulnage Case, or Reasons offer'd for taking away the Office of Aulnage, and changing the subsidy of Aulnage into a Custom. [January, 1690-1.] A broadside.

Reasons of the Decay of the Clothing Trade, Humbly offered to the Parliament : with some Short Proposals of Redress. By a Well-wisher to the Trade, and the True English Interest. 4to, 1691.

An Essay on Wool and Woollen Manufacture. 4to, 1693.

Some Thoughts on the Bill Depending before the Right Honourable the House of Lords, for prohibiting the Exportation of the Woollen Manufactures of Ireland to foreign parts. 4to, Dublin, 1698.

The Interest of England, in Relation to the Woollen Manufacture. In a Dialogue between a Merchant and a Clothier. 4to, 1701.

Proposals humbly Offer'd to the Honourable House of Commons, by the Gloucestershire Clothiers, and other Woollen Manufactories, for the more effectual preventing the Exportation of Wooll, etc. [About 1700.] A broadside.

An Essay towards the Improving of the Hempen and Flaxen Manufactures in the Kingdom of Ireland. By Louis Crommelin, Overseer of the Royal Linnen Manufacture of that Kingdom. 4to, Dublin, 1705, 1734.[1]

An Epitaph, or funerall inscription, upon the godlie life and death of the Right worshipfull Maister William Lambe, Esquire, Founder of the new Conduit in Holborne . . . Deceased the one and twentieth of April, and intumbed in S. Faiths Church vnder Powles, the sixt of Maie next and immediatly following. Deuised by Abraham Fleming. [1580.] A broadside.

The Pleasant History of John Winchcomb, in his younger yeeres called Jack of Newberie, the famous and worthie Clothier of England. By Thomas Deloney. Licensed for the press in 1595. 4to, 1619, 1626, etc. An edit. 8vo, Newbury, 1760.
> See Herbert's *Twelve Livery Companies*, 1836. i., 394.

Thomas of Reading, Or, The Sixe worthie Yeomen of the West. By Thomas Deloney. 4to, 1612, 1623, 1632, 1636, etc.

The Six Clothiers of the West : A play by Richard Hathwaye, Wentworth Smith, William Haughton, and John Day. Mentioned by Henslowe under date of November 12, 1601, but no longer known.
> This drama was doubtless based on Deloney's *Thomas of Reading*, originally printed before 1600, in which year it is not only mentioned in *Kempes Nine Daies Wonder*, but was appropriated by Henry Roberts in a tract entitled *Haigh for Devonshire*. Henslowe also quotes the piece before us as the *Six Yeomen of the West*, the sub-title of Deloney's prose narrative.

The Ancient Honours of the City of London recovered by the Noble Sir John Robinson, Knight and Baronet, Lord Mayor for the year 1662–3, in the true English and man-like exercise of Wrestling, Archery, Sword, and Dagger ; with the Speeches of Mr. William Smith, Master of the Game, and Clerk of the Market upon this solemn occasion. Intermitted twenty-four years, since Garaway was Mayor. [4to, 1663.]
> We have only seen an account of this tract in a note to Herbert's *Livery Companies*, 1836.

The Beau-Merchant. A Comedy written by a Clothier. 4to, 1714.

---

[1] In Burn's *Star Chamber*, 1870, may be found several notices relative to the cloth trade.

CIVIC PAGEANTS.

Londini Emporia; or, London's Mercatura, expressed in sundry Triumphs, Pageants, and Shows, at the Inauguration of the Right Hon. Ralph Freeman, all the charge and expense being the undertaking of the Right Worshipful Company of the Clothworkers. By T. Heywood. 4to, 1633.

The Triumphs of Fame and Honour: At the Inauguration of Robert Parkhurst, Clothworker. Compiled by John Taylor, the Water Poet. 4to, 1634.

London's Triumph, Presented by Industry and Honour: with Other Delightful Scenes, appertaining to them : Celebrated in Honour of the Right Honourable Sir John Ireton, Knight, Lord Mayor of the said City, on the 29th day of October 1658. And done at the Cost and Charges of the Worshipful Company of Cloth- workers. By John Tatham. 4to, 1658.

A Speech made to the Lord General Monck, at Clothworkers' Hall in London, the 13 of March, 1659, at which time he was there entertained by the Worthie Companie. [1660.] A broadside. Written by Thomas Jordan.

London's Triumph: Presented in severall Delightful Scœnes, both upon the Water and Land : and Celebrated in Honour of the truly Loyal and known Deserver of Honour, Sir John Robinson, Knight and Baronet, Lord Mayor of the City of London. At the Costs and Charges of the Worshipfull Company of Cloth- workers. 4to, 1662.

London's Triumphs: Illustrated with many Magnificent Structures and Pageants ; on which are orderly advanced several stately Representations of Poetical Deities, sitting and standing in great splendor on several Scenes in Proper Shapes. With Pertinent Speeches, Jocular Songs (sung bv the City Musick), and Pastoral Dancing. Performed Oct. 29, 1677, for the Celebration, Solemnity, and Inauguration of the Right Honourable Sir Francis Chaplin. Knight, Lord Mayor of the City of London. All the charge and Expenses of the Industrious Designs being the sole Undertaking of the Ancient and Right Worshipful Society of Clothworkers. Designed and composed by Tho. Jordan, Gent. 4to, 1677.

The Triumphs of London: Prepared for the Entertainment of the Right Honourable Sir Thomas Lane, Knight, Lord Mayor of the City of London. Containing A full Description of the Pageants, Speeches, Songs, and the whole Solemnity of the Day. Performed on Monday, the 29 of October, 1694. Set forth at the Proper Cost and Charges of the Honourable Company of Clothworkers. Pub- lished by Authority. By Elkanah Settle. 4to, 1694.

THE MINOR COMPANIES.

The Apothecaries.

BY a charter of 4 James I., April 9, 1606, the Grocers had obtained a renewal of their ancient privileges and powers in relation to the sale of all goods, drugs inclusive, connected with their Gild, and their plenary control of members of the undivided community. No idea was apparently entertained that an early dissolution of the bond between the Grocers and a branch of their corporation was to be expected, or that the grant of 1606 would be the last under which the ancient Company would retain jurisdiction over pharmacy.

But throughout the reigns of Elizabeth and her successor the voice of complaint and remonstrance against the incompetence of apothecaries, and the quality of the drugs sold or dispensed by them, had been gathering strength ; the governing body of the Grocers, through their Wardens, frequently seized and destroyed bad or adulterated wares of various kinds ; and the medical profession exposed the mischief, scandal, and danger of so important a department of medical science being without due technical training and supervision. We have no specific authority for the view ; but it is excessively probable that the opportunities which the eminent apothecary, Gideon Delaune, member of a family illustrious by its attainments in science and letters, enjoyed through his official preferment, about 1615, as Apothecary to the King, had a large share in shaping and maturing the project for severance in the royal mind. It was just such a scheme as James would be apt to patronize. Perchance his son Henry, instead of being poisoned by him, as it has been alleged, was poisoned by some professional empiric ; and we see that in 1614 the City did not improve matters by certain annoyances, to which James's Apothecary at that time, James Garrett, was subjected, and in respect of which he invoked his employer's intercession.

The King, in or before 1614, began to move in the matter, and took credit to himself for having been primarily instrumental in accomplishing a very vital reform. On the 6th December, 1617, a separate charter was given to the Apothecaries, in spite of the opposition of the parent body, which memorialized and argued against the step as an unjust encroachment on their endowment, and prevailed on the Municipality to share the same opinion.

The Apothecaries' grant restrained the Grocers and all other Companies from keeping an apothecary's shop, and from exercising the mistery in London or within a radius of seven miles thereof ; it required every practitioner to have served his full term of apprenticeship, and to have obtained a certificate from the College of Physicians, and it conferred on the Society the power of search, seizure, and destruction over apothecaries' shops in London and within the aforesaid radius.

The new body was entitled to buy, sell, and make drugs ; and here a main difficulty was experienced from the want of corporate resources and the expensive character of the true material. The plan was conceived of facilitating the execution of this very essential part of their functions by creating a Stock, to which any member might subscribe to the extent of a single non-transferable share, and which was calculated to enable them to carry on the pharmaceutical business on behalf of, and in the name of, the Society. But the heavy cost of pure drugs obliged these stockholders to produce or sell at a loss, until their affairs became embarrassed, and the Society itself took over the business, which it still manages in its corporate capacity.

In addition to their own specialities, the Apothecaries to a certain extent trespassed on the province of the Vintner in laying in stocks of the richer sorts of wines for retailing, possibly on the ground or pretext that they were liqueurs for medicinal purposes. Stow specifies more particularly muscadel, malmsey, sack, and bastard.

OLD ARMS.

When the Grocers represented to James I. the prejudice which his movement would entail upon them, he rejoined in a tone and spirit which certainly did him honour. After excepting to other points, the King said : "Another grievance of mine is, that you have condemned the patents of the Apothecaries in London. I myself did devise that Corporation, and do allow it. The Grocers who complain of it are but merchants. The mistery of these Apothecaries was belonging to the Apothecaries, wherein the Grocers are unskilful, and therefore I think it fitting that they should be a Corporation of themselves. They [the Grocers] bring home rotten wares from the Indies, Persia, and Greece, and herewith thro' mixtures make waters and sell such as belong to the Apothecaries, and think no man must control them, because they are not Apothecaries."

The Society was so far fortunate in having James for a friend ; his Majesty would even call this *his* Society ; and in the grant of arms by Camden Clarencieux, the obligations of the Apothecaries, who might otherwise have failed to withstand the influential hostility of the Grocers, were symbolized in the introduction of the two unicorns, the dexter one denoting Scotland.

At one time the Society was one of those among the Gilds of the City, which superintended the King's Beam at the Steelyard ; and the Society probably undertook the charge of the Small Beam, which was calculated for troy weight.

It is deeply to be regretted in the public interest that the apothecary of our days is permitted to tamper alike with his material and his customer, and to deliver prescriptions, which in a heavy proportion of cases are false ; or to tender professional advice, which is often as worthless as it is *ultra vires*. But modern legislation has been rather in the direction of extending and strengthening the authority of the Society, and enlarging its sphere of usefulness ; and in the future Parliament can do no wiser thing than to make it, with proper safeguards, the medium for securing the country against the crying abuse of corrupt pharmaceutical concoctions by all but a few leading establishments.

So far back as 1812 a strong effort was made to organize the medical profession on a sounder basis under parliamentary sanction ; but it was not at that time successful.

The Apothecaries, the Stationers, and the Clothworkers are honourably distinguished in their several ways as the municipal Livery bodies, which recognise and carry out the practical side of their nominal callings, apart from any charitable or fiduciary element and consideration ; and so far as the first Society is concerned it must be obvious that, unless it is courageously and energetically supported, as being the best available machinery for the purpose, in protecting the community against ignorance and fraud, the advance in the other branches of medical and surgical science is sensibly retarded and neutralized.

The Court of Aldermen, manifestly under the Grocers' inspiration, looked unfavourably on the detachment of the Apothecaries ; and as early as 1614, when the matter was already mooted, addressed a petition to the Lords of the Council upon it. The question was referred to two of the Judges, and all the points seem to have been well considered, before the charter passed. But the controversy did not terminate there ; and as late as 1618 the King's letters patent were still unenrolled by the City Chamberlain, and James was maintaining a correspondence with the Corporation on the subject.

The Society is governed by a Master, two Wardens, and twenty-one Assistants. Four ordinary Courts are held in the year, and two special Courts for the swearing in of Examiners or other extraordinary business.

The three grades of the Apothecaries are the Yeomanry or Freemen, the Livery, and the Court. Women are not admitted to the Freedom. Freedom of the City is optional. In 1882 and 1892 the numbers were about 400, of whom the Yeomanry made 250.

This Society, the Stationers, and the Brewers enjoy the distinction of excluding persons not belonging to the vocation. They are all types of the Craft Gild, which must be accounted in some respects as more interesting and technically important than the Gild Merchant.

The members of the Society dine together annually on or about Lord Mayor's Day, and usually invite such members of the Colleges of Physicians and Surgeons, and others, as the Court thinks fit. There used to be a botanical excursion, known as Herborizing Day, once a year, when a second dinner was given ; but this custom has been abandoned ; and it may be predicated generally indeed of the expenditure, that it is exemplarily frugal.

The Hall was acquired under the charter in 1633, and originally consisted of a house and grounds known as Cobham House, then the property of Lady Howard of Effingham ; these premises extended to the Thames on the eastern side of Water Lane, and occupied a larger area than the present buildings, which, with the laboratories, warehouses, and other appurtenances, cover about three-quarters of an acre.

When the Society first came into possession of this estate, it was classic ground on almost every side. There was Baynard's Castle, once held by the Fitzwalters, to whom the site of Grocers' Hall also belonged ; Bridewell, first a palace and then a prison ; the Wardrobe ; and the Theatre, where so many of the dramas of the early playwrights were performed, and of which Playhouse Yard is the sole existing memorial. Moreover, Surgeons' Hall was in the Old Bailey, and the College of

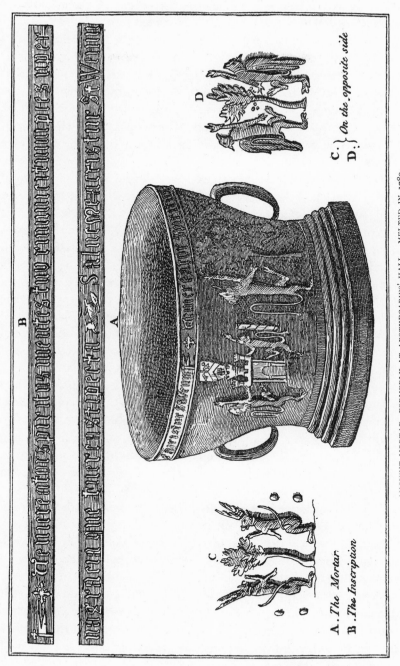

A. The Mortar.
B. The Inscription.

C.
D. } On the opposite side

ANCIENT MORTAR, FORMERLY AT APOTHECARIES' HALL. MELTED IN 1789.

From an engraving in the Gentleman's Magazine for that year (October, 1789).

Physicians in Warwick Lane.   The Apothecaries have alone remained on their original holding, until realities have faded into associations.

Pepys, in his *Diary*, January 29, 1660–1, records his presence at a performance of three acts of *The Maid in the Mill*, by Fletcher and Rowley, at Apothecaries' Hall, and being pleased.   It was at a period when the theatres were not yet fully in working order again ; and the Hall from its vicinage was not an inappropriate substitute for a regular playhouse.   But this is the only incident of consequence which has been handed down to us of the original Hall, which totally perished in the Fire a few years later.

A writer in 1695 describes its successor as " seated almost opposite to the Paved Alley that leadeth to the Ditch side, down steps against Bridewell Bridge."   It was then entered by a pair of gates leading into an open courtyard, paved with broad stones.   The Hall itself was 59 feet in length, 28 in width, and 26 in height.   At the southern end was a screen of Irish oak, 17½ feet high, surmounted by the Society s arms ; and the apartment was wainscoted in the same material to a height of 15 feet.   At the other extremity was the orchestra, or music gallery, surmounted by the royal arms.

The place still preserves an antique aspect and a contrast to the modern life around ; although its owners and occupiers so thoroughly and worthily identify themselves with their own time and its calls.

The famous men who have been members of this body, include many names familiar to the scientific and literary student : Tobias Smollett, William and John Hunter, Edward Jenner, Sir Humphrey Davy, Dr. Sydenham, Sir Spencer Wells, and Sir Erasmus Wilson ; and among those who joined the Society, but owed their celebrity to other gifts, there were Tobias Smollett, Oliver Goldsmith, George Crabbe, and John Keats.

The Physic Garden was originally leased to the Apothecaries by Charles Cheyne, Esquire, lord of the manor, in 1673, for a term of sixty-one years, and was then described as consisting of three acres, one rood, and thirty-five perches ; but in 1731, some time before the expiry of the tenure, Sir Hans Sloane, the new lord, gave the ground to the Society for ever, at a quit-rent of 5*l.* a year, and on condition that it should annually present to the Royal Society fifty well-cured specimens of plants, the produce of the said garden, till such reached the number of 2,000 ; or, by default, the said parcel of ground to lapse to the Royal Society, which should perform the same covenants to the College of Physicians, and finally, if the Royal Society failed so to do, the property should go to the Physicians.

The Apothecaries seem to have had before them more than once in recent times a project for parting with the Garden, and even for migrating to other premises, in order to enable them to profit by the largely augmented value of those in Blackfriars.

LITERARY NOTICES.

The Copie of a Letter sent by a learned Physician to his friend, wherein are detected the manifold errors vsed hitherto of the Apothecaries . . . By T. W. 8vo, 1586.

The ignorance of the early apothecaries is particularly mentioned in the dedication by Dr. Turner of his *Herbal* to Queen Elizabeth in 1568.

A Short View of the Frauds, and Abuses committed by Apothecaries ; as well in relation to Patients, as Physicians. By Christopher Merritt, M.D., F.R.S. 4to, 1669, 1670.

Lex Talionis ; Sive Vindiciæ Pharmacopœorum : Or, A Short Reply to Dr. Merrett's Book, And Others, written against the Apothecaries . . . 4to, 1670.

A Potion for an Apothecary ; Or, the Apothecarye's Portion . . . To the Tune of, Old Flesh. Also the words that were written in the counterfeit Letter, as if they came from her brother out of the Country. [About 1670.] A broadside ballad with three woodcuts.

A Charter granted to the Apothecaries of London, The 30th of May, 13 Jac. I. Translated and Printed for the better information of the said Apothecaries in their Duty to the City of London, the Colledg of Physicians, and Their own Society. 4to, 1695.

The translator was probably Gideon de Laune or Delaune. The tract is inserted in T. Delaune's *Account of London*, 1690.

Physick lies a Bleeding : Or, The Apothecary turned Doctor. A Comedy acted every Day in most Apothecaries Shops in London. And more especially to be seen, by Those who are willing to be cheated, the First of April, every Year. Absolutely necessary for all Persons that are Sick, [or] may be Sick. [Quot. from Juvenal.] By Tho. Brown. 4to. Dedicated to that Worthy and Ingenious Gentleman, Dr. J. B. 4to, 1697.

On the back of the title are the names of the principal actors in this mock-play : John Galen, Tom Galypot, Lancet Pestle, etc. ; the scene is Apothecaries' Hall.

The grete herball. Folio, 1516 [?], 1526, 1529, 1561.
A translation from the French.

A newe mater the whiche sheweth and treateth of ȳ vertues & propryte; o′ herbes ; the whiche is called an Herball. 4to, 1525, 1526.
A translation from a Latin tract called *De Virtutibus Herbarum.*

A new Herball. By William Turner, M.D. Folio, 1551.

The seconde parte. Folio, 1562.

First and seconde partes [and third part]. Folio, 1568.

*** This includes the Book of the Baths of England, and a most excellent and perfect homish Apothecarie, or Homish physic book, translated from the German by John Holybush.

A little Herball of the Properties of Herbes. By Anthony Ascham. 8vo, 1550.

A boke of the propertyes of herbes, the whiche is called an Herbal. By Walter Cary. 8vo, Robert Redman [about 1540].
There are other editions.

A Newe Herball; or, Historie of Plantes. By Rembert Dodoens. Translated by Henry Lyte. Folio, 1578 ; 4to, 1586, 1595 ; folio, 1619. With woodcuts.

A Herbal for the Bible. By Levinus Leminius. Translated by Thomas Newton. 8vo, 1587.

The Herball; or, Generall Historie of Plantes. By John Gerarde. Folio, 1597, 1633, 1636.

Pambotanologia . . . Or, A Compleat Herball. By Robert Lovell. 8vo, 1665.

A Herbal containing 500 Cuts of the most useful Plants which are now used in the Practice of Physick. By Elizabeth Blackwell. 2 vols. Folio, 1737, 1739, or 1751. Folio, with plates.
There was only one edition.

The Composition or making of the moste excellent and vertuous Oil called Oleum Magistrale. By George Baker Chirurgian. 8vo, 1574.

Catalogus arborum, fructuum ac plantarum . . . in horto Johannis Gerardi ciuis & Chirurgi Londinensis nascentium. 4to, 1596 ; folio, 1599.

The practise of the new and old phisicke. By Conrad Gesner. 4to, 1599.

The Vertue and Operation of this Balsame. Made by N. P., Master of Arts, and Minister of God's word. A broadside advertisement. [Charles I.]

Anatomia Sambuci; or, The Anatomy of the Elder. By Martin Blochwich. 8vo, 1677.

Some Observations made upon the Brasillian Root, called Ipecocoanha. 4to, 1682.

Some Observations Made upon the Root called Serapias, or Salep, Imported from Turkey. Shewing its Admirable Virtues in Preventing Womens Miscarriages. Written by a Doctor of Physick in the Countrey to his Friend in London. 4to, 1694.
The two preceding pieces are only part of a series or group of tracts of the same character published between 1663 and 1695, and all described in Hazlitt's Collections.

Variety of Surprising Experiments made of two Incomparable Medicines : Exilir Febrifugum Martis, and Salt of Lymons. By Moses Stringer. 8vo, 1703.

The Armourers and Braziers.

FROM STOW.

DURING some centuries this Association was limited to the former industry, and the Gild is in possession of records, which establish its investiture with a right of search and control over armour and weapons. At successive periods it absorbed certain independent crafts, the Heaumers and other minor divisions of this flourishing industry in those times, when the use of armour, both for infantry and cavalry, and for the horses as well as their riders, was so general. It is concluded that the Braziers, who are said to have been separately incorporated about 1479, did not join them till 1708. The Braziers are described as a distinct body in 1578; but it is possible that from the tendency of the Armourers to traverse the lines of the other craft, the two succeeded in arriving at some unofficial basis of understanding, or co-operated for certain specific objects. The Braziers appear to have absorbed the ancient Fraternity of Potters, whom we have mentioned in the preceding section. As trades always established themselves, before they gave names to individuals, the antiquity of the brazier or brass-founder is shown by the patronymic *Brass-faber*, Humphrey Brass-faber having been one of the Sheriffs of London, and possibly also follower of the vocation, in 1249-50.

The earliest Ordinances, drawn up by the Armourers with the assent of the Corporation, are dated 1322, and provide for the good and sufficient quality of the goods made by this body and offered for sale by them, whereas it had been found that old, worn-out articles were vamped up, and sent into the country beyond jurisdiction, to be sold to the unwary, and that persons of all classes were thus deceived. To meet this evil, supervisors of the craft were appointed; and those, who made the iron or steel parts, were under covenant to deliver each piece whether bassinet, gambeson, or acton, to be lined or covered, to a Linen-Armourer or Taylor. The supervisors had power of search, and might seize any armour on the premises of an armourer or otherwise that was not made according to regulations, which are specially cited in some proceedings at Guildhall in 1578, as though they were still the code in

force and use.   There is no indication of a renewal of these Ordinances.
But the Armourers were gradually rising in consideration and resources, and in or about 1428 established themselves in a place of
business and assembly at London Wall, if they did not at that period
already own likewise the chantry in St. Paul's dedicated to St. George
the Martyr, which is noticed in 1453 as belonging to the Gild.   It is
observable that all crafts, whose employment involved noise and smoke,
as well as an abnormal demand for space, selected as a rule the outskirts
of the metropolis, and fixed themselves, where accommodation was most
plentiful and the interference with the traffic and the repose of the
inhabitants at night was apt to be least serious.

On the 8th May, 1453, 31 Henry VI., the Armourers received their
first charter, in which we see that they are mentioned and instituted as
the Fraternity or Gild of St. George of the Men of the Mistery of
Armourers of the City of London.

At this period they were presumably a far more numerous body than
the Braziers.   In the particulars of the muster of the Crafts for the City
watch, in 1469, they supplied thirty-four men against the Braziers' eight.
On the 8th November, 1559, 1 Elizabeth, the grant of Henry VI. was confirmed by *inspeximus*.   On the 29th September, 1619, 17 James I., in
consideration of 100*l.* paid by the Company, all its privileges, with its
licence in mortmain, were again renewed ; and by his letters patent,
recognising the Armourers, James II. conferred in 1685 a very ample
power of search and presentment over all edge tools and armour, and all
copper and brass work wrought with the hammer in the City and within
a radius of five miles thereof.

The status of the Company in 1619 was probably very subordinate, if
we are entitled to judge from the modest amount—40*l.*—which it subscribed under the Goldsmiths to the purchase of the Ulster Plantation.

It appears that in process of time the Armourers had, as we learn
from the patent of 1685, extended their industry to copper and brass
work, and thus trenched on the province of the Braziers ; and this
circumstance may have led to the fusion which took place in 1708, when
Queen Anne incorporated the two Gilds under the style of the Company
of Armourers and Braziers in the City of London.   There is explicit
reference in this instrument to the development of the Armourers' business just referred to ; and doubtless the present union formed the best
and most satisfactory *modus vivendi*, inasmuch as the governing body
of the combined Crafts was clothed with the largest possible faculty of
inspection and penal restraint.

The charter of Queen Anne is the one by which the Company is
now ruled ; but its ancient privileges have become virtually inoperative,

although it occasionally bound apprentices a few years ago. The Executive is composed of a Master, Upper Warden, Renter Warden, and eighteen Assistants. The Court holds an annual view in May of the Company's estates. According to a statement made in 1882, the pictures, plate, furniture, and armour in its possession were worth nearly 12,000*l.*

Armourers' Hall, at London Wall, used to adjoin Leathersellers' Hall, and is traced back to the earlier half of the fifteenth century. The owners were accustomed to permit its occasional use by other Companies or Fraternities at the ordinary rate of a groat a day. The Founders hired it for two days in 1497.

A FUNERAL CARD.

The Armourers and Braziers have been liberal contributors to the City and Gilds Institute for the Advancement of Technical Education. They subscribed 78*l.* 15*s.* to the preliminary outlay, and appear as annual donors of 525*l.*

The Company has the honour to reckon among its honorary members Henry VI., who gave it its first charter.

In the general lottery of 1567, the posy on the Armourers' ticket, No. 182,833, drawn by Thomas Tindal of London, was "God make all sure for the Armourers." But the prize was only 1*s.* 2*d.* According to information derived from the Loseley MSS., there was a public lottery in 1585, for the disposal of a collection of "beautiful armour;" but nothing definite is known of it, nor is any copy of the scheme or prospectus forthcoming. It was at all events an extremely unusual class of property to offer to competition in such a way at that date.

The Bakers.[1]

THE United Gild of White and Brown Bakers dates its corporate origin from a charter of Henry VIII., 22 July, 1509, under which power was vested in the new body to make, create, build, and establish a certain perpetual Fraternity or Gild of one Master and four Keepers of the commonalty of freemen of the Mistery of Bakers of the City of London and suburbs thereof, with the right to re-elect annually the said Master and Keepers, or Wardens, for the due government of the Society. In 1515, the municipal authorities accorded the Bakers as one Company the nineteenth place in order of precedence.

A second charter was obtained 26 May, 11 Elizabeth, by which a licence in mortmain, to the value of 40*l*. a year, exclusive of the Hall, the authority to plead and be impleaded, and the power of search and amerciament, were conceded. The Hall is mentioned in this instrument as not yet acquired, but as being in the parish of St Dunstan in the East. The Bakers were then presumably in treaty for it. It was in Harp Lane, Tower Street, and in addition to the Hall itself, consisted of certain tenements which have been rebuilt since 1882 at the expense of the Company.

In the Elizabeth, as in the Henry VIII., charter, the White Bakers had taken the initiative in drawing the makers of brown bread, whose business was far more limited and unimportant, into union with them on unequal terms, and the latter body dissented and renounced; whereupon the Queen was advised by the Lords of the Council to recall her patent. This proceeding seems for a time to have caused the matter to drop; but in 19 James I., June 6, 1622, the Brown Bakers succeeded in securing separate incorporation, with a common seal, a Master, three Wardens, and sixteen Assistants, as well as all other usual rights and powers.

---

[1] Some account of the two separate Associations of *White* and *Brown* Bakers has already been given at p. 103.

We hear nothing further of the matter till 1629, when the two bodies were still separate, the White Bakers being assessed for a levy by the City in that year at 25*l.* 16*s.*, the other at 4*l.* 6*s.*, a proof of the relative weight and resources of the disputants, which is confirmed by the proportions contributed by each to the Ulster scheme a few years prior, namely, 480*l.* and 90*l.* In 1654, the Brown Bakers had apparently relinquished their independent quarters at Founders' Hall, Lothbury, as if an union had been arranged; and in 2 James II., the charter was received with the usual restrictions in regard to the oaths of allegiance and supremacy, and conformity to the Church of England, but otherwise in such form as to lead to the belief that it comprehended both sections of the trade. Here we find the governing body fixed at one Master, four Wardens, and thirty Assistants; and the constitution of the Company still follows the terms of this grant in that and other points.

The Bakers, since the Act 3 George IV., cap. 16, altering the law in respect to the supply and sale of bread in London and the environs, have ceased to exercise the ancient right of control, and in fact have no longer any practical connection with this branch of commerce. Nor are working bakers required to join, unless they choose to apply. Women are admissible to the freedom.

The Company possesses a code of bye-laws drawn up 22 February, 1622; but the Standing Orders of 1874 form the present basis of administration. These Orders are publicly read every year on election day, and a copy is handed to each member.

In 1882, there were about 250 freemen and 216 on the Livery. In 1699, the latter is returned at 146, and in 1724, at 189. Between 1871 and 1880, the income considerably increased; but the expenditure was even more than equally progressive. The Court and Livery fines used to be very moderate; but it was found that the applicants grew so numerous as to render a prohibitive scale for the latter expedient, and it has been raised from 16*l.* to 75*l.* The fine for the Court is 50*l.* Down to 1877, the sub-share in the Ulster Plantation was retained, but was in that year sold to the Skinners for 40,000*l.*, payable by instalments. It had been fortunate for the Bakers that the rise in the annual income from this source between 1871 and 1878, owing to the Skinners' capable management, largely enhanced the selling value.

Bakers' Hall, on the eastern side of Harp Lane, is a spacious building, formerly possessing a garden frontage, which is now occupied by warehouses. Stow (1633, p. 138) says that this house or site at one time formed the residence of the Chichley or Chichele family in the person of John Chichley, Chamberlain of London, son to William Chichley, Alderman, and a descendant of the Archbishop of Canterbury of the same name. But it subsequently passed by the marriage of one of the Chamberlain's daughters to Sir Thomas Kirrioll of Kent.

The old structure was destroyed by fire, January 13, 1714-15, when a conflagration at Wapping made terrible havoc in the neighbourhood. It was rebuilt in 1719, and wainscoted in 1722. But the entrance has been diverted southward since the restoration of the tenements facing the lane, and the approach to the Hall through the iron gates is embellished by a series of mural paintings illustrative of the Gild and its craft. We see the concession of the charter: the laying the first stone of the first Hall: the swearing in of the Wardens: a water-scene in the Company's barge: a procession on horseback, representing the Mayor on his way to Westminster [1]: the making of the bread with the ovens formerly in use, and at one period to be seen in the kitchen in Harp Lane: the weighing of it for the assize in the scales of which a specimen is still preserved at the Hall: the Almsgiving.

In the court-room, over the fireplace, are a series of Masters' and Wardens' badges, and in the refectory the Company's banners are suspended from the roof.

A copy of the Bakers' coat of arms, emblazoned in their proper colours, is kept here, and formed the subject, not long since, of a controversy with a well-known confectioner, who was charged with improperly adopting it.

A rather curious circumstance happened in the beginning of 1667, when John Gase, Citizen and Saddler, who also seems to have been in business as a baker, elected to confine himself to the latter employment, and paid his old Company 10l. as a fine on translation, but with the excellent proviso, that he should have the privilege thereafter of supplying the whole of the bread to Saddlers' Hall.

LITERARY NOTICES.

The Assyse of Bread what it ought to waye after the pryce of a quarter of wheete. And also the assyse of al maner of wood, lathe, bourde, tymbre, and the waight of Butyre, and chese. 4to, 1528.

John Rudstone, one of the Aldermen of London, at whose request, and that of Michael English, this the earliest known Assize of Bread was printed, was Mayor in 1528.

This continued, with the *Assize of Ale*, to be published annually down to the last century.

The Assyse of Breade. . . . And also the Assyse of Ale. 4to [1540].

This, as we have stated elsewhere, was republished at regular intervals.

Artachthos. Or a New Booke declaring the Assize or Weight of Bread, not onely by Troy weight, according to the Law, but by Avoirdupois weight, the common Weight of England. 4to, 1638.

The Assize of Bread and Ale. Christopher Packe, Mayor. At the General Quarter Sessions, April 23, 1655. A broadside.

---

[1] The head of the principal figure would, it was hoped at the time, have been that of a Baker; but the Company's candidate was not elected.

The Barbers.

THE earliest vestiges of this interesting Gild, which is popularly associated with the striped pole and the cupping dish, belong to an epoch long anterior to its incorporation in 1461.

In 1308 the Barbers of London presented to the Mayor and Aldermen, Nicholas Le Barbour, dwelling opposite the church of All Hallows the Less, to be their Supervisor; and he was admitted, and swore that he would make scrutiny throughout the whole trade, and distrain upon any that kept brothel, or acted otherwise contrary to law or usage.

In 1357, the Barbers, by reason probably of the necessity of their constant attendance at their places of business in case of sudden illness or casualties, were exempted from serving on juries and inquisitions.

The earliest code of bye-laws for the Barber-Surgeons appears to be that of 1376, which sought to grapple with the mischief done by unskilful persons coming up from the country to practise barbery, surgery, and the cure of maladies; and the Articles forbad any one for the future keeping shop or otherwise working in the craft, who was not approved by the two Masters thereof, duly presented to the Mayor and Aldermen, and sworn before them. At this time the Gild returned two members to the Common Council.

The Barbers stand alone in the single respect of possessing, so far as our present information extends, a copy of the return to the writ of 12 Richard II. (1388), requiring all the Gilds in the kingdom to afford full details of the charters under which they claimed and exercised their powers. The transcript among the Barbers' archives was derived in 1634 from the original document then preserved in the Tower of London, and was transferred in 1648 to a vellum book of ordinances still extant. We seem to be indebted to this proceeding for the survival of the text.

The Gild is represented as being governed at this date by a Master and Surveyors or Overseers, and the Articles closely resemble those of earlier and later periods, and of the other fraternities. They provide for the payment of quarterwages, the appointment to offices and refusal to serve, the distribution of alms, and the maintenance of order.

It is not at all surprising that the City discovered much inconvenience and miscarriage from the union, in the persons of Barbers, of the practitioner in shaving and hair-cutting, and in surgery and physic. But it was not till 1415, apparently, that any formal steps were taken to check this evil, and to prevent the misdeeds and extortions of ignorant and indiscreet men. The Court of Aldermen in this case not only approved the appointment of Masters of the crafts of Barbery and Surgery, but

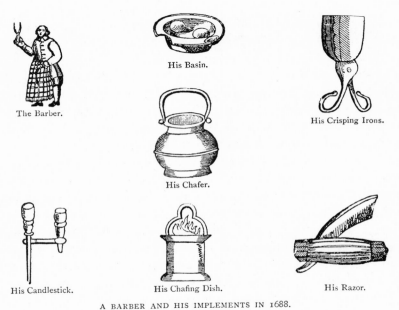

The Barber.

His Basin.

His Crisping Irons.

His Chafer.

His Candlestick.

His Chafing Dish.

His Razor.

A BARBER AND HIS IMPLEMENTS IN 1688.

summoned all the practitioners in the dual employment severally, took their names, and examined them as to their technical capability.

While the Barbers united with their occupation that of surgery and medicine, there were Master-Surgeons, who also formed an Association in early times, and who required, before they could practise in the City, authority from the Corporation. Sometimes they were obliged to tender security.

We also meet with the specialist, who set limbs and bones, and who appears to have been distinct from both. These more experienced persons were often, at the outset, foreigners, from whom, as in other departments of science, the English derived their knowledge of anatomy and medicine. But others were denizens; and in course of time both these and naturalized subjects developed into the important Fellowship which was consolidated with the Barbers by the Act of 1540.

Of the professor of dentistry as a separate and special employment we meet with an example in Stow's *Survey*, under 1554, in the person of John Bricket, Citizen and Toothdrawer, who left funds to provide twelve sacks of charcoal at Easter for ever to the poor of St. Botolph's, Bishopsgate.

The letters patent of 1 Edward IV., February 24, 1461–2, recite that the Freemen of the Mistery of Barbers of the City of London, using the mistery or faculty of Surgery, had long exercised, and still continued to exercise, their skill and labour in healing and curing wounds, blows, and other infirmities, as well as in bleeding and tooth-drawing; but that, owing to certain unexpert practitioners, divers people had greatly suffered; whereupon it was accorded to the said Freemen to be one body and one perpetual community, with power to elect two Masters or Governors,

OLD ARMS.

who should have the right of search and inquisition throughout the City over all freemen being barbers and using the mistery of surgery, and over all foreigners practising surgery, and should oversee what instruments, plaisters, and medicines were used and applied. Every barber, before he presumed to enter upon that vocation, was required to seek approval by the Masters of the Gild, who were to present them to the Mayor for the time being, and all certified barbers were exempted from serving on juries and assizes—a privilege enjoyed by the Craft since 1357. At this date the fellowship was presumably of considerable importance, and tolerably prosperous, as to the muster for the Watch in 1469 it was assessed at 120 men.

This grant, which echoed the complaints and substantially repeated the terms of the bye-laws made 'a century before, was renewed by Henry VII. (December 5, 1500), and by Henry VIII. (March 12, 1512–13).[1] In 32 Henry VIII. an Act of Parliament united the two yet distinct Societies of Barbers and Surgeons, the latter of whom were then a voluntary unchartered Fellowship, under one government and charter by the name and style of the Masters or Governors of the Mistery or Commonalty of Barbers and Surgeons of London, with right of search and supervision over the City and one mile compass, and

---

[1] It appears that in 1515 the number of Barbers practising as surgeons in the City was nineteen. By the municipal order, settling precedence, the Company ranked twenty-eighth.

immunity from bearing armour and service on watches, juries, and assizes.

The Barbers thus stood in the peculiar position of having their proceedings and jurisdiction concurrently directed by a charter and an Act of Parliament, which were to be read and construed together.

In this Act it is set forth " that no person within the City or suburbs, and one mile compass of the said City, using any barbery or shaving, should occupy any surgery, letting of blood, or any other thing belonging to surgery, except drawing of teeth, and that whosoever should use the mistery or craft of surgery should not occupy the feat or craft of barbery or shaving."

Such language seems incompatible with the unreserved amalgamation of the two bodies in 1461, under the circumstances mentioned in the preamble to the charter of that date ; for the statute expressly prohibits the two Crafts from traversing each other beyond dentistry, and leads us to speculate, whether we are not to understand two classes of barber, of which one only really answered to its designation, and was narrowed in its enterprise by the long prevalent general habit of wearing the beard.

The physician and apothecary were alike excluded from the scope of the law, which solely affected the Company of Surgeons and the qualified Barber. The origin of the assumption by the latter of certain functions not appertaining to his normal industry is to be sought in the mediæval usages of the Continent, where the Barbers' Quarter was often invested with special privileges, comprising an exemption from the curfew in view of the contingency of calls for assistance at all hours.

The powers and franchises of the united Company were re-granted 4 Philip and Mary, 2 Elizabeth, 1 James I., 5 Charles I., 25 Charles II., 1 James II., and 8 Anne. By the charter of James I., the radius of jurisdiction was extended to London and Westminster and seven miles compass, and the Company was authorized to make bye-laws, and to appoint lecturers on the principles and rudiments of surgery for the benefit of pupils and beginners. The last provision is of special interest, and it does not occur elsewhere, in the annals of these Gilds, and seems to betray the influence of some professional man of more than ordinary perception.

The probability seems to be, that, the law on the subject notwithstanding, the Barbers practically invaded the province of surgery in conjunction with their ordinary business ; and as the Surgeons in London became a more numerous and influential class, and learned from the Continent many valuable lessons belonging to their profession, the inconvenience and anomaly of the fellowship contracted in 1461, and legally recognised in 1540, grew more and more conspicuous and distasteful. But it was not till 1745 that the Act, 18 George II., cap. 15, finally dissolved the two incongruous constituents,[1] the Barbers paying to the Surgeons a capital sum of 510*l.* and transferring to them an annuity of 16*l.*, and being thereupon re-incorporated under the name of the Master, Governors, and Commonalty of the Mistery of Barbers of London, with a licence in mortmain to the extent of 200*l.* a year.

The Barbers hereby, after the payment of 510*l.* and the surrender of the annuity of 16*l.*, remained in possession of the entire residue of the estate, which seems to prove that, although the Surgeons were the more distinguished section, the bulk of the property in 1745 was vested in their colleagues.

The Act just mentioned now governs the Company, of which the Executive is composed of a Master, three Wardens, and twenty Assist-

FIGURES FROM THE HOLBEIN PICTURE AT BARBERS' HALL.

ants, who are periodically elected from such of the Livery as have served the office of Steward or been fined for it. On the retirement of a Master, it is customary to present him with his badge or jewel of office.

The charter of 1 James I. empowered the Company to frame byelaws—a faculty which it had enjoyed since 1376 by the authority of the Court of Aldermen; but those at present in force exist in a MS. dated January 13, 1708, subject in certain instances to later resolutions of the Court. In 1699 the Livery was officially returned as 195, and in 1724 as 299 (of whom 139 were surgeons, 113 barbers, and 47 of no

---

[1] In some legal proceedings in 1891, the alleged dissolution of the Company of Surgeons in 1796 was disputed, on the ground that the Royal College, established in 1800, had succeeded to the property of the former Society, and that there were existing documents to shew that the latter had a continuous existence down to the institution of the College. This point, however, was ultimately (January 27, 1892) decided adversely to the old Society.

trade). In 1882, there were 120 on the Livery,[1] and 149 of the Freedom, two women included.

The Barbers were sub-sharers of the Ironmongers' Irish Manor of
Lizard, and in 1880 received 196*l.* in respect of their interest. But, as
we have elsewhere stated, the property has since been sold.

Barbers' Hall no longer exists; the site of it is occupied by warehouses; and the existing premises are limited to the Court-room, one
or two other apartments on the ground floor, and one or two rooms
reached by a broad staircase. The Court-room holds the Holbein and
other pictures. The portrait of Inigo Jones, said to be by Vandyke, is

BARBERS' HALL.   THE COURT-ROOM.

more probably a *replica* of that in the hands of the family; yet it is of
interest to the Company, since the father of the great architect was a
Barber-Surgeon.

The unique association with the charter of 1512–13 suggests a few
words of criticism. The painting ascribed to the younger Holbein
represents Henry VIII., in quite middle life, delivering the grant; it is
probably the only specimen of the kind on canvas, although the original
charters of several of the Companies exhibit a similar formality. In
this case, the execution of the picture is not likely to have been con-

---

[1] In 1892, according to Whitaker, the Livery numbered 92.

temporary, and may have been painted for the Barbers many years after the event, as Holbein survived till 1554. We notice that in the policy of insurance it is valued at 8000*l.*, and the Inigo Jones at 300*l.*

Richard Ferris, of Paddington, who was an occasional writer in verse and prose, was Barber-surgeon to Queen Elizabeth in 1563, and appears to have been on terms of friendship with Thomas Gale and other eminent practitioners of the time. He was probably one of the members of the Company who exclusively followed the art of surgery. A person of both his names, possibly his son, was one of the messengers

LOVING CUP IN THE POSSESSION OF THE BARBERS' COMPANY.

of the Queen's chamber in 1590, in which year he undertook a perilous excursion from London to Bristol by sea in a wherry with two companions.

Besides the father of the architect, the Company claims as one of its members the rather famous Sir Humphrey Edwin, who became Lord Mayor in 1698, and was translated to the Skinners. He signalized his year of office by abandoning the usual inaugural ceremony. An elaborate account of Edwin by Mr. Charles Welch is in the *Dictionary of National Biography*.

The father of Nan Clarges, afterward Duchess of Albemarle, was a blacksmith, at the right-hand corner of Little Drury Lane ; and her mother is said to have been one of the five Woman Barbers, who are mentioned as practising in the time of Charles II.

The History of the Company by Mr. Sydney Young, which has lately appeared as a sumptuous volume, will prove an honourable and pleasing memorial of a time when the premises were undivided and the Gild was part of the scene around it.

LOVING CUP PRESENTED TO THE BARBERS BY CHARLES II.

LITERARY NOTICE.

The Tooth-Drawer: A comedy advertised at the end of *Wit and Drollery*, 1661, and of the *New World of English Words*, 1658, as in the press, but not at present known.

*** Compare *Surgeons' Company*.

The Basket-makers.

THIS Company, or Gild, claims to exist by prescription, as no trace of a charter is discoverable. All the papers and property belonging to it were deposited at Guildhall at the time of the Great Fire, and were destroyed. It is surmised that a charter may have been among them; but this is very doubtful. This informal organization, of which we are to meet with several examples, was an enlargement of the principle by which a considerable proportion of the Gilds remained during centuries under the simpler autonomy of Wardens or Aldermen.

The sole very ancient clue to its existence and whereabouts is in a record of the time of Edward IV., which classes it with the Gold and Silver Wire-Drawers, *and other foreigners*, and restricts the quarters of those connected with it to the Manor of Blanche Appleton [or Cha-pelle-ton], Fenchurch Street,[1] whence the infer-ence may be allowable that at this remote period the industry was principally in the hands of persons not free of the City. But from a feature in the constitutional settlement of the Gild in 1569, by the Court of Alder-men, we are tempted to presume that the Craft was subsequently released from this disability, as the incidence of this clause seems to connect its members with Christ Church.

OLD ARMS.

As an ordinary Association, it was established by an order of the Mayor's Court, September 22, 1569, confirmed or renewed January 10, 1585–6, and March 27, 1610. Under this authority the Gild was em-powered to meet biennially in some convenient place within the City, between the Feasts of St. James and St. Bartholomew, and elect two Wardens, who should serve for two years, and be sworn before the

---

[1] The locality is marked by London Street and Fenchurch Street Station.

Mayor in the upper chamber of the Guildhall, to execute their functions faithfully under pain of 5*l.*, one moiety payable to the Chamber of London, the other to the Common Box of the poor of Christ Church. The outgoing Wardens were bound to deliver their accounts within a month to their successors and a committee of five or four of the Gild appointed by the same.

The recognition of the Basket-makers is demonstrated by their appearance among the fifty-five Companies which were assessed in 1602–3 and 1603–4, for corn and money by the City, and which subscribed to the Ulster project in 1615. They held a small sub-share in the Fishmongers' Manor.

The Company consists of a Prime Warden, a Junior Warden, a Court of Assistants, a Livery limited to thirty, and the Freedom, to which women have been admitted. In 1882 four members were carrying on the trade ; and the Clerk is at present doing so. The income from all sources was returned in 1891 at 61*l.*, the same amount as in 1882 ; but in 1892 it had apparently risen to 102*l.*

The Basket-makers have no Hall ; but the Parish Clerks permit them the occasional use of theirs in Silver Street, Wood Street.

The Blacksmiths.

IN looking at this Gild we have to bear in mind that the calling, in which it had at any rate its first root and basis, was formerly of much greater consideration than at the present day, and the followers of it, both here and abroad, were men of wider attainments and higher social standing than their existing representatives. The important and almost fundamental change in their condition and influence has been chiefly, of course, produced by the organic alteration in the methods of locomotion and the distribution of labour. The mediæval smith was, among other matters, an expert in handicraft and dentistry, if not in leechdom ; and as we see in the old tale of *The Smith that forged him a new Dame*, he not unfrequently employed a staff of assistants, and acquired landed property.

The most remarkable aspect, however, in which he differed from his existing namesake was his relationship to the art of horology ; and under our sketch of the history of the Clockmakers we have attempted to explain how, when certain pioneers, unquestionably foreigners, had led the way to an acquisition of the knowledge of this *mistery*, the Blacksmith was the person who learned the lesson and profited by it. His primitive efforts have probably not survived ; but the Clockmakers' and other collections enable us to trace the evolution of the modern masterpiece from the archaic *clepsydra* and bell.

The secondary conception of enclosing the works in a case resulted in the maker seeking alliance with the woodmonger, and in collisions with the chartered monopolist of carpentry.

From the absence of any specific reference to clocks in the bye-laws and charters of the Blacksmiths we may either augur that this branch of their business was included within the general category of iron-work, or that it was very restricted, the finer productions emanating from foreign artificers or being imported. So late as 1680, nearly half a century subsequently to the rise of the Clockmakers as a Gild, the "great church clocks of iron" are mentioned as particularly belonging to the older craft.

EARLY ARMS.

One of the early French *fabliaux* or traditional stories is a humorous anecdote of a blacksmith, who exercised the calling of a toothdrawer, and accomplished his object by attaching one end of a length of wire to his anvil and the other to the tooth of the patient, whose trouble was removed by the unexpected presentation of a red-hot poker. This was in the thirteenth century. But in England, from a very remote date, and in the rural districts, down to recent times, the blacksmith usually officiated as the local dentist ; and we have known persons of high social position who employed no one else.

From the terms of the Act, 32 Henry VIII., we collect that barbers were at that period licensed to draw teeth, but not to exercise any other department of the surgical profession. It need not be said, that the part played by the blacksmith was unofficial.

The bye-laws of the Blacksmiths, while they yet remained unin-corporated, were passed in the usual way in 1372, and seem to have partly arisen out of a prevalent abuse, by which persons requiring this sort of labour clandestinely employed unskilled and unlicensed opera-tives. The first of the articles dealt with this subject of complaint, and directed that henceforth everybody should take blacksmith's work either to Gracechurch Street, to St. Nicholas Shambles, or to a place near the Tun on Cornhill, under penalties. It was also provided that every blacksmith on each piece of large or important fabric should place his mark as a guarantee or voucher, and that no one should be admitted to the trade as a journeyman until he had been approved by one of the Masters or Overseers.

New articles were submitted for approval in 1394, fixing the hours of labour and the season for the annual choice of Wardens, enjoining the use of trade marks, and forbidding any of the trade from making any key from a model thereof in the absence of the old key or the lock, and from sending or taking work to any fair, until it had been warranted by the Wardens.

There is not the slightest probability that the Company was endowed with a charter prior to that of Queen Elizabeth, of April 20, 1571, in which they were united with the Spurriers, and which was renewed and extended by Charles I., February 15, 1639–40, and by James II., March 18, 1685–6.

In 1615 they were sub-sharers with the Vintners in the Ulster scheme; and their payment evinces the possession at that time of moderate resources.

The grant of 1640 conferred the right of framing bye-laws "for the good rule, governing, and correcting of the Freemen of the said arts or misteries within the City of London and four miles of the said City"; and the now amalgamated Gild was clothed with "power to overlook and examine the making of spurs, ironwork, or anything concerning the said arts or misteries" inside the same limits. Under this code the Blacksmiths naturally found themselves drawn into contact with the Ironmongers. But, as we have intimated, they informally infringed on the Barber-Dentist, while in their craft is to be traced the *ovum* of that of the clock and watch maker.

The negotiation and controversy between the Blacksmiths and Clock-makers commenced, so far as we are aware, in 1627, and lasted at least till 1638. The original point in debate was the union of the two bodies under a charter, for which the Blacksmiths entertained the idea of applying in 1628; and when this scheme failed, and the Clockmakers were incorporated in 1631 after full inquiry, the other Company used every effort to hamper its movements and even to modify its powers. They did not content themselves with representations and correspondence, but addressed formal protests to the civic authorities, and engaged in legal proceedings against the rival body. This antipathy, and even rancour, may be construed as a recognition of the influence and success of the Clockmakers, and may have been partly due to chagrin at the error committed in spurning their proffered fellowship. Entries in the Blacksmiths' books, and in the civic archives, seem to form the principal record of a feud, which lasted through so many years, and from which neither party derived any practical advantage beyond the concession in 1636, on the part of the Court of Aldermen, of certain enlarged rights of apprenticeship to the Clockmakers.

There is still another side to the question, as between the Blacksmiths and their fellow-craftsmen ; for the introduction of firearms in the form of guns and pistols, and the necessity for proof of each piece before it passed into the market, which was even then appreciated, prompted the Blacksmiths to enter on a new branch of industry, by way of indemnity for the losses in other quarters ; and the preamble to the Gunmakers' charter, 1637, particularly recites, " that divers members of this and other trades had undertaken to make, try, and prove guns to the great damage of his Majesty's subjects." At the same time, in the latter grant the right of search secured to the Blacksmiths in their own was reserved. The multiplication of privileged bodies was beginning to render cross-lines rather frequent and perplexing.

In a comedy, called *The Whore New-Vamped*, performed at the Red Bull theatre in St. John's Street, in 1639, but not printed, a justice of the peace threatens to bring one of the characters before the Alderman, whereupon the other, after a good deal of abuse, tells the justice that he refers to Alderman the Blacksmith in Holborn—some member at that period of the Company, no doubt.

This, at any rate, may indicate that at that date the Blacksmith enjoyed a certain share of civic importance. Under an earlier year (1622) we have evidence of the membership of a person who possessed some literary taste.

The governing body of the Gild is composed, agreeably to the charter, of four Wardens and twenty-one Assistants. In 1756 the Blacksmiths are said to have a Livery of 220. In 1882, the Livery numbered eighty-one and the Freemen eighty-three. In 1892, the Livery amounted to ninety-two ; and the total income was returned at 684*l.*

Maitland speaks of their pleasant Hall on Lambert or Lambeth Hill. But the Hall was there in Stow's time. He speaks of it as being about the middle of the lane, near the church of St. Mary Mounthaut. It is at present a warehouse.

The Company has discontinued its relationship to the trade, alike in respect to control and pursuit.

Formerly a very interesting piece of antique silver plate, now well known as the Blacksmiths' Cup, belonged to the Fraternity. It was sold in the earlier part of the present century, and was at one period in the possession of Mr. Ralph Bernal, who is said to have paid 35*l.* for it, equal to 1*l.* per ounce. But it changed owners once or twice at an enormously enhanced price, and has now, we understand, found a home in the United States.

LITERARY MEMORIAL.

The Blacksmiths Dreame, written by Dennis Webster, Citizen and Blacksmith of London.   Entered at Stationers' Hall, May 16, 1622.   Not otherwise known.

The Bowyers.[1]

THIS Company rises into notice in 1371 as a voluntary and independent federation, and as having entered with the Fletchers into a certain compact for the maintenance of a good accord by mutual respect for each others' rights and interests.   The proceedings on this occasion prove that on the part of some members of both crafts it had been the practice to manufacture alike bows and arrows ; but the treaty of 1371 ostensibly at least determined this irregularity, and also limited

---

[1] Compare *Stringers*, suprâ, and *Fletchers*, post. The motto of the Bowyers is : *Crecy, Poictiers, Agincourt.*

the hours of work to the day-time, "by reason that bows cannot in any manner be made as well or as profitably for the King and his people by night as by day."

The best and most expensive old English bows were made of foreign yew. In the time of Edward IV. the price for bowstaves was fixed by statute at 3s. 4d. each. But in 1560 the prices had greatly risen through an alteration in the law necessitated by the tariff being found too low, and the best quality was then ordered to go at 6s. 8d. each, the second at 3s. 4d., and the third, made of English yew, at 2s.

OLD ARMS.

It will be seen that not only was the manufacture of bows kept separate from that of arrows, but that a different body of artificers devoted itself to the supply of the strings, the *Stringers* or the Long-Bowstring Makers, a community which eventually became extinct.

This apportionment was conformable with the ancient system of subdivision of labour in the hands of independent unions.

The Fletchers, as we shall find, never received a charter; but the Bowyers, on the contrary, were incorporated, May 25, 1621, and obtained a confirmation of the grant, November 17, 1668.

In the former instrument, the Gild is described as the art or mistery of making long bows, and is stated to have existed as a Fraternity in the City from remote times, but to have at that juncture fallen into decay. The King, desirous of restoring the ancient and laudable exercise of archery with the long bow, allowed accordingly that all such as were free of the City, and used the said trade, should be hereafter one body politic and corporate under the style of the Master, Wardens, and Society of the Mistery of Bowyers of the City of London.

The Society was appointed to have as its government one Master, two Wardens, and thirteen Assistants; and the Master, Wardens, and ten Assistants were authorized to hold office till the Thursday after the Feast of St. James the Apostle, 1622, all subsequent elections to be made as by the charter was prescribed. There was power given to the Court to choose a clerk and a beadle, to require payment of quarter-wages from freemen—8d. a quarter or 2s. 8d. a year—and to make bye-laws. In 1882, there were thirty-six[1] on the Livery, and one freeman.

The only trust or other estate, other than internal revenue and 1000l. stock, is mainly held under the will of James Wood, August 1, 1625,

---

[1] In 1892, according to Whitaker, twenty-seven.

whereby he devised his manor of Isley Walton, Co. Leicester, and other lands, on condition that the Company should establish and maintain certain exhibitions at Oxford and Cambridge with a preferential right reserved to free Bowyers, and should perform other duties, that is to say, should give to six poor brethren at Michaelmas alternately 30s. in money and three yards of broadcloth to make a gown at 10s. the yard ; should repair on election day annually to the parish church of St. Nicholas, Cole Abbey, to hear a sermon, paying to the parson 30s., to the clerk and sexton 1s. 6d. apiece, to the churchwardens 10s. for the use of the poor, to the beadle 2s., and to the good folks whom they might meet coming and going, 15s. in twopences ; and should distribute half-yearly among the yeomanry of the Company 5s., and (through the churchwardens) among the poor of Isley Walton, 10s.

In 1814 the Bowyers acquired a small property contiguous to this, and obtained a licence in mortmain, which perhaps covers both. The latter, however, is in their own absolute right. They now support seven exhibitions of 5l. at each of the two Universities named, and a school, built at their expense, and contribute to other charitable objects. The total income is about 600l. ; but very little is left at the disposal of the Company after the deduction of various charges.

The Company formerly possessed a Hall in Noble Street, but has long ceased to do so. In early days its resources seem to have been extremely straitened. Stow (edit. 1633) affords a certain clue to the quarters once occupied by the Craft, where he writes : " Now betwixt the South end of Ave Mary-lane, and the North end of Creed-lane, is the coming out of Paul's Church-yard, on the East, and the high street, called BOWYER BOW, to Ludgate, on the West, . . ." This position would be at no great distance from Noble Street.

The Brewers.

THE Latin races appear, at the outset, to have uniformly confined themselves, in their choice of a national stimulant, to the fermented juice of the grape, as their Teutonic neighbours acquired the habit of preparing and using a beverage derived from some vegetable substance. Germany reared vines before it learned the art of applying the fruit to other purposes besides that of solid food; but in Britain, where the vine was neither indigenous nor capable of being profitably cultivated in the open air, the natives, at the earliest period of their known history, are found in possession of a drink brewed from the honey of wild bees, or, in other words, mead. This was simply following the universal rule in all parts of the world, by which populations, in the instinctive search for some tonic and exhilarating agent, resorted by necessity, before the intercourse between countries was facilitated, to material close at hand.

The French and English, doubtless, owed their knowledge of the fermented produce of vegetables and cereals to the inhabitants of the North of England—France to her Frankish conquerors and settlers, and England to the Saxons. As the question of malt liquors in France has become a rather burning one, and almost a war-cry, we do not know whether it is prudent to contest the statement of a writer of that country, who quotes the Greek geographers for an account of the familiarity of the Gauls with beer; but the drink which the Greek geographers describe was not beer. It was mead; and there were two qualities of it, suited to the two classes into which the Gaulish community was divided, the rich and the poor.

It is of the greater importance to understand what the early authorities mean when they speak of the Gauls before Charlemagne making
beer, when we see how vague and weakly-founded is the testimony
even of such an author as Lacroix upon this point ; for he says that
in consequence of a great famine, while Gaul was in Roman occupation,
the Emperor Domitian caused all the vines to be destroyed, in order
to render the land available for the culture of cereals, *which would*, says
Lacroix, *render more general there the manufacture of beer*.   A mere
unsupported hypothesis !

He proceeds to tell us that a later Emperor allowed the vines to be
replanted, and that the Gauls gradually lost their taste for any beverage
but wine ; and this was in spite of the fact that in the time of that
very Emperor (Probus) the Germans were beginning to make themselves very troublesome to France, and occupied a good deal of her
territory, so that if the population had had any disposition to adopt
the beverage in use among their Northern invaders, they would have
done so, instead of remaining loyal to grape-juice.

But the truth seems to be, that the Gauls, like the French after them,
were essentially a wine-drinking people ; even when Charlemagne
established his dominion over them, and encouraged the use of beer,
the industry evidently made no progress.   In the thirteenth century,
five hundred years after his time, it was almost in the same stationary
and languid condition.   Lacroix himself admits that at that period
the very few brewers in Paris, notwithstanding the privileges accorded
to them by the King, deserted the capital from insufficient custom ;
and to this day, looking at the increased population, and the large
foreign element in it, it can scarcely be asserted that the French as a
nation have overcome their immemorial predilection for wine.

It is easier to understand how the English became habituated in a
similar manner to malt liquor, or, at all events, to some compound of
vegetable origin, for they had no grapes at hand ; but the Germans
were not only acquainted with viticulture at an early period through a
Roman medium, but were enabled by climatic conditions to cultivate
the plant with advantage and on a wide scale.   Yet the utilization
of the grape was, for an immense length of time, a characteristic of
those populations which could lay claim to a Latin origin ; and not
even the potent influence of the Frankish rulers of Gaul could wean it
from its traditional taste.   Nor is there, in our opinion, much probability
that the French of our day will ever become drinkers of beer, except in
those centres, like Paris, which may be regarded as cosmopolitan, and
in the provinces which are contiguous to the German frontier.

The Franks tried without much result, in or before the Carlovingian era, to naturalize beer on French soil; and to a certain extent the political and commercial relations between France and the Low Countries at a later period led to the introduction of Flemish beer, not as a manufacture but as a rather prominent import. The very fact, however, that a closer intercourse with beer-drinking communities had a periodical tendency to renew a fashion for the liquor, carries with it indirect evidence that it was a fashion and little more; for the demand for Flemish drink seems to have shared the fate of that for the Frankish. Whatever might be the feeling of a limited constituency, or the market created by foreign settlers and visitors, there was never in the old days any general or popular call for what we understand as falling under the category of beer. The Gaul and the Frenchman were at one in preferring the produce of the vine, in its crudest form even, to that of barley or other grain; and it may be fairly suspected that, where recourse was had to a decoction of lentils, vetches, and other cognate material, the explanation was to be found in the absence of the vine from unsuitability of climate.

Lacroix, in his famous work, *Mœurs, Usages et Costumes au Moyen Age*, 1872, devotes some space to this topic; but under the name of beer he classes liquors which we should not consider as belonging to that family.

One indication of the Teutonic parentage of beer lies in the Teutonic origin of the terms which we employ to express it, unless we include the Latin word *cerevisia* or *cervisia*, which some of the later Roman authors, and after them the Germans, who wrote in the same language, apply to a fermented preparation from cereals or vegetables. The French themselves appear to have no corresponding vernacular phrase, and have to make use of such as are obviously mere translations—loans, like the produce itself, from other regions.

Nor are we indebted to the earlier French art for any graphic views of scenes and interiors illustrative of the brewing industry in its varied stages and branches. The Flemings and Germans here again assert their priority, and not only that, but their special and traditional association with this ancient and precious article of commerce and refreshment. The old painters and engravers, who appealed to the tastes and sentiments of those around them, transferred to canvas or to paper objects and costumes which were calculated to awaken an interest in the immediate spectators; and to the woodcutters of Germany and the Netherlands we are indebted for a familiarity with many industrial details, which we should never otherwise have so vividly realized, including glimpses of old-world commercial activity with the operatives at their daily labour.

In an *Inquisitio post mortem* into the goods left by Laurence le
Long, Brewer, of the parish of St. Martin's, Ludgate, in 1335, we find
the brewhouse and three shops belonging to his heir, a minor, valued
at 40*s*. nett, after deducting 22*s*. 6*d*. quit-rent due to the Church of
St. Paul and 13*s*. quit-rent due to the Abbot of Westminster. The
plant of the departed is represented as consisting of two leaden vessels,
one leaden cistern, one leaden tap-trough, one old chest, one mash-vat,
value 18*d*. ; one fining-vat, value 6*d*. ; one trestle for barrels, value 12*d*. ;
three sets of hand-mills, value 4*s*. ; one piece of lead, value 2*d*. ; one
tun and one half-tun, value 8*d*. ; one ale-vat, value 18*d*. ; five *keme-
lynes*, value 10*d*. ; one *clensingbuche*, value 4*d*. ; also one *alegiste*,
value 2*d*.

The stock of a City brewer at this point of time was therefore
humble and limited enough ; and his rent and working expenses were
correspondent. Yet Mother Church took her toll from him in fairly
bountiful measure.

At a Court of Husting of Pleas of Land, held in 1345, the brewers
of the City were interdicted from using the water of Cheap conduit for
brewing ale and making malt, as their requirements had become sufficiently large to encroach seriously on the public supply.

In 50 Edward III. (1376), this Gild returned five members to the
Common Council, six being the *maximum*.

We find it stated that by an ordinance of 7 Henry IV. the freemen of
the mistery were bound to elect yearly eight persons, four for the district
east, and the same number for that west, of Walbrook, to be inspectors
of all matters pertaining to the trade ; but we must add that this was a
movement on parallel lines to that which we have recorded in the annals
of some of the other Gilds, and was an outcome of the demand from the
Yeomanry, as distinguished from the Livery and Court, for a subordinate
share in the executive authority.

EARLY ARMS (FROM
STOW, 1633).

The Brewers' books, in the first half of the fifteenth
century (1418–40), contain numerous entries illustrative of the practice of offering vails or *douceurs* to the
civic authorities, from the Mayor downward, with a
view to secure a lenient interpretation of the law,
where it was a question of meeting a charge or of
disguising an abuse. The gift was usually accepted ;
in one or two recorded instances it was gently refused.
But we hence perceive the commencing difficulty of a
trade dealing with a peculiar industry, in avoiding collision with the
municipal government from a variety of causes, some of which, as the

uncertainty of standard for measures and the dearness of prices, have ceased to operate through legislative changes.

In 1422 the Brewers became involved in a dispute with the Court of Aldermen, in consequence of an alleged breach on their part of the municipal precepts against forestalling, it having been represented by Sir Richard Whittington, late Mayor, that certain brewers, members of the mistery, had ridden into the country, and bought up all the ale, for the purpose of regrating. On July 30, 1422, the Master and twelve of the Company were summoned before the Court, Whittington being present, and fined 20*l.* on this account; but on an exception being raised by the defendants, the Master and Wardens were detained till they found the money or good security, under the surveillance of the Chamberlain.

THE TUMBRIL.

The Mayor and Aldermen, however, going to their dinner, the prisoners demanded of the Chamberlain what they should do; and he bad them go home, and fear not; for this whole matter was only to pleasure Sir Richard Whittington; and we further glean that the ex-Mayor was wrath with the Brewers, moreover, because at their feast on the morrow of St. Martin they had had fat swans served up on the table.

The enforcement of some more efficacious principle of establishing uniformity and precision in the capacity of vessels employed to hold malt liquor, had been long overdue, if we may judge from the complaints made during the reign of Henry IV. to the Mayor's Court; and the evil and reproach were not confined to transactions in gross, but extended throughout "to the displeasure of God, and contrary to the profit of the City." At this period the barrel of ale held by right twenty-seven gallons, the half-barrel, fourteen. The trade was therefore required henceforth to retail their liquor in sealed measures only, and not in their own hanaps, pottles, and tankards ; and the Chamber of London was charged with marking all barrels and half-barrels with the respective legal quantities to be found in them.

In 1423, under the mayoralty of Robert Chichele, ale-sellers were required to retail it in pewter pots, sealed and open, and to have their cups sealed ; and whoever carried ale to the buyer, bore the pot in one hand and the cup in the other.

The origin of the Brewers' Company, like that of other similar associations, is doubtless to be attributed to the necessity, under which all engaged in mercantile pursuits in troubled times lay, of obtaining security from the Government for their property and freedom from molestation in the conduct of their affairs.

The number of persons pursuing this calling in London, even in the remote days to which the commencement of the Gild is referable, must have been comparatively large, although no individual perhaps conducted business on the scale familiar to modern observers ; but the Brewers followed a sufficiently common precedent in sheltering themselves beneath the royal sign-manual when they solicited and obtained from Henry VI., in the sixteenth year of his reign (1437-8), a charter conceding to them certain important privileges, and incorporating them under the title of " The Master and Keepers, or Wardens, and Commonalty of the Mistery or Art of Brewers of the City of London."

There is trustworthy evidence that, at all events within a measurable distance of time, the Brewers had attained a very distinguished rank among the Companies ; for in 1469 their return to the muster for the City Watch was 210, being the highest of all, and ten more than that of the Mercers. In the settlement of precedence in 1515 they rank as the fourteenth Company.

The parent charter of 1437-8 conferred on the Gild the faculty of managing their internal organization, of pleading and being impleaded in the Courts, and of acquiring and holding lands and hereditaments. Under this instrument the Executive was directed to be four Wardens chosen from the Commonalty.

But those of Elizabeth in 1560 and 1563 determined its constitution more precisely, and, among other points, fixed what its governing body was to be—viz., one Master, three Wardens, and the Commonalty ; while the later one of the same sovereign, in 1579, went still further, by reason of the development of the industry, and the then appreciable accession to the ranks of its followers, in placing breweries under the immediate supervision and control of the Masters and Wardens, not merely in the Metropolis proper, but within a circuit of two miles.

On the accession of the Stuarts, in 1603–4, the Brewers do not appear to have moved for a new charter ; and the Wardens were committed to Wood Street Compter for refusing to pay the assessment toward the expenses connected with the royal passage through the City.

The *inspeximus* and confirmation of Charles I., 1641, extended the jurisdiction of the Court to a circuit of four miles (probably from Cornhill), empowered it to make rules and ordinances, and for the first time sanctioned the appointment of Assistants, not exceeding twenty-eight in number, who might hold office for life in the absence of some special and valid reason to the contrary. It was, we presume, this amplification of the functions and authority of the Company which led to a re-issue of the code of bye-laws originally framed in 1580.

The Company surrendered its charter by deed in 1660 and 1684, prior to re-incorporation in the first year of Charles II. and James II. respectively. In the former, a Clerk is authorized. Under the latter charter the radius was extended to eight miles, and the rights of search and quarterage were granted. These rights are defined and regulated by the bye-laws of July 13, 1739, and carry with them larger powers than are practically enforced at the present date. The licence in mortmain is here enlarged to 60*l.* a year, exclusive of all charges.

But the power of search, which was subsequently reduced to four miles, as it stands in the charter of 1641, has long become a dead letter, owing to a multiplicity of legislative and social changes.

The bye-laws of 1739 are still in force without material alteration, except that in 1857 declarations were substituted for oaths.

The Arms of the Brewers, granted 8 Edward IV., and again 35 Henry VIII., 1544, were registered at the College of Arms, August 21, 1801. The grant made July 23, 1469 (8 Edward IV.), are probably identical with those given in Munday's edition of Stow's *Chronicle*, 1633. The motto, " In God is all my trust," which appears on the Arms of the Company, and at which imperfectly-educated persons are apt to sneer, is in strict keeping with the religious atmosphere which surrounded and consecrated all our early institutions, and which carried the sanction and countenance of the Church into all the occupations of life.

The present Executive is composed of a Master, three Wardens, and twenty-six Assistants. The Wardens are styled the Upper, Middle, and Renter Warden. In 1882 there were 320 on the Freedom, and 75 on the Livery.

The Brewers' Company is nearly the only one which admits none but members of the trade or partners in brewing firms. From an early period the Company, with many others, is found trying to deal with what was regarded as an inconvenience or impropriety, the fellowship of persons who had no connexion with the business. It seems to have prospered fairly under a maintenance of this principle; but most of the Gilds which have acquired opulence and power, have done so by a directly opposite policy.

Formerly women were admitted to the Freedom of the Company, for the purpose of obtaining for their sons the advantages of the Aldenham Grammar School; but this qualification is no longer necessary.

The income of the Company is in large measure held in trust, the corporate revenue being comparatively small—about one-fifth of the whole amount, which was returned in 1892 at 17,500*l.* a year.

During the reigns of James I. and his son, the Brewers appear to have had a good deal of trouble in respect to the strength of the liquor brewed by them, which the Board of Green Cloth in 1617 alleged to be above the Assize, that is, 12*s.*, 14*s.*, and 16*s.* a barrel, thereby promoting drunkenness; and the trade complained on their part that the King's purveyors made use of their carts, horses, and men, and did not pay for the goods taken punctually or properly. The Board threatened in 1629 to suppress all brewers not free of the Company.

The Court of Aldermen did what it could to redress matters, and referred the Board to the Company's charter, praying that the beer and ale ordered for his Majesty's occasions might be duly paid for.

So far as the prices charged for beer are concerned, we perceive that even in 1579 the Lords of the Council called upon the City to see what could be done to make the Brewers reduce their tariff.

In 1627 the erection of buildings for the manufacture of alum in the parish of St. Mary Matfellon [Whitechapel], in immediate neighbourhood to certain large breweries, where the beer was brewed for the Navy and others, led to a petition to the King on July 25. The aggrieved parties represented that the new-comers had, ever since their first arrival, boiled quantities of urine for the making of their alum, to the prejudice of the health and convenience of the inhabitants; and had further, by the method of getting rid of their refuse, tended to pollute the wells used for the brewing water. The Lords of the Council ordered the offenders to remove elsewhere within a specified term; but there was a good deal of delay and difficulty, before the nuisance was abated. This incident seems to exhibit an imperfect acquaintance with the art of producing the article, which is ordinarily a sulphate of alumina and potash.

The brewers, until taverns and inns grew more numerous and frequent, were also salesmen, and maintained a retail side, or brewery tap, of which the French *brasserie*, so far as the word goes, is a survival. To many of the minor establishments at the present day a feature of this kind is attached; and of course all the early brewing houses were of this humbler complexion.

Under the civic ordinances of 1371, hostelers, unless they were common brewers at the same time, were prohibited from selling malt liquor save to stranger guests—persons lodging under their roofs; and brewers on their part were not at liberty to vend ale to hucksters for re-sale. The object in either case was to obviate the occurrence of disorders in the streets, as well as to discourage the regrator.

We do not observe any indication of the Hall having been at any period elsewhere than on its present site in Addle Street, a turning out of Wood Street, Cheapside.

In the time of Henry IV., the governing body was charged with the duty of providing a proper place for the transaction of business, to which members might be summoned by the beadle. But in 1420, in the mastership of Thomas Greene, the Company is described as assembling at Brewers' Hall every Monday. That it was occasionally lent to other Companies, which did not possess a seat, is indicated by an entry in the Founders' books of a payment of 8*d.* for two days' use of the room.

The election-feasts were probably more regular, when convenient quarters had been provided for the accommodation of guests. The wives and daughters of freemen were admitted. Brethren paid 12*d.*, sisters 8*d.*, and a husband and wife compounded for 20*d.* A bill of fare of 9 Henry V., gives three courses ; but the order of dishes was irrespective of any modern law of gastronomic or culinary fitness, as fish, soup, game, fruit, and sweets were served up at random. But such a method of distribution was not improbably due to the graduated arrangement of the company at different tables, and a course being allotted to each.

The building in Addle Street was almost completely destroyed in the Great Fire of 1666, and was rebuilt, partly by subscription, partly by pawning the plate (which was never redeemed), in 1673. It is in the form of a quadrangle, surrounding a courtyard, and the entrance is an old-fashioned gateway, which admits the visitor into a broad corridor, and which strangely contrasts with the modern warehouses on all sides. The Hall itself, which is on the first floor, and is reached by an old-fashioned staircase, is a spacious and lofty apartment, with a fine assortment of oak carving and wainscot in good preservation, and portraits of the principal benefactors.[1] The court-room, which is on the same

---

[1] Alderman Ritchard Platt (1528–1609), Dame Alice Owen (1547–1613), Alderman James Hickson (1607–89), Samuel Whitbread, Esq. (1720–96), John Baker, Esq. (1737–1818), and Harry Charrington, Esq., Master in 1813.

storey, is chiefly remarkable for its windows, which resemble the port-
holes of a ship on an enlarged scale. The basement contains the roomy
kitchen and other offices, with a small garden in the rear. In the
kitchen, which is the most ancient portion of the building,[1] one sees
the original spits attached to the large fireplace, and there is a beautiful
leaden cistern, dated 1671, with the arms of the Brewers' Company
upon it. This has been removed to its present situation of late years,
having been formerly, we understand, in a different part of the premises.

The house in Addle Street was, prior to 1860, only in part the freehold of the Company ; but in that year the Dean and Chapter of St.
Paul's, through the Ecclesiastical Commissioners, sold those parcels
which belonged to them, for nearly 3,000l., and the whole is now the
property in fee of the Master, Wardens, and Commonalty.

In the cause of charity and learning, the Company has performed

CREST OR COGNIZANCE OF HICKSON.

very signal services, both within and without the precincts of the City ;
and we ascertain from the official paper before us, as well as from the
account given by Stow in his *Survey*, 1633, how at various epochs
wealthy and benevolent members of the Fraternity felt an honourable
pride in setting apart a portion of their estates to enrich the corporate
fund, and to endow or assist philanthropic objects. Nor did these
benefactors confine themselves to the freemen of their own mystery ;
for we find abundant proof that they contributed to the welfare of the
Church and the maintenance of hospitals.

We may proceed to illustrate the eleemosynary bounties of the Gild
by some extracts from Stow. The first which we give refers to Broad
Street Ward and to the reign of Henry VII. :—

" In the year 1499, Sir *John Tate*, sometime Alebrewer, then a Mercer, caused his
Brewhouse, called the Swan, neere adjoyning to the said Free Chappell, College, or
Hospital of Saint *Anthony*, to bee taken for the enlarging of the Church, which was

---

[1] Mr. Higgins, the courteous and obliging Clerk of the Gild, informs us that it
escaped the Fire of 1666.

then newly builded; toward the building whereof, the said *Tate* gave great summes of money, and finished it in the yeere 1501. Sir John Tate deceased 1514, and was there buried, under a faire Monument by him prepared."

The next instance which we have to mention is that of Dame Alice Owen (1547-1613), of whose beneficent acts the historian of London furnishes us with the following account :—

"Mistress *Alice Elkin*, widdow to Master *William Elkin*, Mercer and Alderman of *London*, was afterwards married to the learned Lawyer, Master *Thomas Owen*, one of the learned Judges of the Land.

[Among other gifts]

Item. The building of the Almeshouses at *Islington*, and purchasing of the Land laid to them, did cost her the sum of one thousand, four hundred and fifteene pounds.

To the Company of Brewers in *London*, to whose trust and care shee hath committed the government and, oversight of the forenamed Almes-houses and school-house at Islington ; as a gratefull remembrance of her love, and that their paines should not goe altogether unregarded, she hath given in plate and money, one hundred pounds.

This worthy woman being borne at Islington, in the time of her childhood, she hapned there to escape a great danger, by means of an Arrow shot at randome in the field, where shee was then sporting among other children, the Arrow missing all the other, pierced quite thorow the hat on her head, and (God be praised for it) did not touch her with any other harme : whereupon, in the Towne of her birth, and where shee escaped such an expected perill, shee made choice to expresse her thankfulnesse to GOD, upon the Altar of her charitable Almes-houses and Schoole."

CREST OF OWEN.

Among the monumental inscriptions formerly existing at St. Botolph's, Bishopsgate, one commemorates the charitable works of another lady :—

"*Hereunder lyeth the body of* Joane Wood, *wife to* Robert Wood, *Citizen and Brewer of London.* . . . *She deceased the* 25. *day of November,* An. Dom. 1600. She gave large gifts and legacies to this Parish, as hereunder is expressed :

At her buriall she gave tenne pounds to the poore.

She gave tenne shillings yeerely for a Sermon on Midsummer day.

For a friendly meeting among the neighbours, forty shillings.

In bread weekly to the poore for ever, two shillings.

Also foure load of Char-coales yeerly to the poore for ever.

To the Parson of the parish yeerely for ever, tenne shillings.

To the Two Church-wardens, tenne shillings to each in like manner.

To the Clerke 6s. 8d. and to the Sexton 5s. yeerely for ever.

For a friendly meeting of the Parson and the parishioners, accompanying him yeerely in walking the bounds of the parish, thirty shillings.

To the poore of the parish, in money yeerely (for ever) to be distributed, eight pounds.

And the remainder of the yeerely rents for the halfe Moone, and halfe Moone Alley, to remaine in the Church Stocke, towards the repairing of the Church."

The name of Alderman Richard Plat is among those which the Brewers' Company, as well as all friends to learning, ought to hold in grateful and affectionate remembrance as that of the founder of the Free Grammar School and Almshouses at Aldenham, in Hertfordshire. He was buried at St. James's, Garlick-Hithe, with the following inscription :—

ARMS OF PLATT.

> "*Here lyeth buried the body of* Richard Plat, *Brewer and sometime chosen Sheriffe of* London. *The Founder of a free School, and six Alms-houses, in* Aldenham, *in the County of* Hertford. *Hee died the* 28. *of November,* 1600. *having taken to wife* Alice Birtles, *the daughter of* John Birtles, *Esquire, and having issue foure sons and one daughter.*"

Roger Bellow, of this Brotherhood, was another friend to humanity and the poor. Stow remarks :—

> "Master *Roger Bellow*, Brewer, hath given the Lease of an house in *Moore-lane*, called the signe of the *Cocke*, the yeerely rent whereof is twenty pounds. Out of the which summe, tenne pounds is yeerely to be given to the poore, at the feast of *Christmas :* And the remainder (except twenty shillings, otherwise by his will disposed) is yeerly to be reserved, for the purchasing of some parcell of Land, towards the reliefe of the poore."

Charles Langley, Ale-brewer, who was buried at St. Giles's Cripplegate, in 1602, left money to be laid out in clothes for his indigent fellow-parishioners annually for ever at All-Hallowtide.

Edward Harvest, Brewer, who died in 1610, besides giving 100*l.* to Christ's Hospital and 50*l.* between Bartholomew's and St. Thomas's Hospitals, and bequeathing large legacies to his kindred, vested in Cripplegate parish both realty and personalty for various purposes, including the repair of the road between Edgworth and Paddington. Harvest, though described as "Citizen and Brewer of London," appears merely to have been a freeman of the Company, as he is called on his monument, "one of his Majesty's gunners."

Two other members of this Gild, Richard Culverwell and William Mascall, left to Bridewell Hospital 200*l.* and an annuity of 9*l.* respectively, and many additions might be made to this roll. No meritorious recipients in the City of London went empty-handed away while the local brewer lived, or when he died ; and the clergy occupied a prominent position among the beneficiaries.

Stow's notice of ancient freemen of the Company does not seem to go further back than 1403, under which year he registers the interment of Benet Gerard, a Brewer, at St. Botolph's in Aldersgate Ward.

Under Downgate or Dowgate Ward, Stow's Continuator (1633)

says : "At the East end of this [All Hallows the more] Church goeth down a Lane, called Hay-wharfe lane, now lately a great Brew-house, builded there by one Pot ; Henry Campion Esquire, a Beer-brewer, used it, and Abraham his sonne since possessed it." The Peacock Brewery in Whitecross Street was another celebrated establishment, and we have already referred to those at Whitechapel. An unique Elizabethan volume by Stephen Batman, preacher, published about 1570, is dedicated "To his moste Louing and friendly Father [in law ?], William Beeston, Brewer."

In the *History of Thomas Hickathrift*, a chap-book founded on earlier legends or traditions, there is a curious mention of the brewer of Lynn, whose servant the hero became, and who, we are told, was in the habit of supplying beer to the people of the Marshlands and of Wisbeach. The description in the story bespeaks a primitive cart drawn by one horse ; and refers to the country thereabout as very sparsely inhabited. It is probably the earliest glimpse which we have of a provincial brewer going his rounds.

LITERARY NOTICES.

Principal muniments of the Company :—

1. The original Charter of 16 Henry VI., Feb. 22, 1437–8.
2. A Pardon granted to the Company in the name of Edward IV. (during the deposition of Henry VI.), Jan. 3, 1454.
3. A grant of Arms to the Company, 8 Edward IV., July 23, 1469.
4. Ordinances of the Company, granted under the hand and seal of the Lord Treasurer and two of the Judges, 22 Henry VII., July 15, 1507.
5. A grant of Arms to the Company, 1544.   35 Henry VIII.
6. A Charter of 4 & 5 Philip and Mary, 1556-7.
7.   ,,   ,,   2 Elizabeth, Nov. 11, 1560.
8.   ,,   ,,   5 Elizabeth, Aug. 29, 1563.
9.   ,,   ,,   21 Elizabeth, July 13, 1579.
10.   ,,   ,,   17 James I., Oct. 2, 1620.
11.   ,,   ,,   15 Charles I., April 6, 1641.
12.   ,,   ,,   1 Charles II., March 18, 1661.
13.   ,,   ,,   1 James II., 1685 (copy).
14. A List of Subscribers towards the erection of the new Hall, 1670.
15. Bye-Laws 22 Elizabeth, June 23, 1580.

⁎⁎⁎ The original code, said to have been given 16 Henry VI., does not appear to exist.

16. Bye-Laws 15 Charles I., July 9, 1641.
17.   ,,   1 George I., 1714.
18.   ,,   July 13, 1739.
19.   ,,   Feb. 13, 1857.
20. MSS. Records and Accounts of the Brewers, 1414-40.

The Beer-brewers' Complaint against the Coopers, 1541.

A Proclamation for Beer and Ale from the Lorde Maiour. Entered at Stationers' Hall in 1557–8.

A Jest of Bottle Ale. Entered at Stationers' Hall, 19 Aug., 1583.

A Booke howe to Brewe all sortes of Beire, &c. Entered at Stationers' Hall, 30 April, 1591.

A Ballad intituled Jones ale is new. Entered at Stationers' Hall, 16 Oct. 1594.

The Unthriftes adiew to Jones ale is new. Entered *ibid.*, 15 Nov. 1594.

Warm Beere; Or, A Treatise wherein is declared by many reasons that Beere so qualified is farre more wholesome then that which is drunke cold. By F. W. 12mo, 1641, 1724.

A Looking-glasse for Brewers. 4to, 1641.

The Brewers Plea; Or, A Vindication of Strong-Beere and Ale. Wherein is declared, the wonderful bounty and patience of God, the wicked and monstruous unthankfulnesse of man. 4to, 1647.

Cerevisaris Comes: Or, The New and True Art of Brewing. By W. Y-Worth. 12mo, 1692.

The Natural History of Bottled Ale. 8vo, Chester, 1710.

A Proclamation concerning certaine Kilnes for the sweet and speedy drying of Mault and Hops at a small charge. 8 Feb. 1636–7.

A Proclamation touching common Maulsters and Brewers. 9 July, 1637. A broadside.

Mault is a Gentleman.

> A pleasant new Ballad to look upon,
> How Mault deals with every man.

A Broadside. [About 1670.]

The Malster caught in a Trap; Or, The Witty Ale-Wife. A ballad. [About 1680.]

Reasons most humbly submitted to the Wisdom of Parliament for taking off the Present duty of Excise upon Beer and Ale, and laying the Duty upon the Original Malt. 4to, 1695.

Reasons Humbly Offer'd to the Honble. House of Commons for Translating the Duty of Excise from Mault-Drinks to Mault. By Robert Murray, Gent. [About 1720.] Large 4to, 2 leaves.

Drinke and welcome: . . . with an especiall declaration of the potency, vertue, and operation of our English Ale. By John Taylor. 4to, 1637.

The Lamentable Complaint of Hop the Brewer and Kilcalfe the Butcher . . . against the restraint lately set out by the Parliament, against Tapsters and Cooks. . . . 4to, 1641.

The Tapster's Downfall and the Drunkard's Joy. 4to, 1641.

The Lamentable Complaints of Nick Froth the Tapster and Rvle-Rost the Cooke. 4to, 1642.

The Ale-wives' Complaint against the Coffee-houses. 4to, 1675.

The Broderers.

OLD ARMS.

THIS Company existed at a date at least three centuries anterior to its formal incorporation in 1561, and was in the time of Edward III. already a body of some consequence. It may be supposed that it represents the original branch of the *Telarii*, distinguished as the Tapestry-Weavers or Tapissers, commemorated by Chaucer. In 1469 the Broderers equipped twelve men-at-arms to watch the City gates, an obligation which establishes a sound and respectable position at the time ; and this view is supported by the circumstance that, twenty years after, they obtained an Act of Parliament to restrain the abuses committed in the manufacture, weight, and package of imported Italian gold-work. In 1501–2, they are found as in the fifty-fifth in sequence without a Livery ; and in the same year mention occurs of the " Queen's Broderer." But they do not occur among the forty-eight Gilds, of which the order of priority was determined in 1515. The later lists do not point to any material improvement in their status.

Among the bequests to superstitious uses made to the Merchant Taylors was one in 1382 of ten marks a year under the will of Thomas Carleton, Citizen and Broderer of London, arising out of his estate in Ad Lane, in the parish of St. Albon, Wood Street, in order that the Fraternity might find a priest to pray for his soul for ever within the Taylors' Chapel at St. Paul's.

Others, not belonging to the last-mentioned Gild, but to a minor one, followed the same practice ; and it may have been because the testator's own Fraternity was destitute of a chantry or other religious establishment specially attached to it.

In 5 Henry VIII. the Broderers occur as conveying property in Gutter Lane to Thomas Foster or Forster, Citizen and Broderer or Broyderer, who executed his will in the nineteenth year of the same reign. It was probably a devise to him for the use of the Gild in the absence of a licence in mortmain. This Foster was, no doubt, the person who gave his name to the lane still so called, and spelled indifferently in early records *Foster, Forster*, and *Farster*.

The charter of 3 Elizabeth, October 25, 1561, established the Gild under the name of the Keepers or Wardens and Society of the Art or Mistery of the Broderers of the City of London, with perpetual succession, a common seal, a licence in mortmain to 30*l.* a year, and the power of pleading and being impleaded. It also conferred the right of search within the City of London and its suburbs, the City of Westminster, St. Katherine's in Middlesex, and the Borough of Southwark, and that of making bye-laws.

This grant was confirmed by *inspeximus* of 7 James I. 20 April 1609, and was revoked by *Quo Warranto* in 1684. In 1686 James II. ratified a new one with the usual political and religious clauses ; but by the Act 2 William and Mary, sect. 1, cap. 8, declaring all the proceedings in relation to the City Gilds void, the Broderers fell back on their original charter.

There are bye-laws made in 1562, 1582, 1609, and 1710. They greatly vary in number and character, the first containing 35 articles, the second, 12 ; the third, 13 ; and the fourth, 3 only ; and the difference in their tenor and object appears to entitle the three later codes to rank as supplementary to the first, rather than as independent series.

At the period of the negotiation between the Crown and the Companies, in 1613–17, for the purchase of the Ulster Plantation, the Broderers were sufficiently thriving to subscribe between 150*l.* and 200*l.* for a sub-share of the Mercers' manor.

But it appears from a petition to Charles I. in 1634 that the trade was then "so much decayed and grown out of use, that a great part of the Company, for want of employment, are so much impoverished that they are constrained to become porters, water-bearers, and the like." The sole fruit of this prayer appears to have been, that the licence in mortmain was augmented from 30*l.* to 100*l.* a year.

The later annals of the Broderers are destitute of general interest. Their control over the trade was called in question in or before 1707 for breaches of discipline and regulations, and eminent counsels' opinion condemned some of the penal bye-laws as invalid save only against freemen.

The Executive consists of a Master, Warden, Renter Warden, two Auditors, and seven Assistants, elected on each Trinity Monday by the Livery. In 1882, the numbers of the Company were returned as 4 Freemen, 31 Liverymen,[1] and the Court, as just described, or an aggregate of 47. In 1699, the numbers were 135, and in 1724, 116 ; but the returns do not specify whether the Court is included. The

---

[1] According to Whitaker, the Livery in 1892 amounted to 39.

total expenditure, exclusively of the cost of three Livery dinners and occasional donations to charities of moderate amount, appears to be about 280*l.* a year, paid in fees and salaries ; in 1874 the Company gave a Scholarship of 50*l.* a year, tenable by a pupil of the City of London School at Oxford or Cambridge. Under the bye-laws of 1609 provision was made for five Livery dinners annually ; but shortly after that date the affairs had begun to decline.

From entries in the minutes in 1874 and 1879 it is to be collected that the Broderers at that time possessed funded property in addition to the product of internal revenue in the shape of fines, and a collection of plate of some value, as a loan of it was solicited by the Education Department for the purpose of making casts for the use of students.

The Company in the last century still preserved their small Hall in Gutter Lane, which they had acquired early in the reign of Henry VIII. It was sometimes let, however, wholly or in part. From 1696 to 1709 the Gold and Silver Wyre Drawers, who were closely associated in business with the present body, continuously occupied it.

The connection with the trade has long ceased ; and embroiderers do not seek membership.

It is tolerably evident that the palmy days of this exceedingly interesting craft preceded its accession to the dignity of a chartered body, in 1561. The best work was perhaps produced between the middle of the fourteenth and the first quarter of the following century. But this industrial art flourished long before the earlier date cited, and its introduction may be assigned with confidence to the eleventh century and to Flemish influence and taste.

The importance and costliness of early embroidered work may be judged from a case which came before the Court of Aldermen in 1304, in which 300 marks sterling are stated to be the value of a cloth, embroidered with divers works in gold and silk, sold to Henry de Lacy, Earl of Lincoln, and another. But we do not hear whether this was of English or of foreign execution.

A charge of fraud preferred in 1374 before the Court of Aldermen by the Wardens of the Tapissers,[1] who in fact preceded the Broderers, demonstrates that the London school of embroidery then aimed at copying the style and texture of the goods of the same class produced at Arras. For it was stated that Katherine Duchewoman, the defendant, had in her house in Finch Lane wrought upon the loom a coster "after the manner of work of Arras," but made of linen thread beneath, and only covered with wool above. The Court ordered that the article should be burned ;

---

[1] See p. 147 *suprà* for some account of this Gild.

but the plaintiffs seem to have interceded for the woman, and saved her piece of handicraft. She was probably warned not to do it again.

One branch of the Broderers' business was the production of the superb palls which some of the Companies still possess, and which were formerly in regular use at funerals. The Merchant Taylors, Fishmongers, Saddlers, Vintners, Brewers, Coopers, Leathersellers, and Founders have very fine specimens belonging to the fifteenth and sixteenth centuries; and there is very slight room for doubt that they were in general use. Under date of October 21, 1547, the Goldsmiths paid 30s. to a Broderer to amend the hearse-cloth, or pall. Herbert suggests that the object may have been to remove any superstitious emblems; but these appliances survive from a far earlier period in an unsophisticated state, even where they have undergone necessary repairs.

Some idea of the cost of these palls may be formed from an entry in the Carpenters' books under 1513, whence it appears that that Company had at one time a cloth of this kind. For the cloth of gold at 2l. 3s. 4d. the yard, 4l. 14s. 9d. were paid; for three yards of black velvet, at 12s. 6d. a yard, 1l. 17s. 6d.; for seven yards and a quarter of buckram, 3s. 10d.; for the fringe, 10s. 4d.; and for the riband, 1s. 8d. The Broderer, for his workmanship, received 8l. The pall, therefore, cost altogether, 15l. 6s. 5d., besides a gratuity of 1s. 4d. to the maker, 2s. 8d. to the herald of arms, who certified to the accuracy of the coat worked on the pall, and 8d. to a scrivener for overseeing the bill, or a gross total of 15l. 12s. 9d. But this was not by any means an extravagant total by comparison.

The Coopers had at least two hearse-cloths, although of the earlier one our knowledge is restricted to the circumstance that in 1563 the Accounts are charged with about 57l. for a new one, presumably to replace it. The particulars are as follow :—

	£	s.	d.
2 lbs. of gold and silver at 54s. the lb.	5	8	0
2 lbs. of Venice gold and silver .	5	8	0
9 oz. of gold and silver	2	0	0
1 oz. of silver	0	5	2
1 lb. of Venice gold	2	14	0
½ lb. of silver	1	11	0
2 oz. of gold and silver	0	10	8
½ oz. of gold	0	3	0
Yellow and white silk, 4 ozs.	0	6	10
Silks of divers colours	1	3	8
1 oz. black ferret silk .	0	0	10
2 oz. yellow silk .	0	3	4
1 oz. Bruges silk	0	1	6
1 oz. ferret silk .	0	0	10
2 oz. yellow and white silk.	0	3	4
1 oz. white silk .	0	1	8

	£	s.	d.
14 oz. purple silk	1	8	0
½ oz. black silk	0	0	9
Purple and yellow silk	0	0	8
1 oz. yellow silk	0	1	8
5½ yards of purple velvet, at 26s. 8d. the yard . . .	7	6	8
Pearls	1	6	0
2 oz. of purple silk	0	12	0
Working 14 oz. of purple silk in fringes	0	6	0
White thread, and thread in colours	0	4	11
¾ and ½ oz. of fringe that was lacking	0	1	9
Yellow cotton made fit for the cloth to keep it from fretting	0	3	6
Canvas	0	5	0
A quartern of yellow kersey	0	0	7
Paper, flour, etc.	0	8	0
Candles for night-work	0	9	0
Paid to the Broderers for their workmanship in the making of the said hearse-cloth in great, with 20s. in reward by consent of the Court	24	10	4
For their bedding for seven months	0	4	4
To the painter for drawing the crest and arms for the cloth	0	3	4
	£57	11	10

It is explicitly stated that the pall of the Founders' Gild, described in the registers as "the Old Hearse Cloth embroydered with Gould and Popish images," was destroyed in 1646 by direction of the Court, pursuant to the Ordinance of Parliament; and the same fate possibly overtook those possessed by the Goldsmiths and other bodies. The Great Fire has not to answer for all.

For these sumptuous articles the London Livery Companies were not, of course, the only customers. They were in demand for all occasions of funeral solemnity, and formed an indispensable feature at the obsequies of every personage of high social standing. The parish church at Dunstable has lately acquired by gift a relic of this description, which was presented about 1516 to the Fraternity of St. John the Baptist at that place by Henry Fayrer and Agnes his wife.

The Broderers enjoyed, besides, a regular custom for ceremonial, festive, and professional habits worn by both sexes, and often worked with rich materials and in elaborate patterns; as well as for the appointments of churches, the vestments of the clergy, and the decorations of the house. They supplied the ornamental garlands worn on special occasions by the Masters and Wardens of the Gilds, caparisons, hammercloths, court-dresses, and hangings, as well as the hilts of swords and daggers, gold and silver lace, fringes, and cords and tassels.

The production of these articles of ornament or use appears to have been particularly expensive. In 1705, the Founders, a poor Company,

paid 14*l.* 14*s.* 6*d.* for a table-cloth with embroidery, inclusive of a further charge for lengthening it and embroidering the arms.

Stow, in his account of St. Botolph's, Bishopsgate, enumerates the
munificent donations of a widow named Price in 1614 to the pulpit
and communion-table of that church; and adds that Humphrey Swan,
Embroiderer of the same parish, embroidered without charge the King's
arms upon the pulpit-cloth so given by Mistress Price.

According to Chaucer, even in ordinary civil life gentlemen adopted
this luxurious and costly class of attire; for, in the *Canterbury Tales,*
he says of the Squire :—

> "Embrowded was he as it were a meade,
>   As ful of fresshe flouers, white and reede."

The present Lord Mayor (Alderman Evans) belongs to the Broderers,
and on New Year's Day, 1892, the Court waited upon his lordship at
the Mansion House, and presented him with a congratulatory address
in a silver casket of antique pattern.

New and Singular Patternes and Workes of Linnen, seruing for patterns to
make all sortes of lace, edginges, and cut-workes. 4to, 1591. Two editions same
year.

Certaine Patternes of Cut-workes. . . . Also sundry sorts of Spots, as
Flowers, Birds, and Fishes, etc., and will fitly serve to be wrought, some with Gould,
some with Silke, and some with Crewell, . . . 4to, 1632, and n. d.

The Butchers.

THE Butchers enjoy the distinction of proved antiquity, as one of
eighteen so-called Adulterine Gilds, which were required to pay their
fines or licences in 1180 in token and recognition of their allegiance to
the Crown. Their Master, in common with those of other ancient
Brotherhoods, was termed the Alderman; and at this time the bearer of
the office was William La Feite.

The Butchers' Gild next occurs as the immediate object of an Act of Parliament (1266, 51 Henry III.) passed, after many ineffectual attempts to stay the evil, to prevent and punish the exposure for sale of putrid or diseased meat. In 1319, butchers convicted of selling meat unfit for human food stood in the pillory, and saw the condemned carcasses burnt beneath them. On the other hand, persons preferring false charges underwent a similar punishment.

In remote days there were two principal markets for meat and poultry in the City: East-Cheap,[1] which comprised occasional attendance at the Stocks in the Poultry; and Newgate Street, or St. Nicholas' Shambles, from the spacious monastic church of St. Nicholas, of which Christ Church marks only a portion of the site. The selection of these two localities was probably due, at the outset, to different causes. East-Cheap, from a period of very great antiquity, was, with the whole remaining area to the water's edge, the busiest of all London

OLD ARMS.

centres, by reason of the great and constant trade which the Thames, the Tower, Smithfield, and the ordinary wants of the citizens, alike created around that quarter. It was to the Middlesex side of the river what the Borough was to the opposite one. In the days of Fitz-stephen the most striking and characteristic scenes might have been witnessed hereabout.

On the contrary, the more westerly colony may not unreasonably be supposed to have originally emanated from a settlement by leave or sufferance outside the walls of the Grey Friars in Newgate Street, and to have been fostered by the steady growth of the demand for produce until its members, long after the disappearance of the old monastery, usurped by degrees the entire quarter, and left only a narrow causeway down the centre of the thoroughfare for vehicles and passengers.

There was a natural drift toward the stealthy growth of stalls and selling rights elsewhere than within the prescribed bounds; apparently with a view to intercept the supplies and catch the custom of Southwark, the East-Cheap men tried to establish stalls on London Bridge. In 1277 a municipal ordinance had restricted the butchers to the appointed localities; and in 1345 the complaint of obstruction on the King's highway was so general, that butchers and fishmongers were ordered to confine themselves to the enclosure called the Stocks on flesh and fish days respectively.

---

[1] East-Cheap was anciently divided into Great and Little East-Cheap, and extended much further westward, being separated from West-Cheap, or Cheapside, only by the Stocks Market and its precincts.

A curious petition of 1331 exhibits the successful opposition of the butchers of the Stocks Market to sales by retail on the part of foreigners, and at the same time procured the assent of the trade generally and the Corporation to the suspension of any who had been bankrupt once or twice, until he had paid his debts in full, and the renewal of the regulation obliging all butchers to reside within the City ; whereas many had houses at Stratford, and neglected their duties as craftsmen and citizens.

A pleasant state of affairs is revealed as existing, when, in 1369, a royal order called upon the Corporation to remove Butchers' Bridge, and to have the slaughtering of animals discontinued at St. Nicholas' Shambles, near Baynard's Castle.   It appears that the animals were slaughtered at the Shambles, and the offal carried through the lanes and streets to the jetty called Butchers' Bridge, where it was thrown into the river ; and the Crown was prayed by many prelates and others of quality to stay such a flagrant nuisance.

Stow says that in ancient times the vicinity of St. Michael's, Crooked Lane, was an ill-favoured spot, where the butchers of East-Cheap kept their stalls.

By an order of later date (1371) the slaughtering of all large animals was directed to be carried out at Stratford or in the village of Knights-bridge—perhaps the earliest mention of this place ; and in 1372 we first hear of precautions against the pollution of the Thames.

But the scheme seems never to have been carried out, although an Act was passed 4 Henry VII. to forbid slaughtering within the City ; and in the reign of Elizabeth the nuisance and danger to health still prevailed.   So great a distance was between the letter of the law and its execution in practice.

Further westward was Butchers' Row, facing St. Clement's Church in the Strand, and at no great distance from Clare Market in the rear. As it lay within the one mile radius specified by the charter of the Company, it is not unlikely that Clare Market was an offshoot from St. Nicholas' Shambles, as Leadenhall was from East-Cheap, and alike subject to the Butchers' Ordinances.

Butchers' Row, which had its namesake in many of our provincial towns, was not exclusively devoted to the Craft, however ; for it was at the Bear and Harrow there that Nathaniel Lee the dramatist drank his last potation.

Leadenhall Market, which became a general depôt for all sorts of goods and a weigh-house, after awhile received the butchers—a detach-ment from the adjacent centre of the trade—and afforded a partial relief to the congestion of the thoroughfare and traffic.   The original building,

Leaden Hall, itself had been given to the Corporation by Sir Richard Whittington in his third mayoralty (1409), and the City exercised a certain jurisdiction over the market. The complex tenure of property, even in 1595, is shown by a letter, addressed by two ladies-in-waiting on the Queen on behalf of the daughter of a bone-setter, who had bequeathed to her fourteen butchers' stalls in Leadenhall, whereof she was debarred from the enjoyment by the municipal authorities.

An inquisition was panelled in 1414–15 (March 14), to delimit the area within which these folks might set up stalls and pent-houses; and the verdict or award was, that by custom they were entitled to sell and stand on both sides of the said street of East-Cheap from north to south, from the Pye on the Hoop to the Saracen's Head, and in length, east and west, from the eastern corner of Crooked Lane to the tenement occupied by William Ivor.

It has been thought that the salesmen of Newgate Street conveyed their offal by the Foss of Houndsditch (part of the City moat) into the Fleet, those of the Stocks Market similarly by Walbrook, and those at East-Cheap down Katherine, subsequently Rother, and eventually Pudding, Lane. The latest denomination of Katherine Lane was due, no doubt, to the existence at one period of emporia for the sale of black-puddings.

In 1343 a piece of land in Sea-Coal Lane, contiguous to the Fleet river, had been granted to the butchers of St. Nicholas' Shambles, on condition that they should keep certain buildings thereon in repair, and send the Lord Mayor a boar's head annually on Christmas Day.[1] This was to provide the Craft with a legal riparian easement. A similar privilege was conceded in 1402 in consideration of a yearly payment of 13s. 4d. to the East-Cheap dealers. But in both cases the operation was to be conducted only at the turn of the tide, in conformity with the statute of Winchester.

At a somewhat later epoch, the transportation of this garbage was limited by order to the night-time, and two Barrow-houses were erected on the banks of the river, at the two points where the Company had ground, for accommodating the noisome matter till the state of the current allowed its committal to the Thames. Each free butcher subscribed toward the maintenance of these receptacles.

No vocation was more amenable to the *Statutes of the Streets against Annoyances*,[2] and accordingly several clauses refer to the City butchers. They were forbidden to scald hogs save in the common scalding-house,

---

[1] Riley's *Memorials*, 1868, p. 214.
[2] Stow's *Survey*, 1633, pp. 665 *et seqq.*

or to sell any measly or otherwise unwholesome pork, to sell any flesh which had been killed above three days in the winter or two in the summer, to cast out the offal of beasts into the public way, and to drive the pudding-cart of the shambles through the streets before nine at night or after five in the morning.

Butchers not free of the City were not allowed to cut any meat for sale at the Stocks market after the hour of noon, and such as they had cut before noon they might sell till vespers ; but they might carry none away. No shop, whether that of a freeman or foreigner, was to be open after daylight.

They are prohibited in the *Liber Albus* from selling the skins beforehand on the living animals ; they are required to bring the carcasses with the hides, and sell them both in the King's market after prime. They were also forbidden to sell tallow or lard for export, in view of the enhancement thereby of the price to home-buyers.

In 1363 the price of best carcass of mutton was 2s. ; best quality of loin of pork, 3d. ; of beef, 5d. ; of leg of beef, 3d. ; a sucking pig was valued at 8d. In 2 Richard II. (1378), the maximum price for a lamb was 6d., and forestalling was unlawful. Nor was any trader at liberty, between November and the ensuing Lent, to discommend other men's meat.

The butchers in the old days suffered, as the fishmongers profited, from the extraordinary frequency of public fasts, and from the discontinuance during Lent, even in Protestant reigns, of the use of flesh. They were required, as we have noticed, to give place to the fishmongers in the market-places on fast-days.

The Company was, nevertheless, in an undoubtedly prosperous condition in the reign of Edward III., in whose 37th year the three branches of the trade made gifts to the King of 9*l.*, 8*l.*, and 6*l.* respectively ; in the 50th of the same King the Company was represented on the Common Council by four members, none sending more than six, many only two.

In 1474 the Butchers made certain Ordinances, and put the same in force, without consulting the Corporation, and were condemned to pay 40*l.* fine, eventually reduced to 20*l.* The act was an offence against the liberty of the City, as interpreted and laid down by a statute of 15 Henry VI., which was subsequently confirmed by the more generally known one of 19 Henry VII., safeguarding the prerogative of the Crown against all rights and exemptions claimed by local bodies.

Altogether, it is difficult to avoid the suspicion that the Company had, with or without licence (it existed illegally in 1180), assumed,—at least in the middle of the sixteenth century, when it acquired its Hall on a long lease,[1]—a regular system of internal government, including a Livery, which the Court of Aldermen was entitled to grant, but of course, not such corporate privileges and powers as it lay with the Crown alone to bestow. The lost archives might have elucidated this point ; the earliest remaining volume combines with all the surrounding circumstances and auxiliary testimony to support the view that an older charter or patent has perished. Yet, on the other hand, certain Gilds remained without any specific title derived from the Crown during an equally long period, or even a longer one ; the Clockmakers were not incorporated till 1632, and had no Livery till 1766 ; the authority for the Coopers' and Leathersellers' Livery could not be supplied to Parliament in 1725 ; and the Basket-makers stand purely and entirely on prescription. It transpires that in 1573 affairs were still progressing favourably ; for in a levy of the corn-tax for laying up stores in the Bridge-house according to an usage and law then in force, the Butchers were assessed at 25l. 10s., the lowest contribution being 6l. 5s.

So far as our existing information goes, it was not till September 16, 1606, however, after a substantial duration of centuries, and the lengthened ownership of a Hall, that the Company applied for a charter, which embodied all the freemen of the art or mistery of Butchers of the City of London, with the customary privileges and a control over the trade in the metropolis and one mile compass. This charter was confirmed in 1608 ; but in 1638, it being found that the jurisdiction was insufficient, it was amplified ; and it was renewed (with modifications) in 1685 and 1749.

The governing body is a Master, five Wardens, and fifteen Assistants. The two grades below the Court are, as usual, the Livery and Yeomanry ; under which title it is explicitly stipulated by the bye-laws of 1752 that freemen are to be entered on the books. In 1699, the Livery is given as 218 ; in 1724, as 130. Since 1834, when the Company numbered 1,600, including women-traders, the ranks have considerably shrunk. The figures in 1882 were : Livery (Court inclusive), 145 ;[2] Freemen, 228.

The Company long carried on its executive government under the guidance of a set of Ordinances drawn up about 1638 ; but these were superseded by a long series of Articles dated as recently as 1752.

The Ordinances of 1752 embrace, amid an assortment of customary provisions, certain special clauses in regard to the respective duties of officers and Yeomen, the holding of Courts, the inspection of slaughter-

---

[1] The possession of a Hall is mentioned in some of the charters as a matter subject to royal licence.

[2] In 1892, according to Whitaker, the figures were 137.

houses and weights, the levy of fines and forfeits for non-attendance, refusal to serve office, combination, the binding of apprentices to none but the true master, and other points ; the observance of a close time for pork between April 20 and August 24, the killing of mainlings and calves under five weeks, the sale of ewe or wether for lamb, and the punishment of hawkers.

But by successive Acts of Parliament in 1824, 1855, and 1863, its authority over the trade was gradually abrogated.   The statute repealed in 1824, and known as the Flaying Act, vested joint powers in the Butchers, Cordwainers, and Curriers, as the three representative bodies severally interested to prevent the unskilful removal of hides, which constitutes one of the Articles in the Ordinances of 1752.

In 1548, in the mayoralty of Sir John Gresham, the Company had secured, on a lease for eighty years, a regular place of meeting in New-gate Street, by a tripartite indenture between the Governors of St. Bartholomew's Hospital, the Wardens of the Company, and the Yeo-manry of the same.   The premises were to the north of the church of St. Nicholas, and were described as "all that the mansion-house, with cellars, solars, and all other appurtenances, called the parsonage or dwelling-house of late belonging to the prior of the late parish church of St. Nicholas in the Flesh-Shambles, being near unto the late dissolved house sometimes called the Grey Friars, now called Christ Church within Newgate."   The rent was fixed at 6l. a year, and the lessees were at liberty to restore or rebuild.   The house was a quadrangle, surround-ing a courtyard or garden, and remained much in its original state when Agas published his map, in or about 1560.

The eighty years' lease expired in 1628; but it was evidently renewed, and doubtless for twenty-one years, at the same rent and for a fine, since on June 22, 1650, the governing body of the Hospital, as we know from an extant minute, again extended the term for a similar period at 70l. fine.[1]   The basement of the Hall, perhaps that fronting what was once nicknamed Stinking, and subsequently known as Butcher Hall, Lane, had been sub-let prior to 1655, as in that year the Company granted a new term of fifteen years to one Michael Shipway.

But the place was swept away, before either lease or sub-lease expired, by the ravages of the Great Fire, which must have equally destroyed the whole of the Company's property in East-Cheap ; and the Butchers were reduced to such straits, that they surrendered their tenure, and prayed to be excused from paying arrears of rent accrued since the calamity.   The Hospital, having secured another tenant at a higher

---

[1] The parchment was dated September 2, 1651.

rate (9*l.*), and the latter having undertaken to rebuild at his own charge, forgave the debt under a minute, dated January 22, 1668–9.

The Butchers rallied from their heavy losses, and determined to erect a new Hall by subscription on the land belonging to them in Scalding Yard on the east side of Pudding Lane, in Billingsgate Ward. This is the edifice of which Maitland (1739) speaks as a very neat and convenient one, and as containing an upper and lower hall, a parlour, and three handsome rooms adorned with fretwork and wainscot. The outlay incurred was still in course of liquidation in 1688. But the Company, owing to the sweeping changes in the vicinity of East-Cheap of recent years, was dispossessed of its second Hall, and has returned to its former haunts in the outskirts of Newgate Street.

It was at a Court held in Pudding Lane on January 12, 1687–8, that Daniel Foe, son of James Foe, Citizen and Butcher, of Fore Street, Cripplegate, attended to apply for his admission by patrimony, and was admitted accordingly, and paid, in discharge of serving all offices, 10*l.* 15*s.* This, of course, refers to the illustrious author of *Robinson Crusoe*, whose connection with the Gild sheds upon it greater glory than an entire catalogue of inarticulate and fugitive names.

Subsequently to the Fire, the Corporation, finding it necessary perhaps to study the public convenience to some greater extent, endeavoured to restrict the butchers and other traders to markets and shops, and even to reform the arrangements for holding markets, so that they might be limited to statutory or usual times. But the resistance to improvement was very strenuous; and even in 1711 we find the City agreeing to enforce its regulations, provided that aggrieved persons would pay the expense; or, in other words, arbitrary compulsion had by this date begun to grow less possible and efficacious.

The Butchers suffered the common misfortune and disadvantage of losing nearly all their papers and muniments in the Fire, and are thus much crippled in any effort to produce a connected and complete record of their Gild. One of their manuscript books of entries, being that which contains the accounts from 1592 to December, 1646, has, however, been fortunately preserved. It includes a great variety of details common to this and other Companies, as payments of fines and charges to or by the Wardens, and receipts under sundry heads, while, of course, many items concern the special craft, such as the cost of wood for scalding hogs, and the repairs of the barrow-houses, where the offal was deposited, and of the furnaces where the scalding was carried out. No barge-money was collected in 1592–3, because, by reason of the plague, the Court of Exchequer was not sitting, and the Mayor was sworn at the Tower-gate.

The receipts of 1592–1646 are arranged under,—

> Quarterages of the Wardens and Assistants.
> Livery.
> Yeomanry.
> Journeymen in the Shambles.
> East Cheap.

Arrears of Quarterage and Barge-money.
Presentments of Indentures.
Ingress money.
Scantling money.
Rentayne.

On all public occasions the Companies were expected to set up their own stands in the line of procession, and attend there betimes. In 1697, when William III. returned from Holland, the Butchers received a precept to be at their station by 9 a.m. The outlay involved in these matters of ceremony was considerable. In 1714, the entry of George I. into London cost 69*l.* 17*s.* 6½*d.* In 1726, Lord Mayor's Day is charged with disbursements of nearly the same amount. For Lord Mayor's Day, 1763, the stand was repaired and re-upholstered, at an expense of 60*l.*, of which the greater part was subscribed among members ; and it served the purpose till 1805, when it realized 20*l.*

LITERARY NOTICES.

A Proclamation Concernynge Bouchers. A broadside, printed by Thomas Berthelet, about 1540.

Reasons tendered by the Free Butchers of London against the Bill in Parliament to restrain Butchers from Grazing of Cattle. A broadside. [1624.]

The Carpenters.

EARLY ARMS.

PRESENT ARMS.

THE original or early associates of the Carpenters' Company belonged to a class which, as a separate and independent body, no longer exists. He was, like the bricklayer, a contractor on his own account, who furnished directly to the employer the estimated cost of work, great or small, from the erection of a cathedral or a palace to that of a cottage, so far as the carpentry was concerned.

The carpenter of ancient times was, in short, a master; and the operative or journeyman carpenter was classed as a labourer. In 1271, the City of London already possessed two Master Carpenters, who were charged with the function of surveying buildings, and who almost beyond doubt were members of what Chaucer in or about 1388 terms "a great fraternity," with its constitution and distinguishing attire.

Under 1303 the name seems to have been on the border-land of a craft and a patronymic, as we meet with such forms as *Wilhelmus filius Wilhelmi de Southwarke Carpentar*, *Philip le Carpenter*, and *Adam le Carpenter;* and we know from the excellent Town Clerk, whose biography Mr. Brewer gave us, that in the next hundred years it was an established family name. From the nature of things, the vocation must have had a pronounced existence in the earliest annals of civilized society; and fraternal union long remained an inevitable corollary of industrial vigour and progress.

Among Riley's *Memorials*, 1868, is inserted the account of William Sunnynge, Carpenter, of moneys expended by him in 1359 as trustee, on the repairs of a house in the parish of St. Michael, Cornhill. Sunnynge in this matter employed not only tilers, paviours, plumbers, daubers, and other operatives, but journeymen of his own craft, to whom he gave 8½*d.* a day.

In the provinces, as well as in London and its suburbs, the Master-Carpenter from a very early period occupied a highly responsible and dignified position, as the controller, under the eye of the architect, of the whole business within his own department.   There is still extant a very curious document relating to the erection of a house in High Street, Bristol, by Stephen Morgan, for Alice Chester, widow of Henry Chester, of that city, draper ; and as it seems to precede in date anything of the ' kind known, we append it entire.   It belongs to the year 1472 :—

" This indenture made between Alice Chester of Bristol, widow, some time the wife of Harry Chester of Bristol, draper, on the one party, and Stephen Morgan of Bristol, carpenter, on the other party, witnesseth that the said Stephen hath covenanted with the same Alice and him bindeth by these presents to make well, workmanly, and surely of good timber and boards, a new House, in the High Street of Bristol, with floors, windows, doors and partitions and all other things of timber work belonging to the same house except laths and lattices, which said new house shall be set between the tenement called the Bull on the one party, and the tenement in which one John a Cork, Corviser [cordwainer or shoemaker] now dwelleth in, on the other party, containing in length 19 feet and 5 inches of size, and in wideness 10 feet and 4 inches ; and the said Stephen shall make in the said a shop, a hall above the same with an oriel [bay window], a chamber above the hall with an oriel, and another chamber above that by the feast of the Annunciation of our Lady next coming for which house so to be made by the same Stephen the said Alice granteth and her bindeth by this present [writing] to pay unto the said Stephen 6l. 18s. 4d. sterling, that is to say, at the feast of the Nativity of our Lord next coming 3l., at flooring of the said house 33s. 4d., and at end of the same work 40s.   Also it is accorded that it shall be lawful to the same Stephen to have and take as his own all the old timber of the said old house without any gainsaying of the same Alice or any other for her or in her name.   In witness thereof the parties aforesaid to these indentures interchangeably have set their seals. Given the 17th day of the month of November, in the 12th year of the reign of King Edward the fourth.—Hardyng."

This indenture, subscribed by the attorney or scrivener, has the seal with the impression of a sword and a Gothic capital I in perfect preservation.

It was not many years subsequently to this curious glimpse into the subject, that we hear of the place of Master Carpenter to the Crown being a Patent office, and being conferred in 1484 on Edward Graveley for life at a stipend of 1s. a day.[1] His successor was probably the Thomas Mauncy, whose name presents itself as King's Carpenter in the household-book of Henry VII., under 1491 and following years ; and there was a continuous series of these functionaries, till the post was apparently merged in that of Surveyor of Works.

The Master Carpenter employed on the timber-work of the Savoy Hospital, toward the close of his life, was Humphrey Coke, who served the office of Warden of the Company in the years 1507–8 and 1511, and

---

[1] This was the scale allowed in 1356 to William of Wykeham as Surveyor of the King's Works and Park at Windsor ; but when he was employed elsewhere, he was entitled to 2s.   The amount, however, was relatively higher.

who is commemorated by Walpole in his *Anecdotes of Painting.* In 1540, John Malyn, a carpenter of foreign extraction, residing at Farnham, was employed by the Goldsmiths to erect a new building in Friday Street ; and the Carpenters' Wardens waited on the Goldsmiths to complain of the proceeding, and demand compensation for the breach of their charter. The Goldsmiths' Wardens were instructed to arrange the business, as best they could.

Again, the name of Mr. John Haines is associated with the works undertaken at Goldsmiths' Hall after the Fire, the completion of which occupied three or four years, and involved for the carpentry alone no less than 1,600*l.* Haines received the order, October 1, 1667, and was

WILLIAM PORTINGTON, ESQUIRE, MASTER CARPENTER IN THE OFFICE OF HIS MAJESTY'S BUILDINGS, OB. 1628.
From an engraving by Fairholt.

to complete his share by the 24th June following. But various causes delayed the matter.

Among the entries in the Brewers' books from 1418 to 1440 is a catalogue of 112 Crafts or Craft-Gilds which existed in London 9 Henry V., 1421–2, and the Carpenters are here the thirty-ninth in order, coming between the Masons and the Pewterers. But this enumeration was probably quite unofficial, as no definite understanding on the precedence of these bodies was reached till the reign of Henry VIII.

That the Carpenters formed a distinct and important Association long prior to 1422, is a proposition at once not easily contested and not easily proved. The late Mr. Jupp held that the Company might be referred back, as a voluntary fellowship, to the middle of the fourteenth century ; and when Maitland speaks of its incorporation in 1344, we apprehend that we should at most interpret the statement as applying to the grant of a royal licence, rather than a charter. In the absence of the former it was not permissible, under the old system at all events, for a Gild to organize itself and assemble in conference ; but with a charter several dispensed for centuries or altogether. It became a question of the measure of jurisdiction and immunity desired.

Nor is it by any means improbable that such a licence may have been accorded anterior to 1344, if we consider the apparent condition of the trade nearly a century earlier on the one hand, and on the other weigh the retrospective significance of the erection of a Hall in 1429, on ground acquired (as usual) through members of the Gild, the arrival in 1438 at a regular official machinery, with books of accounts, and the draft of Ordinances in 1455. The impression produced on the mind of Chaucer, writing in the reign of Richard II., evidently was, that the Carpenters were an established and conspicuous element in the municipal system of the day ; and analogy and arguable likelihood support the few known facts in allowing the claim to high antiquity.

A certain amount of obscurity even hangs over the circumstances under which a charter was ultimately obtained in 1477. For as early as 1466 the Company received permission to use a common seal, and had a grant of arms from Clarencieux,[1] and, nevertheless, payment for the former was not made till 1478, the year succeeding incorporation, so that it may be the case, that the matter was in treaty some years before it was finally settled, and that, as Mr. Jupp suggests, the postponement was due to financial reasons.

The instrument bore date July 7, 1477, and conceded to Certain Men of the Mistery of Carpenters of the City of London the right and power of establishing a Brotherhood or Gild, to be a perpetual commonalty, and to consist of a Master, three Wardens and the Freemen and Freewomen of the said Gild, by the name of the Master, Wardens, and Commonalty of the Mistery of Freemen of the Carpentry of the City of London. The Company so instituted was authorized to elect its officers, who were entitled to make ordinances for the good government of the Society.

The expenses attendant on this enfranchisement amounted, with the cost of the seal, to upwards of 26l., which sum was partly contributed by no fewer than thirty of the brethren. It seems that the funds down

---

[1] Perhaps these bearings might have been identical with the coat in distemper, which was found in 1845 concurrently with the paintings hereafter described, and which had for supporters two naked boys in a recumbent posture. The motto of the Company, *Honour God*, was of much later origin.

to the present time had always been very inconsiderable, but that in 1477 there was a surplus of 12*l.*, possibly arising out of the Warham benefaction in that year; and the subscriptions probably made up the requisite total.   As far back as 1455 the Carpenters had had their Ordinances; but these were now formally exhibited at Guildhall, the eminent scrivener Clifford receiving 13*s.* 6*d.* for making a fair copy. The charter was not enrolled till 1486-7, and we connect with this proceeding a visit paid to the Company's Hall by two officials, Master Tate and Master White, "to see the wrytyng that longeth to the Craft," or, perhaps, in other words, to satisfy themselves that everything was in order.   At the same time a new set of Ordinances was drawn up, and submitted to the Court of Aldermen for approval.

The charter so secured, not without appreciable difficulty, was renewed by *inspeximus* of Philip and Mary and Elizabeth; and 15 July, 5 James I, a new grant on an ampler basis was substituted, conferring on the Company very large powers of search and control.   Charles I. in his 16th year, July 17, sanctioned for the first time a Court of Assistants to the number of twelve or more, the Master and three Wardens inclusive; and in 26 Charles II., October 20, the Company obtained a confirmation and continuance of its powers, with an extension of the faculty of supervision to a radius of four miles from Cornhill.

The normal incidence of the writ of *Quo Warranto* (1684–5) resulted in a re-constitution with one Master, four Wardens, and twenty-two Assistants, under the name and style of the Master, Keepers or Wardens of the Freemen of the Mistery or Art of Carpentry of the City of London; but this change was, as usual, annulled by the Act 2 William and Mary.   The present governing body therefore follows the antecedent grant of Charles II.   A licence in mortmain was separately procured 32 Charles II. enabling the Company to purchase lands to the extent of 200*l.* a year.

In the returns of 1501–2, the Livery (by prescription) is given as 30, and the Company comes twentieth.   In 1509 it is placed twenty-first, and is allowed fourteen yards for its stand; and in 1515 the Corporation made it the twenty-fifth in order.

In 1699, there were 98 liverymen, in 1724, 102.   In 1882 the Livery numbered 134, and the freemen were conjecturally estimated at between 150 and 200.   In 1892, the Livery was returned as 150.

The greater part of the estate seems to have accrued in and after 1587; and for a lengthened term the Carpenters' corporate income was unusually modest.   We have seen that some years elapsed before the negotiation for the first charter was closed.   Whenever any extraordinary outlay was incurred, it invariably involved embarrassment; even in 1664 the expense of certain important additions to the Hall was defrayed by a loan ; and the period of greatest pecuniary prosperity commenced precisely when, owing to the replacement of timber by brick after the Fire, the practical cesser of the jurisdiction over members by the Building Act of 1774, and the disappearance of apprenticeship, the trade began to languish ; and the body, which had once influentially and usefully represented it, was in effect transformed, like most other institutions of the same origin and nature, into a benevolent Society, enabled by the artificial expansion of many of its early acquisitions to dispense with a generous hand both charity and hospitality. Such a rise, development, and climax are not without their moral.

During the years 1831–4 the average income of the Carpenters was officially returned at 2,200l. In 1871, the aggregate had reached nearly 6,000l., and in 1880 it had nearly doubled, being given at 11,318l.[1] This remarkable expansion was due to the development of the London Wall and Lime Street estates. As sub-sharers to the extent of a 1–16th share in the Ironmongers' Irish estate, they received from 1871 to 1880 an annual sum varying from 168l. to 270l., the *minimum* occurring in the last-mentioned year. But this property has of course participated in the destiny of the whole, and has passed from the hands of the original owners by sale.

Such a rent-roll affords a splendid opportunity for philanthropic work, which is now generally recognised as the best justifying ground for the unmolested continuance of these Associations in the presence of new conditions and ideas. Vast internal changes have wrought a revolution in the City beyond all power of prevision and discernment ; and modern opinion prescribes that resources and responsibility shall move in a parallel ratio. The Carpenters pay due homage to this feeling and call, and are doing much in the direction of promoting the trade with which their name and existence are identified. Lectures on architectural sanitation and other subjects calculated to improve our buildings are periodically delivered by eminent specialists in the Hall ; and it is in contemplation to hold there an Exhibition of Carpentry and Joinery.

The history of Carpenters' Hall from its first humble genesis in 1428–9, on a plot of ground without Bishopsgate, leased for 98 years at a rent of 20s. from the Prior of the Hospital and Convent of St. Mary, is a rather long, though not a very eventful one, and exhibits a constant ambition on the part of the government of the Company to enlarge and embellish the mansion-house without a sufficient regard to the claims of antiquity on the one hand and those of harmony on the other. A succession of

---

[1] In 1892, the figures were 11,638l., of which only 956l. were in trust.

architects with conflicting tastes gradually obliterated all that was sacred and interesting both within and without ; and the building, although it escaped the Great Fire, has suffered perhaps more severely at the hands of man.

The original site consisted of a piece of waste and of five cottages in the parish of All Hallows on the Wall ; and, the lease having been formally assigned to twenty-nine members of the Company, the tenements were removed in 1429, and the necessary steps taken to erect the Hall, Almshouses, and outbuildings on a portion of the ground, the rest being reserved for a garden. It is quite clear from the account-books that many years elapsed before the place was rendered complete ; nor can there be any reasonable doubt that the Hall, as it was first designed, was of a very rudimentary model. In 1500, a new parlour was constructed at a cost of 23*l*. 2*s*. 11*d*., the odd pence being for bread, ale, and cheese consumed, presumably when the work was finished ; and 8*s*. 2*d*. of the amount went in improving the garden, which seems to have been laid out in knots, and to have been partly devoted to the growth of kitchen-herbs.

The Accounts comprise repeated charges for seeds, plants, gravel, and labour. We hear of a vine, two walnut-trees, a camomile-bank, roses, a sun-dial, and an arbour. The distribution of these areas was formerly different, and the kitchen and flower gardens, shrubbery and plantation, usually formed one unassorted whole. In the time of Henry VIII., the Carpenters' garden seems to have been kept in order by the Beadle's wife, or under her direction ; and to the same period (1548) is referred the formation of a bowling alley within the precincts.

Under 1561 and 1572 further entries occur relevant to alterations introduced, in some measure at the charge of the Yeomanry ; and in 1579 the Tudor parlour was superseded by a new one, in the wainscot of which were carved panels, one containing the arms, a second the date and Master's name, and the third the names of the Wardens. Yet we must not be quite sure that the old room did not become what is termed below *the little parlour*. In 1588 a gallery was built on the south side of the Hall ; and in 1595 an extension was carried out at the east end, at the unusually heavy charge of 121*l*. 10*s*., which appears to indicate an advance in the value of the corporate estate. At or about this period the block, which was approached through an outer court, is ascertained to have consisted of a refectory, a great parlour, a little parlour, a gallery, a kitchen, pastery and buttery, a Clerk's house, and the almshouses, besides the usual offices, and perhaps an armoury for the weapons and other stores used on public occasions, as we have observed in the account of the Ironmongers. Considerable expense was in-

CARPENTERS' HALL, 1664, SHEWING FRONTAGE TO LONDON WALL.

CARPENTERS' HALL, 1664. THE GARDEN FRONTAGE.

curred in 1608 in glazing the whole of the premises. The bill for this service shews either that there had been, as at Merchant Taylors' Hall, no systematic attempt to introduce glass, or that some special cause had occasioned damage to the windows. It was the year of the great frost. The fairly spacious garden lay in the rear toward Drapers' Hall.

The upper part of the Hall was in 1656 paved, partly at the cost of the Master for the time being, with Purbeck and Dunkirk stone, and in 1664 the last memorable stroke was given to the work of more than two centuries by the addition of a gallery on the west side of the garden, extending to the wall of the Drapers' premises.

The latter perished in the Fire two years later ; but the Carpenters escaped, and in 1666 the Court of the Goldsmiths, whose Hall had been badly injured, met here, while their provisional quarters in Grub Street were being prepared, to discuss the business arising out of the loss of their house-property in the flames.

It was on the western side of the Hall that the series of paintings in distemper, three feet in height, twenty-three in length, and nine feet from the ground, was brought to light in 1845, through the casual removal of the canvas, by which they had been screened from view. These admirable works of art appear to belong to the first half of the sixteenth century, and delineate scenes in biblical history, illustrative of the carpenter's craft, the figures being, as usual, arrayed in contemporary European costume. The object of concealment is not clear, unless it was to preserve them from Puritanical fanaticism. Careful drawings of them from the pencil of the late Mr. Fairholt were engraved in Mr. Jupp's book in 1848 ; and three of the original compartments were transferred by very delicate manipulation to the new Hall.

But the process of alteration, arising from a corporate *cacoethes edificandi*, a chronic passion for bricks and mortar and their customary appurtenances, never slackened, until, in August, 1876, the first stone was laid of a new edifice of a palatial type, and all association with the past was dissolved. The Carpenters of course only followed, after all, the example of other Companies in this last respect. What they did, the Fishmongers, Goldsmiths, Drapers, and Clothworkers had already done ; and the Cutlers have since obeyed the same precedent. Yet, while the existing pile was still perfectly sound, perhaps Carpenters' Hall, from its heterogeneous admixture of all schools of architecture and decoration from time to time, might be said to have parted with nearly every feature of archæological value, when it ultimately disappeared, to make room for the splendid structure which now abuts on Throgmorton Avenue. The building, as it stood in 1664, and the present one, completed in 1880, are figured in Mr. Jupp's monograph ; and no person of

taste can hesitate to pronounce for the former, of which reduced representations are here given by permission. All strikes the eye as crude,
naked, and raw. The ancient almshouses have been transplanted to
Godalming.

In 1500 some feeling had been shown for the garden, which was at
that time open, like that of the Drapers, to the country northward,
although the landscape between London Wall, and Highgate was, down
to the earliest effort made to improve Moorfields (1609), far from
picturesque. But in 1644 the whole area seems to have been in grass,
and the Assistants were allowed to dry their clothes there, and, by
themselves or their servants, to enjoy free ingress and egress for the
purpose at all seasons. A considerable portion of the space was in 1664
appropriated to the formation of the additional gallery; and changed
conditions have effaced this attractive feature in many quarters of the
City within a measurable period.

The Carpenters played their part manfully and loyally in the old days
in contributing to burdens and calls of every description, whether
optional or otherwise. As far back as 1455 the Company is found
paying barge-money. In 1461 there are items in the accounts for
meeting Edward IV.; in 1470, Henry VI.; and in 1476, Edward IV.
again on his return from France. The Mayor and Aldermen were on the
last occasion clad in scarlet, and the rest in murrey; there were between
500 and 600 altogether. The same thing occurs when Henry VII.
enters London, and when his queen is crowned. In 1502–3 the Carpenters take part in the setting out of the Midsummer Watch on the
Eve of St. John the Baptist, a civic custom observed with great pomp
and solemnity by the Corporation and Gilds. It was to obtain a
stealthy view of this imposing pageant, that Henry VIII., at the
beginning of his reign, repairèd *incognito* to Cheapside, disguised as one
of his guard. The observance was last kept in Sir Thomas Gresham's
mayoralty in 1548. The Carpenters' share cost between 3*l.* and 4*l.*
The equipment of the representative body sent to meet James I. in
1617 at Knightsbridge on his return from Scotland, amounted to nearly
as much; it included eight whifflers or fifers.

In 1618, after declining to embark any capital in the settlement of
Virginia, the Company gave a small sum toward the emigration movement to that country. In 1620, they were amerced in 30*l.* in aid of the
abortive Palatine cause; and in 1643 the sale of plate to the extent
of 95*l.* 5*s.* was necessitated by demands for the purposes of the Civil
War. In 1650 the arms of the Commonwealth were set up in Carpenters' Hall and the royal insignia removed and destroyed; and ten
years later the Restoration brought back the old *régime* with its own

special incidence.   The historical connection of the Carpenters with the Crown and its transactions closed with the fall of the Stuarts in 1688.

The troubles of the Company were not limited to the exactions of princes in all their various forms ; for at intervals they were embroiled with other Gilds on points touching the interests and rights of the trade. In 1605–6 a rupture arose with the Woodmongers, by reason of an alleged attempt to draw certain freemen from their allegiance ; and other differences were created between them and the Bricklayers and Joiners through the closeness of the lines on which these craftsmen severally worked, and mutual jealousy of encroachment.   But, on the other hand, the Carpenters and Joiners made common cause, and took concerted and successful action, to resist the incorporation of the yeomen or journeymen Sawyers, then in debate.

The exercise of the power of Search and Presentment under the charter has become a mere matter of history ; but during the active life of the Company the right was very stringently enforced, alike internally and externally ; and so long as a despotic *régime* was feasible, it was carried out in a manner and to an extent which reflected the prevalent notions of relationship between rulers and those whom they ruled.   The Carpenters may be said, from the group of nearly allied crafts whose sphere was so intimately connected with their own, to have been more than commonly liable to trespass.

Their worst enemies as a working Gild and as an industry were, however, the gradual abandonment of timber from the reign of James I. as a main ingredient in architecture, and the tendency of commercial policy toward liberalism ; and then the same operating causes, again, favoured the Company as a proprietary fellowship, by developing general wealth and enhancing the value of central sites within the civic boundaries.

LITERARY NOTICES.

A Table of Boord and Timber measure. By Richard Norwood. [About 1620.]
A broadside.

A Table of the severall Scantlings and sorts of Tymber that shall be used in ȳ future building of all Edifices within the Citty of London and Liberties thereof. 26 Nov. 1666. A broadside.

The Art of Fair Building Experienced in the Figures of Several Uprights of Houses, with their Ground Plots Fitting for Persons of all Qualities.   Wherein is divided each Room and Office, according to their most convenient Occasion. With their Heighths, Depths, and Bredths, according to Proportion.   With Rules and Directions for the Placing of the Dome, windows, . . .   Also A Description of the Names and Properties of the Members belonging to the framing of the Timber-Work, . . .   By Pierre Le Muet, Architect in Ordinary to the French

King, and Surveyor of his Designes and Fortifications in the Province of Picardy. Reviewed and Augmented, in this second Edition, with many Figures of the Choicest Buildings and Edifices, . . . Published by Robert Pricke, for the benefit of all Persons that are contented or take delight in the famous Art of Building. . . . Folio, 1675.

The Clockmakers.

THE knowledge and application of clockwork was not much posterior to the discovery or revival of the art of tempering metal; but it seems to have been primarily confined to the construction of mechanical appliances, such as the famous apparatus fashioned by the necromancer Virgilius, to debar ingress into his castle, in the romance, stated to be of Dutch origin, and printed in the beginning of the fifteenth century.

Tradition refers back the manufacture of *clepsydræ*, or water-clocks, to the third century, and of instruments with metallic works and an index acting with a striking-bell to the eleventh, or even the ninth. The art of horology, known to the Greeks, was brought by modern Europeans to perfection very slowly and gradually. Clocks of primitive fabric were to be seen in the fourteenth century in various parts of England, France, Italy, and Germany; they were automatous, but soon ran down, and entailed great trouble and expense. About 1364 the King of France appointed a Governor of the Palace Clock at Paris. As early as 1393, a similar office existed at Venice, and large sums were laid out in the manufacture and repair of chronometers. These appear to have worked with the bell; and the day was divided into so many bells. The old clock of San Giacomo di Rialto at this period weighed 600 lbs., and was very inefficient. Timepieces of the same character are noted as having existed at Westminster, Dover, and Peterborough in England, and at Bologna.[1]

These ancient horological monuments were doubtless constructed and superintended by special experts in mechanism; and it remained for another craft than the Clockmakers, when the art became more generally diffused, and the demand for timepieces increased in a parallel ratio, to take the initiative in supplying these commodities to such persons or institutions as could afford to defray the relatively large cost. The germ and *prima stamina* of the Gild before us are to be found in the muniments of the Blacksmiths who, both here and on the Continent, once and long occupied a station importantly differing from the workmen of the same denomination familiar to ourselves and our immediate predecessors. Under our account of that Company we have shown the wide scope of labour and enterprise which its members in their varied functions embraced, and have produced ample evidence to establish that the Clockmakers can be considered of recent origin only so far as concerns their existence in an independent form. During many centuries the sun-dial, the hour-glass, and the water-clock sufficed the limited requirements, as they represented the gauge of the mechanical ingenuity, of the nation; and the first departure toward a more intelligent and trustworthy principle came from the worker in metals, who gradually discerned in the malleability and pliability of iron by fire, and in the use of the screw, the means of producing an apparatus for the less troublesome registration of time. We cannot suppose that we possess the most rudimentary efforts of the inventor of clocks with metallic works; but it is sufficient for our present purpose to state that, when the Clockmakers' Company was constituted, in 1631, the science had already made very considerable progress, and the Coffin-Clock was an established fact of some standing. The earliest manufactures of this type were, no doubt, tentative in their construction, and destitute of external embellishment; and the richly decorated cases, which are to be seen in European museums, belong to a later period. The extensive employment of wood for the coffin-clock brought the Blacksmiths into contact with the Woodmongers, just as their long command of the trade in the works not merely postponed the institution of the Clockmakers as a separate Gild, but retarded its development, when it had been actually incorporated, by retaining a share of the commerce in the old-fashioned school of clock and a certain proportion of the operative skill.

---

[1] Hazlitt's *Venetian Republic*, 1860, iv. 344-7.

In spite of charters, the different crafts traversed each other more or less in early times ; and such cross-trading was an everlasting source of friction and discord.

We are enabled by the records of the Court of Aldermen and the Blacksmiths' Company from 1627 to 1631 to judge the combination of agencies which eventuated in the establishment of the Gild at present under notice. At the first-mentioned date, the foreign competition in the English clock trade had become a topic of anxiety and discussion ; and alien manufacturers and artisans were, it is distinctly said, protected by a warrant under the privy seal. The aggrieved freemen of the Blacksmiths' Company, being clockmakers by craft, sought redress, but do not appear to have succeeded ; and the next step taken was an endeavour in 1628 to persuade the Blacksmiths to arrange an amalgamation. This

ARMS, 1739.

alliance the latter declined in January, 1628–9, after a somewhat protracted negotiation ; and the Clockmakers, as the best and perhaps sole means left of improving their position, decided on applying for a charter. During the years 1629–30, several meetings of the trade were held, to consider how the petition should be framed, and in what manner the attendant outlay was to be subscribed. In the course of 1630 72*l.* were guaranteed in writing by sixteen persons, of whom the largest contributor, Roger Johnson, agreed to find 10*l.* ; and the Commissioners for Suits having referred the petition to the Court of Aldermen, and a favourable report having been returned, the process was in due time brought to completion.

The charter was dated August 22, 1631, and founded the Association under the style of " The Master, Wardens, and Fellowship of the Art or Mistery of Clockmaking of the City of London." The tenor of the instrument was unusually comprehensive ; for it admitted to the advantages of the concession all clockmakers within the City, its liberties and suburbs, or residing near the same, whether freemen of the City, or foreigners, or other persons using the art. The chief aim and end of the measure were, therefore, precisely what the petitioners had solicited, surveillance and protection. No one was excluded ; but all were to be under control.

The Company acquired the right of using a common seal, of electing annually from the general body of freemen two or more Assistants, to co-operate with the Master and Wardens, and of making bye-laws for the government and guidance of members, with the power of search and presentment within the City and its liberties, and over ten miles compass.

INITIAL ORNAMENT OF CHARTER.

Its jurisdiction extended to watchmakers and mathematical-instrument makers. There was the usual licence to hold lands and hereditaments in free burgage. But we miss some of the provisions, which occur in other charters, and especially we note the absence of any allusion to the Clothing or Livery, which was not obtained till 1766, notwithstanding the fact that it is made one of the original bye-laws of 1632. In 1652, the Committee for Corporations demanded an inspection of the charter, which was handed back again without comment.

The failure of the treaty with the Blacksmiths had so far, then, borne unexpectedly good fruit; and if the new organization was not in a position to exclude aliens, it was at full liberty to utilize its privileges for the promotion of discipline and efficiency.

The bye-laws, drawn up as a natural sequel, bear date August 11, 1632, and comprise no fewer than sixty-two Articles, to which the only addition was a sixty-third, made in 1796, thirty years posterior to the grant of a Livery, in reference to the refusal of a Freeman to serve on his election as Liveryman.

The authority vested in the Company proved, after all, inadequate to the repression of irregularity and fraud. But the attempt to obtain legislation in furtherance of the object failed from the insufficiency of funds. One source of the weakness of the new Corporation was the absence of a place of meeting and of a properly constituted Livery. It was a Craft Gild, established on a popular basis, and was unprovided with the necessary accommodation for receiving anything approaching a full complement of members; and at the very outset its executive was assailed by hostile criticism and action, which embarrassed the Company year after year.

A serious dispute indeed arose between the Court of Assistants and the commonalty in 1656, relative to the deficiency of a Hall. A section of the freemen complained, among other points, on which they held that the Court did not perform its duty, that there was no proper provision for general assemblies, agreeably to the charter and bye-laws, and that they were often summoned to alehouses and taverns, to the great disparagement of them all ; while the means of supplying this

WARDEN'S BADGE.   MASTER'S BADGE OR JEWEL.

capital want had been otherwise applied. It was further alleged, that apprentices were multiplied beyond reasonable measure, that too much freedom was allowed to aliens, and that the power of search was negligently exercised. This censure was not unanimous, and the Court drew up a vindication of its policy. But the matter ultimately dropped.

The agitation was not resuscitated, and it may under actual circumstances be of insignificant relevance ; but the contention that no proper and reasonable facilities were afforded for the assembly of the freemen of the Gild by the appointment of a common Hall, seeing that the charter was directed to them, both denizens and foreigners, might at one

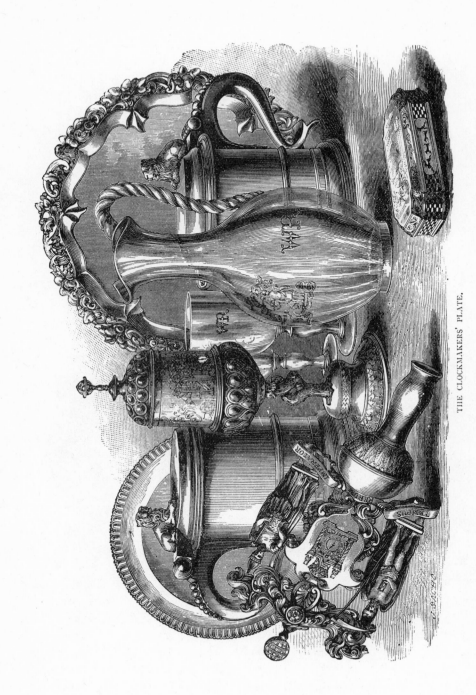

THE CLOCKMAKERS' PLATE.

THE ADAMS CUP.

time, had it been pressed at law, have invalidated the constitution in this, as well as in many other analogous, cases. For here, as elsewhere, the entire commonalty was the electoral body down to the approval of a Livery, and was entitled to a voice in all questions outside general administrative details; and moreover, under one of the bye-laws of 1632, every freeman was to be summoned to attend the quarterly meetings, and to pay a fine on default.

The reproach of convening the members in taverns and such places was perhaps met by the hire from other Companies of their Halls for special occasions. In the Founders' books under August 2, 1702, we meet with this entry, for instance: " The Clockmakers' Company to have use of the parlour for their meetings, at a rental of ten pounds per annum;" and in 1706 the arrangement was still in force, and the Founders were asking for higher terms.

The annals of the Company from the middle of the seventeenth century, down to the point of time when it ceased to exert any interference with the trade, are a somewhat monotonous narrative of the incessant and unavailing correspondence with the City and the Government, in order to procure support in encouraging the native manufacture against the destructive competition of Germany and Switzerland. The Gild had entered on its career in 1631 as the champion of the product of English labour against the undue preponderance of that of strangers; but, as we have signified, the terms of the charter were too wide to favour a monopoly; and to the foreign resident, with his at least equal proficiency and greater thrift, was superadded, in process of time, the foreign importer. These two elements of disintegration, against which the Clockmakers vainly essayed to induce the authorities to proceed, by statute or otherwise, proved in the highest degree injurious to their corporate and individual interests, and deprived the Company of its expected influence and sincere aspirations for good. In common with its ancient foemen the Blacksmiths and the majority of the trading fellowships, which had their daybreak in wholly different conditions of society and feeling, it has found itself reduced to the position of a charitable and hospitable community, with a rather checkered and comparatively brief historical retrospect. It forms one of the group of Gilds whose charter was never renewed. It had its own sorrows; but it avoided the less favourable incidence of notoriety and wealth.

The government of the Company consists of the Master, Wardens, and Court of Assistants, the members of which have, since 1766, been selected from the Livery by show of hands. But although freemen are qualified by the charter and by law, they are never in practice chosen. Therefore the government is here again not strictly in accordance with the constitution. Under the Act of Common Council, those made free of this body were disqualified from joining any other, and a case occurred in 1772, where a clockmaker (Mr. Lotall) who had paid his fees to the Founders in ignorance of this fact, was obliged to apply for release and the reimbursement of his money.

In 1882 the Livery was said to number seventy-three,[1] and the freemen were roughly computed at one hundred.

The estimated aggregate income of the Company from all sources is probably about 1,100*l.* a year, the bulk of which is fiduciary. It is believed that the trusts are loyally carried out ; but the accounts are not published. We understand that a statement of the receipts and expenditure is in preparation for the use of the Court. The particulars furnished in the History, a handsome volume printed in 1881, of which we have been favoured with the loan, are not very full, and do not include the corporate property.

The Clockmakers count on their roll of members nearly all the most distinguished masters of the art, from David Ramsey, the first Master of the Company, to William James Frodsham, F.R.S. The names which are perhaps most deserving of commemoration are those of David Ramsey, Edward East, Ahasuerus Fromantel, father and son, Thomas Tompion, George Graham, F.R.S., John Harris, John Pepis or Pepys, Daniel Quare, and Thomas Earnshaw. Of these and others a sufficiently copious notice will be found in the History of the Company. Charles I. when Prince, is said to have been fond of playing at tennis for an *Edwardus East,* or a watch of East's fabric. Ramsey was a friend of George Heriot, the eminent jeweller of Edinburgh. Pepis, who was Master in 1707, was apprenticed to John Harris. A watch made by him for Lord Baltimore, and in which his name is spelled in two different ways, is stated to be in the possession of a descendant. In the accounts of the Founders' Company, under 1694 is the following :—" Paid Mr. Newton for an eight-day clock . . . £10 0 0."

But a peculiar interest is attached to Tompion and Graham, inasmuch as they were both interred in Westminster Abbey, and a slab placed in the nave to perpetuate the circumstance. This monument remained *in situ* till 1838, or thereabout, when it disappeared ; but, a great stir being made in the papers at the time, Dean Stanley, one of the very few sensible men connected with the Church, caused the missing stone to be found and restored. Its removal was a piece of typical stupidity, bigotry, and insolence.

The Company enjoys the particular, and indeed almost unique, dis-

---

[1] In 1892, seventy-four.

tinction of possessing by purchase and gift a most valuable and representative assemblage of clocks, watches, and other cognate objects,
besides a library of printed books illustrative of the craft.   These collections, in the absence of any other depository, are preserved at Guildhall,
and of the books there is a special catalogue.[1]

Of the corporate plate, and of a few other characteristic items, we
have been enabled by the politeness of the members of the Court to
furnish representations.   The original coat of arms, granted by Clarencieux in 1671, exhibits as one of the supporters the Wild Man, who
occurs so frequently on foreign coins, and who has recently become the
object of archæological research ; but in the bearings now used he is
replaced by a winged figure of Time.

LITERARY NOTICE.

The Artificial Clock-maker.   A Treatise of Watch and Clockwork.   By W. D., M.A.
The Second Edition, enlarged.   12mo, 1700.

The Coach and Coach=Harness Makers.

THE evolution of the carriage in its various types from the cart took
place when the use of a covered and more commodious vehicle for locomotion than either a horse or a waggon suggested itself on a more
frequent and systematic resort to ceremonial progresses or the transit
from place to place of aged or delicate persons.   Even when, in the
sixteenth century, travelling and hunting equipages came into employment here and abroad, the origin of the fashion long remained perceptible in the forms of the new conveyances ; and the most elegant
and costly carriage designed for ladies following the chase betrayed its
parentage alike in the body and the wheels.

---

[1] Compare the account of the Coachmakers' Library, *infrà.*

As early as 1485, nearly a century prior to the reputed introduction of such a luxury by the Earl of Arundel, Henry VII. entered London after his victory at Bosworth in a close chariot, probably of large dimensions, and drawn by several horses. But it is evident that at or about this date the vehicle so called was in more or less general employment ; for in the City Ordinance of 1517, uniting the Pouchmakers with the Leathersellers, the former are said to have among other articles on sale coverings for chariots, or, in the words of the document, " barehidys for coveryng of chariettes."

The institution of coaches and the installation of the Dutchman, Wilhelm Boonen, as coachman to Queen Elizabeth in 1564, soon spread the fashion among the aristocracy of rank and wealth, and made coach-building a profitable and prominent trade ; in 1598, a popular writer of the day affects to represent the fashion as an actual economy, by reason of the great expense which used to be previously incurred for riding equipages. He tells us that a lady of rank, with her gentle-women, maid, and children, could be accommodated, it was reckoned, in a coach at less cost and with more credit, as, in place of a single coachman she required six or eight serving-men to attend her ; and in 1605, according to Stow's Continuator, caroaches or carriages came into ordinary use. The latter, at all events, grew plentiful in James the First's reign, and were viewed by the watermen and chairmen with considerable jealousy.

The present Company was incorporated by charter, dated May 31, 1677, and was appointed to consist of a Master, three Wardens, and a Court of Assistants, chosen from the commonalty or freemen. But, in 1687 and 1694, the Court of Aldermen gave a Livery, which has since continued. The bye-laws, issued in 1677, are with slight variations still in force.

In 1882, the Court consisted of twenty-three Assistants, the Senior, Renter, and Junior Wardens, and the Master. The charter conferred a licence in mortmain, not exceeding 300l. a year, exclusively of the Hall, and the power of search, the latter subject to a warrant of the Court of King's Bench. This right is no longer exercised ; but it originally extended to the Cities of London and Westminster and their suburbs, and over twenty miles' compass. The area under jurisdiction was divided into four Walks : the Middle Walk, Piccadilly Walk, Out Walk, and Low Land Walk, each of which was visited at quarterly intervals, and all shops and factories entered and inspected.

In September, 1881, the numbers were returned at 127, and in 1892 at 117, inclusive. Although the estate is of moderate extent, and yields an amount which fluctuated in the course of ten years between 2,025l.

and 1,279*l.* with an apparent tendency to shrinkage, there seems by careful management to have been a surplus in each of the ten years, 1871–80 ; and these accumulations the executive is evidently disposed to apply to public and practical purposes.

The Company at one period chose year by year Stewards, who were under an obligation to defray the cost of the Court breakfasts and dinners ; but this usage fell into desuetude, and the entertainments given both to the Court and Livery are charged to the general fund.

The present Hall in Noble Street, of which the Coachmakers have, since 1878, let the basement,[1] formerly belonged to the Scriveners, of whom it was purchased, May 13, 1703, with four tenements in Oat Lane, for 1,600*l.* This sum was raised by voluntary subscriptions among 109 members of the Court and Livery, who contributed altogether 2,030*l. 7s. 6d.* In a sufficiently uneventful career, the only incident of a public character was the meeting in 1780 of the Protestant Association, which led the way to the Gordon No Popery riots.

The Hall was refurnished in 1843 by a second subscription of 257*l.* 10*s.* The wording of the charter of 1677, which excepts the Hall from the aggregate annual amount acquirable in real property, might favour the presumption that there had been an anterior one ; but to this there is no explicit reference. In 1864, the Operative Coachmakers' Industrial Exhibition was held in Noble Street ; and the Company has subsequently exerted itself to promote technical knowledge among members of the trade, and to support charities. In the eight years, 1873–80, the former object absorbed out of a limited income 668*l.* 1*s.* 1*d.*, and the latter 437*l.* 15*s.* Special attention may be directed to the details set out in the Parliamentary Returns of 1882 under the head of *Education.*

In 1867, a resolution was formed to rebuild the Hall, which entailed a loan of 3,000*l.*, on the security of the building and the Oat Lane ground rents ; and in the following year the first grant of money was made toward the formation of a Library of Reference, which is now open on Saturdays, and contains, besides books, drawings and photographs of the objects on view at the International Exhibition of Carriages in 1873. With the single exception of the Clockmakers, no other Company has made an attempt of this kind.

---

[1] The practice of appropriating the basement and upper storey of valuable City frontages to different objects was of very ancient origin. The original St. Paul's School (not Colet's), was kept over the *Black Eagle* in St. Paul's Churchyard ; and when William Hobson, the rich and famous Haberdasher, purchased at the Reformation some religious buildings in the Poultry, the rooms over his store were let as chambers.

In 1879, an exhibition of drawings, books, and models was held at the Mansion House; and the Lord Mayor distributed prizes, given by the Coachmakers, to competitors as well as to the pupils of its own Art and Technical School.

Quite recently (1891), there has been a new movement set on foot, under the same courageous auspices, for improving the vehicles of different kinds employed in this country, and the particulars have been published of a competition open to all British subjects resident within the United Kingdom, and of the prizes to be awarded.[1]

LITERARY NOTICES.

A Proclamation for the restraint of the multitude, and promiscuous vse of Coaches, about London and Westminster   19 Jan. 1634–5.   A broadside.

The Coaches' Overthrow. Or, a Jovial Exaltation of divers Tradesmen, and others, for the suppression of troublesome Hackney Coaches.   [1636.]   A ballad.

Coach and Sedan, Pleasantly disputing for Place and Precedence.   The Brewer's Cart being Moderator.   [By Henry Peacham.]   4to, 1636.   With an engraving on the title, representing a coach, a sedan, and a brewer's cart.

To the Right Honble. the Commons of England assembled in Parliament, The humble Petition of the auntient Hackney-Coachmen of London and Westminster. [About 1645.]   A broadside.

A Proclamation to repress the Abuses of Hackney Coaches in the Cities of London and Westminster, and the Suburbs thereof.   1660.   A broadside.

A Proclamation . . . to repress the excess of Gilding of Coaches and Chariots. 1661.   A broadside.

A Copy of a Printed Letter from J. C. to a Post-master in the Country, with Directions about the Management of the Designe for putting down Stage-Coaches.   Folio, 1672.

Stage-Coaches Vindicated : or, Certain Animadversions and Reflections upon several Papers writ by J. C. of the Inner Temple, Gent., against Stage-Coaches.   Folio, [1672].

---

[1] All drawings and models must be delivered by the end of April.   Detailed particulars of the competitions may be obtained from Mr. P. de Lande Long, the clerk of the Coachmakers' Company, Noble Street.

In the first class a prize of 30*l.* by Mr. G. N. Hooper, and others of 20*l.* by Mr. A. A. Clark, and 10*l.* by the Company are offered for the three best models of an improved four-wheel cab suited to the traffic of London, or a four-wheel close cab body with a single or double Victoria body with the same under-carriage and wheels, available for both bodies, so as to provide close carriages for winter use and open ones for summer. In the second class, Mr. G. A. Thrupp offers a prize 6*l.* 6*s.*, to be competed for by technical drawing classes, for the best set of three drawings of the side elevation of any sort of carriage.   The third competition is for working drawings of a pair-horse body brake ; and the fourth for working drawings of an omnibus for private use to carry six inside.   In the fifth competition, Lady Wallace offers 10*l.* 10*s.* among former prize winners only, for a fully-coloured drawing of a Victoria on perch carriage and C springs ; and in a sixth competition Mr. Boulnois, M.P., offers 10*l.* for the model of a gig body.   The prize winners will have the freedom of the Company conferred on them if their drawings or models deserve it.

A Proclamation for restraining the number and abuses of Hackney Coaches in and
about the Cities of London and Westminster, and the Suburbs thereof, and
Parishes comprised within the Bills of Mortality. Whitehall, 25 Nov., 1687. A
broadside.

Reasons to augment the Number of Hackney Coaches, within the Bills of Mortality, from Four Hundred to Six or Eight Hundred; most humbly tendred to
the consideration of Both Houses of Parliament. Folio [about 1690].

The Cooks.

THE Cooks appear to have been originally associated with the Pie-
Bakers or Pastelers; and a common scale or tariff for articles on sale by
them was framed and approved in 1350 and 1378. The prices are of
course very curious, and all deal with roast dishes, except that eggs, ten
for a penny, are included. A charge was made for the paste, pie, and
trouble, where the customer found his material.

This was the community, no doubt, which is mentioned by Fitz-
stephen, Leland, and Stow, as clustering about Thames Street and East
Cheap in the time of Henry II.

In 28 Edward I. (1299–1300) the *publicæ coquinæ*, as Leland calls
them, appear to have multiplied so inconveniently in the neighbourhood
of the wharves, where the wine was unshipped from the Continent, that
the Corporation, on receipt of a royal writ, undertook to remove a
portion of what was popularly known as Cooks' Row, and to erect on
the site warehouses, with vaults and cellars, for the merchants of Bordeaux.

In 1379 regulations were made, prohibiting cooks and pie-bakers from
buying and selling any victuals before ten o'clock in the morning, lest
they might regrate them; from baking rabbits in pasties, from putting
the offal of poultry in the same, from selling beef-pasties as venison, and
from using whole geese, halves, or quarters for this purpose.

The term Pasteler occurs in Stow and elsewhere without any very
definite or clear meaning. The term seems to have been originally

applied to a pie-baker, as distinguished from the ordinary cook ; but he made meat or game pasties, not our modern pastry. The confections sold at a later period by the grocer were sweetmeats.

The Cooks of London were incorporated, as we learn only from an *inspeximus* of George III., by a charter of 27 Edward IV., directed to his well-beloved subjects the honest and free men of the Mistery of Cooks of the City of London, that they, and all of them, should be in substance and name one body and one commonalty perpetual, with power to make two Masters or Governors, two Wardens, and a Court of Assistants to govern the affairs of the Mistery, to have a common seal, and to frame bye-laws and vary the same. A power of search and jurisdiction was conferred over the Cities of London and Westminster, their suburbs and liberties, and a radius of four miles.

In a list of the City Companies, drawn up in 1501–2, the Cooks do not occur ; but the *Pastelers* rank fifty-ninth in the roll, and are classed with those which had no Livery. We take this to be an entry of the *Cooks* under an informal title.

We are able to collect very little of the early history of the Gild, whose records have been lost, till we arrive at a much later reign, and find that in 1614 the governing body applied for a new charter, and obtained it. But the civic authorities came forward to shew cause against its validity, so soon as it was made known that it had been sealed.

It was alleged by the Court of Aldermen (21 May, 1614), that this charter had been obtained by the Cooks " secretly and surreptitiously," with a dispensing *non obstante*, and on their complaint the Commissioners for Suits referred the question to the Lord Chief Justice Coke, who was further authorized by the Lords of the Council to suspend the execution of the charter till further orders.

The Chief Justice reported that the charter was against the common law and the charters of the City, and that it was exceptionable as giving an unlimited power of search, which might lead to abuse. It traversed, moreover, an Order in Council of the 26th March, 1614, as to the limit to be put on the storage of barrels in any one house ; and Coke disliked the *non obstante* clause.

The result was, that for the time the charter stood in abeyance, and it probably lapsed, as there is no further trace of it ; and the Cooks, as we have mentioned, are not in possession of any of their papers, which perished in the Fire, the original charter inclusive.

The present government of the Company is composed of two Masters, two Wardens, and twenty-four Assistants. . The Masters, Wardens, and eight Assistants make a Court. In 1882, the number of freemen, including 98 on the Livery, was 249.[1] During the ten years 1871–80, thirty joined the Livery on their own application.

The Cooks took a sub-share of the Mercers' Manor at the time of the Plantation of Ulster in 1609–15, and have received of late years a fair annual return for their outlay, but with a tendency to shrinkage. In 1882, the Company, whose general income from all sources had then increased through the lapse of a City ground-lease, entertained a fear that its corporate resources would ultimately diminish in consequence of the depression of agricultural rents. From this portion of its revenue it has long been accustomed to apply a considerable yearly sum in pensions to poor freemen and unfortunate members of the Livery, in donations to the National School of Cookery, in the gratuitous instruction of female pupils belonging to the City ward schools in the culinary art, and in supplementing the allowances distributed under various trusts.

One of the sources of charitable endowment is a yearly rent-charge of 28*l.* on the City estate of the Clothworkers' Company, arising out of 500*l.* paid by John Shield to the latter in 1616, and assigned by his will (1617) to the Cooks for certain eleemosynary purposes at the testator's birthplace, East Allandale, within the royalty of Hexham, in the county of York.

The Hall used to be in Aldersgate Street, and escaped the Great Fire. The Saddlers, Stationers, and Painter-Stainers met there, while their own Halls were being rebuilt (1668–70), and Maitland mentions it in 1756. The freehold still belongs to the Company ; but it has been converted to other purposes, and at present swells the corporate receipts. Numbers 10–12, Aldersgate Street, occupy the site, and in 1875 were let on an eighty years' lease at 800*l.* a year.

The participation of the Company in historical events, and its vicissitudes of fortune, are only ascertainable, owing to the loss of its archives, from casual or collateral references. From such material we have already furnished a few notices of its early condition as an unincorporated Fellowship, and there seems to be little more to add. The purely accidental preservation of some of the particulars of a general lottery in 1567 partly helps to shew that many other such social traits have failed to survive. We see from a unique series of printed documents in an old private library, that the City Gilds embarked in the venture, and that Richard Tomson drew No. 268,094 with a motto more commendable for its practical spirit than its metrical accuracy :—

> "We Cooks of London, which work early and late,
> If anything be left, God send us part."

For the Brewers, Armourers, Haberdashers, and other Companies

---

[1] In 1892, according to Whitaker, the Livery numbered 69 only.

there were tickets with similar verses. The balance of money remaining after the provision of the 400,000 prizes (for there were to be no blanks) was stated to be applicable to public works.

LITERARY NOTICES.

This is the Boke of Cokery. 4to, R. Pynson, 1500.

$*_*$ A MS. of this work in the library at Holkham was edited by Mrs. Napier, 4to, 1831. But the lady was not aware that it had been previously printed.

A Noble Booke of Feastes Royall and of Cookerie for Princes Housholds or any other estate. 4to, John Byddell [about 1530].

$*_*$ A reprint of the edition of 1500.

A New Boke of Cokery. 8vo, T. Raynald, [about 1545].

$*_*$ Frequently reprinted.

A Booke of Cookery. 12mo, 1584, 1591, 1594, 1620, 1629, 1634, 1650.

Cookerye for all manner of Dutch Vyctuall. Entered at Stationers' Hall in 1590.

The Art of Cookery Refin'd and Augmented. By Joseph Cooper. 12mo, 1654.

Archimagirus Anglo-Gallicus; or, Excellent and Approved Receipts and Experiments in Cookery. By Sir Theodore Mayerne, Knight. 8vo, 1658.

The Compleat Cook. 8vo, 1662.

The Whole Body of Cookery Dissected. By Will Rabisha. 8vo, 1661, 1673.

The Accomplist Cook; or, The Art and Mystery of Cookery. By Robert May. 8vo, 1660. Fifth Edition, 8vo, 1685.

The Art of Cookery, In Imitation of Horace's Art of Poetry. By Dr. William King 8vo [about 1720].

$*_*$ Copious notices of Cookery-books will be found in Hazlitt's *Old Cookery Books and Ancient Cuisine*, 1836, and in his *Collections and Notes*, 1876-92.

The Coopers.

IN common with many, if not most, of the other Civic Corporations, this Company existed as a prescriptive body from a period legally almost "beyond the memory of man," inasmuch as they seem to be traceable back to the reign of Edward II., and to have been at that period under certain obligations and exemptions, cognate to those belonging to all similar Fraternities in London, and emanating equally from the Lord Mayor and Court of Aldermen.

As the records of disagreement among members of the Crafts frequently form the source of valuable and interesting disclosures in relation to their history, so cases of misfortune and misdemeanour admit us behind the scenes, where in the ordinary course of affairs we should have heard and known nothing. The earliest trace of the London cooper is associated with the seizure of two small stocks for debt in 1310. The insolvents were Robert le Cuver and Alice le Cuver, relict of Walter le Cuver ; they were probably relatives ; and the character of the patronymic shews how close we are to the border-land, where the surname still retained its practical significance. The account sets forth

AN ANCIENT COOPERAGE.

that from the former party were taken two great cuves or tubs, value 19s., one lathe and one lathestock, value 18d., one ale-tun, value 18d., nine hoops, value 5d. ; while the female debtor or partner possessed goods estimated only at 7s. 2d. The estate was worth about 12l. of our money.

In 1396 the Court of Aldermen agreed to proposed Articles for the better government of the Coopers' trade, and particularly for the suppression of a noxious usage by which oil and soap barrels were sold to brewers and others for holding ale and other liquor. The Coopers therefore sought hereby leave to appoint overseers to inspect places of business, so that all unlawful barrels and vessels might be seized, and the holders fined, " for the avoiding of such deceits, for the love of God, and as a work of charity." A renewal of these ordinances in 1409 testifies to the chronic proneness of such provisions to oblivion and neglect, especially where the temptation was powerful.

The Coopers encountered difficulties analogous to those suffered by the Saddlers, in the manufacture by unauthorized persons of tubs and barrels made of unsound or green wood. In 1413, the case occurred, for instance, of a fishmonger, who had had clandestinely constructed in his own dwelling-house as many as 260 vessels, namely barrels and firkins, of wood that was not pure, and was sawn from the middle, and were of untrue measure, the barrels which should have contained thirty gallons holding twenty-eight only, and the firkins $6\frac{1}{2}$ in lieu of $7\frac{1}{2}$. The 260 vessels were taken by order to Guildhall, and after being viewed and certified to be false were burned.

OLD ARMS.

The practice of marking casks, in order to protect buyers of ale and beer against untrue measures, as well as unwholesome vessels, was therefore clearly no superfluous precaution. The delinquent, in the case just reported, may be reasonably suspected of having converted disused fish-casks to the purpose, as the soap-makers applied those which had held soap or oil; and the development of the foreign wine trade opened an additional channel for fraud, by inducing the brewers to purchase for their own purposes casks which did not follow the English standard. The movement in the direction of reform was due to the influence and representations of Sir Richard Whittington, who, as we have demonstrated under the account of the Brewers, had in the later portion of his official career paid far greater attention to these details than some persons at that time found agreeable.

In 9 Henry IV. (1407–8) a decree of the Court of Aldermen made it obligatory on the part of all coopers to bring their goods into the Chamber of London to be marked, prior to output, under certain penalties; and, as a means in each case of verifying the maker, a duplicate of his mark, with his name annexed, was entered on record. But in 1420, 1428, and 1440 the renewal of these regulations told the common tale of lax observance and stealthy infringement. Dishonest artisans or their masters, both freemen and foreigners, were still relying on impunity in employing unseasoned wood and giving short measure, independently of fabricating the official stamp.

This form of security was accounted of sufficient consequence to the trade and the community to become the subject of legislation in later reigns. But the primitive constitution was limited to the authority and protection of the Court of Aldermen, before which the early Wardens, two in number, were sworn. The applications for support in the exercise of their acknowledged jurisdiction were periodical, and denoted the necessity for enlarged powers, which the Corporation never failed to concede.

COOPERS' MARKS, A.D. 1420.

But the extension of the demand for Coopers' work for a wide variety of commercial objects rendered it evident to the overseers of the Craft that the real course was to follow the precedent of other bodies, and place themselves under royal as well as municipal shelter.

As recently as 1488 we find that the Wardens had once more appealed to Guildhall for additional privileges, which were duly accorded with a presumable knowledge of the merits of the case, when, in 16 Henry VII., the momentous step was at length taken of petitioning for a charter,

to which a powerful inducement existed, as we shall subsequently learn
more at large, in the shape of valuable consideration thereupon con-
tingent.   This grant, by writ of Privy Seal, dated April 29th, 1501, and
by authority of Parliament, erected the Coopers into a perpetual commonalty under the style of The Master and Wardens of the Commonalty
of the Freemen of the Mistery of Coopers of the City of London and the
Suburbs thereof, with the usual powers, so far as it lay with the King
to bestow them (*quantum in nobis est*), including a faculty of acquiring,
holding, and alienating real property for the support of the poor men
and women of the Craft, provided that the same was not already held
of the Crown *in capite*, the right of pleading and being impleaded, and
liberty to elect officers and to make ordinances.

The special features of this Tudor charter were its limitation to the
royal prerogative and its claim to parliamentary sanction ; and the
second and governing one of Charles II., under writ of privy seal,
August 30, 1662, preserved the saving clause without the former constitutional stipulation.   But the later grant created a Court of Assistants,
seventeen in number, and appointed the members in the first instance
according to the usual practice.

A grant of arms was made by Thomas Wrythe or Wriothesley,
Garter, September 27, 1509 : Gyronny of eight *gules* and *sable*, on a
chevron, between three annulets *or*, a royne between two adzes *azure*,
on a chief *vert*, three lilies slipped, stalked, and leaved, *argent*.   CREST :
On a wreath a heath-cock, with wings expanded *azure*, powdered with
annulets *or*, in the beak a lily *argent*.   *Supporters :* Two camels *gules*,
bridled *or*, powdered with annulets of the last.   The ancient motto was :
Gaude Maria Virgo ; the modern one is : *Love as Brethren.*

The Coopers received only three charters, that of 1685, pursuant to
the *Quo Warranto*, included ; but various Acts of Parliament affected
and controlled them.   The 23 Henry VIII., cap. 4, vested in the Wardens jointly with one of the Mayor's sergeants, a right to view and gauge
all casks within the City of London and its suburbs, and over two miles
radius from Cornhill, and to affix a mark to each ; and 31 Elizabeth, cap.
8, directed that "for the true gauging of vessels brought from beyond
the seas, converted by brewers for the utterance and sale of ale and
beer," the brewers should not employ any such vessels, before they have
been seen and passed by the Coopers.

The bye-laws of the Company are more numerous than its charters,
and range in date between 1396 and 1741.   They were originally
framed in the first-named year, long before the date of incorporation,
to place a check on certain practices affecting the welfare and credit of
the industry ; in 1407–8, 1409, 1420, 1428, 1440, and 1488, they were

renewed and amplified to meet continued irregularities and frauds in cooperage ; but subsequently to the first charter, when their operation was to a certain extent superseded by a more definite government, they were far less frequently multiplied, and we find only four issues of them in nearly as many centuries, namely, 22 Henry VII. (May 9th, 1507), 3 Elizabeth (June 10th, 1561), 14 Charles II. (May 8th, 1663), and 14 George II. (March 3rd, 1740–1).   The last is the governing code.

The Executive at present consists, under the charter of 1662, of a Master, three Wardens, of whom one is Renter Warden, and sixteen Assistants.   The Upper and Under Wardens are elected by the whole Livery, the Renter by the Court.   This is quite an exceptional practice, and confers on the main body an interest and estate in the Company, which, it is believed, have not proved disadvantageous.

It was not until 1654 that the question of changing election-day from Whit-Sunday to the day following was formally mooted ; and the alteration was not made before 1658.   In the latter year, instead of a potation and cakes after the proceedings, a dinner (not a feast) was instituted at the cost of the Masters and Wardens, each subscribing 40s.

In 1882 the Livery was said to number about 170, and in 1892 it is given as 200, whereas in 1848 it is stated to amount to 318, and the number of freemen was not known.   In the old lists, where the order of precedence is generally unofficial and arbitrary, the Company is variously placed ; in 1501–2 it is thirty-seventh, and is said to have a Livery of 17.   In 1439, 40 paid quarterage ; in 1440, 43 ; in 1442, 46 ; in 1443, 51 ; but the figures fluctuated from year to year.   In 1547, they stood at 152 ; in 1699, at 126.   In 1725 the return to Parliament was 203.

At what date the Company obtained leave to assume a Livery, however, does not seem to be ascertainable ; but it is most likely that it did so, with or without permission, immediately after incorporation. In 1725, during the debate on the Act for Regulating Elections within the City of London (11 George I., c. 18), all the Companies were required to make certified returns of their respective Liveries, and a declaration of the circumstances of the grant ; and the Coopers were unable to state the origin of theirs, merely pleading that it had existed time out of mind, and was specified in the bye-laws of 1507.   They might have gone a little further back, as we have seen, so far as the usage was concerned ; but it is clear that no previous documentary voucher was then, or is at present, forthcoming.   In 1523 the goodman Charley gave 8l. to the use of the "Suit."   In 1540, an annual dinner, whereof the cost was not to exceed 28s. 6d., was ordered for the members of the Livery who attended the Lord Mayor to Westminster or elsewhere to be sworn.

There is a notice in the Accounts, under 1557, of seven young men taken up into the Livery, and paying 2s. each "for their samples." Their proficiency in the Craft was tested by the Wardens prior to admission, and a fee charged.

The fees payable on taking up the freedom by patrimony or servitude are 4l. 16s. ; by purchase, 15l. 13s. 6d. Admission to the Livery by patrimony or servitude costs 22l. 3s. 6d., by purchase, 28l. 1s. 6d, On election to the Court, liverymen have to pay 42l.

Coopers' Hall, in Basinghall Street, was originally erected on a freehold site granted by John Baker, Citizen and Cooper, under his will, April 13, 1490, with all his lands and tenements and their appurtenances in the parish of St. Michael Bassishaw, to the Wardens and Fellowship of the Gild, so soon as it should receive incorporation, and subject to certain religious observances on behalf of the testator. These dispositions in favour of the Coopers naturally stimulated,—concurrently with the recognised need for a more stable and authoritative government,—the desire to secure the charter, which did not, however, come till 1501. That step at once entitled the Company to the property ; but some years evidently elapsed before any definite plan was formed for utilizing a portion of it as a place of meeting and business, in lieu of the inconvenient and undignified practice of assembling at taverns, and of being beholden to the Wardens for the safe custody of the archives.

As in other instances, the Company was indebted to a particular individual, John Heith, Upper Warden in 1543, for initiating, and supporting from his private resources, this most important measure of reform. Heith in fact subsidized the undertaking both in money and material, supplying the principal share of the timber, besides weekly payments toward the wages, and other gifts, and, as the contemporary narrative quaintly and prettily puts it, "praying God to send many more such benefactors to the said Craft."

The building, which was of timber, was not even substantially finished till 1547, when a feast celebrated the eventful occasion, and Heith contributed the venison. The total cost was under 50s.

Those were the days when the street consisted of little more than a few detached mansions or tenements, including Basing Hall, to which it owed its name, and which is associated with some tradition about a dead man and his song, as handed down to us in a popular ballad, although there should by right belong to the house a curious history in connection with its original owners and name-givers, the ancient municipal family of Basing.

The records establish the existence at that time of a refectory, a parlour, a buttery, a pantry, and a kitchen and offices. But the cus-

tomary experience was here repeated to some extent. In 1588, the sum
of 11*l*. 8*s*. was paid out of voluntary contributions for gilding the
Queen's arms in the hall, and fitting up the Company's. The next two
years witnessed additions of some consequence in a little parlour and
cellars, with a house for the Clerk over them. These new premises must
have been of considerable extent, as the bill for their construction was
125*l*. 13*s*. Once more, so late as 1649, 20 dozen spoons, weighing
349½ ozs., were sold to meet the charge of enlarging the Court parlour.

Within a short time of the nominal completion of the Hall, an inventory of the principal contents introduces us to the knowledge of an
armoury similar in character and object to those maintained by some
other Companies. It is tolerably evident that the schedule can only
represent what was considered to be of more particular value, as there
is no reference to the muniments, plate, or furniture ; or the paper may
be no more than a portion of the specification. The armour forms the
most conspicuous feature ; and it is stated in the margin of the document
that at that time (1570) a portion of it was in use for Her Majesty's
service in Flanders, or in other words, for the equipment of the soldiers
supplied by precept. In fact, the only other articles deemed worth
particularizing were :—

> "A wafer with a band and a bosse of silver gilt.
> Three garlands, to choose Master and Wardens, with red ribbon.
> A bearing cloth of blue velvet, embroidered with gold and silver and set with
>   pearls, and yellow cloth to lie between it.
> A box or case to lay the same bearing cloth in.
> Two tables with the pictures of Sir Anthony Knyvett and Dame Avyce his wife."

The bearing cloth was the pall, which replaced an earlier one in 1563,
and of which the details are furnished under the account of the Broderers.
It perished, with many other treasures, a few years after the alterations
of 1649, in the disastrous conflagration, which reduced the Baker site
to a heap of ruins.

The Great Fire desolated the City ; but the Company saved a large
portion of its effects, including its records, plate, pictures, linen, and
pewter. Pending the restoration of the Hall, the meetings were held,
first at the Queen's Head in Bishopsgate Street, and then at the Tylers'
and Bricklayers' Hall in Leadenhall Street. Subscriptions from members and calls to the Livery were forborne, until the charge for rebuilding the premises in Basinghall Street had been completed. The residue
of the plate, special gifts excepted, was sold for 195*l*. 10*s*., of which 70*l*.
went toward the levy for constructing the "London" from the designs
of Mr. Wildgoose.

Between 1669 and 1678 the new Hall was erected, at a total outlay of more than 5,000*l.*, gradually collected in the course of the years 1668–71 from the Court and Livery in sums of varying amount. In 1671, the King's arms were presented by the Master, and placed between the two great windows at the upper end of the Hall. The rooms over the great parlour, with convenient cellarage, were assigned to the Clerk, and reckoned as 20*l.* in his salary.

But the financial position obliged the Company to let the Hall for some time as a Sunday meeting-house, for weddings and funerals, and on any other public or other occasion. In 1672 the accommodation available on Lord Mayor's day continued to be so insufficient, that some of the Livery were obliged to dine at a victualling-house in Thames Street, whither the Company sent the wine and cakes.

Not including the structure, probably John Baker's own place of business, which seems to have occupied the spot in 1490, the existing premises form the third possessed by the Company since its entrance on the bequest in 1501. It is a modern building, which covers only a portion of the area taken for its predecessor, some of the land having been alienated, whereas the second Hall was more spacious than the first to the extent of a plot acquired after the Fire for enlarging the accommodation.

Looking at the price of material and labour about 1670, and the large outlay incurred in replacing the original house, we have not much room for doubt that it surpassed both that which went before and that which succeeded it. Nevertheless, as an impressive monument of energy and piety the timber pile of 1547 stands pre-eminent ; for there the beginning was within the memory of the father or the grandfather, and all the external and internal environments, and all the ingoers and outcomers, were of one vesture.

It may be worth noting, that the last licensed lottery in Great Britain was drawn, in connection with the Glasgow Improvement scheme, at Coopers' Hall, August 28, 1837, just before the passage of the Act 4 Will. IV. c. 37.

The records and accounts of the Coopers have been preserved with unusual care from 1439-40, and depict in a very vivid and interesting manner the progress and growth of the Company itself and the general costume of the successive political systems, under which it has maintained its independence and achieved prosperity. We have merely to glance over the pages of the registers belonging to certain critical stages in our annals, to convince ourselves that it bore quite its full share of oppressive and despotic rule on the part alike of the Corporation and Crown ; but the Revolution of 1688 and a wise husbandry of its resources ever since has enabled the Court to shew a steadily increasing rent-roll, *pari passu* with a constant expansion of the educational and charitable trusts and disbursments. In this respect the Coopers claim precedence even over some of the Great Companies ; and it is the noblest of all pretensions.

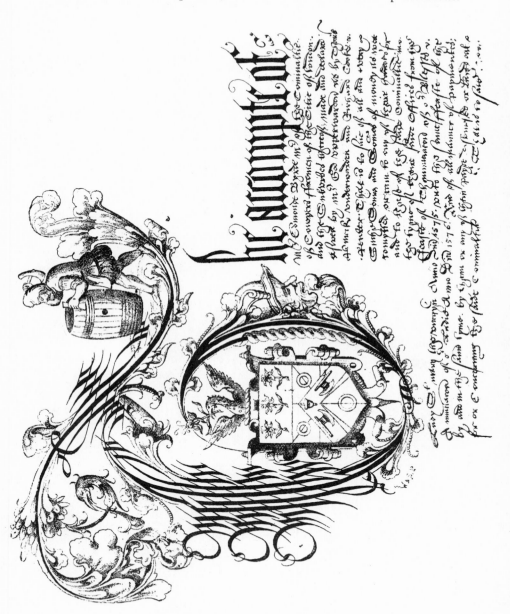

FACSIMILE FROM BOOK OF ACCOUNTS, 1576.

The records between 1439 and 1834, and the Accounts from 1440 to 1598, calendared by Mr. Firth, exhibit a curious and instructive picture in little of the doings and fortunes during three or four centuries, and

admit us to an acquaintance with certain facts which we do not otherwise reach. From an entry under 1440, it follows that at that time the
Fraternity, obeying the general precedent, had already founded a chapel
at St. Paul's, to which one of the Wardens by his will leaves 20s. sterling;
and in the next year a deceased member left " to the support of the
Fraternity," a gown striped with silver, probably for the priest. In 1448,
Richard Samborne paid for admittance by redemption 26s. 8d. In
1455, the outgoing Wardens delivered to their successors one chest with
two keys, one box with a key, a harness girdle, a board cloth, and ready
money amounting to 16l. 13s. 4d. Under 1458, there is an early mention of the mash-tun as a " mashfat ;" but it had been long in use.

The Coopers supplied, with nine other Companies, at the obsequies of
Henry VII. in 1509, two of the Fellowship to walk in the procession,
clothed in black gowns and tippets, besides certain poor men of the Craft
or otherwise in white gowns and hoods, with torches and beads in their
hands.

The practice of calling on every freeman at his admission to present
the Company with a gold noble (6s. 8d.) or a silver spoon of equal value
was inaugurated, it seems, in 1547 ; it was a not uncommon usage, and
led to a large accumulation of plate of this kind, as the newcomers
appear to have generally given the spoon in preference to the coin ; and
periodical sales took place of the surplus stores.

To the Irish Colonization scheme of 1609–13, the Coopers subscribed
140l., and associated themselves with the Ironmongers. The collection
of this sum occupied two or three years. The Company's arms were
set up in 1636 in a glass window of the parish church of St. Albon,
Wood Street. Seven years later the plate, valued at between 150l. and
200l., was sold to defray the share of a levy of 50,000l. on the Companies.

In the year of the Restoration, the Brazil staff was mounted in silver
with the Company's arms, and a cloth gown provided for the Beadle.
Three years afterward a barge was purchased by subscription at a cost
of 154l. 10s., or upward ; and a subsequent entry apprises us that the
vessel had a master, mate, and fourteen watermen. In 1664, the sum
of 600l. was found for the *minimum* quota of a loan of 600,000l. to
the King, and another sale of plate to the extent of 142l. 14s. 3d. was
necessitated.

We find that in 1675 the Common Serjeant was appointed standing
counsel to the Company. A very unusual proceeding is registered in 1671
and again in 1682 ; an Assistant in each case was removed for habitual
neglect and absence.

The only other noteworthy item upon which time has set its mellowing impress, is the loyal and generous conduct of Sir Robert Willimott, Citizen and Cooper, who, upon being elected Lord Mayor in 1743, instead of translating himself, agreeably to the custom of London, to one of the Great Companies, set the precedent of remaining true to his own brethren, who put forth their whole strength on the day, both by land and water, to shew him honour, elected him Master, and excused him from all fines. A prior Mayor, Sir John Fleet, Citizen and Cooper, elected in 1692, had in the usual way joined the Grocers.

Turning to the Accounts, so far as they illustrate circumstances and customs for a century and a half (1440–1598), a majority of the entries are of a normal or common character ; but here and there we encounter an allusion which still has its direct or indirect interest. In 1513, the sum of 16s. 2d. was spent on a supper at the Boar's Head in Cheap, probably for the Court ; and a further 5s. 1d. was disbursed at the Dagger for bread and drink soon after. The Sumner at Paul's is an occasional recipient of gratuities in connection with the Company's chapel or chantry there about the same time ; and periodical payments are made to the priest for the funeral obits, under the will of John Baker (1490), at St. Michael Bassishaw. Wine is furnished on many occasions and for persons of all ranks ; there is a disbursement of 2s. 4d. for a gallon and a pottle of muscadel for my Lord Fiennes, and of 10d. for a bottle of the same for the Lord Chief Baron ; but in 1535 a hogshead of wine offered to the Lord Chancellor, cost 1l. 3s. 6d., and a pipe of Gascony for the Speaker, 3l. 6s. 8d. Altogether, legal charges are constant and relatively heavy, and the vails constitute a standing feature in the outgoings for each year. Nor was the tribute invariably in these graceful forms. In 1576 the Lord Mayor accepts 3l., and in 1584, 6l., and the Recorder, the Judges, the Attorney-General, and others, both principals and subordinates, come in their turn. When the Company dined at Guildhall, they and the rest paid their quota of the expense. Even when we arrive at 1667, we find the Lord Mayor accepting a hogshead of wine for his parliamentary services in opposing the Vintners' monopoly of buying and selling wines in gross.

A clue to the Coopers' possession of an ancient funeral pall, similar to those still or formerly held by the Fishmongers and other bodies, only occurs in 1563, when we have the details set forth of the purchase of a new one, of which the material and workmanship amounted to about 57l.[1]

There is an odd charge in 1531 of 18½d. for the Dutch coopers' breakfast at the Checker tavern, when they attended as witnesses against

---

[1] See the items under the Broderers' Company, *suprà*.

their own countrymen in the trade, who had established themselves in the City as householders and shopkeepers.

The sale of Old Wool Quay for 400*l.* is recorded under 1558, and the contribution of 8*l.* 10*s.* by four members toward the construction of the Royal Exchange in 1566.

A not unusual incident presents itself in 1587, when the Company pays 5*l.* 2*s.* 6*d.* for lands concealed from the Crown. The registration of the arms at Heralds' College costs 10*s.* in 1590. A chain for the Bible is bought in 1591 for sixpence, and in the following year a new Bible and Prayer-book for the chapel or chantry at St. Paul's for 1*l.* 2*s.* 4*d.* There is an interesting memorial in 1593, in the shape of a charge of 12*s.* by a painter for painting the arms in books given by Master Swayne; they were inserted on a spare leaf at the commencement of the volume.

The expenditure on pageants, except in 1743, when the Coopers returned the Mayor, was steadily recurrent, but tolerably frugal. When Queen Elizabeth came to the City in 1570, to dine with Sir Thomas Gresham, the incidental outlay did not exceed 12*s.* 10*d.* But the May-day celebration at Greenwich in 1571, and the expenses attendant on the King's coronation in 1603–4 proved far more costly.

The calls from the Crown for ship-money and equipment of troopers were the most serious in amount, and were usually met by a requisition on the private resources of members of the Livery or Court.

While some of the Companies have unfortunately suffered a more or less serious shrinkage in their resources from the circumstance that the description of property left to or acquired by them has declined in value, others, as we know, have enjoyed a corresponding expansion, owing to the situation of their estates in the City itself or in other urban and central localities. The Coopers' Company belongs to the latter category, because its governing body has seen fit for a lengthened period to apply any available funds to the purchase of City groundrents; these have in some cases vastly grown in their returns; and the owners have not hesitated to devote the increment to public purposes.

For the ten years—1870-9—the receipts from estates in the City of London and the counties of Middlesex, Essex, Surrey, and Kent amounted to 6,493*l.* 1*s.* 9*d.* The almshouses and schools at Ratcliff and Egham are included in this estimate. The property consists of rents and stock; but unfortunately, in a certain sense, the bulk is in trust. In 1882 and 1892 the corporate possessions represented only 2,400*l.* out of 7,120*l.* and 7,400*l.* respectively.

Freemen at the age of fifty-five are eligible for a pension of 10*l.* a year, and at sixty to one of 15*l.* or an almshouse. Liverymen are entitled, in addition, to 20*l.* a year, and also possess the right of voting at the elections of Lord Mayor and Sheriffs, and of the Parliamentary representatives of the City.   The average annual amount paid in pensions or eleemosynary gratuities to needy members is 1,545*l.*

The charitable estate of the Company within the meaning of the Act of Parliament for Chantries Collegiate, 1 Edward VI., cap. 12, was exceedingly limited, insomuch that at this time, in order to redeem the interest in the Baker Estate, and to discharge the whole liability connected with the Obit, Dirige, and Requiem prescribed under the will in 1490, the claim of the Committee sitting at Skinners' Hall amounted altogether only to 9*l.* 2*s.* 10*d.*   The estate had certainly been a profitable accession ; for during the years when the superstitious covenant of the will was fulfilled, the out-payments do not appear to have annually much exceeded 40*s.*

The almshouses and school at Ratcliff St. Mary were originally founded under the will of Nicholas Gibson, Citizen and Grocer (Sheriff in 1538), Sept. 23, 1540 (after the decease of his relict), for fourteen poor men or women, seven to be taken from the parish of Stepney, and seven from the mistery of Coopers or their wives.   But this scheme was enlarged by the benefactions of Henry Cloker, 1573, Toby Wood, 1611, and Henry Strode, 1703 ; and it now provides for eight widows of Stepney, eight widows of freemen, and six poor men of the Company ; the men receive a pension of 30*l.* yearly, and the women, 26*l.* ; they cannot be admitted under sixty years of age.   The school, which is situated in School House Lane, Ratcliff, and which had been restored a few years prior, perished in the terrible fire of July 1794, which destroyed about 500 dwellings and warehouses, but was rebuilt in 1795, and enlarged in 1870 ; it accommodates 300 boys belonging to the parish of Stepney.

It was not until the passing of the Endowed Schools Act of 1869, that public attention was drawn to the justice of allowing girls to participate in educational endowments ; and this Company was amongst the first to give effect to the Act in this respect, by establishing, in 1878, a middle-class Girls' School, which has been successfully conducted at Bow, and now receives over 200 pupils.

By a Scheme of the Charity Commissioners which was approved by Her Majesty in Council on July 30, 1891, the educational endowments of the Ratcliff charity have been amalgamated, however, with that of the Prisca Coborn charity, under the title of "The Stepney and Bow Foundation."   The scheme provides for the removal of the boys' school to the premises of the Prisca Coborn Schools in Tredegar Square, Bow, for boys and girls ; and the management is vested in the hands of sixteen Governors, appointed by the following electing bodies : eight by the Master, Wardens, and Assistants of the Coopers' Company ; one by the London County Council ; one by the School Board for London ; one by the Council of King's College, London ; one by the Council of University College, London ; one by the Vestry of the parish of Bow ; one by the Incumbent and Churchwardens of the same parish ; one by the Incumbent and Churchwardens of the Parish of Bromley in the county of Middlesex ; one by the Incumbent and Churchwardens of the Parish of Stepney.

Seven years after its original endowment by Gibson, but before the Company had, by the remarriage of Mrs. Gibson in 1552 to Sir Anthony Knyvett, and her assignment of the estate thereupon, come into possession, the annual dinner was held at Ratcliff ; and although in the accounts it is styled "the great dinner day of the Company," and was various enough in its character, the aggregate cost was little more than 14*l.*, chiefly defrayed by members out of their own pockets. The prices of some of the constituent items help to explain the modest total : for instance, 18 capons, 15*s.* ; 12 rabbits, 2*s.* 8*d.* ; 12 geese, 16*s.* ; 8 pigs, 5*s.* 4*d.* ; 2 gallons of butter, 4*s.* 8*d.* ; 400 eggs, 8*s.* ; a whole sheep, 4*s.* 8*d.* ; a sirloin of beef, 1*s.* 10*d.* ; 20 lbs. of suet, 3*s.* 4*d.* ; while here and there the figures are almost higher than they would be at present, more particularly spices and sugar. The cook and his man received 11*s.* ; but the minstrels were satisfied with 2*s.*

The almshouses and school at Egham were founded by Henry Strode, Esq., Cooper, in 1703, for the benefit of the parishioners of Egham. There are twelve houses and a school for upward of 100 children. The building was re-constructed in 1828. The inmates of the almshouses have 6*s.* weekly, besides coals, clothing, and medical attendance.

In 1725, William Alexander left to the Company in trust for its poor his freehold estate of Woodham Mortimer, Essex, which at present yields 300*l.* a year, and gives pensions of 10*l.* to thirty members of this Gild.

Stow, speaking of the benefactors to Cripplegate Ward, says :—

"Master *Thomas Busby*, Cooper, gave forty dozen of Wheaten Bread, and foure Loads of Charcoales, to be distributed yeerely forever unto the poore of this Parish, in manner following : The weeke before *Alhallowtide*, one load of Char-coales, and tenne dozen of bread ; the weeke before *Christmas ;* the weeke before the five and twentieth day of January ; and the weeke before *Easter*, the foresaid proportion of bread and coales."

The same authority has transcribed his epitaph in the church, which ran as follows :—

"A Remembrance of THO. BUSBIE,
Citizen and Cooper of London, who
departed this life in the yeere
1575, and was buried
the 11. day of
July.

This Busbie, willing to relieve the poore, with fire and with bread,
Did give the house wherein he dwelt then called the Queenes Head.
Foure full Loads of the best Charcoales he would have bought each yeere
And forty dozen of Wheaten Bread, for poore Householders here.
To see these things distributed, this Busbie put in trust
The Vicar and Church-wardens, thinking them to be just.
God grant that poore Householders here, may thankfull be for such;
So God will move the minds of more, to doe for them as much.
And let this good example move such men as God hath blest,
To doe the like before, they goe with Busbie to their rest.
Within this Chappell, Busbies bones, in dust a while must stay,
Till He that made them, raise them up, to live with Christ for aye."

Besides the lustre shed on the Company by so many philanthropic personages and by those who have been chosen to discharge the duties of the Mayoralty, especially Sir Robert Willimott, it had the distinguished honour of sending to the Court of Aldermen in 1848, in the person of Mr. David Salomons, the first Jew elected to that dignity ; and a banquet was given by the Coopers, to commemorate the occasion, at the London Tavern on the 1st of February in that year, the Master, Mr. James F. Firth, being supported by the Lord Mayor and Mr. John Masterman, M.P.

The Company held an Exhibition in 1888 of Coopers' work at the People's Palace, and published a small catalogue descriptive of the various objects. It possesses a few last-century models and several pictures, chiefly likenesses of distinguished members or benefactors of the Gild ; among these are portraits of Sir Felix Booth and Sir David Salomons. But the most interesting in an historical respect is that of Dame Avisia Knyvett, relict of Nicholas Gibson above mentioned, after whose death she re-married ; the collection includes the original large painting and a reduced copy dated 1540, both part of the salvage in 1666.

The Cordwainers.

THE origin of the Cordwainers is one of those questions which it is almost useless to discuss, and of which one can merely say, that the earliest vestiges disclose a more or less lengthened establishment. But we do not agree with the view, that the Shoemakers' Gild was the parent-body, whence the Curriers and others branched off in course of time, since we hold the present one to have been essentially a community of craftsmen who purchased their material at first of the tanner (*Allutarius*), and subsequently of the leather-seller. In very primitive times, the deficiency of special markets brought the manufacturer,—in this case the tanner,—into direct contact with the retail buyer ; and such relation continued so long as the opportunities for commercial intercourse between the members of the Craft and Merchant Gilds remained more or less limited and difficult.

We therefore deem it a misapprehension to suppose that the Cordwainers were anciently identical with the *Allutarii*, unless we go so far back into the past or *principia rerum*, as to reach a perfectly rudimentary method or system, when the shoemaker may have flayed the beast and tanned the hide. Ordinances for their better government were, so far as we at present are aware, first drawn up and approved by the Lord Mayor in 1271-2, 56 Henry III. They embrace safeguards against the employment of spurious or defective material, the conditions of apprenticeship, the terms on which strangers might be admitted to work at the Craft, and to make sales of goods, and the rule as to the admission of skinners (*corerarii*) to the Fraternity. But the most noticeable feature is, that throughout this parent-code there is no reference to any governing body of the Cordwainers, who appear at this date to have been obliged to hold themselves in direct touch with the Corporation.

Further bye-laws, sanctioned in 1375, touch the ordinary and usual points, as to the attempts of ill-disposed and unqualified persons to impose on the common people, more especially in this case by selling shoes of bazen as cordwaine or Cordovan leather, and of calf-leather for ox-leather. The Articles also provided for the occurrence of disputes, which were to be settled, if practicable, by the good folk of the trade, and limited the sale of goods to the time between prime and noon, and to a certain spot between Soper Lane and the Conduit. Cordwainers were not permitted to open on Sundays, but might serve the common people within their own premises.

In 1395 the Court of Aldermen, in consequence of a dissension between the Cordwainers of London and the Cobblers from beyond sea, estab-

OLD ARMS.

lished a *modus vivendi* by limiting each of these vocations to its own strict province. The proceedings assumed the form of an inquisition of twelve members of each community, and the settlement was by sealed indentures.

In 1409 the Cordwainers and Cobblers re-appeared at Guildhall to procure authoritative sanction to a more elaborate and defined rule of practice for preventing mutual trespass. The most singular feature in this case is the survival of a letter of Henry IV. under the Privy Seal, inclosing a petition addressed to him by the Cordwainers, and praying the attention of the Corporation thereto, in consequence whereof an inquisition was held on the matter. But, the absolute inhibition of the use of new leather to the Cobblers having been found inoperative and unfeasible, they were now left at liberty to employ it for their purposes under certain peremptory restrictions.

The Cordwainers and Cobblers were at this time distinguished as the workers in new and old leather respectively. They seem to have been among the most litigious of the industries, and to have indifferently merited the designation of the Gentle Craft.

A foreign element had thus introduced itself into the trade in the time of Richard II. ; but the strangers seem to have been obliged in the first instance to content themselves with the execution of repairs. Looking forward, as they could not do, we see how in important respects the Continental artificer gradually outstripped and supplanted the English operative.

Returning to the Ordinances of 1272, it becomes manifest,—from a clause which appoints twelve members of the Craft to be overseers for the due preservation of discipline and the enforcement of penalties against defaulters,—that the Gild down to this period had been destitute of any fixed system of government ; and we are unable to assent to the vague proposition, that it was coeval with the Norman dynasty of kings. Even in 1272 the funds arising from amercements and otherwise were made receivable by the Chamber of London, to the use of the commonalty, so that there was still no regular Executive or methodical organization beyond this Committee of twelve persons with stated and narrow functions ; and the Cobblers appear to have possessed, with or without licence, a similar administration.

Two circumstances, which, judging from analogy, may have been connected with each other, happened not many years after the intervention of Henry IV. in 1409 in the feud between the Cordwainers and Cobblers ; for in 1439, April 26 (17 Henry VI.), in consideration of 50 marks (32*l*. 16*s*. 4*d*.), the King, doubtless at the instance of the twelve, conferred a charter on the freemen of the Mistery of Cordwainers of the City of London, whereby they became one body and one Commonalty for ever, with perpetual succession, a common seal, the power of pleading and being impleaded, and a licence in mortmain to the extent of 10*l*. a year. The new Company was invested with the right of annually electing one Master and four Wardens to govern the Mistery, and with a power of search and control over all workers in black and red tanned leather and new boots and shoes within the City of London and a radius of two miles from Cornhill.

This grant does not seem to have been submitted for approval or recognition till the 4–5 Philip and Mary, when it was duly exemplified and confirmed (June 17, 1557). But a patent of 4 Elizabeth (August 24, 1562) includes a provision which demands special notice ; for there, in authorizing a Court of twelve Assistants, these officers are described as twelve discreet and honest persons, chosen according to the ancient custom of London ; and we may reasonably doubt whether this faculty actually went beyond a formal approbation of the Committee of Twelve, which was organized in 1272, and which still existed in 1409 with the same jurisdiction.

The Elizabethan grant likewise extended the title to hold real property to 20*l*. and the radius of search and supervision to three miles, and vested in the Court and Commonalty the power of choosing a Clerk and Beadle, and of drawing up ordinances. The instrument was not enrolled at Guildhall till March 9, 6 Elizabeth.

The Cordwainers succeeded in 10 James I. in securing a considerable

amplification of their privileges and immunities.   The Court of Assistants was raised to sixteen, the licence in mortmain to 200*l.* a year ; and
all the lands thus far acquired were confirmed to the Company.

The only other experience of this character was under the *Quo
Warranto ;* but the charter accorded 1 James II. was, as usual, revoked
by the general terms and operation of the Act of William and Mary,
so that that of 1612–13 at present governs the constitution.

The second point, to which we now have to advert, is the nature of the
means which enabled the Company to consummate the act of incorporation by the foundation of a common Hall.   In the year immediately
following the concession of the first charter, John Yong, a prominent
member of the government of twelve, presented to his brethren a parcel
of land in Great Distaff Lane for the express purpose of facilitating the
periodical assembly of the freemen in council.   Although a gift of land
was not at that period the most serious part of such a transaction,
and the building-material and labour were more costly in proportion
than the site, the possession of a freehold with this specific object
doubtless encouraged an exertion to accomplish the rest.   But the
liberality of the donor did not probably come as a surprise on the
Brotherhood ; and the prayer for a charter in 1439 was influenced by a
confidence in the willingness of John Yong to do his part toward
rendering other conditions suitable and commensurate.

The ancient ordinances, which were in force from the 13th to the
16th century, both while the Gild remained a voluntary Society and
during the earlier period of incorporated life, were finally superseded by
the code of bye-laws made, in pursuance of the charter of 1562, ten
years later ; and these Articles successively gave place to others framed
and approved by the Judges in 1612 and 1749.

The acting charter and bye-laws are those of 1612–13 and 1749
respectively.   Under 1876, the Return made to Parliament mentions " a
Common Hall " as assenting to an augmentation of the fees payable to
the Court ; this was what may be perhaps termed a Grand or General
Committee, of which the Livery, but not " the free men of the Mistery "
specified in 1439, formed part, and which is convened on the last
Thursday in July of each year, for the election of the Clerk and Beadle
and for other current objects, on which the Court is not competent
to adjudicate.   Here we discern, as in the Company last noticed, a
certain, and indeed an important, survival of popular government, which
tends to preserve the constitution from hardening into an oligarchy.
In 1882, the Livery was stated to amount to 96, exclusive of the
Court ; of the Yeomanry, or freemen, no statistics were forthcoming or
procurable.   It is worthy of note that the Livery had not fluctuated

much since 1699 and 1724, when it was 100 and 102; while in 1892 it was returned as 100.

An ordinary sequel to a charter, sometimes a precursor of it, was the grant of arms, which was made to the Cordwainers by Robert Cooke, Clarencieux, June 25, 1579, and exemplified by Henry St. George, Richmond Herald, at the Visitation of London in 1634.

Some of the later history of the Company is associated, as may be supposed, with the crafts which pursued various branches of the leather trade; and even at a point of time much posterior to the early differences and altercations with the Cobblers, occasional glimpses occur of a survival of the old trouble and spirit.

As at present, a good deal existed and was done in the City on sufferance, until the abuse or irregularity was pointed out. In 1580 a representation was made to the municipal authorities, that by assent of the Free Cordwainers, and on payment to them of a certain quarterwage, the Foreign Cordwainers were left at liberty to buy leather at Leadenhall on Mondays, Wednesdays, and Fridays, but that the civic authorities had lately limited this right to Mondays. The Lord Mayor, however, shewed that the Company was not entitled to grant the privilege, and besides, that the Foreigners could, if they chose, make purchases on the other days in Southwark.

The tendency of modern legislation, which almost uniformly and inevitably traverses and effaces the lines on which the Gilds worked and throve, has been to divest the Cordwainers of all practical authority over that industry; and they share the lot of all such communities in continuing to live among traders and thinkers of a wholly different type, with a part to play and a mission to discharge as dispensers of alms and hospitality, but on an entirely different basis from their original and true *locus standi*, as they present themselves to our view and criticism in 1439, in the days of Master John Yong.

Nevertheless, in 1882, one-third of the Liverymen is said to have been practically connected with the business; and in surveying the accounts of expenditure to charitable uses beyond the fulfilment of early trusts, we become satisfied that the Company exercises its discretion with commendable justice and liberality.

The City Regulations of 1350 allowed 6*d.* for a pair of shoes of cordwain, and the same price for one of cow-leather, and for a pair of boots of the two materials mixed, 3*s.* 6*d.*; and the same ordinances forbad the removal of any cordwain or bazen out of the civic bounds on pain of forfeiture, half the value to go to an informer.

Shoes made of improper material were open to confiscation, when the supervisors detected the offence. In 1320, Richard Le Cordwainer and his fellow-officers took possession of a large number of pairs manufactured from bazen or sheep-skin and cordwain, or tawed leather, the latter being a cheap imitation of the Cordovan, which was costly.

From a passage in the tolerably well-known ballad of *The King and the Tanner of Tamworth*, written in the 14th century, we glean that it was the usage of the heads of great families to purchase their own leather, at all events for the repair of the boots and shoes of the establishment and its feudal surroundings, and inferably to employ a cordwainer or cobbler to do the work required. The tanner in the story, speaking of Lord Basset (Ralph, fifth Lord Basset of Drayton, 1299–1343) says to the disguised monarch, his companion :—

> "I know hem not, . . . with hem y hafe lytyll to don ;
> Wolde he never bey of me clot lether to clowt with his schoyn." [1]

In France the Tanners and the Shoemakers were closely associated, as Paul Lacroix shews in his *Histoire de la Chaussure*, 1862.

In the matter of appointments for the feet, we see that in 1639 Londoners and others possessed, in addition to shoes and boots, pumps and slippers, of which the latter is commemorated in the last of Shakspear's Seven Ages of Man.

At what time galoches of leather were introduced, is uncertain ; but we have observed that in 1400 the Pouchmakers secured a monopoly for wooden galoches, which were then represented to be a novelty in London.

The Company acquired the ground for a Hall in 1440 through the generosity of John Yong; it was a locality identified since the thirteenth century with the Craft, whose followers congregated in Corveysers' Street and Soper Lane, with the Curriers, after the abandonment of the former by the Sopers and Pepperers in turn. The Cordwainers are found there in 56 Henry III. and in 9 Henry IV., and Cordwainer Street Ward perpetuates the memory of this colony, which occupied the quarter. But how soon after that date steps were taken to utilize the site in Great Distaff Lane we are without further information than the fact recorded in Harleian MS. 541, where this Company is the twenty-first of twenty-five City Gilds possessing Halls in 1483. As in other similar cases, such an undertaking required much study and courage. The land was only an item ; and the outlay on the charter had been relatively large. The truth is, however, that those most concerned know nothing about the matter, except that the building, doubtless a timber structure, was erected, and in 1577 was replaced by a second with funds supplied by Thomas Nicholson, a Master of the Company.

---

[1] Hazlitt's *Popular Poetry*, 1864, i. 7.

Stow (1633), speaking of the Cordwainers, says :—

"In this Distar Lane, on the North side thereof, is the Cordwayners or Shoo-
makers Hall, . . . Of these Cordwayners I reade, that since the fifth of Richard
the second, (when he tooke to wife Anne, daughter to Wenceslaus, King of Bohemia)
by her example the English people had used piked Shooes, tyed to their knees with
Silken Laces, or Chaines of Silver and Gilt : Wherfore in the fourth of Edward the
fourth it was ordained and proclaimed, that Beakes of Shooue and Bootes should not
passe the length of two inches, upon paine of cursing by the Clergie, and by Parliament to pay 20s. for every paire. And every Cordwayner that shod any man or
woman on the Sunday, to pay 30s."

The Nicholson Hall, again, was lost in the Fire of 1666 with the
entire contents (except the charters and plate), and nearly all the house-
property in the neighbourhood. The pecuniary distress involved in this
calamity obliged the Company to part with forty-four pieces of plate,
including that bought with a legacy of 12l. left for the purpose by the
illustrious Camden in 1623, and with their sub-share of the Ulster estate,
which passed to the Goldsmiths, the tenants-in-chief, themselves sadly
crippled and impoverished.

The Hall was eventually reconstructed at the expense of members of
the Company, and completed in 1670; but the present one is an eighteenth century building, and covers only part of the original area. It
was described by Maitland in 1739, and even by Cunningham in 1850,
as being in Great Distaff Lane ; the extensive changes, a few years later,
have given it a frontage in Cannon Street ; and since 1883 a considerable sum has been expended, out of corporate savings, in alterations and
improvements.

The Cordwainers still retain the warehouses to the east of their
Hall; and very possibly at one time their estate in the City was
much larger. The old Cordwainer Street is lost in Hosier and Bow
Lanes ; and the property of the Company may have formerly extended
to that point eastward.

LITERARY NOTICES.

Acts of Parliament affecting the Company :—

25 Edward III.	cap. 4.		5 Elizabeth	cap. 8.
13 Richard II.	cap. 12.		2 James I.	cap. 22.
4 Henry IV.	cap. 5.		2 William and Mary,	cap. 8.
2 Henry VI.	cap. 7.		9 Anne,	cap. 11.
4 Edward IV.	cap. 7.		9 George III.	cap. 39.
19 Henry VII.	cap. 19.		39–40 „ „	cap. 66.
3 Henry VIII.	cap. 10.		41 „ „	cap. 53.
14–15 „ „	cap. 19.		43 „ „	cap. 106.
22 „ „	cap. 6.		48 „ „	cap. 71.
2–3 Edward VI.	caps. 9 and 11.		5 George IV.	cap. 51.
1 Elizabeth	caps. 8 and 9.		36–37 Victoria	cap. 91.

The Gentle Craft. A most merry and pleasant Historie. By Thomas Deloney. 4to, 1598.

 ⁎ There were numerous editions of the original work relating to the Shoemakers' Craft, as well as abridgments, and narratives founded upon it. Of one of the latter, an edition of 1725 relates to the exploits of a shoemaker called the Green King of St. Martin's.

The Shoemakers' Holiday. Or, The Gentle Craft : With the humorous life of Simon Eyre, Shoemaker, and Lord Mayor of London. As it was acted before the Queen's most excellent Majesty by the right honourable the Earl of Nottingham, Lord High Admiral, his Servants. By Thomas Dekker. 4to, 1600, 1610, 1618, 1631, 1657.

The story is also taken from the above-mentioned novel. Henslowe, in his *Diary*, July 15, 1559, notes the loan of 3*l.* to Thomas Downton and Samuel Rowley to buy this play from Dekker.

A Merry and Pleasant Comedy, Never before Printed, Called a Shoemaker, a Gentleman : As it hath been sundry times acted at the Red Bull and other Theatres with a general and good Applause. By William Rowley. 4to, 1638.

It was afterwards revived at the Theatre in Dorset Gardens. The plot of this play is founded on Deloney's *History of the Gentle Craft*, first printed in 1598.

A Discourse between Upright the Shoemaker, and Master Pattent the Smith, both meeting on the Horse Exchange, in Smithfield, now lately. By A. J. 8vo, 1640.

Crispin and Crispianus : An old popular drama frequently played by the Shoemakers' Gilds before 1643.

It is mentioned by Dr. William King (Works, 1776, i. 180).

The Curriers.

OLD ARMS.

THE first tangible evidence of the status and localization of this body belongs to the fourteenth century, when the Curriers, on the abandonment of Soper or Sopers' Lane by the Pepperers, settled there by the side of the Cordwainers. The industry was in a fairly prosperous condition when, in 1363, the little colony subscribed five marks (3*l.* 6*s.* 8*d.*) toward the French wars of Edward III. But the archives appear to be destitute of any information contributing to illustrate or trace the progress of the Gild during the next half-century, beyond the fact that in 1376 it was authorized to depute two members to the Common Council.

But it is manifest, notwithstanding, that there was a steady onward movement; for in 1415 (September 13) "certain good men of the mistery of Curriers presented to the Court of Aldermen a petition pray-ing for the approval of Ordinances made by the governors thereof; and the request was granted. These Articles provided two Wardens to rule the Craft; enabled the said Wardens to exercise the usual right of con-trol, search, and seizure; forbad the employment by members of any but freemen or apprentices under a penalty of 13s. 4d. and the convention of any assembly by the Yeomanry without the leave of the Wardens; and declared it unlawful for persons of the mistery to make any smouldering fire to the annoyance of the neighbourhood, or to work on any vigil and on Saturdays after noon.

The only other testimony to the proceedings about the same period is the investiture of the Wardens by the Common Council with the nomin-ation of the City scavengers during pleasure. Probably the Gild farmed the revenue.

In 1516 a deed of feoffment executed by Thomas Sterne, one of the Fraternity, placed his brethren after his death, subject to the payment of 2l. a year to his relict during her life, in possession of a messuage called the Boar's Head with four adjoining tenements in the parish of St. Al-phage, in the ward of Cripplegate, contiguous to London Wall, with certain charitable and superstitious stipulations—namely, that the Craft should expend 10s. yearly in charcoal for distribution among the poor of St. Alphage, and a like sum in prayers for the repose of the soul of the testator, whereof 3s. 4d. should be divided among such of the Livery as were in attendance at the said service of Requiem. The mind and intention of the donor in this case were, that the site should be used, and remain, as a common Hall of the beneficiaries for ever; failing which, the whole was appointed to be sold, and the money divided among the poor of the Brotherhood or their widows. The feoffees or trustees were to be periodically renewed in perpetuity, or so long as the original des-tination of the gift was respected.

This sequence of detached circumstances is capable of being employed to establish a few important points. We may be satisfied that at the date when the estate at London Wall was enfeoffed, the Curriers pos-sessed a settled and orderly government by Wardens, a code of Ordin-ances or bye-laws, and a satisfactory standing among their fellow-citizens. The acquisition of the Sterne estate went far to consolidate and centralize the Fraternity; and unquestionably at a very short interval from entrance on the property there was a removal from the neighbourhood of Cheap-side to the quarter which was to become the Curriers' permanent home.

The particulars which we gather in the course of the century relative to this subject are scanty enough, but assist in knitting together something like a connected and consecutive story of the gradual rise to the dignity of a chartered corporation. The acknowledged rank of the Gild as a factor in the branch of trade to which its members applied themselves, is proved by the Acts of the Crown, Court of Aldermen, and Common Council; in 2 Elizabeth (1559–60) there is a particular reference to the oaths to be administered to officers of the Gild and others; and we cannot fail to deduce from this entry, that the power of search, even under royal authority of doubtful force, was exercised outside the craft, and affected Spanish leather-dressers dwelling in and about the City. A licence from the Crown, revocable in five years, if found inexpedient, was granted in 1567, enabling the Wardens, freemen, servants, and apprentices of the Curriers of London to buy or sell leather in all markets and fairs within forty miles of London; under 1581, a complaint lodged in the Court of Aldermen against the governing body, refers to the latter as the Master, Wardens, and Assistants of the Company; and an order of Court was made that journeymen should no longer attend weddings and burials, that a common box should be provided, and that the Assistants should cause quarterage to be collected. Next we arrive (August 8, 1583) at the grant of arms; and in 1587 the Ordinances are revised and a new body of trustees appointed under the feoffment of Thomas Sterne.

These Elizabethan Ordinances are at once significant and interesting, and favour a conclusion presently to be stated. They prescribe that the election of Wardens year by year shall be by the Wardens and Fellowship; that those chosen shall be sworn in the Mayor's Court; that there shall be Assistants to co-operate with the Wardens; that the latter shall have supreme authority over the Company; that no assemblies shall be held without their consent; and that they shall have the right of search and of recovering penalties; finally, that work, save cleaning, shall be suspended on festivals and at noon on Saturdays. There are sundry other stipulations as to apprentices. But the features to be borne in mind are, that the Gild is again described as a Company, that its Hall is named as a place where the entire Brotherhood, as well as every foreigner using the art, is to assemble twice a year, that the Beadle is said to be the summoning officer, and that at these general meetings the Clerk shall read the bye-laws, so that none may plead ignorance of their purport.

It was not perhaps very surprising that the Article touching the election of Wardens should awaken controversy, especially in the presence of such a new element in the Executive as the Assistants; and in 1597 the Lord Mayor was solicited to intrepret the meaning of that particular clause. This duty he discharged by making an order that the outgoing

Wardens should elect two of their successors—one from the ranks of the Assistants, the other not, and that the remaining or junior one should be nominated by the Fellowship.

Let us pause to consider the chain of evidence, thus extending from 1415 to the closing years of the following century. We have cited a series or succession of documents, which set the Curriers before us in the light of a body acquiring by degrees and in turn Wardens (1415), a Hall (1516), Assistants (1581), arms (1583), a Master, Livery, Clerk, and Beadle (1587); and yet we discern no vestige of a charter. The question is, whether we are to infer a prescriptive existence through two centuries, or the loss of muniments by fire or otherwise. The Hall perished in 1666.

Had the Curriers never received a charter, the former view might have been tenable and legitimate. But unfortunately for such an argument, only six years after the constitutional settlement of 1597 James I. accorded one (April 30, 1606), which has been preserved, which recites no other, and which refers to the step as a new phase in the career of the applicants.

The Gild is incorporated by the name of the Master, Wardens, and Commonalty of the Art or Mistery of the Curriers of the City of London, and is endowed with all the customary powers and privileges, of which the only substantial additions to existing jurisdiction appear to be the use of a common seal, the right to sue and be sued, and the usual liberty as to acquisition and sale of lands and hereditaments other than those held of the Crown *in capite*. But special stress is laid on the possession and employment of the common Hall within the City or its liberties.

This was the first and practically the only grant, as that of 1687 was cancelled by the Act 2 William and Mary, c. 8, s. 12. In it a rather material modification of the government is perceptible, as the executive is ordained to consist of a Master, two Wardens (Upper and Renter), and twelve Assistants, the Master and Wardens being eligible from the Livery, but the Renter being customarily chosen by seniority from the Assistants. The Fellowship had been silently disfranchised ; and the popular element in the constitution in course of time was so reduced that in 1882 the number of Freemen was returned at eight, while the Livery, the Court inclusive, was stated to amount to 110. In a Gild which, whatever its primitive complexion may have been, derived from its principal benefactor, Thomas Sterne, in 1516 an estate which yields the bulk of its present income, on terms emphatically recognising and befriending the Commonalty, that class is all but extinct ; and while, if the language of the lease and release of the feoffment of 1516 in 1726 holds good, the charter of 1606 remains valid, the Sterne property vests in the Master, Wardens, and *Commonalty*, the compulsory alternative—the sale of the Hall and its appurtenances—would create an even graver difficulty as to the devolution of the proceeds.

Even where the absence or loss of the Hall may not, as in this case, jeopardize the charter, it seems fatal to the essential attributes and spirit of these institutions ; while, on the contrary, the mere possession of one without the ancient prescriptive accessories strikes us as equally failing to answer all the postulates of fitness.

At the same time, in the official return of 1882, the Company included in its executive staff " a Master of the Household," who was evidently a functionary equivalent to the Wardens of the Yeomanry in some of those bodies which we have had occasion already to describe.   This individual, whose designation only was peculiar, does not occur in any early transactions which have fallen under public notice ; there was a period when such an office, looking at the tenor of Sterne's feoffment, was especially appropriate or pertinent ; and it is somewhat remarkable that his existence, if he was part and parcel of the machinery in former times, does not formally transpire till it has become an anachronism.   The Master is there, but where is the household ?

It may be to the point to add, that during these years the reduction in the number of freemen was apparently influenced by the abnormally large admissions to the Livery, perhaps to assist the Company in its building project, which not only produced a heavy disbursement, but a serious loss of rents from demolished freeholds.

The power of search and connexion with the trade have long ceased. The right of supervision was exercised as lately as 1831.

We have mentioned the destruction of the probably early 16th century Hall in 1666.   At the end of August, 1670, it had not yet been rebuilt, and the Company had *ipso facto* no legal existence.   But at some date prior to 1701 we learn that it had been replaced on a smaller scale and a more limited area, the frontage being apparently left vacant for building.   In 1872–4 the site was again cleared, the materials sold, and temporary accommodation obtained by renting a portion of the Sun public-house facing the street, while a new and more spacious pile was being erected, partly with borrowed money and partly with sold-out stock.   The operations extended from 1872 to 1879 ; and a very singular circumstance occurred.   The premises were actually completed on the approximate site of the former building, without a frontage to London Wall, the Hall being approached through an iron gate and a passage, when, by an arrangement for mutual convenience with the occupants of the adjoining building, the whole structure was taken down, almost before the walls were dry, and rebuilt with an abutment on the main thoroughfare, Messrs. Rylands defraying the outlay and renting the remainder.

There are very few of these institutions which do not offer some novel point of custom or obligation. It may have often occurred, that in either case the origin was casual ; but when the practice began, its continuance was unchallenged. The Curriers during a great length of time were accustomed to place at their meetings, by the side of the Master, a horn whistle, by which the Chair commanded silence ; and when this object was lost, a silver one was substituted from a legacy left for the purpose. But the latter is preserved in a case, and seldom introduced. It has not the sanction of antiquity, and is intrinsically useless.

In a statement of assets and liabilities, applicable to 1880, the new Hall and its contents are reckoned as worth 7,050*l.*, which may represent its cost without representing its realizable value. A small item in the yearly receipts is derived from a sub-share under the Vintners of the Irish Plantation.

In 1834 the Company returned its income at 549*l.* 18*s.* 10*d.*, and its expenditure at 548*l.* In 1870 the former had risen to 804*l.* 5*s.* 9*d.*, and, subject to fluctuations, it reached nearly 1500*l.* in 1880. In 1892, the corrected figures were : corporate revenue, 1,250*l.*, trust, 39*l.* ; which of course involves the treatment of the Hall and its site as the private estate of the Company, instead of being scheduled as held under a very peculiar limitation.

The Cutlers.

OVERSEERS of the trade of Cutlery were appointed by the Court of Aldermen in 1344 with the usual power of search, and in the same year a code of bye-laws was approved, as follows :—1. That no Master or Warden of the said trade shall maintain any one whomsoever against the members ; 2. That none shall make common sales on Sunday, whereas journeymen and apprentices have stolen or wasted their master's property during their master's attendance at church ; 3. That the term of apprenticeship shall be for seven years, and that all masters must be freemen ; 4. That none but a freeman may keep a cutler's shop ; 5. That any declining to be judged by the Warden or Wardens for the time being, shall have liberty to go before the Mayor, and if convicted of wrong done, shall pay half a mark ; 6. That all goods, to prevent deceit, shall be made by day ; 7. That none shall receive the apprentice or journeyman of another, until his term has expired.

Further regulations for the trade were made in 1380, and provide, among other matters, for the harnessing of no knives with handles or gaynes of silver, unless of sterling metal, that in the case of wooden handles none should be coloured, except those of digeon [? boxwood], that no journeyman should receive higher wages than he was assessed to be worth, that all cutlery made in the City should be passed by the Overseers of the Craft, before it was carried out of the City, and that no goods should be sold at evecheapings or in hostelries, but only in cutlers' shops.

At this period the Gild was probably accounted one of the minor bodies in point of importance and membership, as in 50 Edward III. it returned only two members to the Court of Common Council, others sending four and even six.

OLD ARMS.

From some differences which arose between the Cutlers and the Sheathers in 1408, it is to be concluded that the former delivered to the buyer the knife or other similar utensil complete in all its parts, but that, before it was ready for sale, it underwent manipulation at the hands of three (and indeed four) different mechanics or operatives : the blade-smith, the cutler, the sheather, and the furbisher, the last-named contributing the pommel and decorative parts of the handle.

The burden of this grievance in 1408 was, that certain sheathers discredited the Cutlers by supplying unworkmanlike sheaths for knives and other articles ; and a concurrent ground of complaint, common to both crafts, was, that foreigners sold to the Cutlers of London articles bearing forged marks, purporting to come from English bladesmiths. The result was, that the Court of Aldermen sanctioned the appointment of a mixed committee of the Cutlers and Bladesmiths to oversee all goods offered, and to present cases of fraud to the Court.

We have so far .dealt with the few scattered notices, which present themselves in the civic archives or elsewhere ; and even when we reach a somewhat later point of time, we have to lean upon very scanty particulars and suggestions, the Company seeming to have lost its muniments in the Fire, and to possess an unusually slender amount of information as to its early history.[1]

It is stated that charters were conferred by Henry V. in 1415, by Henry VI. in 1422, by Henry VIII. in 1509, by Philip and Mary in 1553, by Elizabeth in 1558, by James I. in 1607, by James II. in 1685, and by Anne in 1703. But these grants may be reduced in a substantial sense to those of Henry V. and James I., since the others were merely confirmations by *inspeximus*, except that of 1685, which contained the usual restrictive and disabling clauses, and was annulled by the statute of William and Mary. The Company is at present governed by the charter of 1607. It does not possess the earlier concessions in any form.

The *inspeximus* of 1422 reveals, according to a statement in the parliamentary return of 1882, a state of great distress among the men of the mistery of the Cutlers by reason of losses at sea, and their inability to subsist, except through the benevolence of well-disposed people ; but there is no further clue to the circumstances under which this depression arose. It must have been temporary ; for in 1451 the Hall in Cloak Lane and other premises were acquired by purchase.

The charter of James I. was granted on the petition of the Company for its better rule and government, and for the prevention of divers abuses practised in cutlery to the loss and damage of His Majesty's subjects. It conferred on the executive the power of making Ordinances for the government of the craft, and of search and correction over the trade in London, and within three miles' radius, and the right to call on the civic authorities and all others for assistance in carrying out the law ; it approved of the constitution of the Company as composed of a Master, an Upper Warden, an Under Warden, and twenty Assistants, of whom all were to be elected out of the Commonalty—the Master and Wardens annually on Trinity Eve, the Assistants for life. The custom long existed of choosing five Stewards from the Livery to provide a dinner for the Court ; but the practice is now varied by the payment of 10*l*. 10*s*. by each of these officers toward that object. The actual course of procedure in electoral matters does not seem strictly to follow the charter, as the Court not only ignores the Commonalty, but assumes the privilege of selecting from the Livery the members of the Committee of Assistance.

---

[1] The Master, Mr. Cheesewright, informs us that he does not possess any means of assisting our researches.

There is one curious feature in the choice of a new Master, however, and it is, that the outgoing Master, with the Wardens and Assistants, having fixed upon two or three meet and sufficient persons in their own ranks, thereupon present them to the Livery ; and the united body, either by a majority of votes or of pricks with a pin on paper, determines which of them shall succeed to the vacancy. The custom of pricking for Master is sufficiently special to merit notice, although it is not limited to the Cutlers, and in the case of the Sheriffs it is so familiar and habitual.

The Company has from time to time made certain bye-laws conformably with the charter of 1607, independently of those submitted to the Court of Aldermen in 1344 and 1380, while it was still unincorporated, and a renewal of the search clause found in the charter of 1607 by the Lord Keeper, Lord Treasurer, and Judges in 1703. This latter ordinance vested in the Cutlers authority to make a quarterly inspection throughout London and within three miles of all shops and other places of manufacture or sale of all manner of swords, daggers, rapiers, hangers, wood-knives, pen-knives, razors, surgeons' instruments and knives, skeynes, hilts, pommels, battleaxes, halberts, or any other weapons or blades, or other thing belonging to the mistery. This control has long fallen into desuetude, and, an Act of Common Council having rendered it obligatory for every cutler in London and the liberties to be free of the Company, the measure was repealed in 1839, at the instance of the Court, from a feeling that the principle was impracticable and unfair. The London branch of this industry, since the first quarter of the eighteenth century, when Sheffield began to develop symptoms of becoming what it is to-day, has been obliged to content itself with sharing the advantages of the steel manufacture, with a constant drift toward a secondary rank ; and the City Livery Company is all but unknown to thousands who have heard of the Master Cutler of Sheffield and the yearly feast over which he presides. The trade has forsaken the Metropolis, which retains only the historical recollection and the antique machinery.

Under the charter of James I. a licence in mortmain to the extent of 100 marks (66*l.* 13*s.* 4*d.*) a year appears to have been obtained ; and in 1839 the amount was raised to 200*l.* a year, of which nearly half was unexhausted in 1882. The Metropolitan Railway (Additional Powers) Act, 1866, s. 43, enabled the Company to lay out in the purchase of land 6,238*l.* paid by the promoters of the line for property in Houndsditch.

In 1501–2, among the Companies having Liveries, the Cutlers are placed twenty-second, with a Livery of 24 ; in 1509, they occur twenty-third in order ; but in 1515 the Company was officially ranked seventeenth. In 1699, the Livery was returned at 110, in 1724, at 125, in 1882, at 88, and in 1892 at 100. In 1882 the number of freemen was thought not to exceed *twelve*.

Referring to the corporate and charitable estates, they have been alike enormously augmented by the common agency of metropolitan development. Under 1417 tenements in Watling Street came into the hands of the Company by feoffment from John Parkes and Thomas Kinton; and from that time a succession of bequests made the Cutlers the owners of property in Cloak Lane, College Hill, Aldersgate Street, Houndsditch, Fleet Street, Fleet Lane, and Ludgate Hill, besides acquisitions of inferior importance in the suburbs and a leasehold at Egham, which has lapsed. The premises at Ludgate Hill are in Belle Sauvage Yard, Boy Court, and in the main thoroughfare, but originally consisted of the Belle Sauvage Inn with all its appurtenances, and the Rose and Crown, which may or may not have been a second hostelry. Messrs. Cassell & Co. are tenants under the Company of the Belle Sauvage Yard tenements, on a lease which had nearly seventy-five years to run in 1882. The Houndsditch property was chiefly acquired under the will of Agnes Carter in 1469-70, and that in Aldersgate Street similarly from John Monk in 1522. In 1566 and 1569 the Bucke Legacy in Fleet Street and the Craythorne estate on Ludgate Hill respectively accrued.

A portion of the Craythorne estate was allotted to the once very necessary and usual object of relieving the poor prisoners in the London gaols, who depended for their maintenance on external alms-givers; and, the fund available for such a purpose, when our prisons were remodelled, ceasing to be required, the Company joined the Mercers in a new scheme prepared by the Charity Commission, and pay over to them the amount for distribution.

In 1451 Thomas Frill executed to the Company a conveyance of messuages on College Hill and in Cloak Lane, which in priority of time followed the entrance upon those in Watling Street, and which derived a special interest from being selected as the site of the Cutlers' Hall, which stood in that part of Cloak Lane demolished for railway purposes, and in the original purchase was said to consist of two houses, the one converted into a seat of business for the Company, and the other into a residence for the Beadle, who was perhaps then, as he has since remained, an officer of more than ordinary consequence, appearing in the modern accounts as the recipient of a higher salary than the Clerk. In Cunningham's *Handbook*, 1850, the Hall is described as No. 6; and in the existing balance-sheets the remaining buildings are numbered 7 to 9 inclusive.

Maitland speaks in 1739 of the second Hall in Cloak Lane, erected after the Fire, as " convenient and beautiful." Very few particulars about it or its precursor transpire. The lane in which it was situated was almost undoubtedly so called from its immediate contiguity to Walbrook, and once adjoined Turnwheel Lane, now completely absorbed by Cannon Street Station, but indebted for its appellation to a similar cause. The present Hall in Warwick Lane, which, judging from the heavy outlay on tavern bills, from 1871 to 1880, occupied, in the arrangements for its purchase from Messrs. Tyler and in its construction, a remarkable length of time, is a handsome edifice ; but is of course destitute of historical interest and contains no archæological objects.

The total income, which in 1871 was under 2,444*l.*, had risen in 1880 to 5,935*l.* 12*s.* 2*d.* with an expectation during the ensuing ten years of a further increase of about 600*l.* a year.[1] In the same period the Company's sub-share of the Irish estate with the Salters shewed a tendency to shrinkage, having been 337*l.* 10*s.* in 1880 against 472*l.* 10*s.* in 1871 and following years. But this loss is relatively immaterial, regarding the expansive capabilities of the London property.

Among the miscellaneous disbursements in the published accounts occurs a yearly item of 3*l.* which is termed " Pepys's gift," arising from a bequest, not of the Diarist, but of a gentleman of that name, a member of the Company in 1840.

The Cutlers elected some time since, when the question of technical education was mooted, to refrain from entering into the movement ; but they promoted an Exhibition of Cutlery[2] in 1879 at a cost of upward of 500*l.*, followed by a series of Technical Lectures, delivered by eminent professional experts at the Hall to large and attentive audiences ; and they appear, moreover, to expend a considerable amount annually in donations. The Exhibition was successful almost beyond the hopes of its patrons ; and an interesting assortment of specimens of ancient work was lent by the owners.

It was about the same time, that the Company decided on appropriat-

---

[1] According to Whitaker, however, the corrected figures for 1892 were 5400*l.* inclusive.

[2] The three classes of goods admitted, were General Cutlery, Surgical Cutlery, Sword Cutlery ; and the points to which exhibitors were recommended to pay special attention were : general excellence of material, temper and workmanship, novelty of style, practical and general utility. There were ninety-four competitors in the three classes, of whom forty-eight were in the first. The jurors were the most distinguished men of the day in the various departments ; one gold and twelve silver medals, and twenty-eight certificates were awarded, and it was estimated that about 15,000 persons visited the show. The Company had reason at the time to believe that the project operated beneficially both on the manufacturers and their work-people.

ing 100*l.* a year to the encouragment of apprentices in the cutlery trade, with a view to secure a succession and school of capable artisans ; and under this scheme bounties were payable to the masters during the term of three years and on its expiration to the apprentice, both in the shape of money and the freedom of the Company, when the report was favourable. It was a praiseworthy effort, but out of touch with the new spirit of commerce and the altered relationships between servants and employers.

The Distillers.[1]

DROP·AS·RAINE   DIS·T·III·AS·DEWE

THE usual accounts of this Company represent its origin as unknown; but there seems little doubt, from the language of the official code of rules and directions drawn up in 1639, that until the charter of 1638 was granted, 14 Charles I., August 9, the followers of the mistery were independent of control, and carried on their operations according to their individual discretion ; nor did the reform of 1638 affect any but the members of the calling in and near the metropolis.

The person, who seems to have been primarily instrumental in promoting the movement for the incorporation of the Distillers, was Sir Theodore de Mayerne, physician to the King, and a gentleman who took a great interest in all matters relating to cookery, preserving, and

[1] This Company made no return in 1880.

similar accomplishments.   He left behind him a very curious MS. of culinary receipts, which was published in 1658.   In the book, hereinafter to be described, he is explicitly called the Founder of this Company.

We have said that the charter was obtained in 1638 ; and in the following year, Mayerne, in conjunction with Dr. Thomas Cademan, medical adviser to the Queen, prepared a series of regulations and bye-laws for the management of the new scheme, with some introductory elucidations of a rather meagre character, relating to the circumstances which had necessitated and encouraged the step.

This volume appeared in 1639, and is entitled :—

"The Distiller of London : Compiled and set forth by the Special Licence and Command of the King's Most Excellent Majesty: For the sole use of the Company of Distillers of London.   And by them to be duly observed and practised."

The preceding leaf is occupied by the arms, which we have engraved above, and a description of them, which is as follows :—

Azure : a Fesse waivie, *Argent ;* between a *Sun* drawing up a *Cloud.*

In the later works of reference the arms are given differently from this, and also more fully :—

Azure : a fesse wavy *argent ;* in chief, the sun in splendour, encircled with a cloud, distilling drops of rain, all proper ; in base, a distillatory double-armed *or*, on a fire proper, with two worms and bolt-receivers of the second.   *Crest :* on a wreath, a garb of barley, environed with a vine fructed, both proper.

Supporters : The dexter, the figure of a man representing a Russian, habited in the dress of the country, all proper ; the sinister, an Indian, vested round the waist with feathers of various colours, wreathed about the temples with feathers, as the last ; in his hand a bow, at his back a quiver of arrows, all proper.   *Motto :* " Drop as Raine Distill as Dewe."—Deut. xxxii. 2.

An address from Dr. Cademan and Sir T. Mayerne immediately succeeds the title, and in it we meet with some slender outline of facts

ARMS, 1739.

connected with the infancy of the institution and the unsatisfactory state of affairs prior to that event.   They tell us that it was a royal mandate, expressly set forth in the Letters Patent, that the rules should be settled and printed.   In fact, the whole thing has a Court flavour ; and doubtless the interest taken by persons of quality of both sexes in these matters tended to accelerate the establishment of the business on a more healthy basis than, if we may credit Cademan and Mayerne, it had till that time occupied.

A second prefatory effort is subscribed by the entire Company, as it existed in 1639, namely :—

Thomas Cademan, *Master.*
Theodorus de Mayerne, *Founder.*

Edward Hooker,
Foulks Wormeleighton, } *Wardens.*
Ralph Triplett,

William Brouncker,	Thomas Dallock,	
Edward Franckton,	Henry Greene,	
Henry Pinson,	Thomas Coe,	
Roger Palmer,	Francis Heath,	
John Brewer,	William Besse,	*Assistants.*
Barnard Fountayne,	John Woods,	
George Snelling,	William Wilks,	
John Bayley,	Henry Boyce,	
Daniel Cage,	Hugh Bowyer,	
John Carnytham,		

In this original list we do not see any mention of a Clerk ; but in the third edition of the *Rules and Orders, etc.*, 1668, the name of John Greene, "one of the Attorneys of his Majesties Court of King's Bench," is represented as holding the appointment ; which is so far interesting, that it shews that at that comparatively early date the civic Gilds appreciated the need of securing the advice of a professional lawyer in the conduct of their affairs.

The process necessary for completing the enfranchisement of the Distillers,—the enrolment of their charter in the Chamber of London,—was delayed, however, to an unexampled extent, the Court of Aldermen declining, in the face of repeated commands from the King and his officers, to sanction the act. The latest communication from Charles I. is dated October 30, 1639; but his directions and threats were unheeded, and the Company was not placed upon the Roll till March 17, 1658.

We have seen that by the original constitution the government consisted of a Master, Founder, three Wardens, and nineteen Assistants, and that a Clerk was subsequently added. The place of Founder probably did not survive Mayerne himself.

There appears to be no mention of the surrender of the Distillers' charter at the Restoration; but they ceded it subsequently and received a new one, May 12, 1687 ; this was confirmed, together with the Rules and Directions, in 1690. The Court of Aldermen gave them a Livery, October 21, 1672.

By an Act of Common Council, July 29, 1774, all distillers within the civic jurisdiction were compelled to be free of the Company ; but this regulation has long grown out of use.

In 1699, the Livery was returned at 108; in 1724, at 127 ; in 1739, at 122 ; and in 1892, at 28.

The fees on taking up the freedom are : by patrimony or servitude,

3*l*. 11*s*. 6*d*. ; by purchase, 7*l*. 15*s*. 6*d*.   Upon admission to the Livery, a sum of 14*l*. 18*s*. 2*d*. is payable ; formerly the amount was 13*l*. 6*s*. 8*d*. The Company holds no trust or charitable property ; but it owns the freehold of the site originally purchased for the erection of a Hall, which was never erected, besides a funded estate arising from the accumulation of surplus income, and certain articles of silver plate presented from time to time by members.

To return for a moment to the book in our hands.   The separate editions, specially printed for the Gild in 1639 and 1668, give the " Characters expressing the quantities, qualities, and kinds of materials and ingredients used in this work " in cipher, which in both the copies before us is alike explained in coeval MS.   But in 1664, Dr. French, in annexing the *Distiller of London* to the third impression of his *Art of Distillation*, 1664, took credit for supplying the terms at length, instead of inserting them " in mysterious Characters and Figures."

At p. 15 (edit. of 1668) we find the following precept :—

" That no Afterworts or Wash (made by Brewers, &c.) called Blew John, nor musty unsavory or unwholesome Tilts or Dregs of Beer or Ale ; nor unwholesome or adulterated wines, or Lees of wines, nor unwholesome sugar-waters ; musty unsavory or unwholesome returned Beer or Ale ; nor rotten corrupt or unsavory fruits, druggs, spices, herbs, seeds; nor any other ill-conditioned materials of what kind soever, shall henceforth be distilled, extracted, or draun into Small spirits, or Low wines, or be any other ways used, directly or indirectly, by any the Members of this Company, or their successors at any time hereafter for ever."

The same subject is taken up again further on, in a passage which refers to the state of trade in 1668.   At p. 51 we read :—

" Whereas upon due examination it hath plainly appeared ; That many insufferable inconveniences have of late fallen upon this Company and their Trade, in general ; by reason of the disorderly and abusive expence and imployment of Brewers After-worts (called Wash) Insomuch that thereby, not only those of this Company that have had no hand therein, but even the *Distillers* themselves that have been the Delinquents, have intollerably suffered both in their Reputation, and great decay of their Trades, by these their alone inconsiderate practices.   For reformation of the present disorders and abuses, and future prevention of the like.   These ensuing admonitions and directions, are strictly to be observed and practised.   *Viz.* :—

" That no Member or Members of this Company, or their Successors, nor any of them at any time hereafter for ever, by any way or means whatsoever, (directly or indirectly) shall or may, use, dispose, convert or imploy, any After-worts (or Wash, made by Brewers or others) into Vinegar, Beer-egar, or Ale-egar, or either of them : or to or for any other use or imployment whatsoever, except only to distill the same into Low wines or Spirits, to be re-distilled into proof spirit, for the uses aforesaid, according to the true interest and meaning of these directions.   As they and every one of them respect their Oaths by them taken (when they were made free, and received into this Incorporation).   And will undergo the penalties provided, or to be provided, by the Ordinances of this Company, or otherwise, to be imposed or inflicted on the Contemners, Neglectors or Opposers hereof."

We have transcribed the foregoing passage as a sample of the character and tone of these regulations for observance by freemen of the Company.

The book ends with " A Catalogue of the Materials and Ingredients used in the precedent Rules," and " The Oath of every Free-man."

The latter runs thus :—

"THE OATH OF EVERY FREE-MAN.

" You shall swear, That you will be good and true to our Sovereign Lord the King's Majesty that now is, and to his Heirs, and Successors, Kings and Queens of this Realme : and in all matters and things lawful and reasonable relating to the said Company, shall be obedient to the Master, Wardens, Assistants, and Governors of this Company for the time being, and their Successors, and shall readily appear upon all Summons by their Beadle or other officer (except you have sufficient cause to be absent), or else you will forthwith pay all such Penalties and Fines, as you shall forfeit according to the Ordinances of this Company for breaking the same : All the lawful Acts, Ordinances and Orders made, or to be made for the weale, rule and good government of the said Company, you shall to your power observe and keep ; . . . and all lawful Councels and Consultations, words, matters, and things which you shall at any time hear or know, spoken or done at any Court or other Assembly of the said Company, that doth concern the government of the Company, Reformation of Abuses, or Regulation of Refractory or Disorderly Persons, you shall not divulge, declare or make known to any Person or Persons whatsoever, whereby the good government of the said Company, Redress of Abuses therein, or Regulation of their Disorderly Members may be hindered, prejudiced or prevented.

" All this you shall faithfully and truly do and performe to the utmost of your power. So help you God, and the Holy contents of this Book.

"GOD SAVE THE KING."

LITERARY NOTICES.

The vertuose boke of the distyllaeyore of all maner of waters. By Jerome of Brunswick. Folio, (1525), 1527, 1529.

The Treasure of Evonymvs, conteynynge the wonderfull hid secretes of nature, touching the most apte formes to prepare and destyl medicines, . . . By Conrad Gesner. Translated by Peter Morwyng. 4to, 1559, 1565.

The Distiller of London. Compiled and set forth by the speciall License and Command of the King's most Excellent Majesty : For the sole use of the Company of Distillers of London. And by them to be duly observed and practized. Folio, 1639, 1668, and with the later editions of French's *Art of Distillation.*
  The List of ciphers in both the folio copies is explained in coeval MS.

The Art of Distillation. By John French, M.D. 4to, 1651, 1653, 1664, 1667.
  To the 3rd and 4th editions is annexed the *Distiller of London,* with the ciphers translated into ordinary characters.

A Description of the Philosophical Furnace, or A new Art of Distilling, divided into five parts. Whereunto is added a Description of the Tincture of Gold, Or the true Avrum Potabile ; Also, The First part of the Mineral Work. Set forth and published for the sakes of them that are studious of the Truth. By John Rudolph Glauber. Set forth in English, By J. F., M.D. 4to, 1651. With diagrams. Dedicated to his Honoured Friend John Jenison in the Bishopric of Durham, Esquire, by J. F.

Introitus Apertus ad Artem Distillationis.   Or, the Whole Art of Distillation Practically Stated.   By W. Y-Worth.   12mo, 1692.
Chymicus Rationalis: Or, The Fundamental Grounds of the Chymical Art Rationally Stated and Demonstrated, By Various Examples in Distillation, Rectification, and Exaltation of Vinor Spirits . . . .   By W. Y-Worth.   12mo, 1692.

The Dyers.

THE Dyers, although they are here placed in the order of the alphabet, are held to rank as the first of the Minor Companies.   At one time, from their lengthened connection with the Shearmen and Fullers on a footing of equality, they strenuously contested precedence with the Clothworkers, when the latter represented by fusion the two other Gilds above named.   But in 7 Henry VIII., by the award of the Lord Mayor, the Dyers were adjudged to follow the Clothworkers, unless the chief magistrate was of this Company, when for the time being they, agreeably to ancient usage, would take precedence of all, if their member chose to dispense with the prescriptive usage of translating himself, on election, to one of the twelve leading Associations.

We have shown how this etiquette practically amounted to an unwritten law, and was not infringed till Sir Robert Willimott courageously declined to leave the Coopers in 1743.

The knowledge of the art of producing colour for all kinds of purposes

OLD ARMS.

at an extremely remote date, is amply demonstrated by the excellence which the illuminator and glass-painter attained in the Middle Ages ; and at a yet earlier date the secret of dyeing wools and woollen goods was familiar to those who pursued that craft, as it was little more than an evolution from the British custom of staining the person with woad or some other pigment,[1] and from the prevailing partiality for bright and

---

[1] During the mediæval period the juices of herbs were employed to stain the features and body for purposes of disguise.

showy colours, the dyer must have found the occupation sufficiently remunerative. The traditional story of the Orkney pirate, who in the eleventh century seized some English vessels bound for Dublin with English cloth, points to the demand in the Irish capital for gaudy and picturesque hues, as part of the booty consisted of scarlet goods, with which Sweyn decorated his ship, and thence christened the expedition his Scarlet Voyage.

We incidentally point out elsewhere, that in Magna Charta, one of the clauses stipulates that there should be only one breadth of dyed cloth throughout England, and that this restriction was abrogated by Edward III.

But apart from the treatment of woollen stuffs, the dyer soon acquired an additional channel for his industry in the dyeing of leather ; and in 1372 an arrangement between the Leathersellers, Pursers of the Bridge, and Dyers, defined their respective duties and obligations. The most curious feature in this transaction is, that with the last-named Craft, of whom three subscribe the Articles, their wives are associated as parties.

The account, which we furnish in its place, of the changes at successive periods in the livery of the Drapers, shews what unlimited means the dyeing trade had acquired by the early part of the fifteenth century, of producing almost every variety and shade of colour, both the " sad " for every-day purposes, and the bright and gay for holidays and feasts.

In the interesting series of scenes in rich stained glass in one of the corridors at Merchant Taylors' Hall, depicting the celebrated feud between the Taylors and the Skinners, we are struck by the lavish and picturesque diversity of costume of the figures, both male and female, which are represented as taking part in the affair at its successive stages, from the first hustle in the streets to the final pacification at the dinner-table, and which merely reproduce the coeval apparel of those concerned.

" Lincoln green " is renowned in the romance of *Robin Hood* and elsewhere ; but that outlaw is represented as possessing a regular store of cloth, both of that colour and of scarlet, in a poem of 1508. Many of our elder writers celebrate *Coventry blue*, or the blue thread which was formerly a staple manufacture there. It was largely used for embroidering on white.

The profuse variety of colours obtainable for costume and decoration is seen from entries in household books of the thirteenth and following centuries. Stow relates that within his memory the Earl of Oxford used to ride into London as far as his mansion in St. Swithin's Lane, attended by eighty gentlemen clad in Reading tawny with gold chains about their necks.

The purple, which was formerly accounted the peculiar distinction of ecclesiastical dignitaries, was obtained from remote times from a small shell-fish (*Bracinium lupullus*) found then, as now, on the Cornish coast.

The dyeing of silks attracted a good deal cf attention in the earlier half of the reign of James I. [1607–16], when various abuses in connection with the business were exposed, and the Projectors desired to force upon the City the appointment of a Viewer of all dyed silks. The Dyers themselves more than once petitioned Parliament against the importation of logwood or blockwood, which, it was alleged, led to a large share of the deception in the process.

The frauds committed in dyeing of silks seem to have been regarded very seriously, and to have been attended by disastrous consequences to the offenders. But it was not the dyer who suffered, in some cases which are reported as having come before the Star Chamber; for although as early as 1516 the Wardens of the Gild were dismissed on this ground in consequence of a complaint lodged with the Chamber by the Lord Mayor, at a later date (1629-32) we find silkmen heavily amerced on the same account. In one instance, the culprit compounded by a payment of 2000*l.*; and in another the informers were awarded 1500*l.* The malpractices in this direction seem therefore to have been both on the side of the dyer and his employers; and the disgraced Wardens owed their punishment to their negligence in not detecting breaches of the law and of the Ordinances of the Gild. In 1635, proceedings were again taken against the silkmen for corrupt dyeing; and here it was the " Governor and Assistants " of the Company who were summoned before the Chamber as the defendants. The presumption must be, that the troubles of the silkmen arose out of their irregular use of dyes and the criminal information filed by the Wardens in consequence.

The Dyers come under notice in 1362, as requiring the offices of the civic authorities to restrain malpractices. The rules which were then made explain the nature of the complaints which had been preferred against certain members of the mistery. They enact that no dyer who dyes wools with woad shall dye any manner of cloth, hats, caps, linen thread, or silk, under penalties; and that owners of wools may know, if they choose, whether their property has been changed, they may take their wools without payment, before the wools are dry; and the owners on their part shall, when the wools are dry, and are of the right colour, pay for the same without fail, or the dyers may make their plaint before the Mayor, according to the Statute of Smithfield.

The Dyers have suffered the double misfortune of having had two conflagrations (1666 and 1681), by which their premises were destroyed or seriously damaged, and they are exceptionally deficient in material for elucidating their early history. What may, perhaps, be termed their political annals are circumscribed within very narrow limits, as we merely hear of a charter granted by Henry VI. in 1471, and of bye-laws approved November 15, 30 Elizabeth (1587), before James I., on the 30th of June (1607), conferred the charter by which the Company is at present constitutionally governed. This instrument, in which it was described and incorporated as the Wardens and Commonalty of the Mistery of Dyers of the City of London, seems, however, to have been mainly an *inspeximus*, and there were probably others in the intermediate period. James II. renewed the grant, 19 March, 1686-7, with the customary restrictions ; and Anne finally ratified the privileges on the original basis, and confirmed the Company's bye-laws, April 26–October 31, 1705.

The Dyers appear, however, to rely immediately, in the management of their affairs, on the Standing Orders, sixty-eight in number, which are set out at large in the parliamentary return of 1880-2, and which embrace every department of the Executive. This code of rules, founded on the earlier bye-laws, is of no further public interest than the particulars which it supplies of the duties of the Bargemaster, which, after the discontinuance of water-pageants, have been confined to the supervision of the swans on the Thames, on behalf of themselves, the Vintners' Company, and the Crown.

These regulations for the swan-herd and his four assistants are the more important, that they may be presumed to disclose to us points of established practice, while many old fashions prevailed. We shall therefore enumerate the principal heads :—1. The appointment of a Bargemaster by the Court from time to time ; 2. His attendance at the Hall on all Court days, and at dinners, if so ordered, when he should stand behind the Renter Warden's chair, in both cases in his livery ; 3. The directions as to surveying the swans and their nests early in May of each year, the inspection of marks, and the pinioning of cygnets ; 4. The service of notice to the Court, to the Crown officer, and to the Vintners, so often as swans should be removed to temporary shelters during frost, alike at the time of removal and restoration ; 5. The allowance of a livery and hat once in seven years ; 6. The payment of 15*l*. a year as salary, and 11*s*. a day during the swan-upping, besides all expenses, which he was bound to enter in a book, and deliver in due course to the Clerk.

The relation of the present Company to the Vintners, who, as we have already noticed, are associated with them in the business, and still christen one of their functionaries Swan-warden, was apparently due to the common proximity of the two Halls to the river side and to each other. But the members of other Companies attended as a matter of compliment ; and in 1598 there is an entry in the Founders' books of 3s. 4d. for baking pies, when the Company, or some of them, went swan-upping.[1]

The administrative machinery of this Gild consists of a Prime Warden, a Renter Warden, and the Assistants, in whom is vested the whole authority, except that the Commonalty, in whose favour the charter was given and exists, has a voice in the choice of the Beadle at the annual general meeting. In 1501–2, the Livery numbered 19 ; in 1699, 200 ; in 1724, 202 ; in 1880, the Court inclusive, about 83; and in 1892, 66. The Company has no exact knowledge of the number of freemen, but 98 were admitted between 1851 and 1880. Under the municipal order of 1515, the Dyers were made the thirteenth Company.

The property chiefly consists of warehouses and tenements in Upper Thames Street, on Dowgate Hill, in Dyers' Buildings, Holborn, and at Leytonstone, in addition to the interest of the purchase-money (39,000l.) paid by the Salters, for the Dyers' sub-share of the Ulster Plantation.[2] An information was filed against the Company in 1831, by a member of the Livery, on the ground of improper user of the Thames Street and Holborn estates, which, it was alleged by the plaintiff, had been left exclusively to elecmosynary objects. The defendants succeeded in clearing themselves from fraud ; but a new scheme was settled in 1833, by which the application of funds from these two sources to charity was still further extended ; and as lately as 1880, the Charity Commission placed the greater part of the Dyers' trust possessions on a new footing. The result justified the challenge and inquiry of 1831, more especially as the Court had withheld with characteristic reticence the true state of affairs, of which it had no reason to be ashamed, as it was subsequently shown that, when the proceedings in equity were first taken, instead of 23l. 19s. 4d. a year, the strict aggregate charge on the trusts concerned, the defendants were paying about 300l. a year on that account. The decree of 1833 fixed the amount at one-half of the Holborn, and one-fourth of the Thames Street income, or altogether about 400l. a year.

The original Hall in Upper Thames Street, near Ebgate or Old Swan

---

[1] At Pattick and Simpson's sale-room in 1877 (February 6, Nos. 290 *et seqq.*) were offered some very curious MSS., containing several hundred swan-marks, principally referring to the river Cam. But one had belonged to the monastery of Crowland, and was described as the Abbot of Crowland's Mark, called *The Scourge.* It was transferred by Sir Walter Mildmay, 2–3 Philip and Mary, to Michael Beale, of Woodhalton, Co. Huntingdon, for 10l., and in 1650 it passed from this family to Talbot Pepys of Impington.

[2] In 1892, according to Whitaker, the total income is 7,000l., of which a seventh is held in trust.

Lane, and not far from London Bridge, disappeared in the Fire of 1666. The site is at present occupied by Dyers' Hall Wharf and Warehouse; but the precise position of the Hall itself is not ascertainable, nor are we aware whether the building was restored on the same spot, and whether a second conflagration in 1681 occurred there.

In 3 Henry VIII. the Wardens of the Dyers laid claim in a petition to the Court of Aldermen to the severalty of Bretaske Lane in Dowgate Ward; but, after due search made in the records, it was declared and adjudged to be a common thoroughfare. Of this lane Stow in his general narrative says nothing. It was probably one contiguous to the original Hall or premises, and was perhaps desired for building purposes. The historian describes a house in Cosin's Lane, once known as Lambard's Messuage, subsequently a dye-house; and there may have been a settlement round the seat of business of such establishments, the supply of water being near at hand.

But it is to be suspected that the Dyers, notwithstanding, closed up the lane; for this is evidently the locality and case to which Stow elsewhere refers, mentioning that in 4 Elizabeth (1561–2) the City Chamberlain was authorized by the Common Council to take down a certain door, and reopen a thoroughfare, in the same Ward.

The Dyers have almost evidently had at successive periods at least four Halls. That in Thames Street, with the double flight of steps leading to an entrance on the first floor, was not the first place of meeting, nor even perhaps the second; and the existing palatial seat is absolutely modern.

The fortunes and transactions of the Company are involved in an obscurity somewhat unnecessarily and tiresomely aggravated by the reserved attitude of the existing authorities. Of the present place of meeting on Dowgate Hill it can only be said, that it is a handsome structure, and that it was formerly part of the Company's property in what was once known as Little Elbow Lane.

LITERARY NOTICES.[1]

The Act 23 George III., cap. 15. For rendering more effectual the provisions contained in an Act of the 13th year of King George the First for preventing fraud and abuse, in the dyeing trade.

The Decree in Chancery, Attorney-General v. the Dyers' Company, Aug. 5, 1833.

Vesting Order and Scheme of the Charity Commissioners as to the Company's Charities, December 10, 1880.

---

[1] Compare Notices annexed to the account of the Vintners.

The Fanmakers.

THE antiquity and Oriental origin of the fan, with the infinite diversity of material and design employed, both in those which were imported from the East Indies and those manufactured in France and Italy, have been rendered even more familiar in quite recent times than before by the attractive volume from the hand of M. Uzanne. In the East, and even in the South of Europe, such an invention was a natural and necessary auxiliary in allaying the heat of a tropical or even a sultry climate ; but in a more northerly region like England it was apt to fulfil an artificial and secondary function; and the ornamental and elegant character which it soon assumed at once opened a new channel to the ingenuity of the artist and converted the fan into an object of fashion and a vehicle for intrigue. The celebrated Colonel Lovelace, in his *Lucasta*, 1649, has some verses " On Lucasta's Fan with a Looking-glass in it ; " it was of ostrich feathers, set with precious stones, we are told, unless this was poetical licence. But it is not necessary to suppose so, as from the notices which have been collected from our early writers on the subject it is to be concluded that no expense was grudged to embellish this appendage to a lady's dress. The handle seems to have often been of silver or gold, or of inlaid ivory, and with the dimensions of the object, which more closely resembled a hand-screen than the fan at present in use, rendered it both weighty and cumbrous. The owner not unfrequently delegated to a servant the task of carrying it abroad.

The probability is that in the time of Elizabeth, when such accessories seem to have been first introduced, either from France or Italy, their use was confined to a limited circle ; but passages in old plays and satires establish that under the Stuarts they became much more plentiful and general, if they were not occasionally employed by the other sex ; and when the Watteau school of painting lent itself to the embellishment of the manufacture, and our social manners were more generally influenced by those of the French Court, fans acquired a prominence and popularity which made their production a lucrative branch of commerce, and exposed their fair purchasers to the attacks of the moralist and lampooner.

The fans imported from the Continent and from India were alike subject to duty, and were consequently expensive commodities when they reached the hands of the retail buyer. This did not sensibly hinder their influx into our ports, where they arrived at regular intervals in the second half of the seventeenth century, in large consignments to the mercers, drapers, and haberdashers of the metropolis and other places along the coast. In London itself the Table of Rates in force in 1680 entitled the riverside porters to charge 12*d.* for each load, which was the scale for foreign goods.

EARLY ARMS.

It was within the period when the employment of fans continued to grow more universal, and the demands of the Excise kept the price of the article necessarily high, that the project was conceived of instituting, on the basis of existing Corporations, a Gild or Company of Fanmakers. Very probably some of those concerned in the movement were foreigners settled in London, and already engaged in the trade ; but the justification for the establishment of an organized Fraternity and the prayer for a charter bespeak a more or less flourishing home industry, rendering common action practicable and advantageous.

It was while a lady of the Stuart family—the last of her name—was on the throne, that the grant was sought and obtained. The charter, which is dated April 19, 1709, and which is the latest in order of time of all such grants, is engrossed on parchment, and contains in the upper left-hand corner, as a sort of initial ornament, a small full-length portrait of her Majesty.[1]

The youngest of all the Companies was designated The Master, Wardens, and Assistants of the Company of Fanmakers, and was appointed to consist of a Master, two Wardens, and seventeen Assistants. In 1882 the Freemen were estimated at 200, and the Livery at 120. The latter is limited to 200; but it is to be remarked that in 1724, when the charter

---

[1] The original instrument was most obligingly shown to us by Colonel Sewell, Clerk to the Company.

had been fifteen years in existence, a return of the Livery Companies omits mention of this one. The actual income is nominal, and is largely dependent on private contributions—a source which has been always employed and recognised, under great emergencies, even by the Great Companies.

But the Fanmakers started at a juncture when there was not sufficient opportunity, prior to the repeal of the duty on foreign imports, to gain a footing and accumulate a common purse; and the exemption of fans from customs was virtually fatal to the welfare of the Gild as a substantial and self-supporting body. The Exhibition, which it promoted in 1878, reflected great credit on the spirit and taste of those concerned, and cost the Company, corporately and personally, no less than 750*l.*

It associates itself, however, with an article of female luxury, of which the fascination does not appear to decline, and the novelty is inexhaustible; and there is no reason why the precedent lately set by the admission of Lady Charlotte Schreiber should not be followed, even to the extent of making the Fanmakers' a true Association of Brethren and Sisteren, who might severally and mutually conduce to its success and prosperous continuance.

In Leadenhall Street Peter Motteux, translator of *Don Quixote*, kept an emporium for East India goods, at the sign of the Two Fans; and it was continued after his death, in 1722, by his widow.

LITERARY NOTICE.

The Fanmakers' Grievances by the Importation of Fanns from the East Indies. A broadside.

The Farriers.

THE Farriers, or, as Stow calls them, Ferrers, are mentioned among the Fellowships which had the right of naming the Keeper of the King's Great Beam at the Steelyard in the thirteenth century. They are also described as Ferriers and *Ferrones;* and somewhat later their French designation, *Maréchaux*, is translated into *Marshals.*

In the first year of Edward I. (1272) Walter le Brun, farrier in the Strand, London, received a grant of the King *in capite* of a piece of ground in St. Clement's Parish for the erection of a forge, on condition that he paid at the Stone Cross annually, in respect thereof, six horse-shoes with the nails appurtenant. The horse-shoes were rendered by Walter himself in the first and second years of Edward I.; and the payment was continued in the fifteenth of Edward II. The property afterward passed to the Corporation. But we see that the craft in its inception started with the functions subsequently discharged by the blacksmith, and doubtless for a long time combined them with those of the horse-leech.

By the civic regulations of 1350, fixing the prices of goods and the wages of operatives, a farrier was not allowed to charge more than he had done before the Pestilence of 1348; that is, for a horse-shoe of six nails, $1\frac{1}{2}d.$, and for one of eight, $2d.$, and for taking off a shoe of six or eight nails, $\frac{1}{2}d.$; but for the shoe of a courser he might ask $2\frac{1}{2}d.$, and for a charger, $3d.$, and for taking either of them off, $1d.$

OLD ARMS.

The Farriers owed their Ordinances to a complaint made in 1356, that certain unskilled ferrons had set up forges in the City, and had occasioned the loss of many horses. Hereupon the Mayor summoned all the farriers, and took steps to prevent a continuance of this abuse. The good folks of the trade were required to elect two Masters to supervise all forges, and the shoes and nails that were employed therein; to provide for cases where surgical treatment was needed, and to preserve the scale of charges which was in force before the Pestilence.

At this epoch they were merely a Mistery and Brotherhood, but exercised the power of binding apprentices, admitting to the Freedom, and controlling the craft; they are designated the Marshals of the City of London; and their two Wardens were presumably elected, as usual, by the Commonalty, subject to ratification at Guildhall.

But our knowledge of this Society and trade is remarkably scanty, partly owing to the almost total destruction of its papers in the Fire; and for the few particulars which we are enabled to furnish we are indebted to collateral sources. In official and other returns of 1501–2, 1509, and 1515, it is not named. In 1531–2 it occurs as having no Livery. But in 1572–3 we observe that property was left to St. Pulker's parish, London, on condition that the churchwardens should pay annually to the Farriers 13s. 4d. for distribution among their poor. The insignificance, indirectness, and solitariness of the gift, so far as charitable uses are concerned, may indicate the obscurity and imperfect organiza-tion of the recipients under Elizabeth ; and the misfortune is that the dole, which is bestowed on the widows of freemen, has consequently undergone no expansion.   In the levy of 1660–1 for the payment of the Forces by land and sea, its members were among the other similar bodies assessed for the purpose.   A code of bye-laws—the next on record to those of 1356—was approved by the Judges in 1676–7.

Tracing back their existence as a constituted Fraternity with a form of government to the middle of the fourteenth century, the Farriers either failed to seek, or omitted to obtain, a charter till the close of the reign of Charles II.   The grant is dated January 17, 1684–5, and does little more than confirm the ancient jurisdiction over the trade, which was now extended to the Cities of London and Westminster and their liberties and a radius of seven miles from either.   There was also a licence in mortmain to the amount of 100*l.* a year, of which a very small proportion has been exhausted.   The Company was directed to consist of a Master, three Wardens, and nineteen Assistants, which is the exist-ing complement.   In 1882 the freemen numbered 94, the Livery, 88.[1] The latter was probably granted by the City on incorporation, but it was for some reason withdrawn, and restored in 1692.   It is unlimited ; but the calls to it seem to be exclusively voluntary.   In the ten years 1870–9 the admissions to the Freedom were principally by redemption ; and the advantages of belonging to the Company are, no doubt, as in the majority of instances, independent of the nominal calling, and are sought by new members on social and electoral grounds.   In 1882 there were only five or six persons who were farriers or veterinary surgeons on the books, although in 1758 the often-quoted Act of Common Council imposed on all operative farriers the obligation of taking up the Freedom of the Company.   Such a principle, equally with the right of search, has been long abandoned as an anachronism.

At the same time there has been on the part of the administrative body a feeling of interest in the welfare and progress of the industry with which the Company is identified, and a desire, as far as possible, to maintain the standard of quality and promote improvements.

Some years since, three prizes were offered with this important object in view : (1) the Freedom of the Company, a gold medal, and 20*l.*, for the best essay on the Treatment of Horses in Health and Disease ; (2) a silver medal and 10*l.* for the best, most economically made, and most useful set of shoes for carriage horses in London over macadam, asphalte, and wood roadways, with special regard to slipperiness from

---

[1] In 1724 it stood at 76, in 1892, 96.

any causes ; (3) a bronze medal and 5*l.* for a similar set of shoes for cart-horses.

The most celebrated of farriers was, we fear, not of the so-named Gild—the joint leader of the Cornish insurgents at Blackheath Field in 1496, where Bishop Latimer's father served on the side of the King. Latimer, as a boy, helped to buckle on his parent's armour before he set out for the battle, as he told Edward VI. in one of his sermons preached before the King, and through him all of us for ever.

LITERARY NOTICES.

Markhams Maister-peece : Containing all Knowledge belonging to a Smith, Farrier, or Horse-leach. By Gervase Markham. 4to, 1615, 1636.
<small>The same writer published several other books of earlier date relating to horses.</small>

The Complete Farriar, Or the King's High-Way to Horsemanship. By Gervase Markham. 8vo, 1639.
⁎ Licensed in 1631.

The Compleat Horseman and Experte Farrier. By Thomas de Gray. Folio, 1639 ; 4to, 1670.

The Coun[t]rey Farrier : Teaching divers and sundry approved Medicines, to Cure all sorts of Cattell : .   .   .   Very useful and necessary for all Country-Farmers, Householders, and generally for all sorts of people. The Second edition, .   .   . 8vo, 1650.

The Anatomy of an Horse. By Andrew Snape, Junior, Farrier to His Majesty. Folio 1683. With engravings.

The Feltmakers.

THIS Association, an offshoot from the Haberdashers, and founded to regulate the manufacture and sale of felt hats, applied as early as 1576, it appears, for a charter, but was opposed by the parent body, and did not succeed in establishing itself till the following reign.

The origin of the Felt manufacture—a method of converting hair or wool into cloth without a loom—is referred back by some to a tradition coupled with the name of St. Clement, who flourished in the second and third centuries ; and St. Clement's Day, the 23rd November, used to be the Hatters' festival. The Saint reduced carded wool to this material, according to the fable, by treading and natural moisture ; but the knowledge of the artificial processes requisite for the purpose was far more ancient than Clement's time.

That the English Feltmakers existed long before their formal union as an independent and distinct Association, we need not doubt. One of the unlicensed bodies, amerced by the Crown in 1180, was that whereof Richard Thedr, *Feltrarius* or the Feltmaker, was Alderman ; and the fine was two marks, being double the amount demanded from the Cloth-workers or *Pannarii*.

Under the name of Feltmongers, they occur in 1501–2, as forty-seventh out of seventy-four bodies, and as the last and least of those possessing a Livery.[1] As the Livery con-

OLD ARMS.

sisted of two members only, perhaps these were the Wardens of the Gild. Once more, in 1515, when the Companies were assigned by the Court of Aldermen to their several places in order of priority, to obviate disputes on public occasions, the Feltmongers retained the rank given to them at the earlier date, except that a forty-eighth Company—the Fruiterers, which came sixty-fourth in 1502—completed the roll, which shut out several important fraternities, the Stationers, Stock-fishmongers, and Scriveners among the number.

Stow [2] tells us that James I., by letters patent of 1604, incorporated this Society by the name of "Master and Wardens and Commonalty of the Art or Mistery of Feltmakers of London :" granting them thereby divers privileges and liberties for the good government of the same Corporation ; and he adds that this was the first Company, which the King incorporated. The charter gave a Master, four Wardens, and twenty-one Assistants, as the governing body.

But although the Feltmongers were incorporated in 1604, they were not enrolled at that time, and in 1612–13 we find the Common Council expressing through the Lord Mayor "a general and free opinion" against the expediency thereof. How this objection and difficulty were overcome, we do not learn ; but the Company held its ground, and not only obtained new charters from Charles II. in 1667 (June 27), and

---

[1] The Fellmongers, mentioned in proceedings at Guildhall in 1394, and in the Leathersellers' Ordinances, 1635, are of course distinct. But the distribution of labour was formerly so irregular and obscure, that it is hard to determine whether they were salesmen or craftsmen, or both.

[2] *Annales*, 1615, p. 855.

1669–70 (January 10), exclusively of an *inspeximus* of George III., December 4, 1772, but in the first-named the grant of 1604 was allowed and confirmed, and in the Skinners' Charters of 1667 and 1685, the right of the Feltmakers' Corporation, or of any other Feltmakers, to cut wools for the manufacture of hats, was specially secured. The right of search and control spread over a four miles' radius.

The Company does not possess the original instrument of 1604. There are bye-laws approved by the Judges in 1667, 1698, 1745, and 1759. By the last-quoted code all persons engaged in the trade were required, in conformity with the Act of Common Council of the previous year, to take up the Freedom.

In 1882, the number of freemen was unknown. The Livery at that date numbered 53, in 1887–8, 61, and in 1892, 65. It is limited to 120.

The Company has long ceased to exercise any practical superintendence over the trade, and chiefly relies (its property of any kind being small) on its honorary Liverymen, among whom there generally are several distinguished public characters. The late Earl of Iddesleigh and the late Mr. W. H. Smith,[1] M.P., belonged to the Gild.

The use of felt as a material for the headdress of both sexes rendered the trade in this description of attire for a considerable period both large and lucrative. The palmy epoch was unquestionably while the business still remained in the hands of the haberdashers ; but the opposition of that body to the separate incorporation may shew that the monopoly was still worth preserving. Throughout the first half of the seventeenth century the contemporary representations of costume satisfy us that the custom for such articles must have remained very regular and extensive even after the Restoration ; but the influx of foreign felt, both in a manufactured and other state, even in the reign of James I., injured the home trade so much as to lead the makers in and near London to remonstrate against the grievance. The establishment of the Hudson's Bay Company in 1670, again, by bringing beaver skins and other furs into fashion, further crippled the members of the Gild, since the fashionable world was apt to prefer the new wares, while the Continental supply answered the requirements of the majority.

The revenue, as we have already hinted, is inconsiderable—from 300*l.* to 400*l.* a year, partly arising from fines and fees, and partly from two properties left in 1692 and 1804 in trust for uses—and leaving little or

---

[1] The founder of the newspaper business, Mr. Smith's father, was a stationer in the Strand, and did not originally sell periodical literature or books. His shop, on the site of the later premises, used to be a long, low-pitched frontage, and lay next door to the Crown and Anchor. One of Mr. Smith's specialities was schoolboys' guinea desks.

no margin after necessary expenses and reasonable hospitalities discharged. In 1876, the Company laid out a small amount in a competition for essays and specimens, with a view to arriving at the most desirable method of manufacturing and applying felt.

There are no relics of any kind in the possession of the Feltmakers. The Beadle's mace is characteristically surmounted by an emblematical hat.

LITERARY NOTICE.

To the most honorable Assembly of the Commons House of Parliament. The humble petition of the Felt-makers in and neare London, praying for the prohibition of the importation of Felts and Hats wrought and half wrought, beyond the seas. [1621.] A broadside.

The Fletchers.[1]

THIS Gild, like one or two others, merely enjoys its rank by prescription, as no charter or Act of Parliament can be produced, whereby it was incorporated. In some form or other it must, from the nature of its employment, have existed literally time out of memory, and in the fourteenth century is found in treaty with the Bowyers on some points of disagreement between them. It was then evidently an established and recognised Fellowship.

In a Romance poem of the fourteenth century, "The King and the Hermit," which has been used by Sir Walter Scott in *Ivanhoe*, the disguised King tells his host, that his name is Jack Fletcher, and the hermit at once suggests that, as he is of that craft, he may perchance help him now and then to a shaft or two.

In 1371, the Bowyers and Fletchers came to Guildhall to seek the approval of the Mayor and Aldermen to a series of Articles drawn up with a view to keeping the two trades distinct, and to preclude the inter-

---

[1] Compare the account of the Bowyers, *suprâ*.

ference of one with the other. It appeared on the face of the proceedings at a Husting of Common Pleas of Land, that certain workmen
served both crafts, and this practice was judged to
be detrimental and improper. It was settled that
all should henceforth elect to which trade they would
belong, and renounce the other ; but all articles in
an incomplete state might be finished and sold within a fixed date.

OLD ARMS.

This case before the Mayor's Court was simply an
effort to reconcile current differences with the allied
craft, and does not touch any principle of status or
government. But the Ordinances of 1403 shew the appointment of
Wardens under the control of the Lord Mayor and Court of Aldermen, with right of search as to all manner of arrows, arrowheads, and
quarels, in the hands alike of freemen and foreigners. No one of the
trade was to offer goods for sale without proper assay ; and the Wardens
on their part were bound to be at all times prepared to make such
assay under penalties. But all manner of folk bringing to the City for
sale broad arrows and bolts were exempt from search. The freemen
were in no case to sell to any foreigner, until it was of certain knowledge that such sale was not to the prejudice of the King and realm.

The Fletchers obtained a grant of arms, 7 Edward IV., and in the
reign of Henry VII. a crest in augmentation, having previously, it is
concluded, had power vested in them to possess a Livery. But all the
ancient registers and ledgers have been lost ; and the earliest extant
records go no further back than 1775.

The governing body consists of an Upper and a Renter Warden and
ten Assistants. There is no common seal, and presumably no licence
to hold real property. The total income is returned at 149*l.* a year, of
which nearly one half arises from the ground-rent of premises erected on
the site of their old Hall in St. Mary Axe.

The Company states that it possesses a right of ancient standing,
though of no present validity, to borrow money from the Bowyers and
Leathersellers. It would be curious to ascertain in what circumstances
such a *liberty* originated, unless it was the absence of a charter, though
it is not difficult to understand how the three crafts would have a running account together.

It has no further direct or other connection with the trade.

There is a palpable indication that the Fletchers formerly enjoyed a
much higher degree of prosperity. We perceive that they had their own
Hall ; and the industrial art, of which they engrossed the profits within
the municipal area, remained during many ages of prominent import-

ance. But they and the Bowyers suffered a common decline when the appliances of war underwent throughout Europe a fundamental change. Even in the time of James I. the Bowyers and Fletchers had evidently survived their prosperity. They, the Musicians, and the Woolmen present themselves in the subscription-list to the Ulster purchase scheme of 1615 as the smallest contributors.

In 1739, the Company consisted of the two Wardens, ten Assistants, and twenty-five Liverymen, of whom the last paid on admission a fine of 10l. They had not then parted with their small Hall.[1]

The Founders or Coppersmiths.[2]

WE are referred to the reign of Edward III., and to the year 1365, for a casual incident, which, as is by no means unusual, constitutes our earliest piece of intelligence respecting the present Association, and at the same time exhibits it in the light of an established Fraternity. The document which embodies the evidence is a petition in Norman-French to the civic authorities from "the Good Men of the Mistery of the Founders of the City of London," and prays for the grant of Ordinances for the management of the Craft. At this point of time and long after, the Founders had no control outside and beyond the detection and presentment of bad material and workmanship.

The goods particularized in this petition are : candlesticks, buckles, spurs, stirrups, straps, lavers, and pots. But we may securely add ewers and basins for various domestic and professional purposes ; and indeed

---

[1] The Hall was in Aldgate Ward. It is thus noticed by Stow :—" So turning backe into S. Mary Axe, they [the bounds] goe upon the East side, from the house of Master Iohn Holding, commonly called *Fletchers hall*"—which reads as if Holding had given or lent his residence at the outset for the meetings of the Company, which was incapacitated from holding it corporately.

[2] We have been indebted to the courtesy and liberality of the Company for a handsome illustrated volume entitled *Annals of the Worshipful Company of Founders*. By William Meade Williams, Master, 1852–3–4. 8vo, privately printed, 1868.

the ewer, as a typical article of manufacture, was the original trademark. The general recognition of the Gild, and its evident length of standing about this time, are evinced by its right in 1376 to accredit two representatives to the Common Council.

We find, about a quarter of a century later (1389) a revival of the regulations of 1365, which, in common with the original Articles, deal with the mischievous practice, which then prevailed, of using light and tender solder for candlesticks, etc., and of making stirrups, spurs, and buckles of defective or fictitious material ; and they guard against irregularities on the part of apprentices, journeymen, and strangers working at the trade. The last-named were required to pass an examination before the Masters or Overseers. Power of search was conceded, as usual, but only in company with a City Serjeant.

EARLY ARMS OR
COGNIZANCE.

The maintenance of subordination among the apprentice class was at once essential and difficult. The Ordinances specify most of the things which these youths were not to do ; but in 1608 playing at bowls, and betting at cards, dice, tables, shovelboard, and other unlawful games, were prohibited. As late as 1684, in the not very cheerful days of the *Quo Warranto*, the Master and Upper Wardens played at nine-pins on the Thames during the great frost ; but perhaps this privilege was reserved for the seniors.

Great stress is laid on *clockwork* being executed only with the finest and purest metal. It is curious that the journeyman is termed a vadlet, an awkward transition from the French *valet*.

There is no reason to doubt that in 1365, if not long prior, the government was in the hands of Wardens or Masters ; but in 1391 the two officers appointed to rule the craft, and to see the Ordinances duly carried out, are named—Thomas Grace and Robert Newman—and were presented to the Court of Aldermen for confirmation.

In 1469, the affairs of the Gild were doubtless not very prosperous, as we meet with it, under the name of *Coppersmiths*, engaging to furnish the modest quota of nine men to the City Watch.

It transpires from an official reply to charges preferred against the governing body at a much more recent period, that in 1472—our next landmark—there was a development of some kind ; for the Court states that in the year cited " we began with twenty-four poor honest men," signifying that such was then the complement of the Executive. Nor does it seem improbable that about this date the Brotherhood—for it was still nothing more—was gaining in consideration and standing, though far from affluent.   The Ordinances of April 2, 1489, justify such a conclusion : they touch upon the exclusive manufacture or fabric of goods by freemen, the scrutiny by the Wardens before the parcels are packed, and their exposure for sale at fairs and by hawkers ; but they are partly occupied by directions as to apprenticeship, masses, burials, and alms.

Here we get a distinct record of a Livery or Clothing, on which, in common with the freemen and journeymen, payments for all religious services are charged, and a sufficient insight to enable us to perceive that the Founders were not remiss in fulfilling the professions on which these Societies based their title and claim to favour.   But while they appear in 1489 to have possessed a Livery, in an official return of 1501–2 they are classed with those who had none, so that it was perhaps not even an acknowledged prescription.   We advance a step further in 1508, when, by reason of the necessity for adjusting certain differences among the members through the good offices of the Corporation, we for the first time trace the seat of the Craft to the neighbourhood of St. Margaret's, Lothbury, and discover St. Clement's Chapel in that church to be at once the receptacle for the common chest and the shrine at which obits, requiems, and oblations were offered.   We also gain a clue, which bears on the glimpse accidentally acquired of the state of affairs in 1472.   For there is in these proceedings of 1508 a highly eloquent indication, that then, as doubtless in the earlier years, the system of government was peculiarly popular, inasmuch as six of the yeomen are appointed to assist in auditing the accounts, and are charged with the custody of one of the four keys of the chest, the other three constructively remaining with the Senior, Renter, and Junior Wardens.

It appears that the Wardens had been involved through the action of one of the Fellowship, John Sandford, in legal proceedings, and had been summoned to the Court of Exchequer to answer a charge of having made some innovation as to the fees payable by apprentices. The matter put the Founders to considerable expense, and was ultimately referred to the Lord Mayor for settlement ; but there seems to have been an unanimous feeling in favour of upholding the Wardens ; for at the meeting held on the 26th October, 1508, " the whole Fellowship, both old and young," joined in praying them to labour, so that the Lord Chancellor might have the irregularity rectified.[1]

---

[1] The question remained open, not merely with this Company, but with several others, at least till 1556, when the Wardens attended at Guildhall to confer with the Lord Mayor and Aldermen thereupon.

The bye-laws of 1515 substantially reproduced those of 1489.

Elsewhere we dwell a little at large on a great stride made approximately in 1534, when the Founders were put, by the bounty of some of their wealthier members, in possession of a site for a common Hall between St. Margaret's Church and Coleman Street. The ownership did not perhaps yield immediate fruit, as material and labour were in those days costlier than land; and if it were the fact that the open area acquired had been a place of interment, the selling value was presumably impaired. At any rate, proceedings before the Court of Aldermen in 1579 afford testimony that some half-century after this occurrence the organization was still feeble and the revenue scanty; and the Lord Mayor was obliged to formulate a scheme for the more punctual payment of quarterages.

Another phase of laxity, the omission to come to the Masters' Feast, was met in 1535 by a regulation that every Liveryman should pay 2s. for his dinner on that occasion whether he brought his wife or not, and whether he came or stayed away.

It is worth while, as a constitutional point, to solicit attention to the fact that the threepence per quarter leviable from the Livery was to be collected by the Junior Warden, but that the twopence payable by the freemen was raised by two of their own number selected from four previously nominated by the Clothing. This practice responded to the democratic feeling otherwise evinced by the Gild; the acuteness of the pecuniary tension seems to manifest itself in the power given to recover by distress.

Perhaps the stricter enforcement of discipline proved beneficial and salutary; for in the course of a few years the Founders, though still unincorporated, seem to have made sensible progress, and to have gained a certain prestige. In 1587 they were invested with the responsible and widely important duty of assizing all weights at a fixed table of rates; and this office led to the appointment of a Sizer, who stamped every weight, before it could be legally used, with the Founders' mark of an ewer, and caused it to be sealed at Guildhall.

This valuable trust, which was amplified in 1599 at the expense of the Plumbers, was succeeded, October 13, 1590, by a grant of arms from Robert Cooke, Clarencieux,[1] and in 1592 (March 28), by the "Ordinances of Elizabeth," so termed, because their comprehensive range almost entitles them to the rank of a charter.

Here several points have to be observed. Not only the Livery, but

---

[1] Viewed, approved, and entered in the Visitation of London, 1634, by Henry St. George, Richmond Herald.

Assistants, are specified ; St. Bartholomew's day, or twelve days before or after, is fixed as the season for elections ; owing to the limited income of the Craft, no one, save a past Warden, is to have more than one apprentice, who shall be bound for eight years, lest the admissions to the Freedom should grow too numerous ; but a past Warden may have two, provided that he employ both on his own work. Each apprentice, before he is bound, is to be " abled " by the Wardens, " in order to see that he is free born and whole of limb for the honour of the City," the master paying hereupon 2s. to the Gild, and 6d. to the Chamber of London. The livery is to be of one suit and colour with hoods of prescribed pattern and hue, and is to be renewed every three years. The quarterages, collected in the manner ordained in 1587, are to be kept in a common box with three locks, of which the Junior Warden shall keep one, the Yeomanry the other two, the box remaining, not in St. Clement's Chapel, but in the common Hall. In 1609, the colours for the livery are said to be black and red.

The tenor of this series of Articles bespeaks an approach to final consolidation. In 1592 the Founders have three Wardens, a Court of Assistants, a Livery, a Hall, and a Cook,[1] with a degree of popularity in the general temper and complexion of the body. But when we trace the Founders a little further, and enter on the next reign, we recognise a somewhat strange phenomenon in the shape of a petition to the Crown by Robert Thompson, Founder, shewing that the absence of a settled government favoured the growth and continuance of many abuses in the Craft, and praying that the said Craft be incorporated for its own and the general good.

The representations of Thompson were referred to the Commissioners for Suits, who obtained a favourable report from the Mayor and Aldermen (Nov. 4, 1613), and ultimately produced the desired effect in a charter of September 18, 1614.

The expenses attendant on the process were defrayed by a loan from Mr. Richard Rudinge, a member, on the security of the estate. The total outlay seems to have been 115l. 14s., of which 100l. represented the payment into the Hanaper, 2l. 4s. a fee to the Recorder for his advice, and the remainder, save 5s. 4d., gratuities to officials, including 11s. to Sir Francis Bacon's clerk. The item of 5s. 4d. was for preparing a written statement of the points which the petitioners desired to be embodied in the charter, which is so far worth noting.

The Gild was constituted a Company with perpetual succession, a common seal, a licence to hold lands of 40l. value by the year, the right

---

[1] On February 24, 1605-6, John Tyffins, of Coleman Street, was appointed Cook during pleasure at 26s. 8d. a year.

of search and prosecution, and a government consisting of a Master, two Wardens, and fifteen Assistants. But a very material change in an aristocratic direction had been effected in the electoral system, which now crossed over to the opposite extreme, by depriving the Livery as well as the Yeomanry of nearly their whole voice in the selection of officers and the management of affairs. A narrow principle of co-ôptation vested in the Court the entire constitutional and administrative authority, and created an oligarchy in the persons of the few more successful and affluent members, who had long previously signalized their presence by the purchase of the freehold occupied by the Hall, as they or their descendants probably did by defraying the cost of the structure. In the present instance the prevailing poverty of the Brotherhood necessarily assisted in enabling the more eminent and fortunate to obtain and preserve an ascendency.

The Gild was incorporated under the style of " The Master, Wardens, and Commonalty of the Mistery of Founders of the City of London," and the letters patent were addressed to " all and every our loving subjects, the Founders of our City of London, and others, the Freemen of the said Mistery ; " but the clauses affecting elections were, as we have intimated, so framed as to neutralize any popular aspirations derived from the preamble.

The composition of the new body embraced all English makers of brass weights, and melters and workers of brass and copper wares, or workers of molten brasses and copper metals, and all annealing, within the City and three miles' compass ; and the executive was empowered to make ordinances, so that they are agreeable to the laws of the land and to the liberties of London, saving the rights of the Pewterers ; and as touching the right of assize, we find it laid down that when the Company's Sizer, who was under oath, had marked weights with the Ewer, they were to be sealed, if of avoirdupois standard, at Guildhall, but if of troy, at Goldsmiths' Hall. Upon the acquisition of arms, stamps of various sizes were employed, the whole coat appearing, when the dimensions of the article permitted.

When Ben Jonson wrote his *Alchemist*, shortly before the formation of the Company in 1614, Lothbury was yet the quarter set apart for this business, and Stow's Continuator (1633) writes : " This street is possessed for the most part by Founders, that cast candlesticks, chafing-dishes, spice-mortars, and such-like copper or laton works, and do afterwards turn them with the foot, and not with the wheel, to make them smooth and bright with turning and scrating (as some do term it), making a loathsome noise to the bye-passers, that have not been used to the like."

The din and smoke in this locality and in Bartholomew Lane must have been highly disagreeable, whatever we may think of the matter, looking back upon the scene from a picturesque point of view. The furnaces were perpetually at work, both in the City and the immediate outskirts ; and the prevalence of wooden buildings made it imperative that the overseers of the craft should enforce all possible precautions against fire.

Of the Ordinances, which closely succeeded, and replaced those of 1592, we shall draw attention to that which directed that on election-day two of the Livery should be nominated to serve as stewards at the Assistants' dinner on Lord Mayor's day, or such other day as might be chosen for the occasion, at which dinner the Livery, as well as the Court might be present, and the former might bring their wives. No one who had not served or fined as Steward, was eligible as an Assistant ; but the same person was not liable to be called upon a second time.

No steps were apparently taken to renew the grant of 1614 previously to the *Quo Warranto* of 1684, except that in 1652 the democratic section of the Company endeavoured to prevail on the Committee for Corporations, by reason of the alleged unconstitutional and arbitrary acts of the Court, to assist in providing them with a more stringent or more clearly worded charter. The papers connected with the business are preserved ; but they do not shew what, if anything, was accomplished. The movement might to a certain extent harmonize with the general tendency of the Commonalty or even Livery ; but it was perhaps in this case prompted and encouraged by the prevailing political spirit ; for the Master and Wardens, in their reply, affirm that these " false, pretending complainers," whom they had " entreated as brethren in love," would " level the government and orders of the Company according to their own perverse, proud and peevish minds."

The Committee possibly shared the view that it was an *ex parte* and ill-founded appeal. Yet it is impossible to disguise the fact that the charter of 1614 was calculated to foster discontent and disunion, while it introduced at the same time, perhaps, the only system of administration compatible with order.

The surrender of the old charter took place in June, 1684 ; and the new one, which cost about 250*l.*, followed the customary lines. The Master appointed by the King under it was the rather celebrated Colonel, afterwards General, Oglethorpe. The Revolution of 1688, as in other cases, restored the *status quo ante.*

The bye-laws, which are now in use, when any necessity arises for reference or exercise, were those passed, however, on February 3, 1783, and offer points of difference from the prior code indicative of a decline in the prosperity and credit of the Corporation. Here we note the requirement of a bond for 500*l.* and one surety from the Master, before he takes office, as a safeguard against the waste or embezzlement of the funds, and whereas the Stewards in the preceding regulations defrayed the cost of the yearly dinner, the amount—not exceeding 10*l.*—was now made a charge on the common purse. The Clerk and Beadle are expressly mentioned as subject to annual election or reappointment ; and at this time the Master, one of the Wardens, or two of the Wardens and nine Assistants, appear to have made a Court.

In returns of 1699 and 1724, the Livery is given as 90 and 136 respectively. In 1736 the Executive consisted of the Master, two Wardens, and twenty-nine Assistants ; in 1746, the Assistants were reduced to twenty-eight. But these fluctuations were often accidental.

It is confessed by those who should be least willing, perhaps, to admit it, that from 1740 to 1840, the affairs, in consequence of impoverishment by the Fire and gradual alterations in mercantile economy, were at a very low ebb, that the income was not over 100*l.* a year, and that a call to the Livery was a phenomenal exception. Except that power without resources is not covetable, this state of things followed the lines of the charter of 1614, which, with the exception of the temporary one of James II., was the only grant to the Company ; but, where the estate was nominal, the absorption of influence and authority by a few was apt either to be short-lived or to react by diverting the scheme from its original and professed objects. The alternative was tried by the Founders, who let their Hall and other freeholds, enlarged their Livery,[1] and increased the scale of fines. The result was thought to warrant the erection of a new place of meeting in 1877 with borrowed money, although in the years 1871–7, both inclusive, the calls to the Livery were only 23, and the fees payable by Freemen and Liverymen, even where the former join by redemption, were moderate. An impulse thus given to the expansion of the Company on new lines in 1853 by an influential member of the Court, does not seem to have been maintained.

The annual receipts in 1880 were stated to exceed 1,660*l.*[2] ; but the expenditure was considerable, and the Company owed 8,500*l.*

It was in that year that a series of prizes was offered, amounting to 87*l.*, for competition in brass and bronze work, and for the best essay on the history of Founding in brass, copper, and bronze. In the execution of the models, beauty, originality of design, and excellence of workman-

---

[1] In 1882, the Livery amounted to 115, in 1892, to 100. In the former year there were only 22 on the Freedom.

[2] In 1892, the figures are 1,900*l.*, of which the trusts make only 90*l.*

ship, were to be studied. These movements are seldom without their share of good ; and the governing body entertained the idea of continuing and extending the encouragement of the art. But we believe that nothing further has been achieved.

We have heard how various trades congregated, at first more or less fortuitously, in certain quarters, to which for convenience or in the public interest they confined themselves. As Cheapside, Cornhill, Bishopsgate, the riverside, had their settlers, so we find that, from time immemorial perhaps, the Founders chose as their seat the area behind the Bank of England, always known as Lothbury, or Lodebury [1] [? Ludbury], and formerly an open area, watered, down to the middle of the 15th century,[2] by the Walbrook, which almost bathed the western side of St. Margaret's Church. Even in the days of Defoe it was a district of comparatively moderate consequence.

The Founders, in fact, formed a colony on this ground, in order to be at a distance from the primitive centre of traffic and habitation, where their employments were calculated to be obnoxious,[3] and probably during at least two centuries presented a spectacle which, from its very humility and rudeness, it becomes interesting to contemplate in the mind's eye. A cluster of poor wooden tenements, roofed with thatch, round St. Margaret's, Lothbury, and in one of these, where the Warden or Wardens dwelt, their place of assembly and consultation.

This spot was their home, their daily haunt. Their thought was for it and of it. They were familiar with every inch of the ground. They had opportunities of knowing the course of events and every turn of affairs. It is the almost invariable incidence and drift in these cases that, where they in the beginning gathered together, there they abode ; for their most solemn associations were with the ground and the holy building erected upon it. It was round this that they had first clustered, and had slowly increased in number and substance ; and they instinctively clang to the place as one breathing a charmed and sacred atmosphere. The ancient nomad instinct was in them no longer. Where their first choice or the exigencies of their position brought them, century after century witnessed their survival, probably their aggrandizement and evolution.

The common practice of the Gilds, until they obtained a regular seat,

---

[1] " By S. Giles Churchyard was a large water, called a Poole : I reade in the yeere 1244, that *Anne of Lodbury* was drowned therein."—Stow's *Survey*, ed. 1633, p. 11.

[2] In 1440 the stream at this point was vaulted over by Robert Large, Mercer, and the church extended.

[3] See the *Statutes of the Streets against Annoyances*, printed in Stow's *Survey*, 1633, No. 25, where the Founders are particularly mentioned.

was to assemble in some religious establishment, at the residence of the Wardens, or at the Hall of another Fraternity. The first allusion to any place of meeting in the present instance is under 1497, when the Brewers' and Armourers' Halls were hired at a groat a day on different occasions, but in each case for two days; on April 12, 1513, certain business was transacted "in Coleman Street," possibly at one of the Wardens' houses; in 1516, Leathersellers' Hall was engaged.

Not as it happened with the Drapers, Ironmongers, and others, a small and poor community, cleaving to the soil whence it sprang, and where its bread was, and its altar, and the ashes of its dead, looked around in quest of a worthier meeting-house and a more commodious repository of its possessions; and in 1534, or thereabout, two houses and a parcel of ground lying between St. Margaret's and what is now Moorgate Street, were purchased by eighteen members of the Gild [1] for the purpose of a common Hall. How long subsequently to this important transaction, denoting a new era in the annals, the object was actually accomplished, we do not learn; but it is abundantly clear that the financial condition of the Founders long after this time was too humble and weak to permit the allotment of common funds to building expenses; and we shall not probably be far from the truth in assuming that they followed the practice of much richer bodies by working piece-meal, and even contenting themselves at first with the available accommodation. The tradition is, that the vacant plot bought with the tenements was the garden or burial-ground of the Friars Austins; and if this had been so, we should have to suppose that the transfer was somewhat later than that usually assigned to it, since, prior to the Dissolution, the monks would scarcely have parted with their garden, and still less with their graveyard. But the fact is, or seems to be, that this is an unsupported theory; and the site of the original seat of government and meeting was not indeed on the eastern, but on the western side of St. Margaret's, toward Coalman or Coleman Street, before Moorgate Street existed.

Not many notices of the building occur. It stood at some distance back from the thoroughfare, the frontage belonging to the Corporation, and appears to have been approached by a lane or alley leading to a spacious paved courtyard. St. Margaret's was immediately to the east of it; in the rear were a few detached buildings in large grounds, with a view of the Moor beyond. We incidentally hear of the basement let as early as 1565 at 4*l.* a year, the refectory, two parlours with a glass window between them, the sizing room, the gowns' room, a paved kitchen, and an inner buttery, where the treasure-chest was kept; but

---

[1] Eight contributed 20*s.* each, the rest, 2*l.* 15*s.*; altogether, 10*l.* 15*s.*

there is no specific account of the house. The refectory and parlours were almost obviously on the first floor, and there was a storey above, where the Clerk probably had his dormitory.

In 1549, a company of players paid 10s. for the use of the place, and a wedding-party was charged only a groat about the same time ; perhaps it was the marriage of a member, as various sums are entered for this sort of service, one of 12s. A Haberdasher, in 1558, gives no more than 3d.

The Hall was lost in the Fire, and was rebuilt by private subscription. The corporate means, however, remained chronically slender, and portions of the building were let off for different purposes and to a variety of persons or public bodies,[1] till in 1846 the whole was rented by the Post Office. But at the same time the Company, by this and various other financial expedients, swelled its income ; and in 1854, the old quarter, which had been the home of the Craft between five and six centuries, was finally abandoned, and a house on the western side of St. Swithin's Lane purchased for 3,500l. under a special licence in mortmain. In 1877, New Founders' Hall, which involved a loan of 8,000l. at four per cent., was erected. The possession of the fee simple affords security for the ultimate freedom from debt ; but of course the Founders' fortunes have entered on a new phase irreconcilable with the Lothbury traditions. They belong to the same category as the Loriners, Needlemakers, and Spectaclemakers, with the special advantage of handsome premises for official and convivial purposes. Historically the curtain falls, as it rose, in Lothbury.

A dispassionate consideration of the few known leading facts relative to the Founders during their five or six centuries of life as a Society in Lothbury and elsewhere, induces us to attach greater weight than at first sight we might be prepared to do, to the statement of the Company in 1652, that it began in 1472 with "twenty-four poor honest men" ; for the paucity of members of more than very moderate means was evidently, down to the middle of the present century, a ruling and chronic feature. Many of the Gilds were poor ; but they either linger in obscurity or have disappeared. Here we have one, which hung on a single thread—a fortuitous and happy investment at the Reformation in a City freehold on the part of certain of its members—and was at last redeemed

---

[1] Among those who had the use of portions of the premises were the Merchant Adventurers, who leased the sizing and gowns' rooms, the Brown Bakers, who occupied the warehouse under the Hall, the Loriners, Clockmakers, Gunmakers, and Ticket-porters, the Society for Promoting Religious Knowledge, preachers, players, and dancing-masters. In 1699, the Scots Church in London took a lease of the Hall and parlour for forty-one years.

from ruin by that agency alone. We have the official admission that the Fraternity or Company was indigent and limited in 1472; we are officially apprised that it was in narrow circumstances from 1740 to 1840; and the sale of plate under pressure is a periodical incidence; but there may have been a middle period of prosperity, for which the vouchers perished in 1666, inasmuch as, although the prime cost, in or about 1534, of the premises in Lothbury was undoubtedly small, and there is no evidence for heavy subsequent outlay, that of the second Hall is computed at nearly 4,000*l.*—an amount which would not have been advanced in the 17th century on the property, and must have come from internal sources as before.

The most ancient book of accounts belongs to 1497, and comprises a schedule of the plate and other effects then in the possession of the Founders. But some of these articles had been acquired at an earlier period, as the collection at present includes two masers attributed to the end of the fourteenth century. In the inventory we observe basons and ewers of latten or laton, a species of fine brass, dishes, table-cloths, and two plain " washing towells." The

THE BOWIN SPOON, 1625.

silver and silver-gilt objects are what are intended, when in a subsequent entry there is a reference to the *Juells* belonging to the Craft ; the term might extend to the vessels employed in St. Clement's Chapel.

From time to time plate, which would have represented a very large and valuable collection, was presented ; but the necessities of the Company, from narrow receipts, irregular payments of dues, constant levies for public purposes, and the severe loss entailed by the Fire in 1666, rendered the periodical conversion of everything of the kind into money indispensable ; and of the entire quantity received not more than four ancient pieces remain.

The plate falling within this category comprises a spoon presented by Humphrey Bowin, with his initials and the date 1625 and three tankards, for the purchase of which Thomas Fisher, Merchant and Founder of London, left 50*l.* by his will, proved in 1708. There are also two masers, one with a cover, ascribed to the reign of Richard II. ; a Venetian glass of the 16th century, richly painted with an allegorical design, and said to have been taken by a yeoman of the English guard at the siege of Boulogne in 1544 ; and a copper chest, probably the one mentioned in the records as given by Mr. Stephen Pilchard, Upper Warden, in 1653–4. The glass, which has a silver foot with the hallmark of 1607, was bequeathed by Richard Wioley, Master in 1631 and 1640, is used on election-day, when the old Master presents it, filled with hippocras, to the new one. There is also a set of six china bowls, the gift of Mr. Thomas King, Clerk to the Company, in 1784, with the arms painted on them ; these are of the ordinary Oriental type, sometimes called *Lowestoft*.

With the excellent monograph of Mr. Williams before us we cannot refrain from annexing a few extracts from the portions of the book which illustrate the share of the Company in public transactions of various kinds.

Upon the visit of Elizabeth to St. Paul's, on November 18 in the Armada year, the Founders were required by precept from the Mayor to attend with their whole Livery in their best apparel at their appointed stand covered with fair blue cloth at eight o'clock in the morning, and there were to be Whifflers[1] in coats of velvet and chains, ten at the least.

In 1614 the Founders associated themselves with the Haberdashers, Turners, and Wax-Chandlers in taking up a 2,000*l.* share of the Irish Plantation, contributing 90*l.*, while the Haberdashers stood for 1688*l.*, the Wax-Chandlers for 120*l.*, and the Turners for 102*l.* The Founders sold their portion in 1686 for 144*l.* 4*s.* 6*d.* It is so far worthy of remark that the tenants-in-chief had realized their own several years before.

---

[1] Young freemen who played on a whiffle, a sort of pipe, and headed a procession. See p. 310 *suprâ* for a representation of one.

In 1627–8 the Wardens of this Company, the Sadlers, and the Glaziers were committed to Newgate for omitting to pay the respective quota toward a loan to the Crown of 120,000*l.* The assessment on the Founders was 90*l.*, and they compounded for 20*l.*

About 1649 we detect a habit of holding the meetings of the Company elsewhere than at the Hall, which was probably let. There are such entries as the following: "Paid at the Three Tuns two severall tymes about our Whifflers and other business concerning Lord Mayor's

THE TREASURE CHEST, 1653.

Day . . . £3 6s. 9d. ;" "Paid upon Midsummer Day at the Dagger [in Cheap] . . . £2 4s. 6d. ;" "Paid upon Bartholomew Day at Islington . . . £5 7s. 10d. ;" "Paid upon — Sepr. at the Ship in Ould Fish St^t . . . £2 13s. 4d. ;" "Paid upon Michaelmas Day at the 3 Tuns . . . £4 2s. 4d. ;" and this state of affairs seems to have continued for some time, as in 1651–2, January 30th, occurs: "A Thanksgiving Day at the Cardinal's Cap [in Lombard Street]."

Under 1652 we find two significant items: "Rec^d of the Gunpowder del^d forth of the Hall, £4 0 0," and "Paid for State Arms in the Glass

Winder, 18s." On June 22nd, 1660, there is a payment of 2l. 4s. 6d. for the King's Arms.

The sale of the plate, pewter, brass, linen, and other effects in 1666-7 at once indicates the consequences of the Great Fire and the rescue of the Company's property. But the Hall was lost, and in order to rebuild it 500l. were borrowed ; 230l. 10s. were raised by fines and sub-scriptions, and 68l. 18s. were realized by 275 oz. 12 dwt. of plate. The first breakfast in the new Hall was held on Lord Mayor's Day, 1671.

It was between 1697 and 1699 that the great scandal arose and con-tinued as to fraudulent practices by officers of the Company, and even by some of the Masters, in relation to the binding of apprentices and admissions to the Freedom ; numerous payments on these accounts were discovered to have been misappropriated by the suppression of entries ; and the books were for a considerable time detained at Guildhall, and an order made that no Founder should henceforth have the freedom of the City. The difficulty was at last overcome, and the disability res-cinded ; but the records afford numerous other cases in which members of the staff were charged with irregularities ; and there was a constant succession of dismissals from the Court for non-attendance or neglect of pecuniary obligations. In 1704 the Company's Staff-head was pawned by the Beadle, and was redeemed for 3l. 5s.

In 1701-3, however, an honourable and capable Master, Noah De-launay, did much to retrieve the affairs of his Gild ; and in the latter year, at the close of his term of office, the Founders were clear of debt.

The objection of the Chamber of London to the same individual belonging to more than one Company was met in 1755 by a proposal that persons exercising the trade, and being of another Company, should enter as *Love Brothers*, paying only 2s. for the King's duty, and not to be eligible for any office. The only instance in which this scheme was carried out seems to have been in 1767, when Mr. Edward Warner, Citizen and Draper, and a founder by trade, paid a guinea and other fees for this honorary distinction. But in 1772 Mr. Lotall, Clockmaker, had his fees returned, because his election as a Founder in the ordinary manner was declared to be irregular and void.

Another singular case occurred in 1773, when, on May 3, at a full Court, Mr. John Cole, a Liveryman elect and afterward Master, insisted on being admitted in proper form ; and the two Wardens accordingly went outside, where Mr. Cole was waiting, and, a Livery gown and hood having been delivered to them, one took the right-hand sleeve of the gown and the other the left-hand one, and introduced into each severally and respectively the arms of Mr. Cole, who, being so gowned, one of the said Wardens thereupon placed a hood on the head of Mr. Cole. Mr.

Cole being now gowned and hooded, one of the Wardens returned into the Court room, and having informed the Company of what had taken place, demanded if they were prepared to receive Mr. Cole. The Company signified their readiness, and, the Beadle opening the folding doors wide, and silence being ordered, a procession was formed, headed by the Beadle carrying his staff, behind whom followed Mr. Cole, with a Warden on either side. Mr. Cole was thus led up and introduced to the Master, who, on learning Mr. Cole's desire, with the whole Court, rose, and the Master taking in his right hand the right hand of Mr. Cole, said : " Gentlemen, I pronounce Brother Cole a Liveryman of this Company." Hereupon all the members of the Court successively shook hands with Brother Cole, and the Master invited him to dine with the Company that day, for which Brother Cole expressed his obligations, but pleaded a prior engagement. Bowing respectfully to the Court, he thereupon took his leave, and gave 2s. 6d. to the Beadle and a like sum to the poor-box.

Among other inconveniences and discomforts attendant on straitened circumstances appears to have been a difficulty in providing Livery gowns on emergencies, although at the Hall there was an apartment appropriated to them. Sometimes they were borrowed from persons who kept them on sale or hire, and who occasionally purchased them from the Wardens when they were sold to cover arrears of fees ; but in 1844, at the opening of the Royal Exchange, when the Founders applied for fifty tickets, the Committee of the Court of Aldermen gave leave to such liverymen as had not gowns, to wear rosettes of the colours of the Company at their stand in the Poultry.

In 1829, in lieu of any external eleemosynary provision, the Founders' Charitable Fund was established, for the relief of distressed and deserving Liverymen and their widows, and upward of 500*l.* were subscribed by the Court and Livery. The interest of whatever principal was collected from time to time was to be distributed twice a year ; but no larger sum than 3*l.* per annum was to be granted without a special order of the Court, and a member of the Court in decayed circumstances or his widow was to take precedence of Liverymen or their widows, and, if the funds permitted, to receive double the said amount.

No other point of particular interest or curiosity offers itself to notice, unless it is the presentation in 1835 by a member of fifty copies of a pamphlet entitled *Affectionate Advice to Apprentices*, of which a copy was to be given to each apprentice on being bound at the Hall.

The Company's accounts, however, throw some light on the nature and development of the staff. At the very commencement, in 1497, William Mivell, or Mepell, is employed, first as Clerk and subsequently as Clerk and Beadle, at 16*s.* 8*d.* a year, an allowance for his gown, and doubtless other perquisites. The salary gradually rises to 3*l.*, 4*l.*, 10*l.*, 20*l.*, 40*l.*, 100*l.* He originally lives at the Hall, when one is obtained, and after the Fire receives a liberal indemnity for losses and rent-money ; but in 1692 he is required to find himself in lodgings, this charge being considered in the emoluments,[1] and a Housekeeper, Sarah Shurley, is appointed, with power to receive all rents arising from the hire of portions of the building.

The first notice of the existence of a Beadle independent of the Clerk is, as usual, of an indirect kind. In 1544 there is a charge of 5*s.* for his quarter's wages. But he enjoys numerous advantages, including a residence, and shortly supersedes the Clerk as the sizer of weights. The Clerk and himself at various times are subject to readjustments of their duties and claims, and are not very unfrequently convicted of embezzlement. The income grows from 1*l.* to 60*l.*, a year, and in 1769 a member of the Court is tempted to resign and to take the post. It is at present worth 146*l.* a year.

The Company thus furnished itself by degrees with a Clerk, Beadle, and Housekeeper, and in 1606 and 1679 appointed a Cook. But this berth probably fell into abeyance when the use of the Hall became more and more restricted through the financial necessity for accepting tenants. It detracted from the characteristic and typical costume of the festive spectacle, where the brethren and the sisteren assembled together in their statutory apparel on the old ground at Lothbury, or even of the official banquet in the Court parlour, when dinners and deliberations were held at unconsecrated taverns—in places of common resort.

FOUNDERS' COMPANY.   MASER WITH COVER (14TH CENTURY).

---

[1] The present Clerk has rooms at the Hall in St. Swithin's Lane, and, in addition to his salary of 100*l.*, is entitled to certain fees.

Tbe fframework Iknitters or Stocking Weavers.

STOW[1] tells us that in 1564 William Rider, apprentice to Thomas Burdet, opposite St. Magnus Corner, London Bridge, happening to see a pair of knit woollen stockings at the lodging of an Italian merchant who had come from Mantua, borrowed them, and made a second pair like them, and these were the earliest articles of the kind manufactured in England.

It was thirty-five years later that, according to the historian just cited, the art of knitting or weaving silk stockings, waistcoats, and divers other things by engines or steel looms was devised and perfected by William Lee, Master of Arts, of St. John's College, Cambridge, who afterward went

ARMS, 1739.

abroad and extended the knowledge of the invention to France, Spain Italy, and other countries.

Under the account of the *Mercers*, we have referred to the adoption by Queen Elizabeth of the fashion of wearing silk stockings about 1560; and her example would naturally be followed. So far as the immediate matter is concerned, it may be sufficient to relate that in 1657 the followers of this trade addressed to the Protector Cromwell: "The humble representation of the promoters and inventors of the art and mistery or trade of framework knitting or making of silk stockings or other work in a frame or engine." The petitioners alleged that the trade of framework knitting was never known or practised here in England or in any other place in the world before it was (about fifty years past) invented

[1] *Annals*, 1615, p. 869.

and found out by one William Lee, of Calverton, in the county of Nottingham, gentleman, who, by himself and such of his kindred and countrymen as he took unto him for servants, practised the same many years somewhat imperfectly in comparison of the exactness it is since brought into by the endeavours of some of your petitioners." They therefore prayed that they might be united and incorporated by charter under the Great Seal of England, whereby their just right to the invention might be preserved from foreigners, the trade advanced, abuses therein suppressed, the benefit of the Commonwealth by importation and exportation and otherwise increased, and hundreds of poor families comfortably relieved by their several employments about the same, who would otherwise be exposed to ruin, having no other calling to live of.

Upon this eloquent and pathetic appeal Cromwell granted the desired charter, June 13th, 1657, and the same was enrolled in the Chamber of London the 14th of July following. The Court of Aldermen did not take so long to consider the expediency of ratifying the act as they had done in prior cases, or a significant hint from his Highness might have been received at Guildhall.

No text of this instrument, however, appears to be extant ; but it was succeeded by one from Charles II. August 19th, 1663, in which the Company is incorporated by the name of the Master, Wardens, Assistants, and Society of the Art or Mistery of Framework Knitters of the Cities of London and Westminster, and Kingdom of England, and Dominion of Wales, with perpetual succession, an exemption from the statute of mortmain to 100l. a year, a common seal, the right of search, and other customary privileges and powers.

The governing body was appointed to consist of a Master, two Wardens, and fifteen or more Assistants, and John Croson, the first Master, was required to take an oath before a Master in Chancery for the due execution of his office. The first Wardens, Court of Assistants, and Clerk (John Hannis) were similarly nominated ; but the election of officers thereafter was to vest in the Company, and to take place on Midsummer Day annually.

The Charter of 1663 was also promptly enrolled (Sept. 24, 1663). But the Court of Aldermen did not grant a Livery till June 9, 1713, and the bye-laws do not seem to have been drawn up and approved by the Judges till 1745.

The peculiarities in the present instance are the omission in the second charter, from political motives, of all recital of the first, the swearing-in of the first Master in Chancery Chambers, and the unprecedented width of scope allowed to the new institution.

In 1678 certain members of the Company united to purchase a site in Red Cross Street for the erection of a common Hall, and so late as 1720 a further amount was raised in a similar manner to complete the arrangement. The result was possibly facilitated by the acquisition of a Livery a few years before. In 1724 this is stated to number fifty-eight, and in 1739 the same; and in the latter year the executive consisted, according to Maitland, of a Master, two Wardens, and eighteen Assistants. The Livery fine was then 10*l*.

It soon came to pass that the large franchise conceded to this body, and carried out under the bye-laws of 1745, was discovered to be injurious to trade; and even in 1753 Parliament ruled that the ordinances governed no one outside the ranks of the Gild. Such a decision paralysed the action of the latter, which ceased almost from that time forward to intervene in the affairs of the trade. In or about 1821 the Hall was sold to the Corporation for 3,628*l*. 10*s*. 3*d*.; and this, with 800*l*. derived from surplus internal income, now forms the entire corporate estate exclusively of a few charities managed by the Company. In 1861 the plate was sold for 79*l*. 16*s*. 1*d*., and the proceeds applied to the repair of the almshouses.

But a system of rigid frugality, which, judging from official returns, has been long observed, may considerably swell the property in course of time. In 1880 there was a surplus of nearly 500*l*.

The sole article of interest or curiosity in the possession of the Framework Knitters is a Master's chair, presented by a past Master in 1681.

The Fruiterers.

OLD ARMS.

ARMS, 1739.[1]

As an Association, the Fruiterers may be naturally supposed to have existed prior to the establishment of a systematic constitution. But we have very little to guide us in forming an opinion on this point, as

---

[1] See these Arms engraved on a very grand scale in Wallis's *London's Armory*, 1677.

the only reference to them of ancient date is in the order of precedence which was fixed in 1515, and here they are placed last in a list of forty-eight. In the rehearsal of the Gilds present at the Mayor's feast in Guildhall in 1531–2 the Fruiterers were represented by two members, and had one mess allotted to them. They are particularly specified as having no Livery. In levies of corn and money on the Gilds between 1602 and 1604 they appear as donors of sixteen quarters and 12s. 9d., the Merchant Taylors heading the list with 936 quarters and 37l. 8s. 9d.

James I., in his third year, incorporated this trade, "for the better order, government, and rule of them," by the name of The Master, Wardens, and Commonalty of the Mistery of Fruiterers of London, with perpetual succession and government, a licence in mortmain to 50l. a year, the faculty of making bye-laws, the right of search and supervision over the City and a three miles' radius, and other usual powers. The executive was fixed at a Master, two Wardens, and five or more, not exceeding twenty, Assistants.

The present governing body consists of the constitutional number. Election-day is on the 25th January, when the Master and Upper Warden are selected from the Court, usually by rotation, and the Renter Warden by the Court from the Livery. The Upper Warden has charge of the charitable funds (which arise almost entirely out of corporate savings), the Renter, of the general accounts.

No code of bye-laws seems to be known anterior to those of 1759. They embrace provisions for the internal government, for the control of the trade, and for the reception and treatment of apprentices.

We do not hear at what precise date the Company acquired a Livery. The official returns of 1699, 1724, 1881–2, and 1892 give it as 37, 57, 99, and 101 respectively.

The earliest glimpse of the Fruiterers, subsequently to their foundation, is connected with the Ulster Plantation in 1613, when they subscribed for a portion of the Vintners' Bellaghy Manor. There is an annual payment on this account of about 3l. 10s.; and the funds and assets of the Company are otherwise derived from fines, fees, and quarterages, which, under the auspices of a thrifty management, have resulted in a very considerable accumulation during many years passed. In 1834 the property was described as mainly consisting of 775l. Bank Stock.

The Company has long ceased to maintain any direct or official connection with the fruit-trade; but of late years it has offered prizes through the Royal Botanic Society for the best English-grown fruit, the exhibitor in all cases to be no other than the grower.

In 1891 Sir James Whitehead, then Master, manifested a warm interest

in the subject, and from his personal influence was enabled to give a
marked impulse to the movement for encouraging fruit-culture. A large
and influential meeting was held in the Egyptian Hall at the Mansion
House to promote local exhibitions all over the country and the delivery
of practical lectures. There was, and yet is, a reasonable feeling, that
the extension of knowledge and industry in this direction might tend to
alleviate agricultural distress, and form a new source of profit for cot-
tagers and other country folk throughout the suburbs and provinces.

Toward the Mansion House fund for this purpose Messrs. Crosse and
Blackwell contributed 105*l.*, Mr. Chaplin, Minister of Agriculture, 21*l.*,
and others smaller sums. The part taken by the Company in the matter,
and perhaps the fragrant associations with it, have assisted in drawing
into its ranks in modern days a highly respectable class of persons,
whose admission-fees sensibly and favourably affect the receipts.

There is an immemorial usage, by which the Fruiterers, on October 7
yearly, present to the Lord Mayor an offering of English-grown fruit
in amicable commutation of the ancient right of the municipal
authorities, as City fruit-meters, to a toll in kind on all produce of this
sort brought into the City. Some eminent firm supplies this prescriptive
due, and there is a regular entry of it in the accounts. The gratuities
to the Lord Mayor's servants inclusive, the outlay is about 24*l.*

There is no Hall; but the meetings are periodically held either at
Guildhall or at the Hall of the Parish Clerks in Silver Street. The
annual banquet on St. Paul's Day (January 25) is a grand and costly
affair; but it is purely a question of subscription among the members
and their friends, and does not represent a corporate charge. The
audit dinner is defrayed out of the Company's funds.

On the whole, the items registered in the books are of ordinary
character; yet one may be particularized as bearing the impress of
antiquity, and it is the payment at each anniversary festival of a sum
of 15*l.*, more or less, to "first-comers," who possibly had their dinner
fees returned to them as a reward for punctuality—a virtue more
appreciable at a period when the guests, who chiefly belonged to the
trade, and resided on their own premises in the suburbs, were apt to
find a difficulty in reaching the place of assembly.[1]

LITERARY NOTICES.

The Frviterers Secrets: Containing directions for the due time and manner of
gathering all kindes of fruite. . . . By N. F. 4to, 1604. Reissued, 4to,
1609, under the title of *The Husbandmans Fruitfull Orchard*.

[1] In the Scriveners' Books are repeated entries of payments to members "for
timely attendance."

A Treatise of Frvit-Trees. Shewing the manner of Grafting, Setting, Pruning, and Ordering of them in all respects. By Ralph Austen. 4to, 1653.

A Book of Fruits and Flowers. Shewing the Nature and Use of them, either for Meat or Medicine. 4to, 1653, 1656.

Herefordshire Orchards. A Pattern for all England. Written in an Epistolary Address to Samuel Hartlib, Esq. By J. B. 8vo, 1657.

Observations upon some part of Sir Francis Bacon's Natural History as it concerns Fruit-trees, Fruits, and Flowers. By Ralph Austen. 4to, 1658.

The French Gardiner : Instructing how to cultivate all sorts of Fruit-trees. . . . Translated (with additions) by John Evelyn. 8vo, 1658, 1672, 1675.

John Evelyn's *Pomona*, appended to his *Sylva*. Folio, 1664, 1670.

A Dialogve : Or Familiar Discourse, and conference betweene the Husbandman, and Frvit-Trees, in his Nurseries, Orchards, and Gardens. . . . By Ra Avsten, Practiser (50 years) in the Art of Planting Frvit-Trees. . . . 8vo, Oxford, 1676.

Plain and Full Instructions to raise all sorts of Fruit-Trees that prosper in England. By T. Langford. 8vo, 1681.

Fruit-Walls Improved. By inclining them to the Horizon. By Nicolas Facio de Duillier. 4to, 1699. With two folded plates.

The Girdlers.

THE remoteness of the origin of this occupation speaks for itself. The gradual call for commodities gave rise to the market of supply; and it was merely secondary and indirect agencies which brought the manufacturers or vendors of articles of use and consumption together, and led them to appreciate the value of union. The name *Ceinturier* had been adopted at an early date as a family patronymic, demonstrating the antiquity and familiarity of the business. In 1 Henry III. (1217) Benet or Benedict Seynturer was one of the Sheriffs of London.

The Girdlers were, doubtless, at the outset, a Fraternity by prescription, as there is testimony that the manufacture to which they devoted themselves was in a flourishing condition even in Anglo-Saxon times, and had indeed reached its climax at or before the Restoration.

They originally constituted a lay union in St. Laurence, Old Jewry, having established themselves there under the tutelary auspices of that church and saint. They possessed Ordinances and a government, the latter most probably in the first place by an Alderman of the feudal type, who was in due course replaced by Wardens.

The antiquity of the Brotherhood is sufficiently proved by the language of letters patent directed by Edward III. in 1327 to "Les Ceincturiers de nôtre Citée de Loundres," wherein the ancient regulations and usages of the craft are approved and confirmed. The royal licence author- izing the Girdlers to elect one or two persons to overlook the rest and prevent defective or dishonest work by no means makes it certain that such an administrative principle was not already in force. But it was not consonant with the dignity of the Crown to admit a defeasance or forestalment of

OLD ARMS.

its authority. Under the designation of *Zonars* it is enumerated among the City Gilds which in 1376 were represented on the Common Council, being entitled to send four members.

The patent above mentioned, which, as we readily perceive, did not pretend to be more than a licence, was confirmed by Richard II. in 1377, and by Henry IV. in 1401. No charter was obtained till the 27 Henry VI. (1448) when the Brotherhood of St. Laurence was incor- porated under the name of The Master and Wardens of the Mistery of Girdlers of the City of London ; and this grant was renewed, 2 Edward IV., 10 Elizabeth, 15 Charles I., and 1 James II. The charter of Elizabeth united together in one corporation the Girdlers, Wyre- workers, and Pinners by the style of The Master and Wardens or Keepers of the Art or Mistery of Girdlers, London. What the motive for this consolidation may have been, does not transpire ; the two other bodies comprised in the proceeding do not seem to have possessed any property or influence ; and the fact may explain their omission from the title. At this period, as we have elsewhere shown, the pins used among us were chiefly imported.

But the three misteries are joined and invited together into one body corporate and politic and one Society and Company for ever. The right of search and a licence in mortmain up to 40*l.* a year were among the concessions.

What may be termed the political history of the Company, sub- sequently to its formation in 1448, seems to have been more than usually devoid of incident ; but this partly arises from the almost total loss of its archives in 1666. Of the little that we are able to collect, the most part is derived from casual or indirect sources.

The Ordinances of the Girdlers, framed by their own body, and approved by the Court of Aldermen, were apparently first formulated in 1344, and were in substance as follows: 1. No man of the trade was to work any manner of tissue of silk, or wool, or of linen thread, unless the tissue was according to the assize, that is, of six quarters; 2. That no man should garnish, or cause to be garnished, girdles or garters with any metal but laten, iron, or steel; 3. That no man should make them barred, unless there were a rowel beneath the bar; 4. That no tissue of sixth, fifth, third, or double size should be garnished without a double point at the buckle in the tongue, and in the bars with a double point down to the rowel; 5. That apprentices should be taken for seven years, and only by freemen; 6. That no man should work on Saturday, or on the Eve of a Double Feast, after noon; 7. That no man should keep his shop open on Sunday, although he might sell on emergency inside the shop; 8. That none should set any woman to work, save his wife or daughter; 9. That none should work by night; 10. That none should make girdles of worse than ox-leather.

The Girdlers were not entitled to *harness* their goods with either of the precious metals, but were obliged, if such a process was desired, to employ a goldsmith, who set his own mark on that portion of the work.

In 1356 the Girdlers obtained from the Crown a power of search and seizure over all goods appertaining to their mistery, when the same were of inferior workmanship or of untrue material. The Gild had represented that its members were injured and defamed by certain men outside the City, who wrought girdles of baser metal than was allowed by custom; and the writ issued in their favour and behalf partook of the character of the grant to the Saddlers in 1272 in being a general licence for the whole realm. But the Saddlers framed a remonstrance against the privilege as obnoxious and unjust, apparently on account of leather saddle-girths forming part of their business, and procured a suspension of the writ till the next meeting of Parliament by Order in Council of the 26th of October in the same year. There is nothing to shew what the ultimate issue was. The transaction serves to illustrate the lax way in which, down to a much later epoch, our Kings, from the ill-organized official system prevailing, were apt to assent to demands of a certain class on the most *ex parte* and imperfect information.

A wide interval elapsed between the municipal regulations for the control and protection of the trade in the fourteenth century, based on customs and principles possibly never committed to writing, and the only code of bye-laws, which we can trace as having been made pursuant to the charter. This is dated May 30, 1682, and was approved in the ordinary manner by the Judges, agreeably to the statute 19 Henry VII., enacted to guard against the authorization of anything contrary to the prerogative or the laws of the realm. In grants made by Henry VI. we find this proviso, however, already introduced.

In consequence of a change of fashion, the practical interest of the Girdlers in the calling cannot be said to have survived the reign of Charles II.; and it has been pointed out that the charter which blended them with the Pinners and Wireworkers, by reason of the successive redistribution of industries and establishment of needlemakers, wire-workers, hook-and-eye makers, lanthorn-makers, stock and wool card makers, tin-plate workers, and others, rendered supervision impracticable, even if it had not become otherwise inoperative.

The governing body is composed of a Master, two Wardens, and seventeen Assistants, according to the charter. The choice of the Master and Wardens is vested in the Livery, and they are occasionally re-elected. A liveryman must have served seven years, before he is qualified to come on the Court. The Clerk, Beadle, and Porter are elected or confirmed at the annual general meeting. This scheme shews a fairly popular constitution.

In 1881 there were 91 on the Livery; and between 1841 and 1880 153 freemen were admitted. The ranks of the liverymen do not appear to undergo much alteration. In 1699 the returns were 85; and in 1724, the same.

The Company refers to its severance from an active share in the united industries, whether commercial or administrative, as a matter of ancient history; but it has been fortunate enough from the fifteenth century to a date within memory to acquire under various wills and other dispositions a series of valuable properties, including the site of its Hall.

These estates lie in the City itself, at Cow Cross, at Hammersmith and Brook Green, and in Ireland. That at Hammersmith is very large, and, with other lands and tenements in London, was given by Henry Flycke by feoffment in 1579 and by will in 1582. The George Inn is specified as a leading feature in the bequest, and was by no means impossibly the best part of it. The Irish estate is a sub-share of the Skinners' manor of Pellipar, and is managed by the latter Company. The Girdlers' income used to be about 700l. a year; but it has since suffered reduction.

The most interesting and the oldest possession, however, goes back to the epoch anterior to the establishment of the Company, and was the ground in the Old Jewry on which the Hall was subsequently built. This important foundation of the prosperity of the Brotherhood was a gift under the will of Andrew Hunt, January 24, 1431–2, and included the area on which the Hall stands, with its appurtenances, and was to be held subject to superstitious and other uses, namely : the performance of masses for the soul of the departed in the Church of St. Laurence, the offering of five wax candles, each of a pound weight, before the image of the saint, twice a year for ever, the Vicar of St. Laurence being joined in the trust to secure the observance of these terms ; the permanent provision of lodging for two decayed members of the Society on the premises, and the payment to one of them of sevenpence a week.[1]

The Hunt and Flycke estates, both of which may be judged to have been of very moderate worth at and long after the period of acquisition, constitute the most important portion of the whole property. The former, represented by the Hall, which was rebuilt and refurnished between 1877 and 1880 at a cost of nearly 10,000*l*.,[2] is of course not remunerative. A shrinkage has been experienced in those directions where the Company owns agricultural land ; and certain improving leases do not fall in till the middle of the twentieth century.

The Company appears to have no objects of historical or archæological value. The only eminent member whom it boasts was Thomas Sutton, founder of the Charterhouse.

The Glass-Sellers.

WE indirectly learn from the patent granted by Elizabeth in 1580 to a Venetian whose name is variously given, for making Venice glasses in Crutched Friars, that at that time there were fifty persons belonging to a Glass-Sellers' Association, who, pleading to the Lords of the Council

---

[1] The Company eventually varied and enlarged this charity by granting pensions of 30*l*. a year to two liverymen and of 10*l*. a year to the widows of two other members.

[2] To meet this outlay a good deal of real and other estate seems to have been sold, including some in Basinghall Street.

the grave injury attendant on the grant to their own trade, succeeded in obtaining a limitation of the sale of the foreigner's wares to his own works or depôt.

We owe to Stow the information that the premises used as a glass-factory had originally been the Hall of Crutched Friars. "The Friers Hall," he says (edit. 1633, p. 157), "was made a glasse-house, or house wherein were made glasse of divers sorts to drinke in." The origin of this establishment is usually assigned to the year 1557; but it was at any rate shortly after the dissolution of religious houses. The same authority adds that on the 4th September, 1575, the place was destroyed by fire. There were at the time stored up for the furnaces no fewer than 40,000 billets of wood, which explains the inability to quench the flames, and implies operations on an extensive scale.

COMMON SEAL.

At this institution, which was constructively rebuilt after the fire, a celebrated literary character, James Howell, writer of the *Letters*, was at one time employed on the staff in the capacity of Steward.

The Glass-sellers, who comprised in their business the manufacture of looking-glasses, do not come prominently under notice in an official way, till, under the usual plea of abuses in the trade demanding a more regular and authoritative control, they obtained a charter from Charles II. in 1664 by the name of the Master, Wardens, Assistants, and Commonalty of Glass-Sellers of London, declaring them, free as well as foreign, in London and its liberties and within seven miles thereof, to be one body politic, with perpetual succession, the right of search with warrant and constable, and other usual privileges. There is particular mention of the art of grinding, polishing, casing, foyling, and finishing of looking-glasses; and we observe a special reservation of the patent rights of Thomas Tilson of London, merchant, for the sole making of crystal glasses and plate and other glass for mirrors, coach-windows, etc., doubtless the works at Lambeth patronized by the Duke of Buckingham, and of those of the Venetian factory above-mentioned.

The charter, dated July 20, 1664, was enrolled in the Chamber of London on the 20th of September following, and the bye-laws were approved on the 28th of November.

It appears that between 1664 and 1684 the Glass-Sellers assumed the title to create a Livery without the usual licence from the Court of Aldermen, but that under the influence of the *Quo Warranto* the custom fell into desuetude, and some members joined the Liveries of other Companies. But about 1710 a revival took place in the state of the glass business, especially in flint and looking-glasses, and the number and character of the Company consequently improved ; and in 1712 a Livery of sixty was granted after the usual formalities.

It is likely that such a concession at that time was fairly commensurate with the commercial standing of the Glass-Sellers ; but in 1825 a compliance with a further prayer for extension, and the carriage of the number to a hundred and twenty, with a 20*l.* fine and other charges, must be simply interpreted as the now familiar process for raising funds, which had first come into operation after the Great Fire, and led to the Act of Common Council of 1697.

In 1724 the Livery numbered, however, only forty; in 1882, fifty-one; and in 1892, 38 ; so that the smaller complement scarcely seems to have been reached.

The bye-laws of 1664 are singularly exhaustive, and provide for a larger development than the Company was destined to attain.   They

ANGLO-SAXON GLASSES.

deal with all the incidence of internal government, including funeral observances and the reception of apprentices, and declare that the meetings are to be held at the Hall *or some other certain appointed place* —an alternative not generally afforded, but perhaps suggested by the discontent in some cases through the absence of becoming accommodation.

The corporate income of the Glass-sellers arises from a small property in stocks, and the fines and fees received from members of the Court, Livery, and Freedom ;[1] its only trust is a scholarship of 50*l.* a year, tenable for four years at either of the Universities, founded by Mr. John Abbott, Master of the Company in 1875, in favour of the City of

---

[1] In 1892, according to Whitaker, the corporate income was *nil* ; but this we apprehend to be an error.   The same authority sets down the trust income as 21*l.*, but does not include the Abbott endowment.

London School. In the Returns of 1834, the average yearly revenue was said to be about 40*l*.

It is highly creditable to a body so modestly endowed, that in 1876 it organized, at a cost of not less than 400*l*., an Exhibition of Glass at the Alexandra Palace, at which medals, certificates, and money prizes were awarded.

LITERARY NOTICE.

The Miserable Case of the Glass-Makers. An undated broadside.

The Glaziers.

ARMS, 1633.

ARMS, 1739.

INDIRECT traces of the Glazier, both as a craftsman and as the member of a Fellowship, frequently occur, long before the formation of the Company under that name. Valid reasons often existed for the delay in seeking a charter, and the least usual one was the reluctance of the Crown to confer it. The two principal difficulties were perhaps the want of union and the want of money ; and we generally find that the movement was ultimately made by one or two leading members of the mistery, who provided the funds and conducted the negotiation. That the art and industry were in a very flourishing state in the time of Elizabeth[1] there is little doubt ; and on the accession of the Stuarts, glass became even more customary in the windows of public and private buildings. There is evidence that for a certain length of time the casements of the Companies' Halls were unprovided with this shelter from the weather, and that the rain was allowed to penetrate into the apartments. But the ancient Glazier did not confine himself to secular work,

---

[1] Young, glazier to the Queen, lived in Wood Street, Cheapside, and it is said that the head of James IV. of Scotland, when his embalmed remains were taken from Shene monastery after the Dissolution, and cast on a rubbish-heap, was severed from the trunk by a workman, and came into Young's possession. The latter kept it for some time, and was struck by its freedom from any offensive odour; but he eventually let the sexton of St. Michael's, Wood Street, lay it in the charnel-house.

and in furnishing painted glass to almost numberless churches and chapels found perhaps the most lucrative department of his occupation. There was no lack of employment, as time passed, however, for the followers of this calling among all classes in the City, who used it for residential or commercial purposes, and the master-glazier might count on receiving extensive orders both from the clergy and laity, alike for new work and repairs. We annex a specification of labour and material supplied in 1608 to the Carpenters' Company :—

THE GLAZIER'S BILL.

		s.	d.
Imprimis for 95 quarrels [squares] of new glass		vij.	xj.
It. In the said Hall, 115 foot of old glass, repaired at 1*d.* a foot ...		ix.	vij.
It. In the little parlour, 18 foot of old glass, repaired at 1*d.* a foot ...			xviij.
It. In the same parlour, 12 quarals of new glass at 1*d.* a quarel ...			xij.
It. In the great parlour, 2 quarels			ij.
It. In the same parlour, 12 foot repaired			xij.
It. In the stairs, 8 foot repaired			viij.
It. In the same stairs, 15 quarels			xv.
It. In the entry, 3 quarels...			iij.
It. In the pastery, 4 foot repaired			iiij.
It. In the same pastery, 5 quarels			v.
It. In the galleries, 50 quarels		iiij.	ij.
It. In the same galleries, 80 foot repaired		vj.	viij.
It. In the buttery, 7 quarels			vij.
It. In the clerk's house, 7 quarels			vij.

The earliest work, serving as a manual for the trade, was published by Walter Gedde in 1615, and about the same date (12 James I.) an Act of Common Council directed that all persons whosoever, using the Art of Glazing within the City and Liberties should thenceforth be subject to the control and search of the Masters of the Craft, and laid down very stringent regulations for the binding of apprentices to none but free Glaziers.

This decree seems to imply the existence in and before 1616 of a Fraternity possessing some kind of government and recognised jurisdiction ; a very few years later (1627-8) irrefragable evidence of such a thing meets the eye in the committal of the Wardens to Newgate for failure to pay an assessment toward a loan to the Crown ; which circumstance may be partly construed by the want of corporate funds ; as in 1602-4 the Gild is at the bottom of a list of subscribers to charges levied by the City as the donor of eight quarters of corn, and 5*s.* 4*d.* respectively. When we come to the date of actual incorporation, 13 Charles I., the preamble of the grant allows in so many words, of course, the antiquity of the art and its rank as an established institution. We learn that the ancient Fraternity of the Mistery or Art of Glaziers had theretofore made many good orders for the regulation of themselves and their calling, and that in several preceding reigns their condition had been advanced and improved.   The present charter therefore erected the existing freemen, in London and within five miles compass, into one body corporate and politic by the name of the Wardens and Commonalty of the Mistery or Art of Glaziers and Painters of glass, and bestowed on them the power to make bye-laws for the guidance of the Craft and the punishment of offenders, a common seal, and other privileges.

This and the one which superseded it, 1 James II., are the only charters in the possession or knowledge of the Company.   The latter seems to be that by which it is governed, save the disabling proviso as to conformity and one or two other points, and prescribes that the executive shall consist of two Wardens and eighteen Assistants chosen from the Commonalty annually on St. Matthew's day.   In 1882, how- ever, the Court was composed of a Master, two Wardens, and only thirteen Assistants.   There were at that time fifteen freemen and thirty- two liverymen.   In 1699 and 1724 the Livery had been 76 and 100 respectively.

Of the original bye-laws we do not meet with the text, but later Articles expressely repealing these were framed at a court held at Loriners' Hall, February 19th, 1749.   They are thirty-two in number, and touch upon the details of management and control.   By No. 12, the person elected Steward was liable to supply the Annual Dinner on Lord Mayor's Day, or pay a fine of 6*l.* ; No. 14 requires the presentment of a proof-piece from apprentices seeking their freedom ; and No. 18 levies 4*d.* from Glaziers whose premises are searched, there being presumably *primâ facie* evidence of something amiss.   It is almost superfluous to add that the search and other like claims are a dead letter.

The corporate estate of the Company is principally derived from in- ternal sources, and 3,700*l* stock, arising from the sale of property in Thames Street and Queen Street, Cheapside, which was purchased, June 6, 1671, for 490*l.*   The trust estate is worth about 50*l.* a year.

The objects of interest are limited to the common seal and the Master's jewel.

LITERARY NOTICES.

A Booke of Svndry Draughtes, Principaly serving for Glasiers ; And not Im- pertinent for Plasterers and Gardiners.   By Walter Gedde.   4to, 1615.

The Art of Glass.   By Antonio Neri.   Translated into English by C. M.   8vo, 1662.   Reprinted, folio, 1826.

Essays of the Strange Subtility of Effluviums, . . . together with a Discovery of the Perviousness of Glass.   By the Honourable Robert Boyle, F.R.S.   8vo, 1673.

The Art of Glass.   Shewing how to make all sorts of Glass, Crystal and Enamel. Likewise the making of Pearls, Precious Stones, China, and Looking Glasses. By H. de Blancourt.   8vo, 1699.   With Plates.
This work includes the method of making Glass Eyes.

The Glovers.

THE Glovers framed their Ordinances, and had them approved by the Corporation, in 1349. They embrace one or two unusual provisions, namely, that no one of the trade shall be admitted to the Freedom of the City without the assent of a majority of the Wardens; 2. That if any servant in the trade shall steal from his master to the value of 12*d.*, more or less, the default shall be arranged by the Wardens, unless the offender elect to be judged otherwise. The remainder of the code offers nothing of particular interest or relevance.

It occurred in the very next year succeeding the issue of these Ordinances, that a case of the breach of them was brought by the Wardens of the Gild before the Mayor's Court. Seventeen pairs of gloves, "vamped up in a false fashion, in deceit of the people, and to the scandal of all the trade," were found upon John Francis of Northampton, with other spurious goods, and were burned by order of the Court in Cheap near the Stone Cross.

In 1372 the Glovers are found among the thirty-one bodies which joined in raising a benevolence amounting altogether to 452*l.* 16*s.* toward the cost of the King's wars in France. In 1464 (October 20) they received from Clarencieux, King of Arms, a grant of a coat of difference, from the terms of which we gather that the Craft then possessed two Wardens Thomas Hoddesden and Nicholas Wright, and the power of making bye-laws. This coat was quartered with one sometimes, but wrongly, ascribed to the Pursers.

In 1488 (April 26) we perceive that the Pursers obtained the sanction of the City to a new set of Ordinances, in which there is no allusion to the Glovers, still a separate, and perhaps weak, community. But ten years afterward we come across a joint petition to the Court of Aldermen on the part of their co-citizens, the Freemen of the two Crafts, representing that time out of mind they have been two separate Crafts, and so have continued to this day, with divers good Ordinances, and many of them. The said petitioners were formerly *of meetly substance* and able not only to live, but to bear their parts toward the charges of the City ; but now of late they have grown both alike sorely decayed both in numbers and property, without means to sustain their Fellowships, or to bear lot and scot. Therefore they pray the Court to grant that they may be henceforth one Craft, under the name of Glovers-Pursers, and be so enrolled ; and the demand was conceded.

We hear no more of the matter till 1501–2, when in a record of the Gilds possessing Liveries the Glovers-Pursers are placed twenty-seventh, with a Livery of twenty-three. Very shortly after (June 7, 1502), they were incorporated with the LEATHERSELLERS, and there the first stage of the independent annals of the Glovers terminates.

But a sufficiently remarkable circumstance is, that, whereas in 1498 the Pursers and Glovers had pleaded their common depression and poverty, in 1502 the former at all events were weighty and influential enough to prevail on the Leathersellers to adopt their special religious observances, and to impress on that important body their own ritualistic idiosyncrasies.

The original Gild or Fraternity of Glovers had in 1464, as we have thus shown, an Executive and coat-armour, and had, thirty-four years subsequently, effected a junction with the Pursers, a more powerful Fellowship, but drawn into peculiarly strict alliance with the other by unity of religious feeling.

Whether the Pursers here mentioned were identical with those " of the Bridge," a Brotherhood possibly as old as 1180, and already associated with the Leathersellers of Cheap in 1372, we cannot be sure ; but in their Ordinances of 1488 the associates of the Glovers seem to connect themselves with the Grey Friars within Newgate, and in 1502 with the Chapel of Our Lady at St. Thomas of Acon in Cheapside. The Leathersellers, on their part, appear to have selected as their place for devotion and offerings the Chapel of St. Mary Magdalen, near Guildhall ; and on their coalition with the Glovers-Pursers in that year the united body transferred their allegiance to Cheapside, or in other words, the Leathersellers deferred in this respect to their new allies. Yet in the Leathersellers' Ordinances of 1635 the *Glovers* and *Glovers-Pursers* are cited (possibly by error) as if they had been distinct.

Only three years posterior to the date just quoted, the members of the Glove Trade, under the auspices of a development of taste for more costly and elaborate fashions in that article of costume, were encouraged to make an effort to recover their corporate independence, their voice in the general Council having perhaps, since the Reformation and the aggrandizement of the Leathersellers, somewhat lost its weight ; and a new Company was constituted by letters patent of September 5, 1638 (14 Charles I.), under the title of "The Master, Wardens, and Fellowship of the Company of Glovers of the City of London."

Its government consisted in 1739 of a Master, four Wardens, and thirty Assistants, with a Livery of 130 paying a fine of 5*l.* 13*s.* 4*d.* ; and at that time it had a Hall in Beech Lane. According to official returns, the Livery in 1699 amounted to 120 and in 1724–5 to 128.

Of the later history of the Glovers little is known, except that in 1882 its entire property consisted of 3,800*l.* stocks, that the Livery fine was 21*l.* and that for coming on the Court 52*l.* 10*s.* The fees on taking up the Freedom are correspondingly high. According to Whitaker, the Livery in 1889 was 14, and in 1892, 90—the latter figure a probable misprint for 9.

The City Regulations of 1350 fixed the price of a pair of sheepskin gloves at 1*d.*, and a superior quality at 1½*d.*, and so upward.

During a lengthened period the trade must have largely profited by the very general demand among both sexes in the upper classes for coverings for the hand for horsemanship, hunting and hawking, as well as for tournaments and occasions of ceremony, and gallantry, and for ordinary use. They were bought for new year's gifts, generally perfumed or inscribed with posies or precepts ; and they were worn by men as favours or tokens. Great expense was often incurred during the Tudor and (more especially) the Stuart reigns, alike in the material and the fabric. To the Ironmongers' pageant for 1566, James Peele contributed, or rather supplied, six pairs of gloves for the children who took part, at 6*d.* a pair.

As Peele was the author of a volume on "Book-keeping," published in 1553, and as he is also mentioned as the writer of the pageant above-mentioned, the Glovers may think it worth while to claim him as a brother, more especially since he was probably related, if not father, to George Peele the dramatist. The family was apparently of a literary turn ; for Stephen Peele, the contemporary stationer, produced several fugitive pieces about 1570.

Ellinda, one of the ladies commemorated in Lovelace's *Lucasta*, 1649, is represented as wearing white gloves trimmed with ermine. In the Museum at Saffron Walden is the

---

[1] A pair of richly embroidered gloves, for ceremonial use, formerly belonging to Louis XIII. of France, is figured from the original by Lacroix (*La Vie Militaire au Moyen Age*, 1873, p. 215).

seventeenth-century lady's glove represented in the text from a drawing by Fairholt.

It is mentioned that in 1580 the haberdashers' shops in London had on sale both French and Spanish gloves.

Furred gloves are named in the Skinners' charter of 1667, and were, it is there said, sometimes irregularly lined or fitted by apprentices.

In *An Abridgment of the City Charter*, 1680, the package duties charged on two of the commoner sorts of imported gloves were, for those with silk fringe and faced with taffeta, per dozen pairs, a penny; for those lined with coney or lamb-skin, or plain, a halfpenny per dozen pairs.

From the same source we learn that glovers "clipping the maund or packet" were chargeable, under the Package Tariff, with the payment of $1\frac{1}{2}d$.

LITERARY NOTICE.

The Gloues deuised for New yeres gyftes to teche yonge people to knowe good from euyl wherby they may learn the x. commaudementes at theyr fyngers endes other good lessons be written within the fyngers, the tree of vertues with her braunches in the right palme and the route of vyces in the lefte, with a declaration of the other pyctures folowinge in meter. God save the Quene. [About 1558.] A broadside with a woodcut.

Tbe Gold and Silver Wyre Drawers.[1]

ARMS, 1739.   PRESENT ARMS.

THE art of drawing wire and thread, formed from the precious metals, was doubtless a development, although an early one, of that which limited itself to copper and iron. Both branches of the trade existed in a thoroughly established state in the reign of Edward IV.[2] The

---

[1] A fuller account of this Company than is practicable in a general work will be found in Mr. Horace Stewart's very useful and elaborate monograph, *History of the Worshipful Company of Gold and Silver Wyre-Drawers, and of the Origin and Development of the Industry which the Company represents.* 4to, 1891. With illustrations.

[2] The wire enclosing the wooden handle of the Walworth dagger at Fishmongers' Hall has the appearance of oxydized silver, and if so is a very early example of this kind of work.

ordinary Wire-workers were at that period, as we have already shown, on an intimate footing with the Pinners, and seem to have occupied the same quarters and used the same ledgers. In 1565 the Wire-workers framed a petition for union with the Chape-makers, by the name of Wiremongers; and in 1569, 10 Elizabeth, they and their old associates the Pinners united with the Girdlers. The Pinners became an independent Company in 1636; but of the iron and copper Wire-drawers we hear no more till, in 1702, an abortive scheme was brought forward for amalgamating them, the Lacemen and Weavers with the Gold and Silver Wire Drawers.

Of the Craft immediately under consideration the earliest notice belongs to the reign of Edward IV. (1461), when the members are included among the foreigners who were obliged to restrict their shops to the manor of Blanche-Appleton (or rather, perhaps, Blanche-Chapelleton) adjoining to Fenchurch, where there seems to have been a sort of market, accredited by Stow with giving its name to Mart (or Mark) Lane. The historian's words are :—" Then have ye *Blanch Apleton*, whereof I read in the thirteenth of *Edward* the first, . . . This *Blanch Apleton* was a Mannor, belonging to Sir *Thomas Roos*, of *Hamelake*, Knight, the seventh of *Richard* the second, standing at the North-east corner of *Mart-lane*, so called of a priviledge sometime enjoyed to keepe a Mart there." The art was clearly of Continental origin, and long remained in the hands of settlers from France or Flanders.

The present Association was probably an outgrowth from the Iron and Copper Wire Workers, who joined the Girdlers, but eventually merged in the Tin Plate Workers. In the list of City Gilds, as they stood in 1501–2, the *Wire Sellers* are said to possess a prescriptive Livery of twelve. Whether the same body, as in other cases, both made and sold the goods, and the Wire Sellers are identifiable with the Drawers, we do not certainly know.

The chief source of demand for the present article of commerce lay in the occupation and requirements of the Broderer, between whose Gild and that under notice an intimate relationship long existed. The Gold and Silver Wire Drawers were the manufacturers of the material which the Broderers so largely and profitably employed, while the fashion for that kind of work prevailed; and when the idea arose of introducing richer tissues in place of ordinary colours in wool and silk, as in the most ancient extant specimens from the eleventh century downward;[1] and the interests and welfare of the two fellowships were necessarily

---

[1] The Bayeux Tapestry is, no doubt, the oldest example which has been transmitted to us of ordinary embroidery.

bound up together. At the same time, the historian of the Company has, perhaps, not kept the two crafts sufficiently distinct, as regards their respective employments and specialities ; and not unfrequently cites the Broderer as if he were identical with the other craftsman who, as a manufacturer, was more directly connected with the Refiners and the Spinners, and whose own particular industry appears to have been apportioned between the working Drawers and the Stuff-men.

There is a considerable amount of confusion and difficulty attendant on the task of tracing the progress of this body of artisans prior to its attainment, in 1693, of a short-lived independence and comparative prosperity.

The pernicious system of patents and commercial farms, which reached its height under the first and second Stuarts, aggravated the troubles of the Craft by placing it between two hostile influences, the jealousy and rivalry of the Goldsmiths on the one hand, and the rapacious court-jobbers and their tools on the other.

James I., equally weak, inert, and unprincipled, vacillated in this case in a singular manner, as he was successively approached by the representatives of one interest or another. The fundamental objection and drawback to the encouragement of the trade in gold and silver wire were the consumption which it involved of English bullion ; and in 1623-4 the King permitted letters patent to pass to certain persons therein named, on condition that they should replace the waste by importing an equivalent amount of foreign metal. These grantees, however, were not the members of the industry, but monopolists ;[1] and on this circumstance being made known, or at least being laid as a grievance before the authorities, the charter was revoked.

The Goldsmiths, who exercised the same mistery, also threw difficulties in the way of the establishment of the members of it with a separate constitution.

The King himself professed to be much scandalized by the abuses involved in the patents ; but he was surrounded by creatures whose sole aim was plunder. Men of all ranks competed for any privilege obtainable by appeals to the royal cupidity or weakness. One of the most greedy, unscrupulous, and persistent of these schemers was Sir Edward Villiers, to whom the King, having exacted from the patentees, in con-

---

[1] In some cases the patentees were guilty of enhancing their profit by alloying the gold and silver with lead. But there was every variety of deception. In 1630-1, a maker of hatbands, named Grymes, was fined by the Star Chamber for using silver mixed with copper thread, and silver and gold mixed with purl and oes of copper double gilt. Burn's *Star Chamber*, 1870, p. 112. Spurious material was at the same time imported from the Continent.

sideration of their charter, an annuity of 1,000*l.*, transferred the payment as an indemnity to Villiers for the loss of other sinecures.

In 1650 an address was laid before the House of Commons by the Refiners and Gold Wire-Drawers of London, praying to be made a body politic, with one Master, three Wardens, twelve Assistants, and a Commonalty ; and in 1662–3 the King was moved by the Queen-mother and the maids of honour to grant the former petitioners a patent, in the name of trustees for their benefit, on account of the corruption of gold and silver lace.   But in neither instance did any substantial fruit arise from these efforts.

The levelling tendency of the Great Fire, and the more liberal temper which marked institutions after the Revolution of 1688, combined with the commencing withdrawal of many of the Great Companies from an active participation in business, made it possible for the Wyre Drawers in 1693 to secure their long-cherished object ; and on the 16th June in that year they were incorporated as " The Master, Wardens, Assistants, and Commonalty of the Art and Mistery of Drawing and Flatting of Gold and Silver Wire, and Working and Spinning of Gold and Silver Thread and Stuffs of the City of London."

The jurisdiction of the new Company extended over London and Southwark, and a three miles' radius from either; and all members of the calling were obliged to be freemen.   The governing body was directed to consist of a Master, four Wardens, and not more than thirty-six Assistants.   Bye-laws were framed by the Executive in January, 1699–1700, and were passed by the Judges on the 17th October following.

At this period the Company, though very far indeed from affluent,[1] was in a tolerably satisfactory condition.   In 1715, 358 were paying quarterage ; and in 1743, when it was proposed to forbid by Act of Parliament the wearing of gold and silver lace, it was publicly stated that no fewer than 6,000 persons (including women and children) were dependent on the trade.

In 1761, additional facilities were acquired for receiving apprentices ; and in 1780 a Livery of 100 was granted.

The grades of membership are, Freemen, Liverymen, Stewards, Assistants, Wardens, Master.   Women are not disqualified from becoming members of the Freedom or Commonalty ; and widows of deceased freemen are entitled to join on payment of 6*s.* 10*d.*   In 1882, there were 52 Freemen and 43 Liverymen.   The Livery was returned in 1892 as 107.   In the ten years 1870–9, there were 21 admissions to the Livery,

---

[1] In the first year of its existence (1694), the total corporate expenditure did not exceed 36*l.* 11*s.* 0*d.*

of which 12 were in 1879. In the same space of time three apprentices were bound.

The Company has 1,000*l.* 3 per cent. stock, producing 28*l.* 10*s.* a year, of which 100*l.* accrued under the will of Mrs. Christian Russell, September 20, 1723. The residue is the accumulation of surplus internal revenue. In 1834 the assets were stated to be 775*l.* four per cent. Bank annuities. In 1892 the income was returned at 65*l.*, 3*l.* in trust inclusive.

The Company had, some years ago, when such schemes were rather popular, the notion of organizing an industrial exhibition of gold and silver wire fabrics, of which it is believed to possess a few specimens, and of which others are in the hands of collectors or in museums. But nothing further has yet been accomplished toward such an object.

It also owns a few official insignia and two or three pieces of silver plate. The arms, of the grant of which there seems to be no precise evidence, first occur in Maitland's *History*, 1739, and are found on the common seal of 1742.

The independent career of the Wyre Drawers in the sense of an executive body was remarkably brief and uneventful, and under existing circumstances their standing is purely social and municipal.

From our first knowledge of them in 1461 as a colony at or near Fenchurch, down to the end of the seventeenth century, there is no intimation or even hint of a Hall. But they appear to have migrated at a subsequent period further westward. Upon their incorporation, they engaged quarters at Plaisterers' Hall in Addle Street, where they remained till 1696, when they removed to Broderers' Hall in Gutter Lane, which they rented till 1709. The expense, however, proved too heavy for their narrow resources, and they have since met at Bracy's Coffee House in Silver Street, at Tom's Coffee House in Wood Street, at the Half Moon Tavern in Cheapside, and other places.

LITERARY NOTICES.

By the King. A Proclamation concerning Wyer, Thread, and other Manufactures of Gold and Silver. [June 16, 1624.] A broadside.

The Humble Petition of the Refiners and Gold Wyer Drawers of London. To the Supreme Authority of this Nation, the Parliament of the Commonwealth of England. 1650. A broadside.

Proposals Humbly Presented to his Highness, Oliver, Lord Protector of England, . . . and to the High Court of Parliament, . . . for the Regulating of the Manufacture of Gold and Silver Thread and Wyer, and for the Passing an Act against Transporting Gold and Silver. . . . Folio, 1656.

⁎ Violet produced other works on this subject. See Hazlitt's *Collections and Notes*, 1876-91.

The Gunmakers.

AT some distance from the opening years of the seventeenth century, the manufacture of manual fire-arms still remained in the hands of persons unconnected with any special Union or Fellowship, and avowedly dispersed among other Gilds, at an epoch when scarcely any division of labour was without its separate organization ; and it further appears that the operation of testing weapons or implements of this class was left to blacksmiths and other incompetent persons, to the discredit of the calling and the public peril. The records of the Brewers and the pages of Stow contain the name of Edward Harvest, Brewer, who died in 1610, and was described on his monument as " one of his Majesty's Gunners." Whether he was also a brewer, or merely free of that Company, does not appear, nor indeed, whether he was a maker of fire-arms or a cannon-founder. But he probably held an official appointment under the Crown, and was one of those who were opposed to the unprofessional gunsmiths. He may have served Elizabeth in the same capacity, as he was her contemporary rather than her successor's.

Just about the time when the long-standing quarrel between the Blacksmiths and the Clockmakers was drawing to a close, the abuses and dangers attendant on the gun manufacture were represented to the Crown ; and it was likewise alleged that the weapons of London fabric were the best of the kingdom, if the existing irregularities could be corrected by the formation of the skilled and experienced makers into a Company with proper authority.

These were the circumstances under which the charter of the Gunmakers was delivered, March 14, 1637–8, to Henry Rowland, Gunmaker, and sixty-two other persons, all freemen of London, practising and using the art, for themselves and all others who might succeed them, by the name of The Master, Wardens, and Society of the Mistery of Gunmakers of the City of London, with a licence in mortmain to 40*l.* a year, a common seal, the right of making ordinances in writing, and of electing officers, and the power of view, gauge, proof, trial, and marking of all hand-guns, such proof or trial to be with good and sufficient gunpowder and weight of bullet of lead sizeable to every several gun. This jurisdiction extended over London and a ten miles' radius ; and all persons making, using, or selling guns, dags, pistols, barrels, or locks, were required to bring them to be examined and marked at the Company's Hall or other meet place appointed. The mark of the Company was to be GP.

The Executive, in addition to the customary functionaries, was ordered to consist of two or more of the Assistants, to superintend the processes of proof and trial, and to be renewed from year to year. Henry Rowland was nominated by the Crown the first Master, and Thomas Addis and John Watson the first Wardens. A special clause was inserted, saving any orders of the Privy Council and Council of War. Ordinances agreeable to the charter were approved, and a Livery granted, in 1670. In the Ordinances, Gunmakers' Hall is named as the place of meeting, and each member is required to contribute 2s. 6d. to the annual dinner. As the Company does not appear to have ever owned any premises except the Proof House at Whitechapel, probably that is the spot intended.

The governing body is in conformity with the charter; but the staff, besides the Clerk and Beadle, comprises the two View and Proof Assistants, and the Proof-master, of whom the latter is not a member.

In 1882 the Liverymen numbered 32 and the Freemen 58. The estate wholly consists of accumulated savings from the profits of the proof business, representing the interest on nearly 30,000l.[1] This is a solitary case in which modern legislation has not interfered with an old institution, and the Gun Barrel Proof Act of 1868 recognises the charter; but the Company's establishment at Whitechapel is subject to the provisions of the Explosives Act, 38 Vict. c. 17. In 1857 the Court of Common Pleas upheld the title of the Gunmakers to stamp manufactures apart from any rights of the Birmingham Proof House.

It may be predicated of this Association that it stands on very peculiar ground, and is a Livery Gild in form rather than in spirit. It has no historical and barely any municipal tie ; there is no religious atmosphere around it, no romantic mystery, no antiquity, no striking personal distinction on the part of any of its members, no impressive vicissitudes. It is a sober, discreet, practical, thriving syndicate, with a single aim and an untiring eye to business ; and it has worked these two hundred years

---

[1] In 1834 the Gunmakers returned their income at over 1,200l. a year. In the years 1870–9 it varied from over 4,000l. to rather under 3,000l. In 1892 it was returned at 2,500l.

and more, down there at Whitechapel, ever since it was a rural hamlet, for the public good and for its own, unaffected by Great Fire, undisturbed by *Scire Facias* and *Quo Warranto*.

The Horners [and Bottlers].

The arms are :—*Argent* on a chevron between three leather-bottles *sable*, and as many bugle-horns, stringed of the first.

THIS Gild certainly lays just claim to the distinction of having been one of the most ancient among those of a similar character founded in the City of London, and it is predicable of it, that its very lengthened

OLD ARMS.

duration as a voluntary Brotherhood was parallel with its greatest prosperity, owing to the more general employment, subsequently to the grant of a charter, of other fabrics for domestic and commercial purposes.

Stow merely says[1]: " As for bottle-makers and horne-makers, the precedent times have remembered them to be of antiquity, and two distinct Companies combined in one ; but I finde no record that they were at any time incorporated."

The fair originally granted by Henry III. in 1268, according to the received tradition—though it has been alleged that it went back as far as King John—to the Horn-makers, to be held at Charlton, near Woolwich, for three days, was first kept in Trinity Week, but afterward changed to the month of October, commencing on St. Luke's Day (October 18). It acquired the name of " Horn Fair," and became in course of time a rather disorderly festival, insomuch that " All is fair at Horn Fair," passed into a popular saying. Here every species of article and utensil formed of the material—drinking-horns, hunting-horns, powder-horns, ink-horns —were on view and sale, and retailers replenished their stocks.[2] We

---

[1] *Survey of London*, 1633, p. 168.
[2] The fair was finally abolished in 1872. " An ink-horn phrase," or " to smell of

shall presently see that two provincial fairs were also important marts for this craft.

In 50 Edward III., the Horners were ranked among the forty-eight Misteries of London, and were represented by two members on the Court of Common Council. In the reign of Henry IV. it was found that the large export of the raw material began to prove very detrimental to the native industry; and by statute 4 Edward IV. c. 8, strangers and foreigners were precluded from buying unwrought horns of butchers, tanners, and others, to the prejudice of freemen of the Company; and the power of search vested in the latter was enlarged to a radius of twenty-four miles from London and to Stourbridge and Ely fairs. The repeal of this Act in the first year of James I. was represented by the Horners to be so fatal to their interests, that in the seventh of the same reign and the third of Charles I. the privileges and powers of the Fellowship were renewed, with certain exceptions as regarded the power of search at Stourbridge and Ely fairs, but with an extension of authority to check the exportation of unwrought horns. An indication of their commencing decline in the fifteenth century is indirectly furnished by their return of eight men-at-arms to the muster for the City Watch in 1469, as this was nearly the minimum quota. They do not present themselves at all in several of the official lists between that date and 1629.

It was not till 13 Charles I. (January 12, 1638) that the Horners, after an existence of nearly four centuries, acquired their charter and bye-laws.

They were incorporated by the name of the Master, Wardens, Assistants, and Fellowship of the Mistery of Horners of the City of London, with a common seal, and the other customary rights; and the Company embraced all free horners within the Cities of London and Westminster, their liberties and suburbs. Authority was also conferred to elect a Master, two Wardens, and ten or more Assistants, and to meet in the common Hall or other convenient place for the transaction of business.

Freemen were bound to reside in London or the liberties, or within seven miles thereof, and to refrain, under a penalty of 40s., from buying or taking any manner of unwrought work within twenty-four miles, and from buying any horns, or parts of horns, of cutlers or other persons within the realm of England and dominion of Wales.

In 1837 the Report of the Commissioners ranks this as the fifty-fourth out of eighty-nine bodies. In 1846, the Court of Aldermen granted the Horners a Livery of 60. The Company is not mentioned in the

the ink-horn," were terms formerly denoting a style which savoured of pedantry or academical conceit.

returns of 1699 and 1724 ; but in 1882 the number of members was given at 13, three freemen inclusive.   In 1892 the Livery is returned as 17, and the total income as 99*l*.[1]

The Horners at present hold no property, but they had at one time a warehouse and sheds in Wentworth Street, Whitechapel, purchased in 1604 on lease at 4*l*. a year for 1000 years, the proceeds of which, on their demolition for public improvements in 1881, were invested in Consols, and appear to realize about 72*l*. a year.   The only other sources of income are the fees, fines, and quarterages.

The only privilege attached to the Freedom or Livery is the right to vote for the parliamentary representatives of the City, if the person reside within twenty-five miles, and for Lord Mayor, Sheriffs, and other civic functionaries under any circumstances.   The fees payable are as follows :—Upon taking up the Freedom, 1*l*. 13*s*. 4*d*. by patrimony or servitude ; 35*l*. by purchase ; upon admission to the Livery, 15*l*. ; upon election on the Court, 10*l*.   There are other minor fees to the Clerk.

It was formerly the practice for certain delegates of the Gild to attend at Leadenhall and other markets or fairs, and buy horns, which were consigned to their depôt at Whitechapel, and divided by lot among the freemen, their widows and orphans, all of whom participated in the monopoly then enjoyed under the charter.

But the premises above mentioned were already let in 1796 at a beneficial rental of 30*l*. a year, and the trading operations of the Company had, at or before that time, doubtless determined.

The practice, however, demonstrates that the followers of the Craft were salesmen by retail as well as manufacturers ; and the probability seems to be that they insensibly succumbed to competition in both capacities with the Pouchmakers and Leathersellers, who dealt in the same goods and enjoyed a more influential standing.

Moreover, about 1570, the establishment of Glass-Houses, commencing with that in the disused Hall of the Crutched Friars, at Aldgate, had the concurrent effect of bringing drinking-vessels of that material into more general vogue ; and the emporium just named was already established on a large scale in 1575, as we may infer from the mere store of fuel on the premises, when it was burnt down in the autumn of that year.   In other words, at the time when the Horners became a corporate body, glass had presumably grown an article in fairly general demand,

---

[1] At the annual Court this year (Feb. 3, 1892), Mr. Samuel Parnwell, C.C., of Queen Street, was elected Master for the year ensuing, Mr. W. S. Chapman, of Aldersgate Street, and Mr. Ellis Hall, Enfield, being respectively appointed Upper and Renter Warden. The Rev. R. F. Hosken, M.A., assistant master at Merchant Taylors' School, was appointed honorary Chaplain.

and was superseding wood[1] and pewter, as well as horn, for many domestic and commercial purposes. The Company succeeded in 1638 to the superintendence of a declining industry.

Horn pots, or other vessels of the same fabric, were employed in the fourteenth century, it appears, to hold wine. In the *King and the Hermit*, a poem of that age, employed by Sir Walter Scott in his *Ivanhoe*, the hermit bids his boy fetch a pot of this material, which is beneath the bed in an inner room, that the king and he may drink together from the contents.

Ink Horn Court, Petticoat Lane, without Bishopsgate, seems to have derived its name from the manufacturers of lanthorns, ink-horns, giggs, spoons, and other things of horn even in Strype's time. The historian's mother lived in Petticoat Lane, over against the sign of the Five Ink-horns.

The Clerk to the Company stated in evidence before the Royal Commission in 1883 that the Company had promoted an Exhibition of Horn Work at the Mansion House in the previous year, and had laid out in the object 200*l.*, the result of accumulated savings. The movement was widely encouraged and assisted ; but it had no influence on the fortunes of the Gild. The collection brought together by the Company from all quarters, and belonging to all periods, was unquestionably very interesting, and it was visited by about 7,000 persons. A descriptive catalogue was printed at the time, with the names of the contributors, among whom were Her Majesty and several members of Archæological Societies.

From a perusal of the *Catalogue*[2] we are apt to form a conclusion that such an industry should be capable of revival ; but the Horners are deficient in the requisite organization, and during sixty years were virtually in the hands of one Clerk, a most estimable gentleman, who remembered Canning, and Peel's maiden speech in Parliament, yet as unlikely a person to advance the desired object as could have been possibly found.

A number of very curious items was lent by various owners, some of considerable antiquity, and prizes were given. We annex from the Londesborough cabinet a representation of a cup made from the tusk of the narwhal, but which was formerly supposed to be derived from the horn of the unicorn. We have before us a punch-ladle of the early part of the last century, with a silver-mounted whalebone handle and a horn bowl. Whistles were also formed of horn.

---

[1] See the account of the TURNERS, *infrà.*

[2] *Catalogue of the Exhibition of Works in Horn, Ancient and Modern, held at the Mansion House, London, October* 18, 19, *and* 20, 1882. 8vo, 1882. We have two editions before us, one purporting to be revised.

Although the armorial bearings of the Horners explicitly testify to the amalgamation with them of the at least equally ancient Gild of Bottlers, the latter are not freely recognised as connected with them. But, whether or not, such was unquestionably the fact long prior to the charter of 1638. The two trades might very well have existed side by side, till the introduction of pottery and glass interfered with the demand for leathern vessels, which, even if the skin was not dressed with oil on the inside, can never have been very satisfactory receptacles for liquor, especially where the fermenting processes remained active after bottling.

The idea of employing skins as vessels for holding liquids is as ancient, at all events, as the Hebrew Scriptures, where the hide of the goat is described as applied to this purpose. In Italy and Spain they employ the gourd or calabash, which becomes as hard and impervious as wood; and in the latter country the sherry is brought to market by the peasants in pigs'-skins, which communicate a peculiar flavour to the wine.

Bottle-makers, or manufacturers of leathern *botels*, are mentioned in some proceedings between the Corporation of London and one Nicholas Burle (1 Richard II., A.D. 1378). This Burle was a dealer in hides, and sold them, among other customers, to bottle-makers. The contention was raised by certain cordwainers or bootmakers, who pleaded that the hides were not only useless to them, but to all other employers of the same material; and two bottle-makers, William Karlille and Thomas Tyrold, deposed that the hides were raw and forfeitable, and were unfit for their business and any other alike, so that the goods were declared forfeited.[1]

The leather bottle was made in a series of sizes, variously designated, from the *bombard* of one and a half gallons to the pint or half-pint. In the time of Charles I., when Thomas Heywood published his *Dissection of a Drunkard*, 1635, the plain bottle is stated to have been chiefly in use among shepherds and country folk; but they had them also mounted in silver in ale-houses, both in the City and suburbs, while at the Court there were the black jack and the bombard, which led to the

---

[1] Riley's *Memorials of London and London Life*, 1868, p. 421.

notion of the Frenchman that we drank our wine and beer out of our boots. In the reign of James I., the Lieutenant of the Tower was entitled to two bombards of wine out of every ship which came freighted therewith to the Thames. A writer of that day, comparing the bottle and the jack, says :—

> When the bottle and jack stand together, O fie on't,
> The bottle looks like a dwarf to a giant ;
> Then have we not reason the jacks to choose,
> For they will make boots when the bottle mends shoes ?

Among the curious tunes formerly in vogue was that of *The Bottle-Makers' Delight*, and it was to this that we are directed to set *A Song in Praise of the Leather Bottle*, published about 1700 on a broad-sheet. The sign of the " Leather Bottle " is still associated with Messrs. Hoares' Bank in Fleet Street, over which it used to be seen suspended.

In the play of *Mucedorus*, 1598, the clown says that he shall go to Thomas the butler for a jack of beer. In the *Serving-Man's Comfort*, by J. M., 1598, where the writer is deploring the decline of ancient hospitality, he inquires, among other points : " Where are the great black jacks of double beer ? " shewing, as we have said, not only that the leathern vessel, like that of glass, was made of various capacities, but that the jack was probably the next size to the bombard.

The late Mr. Thomas Willement, of Davington, Kent, used to shew a jack, which was thought by him to have belonged to Oliver Cromwell. But whether it was strictly a jack or a bottle, we cannot determine, as we never saw the relic.

No doubt, even after the general introduction of glass and hardware for drinking vessels and liquid measures, the fragility of both led travellers, soldiers, officers on the march, and others who had not much room to accommodate their stores, to retain the old leathern cases, of which we yet preserve some trace in our flasks.

Archdeacon Nares, who published his *Glossary* in 1822, observes, in reference to various meanings of the word *jack :* " A kind of pitcher made of leather was similarly called a jack even within my memory." This is, however, not quite explicit, as originally, at all events, the jack was one of the larger vessels of a series.

We see that Mr. Chappell, in his *Popular Music of the Olden Times*, assigns the composition of the famous ballad of the *Praise of the Leather Bottel*, on account of its metrical structure, to a very early period. It was certainly written on the model of the more ancient school of ballad poetry, and is by no means deficient in literary merit. The author is not known ; but he was presumably a layman, who parodied in the exordium and burden of his production the style of many of the familiar effusions of the wandering minstrel of these long by-gone days.   We are afraid that we must print it as it stands :—

The Praise of the Leather Bottèl.

'Twas God above that made all things—
The heavens, the earth, and all therein ;
The ships that on the sea do swim,
To guard from foes that none come in ;
And let them all do what they can,
'Twas for one end—the use of man.
　　So I wish in heaven his soul may dwell,
　　That first found out the leather bottèl.

Now, what do you say to these cans of wood ?
Oh, no ! in faith they cannot be good ;
For if the bearer fall by the way,
Why, on the ground your liquor doth lay
But had it been in a leather bottèl,
Although he had fallen, all had been well,
　　So I wish, etc.

Then, what do you say to these glasses fine ?
Oh, they shall have no praise of mine,
For if you chance to touch the brim,
Down falls the liquor and all therein ;
But had it been in a better bottèl,
And the stopple in, all had been well.
　　So I wish, etc.

Then, what do you say to these black pots three
If a man and his wife should not agree
Why they'd tug and pull till their liquor spill,
In a leather bottèl they may tug their fill,
And pull away till their hearts do ache,
And yet their liquor no harm can take.
　　So I wish, etc.

Then, what do you say to these flagons fine ?
Oh, they shall have no praise of mine ;
For when a lord is about to dine,
And sends them to be filled with wine,
The man with the flagon doth run away,
Because it is silver most gallant and gay.
　　So I wish, etc.

A leather bottèl we know is good,
Far better than glasses or cans of wood,
For when a man is at work in the field,
Your glasses and pots no comfort will yield
But a good leather bottle standing by
Will raise his spirits whenever he's dry.
　　So I wish, etc.

At noon the haymakers sit them down
To drink from their bottles of ale nut-brown ;
In summer, too, when the weather is warm,
A good bottle full will do them no harm.

Then the kids and the lasses begin to tattle,
But what would they do without their bottle ?
        So I wish, etc.

There's never a lord, an earl, or knight,
But in this bottle doth take delight ;
For when he is hunting of the deer,
He oft doth wish for a bottle of beer.
Likewise the man that works in the wood,
A bottle of beer will oft do him good.
        So I wish, etc.

And when the bottle at last grows old,
And will good liquor no longer hold,
Out of the side you can make a clout
To mend your shoes when they're worn out ;
Or take and hang it up on a pin,
'Twill serve to put hinges and odd things in.
        So I wish, etc.

There were other versions of this song with the varying burden :—

And I wish his heirs may never want sack,
That first devis'd the bonny black jack.

The Innholders.

WE have told the early story of this body in the preceding division of the present work, where we speak of the origin and development of the Hostelers, and endeavour to explain the evolutionary process to which we owed the Inn.

Subsequently to the recognition of the Fellowship under its existing title in 1473, as elsewhere noticed, the nearest landmark is the approval of Ordinances submitted to the City authorities ten years later (July 31, 1483). In 1501, 17 Henry VII., the Innholders already possessed a Livery of sixteen, which,—as well as the remainder of the executive system, a Master and three Wardens,—relied upon prescription. In 1509 the Mayor and Aldermen confirmed the rules of the Brotherhood. In 1515 they occur, among the forty-eight misteries then established, as ranking between the Plumbers and the Founders; and in that year (December 21, 6 Henry VIII.) they appear to have been incorporated by letters patent. Our knowledge of this fact is due to the citation of the former grant in the charter of December 21, 1663, 15 Charles II. which at the same time refers to the Act of Common Council passed on the 3rd of May immediately preceding, whereby all persons following the vocation of an innholder within the City and its liberties were bound to take up the freedom of the Gild.

The new charter dissolved the older one, and reconstituted the Fraternity of Innholders of St. Julian le Herberger and all other persons who then, or might hereafter, hold, keep, or occupy any inn, hostry, petty ostry, or livery stable, in the City of London or within three miles of the same, by the style of the Master, Wardens, and Society of the Art and Mistery of Innholders of the City of London, with the customary powers. There was to be a Master, three Wardens, and twenty Assistants.

OLD ARMS.

The standing of the Company, long prior to its elevation to that dignity, must have been very good. We have already traced it back to the earlier part of the fourteenth century, and have collected testimony conducive to the belief that it remained during a vast length of time a flourishing Association under a prescriptive government. The apparent loss of the original charter of 1515 may explain why we are unable to fix the date of the union with the Innholders of the associated Horse-Corsors.[1] Nor can we be actually sure that the two bodies were already united in that year. But they were so in 1520, when, in the precept from the Mayor and Aldermen to the several Companies to contribute toward a provision of wheat, they were assessed together at 30*l.* Sixty-one subscribers made up the required sum of 1,037*l.* 3*s.* 4*d.*, 80*l.* being the *maximum* quota. It began in 1543 to acquire real property by the ordinary indirect process in Coleman Street, Moorgate Street, and elsewhere; and in 1613 accrued the Dowgate Hill and Elbow Lane estate, including the first Hall or its site, followed up by other bequests, concessions, or purchases, among which may be enumerated the lease from the Merchant Taylors for 999 years in 1804 at 20*l.* a year of certain property (7 and 8, Elbow Lane, now 29–30, College Street) contiguous to the Hall.[2]

---

[1] In the North-East and North of England and in Scotland the Corsor is still known as the Couper.

[2] The Merchant Taylors' original seat was here; and probably this transaction refers to the houses erected on the same ground. The disused Hall stood long after the Taylors' migration to Threadneedle Street.

THE TABARD, SOUTHWARK, IN 1720.

THE TABARD (OR TALBOT) IN 1841.

The latter falls under notice in or about the period of its original conveyance (1613) to the new and present owners in relation to a building which was alleged to be prejudicial to it—that is, was probably too close. But the complainants, although they were supported by the Lord Treasurer, were unsuccessful, as it was shown on inspection that the structure was agreeable to the custom of London.

It was only three years after the settlement of the new constitution in 1663, that the Hall perished in the Fire, and was rebuilt. Maitland, writing in 1739, characterizes the second place of meeting as beautiful. But it has since been superseded by a third one, for which between 3,000*l*. and 4,000*l*. were raised by voluntary subscriptions.

THE BLACK BOY, CHELMSFORD.

The Company has received no charter beyond that of 1663, unless we admit that of 1 James II., 28 February, 1665–6, which was revoked by the General Act of William and Mary, concurrently with the Order of Common Council of May 7, 1685, conferring a Livery on the Innholders and other Gilds. Consequently the grant of 1663 is that by which the Company is governed, except in regard to its Livery, which is, as before, by prescription, as virtually acknowledged and ratified by the Act of 1690.

The Livery, which in 1501 amounted to 16, was officially returned in 1699 as 120, in 1724 as 150, in 1880 as 134, and in 1892 at 122. The Court consists of the Master, Upper Warden, Middle Warden, Renter

Warden, and twenty Assistants. There is a considerable trust estate, independently of the corporate income, which during the ten years 1871–80 has shown a tendency to increase, and which will be further benefited by the lapse of leases between 1910 and 1920. In 1892, the aggregate annual revenue was stated to be 1385*l.*, of which 210*l.* were in trust.

In those historical notices which have frequently rendered it possible to judge directly or otherwise the progress and elucidate the growth of

CORNELIUS CATON, LANDLORD OF THE WHITE LION, RICHMOND, SURREY
(ABOUT 1750).

a Company, the Innholders are remarkably deficient. The nature of the calling was perhaps naturally calculated to preclude its members from gaining such prominence as often befell those connected with the ordinary Craft and Merchant Gilds, as the Innholders occupied a somewhat anomalous position, hardly coming within either category.

In a transaction in which the Goldsmiths' Company was concerned in 1531, there is a remarkable mention of Thomas Jones, an innholder at the Star in Bread Street, who was rent-collector, probably for his

London estate, to the Abbot of Reading ; and this person was evidently of substantial character, as he became surety for some articles of value to the Wardens of the Goldsmiths.

Some estimate may be formed of the rateable value of the corporate estate by the assessment of 12*l.* 18*s.* upon the Company for a current ceremonial object in 1629, nearly a century after its incorporation. It was then, if we may form an inference from the comparative amount of its contribution, far from being a rich body, and, although the charter of 1663 gave jurisdiction over the suburbs, was practically limited to persons pursuing the business within the City itself.

This Gild possesses (among other articles of plate) a very fine salt-cellar of the time of James I., which is applied to the special purpose of dividing the Court and the Livery at what are termed Livery dinners. The latter literally sit below the salt.

There seems to be a tendency in one or two quarters to revolt against the ancient prescriptive practice of giving this seat of precedence at table to the Assistants, as the Livery often consists of persons of quite equal social standing.

LITERARY NOTICES.

Articles of Direction Touching Ale-Houses. 4to, 1607, 1608, 1609. With a Proclamation prefixed on the same subject. 4to, 1618.
*** These Articles deal with London and the suburbs.

A Form of License for keeping a common Ale-house or Tippling-house : with the Articles to be observed by the Keeper. [James I.] A broadside.

A Form of License granted by Sir Thomas Walsingham, Sir William Wythines, and others, justices for Kent, for Keeping a common Ale-house in that county. [James I.] A broadside.

Certain Wholesome Observations and Rules for Innkeepers, and also for their Guests, to be fixed upon the wall of every Chamber in the house. By T. W. [About 1630.] A broadside.

A Decree lately made in the High Court of Star Chamber, after consultation had among the Judges. . . . 4to, 1633.
This partly refers to the charges of ordinaries, tavern-keepers, and petty Ostryes or Hostelries.

Taylor's Travels and Circvlar Perambvlation through, and by more then thirty times twelve Signes of the Zodiacke, of the Famous Cities London and Westminster. With the Honour and Worthinesse of the Vine, the Vintage, the Wine, and the Vintoner ; with an Alphabeticall Description of all the Taverne Signes. By John Taylor, 8vo, 1636.

The Honorable and Memorable Foundations . . . of Divers Cities, . . . Also, a Relation of the Wine Tavernes either by their signes, or names, of the persons that allow or keepe them in, and throughout the severall Shires. By John Taylor. 8vo, 1636.

An Useful Table for all Victuallers and others dealing in Beer and Ale Calculating the price of any number of barrels at a certain price per barrel. 1685. A broadside.

Several Orders Made and agreed upon by the Justices of the Peace for the City and Liberty of Westminster, Vpon Monday, the 10 day of March, 1655. Concerning the future Licensing of all Innkeepers, Victuallers, and Ale-house-keepers, within the said City and Liberty. Folio, [1656.]

A Vade Mecum for Malt-Worms: or, a Guide to Good Fellows, being A Description of the Manners and Customs of the most Eminent Public Houses in and about the Cities of London and Westminster. Dedicated to the Brewers. In two parts. 8vo, [1720.] With woodcuts of the tavern signs.

There is a second edition of the First Part. A Third Part was announced, but is not known.

The Joiners.

FROM STOW, 1633.   FROM MAITLAND, 1739.

THAT the Joiners possessed Ordinances before 1309 under the approbation of the City authorities, is proved by proceedings taken in that year; in which it is prayed that the regulations in former use might be renewed, so that the Ordinances were not only framed by the Gild itself, but allowed by the Court of Aldermen at an earlier date; and we find that the governing body was composed of six Wardens or Overseers, whose function it was to examine all goods made, and to affix to them a stamp in token of authenticity. Such a precaution was perfectly necessary, no less than that which restrained a joiner or other artificer from overstepping his legitimate province, as complaint was made that truant apprentices and deceitful persons resorted to the woods near the City, and there made the bows of saddles of green stuff unfit for the purpose, selling them to unscrupulous painters or saddlers, who foisted them on the unwary.

There is no direct allusion to such a thing; but it is to be shrewdly suspected that these practices owed their rise and success to the enhanced cost of saddles, and that the motive was undersale; for in 1350 the King is heard to complain to the City of the dearness of these articles—a serious consideration in the aggregate or for those who had to find cavalry equipments.

In 1376, 50 Edward III., the Joiners were represented on the Common Council by two members, the *maximum* being six. In 1469 they engaged to find for the City Watch thirty men-at-arms, a quota indicative of growing consideration and prosperity ; and in 1515, among the forty-eight Gilds enumerated in an official return, they appear between the Blacksmiths and the Wiresellers. The Company was incorporated by letters patent, 13 Elizabeth, April 14, 1570, as the Master, Wardens, and Commonalty of the Faculty of Joiners and Ceilers or Carvers of London. This grant was ratified July 20 the same year, and these instruments, with the exception of the ephemeral one of James II., are, with the bye-laws, drawn up and approved by the Lord Keeper and the Judges shortly after, the only muniments of the kind in the possession of the Company. The charter of 1570 vested in the commonalty the right of annually electing, on the day of St. James the Apostle, a Master and two Wardens, and gave jurisdiction within the City and over a compass of two miles, rendering freedom of the Company obligatory on all craftsmen. In the contemporary bye-laws, we see that the same principle of election by the whole body of the mistery was extended to the Assistants, twelve in number, whose places were to be filled, as vacancies occurred, from the general body. Some years later, a serious controversy, culminating in a law-suit, originated in the contention of the freemen or Yeomanry that the executive functions ought not, under the charter, to be undertaken by any but craftsmen ; but on the matter being referred to two aldermen as arbitrators, it was settled, adjudged, and finally exemplified under the Great Seal, that the elections of officers should be conducted as heretofore, and that candidates should be taken, irrespectively of calling, from the Court and Livery. These proceedings spread over several years (1613–21), and necessarily entailed heavy expense.

The decision of course preserved the unusually liberal constitution intact ; and the Court of Livery, which meets twice a year, or oftener if necessary, is the body whose voice controls the Master, Wardens, and Assistants.

The bye-laws, originally framed in 1570, were confirmed in 1605 and 1740 ; but in the minor details many alterations have since been made by the Court.

In 1882 the Livery numbered 90 and the freemen about 100. In the returns of 1699 and 1724, the former is said to amount to 190 and 286 respectively. In 1834 the corporate income was about 700*l.* a year ; in 1871, 948*l.*; in 1880, 1,312*l.* ; in 1892, 1300*l.* The Joiners are interested in the Salters' Irish Manor of Magherafelt to a small extent. There is no trust estate.

Stow's Continuator (1633) says: " In Thames Street, on the Thames side West from Downgate, is Greenwitch Lane, of old time so-called, and now Friar Lane, of such a sign there set up. In this lane is the Joiners' Hall, and other faire houses."

The Hall, of which Cunningham [1] mentions the Jacobean doorway and screen as of architectural interest, was in the parishes of All Hallows the Great and St. Martin's in the Vintry. In 1850 it was let to a packer. Joiners' Hall buildings occupy the site. The Company does not seem to know how or whence it acquired the property.

The Joiners as a Craft differed from the Carpenters in being technically limited to the subsidiary adaptation of wood-work to the purpose of forming doors, window-frames, wainscot, and other parts of a building which required to be planed and moulded. This line of distinction was preserved within a measurable period in specifications and estimates ; yet in an official list of 1629 the Planers are entered as a separate body, and as paying their own share of a municipal assessment—about a moiety of the amount paid by the Joiners. The Planers probably retained the same sort of independent rank as the Sawyers, with whom we have coupled them in a brief notice elsewhere. But although from the sum levied upon them they were evidently a numerous and thriving body, this is the only formal or public mention which we have encountered of them. The Carpenter took the whole contract and reserved to himself the roof, with its manifold details ; and the Joiner was his subordinate and servant. But, from the profusion of wood employed in ancient architecture and the exclusive dependence on local labour the calling was necessarily under old conditions a fairly advantageous one.

From the account for rebuilding Ironmongers' Hall in 1587 it is to be inferred that the Joiner by that date had begun to undertake certain carving and designing work ; for one of the charges is, " For cutting of 4 armes and other worke about the parlor," for which the Joiner had 4*l.* 10*s.* 8*d.*—a high figure for ordinary labour of his class.

Naturally the members of the craft varied in qualifications and in the scale of pay demanded. There were the skilled carvers and cabinet-makers and those who merely executed minor repairs. In the Goldsmiths' accounts, July 6, 1666, 24*s.* are paid to Smailes for work done *for the year past.*

At Carpenters' Hall are preserved two interesting specimens of domestic furniture, an octagonal table of carved oak, dated 1606, and a massive carved chair of solid mahogany of later date, both presumably

---

[1] *Handbook to London*, 1850, v. *Joiners' Hall.* It appears more probable that the work belonged to a later period, perhaps about 1670.

the work of early members of the Joiners' craft; similar relics are of course to be found in our museums and private collections; and in the

accounts for furnishing Saddlers' Hall after the Fire we encounter an order for a dozen and a half of Turkey work chairs for the use of the Court.

SPECIMEN OF ELIZABETHAN WOOD-CARVING PRESERVED AT CARPENTERS' HALL.

In 1612–13 the Joiners prevailed on the Corporation to grant to them power of search and survey over the Coachmakers, Trunkmakers, Gunstock, Flask, and Jewel-box Makers, Cupboard Makers, and Box-makers, " so far as their skill and judgment extended."

In 1632 a dispute between the Carpenters and Joiners led to a settlement, by which it was clearly laid down what descriptions of work belonged to each Company, and to the latter were assigned and reserved : 1. All sorts of bedsteads, except boarded bedsteads nailed together ; 2. All sorts of chairs and stools made with mortices or tenents ; 3. All tables of wainscot, walnut, or other stuff glued with frames, mortices, or tenents ; 4. All sorts of forms made of boards pinned or glued ; 5. All sorts of chests, framed, dovetailed, pinned or glued ; 6. All sorts of cabinet cupboards and presses similarly constructed ; and so forth, the Joiner taking in his department shop-windows, doors, picture-frames, sign-boards, coffins of wainscot, pews, pulpits, and all sorts of carved work made without the plane.

But the controversy lingered over a long series of years ; and after the Great Fire there is extant an answer by the Court of Aldermen to a petition preferred by the Joiners, July 9, 1672, in which the Court points out the large field then open to all Crafts, and also mentions that the Joiners, in common with the Wheelwrights, Cartwrights, Box-makers, and others, had originally sprung from the Carpenters.

It is in immediate relevance to this point, that we have to bear in mind the conspicuous part borne by a member of the Joiners' Craft in the political history of the last quarter of the seventeenth century and his tragical fate. Stephen College, known as the *Protestant Joiner*, had a leading share in the important work of re-edification after the Great Fire, and was, from the prices paid to him for his work and from the still surviving examples of it, a man of high standing in his calling. We notice in another place that for wainscoting Stationers' Hall in 1674 his charge was 300*l.* ; and the evidence of his skill and taste are yet before us in an admirable state of preservation.

College or Colledge, who was hanged at Oxford for high treason in 1681, was the predecessor of the more famous Grinling Gibbons, of whose masterpieces so many have come down to us. Gibbons worked not only in London, but was employed by the nobility and gentry throughout the country. There is a good deal of his carving at Pet-worth in Sussex.

The Leathersellers.[1]

THIS distinguished and now affluent Gild, which seems to have evolved from the WHITE TAWYERS (of whom some account has been already furnished), and which in the only place, where its particular province or department is explained, is said to engage itself in the *selling*, *sorting*, *whiting*, and *staking*, of leather, first discovers itself under its new and present name through the appreciable need of protection for its operations and interests. The Company refers the earliest document expressly dealing with its concerns to the closing years of the reign of Edward III. (1372), when the men of the mistery approached the Court of Aldermen with a bill or petition for a more stringent system of regulating the treatment and sale of leather. The record is more than usually curious. It prays that no man of the mistery of Pursers should put leather to sale for other than it was, or foist on the people sheepskin or calfskin scraped and stained as roe-leather, and that no dyer should be suffered to connive at such deceit by taking fraudulent material for the purpose of colouring it. It proposes that, in order to check and punish these and similar abuses, two Leathersellers of Cheap and two Pursers of the Bridge should be chosen by the common assent of the men of the two misteries, and sworn before the Court. The demand was unanimously granted. Four years later, the Leathersellers are returned as sending two of their number to the Common Council.

We hear of the Gild in these days sparingly enough. It was in the year just cited (1376) that it took part in certain parliamentary proceedings taken against one John Peech for monopoly and extortion,

---

[1] We have been indebted for some information respecting this Company to the *History and Antiquities of the Worshipful Company of Leathersellers of the City of London. With Facsimiles of Charters and other Illustrations.* By W. H. Black, F.S.A. Folio, privately printed, 1871.

and we may presume that it was comprised among the "fifty-one of
the more potent misteries" to the representatives of which on the
Common Council an oath was administered on taking their seats at the
board.

Bye-laws were drawn up by the Leathersellers, and approved, in 1398.
They enjoined respect to the authority of the masters of the trade, who
were thereby appointed to be chosen to protect its interests internally
and externally, and to present offenders to the Lord Mayor's Court.
Among the points on which the Articles insist, were that sheepskin and
calfskin were not to be dyed after the same manner as roe-leather; that
no one of the trade should seek to sell lanyers of roe-leather or deer's-
leather secretly or in eve-cheapings; that no man or woman should be
set to work at the trade, unless he or she were first apprenticed and
enrolled, save the wife and children of a freeman; and that none should
work by night with hammer and shears, knife or file; and transgression
against these and other similar ordinances was visited by a scale of
penalties varying from 40s. to 40d.

Between the promulgation of these Articles and the reign of Henry
VI. there was a period of considerable activity as regarded the leather
trade and the attempts of the City and Crown to diminish the irregularities and abuses perpetrated by the several industries connected with
it. Of all these the Leathersellers, whose special province was ostensibly
the sale of the material in gross to others, were possibly less chargable
with the responsibility than those, who were immediately concerned in
preparing the skins on the one hand and in manufacturing them into
goods on the other.

Yet it should be recollected that, as we have seen it to be the case
with the Merchant Taylors, the line between the craftsman and salesman was not in primitive days very distinctly marked; and the most
ancient records of the Leathersellers appear to sustain the view that at
the outset they and the Tanners or Tawyers formed a common body,
from which the merchant Gild eventually segregated itself, and soon
found it advisable to strengthen its hands by an enlargement of its
authority both over its own constituency and over the allied and subsidiary branches of the trade.

While the testimony in our hands points to the White Tawyers as the
ancestors of the Leathersellers, and as their precursors at London Wall,
we cannot help seeing in the Ordinances of 1635, how a gradual process
of incorporation or absorption tended to the aggrandisement and supremacy of the Gild before us, which ultimately, prior to its abandonment
of the practical side, unified all the scattered divisions of labour interested in the treatment of hides and furs.

The early connection of the Leathersellers with the preparatory processes is exemplified by the terms of the lease granted in 1469 to
William Boteler of premises at London Wall as a tan-yard, where 2,600
goatskins and 1,000 kidskins might be dressed yearly, and by the fact
that Boteler was one of the Wardens of the Company in 1471–2.

But prior to the date of a charter, the Ordinances of 1398 were repealed and superseded by others in 1438–9, 1440, and 1443 ; and these
new Articles dealt primarily with the sale of fells or hides, both rough
and tawed or tanned, and with the cognate difficulty attendant on the
control and surveillance of the leather-dyers.

In 1444, August 19, 22 Henry VI., upon the application of Thomas
Bygge and fourteen others, who cited the existing Ordinances, a
regular charter was accorded to the Gild, conferring perpetual succession, a common seal, a licence in mortmain, the power to hold assemblies
and grant liveries, and other privileges, but reserving the presentment
of the Wardens to the Lord Mayor, as heretofore, for approval and
admittance. The main features in the instrument, perhaps, are the
general right of search for bad or false wares, which was extended to
all cities, vills, boroughs, places, fairs, cheapings, and markets throughout the realm, and, secondly, the acknowledgment of a prescriptive
Livery.

At this period the Fraternity was beginning to acquire consequence
and consideration. Within a few months from the settlement of the
charter, it received by feoffment its first parcel of real property at
London Wall, consisting of a messuage with two shops and a garden,
and presumably yielding accommodation for the possessions and meetings of the Gild ; and in 1447 the name meets the eye among eighteen
subscribers of 16*l.* each to the roofing of Guildhall Chapel. In 1469 it
supplied forty-four men-at-arms to the muster for the City Watch ; and
in the following year, under the will of Robert Ferbras, the last feoffee,
the Leathersellers came into possession of the whole London Wall
estate, of which an account is supplied below. In 1502 and 1517 successive orders of the Court of Aldermen sanctioned the union with their
ranks of the Glovers-Pursers and the Pouchmakers, both important
bodies in their respective ways, and both conducive to the commercial
expansion and religious settlement of the Gild, in which they merged.

Some further particulars of these bodies will be found under our
accounts of them *suprâ*.

The accession of the Pursers in 1502 exercised a notable religious
influence ; for in the articles of agreement and union there is, besides
the stipulations that in lieu of the former connection of the Leathersellers with St. Mary Magdalen's Chapel, Guildhall, the joint Fellowship

should be under the patronage of the Virgin at St. Thomas of Acon,[1] the one that their common Hall should likewise be of the Assumption of Our Lady, and that the annual feast should be held on the day of the said Assumption, provided that it fell on Sunday or Monday—if on Saturday, then on the Sunday or Monday ensuing, if on any other day, at such time as the Wardens might appoint. It was also laid down that the united Gild should be partners in the suffrages hitherto performed in the Charterhouse of London on behalf of the Glovers-Pursers, as well as in the light and yearly obit maintained there down to that time by the latter ; that the hangings in the Hall should be made of the stories of Our Lady, and not of the Resurrection ; and that the banners should be charged with the arms of the whole Fraternity, agreeably to an approved pattern.

The work of consolidation was not yet complete ; for in 1517, as we have mentioned, the Pouchmakers followed the example of the Glovers-Pursers, and arranged to join the union, bringing with them a considerable assortment of valuable effects, of which an inventory is extant, besides the advantages accruing from their very extensive and multifarious business. It may be permissible to conjecture that the latest member of the body had some inducement to take the course in a community of religious usages ; for the Pouchmakers, like the Glovers-Pursers, ranged themselves under the protection of the Virgin, and laid equal stress on the Assumption as an object of ceremonial worship and a titular distinction.

The varied nature and scope of the industry pursued by the Pouchmakers, of whom some account is given in the previous section, and who had themselves absorbed the Mail-makers and Galoche-makers, may be easily divined from the enumeration of the goods sold by them, which occurs in the municipal ordinance of 1517 for their alliance with the Leathersellers ; and we seem to discern a clear aim, on the part of those more especially concerned as vendors of leathern utensils or articles, at a federal combination for the common security and profit. In the Ordinances of the Leathersellers, 1635, there is quite an array of trades set forth as having been separate branches, and as then (and long before, of course,) forming part of the Leathersellers' Gild. These were the Fellmongers, Leatherdressers, Parchment-makers, Glovers, Pursers, and Pouchmakers, of whom the last had taken over the two other bodies just named ; and to these we may add the Leather-dyers, often named in earlier documents.

The commodities on sale by the Pouchmakers, at the close of their

---

[1] Where Mercers' Chapel now is.

separate existence, include bellows, lanthorns, sconces, bags of all descriptions, pouches, mails (portmanteaux), budgets (wallets), bow-cases, cloth-sacks, the leathern fittings of chariots, leathern bottles and pots, satchels for carrying food (*garde-viaunces*), and trussing coffers.

The reign of Henry VII. witnessed several measures on the part of the Court of Aldermen or the Common Council for the consolidation and improvement of the leather industry. In 1488, ordinances were made to regulate the sale of tanned leather at Leadenhall, and for the better government of the Pouchmakers and Pursers; and in 1493, 1501, and 1502, others were framed and published for the further guidance and control of the Leathersellers and Pouchmakers.

At the coronation of Henry VIII., the Leathersellers had been reckoned as the eighteenth Company, and had been allotted fifteen yards for their stand to view the procession; but in 1515 they were officially declared to be fifteenth in precedence. Again, at the Mayor's Feast at Guildhall in 1531–2, they were represented by eight members, beside their Wardens—a larger quota than some of the great Companies.

There is an Elizabethan *inspeximus* or confirmation of the charter of 1444, dated June 28, 1559, when William Allen, Alderman,[1] and three other Wardens were the governing body. In this instrument the twofold oversight on the part of all concerned was committed of reciting the grant of 1444 as one of Henry VII. instead of Henry VI., and of confirming the obsolete Ordinances of 1398. It is very singular that the officials responsible on both sides for the matter should have submitted for the Queen's signature such a blundering piece of work.

The acting charter is that of July 24, 1604. Here the Company is designated The Wardens and Society of the Mistery or Art of the

OLD ARMS.

Leathersellers of the City of London; the faculty of electing the Wardens and the twenty-four Assistants, now first instituted, vests in the Court by co-optation upon the retirement or death of the persons named in the grant as the first holders of these offices by his Majesty's appointment; and the fifteenth day after Corpus Christi is declared to be the season for the annual elections thereafter. Vacancies among the Assistants were to be filled up from the ranks of the Commonalty or Freedom. The power of search was renewed, with a limitation to the City of London, its liberties and precincts. The descriptions of leather are specified as "all and singular the several kinds of

---

[1] Afterward Sheriff and (1571) Lord Mayor.

skins and fells in English called buff-leather, shamoy [chamois]-leather, Spanish leather, staggs leather rough or smooth, bucks leather, calfs leather, sheeps leather, lambs leather, kidds leather, frized or grained, dressed or wrought in oil, allum, shoemack or bark, or tawed;" and all parcels sold were henceforth to bear the arms or cognizance of the Company—a stamp bearing the three stags.

The statute, 5 Elizabeth, c. 8., entitled "An Act touching Tanners, Courriours, Shoemakers, and other Artificers occupyeing the cutting of Leather," had ordained that the sale of tanned leather should be restricted to Leadenhall and to Mondays, and to persons intending to work it; and by a later statute, 1 James I., c. 22, which re-enacted the major part of the former, eight searchers and sealers of leather were to be annually appointed by the Court of Aldermen from members of the Cordwainers', Curriers', Saddlers', and Girdlers' Companies.

By an Order in Council, April, 1634, the Lord Mayor was directed to appoint three searchers for Bartholomew Fair; and from the orders published in consequence of the plague of 1593 we learn that it was an ancient usage for the Leathersellers to occupy stations there outside the ring of Smithfield.

In the charters of 1444 and 1559 there had been a licence in mortmain, but not of a sufficient compass to enable the Company to hold the conventual estate at Bishopsgate securely in the presence of all sorts of unscrupulous intriguers and jobbers; and in 1614 heavy charges, including a gratuity of 125*l*. to the King, were incurred in supplying this defect and placing the tenure of the St. Helen's and other property on a clear basis.

With the exception of the charter of 1444, the faulty *inspeximus* of 1559, and the new grants of 1604 and 1614, the Leathersellers do not seem to have ever possessed any concessions from the Crown of a constitutional or permanent character, that conferred by James II., or the surrender in 1685, having been annulled by the Act of 1690.

The only set of bye-laws, posterior to those of 1398 and 1488, is that, which was sanctioned by the Lord Keeper and Judges, 11 Charles I. Mr. Black points out that in the preamble these new Articles are wrongly described as having been made by the Company on Tuesday the 24th, instead of the 14th, April, the Court Book reading *xiiijth*, and the 24th not falling that year on a Tuesday.

In 1591, a very serious dispute arose between the Government of Elizabeth and the City, in regard to the Patent granted by the Queen to Mr. Edward Darcie, of the Privy Chamber, for the Search and Sealing of Leather. The Leathersellers bitterly complained of the hardship and vexation imposed on them by the rigorous execution of the mono-

poly ; and, the Corporation espousing the cause of the Company and
Trade, the Queen offered to revoke the grant on payment of 4,000*l.*

Darcie attended the conference held at the Mayor's house to consider
the matter ; and such high words were exchanged that he committed an
assault on one of the Aldermen, which was reported to the Council as a
grave insult to Her Majesty's Lieutenant, and, of which the knowledge
spreading among the apprentices and others of the City, the offender
had to be safe-guarded out of the precinct.

This imbroglio lasted till 1595.

The present Company in fact shared the common fate of all similarly situated and constituted bodies, and to a certain extent purchased
rather dearly the privileges which conferred on it power and prosperity.
From the periodical exactions of the Crown, apart from more or less legitimate appeals for public objects, there was scarcely any respite.   Even
before the times of the Civil War and Great Fire, with their almost overwhelming incidences and consequences, the Leathersellers were by their
own admission at a very low ebb about 1620, when James I. undertook to
preside in person for the settlement of a dispute between them and the
Earl of March, who sought at the hands of the King a monopoly extremely prejudicial to the Gild.   How it was settled, does not transpire
in the record ; Lord March died in 1624.

The governing body follows the charter of 1604, and is composed of
four Wardens, of whom one is Master, and twenty-four Assistants.   Previously to 1685, there was no *recognised* Livery, although in 1501-2 it
existed by custom, and numbered at that time 33,[1] and in the charters
of 1444 and 1604 an express power was inserted, "to grant Liveries."
But on May 6, 1685 the Court of Aldermen granted one in due form,
limiting it to thirty fit persons, exclusively of the Court as above defined ;
and on the 11th the chosen members were sworn in at Guildhall.   But
the body was enlarged at subsequent dates, and has varied from time to
time.   In 1501-2, we see that it amounted to 33 ; in 1699, it was 169 ; in
1724, 186 ; in 1882, 139 ; in 1892, 141.   A Liveryman must have served
or fined as Steward, before he can come on the Court.   The fines payable by an Assistant and a Master on election (10*l.*) are carried to the
Benevolent Fund, for the relief of distressed members of the Court.
The Steward is bound to find 12*l.* for the dinner on Lord Mayor's day,
and to hand 8*l.* to the Fund.

Upon the election to the Livery it was formerly customary to apprise
the new member of the fact by letter, and to enclose a pattern of the

[1] In the return to Parliament in 1725 the Company confessed its inability to trace
an authority for a Livery.

suit and colour, which he was required to procure, before he presented himself for formal admission. This bore the cognizance of the Company and is attached, in an extant specimen of the early part of the 18th century, to the left-hand margin of the communication.

The property of the Leathersellers, which has largely increased in value since 1834, mainly consists of estates at London Wall, Bishopsgate, Lewisham, and Sydenham, and of a sub-share of the Fishmongers' Irish manor. A very inconsiderable proportion is held in trust, owing to the most important part—the Bishopsgate possessions—having been obtained to the corporate use. In 1882 the corporate revenue was stated to be 16,395*l.*, the trust, 2,333*l.*,[1] whereas in 1834, of less than 4000*l.* a year, 1,500*l.* was set down as trust income. This is another way of saying that in the interval the St. Helen's rental has enormously risen.

But the Company has voluntarily expended large sums in improving and developing its educational charities, and has supported the City and Gilds' Institute and many other undertakings.[2] Some portion of the Bishopsgate estate was derived from Roger Daniel, King's printer, and a Master of the Company, under his will dated April 28, 1625. In Gracechurch Street and Great Eastcheap there were also some early acquisitions. The latter is noticeable merely as having been a messuage then called *The George on Horseback*, left in trust in 1619, and situated in what is at present known as King William Street.

The London Wall estate was composed of two distinct properties obtained at different periods and under different circumstances. What Mr. Black calls the *Western Estate*, at one time constituted the property of William Godale, Citizen and Currier, whose will was proved in 1331, and was left by a later possessor, Nicholas Rumbold, Citizen and White Tawyer, in reversion after the death of his wife, to two of the Brotherhood of White Tawyers, subject to the performance of certain obits in the

---

[1] In 1892 the aggregate income was returned as 18,500*l.*, of which 3,000*l.* were in trust.

[2] In February last, the Company voted and distributed donations of from 5*l.* 5*s.* to 21*l.*, to 140 charitable and other institutions, amounting in all to 1,769*l.* 5*s.*, viz.: General hospitals, 257*l.* 5*s.*; special hospitals, 372*l.* 15*s.*; convalescent homes, 115*l.* 10*s.*; dispensaries, 42*l.*; surgical appliance societies, 36*l.* 15*s.*; orphanages, 199*l.* 10*s.*; homes, etc., for relief in affliction, 126*l.*; homes, etc., for the poor, 152*l.* 5*s.*; benevolent societies, 241*l.* 10*s.*; prisoners' aid societies, 42*l.*; penitentiary societies, 21*l.*; missions, etc., 126*l.*; general, 36*l.* 15*s.* The Company have also given 136*l.* 10*s.* in donations of 21*l.* and 10*l.* 10*s.* among the poor-boxes at eleven metropolitan police-courts. These donations are in addition to grants made from time to time during the year for special objects, such as the City and Gilds' Institute for General Purposes, and for the Leather Trades' School, the Volunteer Patriotic Fund, and other charities.

church of All Hallows on the Wall. The reversioners, however, owing to their incapacity to hold lands, did not succeed on the demise of the widow ; and after a great deal of trouble and delay, and a series of feoffments, the property, with the *Eastern Estate*, devolved on Robert Ferbras, Citizen and Surgeon of London, who conveyed the whole to the Company under his will, November 4, 1470.

The Eastern estate, which was contiguous to the church of All Hallows on the Wall, and which included the site of the first Hall of the Brotherhood, passed into the hands of the Leathersellers in 1470 under the will of Robert Ferbras above-mentioned, the last of a line of feoffees, who had held the property till the Gild became capable under its charter of holding realty to a certain value. Altogether, the possessions in this quarter were fairly extensive upon the union of the two divisions in the manner described. The Hall, which belonged to the eastern one, possessed a parlour, a basement occasionally let to other bodies by the day, the refectory above, adorned with hangings illustrative of the History of the Resurrection,[1] a kitchen, and a garden ; but the latter was alienated in 1477–8. From the lists of plate and other chattels made in 1488 and 1504, we may infer that the other appointments corresponded.

The building was at no great distance from Armourers' Hall, and in fact formed one of a group of such seats, which studded that then outlying part of the metropolis. The isolation was dictated by the nature of the industries ; and the vicinity of the Walbrook rendered the spot convenient for many manufacturing purposes.

The relationship of the Leathersellers to the church of All Hallows was an inheritance from the White Tawyers, who so early as 1346 associated themselves with it ; and the original place of assembly in the present case partook of the composite character, which those of so many of the more ancient Gilds assumed in their inception—that of bodies of a partly religious and partly commercial complexion. It seems to have been their invariable rule to shelter themselves under the tutelary influence of the nearest religious establishment, and even to employ it as a substitute for a meeting-house and a muniment-room.

The fiduciary element equally entered into the primary ownership of the London Wall and Bishopsgate properties ; but the conveyance of 1470 probably released the former from its obligations in a religious direction. Both before and subsequently to the removal to St. Helen's, in or about 1543, portions of the estate at London Wall were sold for

---

[1] Under the agreement with the Pursers in 1502 these were to be replaced by others symbolical of the Assumption of the Virgin.

various reasons; the old Hall itself was divided after a certain interval into tenements; and on the greater part of the land was eventually erected the block known as Leathersellers' Buildings.

The Leathersellers and their predecessors, the White Tawyers, had been settled at London Wall not less than two centuries, when Sir Richard Williams, *alias* Cromwell, Knight, exchanged the manors of Brampton and Hemyngford-Grey in Huntingdonshire with Henry VIII. under letters patent of March 29, 1542, for the site of the dissolved Benedictine Priory of Black Nuns at St. Helen's, Bishopsgate, founded in 1210 by the wealthy goldsmith, William Fitzwilliam, with all the buildings then thereupon; and it happened that, a year later, the Leathersellers having secured the promise of about 350*l.* from John Haselwood toward the object, concluded with Cromwell for the purchase of the Priory and its appurtenances as a common Hall. The negotiation was completed on the 28th April, 1543; and in order to defray the cost (380*l.*) and attendant expenses, some of the tenements at London Wall were sold for 270*l.* The new owners had not entered into actual possession on the 16th October, although they had taken over the premises on the 9th May.

There is not the slightest reason to doubt that the Company contented itself with the place as it found it, employed the monastic refectory as its dining and meeting room, and accommodated the almspeople in some of the disused apartments or offices.

In his will, January 16, 1543-4, John Haselwood, to whose generosity his presumed brethren were under such a weighty debt, records the previous gift to the Master and Wardens of 300*l.*, a bason and ewer of silver of the value of 20 marks (13*l.* 13*s.* 4*d.*), a standing cup and cover gilt of the value of 6*l.*, and a sow of lead weighing 11 cwt. and three quarters,[1] to enable them to purchase the Priory of St. Helen's, Bishopsgate, to make therein their common Hall, and " to the intent and purpose that they and their successors for ever should be bound to me and my executors by a sufficient writing obligatory, to be advised by mine executors, to purchase as much land and tenements or yearly profits for the yearly living and payments to be paid for ever to four beadmen and three beadwomen or almswomen, that is to say, to each of them eightpence weekly, and to every one of them two sacks of coals, each sack containing a quarter, to be delivered to each of them between Hallowmass and Christmas, over and besides their dwelling houses to be provided for them by the Master and Wardens, rent-free, within the site of the said late monastery of St. Helen's."

The premises originally consisted of the dining-hall, with extensive

---

[1] See what we have said under the account of the Plumbers' Company.

crypts and cellars of the most solid and beautiful fabric, the sitting and sleeping apartments of the Prioress and Sisterhood, a garden and a dovecote. The frontage was let to several tenants. This property was designated Little St. Helen's, and lay north of the Church, the close, which was situated to the south, being known as Great St. Helen's.

The Company still retained the Nuns' Hall as their place of meeting and entertainment, when Newcourt compiled his *Repertorium* in 1708. Maitland, writing in 1739, says: "This Hall, considering the antiquity of its building,[1] has some of the best joiners' and plaisterers' work in the kingdom. The screen is magnificent, adorned with six columns of the Ionic order, enrichments, etc., with ceiling of fretwork. The entrance into the Common Hall is up a handsome flight of stone stairs from the courtyard." A printed document of 1799 dwells on the antique fittings of the Refectory, "the Purbeck pavement, the curious and ornamental Gothic embellishments and carving, and the King's coat of arms richly carved and gilt. It was here that in 1769 the wardmote of Bishopsgate assembled, and elected the celebrated James Townsend, Esquire, M.P., subsequently Sheriff and Lord Mayor, their Alderman.

There are no longer any vestiges of this fine old place and its adjuncts. By a resolution of a committee of the Court of the Company in 1797, the entire pile, to the very cellarage, was demolished and swept away two years later. A more ruthless and unpardonable act of ignorant vandalism was perhaps never perpetrated. According to the auctioneer's prospectus the stone and brickwork "arising from a part of the Ancient Priory of St. Helen's, called the Nuns' Hall, founded in the year 1210," was in an astonishing state of preservation. The "curious" were invited to view the site, before it was cleared; and the fortunate result was, that some drawings were made of the crypt, vault, kitchen, and other portions of the structure. These are faithfully reproduced in Mr. Black's most interesting volume.

With that episode the historical career of the Leathersellers terminates. Their second seat in Bishopsgate was at the eastern end of Little St. Helen's, in an old house, which was adapted for the purpose, but which necessitated the resort on occasions, when space was needed, elsewhere. This structure was destroyed by fire in 1819, and a large portion of the contents perished in the flames. Even the common seal was not recovered till some weeks after among the ruins. Some of the Company's papers and parchments were saved,[2] together with a few pieces of plate.

---

[1] The *antiquity* was the reason.

[2] But many were burned, including those connected with the purchase from Cromwell in 1543.

Till the house was rebuilt, the use of Brewers' Hall was obtained, and the new building was not ready for occupation till 1822. It partook of the inadequate character and proportions of its predecessor, or at least its owners became dissatisfied with it, and in 1878 erected a fourth Hall immediately opposite, reserving the other pile for offices.

The Company has severed itself from its primitive Bishopsgate, no less than from its London Wall, traditions, and is on purely modern lines. Even the pump, made in 1679 by Caius Gabriel Cibber in satisfaction of his Livery-fine, has necessarily disappeared with the court-yard, in which it stood, surmounted by a mermaid pressing her breasts. On festive occasions these were made to give forth wine.

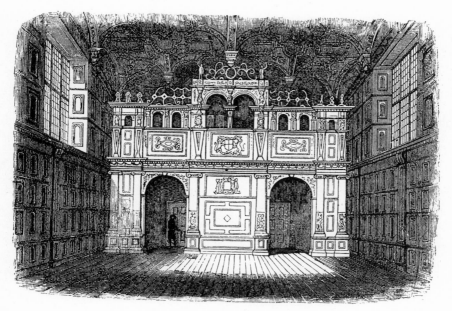

LEATHERSELLERS' HALL IN 1842. INTERIOR VIEW.

The almspeople, on whom Haselwood laid such stress, have been re-moved to Barnet, as their accommodation on the spot was found to be inconvenient. But the Company, in lieu of the amount prescribed for them (12*l*. 2*s*. 8*d*.), now distributes nearly 400*l*. a year among the seven persons periodically chosen to enjoy the benefaction. Yet it may be ques-tioned whether in these larger figures allowance ought not to be made for the fact that a local residence was a distinct *proviso* in the arrangement.

A certain index to the standing and resources of a Gild, both in its corporate and individual or personal capacity, may be found in the power to acquire and retain costly effects in the nature of plate or otherwise. The Leathersellers, prior to their removal to Bishopsgate, possessed a very extensive and valuable assemblage of silver objects and a considerable accumulation of miscellaneous property, the evidences and other muniments inclusive.   There are inventories among the archives of the Company belonging to the years 1488 and 1504, and they are printed at large by Mr. Black.   The ancient collection of plate was kept, it appears, intact till 1545, when it was compulsorily sold to meet urgent pecuniary claims in connection with some portions of the estate.   A second one was doubtless formed by the liberality of private donors or testators ; but there is nothing now in the Company's hands older than 1640.

The Company, like the Fishmongers, Merchant-Taylors, and others, counted among their possessions at an early period one of those funeral palls, which were used to cover the remains of departed brethren, and which were, as we have elsewhere shown, among the more costly and sumptuous of the productions of the Broderers or Embroiderers.   The hearse-cloth of the Leathersellers does not occur in the inventory of 1488 ; and in the first mention of it nothing is said of its texture or appearance.   It is simply described as " a herse-clothe to lay upon corses." In 1556, however, a member presented a new pall of black velvet and cloth of gold, with the images set with pearl and the inscriptions in letters of gold ; whereupon the old cloth was handed over to the yeomanry.

In these, as in other matters the fashion changed, and in 1559, only three years later, another brother gave " a fine herse-clothe, with a case covered with lether, bound with yerne."

The Master's and Wardens' garlands of rich embroidered work, the gift of William Green in 1539, survive as witnesses of the far more numerous treasures, which once existed, and which were either destroyed by use, or perished in the Fire of 1819.   These beautiful examples of early English taste are figured in the History of the Company on a scale almost, if not quite, equal to the originals.

They are thus specifically described in the Company's Books under Sept. 23, 1540 : "*Item* iiij Garlandes of clothe of tycchewe, of the gift of William Grene, both lining and making ; and the Maysters Garland hathe a gyltyde bruche of the Assumption of our Lady, with ij. roo-bucks gyltyde, with a goat and a ram, and ij. bucks' heads of silver parcel gyltt ; and in like manner be the other iij. garlandes with silver broches, according as is afore said.   The which brochys be at the cost of the whole Craft, and be not parcel gyltt as the Masters Garland is, but white silver."

Hence it appears that the brooches were an addition by the Company ; but they were subsequently replaced by the cognizance of the three stags.

The custom of crowning the officers dated long before 1540, however ;

for under 1487–8 it is noted in another of the inventories that " the gud-wyffe Curtes hathe gevyn to ȳ Crafftt a garland of purpull velvett, lynyd wyth red sylver and gyltt ; and on ȳ ffor-frountt standysch a gyltt robuk of silver and gyltt. . . ."

We must be thankful and glad that the specimens of 1540 have been rescued from destruction. Between the two points of time there was beyond doubt a continual succession of these ornamental insignia by gift or otherwise.

LITERARY NOTICES.

A liuing remembrance of Master Robert Rogers, Marchant Adventurer and Leather-seller of London, deceased, who declared the fruites of his faith by his most Christian and charitable workes. And left this life at his house in Bassings Hall the 22nd of September, and was buried in Christ Church on Thursday, 1st October, 1601. A broadside. 1601.

₊ Annexed is a list of his legacies to various charities, amounting to 2,960*l.* 6*s.* 8*d.* To his Company he left 700*l.* in trust for various purposes, including an annual distribution in August of 500 good Kentish billets, or 7*s.* in money, to each of the almspeople.

Leather : A Discourse rendred to the High Court of Parliament. Of the Generall vse of Leather. The generall Abuse thereof. The good that may arise to Great Brittain from the Reformation. The seuerall Statutes made in that behalf by our Ancient Kings. 4to, 1629.

To the Right Honorable, the High Court of Parliament, sitting at Westminster : The Illegal and Immodest Petition of Praise-God Barbone, Anabaptist and Leather-seller of London. 1660. A broadside.

The Picture of the Good Old Cause, drawn to the Life in the Effigies of Master Prais-God Barebone. 1660. A broadside.

A Song in praise of the Leather Bottel. To the tune of the *Bottel-makers' Delight.* A broadside. [Charles II.].

The Loriners.

THIS Fellowship, in common with many others, enjoyed the greatest prosperity, while it remained in the condition of a voluntary Union. It is perfectly manifest that, when its members first occur to our notice,

they were a constituted and recognised body; although in the Ordinances of 45 Henry III. (1260), there is no reference to any antecedent
code, and the four Wardens named in it appear to be a new departure.
The Articles are, moreover, only eight in number, and are confined to
general and leading principles. They provide against working by night,
on Saturday afternoons, and on certain festivals of the Church; that no
old lorinery was to be repaired, unless it was specially so desired by
some chief man or lady of the land, or some good man of the City; that
foreigners, coming to work in the City, should pay half a mark to the
Chamber of London and 2s. at least to the Fellowship's box, and should
agree to observe the Ordinances of the Craft; that, in order to ensure
obedience to the Ordinances, four good men should be elected by the
Commonalty and approved by the Mayor and the rest of the Barons of
the City; and that, by the assent of the whole Craft, a Bridle should be
presented at Easter yearly to secure the maintenance of these provisions.

This instrument was a bipartite indenture, one copy to be on record
in the Chamber of London, the other to be kept by the Gild, and they

OLD ARMS.

were sealed by the Masters of the mistery for
fuller surety. Occasional notices occur of the
renewal or confirmation of these bye-laws, and of the
continuance of the government by Wardens, down
to 1570. In 1511, foreign competition seems to
have begun to make itself sensibly felt; and
agreeably to the protectionist policy then and so
long after predominant, a check was imposed by
the Corporation on the sale of French bits otherwise than in gross to free retailers. The municipal order of 1570
equally deals with this subject, and for the first and last time confers
the right of search in certain cases, but not of seizure. This privilege,
so usual among those bodies which we describe, was never enjoyed
by the Loriners, save in this instance and to this limited extent.

In a document of 1327 they are mentioned as workers both in copper
and in iron. To the muster for the City Watch in 1469 the Gild is
returned as engaging to supply fourteen men-at-arms. The *maximum*
was 210. Returns of 1501-2 and 1531-2 name it among those which
had no Livery.

The memorials of the progress and transactions of this Association
are exceptionally scanty, owing, perhaps, to the absence of a settled
constitution and of a place for the deposit of records. The only charter
granted to it was in 1711, when five centuries or upward had elapsed
from the original rise and existence as a Fellowship. Hereby the Executive was fixed at a Master, two Wardens, and 21 Assistants, and seven

were to be a quorum. The Livery is unlimited, and there is a licence in mortmain to the unusual extent of 500*l.* a year.

The Company, however, has never possessed any real estate. In 1834 its income was returned at about 412*l.* a year, arising from dividends and fees. From the accounts published in 1884 it appears that out of the corporate savings 13,000*l.* in consols and railway stock had then been acquired ; and in 1892 the revenues are given as 1200*l.* a year. But about 1874 a marked impulse was given to the numbers and resources of the Company by the accession of freemen and liverymen for the purposes of social intercourse and of the municipal and parliamentary franchise ; and in 1882 the former were estimated approximately at 1,391 and the latter at 438,[1] figures which at once explain the large increase in the annual receipts. In 1724 the Livery was only 79. Of those Companies, which have entered on such a line of policy and have successfully carried it out, the Loriners and Spectacle-makers probably stand foremost.

In 1891, the Registrations at Guildhall exhibited the maintenance of the electoral ascendency of the Company, the voting power being graduated, for example's sake, as follows :—

Loriners . . .	434 votes.	Fishmongers . . 302 votes.
Haberdashers . .	354 „	Merchant Taylors . 219 „
Spectaclemakers .	317 „	Turners . . . 215 „

The Loriners have had the honour to reckon among their members five passed Mayors, besides Sheriffs and other eminent functionaries. Upon the last occasion (1883) when a Loriner filled the Mayoralty, his brethren celebrated the event by the presentation to him of a handsome and massive loving-cup, 16 inches in height, ornamented at its base with spurs and stirrups, the handles formed of horses' bits and rosettes, and the bits attached to the cup by bridles. On the cover was engraved the coat of arms of the Company.

In 1891 the freedom was for the first time conferred upon the Queen's Loriner, Mr. N. G. Chavasse, successor to Mr. Benjamin Latchford, of Upper St. Martin's Lane, the oldest business of the kind in London.

There was formerly, opposite the northern extremity of Basinghall Street, at London Wall, a Hall belonging to the Gild. It is described by Maitland in 1739 as "small, but convenient." As the affairs in the last century declined, prior to the modern revival, this building was let to a succession of tenants, chiefly for religious purposes, and was eventually demolished. In 1767 we find the Loriners engaging Founders'

---

[1] The Livery fine is 15*l.* 14*s.* 6*d.* In 1892 the numbers were 430.

Hall, Lothbury, for their monthly courts and annual dinner, at 10*l.* a year.

LITERARY NOTICES.

The fower chiefyst offices belongyng to Horsemanshippe. By Thomas Blundevile. 4to, [1566], 1580, 1597, 1609.

*** The fourth book relates to the Ferrer or Farrier. There is a series of woodcuts of bits in use.

Richardi Sadlerii de Procreandis, Eligendis, Alendis, Frænandis, et Tractandis Eqvis Experientia. 4to, 1587.

The Masons.

THE Act 5 Elizabeth (1562–3) may perhaps be the first in which the present trade is specified as a distinct occupation, and persons following it are enabled and even required to take apprentices. We shall supply some testimony below in favour of the belief that the Masons represent in a modified form a Society which once rose to exceptional eminence, and acquired even formidable power. They enjoy the unique distinction of having laid the basis of a social cult, which has immeasurably outstripped its founders, and left behind it the lines which they were content to observe.

But the names of Simon de Pabingham and Richard de Wetham are cited in 1298 as those of two master-masons between whom a reconciliation was effected through the good offices of the authorities, with the proviso that, if either infringed the conditions, he should pay 100 shillings toward the fabric of London Bridge.

Again, in 1332, Master William de Rameseye, who was the master-mason in charge of the new works at St. Paul's, was exempted by an order of the Court of Aldermen from serving on juries, inquests, and assizes, and from being summoned for any purpose, so long as he remained in the service of the Church.

The parent code of bye-laws for the Masons was apparently granted in 1356, and shews that the workmen were divided into two classes, hewers and light masons or setters. The special articles are two :—1, that no one should take work in gross without tendering proper security for its completion ; 2, That all apprentices should work in the presence of their masters, till they perfectly learned their calling. In the Returns of 1376, where the number of members returnable by the Gilds to the Common Council is set forth, the *Masons* are said to be entitled to four representatives, and the *Freemasons* to two, as if they were independent Societies. In later and indeed other Returns the Freemasons are missing ; there may have been an unrecorded fusion, or even a clerical error.

In the list of Craft-Gilds in 1421–2 among the Brewers' archives the Masons stand thirty-eighth among 112. They immediately precede the Carpenters. To the Muster for the Watch in 1469 their return was twenty men-at-arms, a proportion equal to that, not merely of the Painters and Scriveners, but of the Salters. In 1501–2 they occur as forty-first, with a Livery of eleven, and in 1509 as forty-second, in each case being between the Weavers and the Bowyers. When the order of precedence, however, was settled in 1515, they were lifted up to the thirty-third place, between the Curriers and the Plumbers, and left the Weavers and Bowyers far below them. At the Mayor's feast in 1531–2, they rank fortieth, but do not appear to have been numerous, as they were represented by a single member besides the Wardens, and were allotted only one mess. In the reign of James I., when assessments were made on the Companies for sundry public objects, their comparative insignificance is betrayed by the modesty of their quota ; but in 1629, when the City prepared to do honour to the King's coronation, the Masons subscribed 5*l.* 7*s.* 6*d.*, which by comparison signifies intermediate progress.

OLD ARMS.

No charter is at present known anterior to that of September 17 1677 ; but there the petitioners are cited as the Master, Wardens, and Assistants of the Company of Masons. The early accounts among the archives, commencing with 1620, were kept in the name of the Master and Wardens. There was a Livery in 1501–2 ; and the existence of a grant of arms by Clarencieux in 1473 and its purely accidental recovery from oblivion in 1871 [1] may warrant the conclusion that of its other

---

[1] It was found in the possession of a collector at Clerkenwell, and was eventually purchased by the Company for 7*l.* 7*s.* 0*d.*, and presented to the British Museum. The circumstances form the subject of a short paper read before the Society of Antiquaries by Mr. H. H. Burnell, F.S.A., then Master, February 15, 1872.

muniments the Gild has been equally neglectful, or that it was a Company by prescription.

In the *Book in Metre of the Rich Merchant Man called Dives Prag-maticus*, 1563, where all the trades of London are enumerated, including many subordinate callings hardly now recognised, the author, Thomas Newbery, refers to the craft as "free masons"; and in the Accounts the designation *Free Mason* occurs down to 1655–6, when *Mason* only is used. At that time the Society or Fellowship is termed in the records the Worshipful Company of Masons of the City of London. The prefix was, perhaps, intended to denote no more than its position as a privileged and philanthropic body.

The charter of 29 Charles II. (1677), although it does not refer to an antecedent one, mentions the applicants as an organized Association, and rehearses the Act of Elizabeth, acknowledging the trade to be an independent art and business. It declares the existing constituency a body politic with perpetual succession, a common seal, an unlimited licence in mortmain, the right of making ordinances, and the power of search and control within seven miles of the Cities of London and Westminster, wherever any stones to be used in masonry should be brought, in order to see that such be of proper measure and truly wrought.

The bye-laws here authorized were drawn up and passed by the Court of Aldermen and the Judges in the year immediately following, and there was no other grant, save that of James II., subsequently revoked by the Act of William and Mary, and an *inspeximus* of 1 Anne. When the last returns were made, the government was conducted by a Master a Warden, a Renter Warden, and seven Assistants. Three vacancies which had occurred on the Court had not been filled up. In 1501–2, as we have seen, the Livery numbered 11; in 1724 it was returned as 63, in 1882 as 41, and in 1892 as 45. But persons admitted to the Freedom have of late years been forthwith taken up into the Livery, which therefore forms, with the Court, the entire Company.

The total income was stated in 1834 to be about 300*l.* a year; in 1882 it had apparently risen to 400*l.*, and in 1892 to 550*l.* This, with the exception of one charity under the will of Joshua Marshall, a Master of the Company in 1678, is wholly corporate, and proceeds from property in Bishopsgate Street, at Stoke Newington, and in Ireland, the Masons having an interest in the Mercers' Manor. The Marshall benefaction produces about 125*l.* a year for poor freemen and their widows. On the expiration of the Stoke Newington lease in the next century, a further improvement in the receipts may be probably expected; and the accounts for 1871–80 exhibit a tendency to economical administration.

The Hall was formerly in Masons' Alley, Basinghall Street, where Masons' Hall Tavern now stands, and is named by Maitland as the place of assembly in 1739. But it no longer exists. Possibly, if the antecedents of the Bishopsgate property in Masons' Court were known,[1] it might be found that that was an earlier seat of the Company similarly abandoned, and converted to other uses.

The question of assuming the designation of *Freemasons*, or rather, *Free Masons*, suggests one or two remarks. The practice, which might in the absence of the development of the Masonic movement, have attracted no more notice than that of terming the members of another Gild *Free Vintners*, was, as we have seen, followed as far back as 1376, and continued in the books of the Company down to 1655. But it was not recognised in the charter, in the grant of arms, in the bye-laws, or in any Act of Parliament known to us, save the 2 and 3 Edward VI. cap. 15, where the expression signifies no more than a freeman.

Nevertheless, in the excessively ancient institution, both in England and abroad, of a Brotherhood and Sisterhood among members of the Craft and their kin, and the establishment for their government and security of benevolent and philanthropic canons as between themselves, and of injunctions to secrecy in all matters done or said in their lodges and *Chapters* relevant as well to the Trade as to the Fraternity, we have the nucleus of modern Freemasonry, which adopted and remodelled a system appurtenant to archaic society, and of which the Gilds have preserved the only features of enduring value—fellowship and alms.

The earliest English document treating of this subject serves to assist us in discovering how such a superstructure was built on the primitive conception of mediæval trading communities knit together for the sake of protection and support in the exercise of technical and purely civil pursuits.

It is a fourteenth-century poem of a secular complexion, in which the precepts delivered and the terminology are not dissimilar in character and purport from the Ordinances of the London and other Gilds. They comprise the leading principles of conduct on the part of apprentices during their seven years' service, including their confidential obligation, and lay stress on honourable relations among master-artificers. Lodges are mentioned as the seats of the Craft, but not Chapters, which were of ecclesiastical origin. There is no allusion to symbols or cryptography, nor any approach to mysticism. The whole manual is practical and straightforward.

---

[1] An inquiry has been addressed to the Clerk of the Company on this subject through a member, without eliciting any information.

In 3 Henry VI. the influence of the Masons, through what are termed
" their yearly congregations[1] and confederacies," became so marked, and
exercised so great an effect on operative handicrafts, that an Act of
Parliament was passed to forbid these meetings and unions on pain of
conviction and punishment for felony.   At this time the Craft possibly
extended its cognizance beyond the province to which we understand it
as confined, and from the necessity which was felt in the course of the
same reign, of making a proviso that in all Ordinances framed by the
Gilds there should be nothing prejudicial to the rights of the Crown—
a safeguard reduced to legislation in 19 Henry VII.—it may be suspected that the Masons' Gilds all over the kingdom had overstepped
constitutional limits, and brought upon them this statute of Henry VI.,
which was only repealed, so far as it was repealed at all, by 2 and 3
Edward VI. cap. 15, permitting *free masons* to follow their craft in any
town, whether free of it or not, if they were so of some given place.[2]

The Musicians or Minstrels.

THIS was an Association formed some time before its original incorporation, April 24, 1472–3, apparently under the name of the Society
of Minstrels.   The charter does not seem to be in existence ; and the
Company did not seek or obtain another till July 8, 1604, when it was
erected into a body corporate and politic by James I., by the style of
The Master, Wardens, and Commonalty of the Art or Science of the
Musicians of London, with perpetual succession, a common seal, a
licence in mortmain, and other usual privileges, including the power of

---

[1] This expression was used to denote the meetings of the Mercers' Company at the
outset.

[2] But in 1506 John Hylmer and William Vertue, described as *free masons*, were
engaged to vault with freestone the roof of the College Royal of our Lady and St.
George at Windsor Castle.

making bye-laws for the rule and government of the mistery within three miles of London.

Under this grant, the only one at present extant, the Master, two Wardens, and fourteen Assistants were appointed and named ; but we do not observe any person of note among them. William Warren, one of the Assistants, however, had been made Master in 1594, under the old *régime*, and had experienced difficulty and opposition on the part of certain of the members in entering on his position. Beyond the bare fact that there was a previous grant in 1473, and that in 1602–3 it is classed as the fifty-second in rank, the present is the sole trace of the Gild prior to its revival. But we suggest that the *Minstrels' Gallery* in many of the ancient Halls owed its designation to the source, whence the Companies most probably engaged the band or orchestra on festive occasions.

The bye-laws, sanctioned in the charter, were approved by the Lord Chancellor and the Judges August 25, 1606. Besides the ordinary provisions, they are of interest on one or two special accounts. They shew that the Company included Dancing in its province and jurisdiction, and one of the Articles prohibits any freeman from playing on any instrument, morning or evening, under any nobleman's, knight's, or gentleman's window or lodging in London and the suburbs and liberties thereof, without leave of the Court.

These ordinances constituted a Livery unlimited in number. In 1699, it was returned at 17 ; in 1724, at 30 ; in 1739, at 31 ; in 1880, the Court (13) inclusive, at 49 ; and in 1892, at 50.

The aggregate income from rentals was in 1880 stated to be 336*l*, and in 1889 and 1892, 400*l*. This property consists of freeholds at Clapton and elsewhere and Government Consols. But the Company is also supported by occasional receipts from internal sources. In Maitland's time (1739) the fine on admission by patrimony or servitude was 40*s*. It is at present 3*l*. 17*s*. 6*d*.

The Musicians contributed, February 25, 1602–3,—to the assessment on the Companies of 10,000 quarters of corn for storage—5 quarters, the Merchant Taylors heading the return with 936 quarters ; and 14 February, 1603–4, their quota toward the expense of receiving James I. and his Queen on their passage through London was 4*s*., the minimum amount subscribed. They occupy a similarly humble position in 1629, when a levy was raised by the municipality to defray the charges attendant on the coronation of Charles I.

They were co-partners with the Fishmongers in the purchase of the Ulster estate in 1615, and in common with the Bowyers, Fletchers, and Woolmen, were subscribers of 20*l*.

LITERARY NOTICES.

The breffe and playne instruction to lerne to play on the gythren and also on the Cetterne.   Licensed in 1558–9.

The Comendation of Musyke by [Thomas] Churchyard.   Licensed in 1562.

A Briefe and easye instruction to learne the tableture, to conducte and dispose the hande vnto the Lute.   Englished by J. Alford Londenor.   4to, 1568.

The Praise of Musicke.   By John Case, of Woodstock.   8vo, 1586.

Apologia Musices.   By the same.   8vo, 1588.

Diuers & sundry waies of two parts in one, to the number of fortie, vppon one playn-song.   By John Farmer.   8vo, 1591.

The pathway to Musicke, whereunto is annexed a Treatise of Descant.   4to, 1596.

A new Way of making fowre parts in Counter-point.   By Thomas Campion.   8vo, [1613.]

A Briefe and Short Instrvction of the Art of Mvsicke.   By Ralph Bevin.   4to, 1631.

The Principles of Musik.   By Charles Butler.   4to, 1636.

Renatus Des-Cartes Excellent Compendium of Musick.   Translated by Viscount Brouncker.   4to, 1653.

A Briefe Introduction to the Skill of Musick for Song and Violl.   By John Playford.   8vo, 1654.   Often reprinted.

The Division—Violist: Or An Introduction to the Playing upon a Ground.   By Christopher Simpson.   Folio, 1659.

The Well-tuned Organ.   By Joseph Brookbank.   4to, 1660.

A Compendium of Practical Musick in Five Parts.   By Chr. Simpson.   8vo, 1667.   Other editions.

Chelys.   The Division—Viol: Or, The Art of Playing upon a Ground.   By the same.   Folio, 1667.

A Short Explication of such Foreign Words, as are made use of in Musick-Books.   12mo, n.d., and 1725.

Many other works on Music, Musicians, and Dancing, will be found in the General Index to Hazlitt's Bibliography.

In 1662, a licence was granted to George Bayley, of London, musitioner, to make show of a play called Noah's Flood.

The Needlemakers.

THE manufacture of needles, when we had sufficient use for such implements to encourage the formation of a home industry, in competition with the imports from Spain and Italy, should have grown into as extensive a business as that in pins. But the strong organized influence of the Haberdashers, if not of the Mercers and Drapers, seems to have checked the prosperity and independence of both these subsidiary crafts, and although the Needlemakers preserved their *status*, their position was never a prominent or thriving one. The profit went to the shop-keeper.

The very early story of the Devil among the tailors of Birchin Lane, which has been mentioned under the account of the Merchant Taylors, demonstrates the antiquity of the introduction into this country of Spanish needles, with which all the operatives, down to the apprentices, are represented as supplied for the purpose of their work.

Stow mentions in Cheap Ward Needlers' Lane, which has the appearance of a name derived from a craft; and when we look at the Needlemakers' cognizance, above given, we are tempted to speculate whether *Three-Needle Street*, the original name of Threadneedle Street, is not connected with an ancient centre of the industry in proximity to the Taylors and Drapers.

In 1628, the Needlemakers solicited, in common with the Clockmakers, association with the Blacksmiths; but in both cases the proposal seems to have been rejected.

In 1629, they made complaint to the Court of Aldermen of the deceitful manufacture of bad needles with an engine, which was shown by the evidence of experts belonging to the Haberdashers and Taylors to be dangerous to the workmen employed. This engine was the property of aliens residing outside the City, who refused to obey a summons to appear; and it was said that it deprived many of their means of living—perhaps, by economizing labour.

The Company dates back its origin to the reign of Henry VIII. But that is merely an approximate calculation. It was doubtless, like no inconsiderable proportion of these communities, a Company by prescription centuries before its receipt of a charter from the Protector Oliver Cromwell, November 10, 1656. This grant was followed and superseded by a second of February 9, 1664, from Charles II., wherein, on the petition of fifteen persons, all members of the trade, the Company is incorporated under the title of The Master, Wardens, and Commonalty of the Art or Mistery of Needlemakers of the City of London, with the customary privileges, and with a mandate to the Corporation to enroll the said charter, for the better protection and government of the members.

The bye-laws were approved on the 20th June ensuing, and dealt with the right of search, apprenticeship, hawking, and other cognate points.

In 1658, an Act of Common Council prescribed that the Company should be, and was, entitled to exercise the right of search over all practising this art and mistery, and that no apprentices should be bound to other than free Needlemakers, the term of service, whether for seven years or upward, being arranged between the apprentice and his master in each case beforehand ; and all penalties and suits arising out of a breach of this order were to be heard in the Court of His Highness the Lord Protector in the Chamber of London at Guildhall before the Mayor and Aldermen.

A Livery of 50 was granted in 1712. In 1724 it was returned as 44. But in 1874 and 1875 the Court of Aldermen successively raised it to 100 and 200. In 1880 it stood at 116, the number of freemen in that year being estimated at about 150. In 1889 the Livery had decreased to 101, and in 1892 to 90.

There is no property beyond the receipts from internal sources and from interest on accumulated savings. In 1889 the total income was stated to be 250*l.*, and in 1892, 230*l.* The Company some years ago endeavoured to promote the educational cause by subscribing to the City and Gilds Institute.

In evidence furnished to the Royal Commission in May, 1883, the Needlemakers rebutted the imputation, which had been cast upon them, of having attempted to resuscitate the Company on political grounds ; and it was explained that a number of gentlemen, desirous of joining a City Gild, and having heard of the Needlemakers, decided on offering themselves as candidates for election, by which proceeding the Livery was enlarged under the sanction of the Court of Aldermen. The Company had been on the point of dissolution and the question of dividing the available assets was even mooted, when this circumstance occurred, and produced a change of front. One of the witnesses mentioned that he had had the Tin Plate Workers recommended to him ; but he ultimately selected the other. There does not appear to have been any distinct notion in the minds of the new members, that the body, which they thus joined, was more than a social club. The practical side was not considered beyond an unsuccessful effort to revive the needle manufacture at Redditch, in Worcestershire, in which they expended all their funds.

LITERARY NOTICES.

A Schole-Hovse for the Needle. Obl. 4to, 1624.
The Needles Excellency. 4to, 1634, 1640. The former is the tenth edition.
A Proclamation Prohibiting the Importation of Foreign Needles. 14 August, 1687. A broadside.

The Painters or Painter=Stainers.[1]

As early as 1284, a very remarkable entry in the City Records shews, how Nicholas Bacon, painter, had purchased on bond from Hugh Motun sinople, vermilion, and canvas, varnish and verdigris to the value of 20s.

One of the earliest footprints, so to speak, of the Painters is the share which they bore in the long-subsisting feud between them, the Joiners, and the Saddlers. In 1309, representations were made to the Court of Aldermen, as we have already stated in our account of the Joiners, of the abuses in the saddlery trade by the clandestine employment of green wood in the construction of the trees, and the connivance of the painter and saddler in vamping up this worthless material for sale ; and in subsequent years affrays in the public thoroughfares, attended by bloodshed, not unfrequently signalized the strained relations of these

---

[1] See *Some Account of the Worshipful Company of Painters, otherwise Painter-Stainers.* By John Gregory Crace, Master, 1880. 8vo, privately printed, 1880. Mr. Crace, of Wigmore Street, was an eminent decorator and zealous London antiquary. We owe to him the famous collection of drawings and prints relating to London, now in the British Museum.

crafts. Pecuniary matters in the shape of claims and counterclaims sometimes formed the subject of dispute ; and we find the Loriners also
drawn into the quarrel by natural resentment at the interference of the
Saddlers with the metal fittings of the apparatus. The liability to
rupture was augmented by the investiture of each successive person,
through whose hands the work passed, with independent and exclusive
rights, often requiring nice discrimination ; and we have now crossed
over to the other extreme.

In 1467 (June 9), the Mistery of Painters having addressed a petition
to such effect to the Court of Aldermen, their Articles or Bye-laws were
approved, authorizing them to assemble in some honest place within the
City, and elect year by year two true, witty, and honest men free of
the Craft to be their Wardens, and at least six others to be assistant to
them, in governing the Craft, making search for false or bad goods, and
keeping the money, goods, jewels, and other necessaries. Mention is
made of a Beadle, the neglect of whose summons of the brethren to meet
in common Hall was punishable by the levy of a pound of wax, half to
go to Guildhall Chapel, half to the light of St. Luke ; and there was
evidently a Livery by prescription, each member paying 16d. a year
quarterage.

There are the usual stipulations and penalties for the conduct and
control of the trade, besides one or two clauses of interest in respect to
technical points, namely, that no man should work any tinfoil, unless it
were sufficiently wrought with oil colours, and made for colours, and not
for gold, but that where it was used for church-work in any cloth of
gold, it should be truly wrought and gilt ; again, that none should paint
any church work, that is to say, work of entail [? intaglio] but with fine
gold, and no party-gold, unless the customer so wished it. It is curious
that sign-painting for places of business, as well as for inns, enters into
these regulations ; and it is laid down that " no manner of signs hanging
or standing in the weather " shall be wrought with fine gold and with
oil colours.

Looking at these Ordinances of 1467, we cannot doubt that they dealt
with the affairs of a body already in an advanced stage of organization,
which deemed it advisable, after a more or less lengthened period of unrecognised internal autonomy, to seek official acknowledgment as a better
means of maintaining and asserting the authority of their officers within and without.

An Act of Parliament passed at the commencement of the short reign
of Richard III. prohibited the importation by foreign merchants, among
a long catalogue of other goods, of beaten gold or silver wrought in
papers for painters and other purposes.

Two years posterior to the formal proceedings of 1467, the Painters occur as contributors of twenty men-at-arms to the City Watch ;[1] but a circumstance is connected with this record which deserves particular attention. In the same list, the *Stainers* are named as independent furnishers of fourteen soldiers or guards, and while in the return of the Gilds taking part in the obsequies of Henry VII. in 1485, the latter are absent, in 1501–2 we meet for the first time with a reference to the *Painter-Stainers*, who are said in a municipal document of that date to possess a Livery of 18. In the interval

OLD ARMS.

between 1485 and 1502 there had been an amalgamation ; and in the settlement of precedence in 1515 the united Gild is placed twenty-ninth. But its existence and jurisdiction remained purely prescriptive beyond the sanction of its Ordinances by the City. At the Mayor's Feast in 1531–2, it ranked thirty-ninth, and had five representatives and two messes—a proportion which argues a growing measure of importance ; and in the same year it acquired by gift a common Hall, hereafter to be more particularly described.

It was not till 1581 (July 19) that the charter was obtained, incorporating the Fellowship as The Master and Wardens and Commonalty of the Freemen of the Mistery or Art of Painters, commonly called Painters Stainers, within the City of London and suburbs and liberties thereof," with all the ordinary powers as to mortmain, search, and internal government. But no common seal is specified. A Master, two Wardens, *and their Assistants* are mentioned and authorized. The instrument is on one sheet of parchment, with the conventional portrait of the Queen in the upper left-hand corner as a sort of initial ornament. From the Byelaws passed immediately after (January 10, 1581–2) we learn that at the period when the grant of Elizabeth was received, there were two Wardens and twelve Assistants, the Upper Warden, William Herne, esquire, Serjeant-Painter to her Majesty, having however, recently deceased. But the full complement was to be sixteen, besides the Master and Wardens. Elections to vacancies vested jointly in the Livery and Court, and offices might be held for two years or such shorter term as the Livery and Court should determine. No person was compellable to serve as Master more than four times, as Upper Warden more than thrice, or as Junior Warden more than a second time.

These Articles are no fewer than thirty-seven in number, and occupy in the original three large sheets of parchment. The most remarkable are

---

[1] See Riley's *Memorials*, 1868, p. 91.

those which seek to provide for the exclusion from the calling of all incompetent persons, inasmuch as for some time passed the interests of the
Company had severely suffered by unskilful and inexperienced practitioners, not only in the mechanical branch of the art, but in the
higher department of portraiture and landscape.   Some of the stringent
conditions, which meet the eye here, throw light on the testimony of
Stow about this time as to persons, who had not learned the business,
undertaking even to execute portraits of the Queen and nobility, which
seemed fair enough at first sight, but were not capable of bearing examination ; and this criticism applied equally to the materials employed
and the manual skill.

Even although in our early domestic architecture the more ordinary
and mechanical functions of the calling[1] were not yet much brought into
exercise, the field or scope of the Painter-Stainers was remarkably wide,
embracing decorative house-work on the one hand and the highest
branches of the artist's profession on the other.   The fourth clause of
the bye-laws declares " that no person or persons whatsoever, English-
man or stranger, denizen or not denizen, freeman or foreigner, shall at any
time hereafter lawfully scrape, lay, or work anything to be sold with
varnish upon any wood, stone, paper, parchment, or vellum that is
grounded first with any kind of commixture appertaining to the art,
science, or mistery of painting or staining, or with or upon any kind of
colour or colours, oil, size, gum, gleere, glue, or any such-like thing
commonly used in the art or mistery ; " and the paragraph concludes by
describing the Association as in a decadent state.   The seventh provision
touches the discredit and injury incurred by the intrusion of imperfectly
trained limners and painters of what were known as " painted cloths "
and " tables (*tableaux*)."   As it is of special interest, we must transcribe
it :—

"*Item*, it is ordained and constituted, forasmuch as the true workmanship and
knowledge of the said art and mistery of painting and staining cannot be attained, or
the exercise thereof be had, without many years and great diligence, and that, notwithstanding, many unskilful and unable persons in that science do intrude, usurp,
and unlawfully presume to use, exercise, and occupy the same art and mistery, and
having no sufficient skill do enterprise to portrait, counterfeit, shadow, and paint the
pictures, proportions, ensigns, and arms, and divers other great feats of workmanship,
as well of the Kings and Queens, predecessors and ancestors to the Queen's most
excellent Majesty, as of her Highness, as also of divers and many noble, honourable,
and worshipful personages and persons . . .   to the great slander and reproach
of the whole Company aforesaid . . .   that therefore no person or persons before
rehearsed within the said Cities, suburbs, or four miles' compass, shall or lawfully may

---

[1] What appears to have been known as "vulgar painting" is first treated, we believe, by John Smith, in a little volume published by him in 1676, and noticed at the
end of the present article.

occupy, use, or exercise the said art, science, or mistery . . . unless he or they be free of the said art, or have been apprentice or shall be apprentice thereunto by the space of seven years at the least or more, namely with a painter-stainer, or hath heretofore occupied the said science according to the statute of the fifth year of the Queen's Majesty's reign . . ."

The thirty-seventh and last item is "The Oath of the *Baylie or Bedyll*," the former being an exceptional term, and not usually understood in such an alternative acceptation.

The Painter-Stainers, who thus combined industries not perfectly reconcilable from a modern point of view, were in a sufficiently indifferent plight in 1582 by their own admission; and although a special Act of Parliament in the first year of the following reign was declaratory of the charter and bye-laws, their affairs do not seem to have improved in a financial respect during the next half-century. Their contributions to various public objects in 1603, 1604, and 1629, betray very humble resources. Stow's Continuator (1633) re-affirms what the historian himself had stated in regard to the Craft, and tells us that the art of Staining had then departed out of England.

We obtain a glimpse of the Painter-Stainer at work in the account of the expenses incurred by the Ironmongers' Company in 1566–7 at the inaugural ceremony, when Sir Christopher Draper was chosen and admitted Mayor. Under date of October 1 in that year there is a record of a contract with Richard Baker, painter-stainer, for making of the pageant, and all manner of things incident to the same, as well the carpenters' as painters' work, except the children and their apparel. For his labour and skill he was to have 16*l.*, and if he happened to find that he had underrated the prime cost, 40*s.* more.

But Thomas Bullock, a second person of the same calling, was also employed on the occasion to paint the banners and streamers, and "a target-painter" at Aldgate, the escutcheons or arms.

The painter of old days was of course a Master, and occasionally endeavoured, where he thought that his customers were rich, to realize more than a reasonable profit; for we find that in 1629 Nathaniel Glover, the contractor for certain work at Ironmongers' Hall, handed in an estimate for 41*l.*, and accepted 30*l.*

The name of George Knight, painter-stainer in Fenchurch Street, is given in the Coopers' records under 1603 as that of the person who made for the Company a new banner for the coronation of James I. at a cost of 4*l.* 13*s.* 4*d.* A few years before, there is a charge for the painter who drew the Company's arms on a spare leaf in each of the books given to his brethren by Mr. John Swayne.

In his *Diary*, under April 23, 1669, Pepys speaks of having been present at the Council-Chamber, when the cause was being heard between Howard and Watson, alleged inventors of processes in varnishing and lacquer, and the Painters, who claimed that they already performed the same kind of work.   But he omits to record the issue.

The constitution and government were somewhat modified by a charter of James II. substituted for that of Elizabeth; and this appears, contrary to the common practice and experience, to be the acting one.   Under it the Executive consists of a Master, two Wardens (Upper and Renter), and thirty or more Assistants.

A common seal is specified, and the licence in mortmain, which, under the antecedent concession, had been environed by some unusual restrictions in regard to the assent of interested parties, follows the ordinary language.   It deserves notice that one of the Wardens nominated by James was Richard Wallis, the well-known arms-painter, and that on the Court of Assistants occurs the name of Sylvanus Morgan, author of the *Sphere of Gentry* and other works.

In 1502, as we have stated, the Livery numbered eighteen.   In 1699, it is returned as 159 ; in 1724, as 141 ; in 1880, as 144 ; and in 1892, as 130.   In 1880 the Freemen were said to amount to 187.   Of an estate valued in the Parliamentary Returns of 1880 at 3,100*l*. a year, 2,300*l*. are held in trust ; and in 1892 the corporate revenue is said to be reduced to 700*l*.

The Company was a subscriber of very inconsiderable amount to the Ulster project of James I., and was associated in that matter with the Goldsmiths.

We fail to detect any clue to the primitive whereabouts of this Gild. It evidently maintained in 1467 a light or lights in a chapel or chantry dedicated to St. Luke the Evangelist, and he was at the same period its tutelary patron.   The settlement in Queenhithe Ward was a comparatively late event, when the Fellowship of Painters had probably existed at least three centuries.   The forfeiture of wax to the chapel of Guildhall under a certain contingency favours the idea that the earliest home was in that vicinity.

Painters' Hall in Little Trinity Lane, near Cannon Street, a neighbourhood greatly affected in its aspect by modern changes, was previously the private residence of Sir John Browne, Serjeant-painter to Henry VIII. by patent of 1511, and Alderman of London in 1522. Browne had come into possession of the premises in 1504; but the property is traceable back to the beginning of the reign of Henry VI. (1423-4), when it is found described as being situated, with its appurtenances, between the garden of Edmund Salle, clothworker, on the north, the tenement of Ralph Mark, brewer, on the south, the highway of Huggin Lane on the west, and the highway of Trinity Lane on the east.

Scarcely any information has survived respecting the Tudor structure. It is repeatedly noticed in the Ordinances of 1582 as "the Painters' Hall," but naturally without any further details ; and the books of the Company contain no entry relative to it prior to 1630 ; on the 2nd of April in which year it was directed that the wainscoting and beautifying of the Hall should be presently put in hand, the plan of Mr. Paul Isaacson being accepted. We indirectly glean that there was an upper parlour, presumably in distinction from a lower one, and that the former had the arms in the window or windows : for it was resolved to adopt the same course in the window of the refectory, and to set up a record in the same apartment in some prominent position, that these improvements were made at this date. Between 1664 and 1666 the Hall was much used by the Committee for the Relief of the Sick and Wounded in the War ; and Evelyn, who was a member of this body, notes having sat here on the 16th November, 1664, and the 3rd of July, 1666, almost precisely two months before the building was consumed in the Fire. Under the former date he writes :—

"Painters' Hall was lent us to meet in. In the great room were divers pictures, some reasonably good, that had been given to the Company by several of the Wardens and Masters of the Company."

The disaster was not repaired without considerable effort and delay ; and the plate was ultimately mortgaged to meet the cost of reconstruction on the old site. The work was apparently completed in the spring of 1670, when the Hall was let to the German Protestants on Sundays and holy days for two years at 24l. a year. In the Company's books there is an entry under September 30, 1667, shewing that they then met at the Cooks' Hall in Aldersgate Street, of which, in common with the Saddlers and Stationers, they had probably arranged the hire till their own was ready.

The first distinct impression of the aspect of the second building, which is substantially identical with that now standing, is derived from Hatton's *New View of London*, 1708, where the author says :—

"Painter-Stainers' Hall is situated in Little Trinity Lane. It is adorned with a handsome screen, arches, pillars, and pilasters of the Corinthian order, painted in imitation of porphyry, with gilded capitals. The panels of the wainscot and the ceiling [1] are embellished with great variety of history and other painture exquisitely performed, as 1. the portraitures of King Charles II. and his Queen Catherine, by Howsman ; 2. the Fire of London ; 3. Endimion and Luna, by Palmaitier ; 4.

---

[1] The decorations of the ceiling no longer exist ; nor does it seem to be known when or why they were removed.

Orpheus fleaing Pan, by Brull ; 5. a piece of architecture by Trevit ; 6. another, given by Mr. Thompson, the City painter ; 7. Heraclitus and Democritus, by Penn ; 8. a landscape, by Aggas ; 9. Fish and Fowl, by Robinson ; 10. Art and Envy, by Hungis ; 11. a piece of birds, by Barlow ; 12. a piece of fruit and flowers, by Ever-brook ; 13. a ruin, by Griffier ; 14. Cambden's portraiture ; 15. a piece of birds ; 16. The ceiling is fairly painted with Pallas triumphant, with the arts and fame (attended by Mercury), suppressing their enemies, sloth, envy, pride, etc., done by Fuller ; and there are several other pieces in the parlour."

Some of the pictures, at least, mentioned by Evelyn in 1664 were presumably rescued in 1666. But as works of art the specimens at present covering the walls of the refectory and of a small apartment,—which may answer to the parlour of 1708, but has been considerably modernized,—are of very secondary importance.

The character and province of the Company make it easy to understand, how many of the entries in the minute-books are of exceptional interest ; but they do not go back further than 1623.

In January, 1631–2 we meet with the first minute of particular interest. The Master and Wardens were desired by the Lord Chamberlain to view the King's and Queen's barges, 270*l.* being demanded by John De Cretz, Sergeant-painter to his Majesty, for the former, a new one, and 40*l.* for the repairing, gilding, and trimming of the latter ; and to arbitrate as to the value of the work. The award,—signed by the Master, Wardens, three Assistants, and Henry Doddington, material-closer,—was, that the King's was worth 250*l.* and the Queen's 32*l.* In the following year, a similar commission was executed for Lord Goring, who had employed Mr. Buckit to carry out some contract at his house beyond St. James's Palace.

On the 17th May, 1635, we find that,—

" Mr. Inigo Jones, the King's surveyor, was invited to dinner, and very lovingly came, and dined with the Company."

We may annex a few more extracts of peculiar pertinence, some, such as no other Gild could well furnish :—

"February 3, 1635–6. At this Court Mr. John Beston presented as a token and memorial of his love to the Company a Round Salt, with an open cover gilt, waying 37 ounces."

"October 28, 1645. This day a faire silver bread bowle was presented to the Company by Mr. George Willingham (being his gift), with his name and the yeare of our Lord engraven thereon."

It appears that the donor in the latter case gave the plate in remembrance of his wife, and that he had assisted his brethren on two occasions, in 1642 and 1643, when Upper Warden, wherefore they now begged his acceptance of twenty nobles (6*l.* 13*s.* 4*d.*) ; and he signified his intention of devoting the sum to the purchase for their common use of another piece of silver.

When we come to October 26, 1647, there is a singularly interesting item :—

"George Wyld, Doctor of Divinitie, COLONELL RICHARD LOVELACE, Thomas Rawlins, Esqre., Graver of His Majes. Mint, and MR. PETER LILLY, were all made free at this Court."

From an entry under November, 1666, we learn that some of the brass work from the old Hall had been saved, and was sold as old metal, and as we have already seen, as late as August, 1669, the plate was mortgaged to secure loans from members toward the rebuilding fund.

The right of search vested in the Company sometimes involved odd situations or circumstances :—

"March 10, 1673-4. Ordered that the Painter of Joseph and Pottifer's wife and the Fowre Elements be fined 3*l*. 6*s*. 8*d*., for such bad work."

Here is another glimpse of Sir Peter Lely, made a freeman with Lovelace and Rawlins in 1647, and of Greenhill, a less famous artist, but one of great merit :—

"April 6, 1676, Mr. Lilly is desired to paint the King's picture, Mr. Housman, the Queen's, Mr. Wright, the Duke of York's, Mr. Greenhill, the Duchess of York's."

The invitations to the annual dinner in 1687 were signed by Sir Antonio Verrio and Sir Godfrey Kneller.

It has thus become manifest that the Painter-Stainers are entitled to claim a very special and very high place among the Livery Companies of London, by reason of the succession of distinguished individuals, who have not been merely honorary associates, but freemen and officers, in their time. No other similarly constituted body can point to such a muster-roll :—Sir Peter Lely, Sir Godfrey Kneller, Antonio Verrio, Sir James Thornhill, Charles Catton (one of the founders of the Royal Academy), Master in 1761, Sampson Camden, father of the historian, Richard Wallis, Sylvanus Morgan, Richard Lovelace, the soldier-poet, Sir John Browne and William Herne, Esquire, sergeant-painters to Henry VIII. and Elizabeth, and Thomas Rawlins, Engraver to the Mint under Charles I., poet and dramatist.

Morgan the Herald and writer was Master in 1676, and still remained on the Court in 1685. He presented to the Company the portrait of the illustrious Camden, while the latter, in remembrance of his father, Sampson Camden, a liveryman, gave the silver cup, which still testifies to the fact.

LITERARY NOTICES.

The First and Chief Grovnds of Architectvre. By John Shute, Painter and Architect. Folio, 1563.

A Very Proper Treatise, wherein is briefly set forth the Arte of Limning. 4to, 1573, 1581, 1583, 1588, 1596, 1605.

The Armes of all the Companies of the Worshipfull Cyttye of London. Entered at Stationers' Hall, 1 Dec., 1589.

A Tracte, containing the Artes of curious Paintinge Caruinge Buildinge. By Paolo Lomazzo (a pupil of Leonardo da Vinci). Translated by Richard Haydocke. Folio, 1598.

An Idea of the Perfection of Painting; Demonstrated from the Principles of Art, and by Examples. . . . By Roland Freart. Translated from the French by John Evelyn. 8vo, 1668.

The Art of Painting. Wherein is included The whole Art of Vulgar Painting. By John Smith, Clockmaker. 8vo, 1676, 1687, 1705.

Londons Armory Accurately Delineated in a Graphical display of all the Arms, Crests, Supporters, Mantles and Mottoes of every distinct Company and Corporate Societie in the Honourable Citie of London. By Richard Wallis, Citizen and Arms painter of London. Folio, 1677.

In this volume the arms are engraved on a very large scale and in a very finished style; but it does not give all the Companies, although it includes the Newfoundland, Canary, and one or two others of unusual occurrence, as well as the Trinity House and the College of Physicians.

A Short Introduction to the Art of Painting and Varnishing. Probably by John Smith. 8vo, 1685.

A Treatise of Japanning and Varnishing. By George Parker, Varnisher and Japanner. Folio, 1688. With plates.

The Patten Makers.

THE introduction of a contrivance for enabling pedestrians to traverse the dark and filthy lanes and alleys, with which the City formerly abounded, was doubtless due to an observation of the Continental practice of employing the clog. The first tidings which we gain of such a fashion coming into vogue in London is in 1400, when the Pouch-makers' Gild either brought what are termed galoches into use, or obtained the right of controlling the manufacture. This privilege almost necessarily implies that the *galoche* was secured to the foot by leathern straps, as otherwise the Pouch-makers could not have claimed any interest in the matter.

During a certain period the Fellowship, thus entrusted with the liberty of oversight or surveillance, probably limited itself to that function ; but in 4 Henry V. (1416–17) the Pouch-makers and Galoche-makers were united under one government, and so continued in the sixth year of the same reign. But in the ninth year the Galoche-makers no longer appear by name, nor do we know what was their status between 1419 and 1469, when we find the *Patten-makers* a distinct Fellowship, with the power of contributing to municipal obligations. Yet they did not obtain a charter till 22 Charles II. (August 2, 1670), when they were incorporated under the style of The Master, Wardens, Assistants, and Fellowship of the Company of Patten-makers of the City of London, with a right of search over a radius of ten miles, a licence in mortmain to 100*l.* a year, and the power of passing Ordinances. Such Ordinances were drawn up and approved in 1673 ; and in the following year the Court of Aldermen resolved that all persons free of the Company were entitled to the freedom of the City.

The employment of a medium for raising the wearer out of the garbage and mire inseparable from ancient urban life, both here and abroad, dates from a period even anterior to the first mention of the galoche. At Venice the ladies used the *chopine*, of which an illustration may be seen in Mutinelli (*Del costume Veneziano*, 1831), and Coryat furnishes an account of it in his *Crudities*, 1611. In an English play published in the same year (*Ram Alley, or Merry Tricks*) a lady is described as going to church in her new chopines, which were probably ordinary clogs or pattens.

The arguably foreign origin of the patten may be a ground for crediting the statement of Stow, that the Church of St. Margaret Pattens, Fenchurch Street, was so called from that being the quarter where the makers of the article congregated, as we know that the same neighbourhood was the resort and seat of other alien industries, while, as regards the likelihood of such a name being bestowed on a church, we have the analogous case of St. Nicholas Flesh-shambles in Newgate Street.

The charter of the Company fixed the government at one Master, two Wardens, and twelve Assistants. The fine for admission to the Court, originally 10*l.*, has been raised to 50*l.* In 1724, the Livery was returned as 35, in 1880, as 74, and in 1892, as 40. The number of existing freemen is, as usual, unknown.

In 1834 the property was almost nominal (150*l.* Three Per Cents., and 400*l.* Three and a Half Per Cents.) ; but the income and estate profited during many years by the higher scale of fines and by frugal expenditure. The shrinkage of the Livery since 1880 appears to betray, as in many similar instances, a reaction from this temporary and artificial prosperity.

There is no plate worth mentioning, nor any other objects of general interest.

The Pewterers.

The arms of this Company were granted May 20, 1479, and are :—*Azure:* on a chevron *or*, between three cross bars of pewter *argent*, as many roses *gules*, seeded of the second and barbed *vert*. *Crest:* a mount *vert*, thereon two arms embowered, vested and frilled *argent*, holding in both hands a pewter dish. *Supporters:* two sea horses *or*, their tails proper.

THE Company appears to have no motto exclusively belonging to it, but to use that which also appertains to the Brewers : *In God is all my trust.* The two vocations were formerly sometimes found united in the same hands.

The Pewterers existed in all probability, like the other Gilds which we have been describing, long before they were incorporated ; and the circumstance that they had become a more or less numerous and important body was in fact a necessary precursor to the appeal to the Crown for a charter, which might recognise their existing, and protect their future, rights. It is not, therefore, surprising that, in all the instances which we have noticed, incorporation follows at a considerable interval from the proved origin of a Fraternity ; for, in fact, that state of development was a natural outcome from the slow growth of each, and was rather a need of maturer than of early life.

Stow merely says :—

"The *Pewterers* were a Company or Meeting of friendly and neighbourly men, in the time of King *Edward* the fourth ; and in the thirteenth yeere of this King became incorporated, January the 20. And from this King they have been still confirmed by all Princes since : lastly, by King *James.*"

Two agencies appear to have been instrumental in operating favourably on the disposition of the Crown to grant an improved position to the persons engaged within the precincts of the City of London in this vocation : the creation of the Dukedom of Cornwall in favour of the eldest son of Edward III. in 1337–8, with its accompanying tendency to draw attention to the mineral products of the district, and the abuses committed by certain members of the trade in the manufacture of pewter. In the 22 Edward III. (1348), we find a movement on foot for obtaining at the hands of the Corporation some system of inspection over the alloys and workmanship.

The earliest code of bye-laws for the Pewterers seems to be that of 1348, which starts by premising that "the trade of pewtery is founded upon certain matters and metals, such as copper, tin and lead in due proportions, of which three metals they make vessels, that is to say, pots, saltcellars, esquelles (porringers), platters, and other things by good folks bespoken." The Articles provide for the limitation of the trade to skilful workmen and true material, for inspection by the Wardens prior to sale, and for the hours of labour.

OLD ARMS.

We gather from some proceedings at Guildhall in 1350, that the alloy of tin and lead, allowed and recognised by the custom of the trade, was in the proportion of 16 lbs. of lead to 112 lbs. of tin.

The charters of 1474–8 were confirmed, by *inspeximus* or otherwise, by Henry VII. (May 19, 1505) by Henry VIII. (January 4, 1513), by Philip and Mary (Oct. 4, 1555), by Elizabeth (Nov. 20, 1559), and by James I. It was extended by Charles I. (March 14, 1639), and in 1674 Charles II. ratified all former charters. But it was not till the accession of Queen Anne that the Company formally entered on the right of making bye-laws for its own government. The last bye-laws were confirmed in 1766.

In the Founders' charter of 1614 the rights of the Pewterers are specially reserved. This precaution, taken by the Commissioners for Suits, perhaps, when the matter came before them for a report, strikes us as reasonable ; but it is the earliest symptom of a commercial approximation carrying the liability to encroachment or trespass.

Besides the charter and bye-laws, various Acts of Parliament from time to time collaterally prescribed and imposed the rights of search and assay, and those of 25 and 33 Henry VIII. interdict the hawking of pewter by strangers, and give the Wardens of the Company or their deputies power to inspect and oversee pewter throughout the kingdom, to prevent the importation of foreign pewter, and to restrain any freeman, under pain of disfranchisement, from going abroad to instruct foreigners in the mistery.

In 22 Henry VI. (1433) it was represented that a large quantity of faulty tin was brought into the City, the defects of which were not discernible prior to smelting.   Some weight was attached to this complaint, inasmuch as the Corporation in consequence bestowed on some select committee of Pewterers the right and power to assay all such tin as was brought in, and to search for the same.   But it was not till some thirty years later that the followers of this industry received their first charter (1473-4), which confirmed existing rights and established the municipal independence of the Pewterers on a broader and more distinct footing.

The parent charter of Edward IV. (20 Jan., 1473-4) granted to three persons therein named the right of founding and establishing, in honour of the Virgin Mary, a Fraternity or Gild of the Master, two Wardens, and Commonalty or Freemen of the Mistery of Pewterers then dwelling or thereafter to dwell within the City of London or the suburbs thereof, and of the brethren and sisters of the freemen of the same mistery, and of others who, of their own pleasure, were willing to be of the same Fraternity or Gild, to be one body and one community, to be fit and capable in law of acquiring in fee and perpetuity lands and other possessions, to plead and be impleaded in courts, to have a common seal, and to possess the power of extending the right of inquisition into matters touching the mistery throughout the whole realm of England. The last-named privilege seems to have been one which, from its width of scope, met with resistance ; only five years later (18 Edward IV., 1478) a second charter renewed the injunction to all Mayors, Sheriffs, Bailiffs, and others, being the King's officers, lieges, etc., to proclaim searches by the officers of the Company, and to be assisting to them therein.   There is little doubt, however, that at this period, and long afterward, evasion and deceit were extensively practised beyond the immediate limits of the metropolis, and that no really effectual system of control and surveillance was readily or generally established.

The Gild, subsequently to incorporation, had to contend with irregular practices, and to guard against trespass and fraud, both within and without.   As early as 1555, it was ordered that no member should buy tin of any tiler, labourer, boy, woman, or other suspected person, or between six and six ; and the Company in its palmy days neglected no precaution to maintain the character and reputation of the English pewter, which was largely used in private houses, in place of the more precious metal, insomuch that it was common during the Stuart era to speak of a person's " pewter," where we now should speak of his plate.

In his poem of *London Lickpenny*, composed about 1425, Lydgate speaks of the clatter of pewter pots in the neighbourhood of East

Cheap. In the early inventories of the Companies, as well as in those of great houses, vessels and utensils of this material are of constant occurrence. At the Inns of Court, down to a recent period, the members dined off pewter.

Toward the close of the reign of Elizabeth (1598) letters patent, obtained after four years' negotiation, confirmed the privilege of charging a royalty on the smelting and casting of tin. This concession seems to have arisen from the pressure of foreign competition, which seriously affected the export of bar-tin.

In 1629 the importance of pewter for domestic and even ornamental purposes had grown to such an extent, that the Company made suit to the Board of Green Cloth to be placed on the same footing as the Goldsmiths, in regard to the proper marking of articles of pewter, for the protection of buyers and owners, from whom it was frequently stolen in large quantities, and transported by brokers beyond sea in barrels. The stamps on early utensils in this material, placed in pursuance of this appeal, and of an order made thereupon, probably differed from time to time. On a spoon of seventeenth-century fabric before us occurs a T crowned. The danger of the course recommended was illustrated, however, by cases, where the Goldsmiths' silver-plate mark was fraudulently placed on vessels of the baser metal by the negligence or oversight of the Wardens.

At the same time, the prosecution of the business within the precincts of the City was not unattended by inconvenience and discomfort, and it was found requisite to limit the times for carrying it on in order not to disturb the inhabitants during hours of rest. In the *Statutes of the Streets against Annoyances*, printed by Stow, No. 25 enjoins that " No Hammer-man, as a Smith, *a Pewterer*, a Founder, and all Artificers making great sound, shall not work after the houre of nine in the night, nor afore the hour of foure in the morning, under paine of three shil. foure pence."

The Pewterers had their full share of participation in all the troubles and exactions from which their fellow-citizens so grievously suffered during the various intestine disorders and foreign wars from the 15th to the 17th century, and seem to have experienced a lengthened interval of depression.

To a certain extent the contribution of personal service and money for the King's wars constituted a part of the old feudal relationship between the Crown and its subjects ; but the City of London was thought at all times a legitimate prey in all cases of extraordinary levies, and was impoverished all round by the calls on every side for assistance both in coin and kind. Indeed, had it not been for the phenomenal expansion of the country at large and of the metropolis itself as the centre of trade, the Companies could never have rallied in many instances from the blow inflicted on their financial prosperity by the Civil War and the commercial stagnation which it produced.

The Pewterers are the fortieth of the 112 Craft-Gilds enumerated in a list among the archives at Brewers' Hall (1418–40), apparently drawn up in 1421–2. But, as we have before mentioned, the order of precedence here is not to be taken as authoritative ; and indeed in 1515, when this principle was settled by the Court of Aldermen, they were directed to rank as sixteenth.

In 1469 they are found contributing sixteen men to the muster for the City Watch. In 1509, at the coronation of Henry VIII., they were allotted twelve yards for their standing to witness and honour the procession. In 1531–2, at the Lord Mayor's feast held in that year, the Company is placed between the Leathersellers and the Cutlers. Once more, in 1602–3 and 1603–4, and 1629, upon the occasion of municipal assessments in aid of public objects, they are rated on a scale, which enables us to presume that they were then in a fair pecuniary position.

In the contributory acquisition of the Irish Estate in 1613–18 the Pewterers took a sub-share of the Ironmongers' manor, which is now sold.

The Executive is composed of thirty-two members, the Master and Wardens inclusive. All members of the Court must qualify themselves before election by having served or fined as Steward. The Livery, of which we first hear in 1501–2, then consisted, according to an official return, of 25 ; in 1699 it amounted to 108, in 1724, to 91, in 1882, to 70, and in 1892, to 74.

The Master and Wardens are elected in August of each year. The members of the Livery come on to the Court in their turn. The fees payable are :—On taking up the freedom by patrimony, 9s. 2d. ; by servitude, 3s. 4d., stamps not inclusive ; by redemption, 105l. ; on admission to the Livery by patrimony or servitude, 20l.; by redemption, 105l.; on admission to the Court, 20l., besides Steward's fine, 20l. Freemen and their widows and orphans are entitled, according to their age and standing, to pensions varying from 12l. to 66l.

The average income for the ten years from 1870 to 1879 was returned to Parliament as 3623l. 8s. 8d., of which all but a fraction is corporate estate. In 1834 the revenue was about 1300l. a year. In 1892, it is given as 4050l., of which 250l. only are held in trust. The Company owns a variety of leasehold properties in the City of London, and rent-charges on estates in London, Essex, and Suffolk, together with interest amounting annually to 415l. 15s. 10d. on Consols and Reduced Three Per Cents. During many years, the Company has liberally contributed to the City and Gilds Institute and other benevolent and useful public objects.

Among the charitable trusts enumerated by Stow and others are the following :—

Alderman Catcher gave property in trust to Christ's Hospital ; 40s. to be distributed among five poor men of this Company.

Ralph Stray bequeathed, 2nd Nov., 1602, all his freehold lands, etc., in Suffolk and elsewhere, to Edward Catcher and his wife for their lives and that of the survivor, with remainder to their son, Ralph Catcher, and his heirs male, etc., provided they paid yearly for ever 40s. to this Company, 20s. to be given to poor freemen.

" *Lewis Randall*, Pewterer, but a Brewer by his profession, of his owne free cost and charge, paved (with faire free stone) the East Ile of Christ's Hospital Cloyster, and renewed all the Armories of former liberall Benefactors to that house wherof him-selfe was one of the Governours.

Hee gave beside 50 pound [in 1616] to the Treasurer, that the poore children there maintained, might eate roste-meat, at dinner, on every Saint *Mathias* day, if it fall out of Lent. But if it fall in Lent, then they are to eat good and well made Furmenty, both at dinner and supper."

Thomas Scattergood devised, the 21st of August, 1776, 600l. in trust, to pay five poor men and five poor women 2l. each yearly ; 18l. is divided under this trust.

John Jones gave, in 1780, 600l. Three per cent. Consols, the yearly interest to be paid to nine poor men and nine poor widows of this Company ; 18l. is divided by the Court of Assistants.

George Mullins bequeathed, 1874, 1000l. for the benefit of the poor freemen of the Company.

John Robins gave, 28th of April, 1648, the rent of a house in Barbican, to pay 8l. a year each to four poor freemen of the Company. Residue to the Company. This charity realises 65l. a year.

Thomas Swanson, 10th June, 1783, gave funds in Consols, by which 30l. is annually divided between six poor widows of pewterers.

Issac Smith, 4th of Oct., 1855, gave 500l. Consols, by which 30s. each is given annually to five poor freemen and five poor widows.

There are other bequests out of which donations are periodically paid to objects connected with technical and other education, and in some cases the Company augments the income arising from its old benefactions out of its own funds, or rather transfers from one source of revenue to another according to circumstances and requirements.

The old Hall in Lime Street was built on a piece of land given to the Gild by Mr. W. Smallwood in 1487, he being then Master ; it occupied the site of six tenements, and it was destroyed in the fire of 1666. A second Hall was subsequently erected ; but this, again, has been transformed into a warehouse, and a modern structure substituted on a portion of the ground. The Company has no objects of interest, beyond a few early specimens of pewter and a representation of a sundial, with a spider and a fly underneath it, let into one of the windows of the present dining-room, and said to have been rescued from the original edifice. In 1882 the corporate plate was returned at 278 oz.

We learn from some proceedings between the Corporation and the Pewterers in 1604 that it was then held customary for the Master to take charge of the plate and other articles of value belonging to a Company, and to give bond for the same.

The earliest record of a corporate dinner occurs in 1559; it included the Court, Livery, Freemen, and their wives, and the Master and Wardens were at liberty to invite guests.

LITERARY NOTICES.

The Olde Lawes and Statutes of the Stannarie of Devon, as many as were in Force, and heretofore imprinted. Whereunto are added certayne other newlie made in the Yeare of the Reigne of our Sovereigne Ladie Queen Elizabeth the xvi. 4to, 1574.

A Declaration of sundry Grievances concerning Tinne and Pewter, worthy the serious consideration of the Honourable Houses of Parliament, in the behalfe of the Pewterers and People of the three Kingdoms. By J. S. 1646. A broadside.

The Liberties and Cvstomes of the Lead-mines within the Wapentake of Wirksworth in the County of Derby. Composed in meeter by Edward Manlove, Esq.; heretofore Steward of the Burghmoot Court for the Lead-mines. 4to, 1653, 1708.

Aggravii Venetiani, &c.; Or the Venetian and other Grievances. Together, with a Proposal for raising the Price of Tin in the Counties of Cornwall and Devon. 4to, 1697.

Laws and Customs of the Stannaries in the Counties of Cornwall and Devon, Revis'd and Corrected according to the Ancient and Modern Practise. By Thomas Pearce. Folio, 1725.

The Plaisterers or Pargettors.

THE most ancient document illustrating this Gild is a contract made by Adam le Plastrer, citizen of London, for plaistering the Hall of Sir John de Bretagne, Earl of Richmond, in 1317. Herein the contractor binds himself to find the plaster of Paris, and to complete the work with the tewels or flues within eight weeks on the security of all his goods.

Here the calling conferred the surname. But we have to traverse nearly two centuries, before we arrive at the period, when it assumed a definite corporate form ; nor are the casual notices of its followers so frequent as in the case of other trades. In the late Mr. Fairholt's *Dictionary of Terms in Art*, an excellent account of Pargetting, of which we have cited probably the most ancient English illustration extant may be found. That accomplished writer and artist seems disposed to trace the invention to Dutch influence.

The Plaisterers of London obtained their first charter 16 Henry VII. (March 10, 1501–2). It incorporated them as a Gild or Fraternity in Honour of the Blessed Virgin Mary of Men of the Mistery or Art of Pargettors in the City of London, commonly called Plaisterers, with a common seal, perpetual succession, and other customary privileges. The right of search was conferred and was subsequently extended to a radius of two miles from the City ; but the power of conviction and amercement rested with the Mayor's Court ; the Company could only present offenders. Search-days were appointed as lately as 1832 ; but the practice has long wholly determined.

OLD ARMS.

The Company received a grant of arms, January 15, 1546–7, and the approval of its bye-laws about the same time. The charter of Henry VII. was renewed 2 and 39 Elizabeth, 2 James I., and 19 Charles II. Of these only the second and fourth are preserved. The Ordinances were renewed in 1586 and 1765, of which the latter is the acting code.

The Executive consists of a Master, two Wardens (an Upper and a Renter) and 27 Assistants. In 1699, the Livery was returned as 87 ; in 1724, as 70 ; in 1880, as 60 ; and in 1892, as 50. In 1880, it was supposed that there were 25 freemen.

The references to the Plaisterers in official returns are very scanty, and uniformly shew them to have been a body of very subordinate weight and resources.

Perhaps the most signal prominence, which they ever obtained, was in the course of the reigns of Elizabeth and her immediate successor, when the fashion for ornamental and elaborate work of the description, in which they engaged, was at its height, and when the temptations to encroachment by other trades was proportionately strong. From 1585 to 1613 the Court of Aldermen and the Privy Council had before them intermittently a dispute between this Craft and the Tylers and Brick-layers, arising out of an alleged trespass by the latter ; and regulations of greater stringency were found requisite to prevent a collision.

But a very material point and principle of commercial usage transpire in another case, which occurred during the earlier portion of the reign of Elizabeth. In or about 1574, the Plaisterers represented to the Carpenters' Court that two freemen of the latter Craft had illegally interfered with their rights by executing Plaisterers' work. One of the offenders was convicted, and obliged to lodge security for trial in Court ; but the other put in a plea, that he had been employed on *Queen's work*, or, in other words, on a Crown contract or order, and was excused accordingly. This may have been a purely isolated instance ; but if it is anything more, it shews that the royal authority traversed that of the Gilds even in such minor particulars. In the Coopers' Books under 1580 there is a reference to press-money for the Queen's work on Tower Hill, which the Wardens had paid to certain foreigners ; but this was outside the jurisdiction, and it is not stated what the service precisely was.

On the other hand, the statute of 1 James I., cap. 20, restrained Plaisterers, their apprentices and servants, from interfering in any manner with the trade and occupation of a painter or painter-stainer.

The three vocations just specified were naturally prone to overstep the boundaries of each other.

The plaister employed in ancient buildings was composed of lime, free from iron, gypsum, and hay or straw. Other ingredients at present enter into it, as chaff, cow-hair, lias, and cement. The early practitioner entirely relied on hand-moulding, and we can easily judge from extant specimens, both in this country and abroad, that he not unfrequently, where cost was not regarded, attained consummate excellence in workmanship and taste.

Apart from a moderate income produced by accumulated savings, a small sub-share of the Fishmongers' Irish estate, and one or two bequests, the Plaisterers own the freehold in Addle Street, occupied by premises now let on lease, but during a period of nearly three centuries used as a common Hall. The property devolved upon them under the will of William Elder, May 14, 1545, "to hold to the Master, Wardens, and Fraternity, and their successors, for ever, quietly and in peace." It is subject to a quit-rent of eightpence a year payable to the Merchant-Taylors.

The position thus acquired under Elder's will was doubtless applied to the purpose intended and prescribed. But the Company followed the common precedent of lending or letting a portion to other bodies. The Pinners or Pinmakers hired it till 1598 or thereabout, when they removed to St. Mary at Hill, owing, according to Stow, to a decline in their trade. From 1693 to 1696 the Gold and Silver Wyer Drawers met here. Maitland, writing in 1739, describes the Hall as a handsome one.

This body has been a liberal subscriber to the City and Gilds Institute and to the Science and Art Department, South Kensington, in connexion with the award of prizes for the higher class of plaister-work.

Among the benefactors of Christ's Hospital and other institutions, Stow enumerates Hugh Coppe, Plaisterer, who gave to the first charity 100*l.*, and to St. Bartholomew's and St. Thomas's 10*l.* each.

The Playing-Card Makers.

EARLY ARMS.

PRESENT ARMS.

THIS is one of the Associations of comparatively late origin, which has never possessed any substantial standing as a trading body, and has within a measurable distance of time bidden for popularity and the means of subsistence by opening its ranks to all comers.

The charter was obtained October 22, 1628, and was followed by bye-laws or ordinances of February 19, 1630-1. The former,—which recited in the preamble that the home-trade was injured by the importation of foreign playing-cards and by the abuses committed by those engaged in the manufacture here,—vested in the Company the power of making bye-laws and of search and supervision within a radius of ten miles, and constituted a Master, two Wardens, and sixteen Assistants, the governing body. There was a licence in mortmain, which has never been exercised; but there is no mention of a common seal and some other points generally comprised in these grants.

The property is almost nominal, arising from fines and accumulations of current income; in 1834, the entire corporate estate was derived from the interest of 700*l.* Consols. In 1880 there was only one freeman; and the Livery was returned as 23. In 1889 and 1892 the latter body numbered 75. It is limited to 100; and the fine is 15*l.* 15*s.* 0*d.*

Although the Playing-Card Makers are wholly dissociated from the calling, the Gild is one of the favourite objects of selection by gentlemen desirous, on social and other grounds, of enjoying the advantages of membership.

LITERARY NOTICES.

Certen Poesies vpon the Playing Cards. Entered at Stationers' Hall in 1588.

The Play of Cards, an unpublished Drama of the Seventeenth Century, mentioned in Harington's *Apologie of Poetrie,* 1591.

Order by the Committee, Appointed by Parliament for the Navy and Customs, on the Complaint by the Cardmakers of London, likely to perish by reason of divers merchants bringing in Playing Cards into this Kingdome. 1643. A broadside.

The Royall and Delightfull Game of Picquet. Written in French, and now rendered into English. 12mo, 1651.

The Royal Game of the Ombre. Written at the Request of divers Honourable Personages. 12mo, 1660.

Geographical Cards. 12mo, 1676. 52 leaves and the title-page.

A Proclamation, prohibiting the Importation of Foreign Playing Cards, and for seizing such as are or shall be imported. Whitehall, 7 November, 1684.

A New Pack of Cards, representing (in lively Figures) the two late Rebellions. 12mo, [1685.]

The Plumbers.

ARMS (FROM STOW).   ARMS (FROM MAITLAND).

THIS is another of those very numerous instances, in which a Brotherhood had tangible and recognised existence, and even an organized system of government, centuries prior to the grant of any incorporation. Yet there is no reason to believe that the Plumbers of London at an early period formed a very important or influential body, since to many of the purposes, for which lead was subsequently used, it was not at first applied. The most ancient regulations for the Craft, however, shew that even in the fourteenth century it was beginning to grow more common to roof with lead in the case of cathedrals, churches, and public buildings generally, and that the quality of the material employed at once rendered such work expensive, and necessitated exceptional safeguards against dishonesty.

The most flourishing period of the plumbing industry and of the Fellowship connected with it was that, when London abounded with palatial edifices, both religious and lay, and when nothing but true lead was made on the casting benches. The value of this commodity, containing an appreciable proportion of silver quartz, and weighing about 14 lbs. to the foot, is not to be estimated by a modern standard, when our roofs and watersheds are supplied with a poor and fictitious substitute.

Even in the mediæval time, however, there was another side to the question. As trades multiplied and grew, many of them demanded for working or technical purposes vessels and utensils of this material. One of the earliest inventories which has come down to us of a brewer's plant (1335) enumerates several items made of lead, which had been acquired for cisterns and other receptacles; but the valuation of them is sufficiently humble, leading me to infer that the calling was not one likely to accumulate wealth in the hands of its followers.

At the Reformation, the ecclesiastical foundations demolished for the clearance of the sites and the sale of the materials, where the existing buildings could not be utilized, yielded an immense store of the finest and purest lead, which was available for re-employment. Under the beneficiary dispositions of John Haselwood in 1543 in favour of the Leathersellers' Company, we see that the donor included in his gift a *sow* of lead, weighing no less than 11 cwt. and three quarters. This was just at the juncture, when a large number of religious houses had been dissolved within the metropolis; and the rather unusual present was doubtless the product of the dismantlement of one or more of these establishments. Even when, about fifty years since, the roof of Canterbury Cathedral was removed, it was a saying (if nothing more), that there was enough silver in the old one to pay for the new.

The Ordinances or bye-laws of the Plumbers were first framed in 1365, and approved at their request by the Mayor and Aldermen. They rehearse some of the customary conditions, but also deal with the use of lawful weights, the price of labour, the restraint of engrossers, the purchase of old lead, the stripping of lead from roofs, and the inveiglement of a customer away from one of the calling by members of other trades. Any plumber convicted of theft was liable to dismissal from the Fraternity. It seems brotherly to excess, that no one was at liberty to carry out a work alone, if any of his fellow-craftsmen desired to take a share of the labour and profit.

A rather curious case occurred in 1371, in which certain plumbers, who held on hire a vacant place in East Cheap for the purpose of a melting-furnace, were summoned for a nuisance, but proved to the satisfaction of the Mayor and Aldermen, that it had been so used for forty years passed, and was not so noxious as had been represented. But they were required to carry their shaft higher.

The Ordinances of 1365 enumerate among the articles, which the plumber of those days furnished, gutters, conduit-pipes, tap-troughs, furnaces and belfries, but omits roofing and cisterns. The application of lead to the latter must have long preceded this date, however, while tiles had not very long replaced, on the other hand, the primitive thatch.

The annals of the Plumbers are neither eventful nor interesting. It is evident from casual glimpses, which we indirectly gain of their progress, that they always remained a body of secondary weight and rank. In 1469 we find them undertaking to provide eight men-at-arms for the City Watch against the *maximum* of 210. In 1501–2 a municipal return makes them the thirty-second Gild, with a prescriptive Livery of twelve ; and when the order of precedence was settled in 1515, they occur thirty-second. During the reign of Henry VIII. from 1509 to 1532 they maintained a respectable position ;[1] but at the commencement of the Stuart government (1602–4) they had apparently somewhat receded in wealth and estimation. In 1599 they lost the privilege of assize of certain weights, because their fee was judged by an award delivered in that year to be excessive, and the duty was assigned to the keeper of Guildhall, assisted by two members of the Gild of Founders, who engaged to perform it for a reasonable consideration.

Nevertheless, in 1611, the Plumbers, then, if we may judge from their contributions to public objects, a Society of very limited pecuniary resources, obtained the only charter ever granted to them, in which they were declared to be one body corporate and politic, in deed, fact and name, under the style of The Master, Wardens, and Commonalty of the Freemen of the Mistery of Plumbing of the City of London, with a common seal, a licence in mortmain, the power of electing officers, and the obligation to secure for the Company a council-house within the City or its liberties.

The proceeding, of which the cost was probably borne, as usual, by a few prominent members of the Gild, purports to have been prompted by a desire to reduce to a better rule and order the men of the Mistery, and all those who then exercised, or might thereafter exercise, the art of plumbing, or use the materials pertaining to it ; and it is energetically described as a step taken " for the utility, advantage, and relief of the

---

[1] Stow (*Survey of London*, 1633, p. 908) prints the epitaph at St. Magdalen's, Bermondsey, of John Borwet, Esquire, sometime Sergeant Plumber to Henry VII. and his son. He died December 7, 1525.

good and honest, and for the terror and correction of the evil, deceitful, and dishonest."

There is no reference to Assistants or to a Livery, although in 1501–2 the Fellowship had already possessed the latter by right of custom ; and the Executive to this day is composed of the Master, two Wardens, and a certain number of the commonalty—in 1882, six. In 1699, the prescriptive Livery amounted to 54 ; in 1724–5, to 65 ; in 1882, to 50 ; and in 1892, to 40. Between 1871–80 there were no calls. In 1882, the number of freemen was estimated at 50.

The property of the Company consists of a freehold in Great St. Helen's, a sub-share in the Vintners' Irish manor, and the interest of 10,000*l.* arising from the compulsory sale of the Hall in Chequer Yard, Dowgate Hill, to the South-Eastern Railway.

Stows' Continuator (1633) does not specify Chequer Yard, but mentions Chequer Lane or Alley ; nor does he refer to the Hall, which is particularized as a *desideratum* in the charter. Maitland speaks of it in 1739, and again in 1756, as a small one.

In recent years, the Plumbers have manifested considerable interest in the cause of technical education and the sanitation of dwellings and other buildings by improved principles of sewerage. As lately as 1891, the Master and Wardens entertained the Lord Mayor and a distinguished circle at dinner, at the Cannon Street Hotel, in furtherance of this desirable object, and the following resolution was carried :—

" That this conference of representatives of educational authorities, master and operative plumbers, of County Councils and others, is of opinion that the technical education of plumbers is a question of national importance, the provision of which is exceptionally difficult and costly, and that it is expedient that its special claims for money help should be brought before the attention of the County Councils, and Municipal Corporations, and Township Commissioners." [1]

But whatever one or two individual members may accomplish, the influence of the Company in the direction of public control has long determined ; and the almost universal debasement of the material in use, as well as the too frequent incompetence of the artificer, must be reformed, before any substantial benefit can accrue to the community from the movement directed by this ancient body. The great drawback to progress is the dishonest District Surveyor, whose eyes are furnished with golden shutters at the expense of the equally dishonest builder.

---

[1] See *Revived Guild Action*, by George Shaw, Past Master. 8vo, 1878 ; second edition enlarged, 8vo, 1890.

The Poulters.[1]

OF the ancient poultry market in the thoroughfare still bearing the once significant name, Conyhope or Coneyhoop Lane, one of the original abutments of Grocers' Hall, constituted part, and was probably the place where the live rabbits were offered for sale, as at Leadenhall now, in hutches.

The Poulterers had also a scalding-house close by the Stocks, but on the opposite side of the street, and east of St. Mildred's Church, in a narrow turning called Scalding Alley.

Stow's Continuator (1633) observes that *Scalding-Wike*, by the Stocks Market, was so called, because the Poulters dressed and scalded their poultry there. This was another appellation for the same locality.

The same writer elsewhere apprises us that the followers of the trade dwelled between the Stocks Market and the Great Conduit, but subsequently removed to Gracechurch and Newgate Streets.

What is now still called the *Poultry* was formerly the scene of a somewhat complex trade in poultry, fish, and butcher's meat ; and at length the thoroughfare became so congested, that arrangements were made, whereby the poulterers were ordered to sell their goods in their shops, and that, as to the two other crafts, the fishmongers should take turns with the fleshers to hold their market in the enclosure called the Stocks and in the contiguous pent-houses on fish-days and flesh-day respectively.

Cases arose in which these several trades suffered forfeiture of their stocks by contumacy. So far as the Poulterers were concerned, the difficulty may have been relieved by the poultry market at

---

[1] See *The Charter of the Worshipful Company of Poulters, London : Its Orders, Ordinances, and Constitution. Also, Acts granted by the Corporation of London. With a List of the Estates and Charities belonging to and under the direction of the Court of Assistants of the said Company.* 4to, privately printed [1872].

Leadenhall. But new regulations on this subject were published from time to time to suit varying opinions or exigencies.

In 1357 the Poulters freemen of the City were forbidden to stand " at the carfukes of the Leden-halle with Rabbits, fowls, or other poultry ;" and they were required to offer them for sale along the wall toward the west of St. Michael's, Cornhill.

In 1375, the Court of Aldermen made an order that foreign poulterers, who entered the City by Newgate or Aldersgate, should sell their goods on the pavement in front of the Friars Minors near the Fountain, and that freemen of the trade should stand before the Church of St. Nicholas Flesh-Shambles in Newgate Street. The aim was to prevent collision and discord between the two.

A case occurred,—one of many,—in 1381, where William Fot, a poulterer, offered eighteen pigeons for sale on the Thursday next after the Feast of St. Austin, in contempt of the City and deceit of the people, for that the same were putrid and an abomination to mankind ; and the said William was put into the pillory on the averment of four cooks of Bread Street that the birds were putrid when exposed for sale.

OLD ARMS.

From a very remote period,—certainly from 1350, —the Corporation reserved the right of fixing the prices of victual sold within the City, and we possess the printed tariff established and advertised for this description of food from 1572 onward.

An interesting point is, that the salesman was expected to establish his authenticity by wearing a recognised garb, for one of the " Laws of the Market" inserted by Stow in his *Survey*, but separately printed more than once, prescribes " that no Poulters shall deceivably occupy the market, to sell any stale victuall, or such as bee Poulters of this City for to stand in strange cloathing so to doe under paine of forty shillings and the forfeiture of such victuall."

The Poulters claim an existence as a voluntary Association as far back as 1345 ; and there is no reason, why they should not have subsisted even earlier. But they were not incorporated till 19 Henry VII., Feb. 23, 1504. This charter was renewed Feb. 22, 30 Elizabeth, and 13 June, 6 Charles II. ; but all these grants, with one of James II., are stated to have perished in the Great Fire. The acting charter was obtained from William and Mary, May 6, 1692.[1]

---

[1] In the years 1763 and 1820 the charter was supplemented by Acts of Common Council. The power of search, conferred by the royal grant, has long ceased.

The quota of ten men returned to the muster for the City Watch in 1469 bespeaks the poulters at that date a somewhat insignificant body in point of numbers, if not of influence ; and the same estimate is deducible from the periodical recurrence of their name in connection with various public calls and events. They present themselves in 1501–2, on the eve of the application for their first charter, as the 44th Gild with a customary Livery of 10, and in 1515 they are officially ranked as thirty-fifth.

The epoch of highest prosperity was perhaps about 1724, in which year the Livery was returned at 127. In 1882, it had receded to 57, and in 1892 to 40, the entire Company at the later date counting scarcely 100.

The government is composed, agreeably to the charter of 1692, of a Master, two Wardens (Upper and Renter), and Assistants, and manages the corporate estate on behalf of the Company and the trust funds subject to the approval of the Charity Commissioners. Election day is Ash Wednesday.

The income of 600*l.* a year or thereabout appears to arise from dividends, rents, and fines. The Company has a small interest in the Vintners' Irish manor of Bellaghy. The greater part of the revenue derived from dividends is in respect of 11,889*l.* 16*s.* 5*d.* paid by the Great Eastern and North London Railways for the compulsory purchase of freeholds in Dunning's Alley, Bishopsgate Within, where the Hall may have once been ; the receipts from this source are about 400*l.* a year.

The property seems to have come into the possession of the Company under the will of Thomas Nepton, May 6, 1718, subject to certain trusts, which upon the death of his relict, Anne Nepton, in 1728, were by her varied and enlarged, the ultimate beneficiaries being charged with the payment of 40*l.* a year to the poor of Barking, Essex, a like sum to the poor of St. Botolph, Aldgate, and 20*l.* a year to Shoreditch School, and the residue to be divisible between the poor of the Gild and the fees of apprenticeship.

Robert Warden, by his will dated June 3, 1609, gave the Company a house then known under the sign of the *Pepper Queen*, in the parish of St. Peter on Cornhill, and situated at the junction of Cornhill and Bishopsgate Street, on condition that they should pay 3*l.* 12*s.* a year to the parson and churchwardens for the benefit of the poor. The payment has been increased since that time ; in 1872, it was 8*l.* 2*s.* 6*d.*

LITERARY NOTICES.

Certain prices set upon Fowl by the Lord Mayor in the year 1572. A broadside printed in or about that year by John Day.

By the Mayor. Rates and prices of all sorts of Poultry, set down by the right honourable Ralph Freeman, Lord Mayor. . . . to be observed and kept by all and every the Poulterers and other persons whatsoever . . . 1633. A broadside.

A Proclamation by the Lord Mayor on the same subject. [1633-4.] A broadside.

The Saddlers.

OUR TRUST IS IN GOD

THE earliest traces of this community exhibit them as an Association gathered together in very remote times under the eastern boundary-wall of the conventual church of St. Martin le Grand, founded by one of the kings of Kent in the eighth century, and endowed by the Normans with new privileges and the right of sanctuary.

A more happily chosen spot for what was in course of time known as the *Saddlery* nowhere existed ; for the immediate contiguity at once carried with it a religious atmosphere and a practical safeguard.

The Saddlers may contest with the Weavers the palm of antiquity ; but while the latter have no special claim to attention beyond their precedence of origin, we here hold in our hands the interesting means of identifying the intimate link quite as far back into the past between a collegiate and a trading Brotherhood, the bond of amity which the convent formed and maintained with the occupiers of the neighbouring commercial quarter. Time has played his too common part with both alike. In the room of the monastery it has placed the General Post

OLD ARMS.

Office ; of the Saddlery nothing survives but the modern Hall in Foster Lane.

The great church and its adjuncts disappeared at the Reformation, the

older Hall of the Gild in 1666. It is to one of the muniments removed from the former that we derive our earliest clue to the genesis and home of the Fellowship under notice. A mutilated document of the twelfth century, which has long been more or less generally known by repute, but of which a subsequent and complete transcript was more recently brought to light, bears unique witness to a convention made in 1154 between two bodies so dissimilar, yet apparently so closely knit together in charity and goodwill.

This compact testified to the then well-established relations of the monks and gildesmen to each other, and is a sort of exemplification of the mutual tie. The Saddlers are reminded of their acknowledged right to participate in all the benefits arising from the services performed in the church both by night and by day, and of the fact that two masses are said every week, one for the living and the other for the departed of their congregation, and that their members are entitled to equal privileges and honours with the holy brethren themselves at their obsequies and burial. In consideration whereof the Saddlers are enjoined to conform to the usage in the days of their Alderman Ernaldus, and to pay for each reception of a deceased brother in the churchyard and the ringing of the bell the sum of eightpence.

A piece of parchment, such as this before us, is a remarkable title-deed; for it fixes the original settlement of the trading colony in the vicinity of Cheapside or West Cheap as much prior to 1154 as we may be warranted in interpreting the language of the memorandum to convey. That the Gild in the present stage of its existence was ruled by an Alderman of proprietary rank, is not more than the prevailing custom and principle of those days ; and when we recollect that, before other methods of conveyance came into vogue, riding was the sole and universal medium of transit, nothing can be more natural and secure than the conclusion that the saddle in some shape closely succeeded the utilization of the horse for both sexes and all classes. But in this case we ought to be rather proud of owning the absolute voucher for the institution of the trade in London, for a knowledge of the locality, which constituted its primitive seat, and for the highly characteristic alliance between its freemen and their nearest, most pacific, and yet most powerful neighbours.

It proceeds from the dearth of such records that we are enabled to learn so little of the remoter history of our institutions and our country. With the solitary exception just mentioned the annals of the Saddlers present almost a blank during two centuries ; they are not enumerated in 1180 among the eighteen adulterine bodies associating and assembling without authority.

A charter was granted to the followers of the industry in 1272 ; but it was of a general scope, and applied, not to the City of London only, but to the kingdom at large, prescribing and authorizing that in every borough, city, or town, where saddlery was practised, two honest and discreet men should be chosen to survey the Craft. This instrument was repeatedly renewed, and, as we shall perceive, long ran parallel with the special grant to the London body.

We discern in the step here taken, however, one or two important considerations. The charter of course embraced London, and substituted there, as well as probably in the provinces, an Executive of two elective Wardens for the archaic feudal Alderman, whose tenure was at least for life, if it was not for a time hereditary ; but its language seems to favour the supposition, on the other hand, that it was the first formal embodiment of the trade under responsible control and royal licence ; and we are tempted to speculate, whether the peculiar footing on which the Saddlers stood with the monastery of St. Martin did not shield them from cognizance in 1180, as they present themselves to our view only a few years before in a fraternal light, using a common place of worship and a common place of interment. Beneath the stones of the Post Office reposes the mingled dust of canon, monk, and saddler, more closely united in death even than in life, and more inseparable.

In the first year of Edward I., then, it may be fairly presumed that the Saddlers were provided with a more modern and practical administrative system, although their friendship and intercourse with the monks of St. Martin still continued unaltered. In that quarter it was easier to preserve concord than in others, where commercial interests intervened. In fact, as it has been in our accounts of many other Gilds, we are chiefly indebted for our acquaintance with the progress and doings of this one in ancient days to its differences with those trades, which by their nature were more or less allied to it, more especially the Joiners, who claimed the monopoly of making the timber-work or trees of saddles. Between 1309 and 1327[1] a considerable revelation incidentally occurs through the exposure by the Wardens of the Saddlers of the frauds or enroachments committed by dishonest members of their own Gild in concert with the Joiners, Loriners, and Painters. In 1320 the Ordinances obtained by the Loriners in 45 Henry III. were condemned, and committed to the

---

[1] In the *Book of Expenses of Thomas, Earl of Lancaster*, for 1313–14, we meet with two entries exhibiting the charges at that time for this class of article in a princely household :—

"*Item*, Saddles for the Lord's Liveries in summer, 52*l*. 6*s*. 8*d*.

Item, for one Saddle for the Earle, of the Prince's Armes, 40*s*."

Cardinal Wolsey maintained a saddler on his establishment.

flames in Cheapside.   This was an unusually severe rebuke, as it in a
certain measure disfranchised the Gild by placing them out of the pale
of the law ; and it had its natural sequence in active hostilities.

In 1327 parties of Saddlers, Joiners, Painters, and Loriners assembled
in force with arms, both in Cheapside and in Cripplegate, on the 20th May,
by reason of some " rancour and dissension " among them, because the
Saddlers desired to restrain the others from selling to any but themselves
and were, moreover, greatly indebted to the Loriners and the rest for
work done.   Considerable bloodshed ensued, and much difficulty occurred in effecting a pacification, which was reduced to writing, and is
still extant.   The Saddlers were adjudged by a committee of arbitrators
to be in the wrong ; and we must allow that committee to be more conversant with the facts than ourselves.

It comes to this, that the early life of all similarly organized communities, when it emerged from the stage of obscurity, entered on that
of jealous inquisition, turbulence, and deceit.   We should be far more
ignorant of their career, had their proceedings been really on the lines
of brotherly and religious association, which their charters, ordinances,
and professions specify.

We do not meet with any code of bye-laws for internal government
anterior to that of 1365 ; and the knowledge of these Articles is entirely
due to their ratification by the Court of Aldermen on the prayer of the
Wardens and their consequent enrolment in the Chamber of London.
They indicate, in the first place, the regulations, which had probably
long been in force in the trade, and secondly the feeling that, as the
volume of business increased, and details became more complex, the
official sanction and acceptance of these canons were imperative on a
variety of accounts.   In soliciting their confirmation, the Wardens declared them to be for the common profit of the realm and the honour
and preservation of their mistery.   They bespeak the possession by the
freemen and even journeymen at this date of a more than customary
measure of weight, as several of the stipulations are calculated to protect the *vadlet* (valet) or servant equally with the master or employer.

Meanwhile, the *general* royal licence accorded to the trade in 1272
had been renewed (1364) by Edward III., and with the Ordinances or
bye-laws just cited placed the Craft on a tolerably secure footing.   The
principal cause of anxiety and discontent about this period was due to
the arbitrary proceedings of a Mayor (Sir Nicholas Brember), who un-
happily acquired phenomenal ascendency for the time being, and during
his four years of office (1377–83–4–5) exercised a sort of despotism
over the City.   His career was brought to a close by his attainder and
execution for high treason ; but the Saddlers distinguished themselves

in this case very signally, by a special address to the Crown on behalf of themselves and the rest of the municipality.

At length, when they had subsisted during the greater part of three centuries as a Fellowship—if they did not make out their title to an even Anglo-Saxon origin—the first charter of incorporation was obtained from Richard II., March 20, 1394–5, at a cost of 60*l.*, an amount which may explain the delay in approaching the Crown. The grant was, after all, not of a very elaborate character, and was confined to the constitution of the men of the mistery as a perpetual commonalty, the appointment of four Wardens, and a licence in mortmain to purchase lands and hereditaments of 20*l.* yearly value, for the sustentation of the poor, aged, and sick of the Company. The exordium of the concession is couched in terms, which imply on the part of the beneficiaries an almost pathetic appeal for the relief of their needs through the arrival of many at venerable estate and the fall of others into great poverty, insomuch that the pious Brotherhood was solicitous to have it in its power to alleviate their condition. Yet in 1364 this body had contributed 100 shillings to Edward the Third's French wars, and in 1377 sent four members to represent it on the Common Council. This instrument was viewed, exemplified, and confirmed by Edward IV., May 5, 1463, by Henry VII., October 28, 1495, and by Henry VIII., June 11, 1540.

Elizabeth in her first year (November 9, 1558) reincorporated the Company under the name of the Wardens or Keepers and Commonalty of the Mistery or Art of Saddlers of the City of London, and named and appointed four Wardens to hold office till the 14th of August, 1559, with power to summon and hold an assembly within their common Hall of the Wardens and freemen of the mistery, and eight of the same freemen to be Assistants. The Wardens and eight Assistants formed a body qualified to consult and decide on all the offices of the mistery; and a casting vote was given to the Senior Warden. The grant conferred the right of search and of making bye-laws.

We distinctly perceive the survival in this Elizabethan grant of the popular constitution of 1365 and 1395 ; and the Ordinances of 1560–1 naturally followed the tenor and language of the charter. But we must retrace our steps a long way, in order as clearly as possible to understand how an organic change was impending.

In common with the Merchant Taylors and a few other bodies, whose history in outline we have already given, the Saddlers, from a remote date not capable of exact fixture, appear to have acquiesced in the assumption and enjoyment by their Yeomanry of certain valued prerogatives, including overseers with definite jurisdiction and the right to hold periodical religious observances akin to those celebrated by the Livery and Court. Their Wardens assisted in the preparation of the yearly Feast on St. Bartholomew's Day (August 14), when the journey-men were "treated."

Immediately after the concession of the parent charter in 1395, we are almost entitled to presume that a fresh issue took place of bye-laws to meet the altered circumstances. The text, however, we do not seem to possess ; and it was probably on the conditions laid down in them that the question turned in 1396 as to certain privileges of the Yeomanry. In that year, what is described as an unlawful combination among this body occurred, and the alleged offenders, on being summoned to Guild-hall, appeared by their Wardens, who pleaded that "time out of mind the serving-men of the trade had had a certain Fraternity among them-selves, and had been wont to array themselves all in like suit once in the year, and, after meeting together at Stratford on the Feast of the Assumption, to come thence to the church of St. Vedast in London, to hear mass in honour of the Virgin."

But the Court disallowed the plea, and commanded the said yeomen-saddlers henceforth to refer all questions among them to the Wardens of the Company.

This was really the beginning of the end, although the end was yet far off. In 1606–7, March 20, an *inspeximus* of the charter was pro-cured from James I., and this act was followed by the ratification under the hand of the Lord Treasurer and the Judges of a new set of Ordin-ances, dated April 17, 1608. The interval of a twelvemonth may well have been employed in carefully and thoroughly considering the step, which the Court proposed to take ; for in this code the whole electoral power, and the entire authority, was constructively vested in the Wardens and Assistants, since all mention of the summons and admittance of the Livery and Yeomanry to the Hall before the election was suppressed.

The executive and sovereign oligarchy was of course too wary to deprive the freemen of the mistery, on whose behalf the charters had been solicited and conferred, of all show of jurisdiction and interest ; but their part henceforth was purely ceremonial ; and their Wardens, whom we still trace in 1632, limited themselves to attendance in Hall to hear the result of the election and the arrangement of subordinate de-tails, more especially in connection with the Yeomanry dinner or Steward's Festival. In 1624 it was prescribed that the "bringing home" of the Wardens of the Yeomanry, which had long grown out of use, should be altogether abolished, by reason of disorderly proceedings, which were apt to arise. This ceremony, admitted to be of lengthened continuance, was perhaps the one which led to the disturbances in 1396.

On Election Day, 1646, the Livery attempted a *coup de main*, and pressed for a share in the appointment of the new Wardens ; but their demand was successfully resisted.

In 1669 the bye-laws of 1608 were approved by the Judges, and on December 24, 1684, Charles II. gave a new charter, allowing—with the customary political and religious disabilities—all the powers and benefits contained in that of 1607.

Thus the constitution, which had at the outset, and more or less down to 1560, been emphatically popular in its complexion, became in and after 1608 strictly and irrevocably aristocratic. The experience in this and other cases, where the same revolution occurred at a later period of time and with less signal completeness, was that the very essence of the principle which called the Gilds into existence—the welfare of the freemen and freewomen both in health and infirmity, and their support in old age or indigence—was largely inimical to altered circumstances, even while it must have been manifest that such alteration was solely due to the incidence of origin and conditions of tenure.

The Saddlers may be regarded as a very striking type of the aristocratically constituted Gild ; and in this respect it offers an instructive contrast to one like the Coopers' or even the Cordwainers', where the suffrage has not been so narrowed, but where, on the contrary, there is an unusual measure of liberalism. The violent departure from the primitive form of organization in the case of the other body is apt to strike us as a reaction from the self-asserting and unruly policy of the Yeomanry in early days, and such a radical change was perhaps facilitated by the gradual discouragement of applicants for the Freedom. In more modern times, trade disputes, which still occasionally arose, were arranged in a manner more consonant with advanced ideas. Not so long ago, the Saddlers quarrelled with the Joiners, because the latter claimed the right of making the trees of the high-peaked saddles then in vogue. Down to 1822, the interposition under the power of search was practically carried out in the case of a saddler in Holborn, who was summoned by the Court on the ground that he had on sale sundry saddles made of improper material ; and the goods were seized and destroyed.

The introduction of the coach in various forms was entertained by the Company with misgiving and dislike, as it foreshadowed in their view a gradual decline in the call for saddle-horses. But the apprehension was more or less chimerical, and in the Civil War, if the taxation proved onerous, the supply of stores for the army partly counterbalanced the claims upon their loyalty and funds.

We have observed that so long ago as 1356 the Gild exhibited great jealousy and intolerance of the slightest intrenchment on its rights ; and as time went on, the category of articles in which the members claimed an interest grew more and more extended, comprising pillions, stirrups, straps, leathern cans, horsecloths, and even mails (the ancient portmanteaux), and other travelling appliances. In fact, the saddler's shop gradually acquired the aspect of a depôt, where buyers might obtain not only horse-furniture but a certain section of necessaries for a journey by road.

The Company was under the common necessity of compounding with the assignees of the Crown in 1547–8 for its property held to superstitious uses, and to effect this purpose had to part with other estate of approximate value, owing to the insufficiency of corporate income.

But from this time forward, nevertheless, it appears as a contributor to nearly every public solemnity and burden. There is an amusing entry in the Books where some of the Yeomanry were deputed to attend the Queen from Hyde Park Corner to St. James's Palace in 1584–5, of a fine of 8s. 8d. levied by the auditors, because the torch-holders "prodigally and lasciviously " wasted the lights by burning them the whole of the way homeward. In 1609 a subscription to the enterprise for settling Virginia was raised among the Livery, and subsequently reimbursed ; this method of discharging engagements was not unfrequent. Somewhat later, 390l. were invested in a sub-share of the Salters' Irish Manor, the other holders from the tenants in chief being the Dyers, Cutlers, Joiners, and Woolmen. The interest has determined by sale to the Salters.

In the Books from 1609 there are charges for attending the Lord Mayor's Show. At first the Saddlers hired a barge ; but they afterward acquired one ; and in 1671 Alderman Dashwood presented 100l. to purchase bunting. Part of the amount was spent in a canopy, however.

Of the etiquette observed at burials we have numerous illustrative memoranda. The whole Fellowship attended the obsequies, first at St. Martin's, and after the Reformation at St. Vedast's, Foster Lane. The " funeral baked meats " were supplied at the expense of the departed, unless his means were inadequate. In 1624 an order was made that the distribution to the Livery " in the streets," that is, in the short distance between the Hall and the Church, of comfits, bread and wine, should be discontinued.

The Saddlers possess an ancient pall of crimson velvet with the edges worked in gold, which used to be laid over the coffin of each deceased member, when his brethren followed him to the grave. It is still placed on the table, when a new comer is sworn, as a token of the vacancy.

The habit of wearing one suit of Livery is evidently of great antiquity. In 1396 the Yeomen-Saddlers claimed their established right to an uniform vesture on Assumption Day; and in the Elizabethan Ordinances (1560-1) the clothing was directed to be such " as shall seem meet and convenient for the worship of the City and the honesty of the Fellowship." At a call to the Livery in April, 1664, the clerk repaired to the persons elected to deliver them the patterns of the cloth for their gowns and hoods, which were to be provided against admission-day, when the Senior Warden personally invested each of the new members with his hood. But the colour of the Company is not stated. This we know to have been elsewhere a point of infinite interest and moment.

The Executive body has almost invariably followed the charter in consisting of four Wardens and a Court of Assistants. From 1737 to 1751, Frederick Prince of Wales was Master of the Company; but after his death the Senior Warden was termed Prime Warden, and the other three, Second or Key Warden, Third or Quarter Warden, and Fourth or Renter Warden, with whom was associated at one time an Under-Renter, ostensibly as an auxiliary to the Junior Warden. The name does not appear after 1609; but in 1634 two Cup-fillers were nominated to take charge of the table-linen or napery and other similar effects.

The bye-laws were made and renewed with variations and additions, *probably in or about* 1397, and certainly in 1560-1, 1608, 1624, and 1669. In estimating their character and tone we are always to recollect that their legality depended on their freedom from any provisions derogatory to the Crown, and that they passed the scrutiny of the Corporation, before they could have effect. Whatever we may think of them, they reflected the mercantile and social genius of the period; and this may be taken to be a general criticism.

In 1501-2 the Saddlers numbered 33, and are placed nineteenth, between the Butchers and the Carpenters. In 1509, they are the twentieth company according to the list drawn up on the occasion of the coronation of Henry VIII. and Catherine of Arragon, and had 14 yards' space allotted to them in the line of procession, the *maximum* being 26 yards. In 8 Henry VIII. the order of precedence was officially regulated, and the Saddlers have the twenty-sixth place, between the Carpenters and Cordwainers; yet in the 23rd of the same reign, in the arrangement at the Lord Mayor's feast in Guildhall, the Company appears as twenty-first, between the Fullers and the Brewers, although it was allowed to send only 4 members, besides the Wardens, against the Fullers' 9 and the Brewers' 12.

In 1537 the Saddlers numbered 60, including three freewomen. At a late period their relative standing and wealth are gauged by their assessment for corn in 1602–3, and for the ceremony of welcoming James I. into London. In the former case they contributed 90 quarters against the Carpenters,' Cordwainers' and Coopers' 70 ; and in the latter 3*l.* 12*s.*, a higher amount than the three others just named and indeed than a majority of the Minor Gilds.

In 1882 the liverymen were returned as 92, the freemen as 33, and the free sisters as 6. Of late years the admissions have been almost exclusively by patrimony or redemption, and those not at all numerous. The Act of Common Council, passed in 1722, by which all persons carrying on the business in London were required to belong to the Company, was operative in 1882 to the extent of 22 members. But the tendency of all such protectionist regulations has been to fall into practical disuse.

At the same time, owing to the abnormal increase in the value of freeholds situate in prominent City thoroughfares,[1] the financial position in the ten years, 1870–79, is shown to have been steadily progressive,[2] and the Saddlers have borne some part in encouraging technical and general education, if not on a scale commensurate with their means and consequent responsibility. In 1873–4, two exhibitions of Saddlery were held at the Hall, and prizes offered for the best work.

There is this peculiar feature about the charity estate of the Saddlers, derived from several benefactors, that the Company found itself unable to apply the income in many cases to the intended objects, from the absence of qualified recipients, and was obliged to seek the approval of the Commissioners for new schemes.

As recently as 1859 the almshouses for poor Saddlers, designated Honnor's Home, were erected at Spring Grove, Isleworth, from funds arising out of the residuary estate of Young George Honnor, Citizen and Saddler, left to the Company in 1769 for the relief of decayed Masters, Wardens, or Assistants. No application having occurred,

---

[1] The estates, according to the official returns of 1834, are situated in Cheapside, Wood Street, Aldersgate Street, Southwark, Milford Lane, Strand, Harrow, Maidstone, and Stistead (Essex). The possessions in the City included several taverns : the Dolphin and Mermaid in West Cheap or Cheapside, the Golden Bull, and the White Lion and the Goat in East Cheap, the Talbot in Wood Street, the Crown at Holborn Conduit, and the Adam and Eve without Temple Bar.

[2] In the first-named year the total income is returned at 7,561*l.* 7*s.* 8*d.* ; in 1879, at 10,243*l.* 10*s.* ; and in 1892, at 11,200*l.*, exclusive of 1000*l.* trust ; and there appears to have usually been a considerable annual surplus.

the money accumulated, and in 1855 had reached nearly 18,000*l.*; and under the authority of the Charity Commission the scheme was varied.

The first vestige of a Hall is of an indirect kind, being in the form of a bequest by William de Lincoln, Citizen and Saddler, and one of the Wardens for 1363, under his will proved in 1393, of the sum of 10 marks toward a common Hall, provided that the same be built within three years. The position of the testator, and the natural desire to give effect to his intentions, go some way in the direction of convincing us that something was done accordingly; and there is the additional argument that the clause in the will was dictated by a knowledge of the wishes of his brethren, and responded to conversations held in his lifetime on the subject, somewhat in the same manner as with the Coopers the erection of a Hall resulted from the initiative of one of the Wardens. A positive proof of such a possession must, however, be carried forward to 1545; and it first presents itself under very inauspicious circumstances, as the theatre of the disgraceful proceedings connected with Anne Askew, who was tried here. In the charter of 1558, the " common Hall " is particularly specified. But the Company appears to have no records tending to elucidate its history, and it perished in the Fire. Such lead and iron as could be obtained from the ruins were stored up in the vaults of the Mermaid Tavern for use in a new building, which was eventually entrusted to Mr. Thomas Davis, Mr. Hodgkin, and Mr. Braithwaite. But subsequently, when the full amount of the losses was ascertained, all proceedings were adjourned; the material, with most of the plate, was sold; the Wardens were instructed to endeavour to procure purchasers for the Maidstone estate, and not merely was the staff reduced, but some of the pensions were suspended. The Court temporarily met at the house of one of the Assistants in Bishopsgate.

The plate realized consisted of 281½ ounces of gilt plate, which fetched 5*s.* 6*d.* per ounce, and 427½ of white or plain; the whole produced 184*l* 12*s.* 9*d.*, which went to defray certain outstanding debts.

Steps were taken in 1668, however, to replace the Hall, which was not ready for occupation till 1670; and the meetings were held in the interval at Christ's Hospital and at the Cooks' Hall in Aldersgate Street. But when the work had been finished, the Company was compelled by its straitened position to offer a portion of the new premises to other public bodies or to whomever would hire the accommodation, except to conventicles, dancing-masters, and the like. This state of things lasted till 1721, and from the ceremonies connected with interments of members taking place there, a rather odd practice arose of

letting the apartment to others.   The low financial plight necessitated
and excused such expedients.

The facts known about the second Hall are singularly few.   Hatton,
writing in 1708, refers to it as adorned with fretwork and wainscot.
Under 1714 mention occurs of a cupola or lanthorn.   It had no outlet
from Cheapside, but was approached by a small passage called Saddlers'
Hall Court, in which the Clerk had a house.   In Maitland's time
(1739–72) it had been completed in all respects, except the wine-cellar,
which was formed below the front yard in 1805, and he says of it :
" Saddlers' Hall is situate near the end of Foster Lane in Cheapside, in
the upper end of an handsome alley, at the entrance of which is an
ornamental doorcase and an iron gate, and is a very compleat building
for the use of such a Company."   He adds that the Company's Arms
were carved in stone over the gate next the street.

These descriptive notices are the more necessary, that in 1815 the
edifice was partly, and in 1821, totally, destroyed by fire.   The furniture,
wine, plate, and painted glass windows were saved, although the last
were seriously damaged, and the ruins were sold by auction as building
material.

The first stone of the third Hall was laid March 7, 1822.   The
building, which has entrances both in Cheapside and Foster Lane, abuts
on the church of St. Vedast Foster and St. Michael-le-Quern, near the
General Post Office, and the Members go thither in procession every
August, attended by their chaplain, to pay a thank-offering to God, and
to testify to the loyal discharge of their duty toward the poor of the
Brotherhood.

In casting our eyes down the list of former eminent members, honorary or otherwise, of this Craft, we arrive at 1653 without meeting with
any one of special note.   In that year, Alderman Dashwood, a benefactor of the Company, and ancestor of the Dashwood, De Spencer,
and Brooke families, was Master ; and the only other name is that of
Richard Earlom, the famous engraver, whose father, William Earlom,
appears under 1791.   But we do not suggest that throughout the long
catalogue there are not many personages, whose memory ought to be
very dear to the Gild, as those who made it, and enabled it to become
and to remain what it is.

The Company possesses a few paintings, including a portrait of Pitt,
by Romney, one of Queen Anne by Clostermans, and a picture
attributed to Ostade.   They also have a considerable collection of
plate, which, with the two exceptions retained in 1668, has accumulated since that date.   The Cocoanut Cup is probably the most ancient
and the most important piece ; but there are several others of 17th

century fabric. Beyond the loss of the bulk of the original collection, the common practice existed of selling from time to time the spoons accumulated by the usage of each freeman presenting one on his admission, only as many being retained as were judged requisite.

THE RICH CUP.

There are also in the Hall an ancient treasure-chest of Flemish workmanship, with a most elaborate lock, a ballot-box or *cadet*, which was once used for elections, and a MS. copy of the Gospels, on which the officers of the Company are still sworn.[1]

The Scriveners. [2]

THIS fellowship was originally known and described as The Fraternity or Mistery of the Scriveners or Writers of the Court Letter of the

---

[1] An interesting account of this Gild, by Mr. J. W. Sherwell, the Clerk, 8vo, 1889, has been lent to us by that gentleman. There appeared in 1861 a pamphlet by Mr. J. B. Burton, "Twenty-five Years a Liveryman of the Company of Saddlers," entitled: *The Saddlers' Company, and the Rights of the Livery. Being An Address to the Livery of London.* It deals with the question of the absorption of executive authority by the Court.

[2] There is no material for a history of this Company beyond the parliamentary returns, the *Case* printed in 1749, and casual or indirect references. All the ancient papers, except the Minute Book, were lost in 1666.

City of London, and is supposed at one time to have been associated with the Limners, who constituted the germ of the Stationers' Company. As early as 1357 we find its members exempted, under their original designation of Writers of Court-hand and text-letters, from serving on juries or inquisitions, and only required to attend at Guildhall if summoned on special business. They were then plainly an organized and respectable Union or Gild, with some system of internal management. They obtained their bye-laws in 1373–4, and a rather lengthy preamble recites the need and demand for great vigilance in preventing any but skilled men from following the craft, or receiving work. They expressly laid down the rule, that every Scrivener should set his name to the deeds, which he copied.

Here we discover an unusually early notice of a Livery and of the rules to be observed in purchasing it. Every sworn brother was bound to provide a suit against Whitsuntide, to pay a noble of gold in advance at the beginning of Lent, and the rest as soon after delivery of the cloth as possible ; but the vesture seems to have been renewed only every two years, and to have been principally worn on the Feast of Pentecost.

Other Ordinances were passed by the Court of Aldermen in 1390 and 1440. They related to apprenticeship, the examination of all craftsmen keeping shop, to ascertain their fitness for making evidences and muniments, to the necessity of a licence from the Wardens, before any could be enfranchised, and to the restriction of all freemen to a single shop. The Craft put forth additional bye-laws in 1497 and 1557, by the former of which apprentices were required to satisfy the Wardens as to their "congruity of grammar" ; and there is the noticeable circumstance that at this period the meetings were held at the mansion or dwelling-house of one of the Wardens, and that the minutes were entered in a book called the Common Paper.

The Scriveners of London enjoyed a large and growing share of consideration from the fifteenth to the seventeenth century, or in other words, during the time when they represented a calling rendered lucrative by the extensive demand and the special skill required, and developed by degrees into a machinery for conveyancing and finance. A succession of able and enterprising men imparted to the pursuit in the course of time an almost entirely new character.

The growth of the avocation naturally opened the way to occasional cases of fraud and crime. In 1367, Robert de Edensore, Scrivener, was put in the pillory for forging a deed of entail ; in 1376, William Grendon called *Credelle*, Scrivener, was imprisoned for making false indentures of apprenticeship ; and, once more, in 1391 a member of the Gild was pilloried for forging title-deeds. It was a very gross case, and the punishment seems disproportionately light. The profession was even now numerous, and held within its ranks various grades and types, of which the lower were already prepared to lend themselves to any transaction whatever.

In 1473, we come across Clifford the Scrivener as a person mixed up with a law-case between the Goldsmiths and another party, and 6s. 8d. was paid for the search of his books to inspect a deed relevant to the case. This person figures in many transactions about the same period ; and it was a time when his profession was beginning to acquire influence and rank. Four years earlier (1469) the Gild, of which he was a member, found twenty soldiers to bear a part in guarding the City Gates. It was a fairly large proportion for an unincorporated body.

A curious Star Chamber case in 35 Elizabeth proves that this calling was not always proof against the attractions of political notoriety. Short, a Scrivener, was in that year sentenced to the pillory, imprisonment, and exile for having published a seditious libel, warning the Flemings and Frenchmen resident in London to depart, lest the apprentices and craftsmen should take their lives from jealousy of their interference with native labour. But it was under the Stuart *régime*, that the highest point of power and prominence was attained ; and on the 28th January, 1617, the charter was obtained, constituting the Craft one body corporate and politic under the name of The Master, Wardens, and Assistants of the Society of Scriveners of the City of London, with perpetual succession, the right of survey and oversight within the Cities of London and Westminster and suburbs thereof, the Borough of Southwark, the precinct of St. Catherine by the Tower, and all other places within three miles' radius, and the power and obligation to secure a Common Hall or Council-house.

This is the only grant now in the hands of the Company, that of James II. having been apparently lost or destroyed. But the latter was revoked by the often-cited Act of William and Mary.

The government consists, in conformity with the charter of 1617, of a Master, two Wardens, and twenty-four Assistants. The Master and Wardens are annually elected on the Tuesday next after the Feast of St. James, or at any other more convenient time. The Company usually dines together on Lord Mayor's Day.

The bye-laws of 1374 and 1440 were virtually repealed by others successively made, and approved by the Judges in 1619 and 1635. In those of 1635 persons chosen Assistants, and fined for renouncing, were still liable to act as Stewards, under a penalty of 10l. ; but for the stewardship the whole commonalty was eligible.

In the reign of James I. the Scriveners appear to have been in a fairly prosperous condition, as (in association with the Ironmongers) they subscribed to the Irish project of James 570*l*., an amount exceeding that found by the Carpenters, Coopers, Cordwainers, Barbers, and other bodies, which subsequently far eclipsed them in eminence and wealth.

Under 1626, Stow notices the bequest by Nichlas Reive, Scrivener of Cornhill, to the use of the poor of St. Botolph's, Bishopsgate, of a sum of 406*l*. 5*s*., the proceeds of which, invested in lands at Stratford-at-Bow, were in 1633 25*l*. a year.

Three years later, out of corporate money, 21*l*. were applied to a municipal assessment for defraying the expenses of the City on account of the coronation of Charles I.

The business of the early Scrivener was not confined to writing and conveyancing ; but the profession gradually included the duties of a banker and an agent. Through their original vocation, which brought them into necessary contact with persons of property, they became the factors for those, who had money to invest or estates to deposit as security for pecuniary advances.

OLD ARMS.

In achieving success, where great tact and discretion were indispensable, comparatively few of course rose beyond a moderate height. But in the time of James I. one Abbot monopolized a large share of this employment, so readily susceptible of becoming lucrative under favourable conditions, and at his death left his fortune and interest to his nephew, afterward the celebrated Sir Robert Clayton, and one Morris, of whom the latter, having no issue, bequeathed his share to his partner.

Clayton inhabited a noble brick mansion in Old Jewry, where Evelyn was frequently his guest. The Diarist describes the cedar dining-room, painted by Streeter with the History of the Giants' War, and alludes more than once to the vast wealth and princely hospitality of Clayton, who had among his clients and visitors all the leading personages in the kingdom, from the royal family downward. He was Sheriff in 1672 and Mayor in 1679, and served both offices with unsurpassed liberality and magnificence ; he was at this period a member of the Drapers' Company, to which he had translated himself on his accession to the mayoralty. Evelyn notes going to his house, while he was Mayor, with the Countess of Sunderland, and subsequently dining at his table with the Earl of Ossory on a private day ; " but the feast and entertainment," he says, " might have become a king." He purchased at Marden, near Godstone, of the Evelyns a tract of land, which he changed at enormous cost from a barren warren into a splendid estate, whither some of the furniture and decorations from the Old Jewry were subsequently removed by the family.

But the evolution of the normal Scrivener, though striking, from a mere court-letter-writer into a conveyancer and financial agent, never attained in a second instance the proportions which it fortuitously assumed in the case of Clayton, who combined great capacity with unrivalled opportunities.

Clayton was in fact during the whole of his earlier life a Scrivener by calling and freedom, but in reality a banker and financier on the largest scale, and, as we have stated, a Draper by transfer. At Drapers' Hall there is a fine portrait of him by Kneller in his official robes, with the mace lying on a table by him.

The provincial Scrivener, especially where he was established in a prominent and busy centre, soon grew into lucrative practice, and became a member, like his London contemporary, of a Livery Gild, or at least of a religious and social Brotherhood. In the 15th century, the Scriveners of York bore their part in the series of miracle plays exhibited in that city; the subject selected by them was the Incredulity of St. Thomas.

One employment of the Scrivener, though possibly confined to juniors, was superseded by the progress of education; it was that of making out or certifying accounts, where the transaction involved matter of record; and it is also shown by an entry in the Vintners' Books under 1507, that the members of this craft were the persons who translated into English, for the information and use of those concerned, charters and other documents originally written in other languages.

The modern Scrivener has returned to the lines, which originally limited his employment and competence. He does not fulfil any duties outside those of a notary and writer; and the law-stationers frequently undertake the latter branch of the profession. The outlets, which a wholly different distribution of commercial industry lent to the more enterprising members of this calling, no longer exist.

The decline in the affairs of the Company probably commenced during the lifetime of Sir Robert Clayton, who had, as we know, severed his connection with it some time before his death. In 1703 the Hall in Noble Street, acquired in 1631 (with other property) for 810*l.*, was sold to the Coach and Coach Harness Makers under circumstances already explained. An unsuccessful attempt was made to procure an Act of Parliament compelling all conveyancers to take up the freedom.

From the rent of the remaining estate in Noble Street,[1] dividends on savings, and internal income, combined with frugal expenditure, the Scriveners succeed, however, in maintaining their ground, and increasing their capital out of surplus income compatibly with occasional donations to charities ; and had it not been for their failure to sustain their pretensions in regard to the Irish property, their financial position at the present time would have been considerably stronger.

It appears from some evidence given in May, 1883, by the Clerk to the Company before the Royal Commission, that so far back, as January 10, 1626, this Gild believed that in acquiring by purchase out of its own funds an allotment from the Skinners of their Irish estate, they had become the absolute owners of the fee, and formed the expectation that from the accruing profits they would be enabled to erect a Hall and carry out other works and repairs. A member of the Court of Assistants at this time was the father of Milton, and his signature is among those appended to a resolution to the said effect.

Thus the same misunderstanding, which arose between the Skinners and their other partners in this business, existed equally here ; but the present Company was in less capable hands, and did not act with the same firmness. If the Scriveners had succeeded in their pretensions, their claim against the tenant-in-chief would have amounted by analogy to nearly 20,000*l.* On the other hand, they have profited by the excellent management of the Skinners, and derive a very handsome yearly return for their original outlay.

For the seven years, ending in August, 1830, the Company returned its average annual income at 429*l.* to the Royal Commission of 1834 ; but through investment from time to time of surplus internal income and the rise in the value of the Irish estate, in which it is interested, the receipts shew a considerable advance, although since 1874 there has been a decline from the *maximum*.

The Livery, which affords a certain criterion of the standing of these bodies, and which here was prescriptive and unlimited, has fluctuated at different periods. In 1699 it was 45; in 1724, 37; in 1739, 53; in 1882, 22; and in 1892, 50. In the present case, the numbers are kept up by the provision of the Act 41 George III. cap. 79, s. 13, requiring every notary

---

[1] Nos. 12, 13, 14, and 15. The original deed of conveyance has not survived ; but in a lease of 1864 the property is specified as "All those four messuages or tenements situate and being in Noble Street in the parish of St. Mary Steyning, in the City of London, fronting towards the west on the said street, two of which said messuages or tenements are situate on the north side and two on the south side of the great gateway or entry leading out of Noble Street aforesaid to Coachmakers' Hall, and one of which said messuages or tenements extends over the said gateway."

public within the City and its Liberties to belong to the Company. In 1739 the Livery fine was 5*l.* ; in 1882, 15*l.* 2*s.* ; in 1892, 15*l.* 15*s.*

LITERARY NOTICES.

The Case of the Free Scriveners of London : Set forth in A Report from a Committee of the Court of Assistants of the Company of Scriveners, London : To the Master, Wardens, and Assistants of the Company. At their Court holden the 23rd Day of June, 1748. 4to, 1749.

Reprinted in Parliamentary Return of 1884, *Scriveners' Company, Appendix A.*

The Incredulity of St. Thomas : One of the series of miracle-plays, acted by the Scriveners of York. Printed from the original MS (fifteenth century) in Croft's *Excerpta Antiqua,* 1797, by Collier, in the *Camden Miscellany,* vol. iv., and in the collective edition of the Plays.

The Shipwrights.[1]

OUR earliest information respecting this Company reaches us in the shape of a reference to Ordinances devised for the government of the Gild as an unchartered body in 1428, 1456, and 1483. The Shipwrights who, from the very nature of their Craft, bespeak themselves of great antiquity, appear at the outset to have been a Brotherhood of SS. Simon and Jude, established at the river side in Southwark or Bermondsey ; and in 1661 it claimed an existence of four centuries. The Ordinances rehearse that it is not unknown to all the brethren and sisters that

---

[1] See *A Short Account of the Worshipful Company of Shipwrights.* By Reginald R. Sharpe, B.C.L. 4to, 1876.

the Fraternity of SS. Simon and Jude hath been holden in London by the Craft of Shipwrights time out of mind ; they chiefly deal with apprenticeship and other points of internal government ; but they also contain an injunction to members to view and search that the brethren of that Fraternity do use in their said trades good and seasonable timber, and do their work workmanlike as appertaineth.

In 1428 we find that Robert Proufote and John James were sworn Masters of the Mistery. At this time and long after, the religious side was very prominent ; and in the Company's *Repertory* or Minute-Book, commencing with 1456, the opening passage or entry is : " The yeare of thincarnation of our Lord Jesus Christ One thousand fower hundred fiftie and six, and the yere of Kinge Henrie the sixt after the conquest the five and thirteth is founded and ordeyned by the artificers of Ship-wrights in the Citie of London a fraternitie in the worshipp of Saint Symon and Jude, and the feaste of the same yearelie to be solempnized by the same artificers perpetuallie through the grace of God and helpe of devotion of Christen people to be kept and augmented and there-uppon diverse Articles appointed as followeth hereafter."

We only know, or at least infer, that bye-laws were framed in 35 Henry VI. from an allusion to them in a petition from the Company in or about 1613 to the Corporation. There mention occurs of " certen ordynaunces instituted for the good government of the said Guilde in the xxxvth yere of the reigne of King Henry the sixt [extant in Guildhall]" ; but nothing further is ascertainable of such a code. Like other muniments of the Company, it may occur in some unexpected manner, or it may have been lost in the Fire of 1666.

The Association obtained a charter,[1] 23 April, 1605, 3 James I. under the title of the Master, Wardens, and Commonalty of the Art or Mistery of Shipwrights, London. The governing body seems to have originally consisted of a Master, two Wardens, and sixteen Assistants, without a Livery. The Court has comprised since 1777 a Master, four Wardens, and about twenty-five Assistants. In 1830 the Livery was extended to 200 ; and in 1892, according to Whitaker, it numbered 245. The power of search, presumably conferred by the instrument of 1605, was exercised at least down to 1746.

A grant of arms was made to the Shipwrights by Camden Clarencieux in 1605, almost concurrently with the charter, and is at present in the Company's possession. It had been long mislaid, and was at last dis-

---

[1] This is now in the Record Office. In the Accounts for 1661 are charges paid for searching for it in the Tower and at the Rolls ; but it was not recovered till 1782. See Sharpe, pp. 7, 17.

covered (Colonel Sewell, Clerk to the Company, informs us) by accident in the hands of children in a nursery. But they had luckily not had time to exercise their ingenuity upon it ; and it is in perfect preservation.

ARMS, 1739.

It happened, a few years after the incorporation that the King, with that remarkable alacrity for acceding to any proposal involving a pecuniary advantage, which he and his son equally displayed, accorded a charter (May 6, 1612)[1] to the foreign shipwrights, who were located in the same neighbourhood, and that the latter attempted, by virtue of the power alleged to vest in them thereby, to levy dues on the older Fraternity. The difficulty and friction lasted from 1613 to 1683 in spite of decisions by the Court of Aldermen, the Lords of the Council, and the Admiralty in favour of the present Company ; and one result appears to have been, that the corporate funds were during nearly the whole of this lengthened interval at a very low ebb.

Nevertheless in 1660 the Gild found 10l. 3s. 6d. toward the cost of celebrating the coronation of Charles II. by the civic authorities.

It appears that it was subsequently to 1605, that the Shipwrights migrated from the Surrey side,[2] where they lay not very far from the foreign settlement at Rotherhithe, to the Middlesex shore at a point near Ratcliffe St. Mary ; for the report of the Select Committee appointed to inquire about 1615 into the question in dispute between the Free and Foreign bodies, explicitly states that the former had always preserved their freedom of the City, even after they were compelled to leave their yards adjoining the River Thames, and to cross the River, without the City's Liberties, to Ratcliffe.

The practical conclusion of the attempt of the Foreign Shipwrights to override the others was their failure, in 1683, to obtain a new charter with enlarged powers.

The City did its part toward the support of the pretensions of the Company in more than one way. In 1620, it passed a set of Ordinances for the more effectual management of the affairs of the mistery. As early as 1631, it permitted it to admit twelve members by redemption, and in 1661 as many more. It gave it a Livery (1782), and enlarged it (1830) from 100 to 200 with a fine of 21l. It passed (1808) an Act obliging all

---

[1] Now in the Record Office.

[2] The Shipwrights may have removed farther away, as the population within the Liberties increased, for the same reason that the Ironmongers, Founders, and other noisy or troublesome businesses established themselves on the outskirts of the City.

persons engaged in the trade to become freemen. Yet the Shipwrights can never be said to have possessed a substantial constitution ; and they survive at the present moment mainly by the artificial scale of charges, which they impose upon members, the fee for coming on the Court being 50*l.*, and that for serving as Master or Warden, 36*l.* 15*s.* The freedom by redemption costs 9*l.* 5*s.*

In 1882 the freedom was said to number 400 ; and a fair proportion of the members of this division belonged to the trade, as those of the Livery and Executive did to the naval profession or the Admiralty Department. The Shipwrights' Company's Competitive Exhibition of 1877 was doubtless a judicious movement, and repaid the outlay by bringing the promoters into more general public notice.

The funded property of the Company in 1834 was returned at 2,400*l.*, and in 1882 at 4,384*l.*[1] The remainder of the income is derived from internal sources ; nor is there any apparent clue to the proceeds of the Hall, which used to be near Ratcliff Cross. There is no real estate ; nor is there the usual licence in mortmain under the charter. During the years 1876–8 the expenditure shewed a sudden inflation, but in 1879 began again to decline, leaving at the same time a very reduced amount to carry over.

Stow does not specify the Hall, which Maitland (1739) apprises us was once near Ratcliff ; but the former writer observes : " The first building at Radcliffe in my youth (not to be forgotten) was a faire Free Schoole, and Almes-houses. . . . But of late yeeres, Ship-wrights, and (for the most part) other Marine men, have builded many large and strong houses for themselves, and smaller for Saylers, . . ."

The Shipwrights appear at one period to have supplied barges to the Companies on festive or ceremonial occasions. In the Carpenters' Accounts under 1547 there is the item : " Paid to Moule the Shipwright for a barge to Westminster . . . xiiij*s.*"

Among the members of the Company may be noted the celebrated George Whitehead, who subscribed to the substance of the declaration on admittance, *the oath excepted*, and Thomas Ward, Citizen and Shipwright, Sheriff in 1829.

The Shipwrights possess a chest for their muniments somewhat similar to that belonging to the Founders, and figured at p. 501. It is described in 1696 as in the hands of the Wardens, and in 1728 as having four keys, of which two have been since lost. It is probably less ancient than the Founders' chest ; but a receptacle of the same character existed as far back as 1620, as it is named in the Ordinances of that date.

---

[1] Whitaker for 1892 returns the income as 830*l.*

The Spectacle=makers.

ARMS, 1739.   PRESENT ARMS.

THE antecedents of the present Company are admittedly obscure and scanty. The charter dates from 1629, and gave as the governing body a Master, two Wardens, and eight Assistants, a constitution which betrays at that time an unimportant industry and union. By an Act of Common Council, July 1, 1658, all persons in the trade were required to take up the freedom. A Livery was granted in 1809, and is at present limited to 400. By a resolution of the Court, March 26, 1868, a member of the Livery might be elected to the office of Renter Warden, when it should happen that all the members of the Court had already served. The qualification for belonging to the governing body is that the candidate shall be a Liveryman.

The Spectacle-makers are one of the most numerous of the City Companies. In 1882, there were 1,300 on the Freedom and 400 on the Livery. In 1892 the latter was returned at 356, and the income at the interest on 2,100*l.* corporate property, and 1166*l.* trust, estate. Of the last, 40*l.* a year arise from 1,000*l.* 4 per cent. railway stock left by Sir William Tite in 1863. The bulk of the means of expenditure is therefore current internal revenue. In 1834 the average annual receipts were stated to be 364*l.* ; in 1870, the figures were 859*l.*

The Company is one of those which mainly depend on the modern movement, on the part of persons wholly unconnected with the trade, for joining a Society, which confers social and municipal advantages ; and its financial welfare consequently hangs on the continuance of such a taste or demand.

Although those connected with the Gild do not appear to have any information throwing light on its earlier history, and the registers prior to 1666 are no longer in existence, it is obvious that from a very remote period the calling was more or less extensively pursued. In 1644, as we see from a notice annexed, some sort of magnifying lens was introduced.

In Newbery's *Dives Pragmaticus*, 1563, we find the Spectacle-makers recited among the other traders, who would be obliged to resort to a supposed universal provider of wares :

"Al Spectacle makers, for dim sighted eyes."

And further on he speaks of "spectacles made of fine Burral [crystal] glass." But in the biography of Carlo Zeno, an illustrious Venetian statesman and hero, who died at the age of 84 in 1418, we are expressly informed that he never wore artificial aids to his sight ; which is another way of saying that such appliances were then in ordinary use in Italy.

LITERARY NOTICE.

A New Invention ; Or A Paire of Cristall Spectacles, By helpe whereof may be read so small a print that what twenty sheetes of paper will hardly contain shall be discover'd in one. 4to, 1644.

With an engraving of a Multiplying glass or lens in the centre of which is an eye.

The Second Part of the Spectacles. 4to, 1644.

The Stationers.[1]

THE Fellowship of Text-Writers, which is traceable back to the middle of the fourteenth century, and which originally confined its duties to the preparation of deeds, indentures, and other legal documents, is believed to have gradually formed itself into two branches, which for some length of time continued under one government. Of these one adhered to its primary calling and province, while the other engaged in the writing, binding, and selling of books. The former acquired the

---

[1] We have to acknowledge ourselves much indebted, in drawing up the present account, to a pamphlet by Mr. C. R. Rivington, Clerk to the Company, entitled : *The Records of the Worshipful Company of Stationers*, 8vo, 1883, for facts and suggestions used in this account of one of the most interesting of the Gilds of London. Mr Rivington, at the same time, placed at our disposal several of the illustrations which accompany the text.

designation of *Scriveners*, the latter of *Stationers*. The Scrivener at the outset probably depended on the Stationer, who had better opportunities of procuring commissions, for his custom ; and the *prima stamina* of the present interesting Association may be referred to their employment of the Stations at the Crosses in Cheapside, whither they or their representatives resorted, during certain hours of the day, from their quarters thereabout.

These Stations soon became objects of commercial competition. So early as 1379 a lease of them was granted to eleven women, therein named, by the Mayor and Aldermen at a yearly rent of 13s. 4d., and one of those at the Broken Cross in St. Paul's Churchyard to seven others, of whom some paid 10s. and others 6s. 8d. a year. These were dealers in small wares.

It further appears that the Corporation gave the rents to their Common Huntsman, John Charney, during pleasure, to an amount not exceeding 10l. yearly.

The first clear manifestation of a branch of Text-Writers, who were not Scriveners in the usually accepted sense, is discovered in 1403, when the Corporation acceded to a certain Ordinance " of the Writers of Text-Letter, Limners, and others, who bind and sell books," whereby two Wardens were appointed to oversee *the said trades*, one representing the *Limners*, the other the *Text-Writers ;* whence we gather that the entire industry in all its departments was so far under the same control. From many indications, however, the Scriveners and Stationers must be held to have severed their constitutional alliance long before they became corporate bodies, and while, from the gradual multiplication of legal forms, the Scrivener grew at first the more flourishing and affluent craft, both in their turn acquired independent prominence and wealth.[1]

The term *Limner* itself may be thought to embrace, not elaborate pictorial design, but those ornamental embellishments which often accompany ancient records and documents in the shape of initial letters and floriated or other decorative borders.

Prior to its incorporation, the present Company had existed during upward of a century and a half as a Fraternity, whose functions and scope are involved in acknowledged obscurity. At what precise period the Stationers, like the Apothecaries' Society, developed into printers holding a common stock, or by what

OLD ARMS.

---

[1] Ultimately the Stationers gained and preserved an ascendency, because the most lucrative features in the Scriveners' earlier business—conveyancing and financing—passed away from them.

successive stages that process was accomplished from a rudimentary life, which limited itself to the sale of literary and other cognate wares at stations (in Cheapside and the vicinity) answering to the *columnæ* of the Romans, we are equally ill-informed. The miscellaneous objects which the primitive Stationer sold, were not much more perishable and fugitive than the popular productions which were issued at one or two pence, and cast away after persual. It is a comparatively recent discovery, that even at Oxford as early as 1520 ballads and other trifles were procurable at such marts as that of John Dorne, the inventory of whose stock survives.

We infer that the original usage, when the Stationer rose to a higher grade, was for each member of the Brotherhood to subscribe to the general fund, and for such work as was obtained to be apportioned among them, the profit being divisible in proportion, save as much as was deemed necessary to defray expenses of management and to support a common box.

But, even after the organization of the Company in 1556, the old system continued, and constituted a second collateral union, namely, the Partners in the Stock, which is now, and has long been, an exclusively English one.

" Formerly," observes Mr. Rivington in 1882, " there were several stocks—there was a Latin stock, an Irish stock, a ballad stock, and a Bible stock. About 1601 the Company obtained a grant from the Crown giving them the exclusive right of printing certain publications, and that was amalgamated with the English stock." In 1882, this had a capital of between 41,000*l.* and 42,000*l.*, which was held among 306 members of the Company.

" The capital," Mr. Rivington continues, " is divided into certain shares, which are held just in the same way as the shares of ordinary Companies, and the profits of the stock and property belonging to the stock are appropriated thus :—a certain amount is distributed among the poor of the Company (it used to be 100*l.* a year, but now [1882] it is 400*l.* a year), and after paying that the nett profit is divided . . . each half year. The members of the Company under the bye-laws have a power of disposing of the shares to their widows, but to no other persons."

The antiquity of the Stationers as a Gild or Brotherhood has been referred back to 1403 ; Wynkyn de Worde is supposed to have been a member at a later point in the same century ; and there is a tradition, that the custom of registering copies commenced some time prior to the incorporation in 1556.

But the Stationers do not present themselves in many of the official returns, which furnish in an indirect manner a clue to the progress and standing of these bodies at various and successive periods. Already, however, in 1469 they were sufficiently affluent to defray the cost of equipping two-and-twenty guards for the City gates. In 1501–2 they ranked as the fifty-third Company or Association, but are noted as having no Livery. In 1515, when the precedence is arranged by the City, they are not mentioned.

The motive for viewing favourably the petition for a charter in this case was the aim of the Government of Philip and Mary at the establishment of a restraining power or censorship over the liberty of the press, and the preamble of the grant[1] runs thus :—" Know ye, that we, considering and manifestly perceiving that certain seditious and heretical books, rhymes, and treatises are daily published and printed by divers scandalous, malicious, schismatical, and heretical persons, not only moving our subjects and lieges to sedition and disobedience against us, our Crown and liberty, but also to renew and move very great and detestable heresies against the faith and sound doctrine of Holy Mother Church, and wishing to provide a suitable remedy in this behalf——"
It was under these circumstances that the Gild was erected into a corporation under the title of The Master and Keepers, or Wardens and Commonalty of the Mistery or Art of a Stationer of the City of London. Thomas Dockwray was the first Master, and John Cawood, royal printer, and Henry Cooke the first Wardens.

As a matter of course, the power of search and seizure was a prominent feature in this concession, of which the cost to the grantees was somewhat over 20*l.*, an item of 9*s.* being incurred in consequence of the first draft submitted being rejected or altered.

On the 10th November, 1559, Queen Elizabeth confirmed the charter. It was temporarily held in abeyance by *Quo Warranto* in 1663 and 1684, but ultimately restored by the Act of 1690. The writ of 1663, however, was not so much a measure of hostility in the ordinary sense and direction, as the result of a belief that the Company was not sufficiently vigilant and strict in its capacity as a curb on the press, and connived at the publication of inflammatory or scurrilous literature.

The Ordinances date from the epoch of incorporation, but exist only at present in the form of printed pamphlets or books, of which there were issues in 1678, 1682, and 1741. There were various decrees of the Court of Star Chamber in support of the executive and penal jurisdiction of the Stationers ; and many Acts of Parliament, besides that of

---

[1] The original instrument was lost in the Fire of 1666 ; but the Company has a transcript.

2 William and Mary just-named, bear upon the matters, whereof they took cognizance.

Perhaps one of the earliest distinct glimpses of the resources of the newly-incorporated body is that due to a demand from the Lord Mayor in 1563 for a return of the Company's lands, plate, jewels, and stock of money, doubtless with a view to an assessment ; and the answer was, that they had nothing of the kind, only a house with effects for necessary use, when they met together.

The Stationers were harassed and injured, in common with other Associations, by the system of granting patents to persons who were not freemen for a valuable consideration paid to the Crown or to some one in power. About 1620 they found their existing privileges as regarded the sole right to print certain matters invaded and challenged by the monopoly created in favour of three individuals, of whom one was an alien. This syndicate did not actually print, but assigned the work to others at a price. From such evidence as is within reach, this particular abuse does not seem to have been of long duration.

During the first half of the seventeenth century, the position of the Company was well maintained in spite of all political disturbances and requisitions. In returns of 1602–3, 1603–4, and 1629, it manifested itself capable of subscribing liberally toward public objects, where the party assessed had no option but to pay. The Civil War, however, seems to have weakened the corporate resources, and in 1643 the stock of plate was sold to meet liabilities amounting to about 1,500*l.*

The administrative system is conformable with the charters. But the Renter Wardens used to be required, in addition to their normal functions, to discharge the office of stewards, and to become responsible for the cost of a dinner—an obligation which was often resisted. In the old days it was customary to crown the Master and Wardens with garlands in the same manner as the Grocers, Fishmongers, and Leather-sellers ; and each Master, on the expiration of his term of office, presented a piece of plate of the weight of 14 ozs. at least.

The fines for the Livery and Court are 70*l.* and 80*l.* respectively. Admission to the Freedom by patrimony costs 5*l.* ; by redemption, 30*l.* But all freemen must belong to the Mistery. In 1882, 445 freemen were on the books. In 1629 the Livery was returned as 226, in 1724–5 as 214, in 1882 as 312, and in 1892 as 282. The late Mr. W. H. Smith, M.P., was an honorary liveryman. About 100 apprentices are annually enrolled at the Hall. The choice of the Saturday after St. Peter's Day for elections may have arisen from the early association of the Gild with Peter College.

We have mentioned that in the municipal order of 1515, prescribing

A WATERMAN.

THE STATIONERS' BARGE.

the sequence of the Gilds, the Stationers are absent ; but in 1561 they were made the thirty-seventh in priority, and received a Livery for the first time, the colours being scarlet and brown-blue.

Unusual punctilio used to be observed in regard to the use of the livery on all Court days and other occasions of ceremony. In 1582 the Court of Common Council prohibited the embellishment of livery gowns in general with embroidery and lace ; in 1635, the Assistants and Livery having appeared in public at the Hall and elsewhere upon solemn anniversaries or meeting-days in falling bands, slashed doublets, and other indecent apparel not suitable to the habit of a citizen, the Assistants were ordered in future to attend in ruff bands, and the Livery were enjoined not to wear falling bands or other unseemly raiment, on pain of forfeiting 11*d*., either when they presented themselves at the Hall, or followed a brother to the grave. Nay, even so late as 1819, the Court of Aldermen prescribed, that livery gowns should be decently faced with fur.

The contention as to precedence was not limited to ordinary processions and the distribution of the guests at banquets. It extended to the stands erected in Cheapside and other thoroughfares to view or honour the passage of royal personages to and from the City, and even to the Companies' barges on the river. In 1738 the Court of Aldermen decided that the barge of the Company to which the Senior Sheriff belonged should precede that of the Company of the Junior one ; but in 1761 the Stationers were permitted to take the lead on the river by virtue of being the youngest possessor of a barge. They had had theirs since 1679 ; and it used to be considered the handsomest of the whole series.[1]

The income is derived from the following sources :—

1. Dividends on Government Annuities and Metropolitan Board of Works Consols.
2. Rents from freehold and leasehold property.
3. Gifts made to the Company under wills.
4. Quarterages, fines, and fees.
5. Voluntary contribution toward the expenses by the parners in the English stock.

In 1833 the receipts were officially given as 2,542*l*., and the expenditure as 1951*l*. In 1892 the revenue had increased to 4,700*l*., 1,600*l*. in trust inclusive. The advance therefore was inconsiderable, as the figures for the earlier year applied only to the corporate estate. About 1873 a house in Darkhouse Lane, Billingsgate, required for the enlargement of the market, was bought by the Corporation for 3,655*l*. ; it had been a bequest to the Stationers in 1575 by Jane Kevall, and

---

[1] It has long been sold, and is now the club boat on the Isis at Oxford. The cost of these vessels was very heavy. In 1663 the Coopers laid out 154*l*. 10*s*. on theirs.

STATIONERS' HALL IN 1670.

STATIONERS' HALL IN 1842.

Reginald Wolfe.

DEVICES AND MONOGRAMS OF EMINENT STATIONERS.

Hugh Singleton.

Richard Smith.

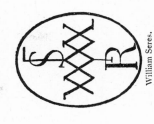

William Seres.

Christopher Barker.
(From Gascoigne's *Glasse of Government*,
1575.)

Richard Tottell.

DEVICES AND MONOGRAMS OF EMINENT STATIONERS.

Robert Wyer.

Richard Jones.

was subject to an annual payment of 5*l.* to the parish of St. Mary-at-Hill. In the funded property is included the purchase-money by the Skinners of the Stationers' sub-share in the Irish Plantation.

The Skinners, as one of the twelve Great Companies, had one of the shares of the Irish property allotted to them at the proportionate cost of 5,000*l.* But by way of lightening the burden, they allowed three of the Minor Companies, the Stationers, Bakers, and Girdlers, to take sub-shares from them again. The Stationers', portion appears to have cost about 800*l.* When it happened that a long life-interest ran out, a dispute arose as to the title to the fee, and the Skinners assumed that they were the freeholders of the whole estate ; but in this view they were successfully challenged, and eventually the Stationers, adroitly turning to their own account a very favourable report by certain members of the Skinners' Company, obtained a large sum to be quit of their venture.

The Company educates 180 boys at its school in Bolt Court, Fleet Street, the yearly fee on the foundation being 24*s.* It subscribes 125*l.* a year to Guy's Hospital, and distributes many charities of various amounts without any charge to the funds concerned. It also supports its own poor.

The present Hall appears to be the fifth seat of the Company since its rise into notice in the earlier half of the sixteenth century. The Stationers, at least, cannot be traced further back as a body in possession of a place of meeting than certain quarters in Clement Court, Milk Street, Cheapside, a spot convenient for their special purposes. Whether this was the original establishment, is extremely doubtful ; the site still belongs to the same owners, and produces a handsome rental as a warehouse. Hence, about 1550, the Fraternity removed to Peter College, at one time an institution connected with St. Paul's Cathedral, and at the Dissolution converted by William Seres into a printing-office. It stood at the south-west angle of the churchyard,[1] and adjoined the Dean's Yard. In 1582–3 the accounts include payments for repairs, among which is an item of 4*d.* for cleaning the Yard.

If the Stationers were as constant to their former Hall as to the one to which they thus succeeded, and which they probably adapted to their own wants, rather than rebuilt, their tenure of the premises in Milk Street might be thrown back to the middle of the preceding century. For it was only after an experience of nearly sixty years, that the Company decided on another change, and in 1606 let, not probably

---

[1] See Herbert's *Typographical Antiquities*, 1785, p. 687. The writer supposes that the exact position of Peter College was marked by that of *Paul's College*, used, when Strype's *Stow* was published in 1720, to accommodate the choristers attached to the cathedral.

the whole house, but the frontage to Mr. Edward Kynaston, a vintner, who converted it into the Feathers Tavern.[1] Five years later, Aberga-venny House and certain appurtenances, at that time comprising in its area the ground between Amen Corner and the Chapter House estate to the north, St. Martin's, Ludgate, to the south, the City wall to the west, and the garden of London House to the east, was acquired, with a portion of the Bishop's garden [2] now occupied by the east side of Ave Maria Lane.

Here thenceforward the Company made its home. We seem to have no means of acquainting ourselves with their transactions from 1611 to 1654, when the premises had fallen into such bad repair, that the Livery dinner on Lord Mayor's day was held elsewhere, and the interest or copyright of Foxe's *Book of Martyrs* [3] was sold toward the expense of re-construction. But in 1666 the Hall was reduced to a wreck, with the contents and even the common seal, the registers excepted ; [4] and the loss was not repaired till 1674, the meet-ings and business being temporarily transacted at the Cooks' Hall in Aldersgate Street or at St. Bartho-lomew's Hospital. The Company agreed with the celebrated Stephen College, the "Protestant Joiner," to wainscot the new Hall for 300*l*. "with well-seasoned and well-matched wain-scot, according to a model delivered in."

ORIGINAL COMMON SEAL,
LOST IN THE GREAT FIRE.

From 1667 to the present time the Hall has been occasionally let or lent to various public bodies for sundry purposes. The Surgeons' Com-pany were permitted to use it in 1745, provided that no dissecting oper-

---

[1] In 1671 the Company sold the property to Sir William Turner for 420*l*.

[2] This part of the purchase was afterward resold.

[3] "*The Book of Martyrs* was frequently reprinted, and was so highly appreciated that, when in 1631 it was out of print, some persons of quality, being desirous that it might be reprinted for the general good of the kingdom, threatened to print it themselves, if the Company did not immediately issue a fresh edition. A copy of the best paper, ruled, bound in Turkey leather gilt, with the King's arms stamped on it, was presented to His Most Excellent Majesty Charles the Second in 1660, as a token of the Company's duty and submission to his royal person and govern-ment."—*Rivington*.

[4] Mr. Rivington presumes that they were in the custody of the Clerk at his house on Clerkenwell Green.

ations were conducted there. It has been at intervals the scene of
concerts, lotteries, Freemasons' meetings, and complimentary dinners.

The long obsolete usage, by which each retiring Master gave the
Fellowship a piece of plate of fourteen ounces weight at the least, may
be taken to have been one dating at all events from the foundation of
the Company, as the collection is shown by the extant inventory to
have included a silver-gilt spoon presented by Thomas Dockwray, first
Master. It is not pleasant to have to add that all these treasures,
consisting of spoons (one dated September 11, 1560), salt-cellars,
bowls, and cups, were sold to meet financial exigencies in 1643, to Mr.
Nowell, a goldsmith, in Foster Lane, except Mr. Hulet's standing
cup.

Owing to the fortunate escape of the registers in 1666, the Company
possesses not only the entries of publications which have been printed
from 1557 down to 1640 by Professor Arber, but its account-books from
the commencement. The earliest of the series was presented by a
member of the Court ; and each side of the leather binding, which is well
preserved, is embellished with the figures of animals. The volume opens
with the receipts and disbursements of the Master and Wardens from
1554 to 1557. Thomas Berthelet, the eminent printer, was Master in
the former year, but died within the twelvemonth ; and his wife Margery
gave the Company 13*s.* 4*d.*, "for a rewarde for comynge to the sayde
Barthelet his buryall."

Not the least curious feature in the Court Records is the account of
suppressed works, and of incidents connected with the trade. In 1595
various little French books and other printed matter were burned by
order of the Primate. In 1602 Stow was awarded 3*l.* and forty copies
for his pains in the *Survey of London*,[1] and 20*s.* and fifty copies for his
pains in the *Brief Chronicle*. Under 1614 his Grace of Canterbury
directs the suppression of Raleigh's *History of the World*. The same
fate befalls Lithgow's *Travels* in 1616. In 1634 Prynne's *Histriomastix*
is erased from the books. In 1646 *The Women's Parliament*[2] is suppressed, "being very lewdly written, and tending to corrupt youth."
The original MS. and whole impression of Buchanan's *History of Scotland* are seized.

An enumeration of the more distinguished members of the Gild almost amounts to a rehearsal of the already familiar names of our cele-

---

[1] Compare *Merchant Taylors' Company*, suprâ, p. 271.
[2] If this refers to the Ladies' Parliament by Henry Nevile [1647], the proceeding
was not unwarranted, as the tract is extremely coarse. A copy is among the King's
Pamphlets in the British Museum. But the piece entitled *The Parliament of Women*,
1640, 1646, 1656, etc., is not specially exceptionable.

brated printers and publishers from the closing years of the fifteenth century. It is highly probable, though there appears to be no distinct evidence of the fact, that both Richard Pynson and Wynkyn de Worde were among the associates of the unincorporated Fellowship. But we know that Thomas Berthelet, Reginald Wolfe (four times Master), John Cawood, Richard Jugge, Richard Tottell, and other equally famous men belonged to the Company ; and at a later date the roll of worthies embraced the Harrisons, the Days, the Nortons, the Barkers, the Rivingtons, the Nicholses, and many more. It was John Norton who left 1,000*l.* in 1612, to be lent to poor young men of the Company, which amount was invested in houses in Wood Street, and now forms part of the endowment of the Stationers' School. We must not overlook Richard Field, son of Henry Field, of Stratford-upon-Avon, tanner, Shakespear's fellow-townsman, and the publisher of his youthful productions. Field married

MARK OF RICHARD TOTTELL.

MARK OF JOHN DAY (1548-71).

the daughter of Thomas Vautrollier, and the poet is supposed to have profited by some of the classical or historical books which proceeded from both presses. Several of these presented during their masterships pieces of plate or sums of money for charitable and general purposes. Sir Thomas Davies, Master in 1668-9, became Lord Mayor in 1677, and on his translation to the Drapers gave his old associates two silver cups. His copy of Stow's *Survey of London*, 1633, contains an extra leaf with his arms emblazoned in their proper colours, and is in the possession of the writer. Thomas Parkhurst, Master in 1703, by a gift of 37*l.* to purchase twenty-five Bibles and Psalms for annual distribution, founded the custom of making a donation of a copy of the Scriptures to each apprentice bound at the Hall.

The catalogue might be greatly extended ; but we must content ourselves with mentioning Samuel Richardson the novelist, Master in 1754 and Jacob Tonson, great nephew of Dryden's Tonson, and High Sheriff of Surrey in 1750, and Henry Sampson Woodfall, printer of the *Letters of Junius*. The last was Master in 1797.

Besides Sir Thomas Davies, Mayor in 1677, the chief magistracy has been held by other Stationers, in the persons of Sir Stephen Theodore Jansen (1749-50), Thomas Wright (1777), William Gill (1780), John Boydell (1783), William Domville (1803), Christopher Magnay (1816), William Venables (1824), John Crowder (1829), John Key (1830), William

TITLE-PAGE OF LYDGATE'S *Vertue of the Masse.*
Printed by Wynkyn de Worde.

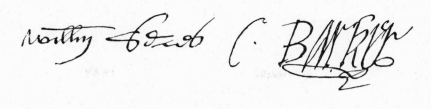

AUTOGRAPHS OF EMINENT STATIONERS OF THE 16TH CENTURY.

Magnay (1847), Francis Graham Moon (1855), Sydney Hedley Waterlow (1872), and Francis Wyatt Truscott (1879).

Several who did not attain the Mayoralty were members of the Court
of Aldermen, and served as Sheriff. Since 1800 three generations of
Rivington have held the Clerkship, which involves not merely the ordinary business of the Company, but that arising from the English Stock.[1]

LITERARY NOTICES.

The Orders, Rules, and Ordinances, Ordained, Devised, and made by the Master
and Keepers or Wardens and Comminalty of the Mystery or Art of Stationers of
the City of London, for the well Governing of that Society. 4to, 1678, 1682.

Charters and Grants of the Company of Stationers of the City of London ; containing an Account of the Freemen's Rights and Privileges ; with an Appendix. 8vo,
1741.

A Proclamation of the Queen against the printing of books, ballads, rhymes, and
interludes. 18 August, 1553. A broadside. Rivington's *Stationers' Records*, p. 3.

A Proclamation of the King and the Queen against Diuers Books. Given at Our
Manor of Saint James, the sixth day of June, 1558.

Ordinances decreed for reformation of diuers disorders in printing and vttering of
Bookes. 29 June, 1566. A broadside.

        ⁎ This is a reprint, perhaps about 1620, of the original sheet.

A Patent to Raffe Bowes and Thomas Beddingfield to import Playing Cards into this
Kingdom for twelve years, and dispose of them in large or small quantities, any
Act formerly made notwithstanding. 13 June, 13 Elizabeth [1571].

The Whole Rate of mouldes belonging to the olde forume [? font or form] of
plaienge cardes, commonlie called the Frenche Carde, by warrant from Mr. Warden
Coldocke. Entered with the Jew Cisian [? douze sixième] dozen and all other things
thereunto belonginge. Entered at Stationers' Hall, to Ralph Bowes, Esquire, Oct.
28, 1588.

The Case of the Booksellers Trading beyond the Sea. A broadside. [James I.]

A Generall Note of the prises for binding all sorts of bookes, 1619. A broadside.

The same. . . . 1646. A broadside.

An Abstract of his Maiesties Letters Patent granted unto Roger Wood and Thomas
Symcocke, for the sole printing of paper and parchment on the one side. 4to,
1620.

To the Most Honourable Assembly of the Commons House of Parliament. The
Binders of Bookes in London doe most humblie shew complaining of the Com-
pany of Goldbeaters, and of their monopoly of the importation and sale of
Gold Foliat. [1621.] A broadside.

To the Right Reverend and Right Honourable the Lords Spiritual and Temporal,
assembled in Parliament, An abstract of the general grievances of the poore Freemen and Journeymen Printers, oppressed and kept in seruile bondage all their
lives by the Vnlawfull Ordinances of the Master and Wardens of the Company,
which they fortifie only by a Warrant dormant. A broadside. [About 1630.]

---

[1] The background in Hogarth's print of the *Industrious Apprentice*, represents
the members of the Stationers' Company marching down Paternoster Row, on their
return from the Lord Mayor's Show.

A Proclamation to inhibit the sale of Latine Bookes reprinted beyond the Seas, hauing been first printed at Oxford or Cambridge. 1625. A broadside.

A Decree of the Star-Chamber, concerning Printing. 11 July, 1637. A broadside.

The **Humble Petition** of the Stationers, Printers, and Booksellers of the Citie of London, on the introduction of a Bill for reducing the Printers to a certain number, and for the avoiding of unskilfull printers. 1641. A broadside.

S.intilla, Or, A Light Broken into darke Warehouses. With Observations upon the Monopolists of Seaven severall Patents, and Two Charters. Practised and performed by a Mistery of some Printers, Sleeping Stationers and Combining Booksellers. [By Michael Sparke.] 4to, 1641.

T**ɔ the Honourable House of Commons** in this present Parliament assembled. The humble Petition of the Company of Stationers of the City of London. [January, 1643.] A broadside.

To all **Printers,** Booke-sellers, Booke-binders, Freemen of the Company of Stationers. 13 June, 1645. A broadside.

*** It may be remarked that there are numerous other publications relative to the press and to printers, but not sufficiently relevant to the Stationers' Company to necessitate or warrant their insertion here.

The Tallow Chandlers.

WE do not receive any intelligence of this body before 1426, when it was associated under the style of The Master and Wardens of the Mistery or Craft of Tallow Chandlers, in letters patent of Henry VI. for the search and destruction of all bad or adulterated oils.

Here we consequently meet with another instance, where, in the absence of any licence or charter, a commercial Fellowship established itself with a regular organization, and was evidently recognised as such. The acknowledged standing of the Tallow Chandlers is still further confirmed by a grant of arms[1] from John Smert, Garter King of Arms, in 1456 to John Priour, John Thurlow, William Blackman, and Richard Grenecroft, Guardians, and several other notable men of the trade, and

---

[1] Supporters were added in 1602, upon an application to William Camden, Clarencieux King of Arms.

of the Company of Tallow Chandlers, or *Chandeliers de Suif* of the City of London, on behalf of and in the name of their whole confraternity, one of the members of the City of London, having sworn Wardens or keepers, and other officers authorized to make, constitute, and put in force among themselves rules and good ordinances for the separate conduct of their own trade.

OLD ARMS.

The Tallow Chandlers, having thus already clothed themselves with many of the attributes of a corporation, thought fit, for the better security of the vocation which they followed, and for the more ample and complete exercise and enjoyment of their powers and position, to proceed in 1462, 2 Edward IV., to the crowning step of procuring a charter from the King. The instrument is dated March 8, and is directed "To our beloved and faithful subjects, the Freemen of the Mistery or Art of Talough Chaundelers of our City of London." It confirms, rather than confers, certain rights and privileges in relation to the choice of officers, the power of holding realty, a common seal, the title to sue and be sued in courts, a licence in mortmain to ten marks a year,[1] and the liberty of search and correction.

Of all these matters the grant was a recognition ; as the Gild had manifestly assumed authority and jurisdiction to the full extent of the royal concession, save the licence in mortmain and the common seal. There is no mention of a Livery even in 1462, yet this, again, existed at that time almost beyond doubt ; and in 1501-2 is returned as thirty-six. It was possibly considered as falling under the general sanction of established forms and practices. In 1469, within a very short space after the incorporation, the Company was able to supply to the City Watch the large quota of sixty men, and in 1515 it was officially ranked as twenty-first in order.[2]

The charter was renewed by succeeding sovereigns (November 15, 1517, 8 Henry VIII. ; February 18, 1549, 2 Edward VI. ; June 7, 1557, 4 and 5 Philip and Mary; March 3, 1561, 3 Elizabeth; and March 6, 1606, 3 James I.). Letters patent of James I. March 6, 1620, confirmed the Tallow Chandlers in all their lands and hereditaments theretofore

---

[1] This was enlarged in 1831, 1856, and 1865, to enable the Gild to hold more recent accessions of property in trust, including that accruing under the will of Mr. Roger Monk in 1831.

[2] In the grant by Camden of supporters to the Arms in 1602, it is laid down "that the Company are to take their place after their ancientry at all feasts and other solemn processions as the *seventeenth* Company of the City, which he found, according to the date of their patent, to be anciently recorded."

acquired, and finally settled all controversy as to the possessions in Dowgate Ward, the Hall doubtless included.[1]

The power of search, which was successively fixed at two and three miles' compass from the City, formed the subject-matter of two or three public acts, beginning with an indenture of 1559, in which existing letters patent of Elizabeth are cited. The latter are no longer known ; but they probably corresponded with others of April 15, 1577, where the Company is empowered to search for, weigh, and measure all soap, vinegar, barrelled butter, salt, oils, and hops within the City and suburbs, and mark all good vessels with the Rose and Crown Imperial. By Act of Parliament the Wardens were further entitled to seize and destroy all adulterated and spurious oils ; but the legislation is said to have proved inoperative, because no reward was offered on conviction to the informers. From the Drapers' accounts of 1516 it is inferable that the Tallow Chandler of those days, in addition to his own special wares, dealt in a multifarious assortment of domestic necessaries, such as mustard, red and white vinegar, verjuice, oatmeal, fine salt, packthread, lathes, gally-pots and pans, and brooms. We here recognise the parentage of the modern chandler's shop and its almost inexhaustible resources.

During the former half of the seventeenth century, the Company appears to have maintained an excellent ground among the bodies of secondary rank. It joined the Drapers as a sub-sharer in the Ulster project, and so far occupied the exceptional position of being not merely the only coparcener, but of offering the sole instance in which one of the great Companies associated itself thus exclusively with one of the minor.

In 1629, to a municipal assessment the Tallow Chandlers exhibited a gauge of their comparative prosperity by a contribution of 12l. 18s. It is more difficult to divine the source of the commercial intimacy between the present Fraternity and the Drapers than that between its members or Executive and the Salters, where salt is continually specified as one of the articles over which the Tallow Chandlers exercised control, and in which they dealt ; and, in fact, the most ancient ordinances of the latter, while they still remained unincorporated, were drawn up in conjunction with the other Gild, being described as " Ordinances of the Salters and Tallow Chandlers."[2] The two Societies were evidently at one epoch in rather close relations ; and we shall see that their head-quarters and Halls were adjacent.

---

[1] Not, we apprehend, the property held to superstitious uses, within the meaning of the Act of Edward VI., for such there is no trace, the trust-estate being of purely modern origin.

[2] Compare p. 295, *suprâ*. These ordinances were most probably the reduction to form of a compact between the two Fellowships.

Beyond the Ordinances above-mentioned, the Tallow Chandlers possess one set of bye-laws, framed and approved in 1639, and extending to no fewer than sixty-six articles. They deal with points of internal government, as elections, which are appointed to be held on the day of the feast of St. John the Baptist, or within twenty days thereof, the Master, in cases of an equality of votes, having a casting voice or prick on the paper: fines, Livery, oaths, election-dinners: the duties and powers of the two Wardens of the Yeomanry, who were to provide at their own cost four quarter-suppers in the common Hall: the choice of Whifflers, or associates from among the junior members, to attend and wait upon the rest: the appointment of a Beadle: the provision of a common chest: the conditions under which search could be conducted and the payment of search-money by persons' of other Companies, who pursued the trade of a maker or seller of candles: and the ordinary stipulations as to apprenticeship.

The Yeomanry clearly constituted a very important and influential element, and possessed their own parlour with two locks and keys kept by their Wardens, and an independent store of plate, pewter, linen, and other effects, which, by one of the clauses, were to be surrendered in the contingency of the dissolution or suspension of the separate Executive at any time.

The voluminous character of the bye-laws of 1639 may be construed into an evidence of the substantial standing of the body, whose members they affected and governed; and probably we have now reached the period when the Company was at the zenith of its power. The Civil War and the Great Fire combined to weaken it; and perhaps the more general employment of wax for candles formed an additional cause of decline. The charter of 28 Charles II., July 29, 1677, expressly dwells on the increase of buildings in London and on the number of hands engaged in the candle manufacture, but at the same time speaks of the diminution of the Company. It recognised and allowed all its rights and privileges, and made it obligatory on all members of the trade within a three miles' radius to take up the Freedom.

This, with the exception of the general *Quo Warranto* episode and its normal consequences, concludes the transactions with the Crown. The right of search has not been put in force since 1709, and it has become optional on the part of freemen to come upon the Livery.

The government consists of the Master, Deputy Master, four Wardens, and fifteen Assistants; but the number of the Court is not defined by the charters and bye-laws. In 1699 the Livery was returned as 113, in 1724 as 178, in 1882 as about 120, and in 1892 as 102. The Livery fine, which in 1639 was 3*l.* 6*s.* 8*d.,* is at present 27*l.* 5*s.* 0*d.,* and that for the Court 200*l.*

The trust income is about 220*l.* a year ; but of the corporate receipts there are no particulars. They are probably not much larger than they were in 1882. But they enable the Company to pay about 400*l.* in salaries, besides taxes and other incidental outlays ; and while in 1620 it was thought desirable to quiet the title to certain London properties —probably the Hall and other messuages destroyed in the Fire—by incurring the charges attendant on special letters patent for that purpose, the new licences in mortmain obtained in 1856 and 1865 appear to have been connected with fresh corporate acquisitions.

The Tallow Chandlers gave 315*l.* by three instalments to the City and Gilds' Institute.

Tallow Chandlers' Hall on Dowgate Hill, to which there is repeated reference in the bye-laws of 1639, but of the antecedents and origin of which we learn next to nothing, was destroyed in the Fire with the other freeholds named in the Patent of 1620, rebuilt in 1672, and thoroughly restored on the 17th-century model in 1871. A portion of the ancient quadrangle has been let for building, and doubtless constitutes, with a few rents and the fines and fees, the actual private revenue.

There is no room to question that this neighbourhood was the seat of the industry from very remote times, and that Candlewick Street [1] derived its name from this source, as Scaldingwike in the Poultry did from an analogous circumstance. The Hall was at once situated in convenient proximity to the works where the manufacture was carried on and to the water-way, which equally brought the raw material, and helped to distribute the produce.

---

[1] Stow (edit., 1633) says that in old records he had seen it spelled *Candlewright* Street, and adds that it was the place where candles, both of wax and tallow, were made. Yet the two productions seem to have been always kept distinct.

The Tin-plate Workers.

EVIDENCES of the great antiquity of this craft and art, which were known to the Romans, and possibly introduced by them to us, have been found in excavations of Anglo-Saxon remains, belonging to the sixth, seventh, and eighth centuries. The material was employed for a variety of purposes, including the metallic fittings of wooden utensils and implements of war or appliances for the protection of the person, as for example in the bosses of shields, as well as for the coating of coins and other small objects.

The Tin-plate Workers are supposed to have originally been an offshoot from the Girdlers, when the centralizing movement, which had at first operated so powerfully in combining branches of the same trade in one body and government, experienced a reaction, and a series of minor industries, such as this before us and several others, subdivided themselves into independent unions and Companies.

But the first intimation of the present Fraternity occurs in the reign of Edward IV., where, under the appellation of *Wire Workers*, it associated itself with the Pinners, and kept its accounts in the same books or ledgers. In 1569 this bipartite body took advantage of the incorporation of the Girdlers to seek shelter beneath their charter.

OLD ARMS.

There is considerable difficulty in ascertaining whether or how far the Tin-plate Workers are to be regarded as the representatives of the *Wire Sellers* and *Wire Drawers*, as well as of the Wire Workers. At various periods we find mention of communities bearing these several names ; and it is not easy to avoid surmising that the allusions are to one and the same industry. In 1469, for instance, the Wire Drawers are said to furnish two men to the City Watch; while in 1501–2 a municipal return gives the Wire Sellers a prescriptive Livery of twelve.

Again, although the Wire Workers and Pinners were so intimately connected in the fifteenth century, and apparently employed one place of business, they never present themselves together in returns or otherwise; nor were the former, on the amalgamation with the Girdlers, 10 Elizabeth, specified in the charter by name. Later in the same reign, the Pinners were evidently independent, and then or soon after owned their own Hall; and in 1636 they secured a separate charter. But of the Wire Workers we gain no tidings, until in 1670, 22 Charles II., it is on record that they, too, were incorporated, and in 1678 possessed bye-laws.

The affairs are managed by a Master, two Wardens, and eight Assistants. The trust income consists of the interest on 1,145*l*., derived under the wills of Mr. John Miers and Mr. John White; the proceeds of the former bequest, which are applied in pensions, are augmented by grants out of the Company's own funds from quarter to quarter; and with the latter (1,000*l*.) it has been proposed to erect almshouses. Of the corporate estate no particulars are forthcoming. A fine of 31*l*. 10*s*. is payable by each liveryman on his election to the Court; but no charges are made, as in other cases, on promotion to the higher offices. In 1882 the Livery was returned as about 77, in 1892, as 71.

The Company has organized two Exhibitions of Tin and Wire Work at its own expense since 1878.

The Turners.

THE few scattered notices relative to this Company almost exclusively belong to the epoch anterior to incorporation.

In 1310 several Turners at different addresses in the City were sworn to make no other measures than gallons, pottles, and quarts, and no false measures, as chopyns and gills, either in the form of boxes or otherwise. It may be worth while to add that these persons were Henry the Turner, dwelling in Wood Street; Richard the Turner, John the Turner in St. Swithin's Lane, Candlewick Street; William the Turner, without the Gate of Bishopsgate, and Richard le Corveiser, dwelling in Wood Street. They were perhaps the leading or even only members of the calling in London at that date, and with one exception they derived their surname from their business.

OLD CREST OR
COGNIZANCE.

In 1347, it was found requisite to place some further restrictions on the Turners of London in regard to the material of which they made their liquid measures, which were often of unseasoned wood, and also to regulate the marks upon them, which were to be placed on the bottom of each vessel outside. The measures were at the same time to agree with the standard of the Ward, in which it was proposed to sell and use them.

Some false utensils of this kind were burned in Cheapside in 1370 near the Stone Cross.

An order of the Court of Aldermen, prescribing the prices to be paid to various persons or trades for supplies to be presented to the King in 1418 in aid of the operations against Rouen, mentions 2,500 wooden cups or mugs, for which the Turners were to receive 4s. per hundred, or 100s. altogether. They were for the use of the troops forming the siege.

These drinking-vessels of wood, turned on the lathe, also entered into the regular stock of the early innholder, and before they were more generally made of silver, passed through the intermediate stage of being simply bound or mounted with that metal. The call for such articles on the part of the retailers of wine and beer, as well as presumably for military and other public purposes, cannot have failed to constitute a very valuable element in the turners' business, before pewter and earthenware were brought into general use.

The first and only known charter of the Company was granted June 12, 1604, and conferred a licence in mortmain to the value of 20l. a year beyond all charges and reprises, which has never been exercised ; the right of search in London and within five miles radius, which has long fallen into disuse, since the City divested the Turners of the power of marking vessels ; and other usual privileges.

No bye-laws appear to have been drawn up till 1823.

The Executive is composed of a Master, an Upper and Renter Warden, and twenty-four Assistants. The Livery is unlimited. In 1699, it stood at 112 ; in 1724, at 127 ; in 1882, at 239 ; and in 1892, at 193.

There is no trust property, and the corporate estate, which was returned in 1882 as 718l., and in 1892 as 700l., arises from fees, fines, and interest on 1,787l. Scinde Railway Stock, the last-named source being probably the product of the sale of the Hall, which formerly existed on College Hill. There is source for the apprehension that the financial position of the Company will not improve.

Since 1870 there have been annual Exhibitions of Turners' Work at the Mansion House, the outlay involved in the first year being entirely defrayed by Mr. Secondary Potter, then Master, and since that time by voluntary subscriptions from Lady Burdett Coutts, Mr. Samuel Morley, M.P., and many others.

The prizes awarded, and usually distributed by the Lord Mayor, are for the best specimens of work under the following categories :—

1. Beauty of design, symmetry of shape, and utility and general excellence of workmanship.

2. Exact copying, so that two objects produced (such as two cups, vases, boxes, or other articles) may be facsimiles in every part, as well as in measure of capacity.

3. Fitness of the work and design for the purpose proposed, as, for instance, turned work for portions of domestic or church furniture.

4. Ability to turn, whether circular or oval, both in hard and soft wood.

5. Novelty in application or in design.

⁎ Carving and polishing are admissible, and, if skilfully done, any additional effect produced will be considered ; but it must be subsidiary to the turning.

The Tylers and Bricklayers.

THE substitution of tiles for thatch in City houses necessarily tended to develope the Tylers' industry. After the Fire of 1212, the roofs of reed or rush, which were then general, were declared unlawful, and were to be replaced with tiles and other material. But of course the system was not altered either with promptitude or with uniformity. In 1245, a further order was published by the Mayor, that all houses in the principal thoroughfares should be covered in future with slates or tiles. In 1302, we find Thomas Bat indemnifying the City from peril in respect of his property in St. Laurence Parish, Cannon Street, and agreeing to tile the roofs of the premises by the ensuing Pentecost.

The early English bricklayer, who belonged to the Gild of Tylers and Bricklayers, was not an operative, but an employer of operatives, often on a very large scale. He was the contractor for the entire brickwork of a structure, as we see in the negotiations and estimates for rebuilding or restoring some of the Halls after the Fire. For instance, it is easy to see in the account of the arrangements for making good the portions of Goldsmiths' Hall in 1666, that Mr. Burridge the bricklayer plays a prominent and responsible part, and had all that share of the contract to carry out under the supervision of Jarman the architect. Luck the bricklayer and Bell the carpenter seem to have similarly treated for the principal portion of the work of restoration at Painter-Stainers' Hall after the Fire, when the designs had been approved.

Doubtless, the colleague of Jack Straw in the rebellion or riot in 1381, consequent on the enforcement of a poll-tax, was a member of this Brotherhood at a period prior to its incorporation with the Bricklayers in 1568. He was not a peasant or a labourer, but a master-tyler ; and much in the same way Stow and Speed the historians were rather members of the Merchant-Taylors' Gild than tailors in our modern conventional sense.

It is usually represented by the biographers of Benjamin Jonson that his stepfather was a working bricklayer, and obliged the future poet to follow the trade for a brief time. But, from all the known associations of Jonson, this statement and notion seem to be eminently improbable ; and the far more likely case is, that the mother's second husband was a member of the Company, and that the poet became free by patrimony. It may have been through this channel that Jonson became acquainted with Inigo Jones, who, as a professional architect, might have come into contact with the elder Jonson in the ordinary way of business, as he would take the entire contract for brickwork in new buildings. The Tylers and Bricklayers were in fact specially excluded from the provisions of the scheme prepared in 1636 for establishing a Gild of Retailers of London and Suburbs. The followers of these vocations were, in fact, regarded as contractors rather than shopkeepers.

OLD ARMS.

We have to traverse centuries without meeting more than the most occasional and fortuitous information respecting the body whose name stands at the head of the present article. In 1501–2, an official list assigns it a customary Livery of 22, and in 1515 it is ranked as the 38th Company, though unincorporated. Again, at the Mayor's Feast in 1551–2 it was represented by one member, besides the Wardens, and was allotted a single mess.

These statistics establish the possession during the fifteenth and first moiety of the following century of substantial rank and resources ; yet, like many other Associations, the Tylers and Bricklayers do not seem to have been anxious to consolidate themselves to any further extent by the agency of a charter ; and when at last, in 1568, they obtained one, it conferred, so far as we can judge, very little beyond existing prescriptive rights and executive powers.

It was succeeded by the publication of Ordinances in 1570 and in 1571, curiously enough, by a second charter from Elizabeth, authorizing the search for defective bricks, tiles, and other cognate material, the appointment of a Beadle and a Clerk, the administration of oaths, regulations for apprentices, and other points. Both here and in the antecedent grant the customary title to frame and impose rules for the government of the Fraternity is said to have been vested in the Wardens or *Custodes* time out of mind. The charters of 1568 and 1571, with a third of James I., dated from Gorhambury, April 20, 1604, constitute the entire recognised series, as that of James II. was involved in the common operation of the Act of 1690. The grant of 1604 specifies a common seal, a licence in mortmain, the faculty of suing and being sued, the election of officers (a Master and two Wardens), the levy of fines, and the correction of bad work in London and over a radius of fifteen miles.

Besides the bye-laws of 1570-86, which have been lately printed, it is augurable from a printed document of 1614, cited below, that others were framed on the lines of the charter of 1604 ; and the Company was affected by an order of the Court of Common Council, July 1, 1658, and a royal one of January 25, 1723.

The government, following the acting charter of 1604, consists of a Master, an Upper Warden, a Renter Warden, and twenty Assistants. The Renter is elected from the Livery, the others from the Court.

We have noticed that in 1302 there was a prescriptive Livery of 22. In 1699 the numbers were officially returned as 73 ; in 1724, as 99 ; in 1882, as 78 ; and in 1892, as 73. In 1882 there were about 90 on the Freedom.

In 1834 the income was stated to be about 600*l.* a year ; and at that time the Company included many members of the trade. In 1882 and 1892 the receipts amounted to about 670*l.*, not reckoning 170*l.* trust estate. During the ten years 1870-79 there does not seem to have been much fluctuation ; but it was anticipated in 1882, that when certain leases of the property in the City and suburbs fell in, the figures would improve ; and the good intentions of the Executive may, under such circumstances, be more fully exercised in the direction of educational grants. An important factor in the returns is the house No. 22, Throgmorton Street, of which the term will expire about 1895, and which was let in 1881 at 125*l.* reserved rent, and 2,200*l.* fine.

One item in the yearly revenue is a sum of about 4*l.*, derived from a sub-share in the Vintners' Irish manor. The payment represents little more than four per cent. on the outlay of 80*l.* in 1615, and must therefore be said to have been a rather poor investment, looking at the returns of the Salters and Skinners. The character of the contribution, at the same time, imports at that juncture comparative prosperity, and in 1629 the quota found for the civic arrangements for celebrating the coronation of Charles I.—4*l.* 6*s.*—argues a fair medium standing.

Comprised in the Leadenhall estate is the former Hall of the Company, now occupied by the City of London College. The building lay at the western extremity of Aldgate ward, not far from Fletchers' and Ironmongers' Halls. It is mentioned by Stow and Maitland ; but of its early history nothing is recorded. It escaped the fire in 1666, and the

Coopers met here for some time, while their own seat of business was unavailable.

The property at Wapping is believed to have been received from some member of the Gild connected with Chipping Norton, to the church-wardens of which place 4*l.* a year are payable in respect of that portion taken by the St. Katharine's Docks Company and now represented by 799*l.* 12*s.* Consols.

Finally, the Tylers and Bricklayers hold in trust certain houses at Islington, where their Almshouses are situated, and a rent-charge at Whitechapel, acquired under the will of Francis Field in 1669. The rents are applied to the support of poor freemen and their widows, and are occasionally supplemented by votes from the corporate funds.

The date of the grant of arms and supporters is not known to us. The bearings are given by Wallis in *London's Armoury*, 1677, as those of the Bricklayers alone.

LITERARY NOTICES.

The Petition of the Tylers and Bricklayers of London, praying that it may be enacted that the Assize of Bricke and Tyle and the measure of Lyme and Sand, may be observed in London and in all places within fifteene miles compasse thereof, according to the Ordinances established by the Master and Wardens of the Company of Tylers and Bricklayers of London. [1614.] A broadside.

The Idol of the Clowns; or, the Insurrection of Wat the Tyler. By Francis White, of Gray's Inn. 12mo, 1654.

** In Harl. MS. 6466 occur the statutes of the Tylers of Coventry, made in the 14th century.

The Upholders or Upholsters.[1]

ARMS (FROM STOW, 1633).

ARMS, 1739.

THE Upholders were originally dealers in second-hand clothes, and were otherwise called Fripperers. They are particularly noticed as having occupied the shops in and about Cornhill, when these were vacated, toward the close of the fourteenth century, by the Drapers.

---

[1] Stow (*Survey*, 1633) adopts the latter form of the name.

An official document of 1532 denominates them the *Clothing Up-holders*.

But it would seem from the ancient and intimate relationship between the Upholders and the Skinners, that the former applied themselves at the beginning, at least, more particularly to some branch of the trade in peltry, perhaps to the purchase and resale of second-hand skins and furs.

It is obvious from an inventory, which exists among the City Records, of the stock of Stephen le Northerne in 1356, that he was not an iron-monger, as Riley names him, but a store-dealer, since the contents indicate a commerce in cushions, portable cupboards, curtains, weighing machines, wooden bedsteads and testers, feather beds, sheets, carpets, chequer-boards, doublets (paltoks), armour, planks, combs, shoe-horns, jordans, and other miscellaneous utensils or commodities. On the other hand, there is a large assortment of ironmongery for domestic, industrial, and farming or gardening purposes : trivets, sledge-hammers, puncheons, augers, pitchforks, ship-hinges, latches and bolts, goldsmiths' anvils, andirons, hatchets, pickaxes, and a variety of such items, some under archaic designations, which are not readily identifiable ; one of the articles is said to be "worn out." This was our modern broker's shop. It was situated in the parish of St. Michael, Cornhill, where at one period the upholders or fripperers, as Stow tells us, concentrated themselves.

The trade had begun to settle in Cornhill before the time of Lydgate probably, as in his *London Lickpenny*, written about 1425, he refers to the loss of his hood in the crowd at Westminster and its exposure for sale shortly after at a dealer's in the more easterly quarter. He in fact charges the mistery with being habitual receivers of stolen goods.

Riley appears to consider that the original upholder was also an undertaker ; and it may be that, from being at first a fripperer, as Stow terms him, or dealer in second-hand clothes and other goods, he in some cases rose to the dignity of a furniture-warehouseman, who still combines with that business the function of attendance upon funerals. The furniture-dealer suffered a further evolution, and became a cabinet-maker, or at least a cabinet-maker's salesman.

The members of this fraternity, by a natural drift toward the exten-sion of a not very definite class of commerce, gradually became pawn-brokers, costumiers, and wardrobe-men. They purchased cast-off clothing, took goods in pledge,[1] as the Goldsmiths did on a different

---

[1] Cases are recorded of the officers of one or two of the minor Gilds, under pecuniary stress or otherwise, hypothecating the corporate effects.

scale, and lent apparel on hire. The Companies which were deficient in Livery-gowns, procured them here, and the Wardens occasionally sold, in satisfaction of quarterages, the gowns of defaulting members at these rather incongruous and not too inquisitive establishments.

Yet, whatever may have been the incidence of their vocation, the present body undoubtedly rose at an early date to high consideration, and acquired a substantial standing among the minor Gilds of the City. In 1465 they obtained a grant of arms. Four years later, they contributed to the City Watch four-and-twenty guards; and in 1479, Sir Bartholomew James, son of Edward James, Citizen and Upholder was Lord Mayor.

There had evidently been a lapse of more than a century and a half, during which the Upholder steadily maintained his ground as a merchant and as the component part of a Fellowship, when from an entry in the Skinners' books (February–March, 1605–6), it appears that in 4 Henry VII. an indenture tripartite was made between the Master and Wardens of the Skinners of the first part, the Upholders of the second part, and the Chamberlain of London of the third part, whereby the Upholders were admitted into the Skinners' Fraternity. This was a compact on the lines of the old commercial alliance between the two Associations as touching a certain branch of the peltry industry; and although we have not seen the text of the treaty or agreement, it was doubtless either temporary or special, and did not extinguish the independent existence of the less ancient community; for in 1502 the Upholders appear in one of the municipal lists as fifty-second in order, but without a Livery. They had been amalgamated with the Skinners merely for specific purposes—perhaps for municipal protection and convenience.

But when we reach the second year of Charles I., and find the Upholders at length in possession of a charter, it is somewhat remarkable that by some of its terms a right of supervision is granted over work executed by the Craft, whence it may or must be deduced that in 1626 the new Company counted among its constituency some, at least, who were manufacturers—possibly of furniture and coffins. At this date the position and resources are indicated by the subscription of the rather moderate sum of 2*l*. 7*s*. 3½*d*. toward the outlay incurred by the City in connection with the coronation of Charles I. in 1629.

The governing body is composed of a Master, Wardens, and Court of Assistants. The Court calls up members from the Livery, which is unlimited, at its discretion.

In 1699 the Livery was returned at 121, in 1724 at 144, in 1739 at 131, in 1882 at 38, and in 1892 at 33. In 1739 the fine was 4*l*. 10*s*.

But all fines and fees have long been abolished, and the income arises from the interest on 8,350*l.* (320*l.*), realized by the sale of the land on which the Hall and other houses formerly stood, exclusively of Jackson's Charity, which distributes 20*l.* a year among poor members.

The Wax Chandlers.

THE occupation of the Wax-chandler was divided between ordinary customers and the supply of his wares to churches and chapels, public schools, and other establishments. The latter branch of the business must have long remained by far the most extensive and profitable. The terms of almost every ancient will mention the employment of tapers of all kinds of this material for use in the offices of the dead. The produce of the hive was naturally viewed as the fittest medium for the twofold purpose of light and purification ; and even in the statutes of St. Paul's, Dean Colet laid down a rule, followed elsewhere, that the boys were to provide in the winter time a wax candle.[1]

Swarms of bees were sometimes left to churches for the purpose of supporting lights ; and these institutions during the mediæval period grew very numerous, so that the present resort to the practice even in the Papal Church must be considerably more sparing than formerly, when we hear of the summer-game light, the young men's light, the bachelors' light, the married men's light, the maidens' light, the young men's light, the children's light, the wives' light, the plough light, the hoglers' light, the tuckers' light. It seems not improbable that, where the means of obtaining the material existed on the spot, religious bodies manufactured their own tapers and candles, and perhaps maintained on the staff some one versed in the mistery.

The very derivation of our term *ceremony* (*cera*, wax) at once power-fully indicates the universal prevalence of the material in all religious

---

[1] At Merchant Taylors' School, as recently as 1850, each boy was expected to bring a candle with him on Probation Day ; but tallow was permitted.

formalities, and the consequently enormous custom for it at the hands of the clergy, independently of its consumption in civil life and for legal or constitutional purposes.

Again, where acts of penance or expiation were enjoined, a normal feature was a waxen taper in the hands of the offender. Here the notion of purity and light was equally present.

The torches so largely and habitually required for processions and pageants, and in the precincts of theatres, in the almost total absence of other provision for lighting the streets, formed a further source of demand ; in these cases, with the wax was mixed a certain proportion of resin, in order to prolong the supply of flame. And there seems to have been a usage, by which the chandler sometimes let the torches on hire, and charged only for as much as was consumed.

The Companies, as bodies extensively concerned in religious celebrations, were at all times large and constant customers to the wax chandler, through whom they supplied the altars of the churches and chapels with lights, and from whom they also hired torches on festive and other occasions. A species of wax—saffron wax—was employed by the Broderer in his work, as we learn from the account of the material and ingredients purchased for the hearse-cloths of some of the Companies.

At a very remote period the high price of wax rendered it barely available for common use or for purposes where tallow or oil would suffice. But the tariff gradually declined from the middle of the thirteenth century, when the price was 1s. per lb., to 1490, when it had fallen to a fourth of that amount.

The relative costliness and importance of wax and tallow are illustrated by two entries in a book of accounts of the Cofferer of Thomas Earl of Lancaster, 7 Edward II. (1313–14) :—

> "For 1714 pound Waxe, with Vermilion and Turpentine to make red Wax £314 7 4½.
> "For 1319 pound of Tallow candles for the houshold, and 1870 of light for Paris-candles, called Perchers, £31 14 3."

Here we gain a glimpse at an early date of the large consumption of both sorts, calculated on the demand for one baronial establishment for a twelvemonth ; and it also appears that coloured wax had been introduced.

The early prices of wax candles, torches, and tapers may be judged from innumerable entries in household and other accounts. Among the expenses for the funeral of Sir John Finkell, Draper, in 1519, occur :—
"To Stephen Ward, wax chandler, for 24 torches, of 24 lbs. a-piece ; 4 tapers of 14 lbs. a-piece ; and two branches of white wax, goodly

made, together with four mighty high standard candlesticks, clean gilt, 54s. 4d."

The Gild of WAX CHANDLERS has bye-laws extending back to 1358,

OLD ARMS.

when, as is expressly recited in the preamble of the earliest Articles, certain abuses in the trade demanded correction. The code describes the Fraternity as "all the Wax-chandlers who are dwelling within London and in the suburb, as well freemen as foreigners, who shall make torches, cierges, prikets, great candles, or any other manner of wax-chandlery for sale." It provides for the appointment of supervisors, who are to be two or four of the most lawful folks of the trade.

This code was renewed and enlarged in 1371, and the later issue enters into some instructive particulars as to the prices charged for articles, as well as into the rather extensive practice of letting out torches for funerals and other occasions. Chandlers made torches for parties bringing their own wax and wick, or paying extra for the wick. It was likewise provided that every chandler should have his own mark to set upon his work.

There seems to be no trace of any approach to the municipal authorities before 1358 or between that date and 1371. On the former occasion the Gild was left at liberty to fix its governing body at two or four Wardens; and from the circumstance that in 1371 two, Walter Rede and John Pope, were appointed, it may be presumed that the lower number was preferred, as it has been retained to the present day.

The Wax Chandlers, who had scarcely become, at the close of the fifteenth century, so important and conspicuous a body as the nature of their industry might have prepared us to expect, owing in part, it may be, to an appreciable share of the custom of the Church being diverted by the agency above-mentioned, obtained from Richard III. in 1483 their parent charter, in which their humble standing is argued by the extent of their licence in mortmain—five marks, or 3l. 13s. 4d. a year, and in the succeeding year a grant of arms.[1] The charter was renewed several times[2] by *inspeximus* down to 15 Charles II., which is the acting one; and bye-laws, the earliest after those of 1371, were approved by the Judges, June 28, 1664. By the charter of 1663 the power to hold real property was considerably extended.

Some years prior to the first charter the Company undertook (1469)

[1] A further grant was made in 1536, 28 Henry VIII.

[2] June 7, 4 and 5 Philip and Mary, 2 Elizabeth, and 2 James I. There was the ordinary incident of the *Quo Warranto* and its reversal by the Act of 1690.

to supply 21 men to the City Watch. In 1502 it is stated to have a Livery (by prescription) of 17 ; and in 1515 the twentieth place was appropriated to it by the Corporation in all public acts and ceremonies, the Tallow Chandlers following immediately after.

The first acquisition of property was apparently the land on which the Hall has always stood, and which can be traced back as far as 1493. In 1543 tenements in Coleman Street came into the hands of the Company under the will of Robert Brocket ; and it possesses other estates in Upper Thames Street, Sugar-Loaf Court, Old Change,[1] and Aldersgate Street, partly obtained by gift and partly by purchase. In 1892 the total income was returned as 1,600*l.*, of which 230*l.* represented trusts.[2]

The Company is governed by a Master, two Wardens (Upper and Renter), and twenty Assistants. The Master and Wardens hold office for two years.

The Livery is unlimited. We have noted that as early as 1502 it existed by custom. In 1699 it amounted to 79 ; in 1724, to 101 ; in 1882, to 41 ; and in 1892, to 27. In 1882 twenty-five persons were said to be on the Freedom, to which women are admissible.

The connection with the trade has long determined.

The Hall, to which we have already adverted as being situate in what is at present known as Gresham Street, originally lay in Ingane Lane, subsequently called Maiden Lane, and while the licence in mortmain was only 3*l.* 13*s.* 4*d.* a year, namely in 1493, was already in the hands of the Company, held in feoffment, we may infer, as in other instances, until enlarged powers were conferred. It was there, of course, in the days of Stow, who says nothing about it, and disappeared in 1666. The present structure, which immediately faces Haberdashers' Hall, is perfectly modern and of limited area.[3] It must be at least the fourth building which has occupied the ground. Of the exterior of the one which was erected after the Great Fire, we have before us a beautiful water-colour drawing by Shepherd, made in 1811.

---

[1] A warehouse and premises, purchased as recently as 1790.

[2] The corporate funds were, it is officially stated, considerably reduced by the Chancery proceedings of 1878 in relation to Kendal's Charity. Yet in 1834 the proceeds of the London property were given as only 668*l.* a year, and internal sources are almost wholly unproductive.

[3] In 1882 its rateable value was returned as 417*l.*

The Weavers.

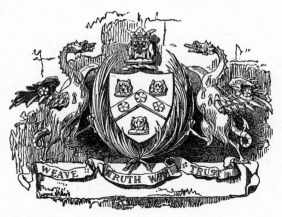

As the FOUNDERS lay claim to descent from Tubalcain, the son of Lamech and Zillah, so the Weavers are entitled to trace their origin so far back as Naamah, daughter of that pair, and sister of the first artificer in brass and iron.

The priority of the existence of Craft and other mercantile associations to any existing record of them seems to be a warrantable inference from the universal tendency of such bodies to knit themselves together at an early stage for purposes of protection and government, and from the testimony which they have supplied to us, in the notable case of the Pipe Rolls entries of 1180, of continuing to grow, and to assume, by virtue of a sort of lax prescription, rights and privileges requiring the sanction of the Crown, and involving them by default in amercements.

It is of course impossible to determine how long the eighteen "Adulterine" Gilds had been exercising usurped authority, when they were detected and fined in 1180, although the political circumstances might have favoured their escape from observation. When we look at the obscure and humble beginnings of even the Greater Companies, it is perfectly likely that they did not, as a rule, care to seek formal recognition until they had something to gain by the step, and something to lose by neglecting it; and the light manner in which the offenders were treated in 1180 shews perhaps at once, that they were not judged very guilty or very important. Their significance as political factors and as financial resorts was yet to come.

This view may be further substantiated in the present case by the logical conclusion, that the art of weaving, with which were associated the subsidiary processes of spinning and carding, preceded that of dyeing the product, and that the most ancient woollen manufactures were plain, while in a more or less rude form they probably rank among the features of the most primitive English life when our distant forefathers had renounced the use of skins.

At the same time, if the traditional legend of Sweyn of Orkney, narrated under the account of the DYERS, be entitled to credit, the art of communicating attractive tinctures to articles of apparel or use did not follow far behind the introduction of the textiles themselves, and in fact it transferred to the garments the bright and striking hues with which at the outset the Britons decorated their persons.

In the reign of Henry VI. the Court of Aldermen certified to the Crown on the back of a writ in Chancery, that "from time beyond the memory of man there were used and approved in the City three Misteries, distinct and separate each from other, to wit, the native *Telarii* of woollen cloths of and for Tapestry, the native *Telarii* of woollen cloths of and for Drapery, and the native *Telarii* of and for Napery." It is added that the second of these had had a Gild of their own long before the statute of 11 Edward III. (1337–8).

Maitland says: "The Company originally consisted of the Cloth and Tapestry Weavers, who, by Act of Parliament of the seventh of Henry IV. were put under the government and correction of the Lord Mayor and Aldermen of this City."

 HE *Telarii*, or Weavers, are perhaps to be considered the most ancient of the Anglo-Norman Gilds, and in point of fact to have been substantially in existence before the Conquest. But the earliest tangible reference to them is a recitation of a charter of Henry I. (1100–35) in one of his grandson Henry II. (1154–89), wherein the King makes known to all concerned,[1] that he has granted to the Weavers of London to have their Gild there, with all liberties and customs, which they had in the time of Henry his grandfather, and in such

---

[1] Stow (*Survey of London*, by Howes, 1633, p. 297) gives as follows the text of the licence of Henry II. :—

"Henry, King of England, Duke of Normandy and of Guian, Earle of Anjou, to the Bishop, Justices, Sheriffs, Barons, Ministers, and all his true Lieges of London, sendeth greeting : Knowe ye, that we have granted to the Weavers in London their Guild, with all the Fredomes and Customs that they had in the time of King Henry my Grandfather : so that none but they intermit within the City their Craft, but he be of their Guild ; neither in Southwarke, or other places pertaining to London, otherwise than it was done in the time of King Henry my Grandfather. Wherefore I will and straightly command, that over all lawfully they may treat, and have all aforesaid, as well in peace, free, worshipfull, and wholly as they had it ; freer, better, worshipfullier, and whollier, than in the time of King Henry my Grandfather. So that they yeeld yeerly to mee two Markes of Gold, at the Feast of Saint Michael. And I forbid that any man to them doe any unright, or disease, upon paine of ten pound."

sort that none, unless by their leave, or that it be done by one of themselves, shall intermeddle with their ministers [government] within the
City or in Southwark, or in the places adjoining, as was ordered in the
reign of his grandfather.   A penalty of ten pounds was incurred by any
offender against this regulation ; and the Gild on its part engaged to
pay to the Crown two marks of gold every year at Michaelmas.[1]

This concession of Henry II., which was given at Winchester, exhibits
the Weavers in the light of a body of long and generally recognised
standing ; and Stow affirms that in the 31st year of the same reign
(1184-5) there was a second instrument executed in favour of the same
Association.   " Also I reade," he says, " that the same *Henry* the second,
in the 31 of his reigne, made a Confirmation to the Weavers, . . .
wherein it appeareth, that the said Weavers made woollen cloth, and
that they had the correction thereof.   But amongst other Articles in that
Patent it was decreed, That if any man made cloth of *Spanish* wooll,
mixed with *English* wooll, the Portgrave or principal Magistrate of *London* ought to burn it . . . " ; and the historian proceeds to give an
account of the Statute passed in 1197 for the further regulation of the
woollen trade.

The two patents of Henry II. were followed by an *inspeximus* dated
from London, April 8, 27 Edward I.   But in 14 Edward II. (1320-1) a
Scire facias issued, requiring the Fraternity to shew by what authority
it exercised its rights and privileges, including the election of bailiffs
and ministers (subject to the approval of the Court of Aldermen), the
holding of weekly Courts for the transaction of current business, the
immunity from interference in the conduct of their Craft and from the
jurisdiction of the Courts in matters relevant to the Gild, the view of
tools and implements, and the distraint on them for arrears of quarter-
wages or other dues payable by members, the exclusion of strangers,

---

[1] In the time of Henry I. according to Maitland, this Gild paid sixteen pounds a
year to the Crown by way of tribute or fee.

The tribute or fine imposed on the Weavers for payment at Michaelmas is not
readily convertible into our modern currency ; and it will be more prudent 'to satisfy
ourselves by the light of collateral evidence, that it was a heavy amount and possibly
beyond the resources of those who engaged to discharge it.   A charter of John revoked that of Henry II. in favour of the Corporation, which seems to have undertaken
to give twenty marks (of silver) in lieu of eighteen, renderable at the same period
(Michaelmas) in order to determine the contract between the Crown and the Weavers.*
The fact seems to be, however, that the municipal authorities found themselves
equally unable or unwilling to fulfil the agreement, as in 4 John (1202-3) they owed
the King 60 marks, or three years' arrears ; and the practical result was, doubtless, that
the Gild continued to flourish, and to constitute a source of jealousy and soreness to
the City at large.   So far as we are now concerned, this mainly serves to establish its
importance.

* *Pro Gildâ Telariâ delenda, ita ut de cætero non suscitetur.*

the dismissal of defaulters or delinquents, with the forfeiture of his tools, at the discretion of twenty-four of the Gild, the power claimed of supervising all cloth of Candlewick [Cannon] Street, whether it was suspected, or not, of being bad, or of being of mixed Spanish and English wool, the suspension of work between Christmas and the Purification, as well as after dark.

This rehearsal of inquiries, or inquisition, admits us by inference to a fuller knowledge of the position of the Weavers than we should gain by any direct testimony ; and the answers of the jury of twelve empanelled to give their verdict form a supplementary fund of information in the same way. The jurors found that it was in 1320–1 the established usage of the Fraternity to hold their Court, not weekly, but at three-weekly intervals, and that there was no right of external interference with them and their proceedings ; that thirty years since there were 280 Burrillers or *Astilamenta*, but that at present there were only 80, whereof the majority were employed by the Weavers on terms disadvantageous to the community ; and that the Ordinances of the Weavers in regard to the control and punishment of members of the Gild by a verdict of 24 of the governing body were *ultra vires*.

How this matter was ultimately adjusted, does not appear ; but the recognition of the Crown was not withheld very long ; and in fact, as we see from the list of charters and royal licences given below, the Gild took advantage of the opening of a new reign in 1327 to secure a regular constitution.

The Ordinances of the Weavers, attributed to the time of Edward I., present internal testimony of the existence of prior codes ; they are of unusual interest as the probable germ of those of the Clothworkers, who, through the Shearmen and Fullers, trace their pedigree from this more ancient Brotherhood.

At this time, the governing body consisted of Bailiffs, a Clerk, and a Serjeant, the last-mentioned having to conduct searches. Courts, composed of the Lord Mayor or four deputies, were to be held each week, and a general meeting of the Gild once a year. Of course, much of the space is devoted to technical details as to the composition and mixture of cloths, their weight and breadth, the processes of fulling, dyeing, and so forth ; but some of the articles relate to the obligations of widows of freemen, who on re-marriage to a non-freeman, must quit their late husbands' premises ; to the legal privileges of the Craft in exemption from the jurisdiction of the ordinary Courts in matters touching the trade, and to the stoppage of goods at the City gates, unlawfully sent to be fulled or dyed outside the bounds.

But Edward III., whose foreign wars were far from being unmitigated misfortunes, was the first who gave a decided stimulus to the English Weavers by relaxing certain archaic restrictions in regard to the working of the material employed, and by inviting (1330) foreigners to settle in London for the purpose of instructing his subjects in a more ample and thorough knowledge of the mistery, while, on the other hand, agreeably to the commercial theories, nay, demands of the period, he interdicted the importation of foreign cloth and the export of native wool.

Cognizance is taken on a former page[1] of the *Flemish Weavers* and the *Alien Weavers*, two Societies, which co-existed in London with each other and with the English Fraternity. No moral doubt can be entertained that the art and industry, which they pursued in common, and with which the Fullers and Shearmen, and eventually the Clothworkers, were connected, was of foreign origin, and was introduced into London and even into some parts of the provinces, as Oxford, Beverley, Newcastle-on-Tyne, at an epoch beyond any existing record, seeing that the English associated Weavers themselves were of more or less lengthened standing, when (by allowable presumption) the charter of Henry I. was conferred.

A further step in the direction of improving and regulating the woollen trade was the removal of the Staple from Calais in 1361 to Westminster and eight other places in England, each district being governed by a Mayor and two Constables, and being exactly defined. That of Westminster extended from Temple Bar to Tuthill Fields ; in 1378, it was removed to Holborn, where the name is still preserved ; its proceedings were conformable to the law merchant ; and it took cognizance not only of wool, but of the four other staples, woolfells, leather, lead, and tin. Occasionally the Lord Mayor coupled with his own office that of Mayor of the Staple, as we note in the case of Sir John Allot, Fishmonger, so late as 1590.

As early as 1367, at least, the Hosier, or salesman of certain of the goods made by the Weaver, occurs not only as a separate trade, which it has since remained in name rather than in fact, but as one which counted among its members men of substance and standing ; and, from a case which came in the year specified before the Mayor's Court, we might be further entitled to conclude that Hosier Lane was at the outset a seat of the business, if Stow had not stated such to be the case. John Flaundene was at this period, it appears, in possession of various

---

[1] It is not surprising that the foreign element, composed of settlers who constantly quarrelled among themselves, came into collision with its English pupils ; and in the second year of Richard II. articles of agreement were drawn up with a view to the promotion of a *modus vivendi*.

tenements in Cordwainers' Street, Holborn, and Hosier Lane. The property was evidently important and extensive.

It is difficult and hazardous to form any deductions from the official records of the City and of the Weavers themselves as to the position and fortunes of the Gild, when we arrive at a later period. The first formal charter was received in 1327, when the Fraternity had been "time out of mind" an organized body with a government by Bailiffs; and down to 1469, when they furnished the heavy quota of 60 to the City Watch, or even down to 1502, when we find them in possession of a customary Livery of 30, there seems to have been some survival of the old prosperity and prestige. But in the municipal order of 1515 they appear as the forty-fourth of 48 Companies, and at the Mayor's Feast in 1532 they occupied a very humble position.

On the other hand, they found 100*l.* in 1615 as partners in the Vintners' Irish manor of Bellaghy, and in 1629 they were assessed at 5*l.* 7*s.* 6*d.* toward the arrangements of the City for doing honour to the coronation of Charles I.

But there is no question that a variety of influences had operated before this date to weaken their resources and impair their practical authority, although the casual or collateral traces of their movements are exceptionally scanty. A system or school of manufacture, more contemporary in its spirit and more commensurate with the public requirements, had grown up outside the ranks of the Weavers, and had pushed them into the background,[1] independently of the formidable competition of the East India trade with the native silk-looms.

The charters or licences granted to the Weavers form a remarkably long series, beginning with those of Henry II., in one of which a licence or other patent of Henry I. is recited, and comprising renewals by *inspeximus* of 31 Henry II. (1184–5), 28 Edward I. (April 8, 1300), 1 and 39 Edward III. (1327 and 1366), 1 Henry VI. (Oct. 15, 1422), 31 Henry VIII. (Nov. 7, 1540), 2 and 3 Philip and Mary (Feb. 18, 1555), 1 Elizabeth (15 Nov. 1558–9), 2 James I. (May 23, 1604), and 2 Charles I. (Nov. 20, 1626). New grants were received in 14 Charles I. (July 4, 1638), 1 James II. (Oct. 24, 1685), and 6 Anne (Nov. 17, 1708).

The code of bye-laws, by which the Company is governed, bears date March 15, 1737, and was approved by the Judges in the usual manner on the 24th March ensuing.

In the Ordinances of the Gild, made and approved in the reign of

---

[1] The Weavers, with the Tylers and Bricklayers, were excepted from the proposed charter of 1636 in favour of the Retail Trades of London and the Suburbs, for the probable reason that they worked for the trade only, and were not salesmen.

Edward I., the Weavers are described as consisting of Bailiffs and a Commonalty; and in 1502 there was a Livery of 30. In 1699, the Livery was returned as 180; in 1724, as 263; in 1882, as 101; and in 1892, as 77. But the figures of 1724, if not the rest, seem to suggest that we have there the inclusive aggregate of the Company; and the same remark applies to 1739, when the numbers were given as 279. At the last-mentioned date, there were two Bailiffs, two Wardens, and sixteen Assistants. The Livery fine was then 6*l.*

In 1882 the Executive corresponded to that existing at the earlier period, except that the number of Assistants was 18. The staff is composed of the Upper and Renter Bailiff, the Upper and Renter Warden, the Clerk, the Surveyor, and the Beadle.

Of the corporate property no particulars have been divulged; but in 1892 the trust-estate amounted to 360*l.*

Of the Hall in Basinghall Street, which has been long since relinquished, Stow (1633) affords no more than a cursory mention. Maitland (1739) describes it as a handsome one. It appears to have stood between Masons' and Girdlers' Halls.

ARMS, 1633.

The former frequenters of Spitalfields have left a record of their impressions, when they strolled through this once primitive and characteristic locality, and listened to the weavers singing at their looms. Brayley speaks of this as a practice, which they had introduced from their original homes in the Netherlands and other parts. As ordinary conversation was more or less apt to interfere with their work, it is easy to understand how they acquired a habit of chanting or reciting ditties and rhymes of a popular cast to relieve the monotony of their labour.

Some of the members, on the establishment in 1741 by John Immyns, an attorney, at the Twelve Bells in Bride Lane, of the *Madrigal Society,* joined the institution, and it also counted several artisan clothworkers from the same musical predilection. In the *First Part of Henry IV.,* Falstaff is made to exclaim, " I would I were a weaver, I could sing all manner of songs!" and in the *Silent Woman,* by Ben Jonson, one of the characters accounts for a cold contracted by the minister, by saying that he got it by sitting up late and singing catches with clothworkers.

LITERARY NOTICES.

The Weaver's Song in the Praise of Love and Friendship. [About 1600.] A ballad.
A Breviate of the Weavers' Business before the Honourable Committee of the House of Commons in the Star-Chamber. [July 28, 1648.] 4to, 1648.

Minerva, Or, the Art of Weaving. Containing the Antiquity, Utility, and Excellency of Weaving. By R. C. 8vo, 1677. In verse.

Strange and Fearful Newes from Plasto, neare Bow, in the House of one Paul Fox, a Silk-weaver, where is dayly to be seene throwing of Stones . . . Cutting his Work in Pieces. 4to, n.d. [About 1680.]

The Weavers' and Clothiers' Complaint against the East India trade. 1699. A broadside.

The Wheelwrights.

IN 1669–70, a petition was addressed to the Crown by the Wheelwrights of London, setting forth that certain foreigners undertake the profession and trade of a wheelwright, notwithstanding they are ignorant and unskilful therein, and altogether incapable of making the works used in and about the said City, whereby much mischief happeneth to persons in the streets, by falling of carts and coaches, and great damage to merchants and others in their goods, as also loss and danger to gentlemen, occasioned by the ignorance and ill-work of the said foreigners, that never served to the said profession; and that other great inconveniences and misdemeanours are used and practised in the said art and trade; and accordingly praying that the petitioners might be formed into one body politic for the prevention thereof.

A charter, dated February 3, 1670, was the fruit of this representation. It constituted all persons employed as wheelwrights within the City and five miles' compass one body corporate and public under the style of The Master, Wardens, Assistants, and Commonalty of the Art and Mistery of Wheelwrights of the City of London, with a common seal, the right to sue and be sued, a licence in mortmain to 40*l.* a year,[1] the power of search in conjunction with an officer of the City,[2] and authority to appoint a Clerk and Beadle.

The instrument nominated the Master, two Wardens, and eighteen

---

[1] This faculty has never been exercised.

[2] All justices of the peace and others were enjoined to be assisting to the Company in carrying out these letters patent.

Assistants, and provided that they should thereafter be elected annually on the Thursday following Michaelmas Day. It concluded with the stipulation that, in case the present concessions, or any of them, should prove to be contrary to public good and benefit, the Crown might, under writ of Privy Seal, determine it or them wholly or in part.

The bye-laws, interpreting the charter and governing the internal arrangements, are dated October 12 immediately ensuing. They are of the normal tenor, except one, which inflicts a penalty of 5*l.* on any member refusing to serve, if the Company is required to furnish his Majesty's train of waggons or artillery. There is also a peculiar inhibition against making wheels in any brewer's or coachmaker's shop—that is, on their premises. In a renewal of these Ordinances, April 3, 1714, the two special provisions do not occur.

Under the power of search, which was first carried into effect in 1671, the area under jurisdiction was divided into the North and South sides, and two searches were usually made every year. The principle has been abandoned since 1750. For the north side a warrant was obtained from the Recorder.

The payment of quarterwages and fines appears to have long remained optional and precarious, and the financial position of the Company was of course correspondingly weak. There being no Livery, the fines amounted to a very inconsiderable sum, and there was no corporate estate. The control over the journeymen was also very imperfect, and about 1720 a movement, which continued with intermissions till the end of the century, began for shortening hours of labour and advancing the rate of wages. The Court had the support of the Justices, as well as counsel's opinion on their side, and even went so far as to indict some of the agitators. But no practical remedy was obtained, and the controversy dropped. It is easy to discern throughout a want of consolidation and central authority. At first, no steps seem to have been taken to secure discipline or enforce rules ; and then arrived the period within the experience of all these Societies, when the operative element began to think and act for itself. A jacobinical spirit animated even the lower section of the City Companies, as the second moiety of the eighteenth century was reached.

In 1882, of 150 members of the Wheelwrights' Gild only four belonged to the trade ; and the tie has now become purely nominal.

The Company is governed agreeably to the only charter. A Livery, which formed no part of the original constitution, was mooted in 1734 ; but the application to the Court of Aldermen was not made till 1773. It was limited to 100, and twice enlarged—in 1792, to 150, and in 1817, to 250. It has never reached, however, the lowest *maximum*. In 1882 it numbered 105, and in 1892, 120, *the Court* (21) *inclusive*.

There were in 1882 about 45 on the Freedom. Freewomen were formerly admitted by apprenticeship; but a freewoman transmitted no right to her children, and conferred none upon her husband. It was necessary that she should be bound to a man-milliner, or, in other words, to a trade which she could follow: her master, though free of the Company, probably not belonging to the Craft.

The income was returned in 1892 as 300*l.*, partly arising from invested surplus,[1] and partly from internal sources.[2] There are no actual trusts; but the Wheelwrights treat as such the sum of 155*l.* paid by two members many years ago—105*l.* by Sir William Leighton, on translation to the Fishmongers, and 50*l.* by Mr. William Leedham, on excusing himself from serving as Master.

Although the resources are so limited, a yearly amount is disbursed in payments to the poor; and the Company made donations of 100*l.* to the Indian Famine Fund and of 210*l.* to the City and Gilds Institute.

In the year succeeding the charter, "for the preservation of amity and brotherly love in this Society," four stewards were chosen to provide an annual dinner at their own expense for the Court and their wives. The number was subsequently reduced to three. This rule, in spite of great opposition and difficulty, was enforced down to 1693, and heavy fines levied on those who refused or failed to comply with it; but the practice has been since varied by calling upon the Master and Wardens to entertain the Court on or after each yearly election, a subscription being raised for the purpose, while a Livery dinner is given out of the general funds.[3]

In the accounts for 1873, an item of 65*l.* 11*s.* appears for a "badge of the Company's arms." This is presumably the Master's badge specified in the returns among the corporate possessions, which also comprise a few pieces of plate. *Three Livery gowns* are particularized in the inventory; these were for the investiture of new members; but on occasions when the whole body might be required to assume the distinctive garb, a supply in this, as in all other similar cases, would be necessarily hired. To keep a stock in hand for such contingencies, once more frequent and habitual, was the *rôle* of the early Upholder.

---

[1] In 1882 this had reached 3,400*l.* in Dominion of Canada 4 per cents.

[2] Chiefly Assistants' and Liverymen's fines. The former is 15*l.*, the latter 21*l.*

[3] In 1870 the Master's dinner cost 25*l.*, and the Livery dinner the same. But the outlay on both accounts from that date to 1879 shewed a chronic tendency to increase. In 1879, the aggregate amount collected was 225*l.* 3*s.* 8*d.*

The Woolmen.

THE Woolmen are doubtless entitled to claim as belonging to their Gild the Wool-staplers, who may be traced back to the time of the earlier Plantagenets, and who acquired eminence and wealth in the reign of Edward I. One of the most distinguished persons of that period, who engaged in the traffic both for home-trade and for export, was Gregory de Rokesley, eight times Mayor, and a man of honourable and courageous disposition. He united with his business as a gold-smith and his office as general Assay-master of the King and Keeper of his Exchange, to say nothing of his municipal functions, large trans-actions in wool; and in 2 Edward I. his name stands at the head of a list of fifty-seven Staplers, who were licensed to export the commodity beyond sea.

The Woolmen are, at the same time, almost unquestionably identical with the *Woolpackers*[1] and *Woolwinders;* and the body occurs under all these designations. By a proclamation dated in the reign of Charles II. the Wool-combers were placed under their jurisdiction.

In the recent account of the WEAVERS, as well as in the annals of other Associations connected with the wool trade, we have collected rather copious particulars of the periodical ordinances and statutes made on their behalf from the reign of Henry I.

In 1291–2, Edward I. founded the fair and market at Sandwich, "where," says *A Chronicle of London* (1089–1483), "alle the wolles of Engelond schal be brought, and there sold;" and according to the same authority, in the 24th year of the same reign (1295–6), "the kyng lete areste alle the wolles of Engelond, wolle felles and hydes."

The Statute of 27 Edward III. cap. 23 vested in this body the right of appointing licensed persons to wind wools; and in the 25th of the same reign, while the influence of the Livery Gilds or voluntary associa-tions temporarily drew into their hands a preponderance of the electoral power in the City, the Woolners or Woolmen were among thirteen bodies who received a precept from the Mayor to delegate representa-tives to Guildhall to confer with him on current affairs, or, in other

---

[1] Compare p. 153, *suprâ*. The arms of the *Wool-packers*, as given by Stow, 1633, correspond.

words, to attend the Common Council ; there is no apparent order of precedence ; and the Woolners are the sixth in the list. A similar summons was received by the Gilds in 1376.

In 1386 the cargoes of wool seem to have been usually discharged at what was then already known as Wool Wharf, on the riverside in Tower Ward, and in the year named a weighing house, with accommodation for comptrollers and clerks, was built there by John Churchman.

As the Pepperers and Corders had the nomination of the custodian of the Great Beam or Balance for weighing avoirdupois, the Woolners or Woolmen, at least at one time, were entitled to submit to the Court of Aldermen the name of the keeper of the Small one for Troy or goldsmiths' weight, of 12 ounces to the pound.

We hear very little indeed of this industry, when the earlier period of its existence and duration has passed ; and it evidently shared the fate of the weaving trade, and through similar agencies, having equally, before it rose to the rank of a corporate institution, outlived its importance and prosperity.

Even in 1469, in a return where nearly all the then existing Gilds are mentioned and assessed, it does not occur ; in 1502, it ranked fortyfifth (out of 74) with a prescriptive Livery of eight ; and in 1515 it was officially declared the forty-fifth in order among forty-eight associations enumerated.

Sir John Crosby is described by Stow as a Woolman. "Then have ye," says he, "one great house, called Crosbie Place, because the same was builded by Sir Iohn Crosbie, Grocer and Woollman, in place of certaine Tenements, with their appurtenances, letten to him by Alice Ashfield, Prioresse of S. Helens, and the Covent, for ninety nine yeeres, from the yeere 1466. unto the yeere 1565. for the annuall rent of eleven pounds six shillings eightpence."

This passage and reference are so far serviceable, that they shew how some combined transactions in wool and the fellowship of the Gild with another and more lucrative calling. But we may likewise conclude that the Woolmen gradually absorbed the Staplers, the Packers, and the Winders,[1] as well as the Combers, and in fact acquired for what it was worth a general control over the wholesale market.

In a petition, which it had occasion to present to the Court of Aldermen in 1825, the Woolmen represented themselves as an ancient Company by prescription, which at various times had been acknowledged as such, and had been called upon in conjunction with others to perform suits and services for the protection and honour of the City.

---

[1] Down to 1779 every Woolwinder required a licence from the Company.

We have to rely, however, on these and other indirect evidences in forming a narrative and estimate in the present instance, as the papers of the Gild appear to have almost without exception perished in 1666, when the Hall was burned down.

The charter is said to have fallen a prey to the flames ; but the Ordinances, by which, agreeably to analogy, it was perhaps closely followed, have been preserved ; and they bear date in 1587. These regulations define the constitution of the governing body, the duties of the Clerk and Beadle, and are of the usual character.

The Executive consists of a Master, two Wardens, and eleven Assistants. The Master and Wardens hold office for two years, and are unpaid. It is a curious survival, that Assistants, on refusing to serve as Warden, are fined *five marks*. Votes are taken in the ordinary way or by pricks upon paper.

In 1825 the Court of Aldermen granted a Livery of 40. The fine is 21*l*.[1] In 1882 the number returned was 31 ; in 1892, 24.[2] The gross annual revenue seems to fluctuate between 300*l*. and 400*l*, In 1871 it was 303*l*. ; in 1880, 444*l*. ; in 1892, 334*l*.

The Master has the right to nominate year by year two poor members of the Company as pensioners under Vernon's Charity, administered by the Merchant Taylors. The alms to the Woolmen's pensioners are distributed on the 16th January by the Master and Wardens, and each recipient has half a guinea in lieu of a dinner.

The accounts are not published ; but as in the ten years 1871-80 internal sources only realized an average of about 32*l*. a year, it follows that the difference arises from corporate estate, probably in the shape of periodically invested surplus and of the proceeds of the sale in 1827 of tenements in Mark Lane required for the Corn Exchange.

The convenient proximity of that spot to Wool Wharf or Quay, and the admitted fact that the Company lost a Hall in the Fire, suggests the speculation whether the place of assembly did not stand on the site of the premises demolished in 1827, and whether the circumstances of the Woolmen did not preclude them from rebuilding it. Under April 3, 1672, there is a memorandum in the Founders' Books, "that the Company of Woolwinders have liberty to meet at Founders' Hall two days in the year, and to sett a chest or trunk in some convenient place to putt their papers in, for which they shall pay forty shillings. The

---

[1] In 1882, 34 were said to be on the Freedom.

[2] But in 1882 of the 31 liverymen four had not presented themselves within twenty years. In 1892, the number was returned as 24. The fine on coming on the Court is 10*l*. 10*s*., for refusing to serve as Master, 5*l*. Assistants receive 21*s*. for each attendance ; but the higher posts, as we have said, are honorary.

nature of the arrangement indicates that the practice then was, as at present, to hold two general Courts in the year ; and the Founders' tenants have been ever since dependent on the same kind of accommodation.

A FEW GENERAL LITERARY NOTICES.

The Ordynal or Statute, concernynge Artyficers, Seruanntes, and Labourers. 8vo (about 1535.)

There is more than one edition.

An Acte touching dyvers orders for Artificers, Laborers, Servantes of Husbandrye and Apprentices. 5 Elizabeth, Cap. 4.

Repealed and mainly re-enacted by Act 1 James I, c. 22.

A Briefe Description of Ireland: made in this year, 1589, by Robert Payne, vnto xxv. of his partners for whom he is vndertaker there. 8vo, 1589, 1590.

Reprinted by the Irish Archæological Society. Payne was a surveyor and land-agent. He is also the author of the Vale-man's Table, 1583.

A Collection of Svch Orders and Conditions, as are to be obserued by the Vndertakers, Vpon the Distribution and Plantation of the Escheated Lands in Vlster. 4to, 1608, 1609, 1610.

The three points with which these Orders deal are : 1. What the British Vndertaker shall have of his Maiesties gift ; 2. What the said Vndertakers shall for their part performe ; 3. In what maner the same performance shall be.

The Speech of a Warden to the Fellowes of his Companie. Touching the great affairs of the Kingdome. Published by Antibrownistus Puritanomastix. 4to, 1642.

Midsummer-Moon: or, the Livery-man's Complaint. By Tho. Thompson. 4to, 1680.

The True Friends to Corporations Vindicated. In Answer to a Letter concerning the Disabling Clauses lately offered to the House of Commons for Regulating Corporations. 4to, 1690.

INDEX.

Exchange 181, 182 ; Queen Elizabeth dines with him 445.
Gresham, William 181.
Greshams, The 181–2.
Grey Tawyers, The 147.
Grocers' Company, The 187–94 ; Administrators 64 ; Articles of Merchandise 189 ; Bibliography 194–7 ; Complaint against their Drugs 347 ; Connection with Irish Estate 190 ; Court of Assistants 188 ; Eminent Members 194 ; Enmity towards Grocers 348–9 ; Financial Embarrassments 191 ; Foundation 130 ; Hall 193 ; Losses by Fire of London 191 ; Numerical Strength 192 ; Ordinances 188–9 ; Origin 187 ; Philanthropic Works 192 ; Privileges 71 ; Right of Search 189-90 ; Severance from Apothecaries 190 ; Staff 193.
Gunmakers' Company, The 528–30 ; Charter 528 ; Hall 529 ; Income 529 ; Numerical Strength 529 ; Ordinances 529 ; Powers 70 ; Proof House, Whitechapel 529.
Guy, Thos., Founder of Guy's Hospital 183.

Haberdashers' Company, The 285–92 ; Almshouses 290 ; Articles of Commerce 287 ; Bibliography 291–2 ; Charters 286–7 ; Connection w. Irish Estate 288 ; Constitution of Court 288 ; Hall 288–90 ; Ordinances 288 ; Origin 285 ; Schools 290 ; of St. Katharine the Virgin and of St. Nicholas 115 ; Shop-contents in 1378 115–6.
Haines, John, Carpenter 407.
Hall, The Common 3, 80, 81.
Hall-Moots, Bakers', Objects of 104 ; Fishmongers' 221.
Halliwell Chalice, The 129.
Halliwell, Geoffrey de, Pepperer 191.
Halls, The 46.
Hannis, John, Framework Knitter 506.
Hanseatic League, The 164-6.
Harris, John, Clockmaker 425.
Harvest, Edw., Gunner and Brewer 388, 528.
Haselwood, John, Leatherseller, Bequest of 557.
Hatband Makers' Society, The 116–7.
Hatherley, Sir John, Lord Mayor 303.
Hatters, The 117.
Haymongers, The 117–20.

Heath, John, Clothworker 339.
Heathcote, Sir Gilbert, Lord Mayor 328.
Heaumers, The 117, 355.
Heith, John, Cooper 439.
Helmetry, Trade of 117.
Hend, John, Lord Mayor 206, 210–1.
Herbert, W., *Hist. of the Twelve Great Companies* 52.
Herne, William, Sergeant-Painter 581.
Hewer, William, Clothworker 339.
Heyward, James, Linen Draper 121.
Heywood, Thomas, Dramatist 534.
Hicks, Sir Baptist, Visc. Campden 181.
Hickson, James, Brewer 385.
History of Thomas Hickathrift 389.
Hobson, William 290–1.
Hoddesden, Thomas, Glover 520.
Hodgkin, Mr., Saddler 611.
Honnor, Young Geo., Saddler, Bequests of 610–1.
Honnor's Home 610.
Hook, Charles, Schoolmaster 241.
Horn, Andrew, Author of *Liber Horn* 217, 219.
Horn Fair 530.
Horners' Company, The 316, 530–7 ; Charter 531 ; Connection with Bottlers 534 ; Decline 532–3 ; Exhibition 533 ; Fairs 530, 531 ; Fees 532 ; Income 532 ; Numerical Strength 532 ; Order of Precedence 531 ; Privileges 531–2.
Horse-Corsors, Union with Innholders 538.
Horse-dealers, The 155.
Hospital of St. Thomas of Acon 169.
Hostler, Origin of the word 118–9.
Hostelers, The 117–20.
"Hot Cross Buns" 104.
House of Black Nuns 246, 267.
Housman, Mr., Painter 581.
Howard, William, Clothworker 338.
Howard and Watson, Painters, Trial between 578.
Howell, James, Author 208, 515.
Howell, Thos., Bequest of 207–8, 210 ; Will 207, 211.
Hudson's Bay Company 163.
Hulet, Mr., Stationer 636.
Hungerford, John, Shearman 136.
Hunt, And., Girdler, Bequest of 513–4.
Hunter, John, Apothecary 352.
Hunter, William, Apothecary 352.
Hurers, The 120 ; Bibliography 121.
Hurriers—*see* Hurers.